Black Africans in Renaissance Europe

This highly original book opens up the almost entirely neglected area of the black African presence in Western Europe during the Renaissance. Covering history, literature, art history and anthropology, it investigates a whole range of black African experience and representation across Renaissance Europe, from various types of slavery to black musicians and dancers, from real and symbolic Africans at court to the views of the Catholic Church, and from writers of African descent to black African 'criminality'. The main purpose of the collection is to show the variety and complexity of black African life in fifteenth- and sixteenth-century Europe, and how it was affected by firmly held preconceptions relating to the African continent and its inhabitants, reinforced by Renaissance ideas and conditions. Of enormous importance both for European and for American history, this book mixes empirical material and theoretical approaches, and addresses such issues as stereotypes, changing black African identities, and cultural representation in art and literature.

T. F. EARLE is King John II Professor of Portuguese Studies at the University of Oxford.

K. J. P. LOWE is Professor of Renaissance History and Culture, Queen Mary, University of London.

Black Africans in Renaissance Europe

edited by

T. F. EARLE AND K. J. P. LOWE

CAMBRIDGE
UNIVERSITY PRESS

CAMBRIDGE
UNIVERSITY PRESS

University Printing House, Cambridge CB2 8BS, United Kingdom

Published in the United States of America by Cambridge University Press, New York

Cambridge University Press is part of the University of Cambridge.

It furthers the University's mission by disseminating knowledge in the pursuit of education, learning and research at the highest international levels of excellence.

www.cambridge.org
Information on this title: www.cambridge.org/9780521176606

© Cambridge University Press 2005

First published 2005
3rd printing 2007
First paperback edition published 2010

A catalogue record for this publication is available from the British Library

ISBN 978-0-521-81582-6 Hardback
ISBN 978-0-521-17660-6 Paperback

Contents

List of illustrations   *page* vii
List of contributors   xii
Acknowledgements   xiv
Notes on the text   xv

Introduction: The black African presence in
Renaissance Europe   1
KATE LOWE

PART I   CONCEPTUALISING BLACK AFRICANS

1   The stereotyping of black Africans in Renaissance Europe   17
KATE LOWE

2   The image of Africa and the iconography of lip-plated
Africans in Pierre Desceliers's World Map of 1550   48
JEAN MICHEL MASSING

3   Black Africans in Renaissance Spanish literature   70
JEREMY LAWRANCE

4   Washing the Ethiopian white: conceptualising black skin
in Renaissance England   94
ANU KORHONEN

5   Black Africans in Portugal during Cleynaerts's visit (1533–1538)   113
JORGE FONSECA

PART II   REAL AND SYMBOLIC BLACK AFRICANS AT COURT

6   Isabella d'Este and black African women   125
PAUL H. D. KAPLAN

7   Images of empire: slaves in the Lisbon household and court of
Catherine of Austria   155
ANNEMARIE JORDAN

8   Christoph Jamnitzer's 'Moor's Head': a late Renaissance
    drinking vessel   181
    LORENZ SEELIG

PART III THE PRACTICALITIES OF ENSLAVEMENT
AND EMANCIPATION

9   The trade in black African slaves in fifteenth-century Florence   213
    SERGIO TOGNETTI

10 'La Casa dels Negres': black African solidarity in late
    medieval Valencia   225
    DEBRA BLUMENTHAL

11 Free and freed black Africans in Granada in the time of the
    Spanish Renaissance   247
    AURELIA MARTÍN CASARES

12 Black African slaves and freedmen in Portugal during the
    Renaissance: creating a new pattern of reality   261
    DIDIER LAHON

13 The Catholic Church and the pastoral care of black Africans
    in Renaissance Italy   280
    NELSON H. MINNICH

PART IV BLACK AFRICANS WITH EUROPEAN IDENTITIES
AND PROFILES

14 Race and rulership: Alessandro de' Medici, first Medici duke
    of Florence, 1529–1537   303
    JOHN K. BRACKETT

15 Juan Latino and his racial difference   326
    BALTASAR FRA-MOLINERO

16 Black Africans versus Jews: religious and racial tension in a
    Portuguese saint's play   345
    T. F. EARLE

Bibliography   361
Index   401

Illustrations

1 Christoph Weiditz, *Black Slave with a Wineskin in Castile*,
1529 (photo: Germanisches Nationalmuseum, Nuremberg).   *page* 26

2 *Sketch of the Slave-trader John Hawkins' Crest*, late sixteenth-century
(photo: College of Arms, London).   27

3 Anonymous, *Chafariz d'el-Rei in the Alfama District, Lisbon*,
c. 1525–30 (photo: private collection, Lisbon).   30

4 Anonymous, *Chafariz d'el-Rei in the Alfama District, Lisbon* (detail of
black African being arrested), *c.* 1525–30 (photo: Lisbon, private
collection).   31

5 Jörg Breu the Younger, *A Duel with Two Sickles*, *c.* 1560 (photo:
Bayerische Staatsbibliothek, Munich).   34

6 The Master of Frankfurt, *The Archers' Festival in the Garden of their
Guild* (detail of black pipe and tabor player), *c.* 1493 (photo: The
Warburg Institute, London).   36

7 Christoph Weiditz, *Drummer at the Entrance of the Emperor*, 1529
(photo: Germanisches Nationalmuseum, Nuremberg).   38

8 *John Blanke, the Black Trumpet*, Great Tournament Roll of
Westminster, 1511 (photo: College of Arms, London).   40

9 Anonymous, *Chafariz d'el-Rei in the Alfama District, Lisbon* (detail of
African/European couple dancing), *c.* 1560–80 (photo: private
collection, Lisbon).   42

10 Jan Mostaert's *Portrait of a Moor*, c.1525–30 (oil on panel,
30.7 × 21.2 cm). Reproduced by permission of the Rijksmuseum,
Amsterdam.   45

11 Amédée Féret and Charles Mauduit, *Frieze in the Church of
St Jacques in Dieppe*, 1833.   49

12 Pierre Desceliers, *World Map*, 1550 (photo: British Library,
London).   53

13 Detail of Africa from Pierre Desceliers, *World Map*, 1550 (photo:
British Library, London).   57

14 Detail of Africans with enlarged lips from Pierre Desceliers, *World
Map*, 1550 (photo: British Library, London).   60

15 Hans Holbein, *Typus cosmographicus universalis* in Sebastian
   Münster, *Novus orbis regionum ac insularum veteribus incognitarum . . .*
   libellus (Basel, 1532).   62

16 *African with Lip-plate*, post-card (photo: Touly).   63

17 *Fabulous Beings*, Syon College Bestiary, c. 1277 (Los Angeles, The
   J. Paul Getty Museum).   66

18 *Man with Elongated Lower Lip*, in Hartman Schedel, *Liber cronicarum*
   (Nuremberg, 1493).   68

19 *Africans with Elongated Lips*, in Claudius Ptolemy, *Opus*
   Geographicae (Strasbourg, 1525).   69

20 Woodcut from the broadside *Coplas de como una dama ruega a un*
   negro que cante en manera de requiebro (Seville, Cromberger, c. 1520?).   76

21 Andrea Mantegna, *Judith and her maidservant with the head of*
   Holofernes, February 1491/1492 (photo: Alinari).   126

22 *The False Frederick II and his African Retainers*, from Clement
   Specker 'Chronik', 1476 (photo: Burgerbibliothek, Bern).   128

23 Andrea Mantegna, detail from *Oculus* of the Camera Picta,
   c. 1465–1474 (photo: Alinari).   129

24 Andrea Mantegna, *Adoration of the Magi*, c. 1464 (photo: Alinari).   131

25 *Assassination of Giangalezzo Sforza*, from Lorenzo dalla Rota,
   Lamento del Duca Galeazzo (Florence, 1505) (photo: Paul H. D.
   Kaplan).   138

26 Andrea Mantegna, *Judith*, c. 1495–1500 (photo: National Gallery
   of Ireland, Dublin).   140

27 Andrea Mantegna, *Judith*, c. 1500–5 (photo: Christine Guest,
   Musée des Beaux-Arts de Montréal/The Montreal Museum of
   Fine Arts).   142

28 After Andrea Mantegna, *Judith*, 1490s (photo: National Gallery of
   Art, Washington, DC).   143

29 Andrea Mocetto after Andrea Mantegna, *Judith*, c. 1500–5 (photo:
   National Gallery of Art, Washington, DC).   144

30 Andrea Mantegna and heirs, *Judith*, after 1506 (photo: Paul H. D.
   Kaplan).   146

31 Correggio, *Judith*, c. 1510–2 (photo: Musées de la Ville de
   Strasbourg).   147

32 Andrea Mantegna, *Adoration of the Magi*, c. 1497–1500 (photo:
   The J. Paul Getty Museum, Los Angeles).   148

33 Giovanni Maria Falconetto, *Leo (July)*, c. 1520 (photo:
   Paul H. D. Kaplan).   150

34 Correggio, *Allegory of Virtue*, c. 1523–30 (photo: Service photographique de la Réunion des Musées Nationaux, Paris).   151

35 Titian, *Laura Dianti and her Page*, c. 1523 (photo: Paul H. D. Kaplan).   152

36 Albrecht Durer, *Portrait of Katherina*, 1521 (photo: Paul H. D. Kaplan).   153

37 Attributed to António de Holanda, *Scene with a Black Slave in the Household of a Wealthy Patrician*, Book of Hours of King D. Manuel, 1517–38 (photo: Arquivo Nacional de Fotografia/Instituto Português de Museus, Lisbon).   157

38 Attributed to Cristovão de Figueiredo and Garcia Fernandes, *The Santa Auta Retable: The Encounter of Prince Conan and St Ursula*. (detail with black musicians), 1522–5 (photo: Arquivo Nacional de Fotografia/Instituto Português de Museus, Lisbon).   158

39 Anonymous, *Chafariz d'el-Rei in the Alfama District, Lisbon* (detail with black cavalier), c. 1560–80 (photo: private collection, Lisbon).   160

40 Vasco Fernandes and Francisco Henriques (?), *The Adoration of the Magi*, 1502–6, detail of Tupi Indian (photo: Arquivo Nacional de Fotografia/Instituto Português de Museus, Lisbon).   163

41 Mandate signed by Catherine of Austria for clothes given to Duarte Frois for his work (detail with his signature), 1 February 1552 (photo: Instituto dos Arquivos Nacionais/Torre do Tombo, Lisbon).   164

42 Mandate signed by Catherine of Austria for clothes given to Pero Fernandes for his work as housekeeper (detail with his signature), 20 June 1556 (photo: Instituto dos Arquivos Nacionais/Torre do Tombo, Lisbon).   166

43 Garcia Fernandes and Jorge Leal, *The Birth of the Virgin* (detail with a black lady's servant), early sixteenth century (photo: Colecção António Trindade, Lisbon).   168

44 Workshop of Simon Bening, *Scene of an Aristocratic Hunting Party including a Black Attendant*, Month of May, Book of Hours of Infante Ferdinand, 1530–4 (photo: Arquivo Nacional de Fotografia/Instituto Português de Museus, Lisbon).   170

45 Cristóvão de Morais, *Portrait of Juana de Austria with her Black Slave Girl*, 1553 (photo: Institut Royal du Patrimoine Artistique, Brussels).   177

46 Christoph Jamnitzer, *Moor's Head*, Nuremberg, *c.* 1600 (photo:
    Bayerisches Nationalmuseum, Munich).   182

47 Christoph Jamnitzer, *Moor's Head*, Nuremberg, *c.* 1600 (photo:
    Bayerisches Nationalmuseum, Munich).   183

48 Christoph Jamnitzer, *Moor's Head*, Nuremberg, *c.* 1600 (photo:
    Bayerisches Nationalmuseum, Munich).   184

49 *Young Moor representing the Pucci Coat of Arms*, Giovanni da San
    Giovanni, called Mannozzi, Florence, first half of the seventeenth
    century (photo: Gabinetto fotografico, Soprintendenza speciale
    per il polo museale fiorentino, Ministero per i beni e le attività
    culturali, Florence).   186

50 Niccolò Fiorentino or workshop, *Portrait medal of Filippo Strozzi*
    (reverse and obverse), Florence, *c.* 1489 (photo: The Warburg
    Institute, London).   187

51 *Portrait Medal of Alessandro Strozzi* (obverse and reverse), Florence,
    1593 (photo: The Warburg Institute, London).   188

52 *Head Relic of Saint Vitalis*, 1517 (photo: Bayerisches Landesamt für
    Denkmalpflege, Munich).   192

53 Workshop of Andrea Riccio, oil lamp, Padua, *c.* 1500 (photo:
    Bayerisches Nationalmuseum, Munich).   194

54 *Black Prisoner*, Northern Italy, first half of the sixteenth century
    (photo: Kunsthistorisches Museum, Vienna).   196

55 *Black Venus*, Flanders or France, late sixteenth century (photo:
    Kunsthistorisches Museum, Vienna).   197

56 *Head of a Black African*, Flanders, second third of the seventeenth
    century (photo: Herzog Anton Ulrich-Museum, Brunswick).   198

57 Pietro Tacca, *Black African Slave* on the pedestal of the monument
    of Grand-duke Ferdinando I of Tuscany, 1615–23/4, Livorno,
    Piazza della Darsena.   200

58 Pietro Francavilla and Francesco Bordoni, *Black African Slave*,
    Paris, *c.* 1614–18 (photo: Service photographique de la Réunion
    des Musées Nationaux, Paris).   201

59 Nicolas Cordier, *Head of a Black African*, Rome, *c.* 1610 (photo:
    Dresden, Staatliche Kunstsammlungen, Skulpturensammlung).   202

60 Francesco Caporale, *Bust of Antonio Emanuele Funta, called Nigrita*,
    1608, Rome, Santa Maria Maggiore.   204

61 Miseroni workshop, *Cameo with Black Diana*, Milan, last quarter of
    the sixteenth century; Andreas Osenbruck, mounts, Prague,
    c. 1610 (photo: Kunsthistorisches Museum, Vienna).   205

62 Lourenço de Salzedo, *Christ carrying the Cross* (original, and now restored, detail of three Marias), 1570–2 (photo: Instituto Português do Património Arquitectónico e Arqueológico, Lisbon).   276

63 Workshop of Agnolo Bronzino, *Portrait of Alessandro de' Medici*, after 1553 (photo: Alinari).   311

64 Workshop of Girolamo Macchietti, *Portrait of Duke Alessandro de' Medici*, 1585 (photo: Gabinetto fotografico, Soprintendenza speciale per il polo museale fiorentino, Ministero per i beni e le attività culturali, Florence).   312

65 Giorgio Vasari, *Alessandro de' Medici*, 1534 (photo: Alinari).   314

66 Giovanni Stradano (design), Benedetto di Michele Squilli (execution), *Clement VII selects Alessandro de' Medici as Duke of Florence*, 1573–4 (photo: Alinari).   315

67 Francesco da Sangallo, *Portrait Medal of Alessandro de' Medici and Cosimo I de' Medici* (obverse and reverse), sixteenth century (photo: Alinari).   319

Contributors

Debra Blumenthal, Associate Professor, Department of History, University of California, Santa Barbara, USA.

John K. Brackett, Professor of History, University of Cincinatti, USA.

T. F. Earle, Professor of Portuguese Studies, St Peter's College, University of Oxford, UK.

Jorge Fonseca, former Director, Biblioteca Municipal e Arquivo Histórico de Montemor-o-Novo, Portugal.

Baltasar Fra-Molinero, Professor of Spanish, Bates College, USA.

Annemarie Jordan, Private Researcher, Jona, Switzerland.

Paul H. D. Kaplan, Professor of the History of Art, Purchase College, State University of New York, USA.

Anu Korhonen, Academy of Finland Research Fellow at the Renvall Institute, University of Helsinki, Finland.

Didier Lahon, teaches African History in the Universidade Federal do Pará, Belém, Brazil.

Jeremy Lawrance, Professor of Spanish, University of Nottingham, UK.

Kate Lowe, Professor of Renaissance History and Culture, Queen Mary, University of London, UK.

Aurelia Martín Casares, Professor of Anthropology, Universidad de Granada, Spain.

Jean Michel Massing, Professor of the History of Art, King's College, University of Cambridge, UK.

Nelson H. Minnich, Professor of Church History, The Catholic University of America.

Lorenz Seelig, former Keeper of Metalwork and Deputy Director, Bayerisches Nationalmuseum, Munich, Germany.

Sergio Tognetti, Ricercatore di storia medievale, Università degli studi di Cagliari, Italy.

Acknowledgements

The editors wish to thank the following organizations for financial assistance received during the course of the project which has resulted in the present book: The British Academy; the Comissão Nacional para as Comemorações dos Descobrimentos Portugueses, Lisbon; the Faculties of Medieval and Modern Languages and of Modern History at the University of Oxford; the History Department of Goldsmiths' College, University of London; St Peter's College, Oxford and the Society for Renaissance Studies.

The editors are also very grateful to all the contributors to the book, who made the project such a pleasant and fruitful experience, and to the anonymous readers for Cambridge University Press, whose thoughtful and sensible suggestions were much appreciated.

Finally, we should like to thank William Davies, lately of Cambridge University Press, for his good humour, unfailing patience and steadfast encouragement. Michael Watson, who took over responsibility for the book as it was delivered to the Press, remained calm and clear-headed at all the vital moments.

Sergio Tognetti's chapter was translated by Kate Lowe and Didier Lahon's by Jane Jones and T. F. Earle.

Notes on the text

Please note that as this book engages with a subject that has only recently been considered of universal interest, the terminology is still emergent. It has been influenced in the past by different 'national' traditions, and translation of some of these terms into English is approximate. There has also been discussion about the significance and import of some of these European labels. Occasionally choices have had to be made in the interests of clarity; an example of this is the word 'slave', which has been used throughout (even though the word 'captive' is often preferred by Iberian scholars). Sometimes we have been forced to choose what appears to be the least bad option, and on this basis – in the absence of a better alternative – we are using 'mulatto' to describe a person of mixed black and white parentage. This is the Anglicised version of the Portuguese and Spanish word *mulato*, which was often used to mean 'mule' in the fifteenth and sixteenth centuries. Although its depreciative quality when applied to human beings at the time is obvious, we of course have stripped away any sense of that in our usage.

A variety of different words could signify a black African or person of African descent in fifteenth- and sixteenth-century documentation in Europe, and these varied according to locale and according to the level of knowledge of the person concerned. One major difficulty is that black people in Renaissance Europe were routinely distinguished according to their skin colour or their supposed religion rather than according to their place of birth or language, and consequently it is usually impossible to know (without additional documentation) whether an individual had been born in Africa and brought to Europe as a child or an adult, or was second generation and had been born in Europe. In the interests of keeping the word length of this book under control, the reader should understand that in most cases when the term 'black African' has been used, it could also denote a second-generation person of African descent.

The issue is further complicated by the use of Latin in some documents as opposed to the vernacular (Portuguese, Spanish, Italian etc.) in others, and conventions could differ between languages. Some words were (in some places) rather vague, and may or may not have denoted someone from sub-Saharan

Africa – for example, someone described as a *moro* (Moor) in many parts of Italy may or may not have been black. Even the phrase 'moro nero' might not have referred to a person from sub-Saharan Africa but to a dark-skinned North African. All over the Italian peninsula, however, the words 'moro negro' definitely referred to a black African. *Nero* as a noun did not necessarily denote a black African (although it often did, especially when used in opposition to bianco or white), but the noun *negro* always indicated a black African.

Portuguese also has two words meaning 'black', *negro* and *preto*. A correct writer, the historian João de Barros, using a formal register, never used *preto* to mean a black human being or animal – it was applied only to inanimate objects. In informal language *preto* did refer to people and was depreciative, as it still is today, because it emphasised blackness rather than humanity. In Spain, precise meaning varied from place to place: for example, in Valencia, the word *moro* signified a North African Moor, and *negre* was the word consistently used for a black African, whereas in Granada the word *negro* could include (amongst other groups) both sub-Saharan and North Africans.

Conversely, the word 'Ethiopian' in all the vernaculars and in Latin did not necessarily signify someone from Ethiopia but was more generally used to refer to someone with a black skin from Africa; the same is true of the phrase 'from Guinea' or people described as 'Guineans'. In Italian, someone described as an *africano* usually came from sub-Saharan Africa, but someone described as 'da Africa' (from Africa) could have come from any part of the continent. Finally, and still more confusingly for the uninitiated, other words whose meaning should have been fixed were also fluid and flexible, so that *indiani* in a Roman context could equally refer to either people from India or people from Ethiopia (the land of Prester John of the Indies). Given all this diversity, we have not attempted any standardization but have left it up to individual contributors to define their own terms and set the parameters of their own discussions. For further elucidation of some of these terms, please see the relevant discussion in Tognetti (pp. 217 and 219), Blumenthal (p. 229), Martín Casares (p. 248), Minnich (p. 282) and Brackett (p. 303).

Two further terms appear in some Italian notarial documents, making the distinction between a black African who was *selvaticus* (wild or savage, that is someone who came directly from Africa) and one who was *casanicus* (domesticated or home-born, that is someone who had been born in Europe). This may be correlated with the discussion of those people who only spoke African languages as opposed to those who spoke a European vernacular. The most commonly used term here for Africans who could not speak Portuguese was *boçal* (Spanish *bozal*) but the word could also be used adjectivally (and pejoratively), approximating to 'just off the boat' or 'straight from the bush'. Those black people who could only speak Portuguese or Spanish badly had their 'pidgin' described as 'fala de preto' or 'habla de negros'. For discussion and use of these terms, see Lawrance (pp. 72 and 83), Blumenthal (p. 230), Martín Casares (p. 251) and Earle (p. 346).

A final note is necessary about the numbers of black Africans in various parts of Europe in the fifteenth and the sixteenth centuries. This is a vexed question, but because of all the difficulties inherent in their study, it is highly unlikely that estimates will ever be very precise. Numbers were highest in Portugal and Spain. For estimates for Portugal, see Fonseca (pp. 115–16) and Jordan (p. 157), for estimates for Spain see Lawrance (p. 70) and Martín Casares (p. 250), and for some discussion of the situation in Valencia, see Blumenthal (p. 229). Elsewhere in Europe, numbers were considerably lower, but could still be significant.

Introduction: The black African presence in Renaissance Europe

KATE LOWE

The origins of this volume lie in my previous edited volume on *Cultural Links between Portugal and Italy in the Renaissance* (Oxford, 2000). While writing the introduction to that book, I thought I should include a few sentences on black Africans in fifteenth- and sixteenth-century Lisbon, and in the course of preliminary reading (some of which was kindly suggested by Annemarie Jordan), I realised that Lisbon was the tip of the iceberg as far as Europe as a whole was concerned, and that little work had been done on the subject anywhere (one notable exception in English is A. C. de C. M. Saunders, *A Social History of Black Slaves and Freedmen in Portugal, 1441–1555* (Cambridge, 1982), which was presciently ahead of its time). It was with this in mind that I conceived of the idea of a conference that tried to look at the subject from the vantage points of several European countries, and from differing interdisciplinary perspectives, and invited Tom Earle to join me as co-organiser, in order to have complementary specialisms on Renaissance Italian history and Renaissance Portuguese literature. The conference took place at St Peter's College, Oxford in September 2001, with 18 speakers, 5 each from the UK and the US, and 8 from mainland Europe. The range of disciplines centred on history, with 3 'ordinary' historians, 1 economic historian, 1 church historian and 2 cultural historians, but also included 3 art historians, 1 museum curator, 2 social anthropologists and 3 literature specialists. It is worth noting that although we were all Renaissance scholars, only some of the participants, notably Jorge Fonseca, Paul Kaplan, Aurelia Martín Casares, Didier Lahon and Baltasar Fra-Molinero, had been working and publishing on various aspects of the European history of black Africans for years, whereas others (including me) were relative newcomers to the field. The conference proved eye-opening in terms of the cross-country connections that could be made as well as in terms of recurrent interdisciplinary themes. We planned an edited volume from the beginning, and in the intervening period the participants have reworked and expanded their papers into chapters.

The present volume therefore concentrates on the greatly overlooked subject of the consequences (mainly for the Africans themselves but also for Europeans) of the introduction of considerable numbers of enslaved sub-Saharan Africans into Europe in the hundred and fifty years succeeding the so-called voyages of discovery, that is in a period very roughly co-terminous with the Renaissance. It is of course absurd to treat black Africans as a homogeneous group in the fifteenth and sixteenth centuries, just as it is absurd to talk of Europeans in the Renaissance period. These concepts only have value as oppositional or contrasting terms, which is how they are being used here. No such place as a generic 'black Africa' existed or exists; Africa was/is a vast continent, full of cultural, social, religious, linguistic and ethnic diversity, and of regional difference. But the process of removing Africans to Europe in the Renaissance period served to rob them of these distinguishing features, taking away their old, nuanced identities and providing them instead with new, one-dimensional European ones by labelling them all as 'black Africans'. Arrival in Europe as slaves meant the systematic erasure of all the more significant aspects of their past, starting with their names, their languages, their religions, their families and communities, and their cultural practices, but it did not erase their appearance. Hence the use of the term 'black Africans' and, in order to maintain parity of terminology, the use of the similarly non-existent construct 'Renaissance Europeans'.

Although the vast majority of black Africans in Renaissance Europe were slaves, it was perfectly possible for sub-Saharan Africans not to be slaves in fifteenth- and sixteenth-century Europe, and significant exceptions to the rule were African ambassadors and Ethiopian pilgrims (who benefited from Ethiopian churches and communities at Nicosia and Rome).[1] The possibility of manumission also always existed, and within a few years, the first of these Africans were freed, and communities of freed (but usually poverty-stricken) black Africans lived cheek-by-jowl with the constantly renewed larger numbers of black African slaves. Yet the words Renaissance and sub-Saharan African appear to have no obvious connection; indeed, it could be argued that they stand in almost complete opposition to each other. But the reality may be more complex. For example, while it may be true that (although the Renaissance was a period in which great store was set on literacy) most non-literate, enslaved West Africans transported to Europe received no education and therefore remained non-literate, this volume highlights several sub-Saharan Africans in Renaissance Europe with varying degrees of literacy and literary ability. The chapter by Jordan adverts to a black African who could

---

[1] On Rome, see P. Mauro da Leonessa, *Santo Stefano Maggiore degli Abissini e le relazioni romano-etiopiche* (Città del Vaticano, 1929), and on Nicosia, Renato Lefevre, 'Roma e la comunità etiopica di Cipro nei secoli XV e XVI', *Annali Lateranensi*, 11 (1947), pp. 277–94.

sign his name, that by Fonseca mentions black Africans who were taught Latin, and those by Fra-Molinero and Earle signal black African writers. It is our intention in this volume to consider this seemingly troubled juxtaposition by examining how the variety and complexity of black African life in Europe between 1440 and 1600 was affected by Renaissance ideas (including firmly held classical and medieval preconceptions relating to the African continent and its inhabitants) and Renaissance conditions. In other words, we want to understand why the reception of black Africans was as it was in Renaissance Europe.

At first glance, it might seem astonishing that the black African presence has been so completely ignored. The reasons for this are manifold, but an absence of material is not one of them. Far from being genuinely invisible, the traces of these fifteenth- and sixteenth-century black Africans can be found in almost every type of record: documentary, textual and visual; secular and ecclesiastical; Northern and Southern European; factual and fictional. The reasons for their perceived invisibility lie elsewhere, in the realities of national politics, in the still-evolving effects of European colonisation and in the straightjacket of fashionable or acceptable historical scholarship. The long history of black African settlement in many parts of Europe was denied for political and racial reasons, and the topic was successfully buried until the end of the twentieth century. So in general and with a few high profile exceptions, although copious material existed, each archival reference or image relating to black Africans in Europe brought into the public domain was treated as an isolated case. The fiction that not much material existed on this topic was aided by the nationalistic practices of European historians. European countries have tended to write their own history or the history of their major cities or areas, and it is very rare for problems to be studied in any depth on a European basis. In any case, non-nationals (or those viewed as outsiders) would not have been included even in national studies. Occasional historical studies that include sections on black Africans in the fifteenth and sixteenth centuries have emerged from Portugal[2] and the discrete parts of Spain,[3] the

[2] See, e.g., Pedro de Azevedo, 'Os Escravos', *Archivo Histórico Portuguez*, 1 (1903), pp. 289–307, and António Brásio, *Os Pretos em Portugal* (Lisbon, 1944), published by the Agência Geral das Colónias. More recently, José Ramos Tinhorão, *Os Negros em Portugal. Uma Presença Silenciosa* (Lisbon, 1988) was an important book.

[3] See, e.g., José Ramos y Loscertales, *Estudios sobre el derecho de gentes en la Baja Edad Media. El cautiverio en la Corona de Aragon durante los siglos XIII, XIIV y XV* (Saragossa, 1915), Antonio Domínguez Ortiz, 'La esclavitud en Castilla durante la Edad Moderna', in C. Viñas y Mey, ed., *Estudios de historia social de España*, 5 vols. (Madrid, 1949–60), and Vicenta Cortes, *La esclavitud en Valencia durante el reinado de los Reyes Católicos (1479–1516)* (Valencia, 1964).

two areas with the largest black populations, but usually in the context of examining slavery in these countries. However, these studies have been against the grain, and indeed until very recently most received little attention, because while the institution of slavery was considered worthy of investigation and analysis – as were slaves as objects – slaves as people were not thought to have enough agency to be suitably valuable research subjects during much of the nineteenth and twentieth centuries. Certainly in this respect cultural power – the power to define others – was indubitably linked to the political power to dominate, and the continuation and expansion of the European colonisation of Africa in the twentieth century was obviously detrimental to an interest in the study of enslaved sub-Saharan Africans in fifteenth- and sixteenth-century Europe.

Each discipline has its own internal rules and rhythms, and much more research on black Africans in fifteenth- and sixteenth-century Europe has focused on their representation in art and literature than on their historical realities, with Othello and the dramatic representation of Africans,[4] images of the black Magus[5] and Golden Age Spanish literature[6] receiving particular attention. The series of books on *The Image of the Black in Western Art*, sponsored by the Menil Foundation in Paris,[7] was very influential in flagging avenues that could profitably be explored (and Kaplan and Seelig have written on symbolic representations of black Africans). It is always pleasanter to dwell on those in positions of power than to confront slavery, which is precisely why the phenomenon of European slavery is often played down or obliterated. Politics have intruded here too, because the Fascist pasts of many European countries in the twentieth century (and their concomitant racist views) have precluded or impeded 'objective' scholarship for long periods of time. But the connections between these often slightly glamorous representations and real Africans have not been explored at any level. It has not helped that most black Africans who were not slaves were poor, and the poor until relatively recently were also not considered a topic that would respond well to scholarly investigation.

While they are not at all invisible, it cannot be denied that carrying out research on black African individuals in Renaissance Europe does

---

[4] See, e.g., Elliott H. Tokson, *The Popular Image of the Black Man in English Drama, 1550–1688* (Boston, 1982).

[5] E.g., Paul H. D. Kaplan, *The Rise of the Black Magus in Western Art* (Ann Arbor, 1985).

[6] E.g., Baltasar Fra Molinero, *La imagen de los negros en el teatro del Siglo de Oro* (Madrid, 1995).

[7] Ladislas Bugner (general ed.), *The Image of the Black in Western Art*, 4 vols. in 6 tomes (New York, 1976 – Houston, 1979).

present certain difficulties, mainly related to the combined 'drawbacks' of enforced Christianisation, legalised inferiority, fifteenth- and sixteenth-century European inability to appreciate cultural difference, and a preoccupation with differences in skin colour. The most obvious difficulties stem from naming practices. The vast majority of black Africans were renamed at the start of their new lives in Europe, although a small minority managed not to be.[8] When they were baptised, they were given Christian names (usually from a small pool of the commoner saints' names) (see Jordan, chapter 7, and Tognetti, chapter 9). Many slaves or freed black Africans never graduated to possessing surnames, which also hampers secure identification. Most black Africans were slaves, and consequently were recorded as the possessions of other people. One of the most basic 'rights' enjoyed by slave owners was that of naming their slaves, and their naming practices often obfuscate the historical record, for a further tranch of slaves were given exactly the same names, both first names and surnames, as their owners, presumably so that their ownership was in no doubt. When sold to a new owner, they took the new owner's surname. This practice may have been a precursor to that whereby servants were known by the family surname. The effect was to make it very difficult to distinguish between master and slave in a document except through context. Precisely the same mindset and process were responsible for the naming of the Congolese 'royal family' and nobility: when the Manicongo (the Congolese 'king') Nzinga Nkuwu and his 'queen' were converted to Christianity and baptised in 1491, they took the names of the king and queen of Portugal, D. João and D. Leonor, their children were given other Portuguese royal names, and their relations and chiefs took the names of members of the Portuguese nobility.[9] As well as signalling a hierarchical relationship in Europe, taking or being given an identical name to a patron or owner was obviously construed as a sign of respect to the socially superior party.

Another huge problem in terms of identifying and tracing black Africans arises because most Europeans in the fifteenth and sixteenth centuries were completely incapable of distinguishing between different parts and traditions

---

[8] See José Leite de Vasconcellos, *Antroponímia Portuguesa: Tratado Comparativo da Origem, Significação, Classificação e Vida do Conjunto dos Nomes Próprios, Sobrenomes, e Apelidos, Usados por nós Desde a Idade-média até Hoje* (Lisbon, 1928), pp. 368–74 for servant and slave names in fifteenth- and sixteenth-century Portugal, and P. E. H. Hair, 'Black African slaves at Valencia, 1482–1516: an onomastic enquiry', *History in Africa*, 7 (1980), pp. 119–39 on black African slaves' names on arrival at Valencia in the late fifteenth and early sixteenth centuries.

[9] António Brásio, ed., *História do Reino do Congo (MS 8080 da Biblioteca Nacional de Lisboa)* (Lisbon, 1969), pp. 66–71.

of the African continent. European ignorance of Africa was almost complete, and very few Europeans at this date had ever been to sub-Saharan Africa. To the majority of Europeans, the defining feature of Africans was their skin colour, and nothing else – whether area of origin,[10] religion or previous occupation – mattered, and consequently nothing else was recorded. Without clearly differentiated names and without other identifying markers, descriptions of skin colour take on a paramount importance. However, as stated in the Notes on the text (pp. xv–xvii), the terminology of both outsider status and skin pigmentation was fluid and imprecise, and most of the time it is impossible to find out if the *moro* discussed (as it were) in a letter in February 1486 is the same person as the *nero* recorded in a will of 1494. These difficulties are a further reason why research into representations of black Africans (where these difficulties do not exist) is more advanced than studies of their lives.

An informed understanding of the black African presence in Renaissance Europe is vitally important to many cultural and historical narratives for a number of reasons. It is important for Africans and Europeans because it focuses on the moment when significant numbers of black Africans were first transported into Europe, and it is therefore legitimate to search here for the beginnings of individual and institutional prejudice and discrimination, as well as for the beginnings of acceptance of difference, successful assimilation and the first attempts at formulating black perspectives and creating black identities among communities in Europe. It is important for Americans searching for the antecedents of the inhumanity of American and Caribbean plantation slavery. And it is important to everybody, because it is such a crucial, early episode of black African diasporic history.

The four sections of the book correspond to four distinct areas worthy of investigation, but there are many others. It seems more worthwhile to comment on a few themes raised across these sections rather than reiterate individual contributors' findings. The first question to be addressed (and the most frequently asked question by those outside the field) is whether 'racism' in any generally accepted contemporary sense existed in fifteenth- and sixteenth-century Europe, a period in which the modern concept of 'race' is not generally believed to have been formulated.[11] As the reader will see, forms of 'racism'

---

[10] Aurelia Martín Casares, *La esclavitud en la Granada del siglo XVI: género, raza y religion* (Granada, 2000), pp. 151–5 considers the places of origin and ethnographies of sub-Saharan African slaves in Granada in the sixteenth century.

[11] Different disciplines take different views on this matter. See *The William and Mary Quarterly*, third series, 54: 1 (1997) devoted to 'Constructing race: differentiating peoples in the early modern world'.

are discussed by several contributors (notably Lowe, Lawrance, Korhonen, Fonseca, Lahon, Brackett and Earle) and alluded to by several others, and various answers are posited. It is of course not really the right question, because scientific racism (which is the starting point for most modern discussions of racism) was not articulated fully until the nineteenth century, and therefore technically the answer is clearly no. It seems preferable to adopt an approach that does not read the present onto an historical situation but also that does not ignore the fact that there is something very familiar about the scenarios under discussion.

It does however seem clear that African ancestry and possession of a black skin led directly to all sorts of differentiation, prejudice and discrimination, and most of the contributors have signalled their interest in these historical forms of differentiation (evinced for whatever reason and with whatever attempt at justification) between Africans and Europeans. It should be stated immediately that differentiation of various sorts was also commonplace with regard to various other minority groups, often on the basis of religion (e.g. Muslims and Jews) and ethnicity (marginal Europeans such as peoples from around the Black Sea, and other non-Europeans, such as Amerindians and Japanese). There are two points to be made here about differentiation relating to black Africans. The first concerns processes of differentiation, and the second moments of differentiation.

There were two major, defining processes of differentiation for black Africans in Europe at this time. The first was a legal differentiation that had meaning for all new captives transported from sub-Saharan Africa – slave status was enshrined in law across Europe. In most areas, Roman law definitions and restrictions on slave rights and behaviour were already in operation, and were not modified when the changeover from a mostly white slave class to a majority black slave class occurred. However in some countries, for example, in Portugal under King Manuel, new legal codes were introduced aimed specifically at legislating for circumstances arising from the new influx and population of slaves. The royal legislation on slavery enacted between 1481 and 1514 was collected and included in the *Ordenações Manuelinas*, first published in 1514, with a definitive edition of 1521.[12] Legalised inferiority was therefore a very basic and very potent process of differentiation for black African slaves. A second defining process of differentiation was cultural (it could apply to either enslaved or free Africans), and took place because

---

[12] A. C. de C. M. Saunders, *A Social History of Black Slaves and Freedmen in Portugal, 1441–1555* (Cambridge, 1982), pp. 113–33, esp. 113–14.

of European late medieval and (particularly) Renaissance notions of civilisation and barbarism. The European definition of civilisation depended upon an Aristotelian typology for assessing alien people, and dividing them into the civilised and the barbarian. Civilised people could be distinguished from barbarian people on the basis of a number of factors concerning hierarchical structure, social organisation and collective memory, made manifest by the construction of civil society in the guise of the foundation of cities, the establishment and implementation of written laws, the existence of written histories, adherence to rules governing inheritance and the institution of marriage, correct commercial relations and the use of clothes as differing status indicators.[13] In general, this exclusive Aristotelian taxonomy allowed Europe to categorise itself (and its inhabitants) as civilised and Africa (and its inhabitants) as uncivilised, but even when evidence was found in (for example) the Congo of many of these Aristotelian prerequisites, the taxonomy could be ignored and Europeans could still define the Congloese as barbarians. A very immediate and obvious difference that allowed the process of cultural differentiation to be set in train was the difference in skin colour between Europeans and sub-Saharan Africans.

In addition to distinguishing between various processes of differentiation, it is salutary to examine moments of differentiation between black Africans and white Europeans in the Renaissance. Some of the most crippling of these for black Africans were highlighted by formal and informal exclusionary practices. For example, certain formal exclusionary work practices had the force of law, such as guild regulations that sometimes, as in the charter of the goldsmiths of Lisbon, forbade the inclusion of slaves; the charter of the pie-makers of Lisbon, however, banned slaves and free Moriscos but allowed free and Christian black Africans and mulattos to be considered for inclusion.[14] Informal exclusionary practices appear to have been routinely practiced by the Catholic Church, both in relation to sub-Saharan Africans in Africa and to black Africans in Europe, so that in the fifteenth and sixteenth centuries there is a dearth of black priests, monks or nuns (who were not lay brothers and sisters) (see Minnich, chapter thirteen), only one black African bishop, the Congolese D. Henrique (who was ordained as bishop of Utica on the understanding that he could not have a European diocese or flock, but 'only' an African one), and no black cardinal. The first black saint – known as San

---

[13] Jeremy Lawrance, 'The Middle Indies: Damião de Góis on Prester John and the Ethiopians', *Renaissance Studies*, 6 (1992), pp. 306–24 at 322–3.

[14] Saunders, *A Social History*, pp. 74–5.

Benedetto il moro – lived in the sixteenth century but was not canonised until 1807.[15]

The detail that no marriage alliances were concluded between African and European rulers in this time period is also an indication of differential practices, as alliances were concluded between the ruling houses of virtually all European powers. As far as is known, the question of marriage was only raised on two occasions. A pair of marriage alliances (involving a reciprocal double marriage) was proposed between the ruler of Aragon, King Alfonso V, and the ruler of Ethiopia, the emperor Ishaq, in 1428: Ishaq was to marry Alfonso's sister, Joana d'Urgell, and the Infante Don Pedro was to marry an unspecified Ethiopian princess. Whether these proposals were ever a concrete reality is unclear, but for unknown reasons nothing came of them.[16] A letter from Queen Eleni of Ethiopia to King Manuel, probably in the second decade of the sixteenth century, also suggested marriages between their sons and daughters, without being more specific.[17] Black African slaves (and in many cases freed black Africans) were also very often excluded from common welfare and a common humanity by being denied access to marriage, family and community. Other moments of differentiation can be observed when white Europeans and black Africans came into competition with each other, whether in terms of occupation, or as witnesses giving testimony, or as sexual partners. Finally, much can be learnt from moments when casual differentiation is turned on its head, such as in the offhand comment Olivares made to Philip II of Spain when reporting an audience of Pope Sixtus V with the English cardinal William Allen in 1588: 'he treated him like a black man'.[18] All these processes and moments of differentiation expose the fact that differential behaviour based upon perceived difference (of whatever sort) was the norm in Renaissance Europe. Both Elizabeth I's letter and warrant of July 1596 and her proclamation of January 1601 ordering the expulsion of all black Africans (described as 'Blackmoores', 'Blackamoores' and 'Negroes') from England,[19] and the introduction of the concept of 'purity of blood' (*limpieza de sangre*) that

[15] On S. Benedetto il moro's canonisation saga, see Giovanna Fiume and Marilena Modica, eds., *San Benedetto il moro: santità, agiografia e primi processi di canonizzazione* (Palermo, 1998).

[16] Peter P. Garretson, 'A note on relations between Ethiopia and the Kingdom of Aragon in the fifteenth century', *Rassegna di studi etiopici*, 37 (1993), pp. 37–44, esp. 41–2.

[17] Sergew Hable-Selassie, 'The Ge'ez letters of Queen Eleni and Libne Dingil to John, King of Portugal', in *IV Congresso internazionale di studi etiopici*, 2 vols. (Rome, 1974), I, pp. 547–66 at 557 and 566.

[18] *The Letters and Memorials of William Cardinal Allen (1532–1594)* ed. by Fathers of the Congregation of the London Oratory (London, 1882), p. 309: 'le trato como a un negro'. I am gratful to Stefan Bauer for this reference.

[19] Peter Fryer, *Staying Power: The History of Black People in Britain* (London, 1984), pp. 10–12.

took hold on the Iberian peninsula in the sixteenth century,[20] relied heavily upon already accepted antecedents.

The part skin colour played in this differentiation was crucial for sub-Saharan Africans.[21] In the intensely status-conscious and hierarchical societies of fifteenth-century Europe, powerful stereotypical representations of the 'other' (the Jew, the Moor, the African) were already elaborately crafted from classical and medieval sources (see Massing, chapter 2), and it is not difficult to locate the sub-Saharan African within this taxonomy. Later, Jews and black Africans may have clashed over their place in this pecking order (see Earle, chapter 16), as happened in other eras and situations when two 'immigrant' communities competed for resources and survival. However, what must have been truly remarkable was the unprecedented spectacle of 'blackness' (see Korhonen, chapter 4), presented first at Portuguese ports and later at Spanish ones when the first shipments of black Africans started to arrive in the 1440s (see Lahon, chapter 12). The reality of blackness swept away some previous notions about black skin and reinforced and transformed others. African blackness was at that moment presented in a peculiarly reductive and pre-emptive way. The Portuguese royal chronicler Gomes Eanes de Zurara, writing c. 1453–4, has left an eye-witness account (probably an amalgam of a lost narrative of Afonso Cerveira and his own memory of slave auctions)[22] of the landing of the first sizeable group of black Africans – about 250 – at Lagos in the Algarve on 8 August 1444.[23] Even allowing for the superlatives of rhetorical convention, the homecoming scene enacting the consequences of conquest was extraordinary. The local inhabitants were given a holiday from work and were encouraged to play their part in the spectacle by being the awed audience. The captive, conquered black Africans were virtually or completely naked, and in chains. The free, triumphant white Portuguese separated their human booty into five equal groups, in the process dividing family units, whereupon the Africans began to scream and cry, and some began an African chant. Zurara and the audience of the day supposedly were moved by

---

[20] On this, see Albert A. Sicroff, *Les controversies des statuts de "pureté de sang" en Espagne du XVe au XVIIe siècle* (Paris, 1960), esp. pp. 63–139.

[21] See Steven A. Epstein, *Speaking of Slavery: Color, Ethnicity and Human Bondage in Italy* (Ithaca and London, 2001), p. 108 for a discussion of the range of skin colours used to describe fourteenth-century slaves in Florence.

[22] On Zurara's account, see Peter Russell, *Prince Henry 'the Navigator': A Life* (New Haven and London, 2000), pp. 239–45.

[23] Gomes Eanes de Zurara, *Crónica dos Feitos Notáveis que se Passaram na Conquista da Guiné por Mandado do Infante D. Henrique*, ed. Torquato de Sousa Soares, 2 vols. (Lisbon, 1978–81), ch. 25, II, pp. 145–8.

the Africans' suffering (although Zurara analysed it in terms of fate), but the behaviour of Lançarote da Ilha, the commander of the slave raid and royal tax-collector in Lagos, was reinforced when Prince Henrique spontaneously knighted him on the field where the scene had unfolded.[24] The message could not have been clearer: it was not only permissible but right for Europeans to capture and enslave black Africans, and to treat them in an inhuman way; it was also financially rewarding and led directly to royal favours. This textual representation of 'blackness' and rendition of the place of black Africans in European society forcefully articulated a link between Africa, black skin and slavery that was to take hundreds of years to uncouple.

Nevertheless, 'blackness' proved a slippery concept for Europeans who already believed that some of their own number (for example, Southern Italians) were dark-skinned and consequently less than ideal. There were many gradations of 'white' just as there were many varieties of 'black', and classification of these often subtle differences could be challenging. Zurara classified the 1444 Lagos arrivals into three different shades of skin colour – white, mulatto and black – although how he achieved this classification is less transparent.[25] Contradictory notions about the value of a black skin can be found across Renaissance Europe – most of the time a lighter skin meant a higher price for a slave (see Tognetti, chapter 9), but occasionally a knowledgeable owner at a court requested a slave with the blackest possible skin (see Kaplan, chapter 6) – usually inflected by considerations of social status and function. The appearance of significant numbers of people of mixed African and European descent in Europe (mulattos) from the mid-fifteenth century onwards, as a consequence of the Portuguese slave trade with West Africa, was another novel feature that complicated the issue, demanding new reactions and presenting new skin shades. It also presented new legal dilemmas if one of the couple was free or freed. According to Roman law,[26] the legal status of the child followed that of the mother. According to the Florentine statutes of 1415, however, if a free man impregnated another person's slave, although the father was obliged to pay the costs of food and the birth, and to pay compensation to the owner, the child was to have the free legal status of its father rather than the slave status of its mother.[27] And in social terms, were people of mixed descent to be treated in a similar way to their white

---

[24] Zurara, *Crónica*, ch. 25, II, pp. 152–3.   [25] Zurara, *Crónica*, ch. 25, II, p. 146.

[26] On the vital question of how people became slaves (including by being born to a slave mother), see W. W. Buckland, *The Roman Law of Slavery: The Condition of the Slave in Private Law from Augustus to Justinian* (Cambridge, 1908), pp. 397–436.

[27] Thomas Kuehn, *Illegitimacy in Renaissance Florence* (Ann Arbor, 2002), p. 79.

parents or to their black parents (or more concisely but less accurately as white Europeans or black Africans)? And how much was their treatment a result of their skin colour and how much a result of acknowledgement of paternity and status?

Black skin also elicited considerable discussion as to its causes. For example, debates concerning the reason for black skin abounded both among intellectual elites and within popular culture,[28] without resolution, as an understanding of skin pigmentation lay in the future. It is instructive, too, to examine jokes or puns in connection with naming practices and to investigate white nicknames for people of African descent in Europe. It appears to have been considered humorous to give black Africans the 'surname' Blanco or White or a variation of it (see Lowe, chapter 1, and Martín Casares, chapter 11), and to invent nicknames for black slaves that alluded to their skin colour, such as Nerone and Moretto. Presumably the joke lay in the very visible 'mistake' which was obvious to everybody, but which the African was humiliatingly forced to repeat and internalise. But at least all this talk and observation of 'blackness' may have forced some Europeans to ponder what their own 'whiteness' signified.

A further important issue is the relationship between Christianity and slavery, and between conversion (forced or genuine) to Christianity and the attainment of freedom. Although occasional individual popes criticised the slave trade, the Catholic church as a general rule gave its blessing to the trade in humans, albeit with minimal restrictions. In 1455 Pope Nicholas V in his papal bull *Romanus pontifex* pronounced that it was permissible to acquire black Africans from Guinea as long as efforts for their conversion were made,[29] and Zurara mouthed the church's line when he constantly justified the Portuguese enslavement of West Africans on religious grounds, as he did in the scene described previously. Conversely, popes decreed that people who were already Christians should not be enslaved (see Minnich, chapter 13), although in practice the Christianity of Orthodox Christians from the Eastern Mediterranean and around the Black Sea seems to have been considered of little value, as they were frequently enslaved by Southern Europeans in the centuries up to 1450 (see Tognetti, chapter 9). With the advent of large numbers of black African

---

[28] William McKee Evans, 'From the land of Canaan to the land of Guinea: the strange odyssey of the "Sons of Ham" ', *American Historical Review*, 85 (1980), pp. 15–43, and Benjamin Braude, 'The sons of Noah and the construction of ethnic and geographical identities in the medieval and modern periods', *The William and Mary Quarterly*, third series, 54: 1 (1997), pp. 103–42.

[29] Antonio Joaquim Dinis OFM, ed., *Monumenta Henricina*, 15 vols. (Coimbra, 1960–74), XII, pp. 72–9 esp. 76–7.

slaves, the contours of those defined as being inside the community (who therefore could not be enslaved) changed, and further adjustments ensued to legitimise the enslavement of people of African descent born in England, and those of mixed African and European descent.[30]

It may be useful to recap schematically a black African's trajectory from slave to freed person in relation to their standing in the Christian church,[31] although there was significant regional variation. When enslaved 'pagans' and Muslims converted to Christianity, the fact that they had been baptised was not sufficient to free them. Some slaves believed that it should have been (see Minnich, chapter 13), but the ecclesiastical authorities did not agree. In general, the owner of a slave was entitled to financial compensation if a slave were freed, but even when suitable funds were available, the owner could refuse to allow the freedom of her/his baptised slave to be purchased. In several Southern European cities, including Granada (see Martín Casares, chapter 11) and Valencia (see Blumenthal, chapter 10), there were black confraternities (usually Dominican) that tried to raise the money necessary to negotiate the release of various slaves. But only in Lisbon was there for a period a black confraternity – composed of both slaves and freed people – whose members could, in specified circumstances, demand the manumission of black slaves, and this special right was hotly contested by the slave owners, who campaigned successfully for this privilege to be rescinded (see Lahon, chapter 12).

Another important issue is that of identity. Sub-Saharan Africans were captured, enslaved, and transported to Europe against their will, where their 'Africanity' was constantly used against them. Over time, their identities became more and more blurred (or took on more and more 'European' features), as they came to grips with new countries and cultures, learnt to speak new languages (see Lawrance, chapter 3), engaged with new occupations, had children from/with European partners, and sometimes gained their freedom. It was only to be expected that familiarity with aspects of European life and culture would allow black Africans to circumvent the worst excesses of stereotyping or prejudice. But the speed with which newly-arrived black Africans adapted to European institutions and legal systems, and became skilled at organising their own confraternities for the good of the black communities and at fighting cases of injustice through the courts (see Blumenthal, chapter 10, and Lahon, chapter 12) is also noteworthy, and indicative of great adaptability and enterprise. Black Africans who were transported to Europe as children

---

[30] Cf. Alessandro Stella, *Histoire d'esclaves dans la péninsule ibérique* (Paris, 2000), pp. 27–42.

[31] This paragraph was suggested by one of the anonymous readers for Cambridge University Press.

and second-generation Africans and mulattos born in Europe obviously felt sufficiently at home to create their own images of themselves and to use their identities to challenge directly or indirectly European notions of hierarchy (see chapters by Lowe, Brackett, Fra-Molinero, Earle).

A final point concerns future directions for research. It is our hope that the present volume will start the ball rolling by showing some of the possibilities for historical research, and by stimulating and encouraging others to follow in our footsteps. More original research is needed across the board but – in my opinion – two areas appear particularly likely to yield good results. First, collaboration between historians of fifteenth- and sixteenth-century Europe and historians of fifteenth- and sixteenth-century West Africa would greatly increase our understanding of black African cultural history in Europe, and allow a much more nuanced calibration of cultural life. The second is that it would be helpful to have an intensification of historical investigation centring on those records which, for all their drawbacks, both allowed some notional black African voices to be heard, and permitted some recreation of the biographical details of black Africans in Europe (for example, some trial documentation (civil, criminal and Inquisitorial) and confraternity records, or some exceptional data such as the documents of the Bailía in Valencia).[32] Recognising the black African presence in Renaissance Europe in all its complexities necessitates archival, textual and visual investigations that move the discourse beyond the methodologies and conceptualisations that have forged both the canon of Renaissance scholarship and current studies of the African diaspora.

---

[32] Vicenta Cortes, *La esclavitud en Valencia durante el reinado de los Reyes Católicos (1479–1516)* (Valencia, 1964), pp. 217–471.

PART ONE

Conceptualising black Africans

The stereotyping of black Africans in Renaissance Europe

KATE LOWE

This chapter is concerned with the patterns of reasoning whereby black Africans in Renaissance Europe were categorised or stereotyped in a variety of ways, and with the practical consequences of this stereotyping. The original English meaning of the word stereotype was a printing plate cast from a mould, and the secondary (and much more widespread) figurative use is of an unduly fixed mental impression. At a more theoretical level, most discussions of stereotyping start with Gordon Allport's 1954 definition: 'an exaggerated belief associated with a category . . . [whose] function is to justify (rationalize) our conduct in relation to that category'.[1] This definition introduces the two main aspects of stereotyping which will be discussed here. The first is that stereotyping does not allow differentiation between individuals within a category, thus leading to automatic and unthinking reactions. The second is that the process of justifying exaggerated beliefs can cause even a positive stereotype to have negative implications.

Although stereotypes relating to black Africans undoubtedly existed before the Renaissance,[2] it appears to have been detrimental to the European perception of the black African that the first sustained influx of black African slaves into Europe, and the consequent change from the widespread use of white slaves[3] to the widespread use of black slaves within Europe, took place at this momentous time of white, European self-definition. The first cargoes of captured or sold black Africans were taken from the West coast of Africa to

---

I should like to thank Sydney Anglo, Ian Bavington Jones, Trevor Dean, Tim Duke, Tom Earle, Paulla Ebron, Michael Fend, Jan Piet Filedt Kok, Annemarie Jordan, Amanda Lillie and Eugene McLaughlin for their help in the preparation of this chapter. I am using the constructs 'black African' and 'Renaissance European' in a similar fashion to how they were used in the introduction.

[1] Gordon W. Allport, *The Nature of Prejudice* (Boston, 1954), p. 191.

[2] See, e.g., Lloyd A. Thompson, *Romans and Blacks* (London and Oklahoma, 1989), esp. pp. 86–156. Frank M. Snowden, Jr has an altogether rosier view: *Blacks in Antiquity: Ethiopians in the Graeco-Roman Experience* (Cambridge, MA, 1970) and *Before Color Prejudice: the Ancient View of Blacks* (Cambridge, MA, and London, 1983).

[3] Iris Origo, 'The domestic enemy: the Eastern slaves in Tuscany in the fourteenth and fifteenth centuries', *Speculum*, 30 (1955), pp. 321–66.

Portugal in the 1440s, and the subsequent 100 to 150 years witnessed record numbers of sub-Saharan Africans uprooted and transported to Europe to be slaves. It was precisely at this juncture that the whole idea of civilisation became critical to the European self-image, that certain European notions of civilisation hardened into belief systems, and that various sets of European behaviours were labelled as civilised and various other sets of non-European behaviour were (by contrast) labelled as uncivilised. The exact chronology of this hardening and labelling, and its relationship to the physical 'discoveries' both of black Africa and of the Americas and to the categorisation of their indigenous populations, has not been sufficiently examined. However, the intention here is rather to investigate one very significant and long-lived outcome of this process: how the stereotyping of black Africans was used in Renaissance Europe – verbally, textually and visually – as an analytical category that excluded sub-Saharan Africans from much of mainstream European life and culture during that period. This process was multi-layered and had many components, in addition to the obvious one of standardised inferiority imposed by the condition of slavery. It is also of interest that occasionally black Africans, by conforming to Renaissance norms of dress and behaviour, and appearing to assimilate to European cultural life, may have been able to neutralise these stereotypes and both project themselves, and be accepted, as 'honorary' Europeans, who just happened to have black skin.

The sources used in this chapter are from a wide variety of different cultural contexts – including travel journals and descriptions, costume books, fiscal, legal and notarial records, genre and court paintings, joke collections, and books on behaviour – in order to try and circumvent some of the difficulties inherent in studying people who have moved from an oral to a literate culture. The images have been chosen for their verifiably high degree of detail and 'accuracy' in terms of dress and circumstances, in the belief that the black Africans represented in them are similarly carefully depicted and can be taken as a good approximation of 'reality'; wherever possible, visual descriptions have been backed up by documentation.

It is clear first of all that crucial aspects of this stereotyping can be found in fifteenth- and sixteenth-century reports by Europeans on voyages to Africa. Contemporary Europeanists are aware that these reports are very 'flawed', and that the descriptions of African behaviour (for example) often succeed merely in showing just how limited Europeans were as observers of non-European societies and as analysts of non-European behaviours. The absence of written records by fifteenth- and sixteenth-century Africans, which could have served to counteract and correct the European descriptions, compounds these problems. However, the necessary next step of trying to integrate what is known about West African societies in these centuries[4] with what is known about the black Africans reduced to slavery in Europe has not taken place, and most European Renaissance historians remain woefully ignorant of African historical cultures and traditions. In addition to highlighting and explaining difference, integration of these two distinct bodies of knowledge would also draw attention to similarities, and could lead to new slants on the processes of stereotyping. It is likely that the bunching of a proportion of skilled black Africans in certain occupations in Europe is as much a reflection of the fact that these skills were valued in African society and had already been acquired there as a reflection that they were considered and labelled as suitable or acceptable skills for black Africans in Europe. It is commonly accepted that very little can be known of the background of black Africans reduced to slavery in Renaissance Europe, but (for example) some of the high numbers of musicians may be traceable to certain West African courts. It may be possible to link European accounts of slave raids in these areas and descriptions of the capture of whole courts to the arrival of some of these musicians in Europe, and their documentation in European records. While these thoughts have to remain at the level of speculation, this type of speculation serves a valuable purpose in stressing that black Africans transported as slaves had a life prior to their arrival in Europe, and that the tenor of this life, and its subsequent absorption into a stereotype, should be considered wherever possible.

Much of the stereotyping of Africans that took place in Renaissance Europe should also be placed in the context of the changes in cultural meaning that occurred during the physical displacement from Africa to Europe. Actions and behaviours imbued with neutral or positive meanings in African settings were routinely assigned negative ones in European settings. The most pertinent question here seems to be: why was there a 'European-wide' reaction? How is it possible that different European peoples with different cultural traditions reacted in overwhelmingly similar ways to the arrival of black Africans? One answer is because they perceived them to be in opposition to the particularly Renaissance vision of white, European culture and civilisation. In an attempt to investigate this European phenomenon, this chapter will analyse specimen material from across much of Europe, but it will include many documentary examples from Italy, in line with my specialisation in Italian history.

---

[4] See, e.g., Barbara Winston Blackman, ' "From time immemorial": historicism in the court art of Benin, Nigeria', in Christian Heck and Kristen Lippincott, eds., *Symbols of Time in the History of Art* (Turnhout, 2002), pp. 27–39.

The first cluster of stereotypes centres upon the appearance of black Africans. Most obviously and unavoidably, sub-Saharan Africans were set apart by their skin colour, causing them to be characterised first and foremost as non-European 'others', and to be described in opposition to the defining characteristics of white, European appearance. There were many different variations of black skin colour across the African continent, and many different phenotypic traits, but in Europe these differences were elided. A so-called black skin was almost uniformly condemned, and it was impossible for black Africans to escape from the negative implications of their skin colour.[5] Black and the devil were firmly allied in the popular imagination; in folklore beliefs, stories and sayings about people with 'black' skin provided a cultural context for prejudice, and sneezing when a black African appeared was in Spain a primitive practice for warding off the devil.[6] Perhaps the easiest way to begin to understand what this stereotyping with regard to skin colour might have entailed is to realise that manumission could not free black Africans from slavery because society at large equated black skin colour (of whatever hue) with slavery, and many freed ex-slaves were apprehended as fugitives and were forced to negotiate their freedom all over again through the courts. As most slaves were non-literate and were operating within a culture that set a particular premium on literacy and legal documentation, the odds of obtaining freedom a second time were stacked against them, and only a handful managed. For instance, a Lucchese notarial document of 5 March 1470 reveals the case of a black female bought for 52 florins from a Lucchese broker in Palermo by an artisan in Lucca. She protested that not only had she been born free, but that her parents had also been free, and that she had been sold illegally. The magistrates in Palermo supported her case and she was freed.[7]

Although the majority of black Africans in Renaissance Europe were slaves, some were not. Free-born black Africans or people of black African descent were relatively rare, freed black African ex-slaves were relatively common, and people of mixed race (some free and some enslaved) were also relatively common. So within a generation there were multiple possibilities relative

[5] Steven A. Epstein, *Speaking of Slavery: Color, Ethnicity and Human Bondage* (Ithaca and London, 2001), pp. 22–3, has a fascinating section on the discussions of the words connected to *albus* (white) and *niger* (black) in the thirteenth-century Latin dictionary compiled by Giovanni Balbi.

[6] Eileen McGrath Grubb, 'Attitudes towards black Africans in imperial Spain', *Legon Journal of the Humanities*, 1 (1974), pp. 68–90 at 83.

[7] 'Notizie di un archivio privato utili alla storia pisana', *Bullettino pisano d'arte e di storia*, 1 ([November], 1913), pp. 217–9 at 219.

to legal status for people of black African descent, yet Europeans persisted in imagining all black Africans in Europe as slaves. So the first, most fundamental and most deep-seated stereotype (one that was patently incorrect) was that all black Africans in Renaissance Europe were (and by extension were only fit to be) slaves.

The stereotype that routinely equated black skin with inferior legal status was a European creation, because although slavery existed in both North and sub-Saharan Africa, most black people in Africa were not slaves. From this point of view, black Africans were perceived differently to other ethnic or religious minority groups in Europe, such as Jews or Muslims or gypsies or Amerindians, because none of these groups was assigned slave status as a group, although in some cases numbers of individuals were. Part of the reason for this may lie with Europeans' categorisation of animist or Muslim sub-Saharan Africans as uncivilised 'savages', not only on account of their ignorance of Christianity, but also on account of such factors as nudity. Nearly all of the European writers who travelled to West Africa and saw Africans *in situ* comment on the nakedness or near nakedness of black Africans, often with a reference back to the so-called state of nature, and often describing the material with which they covered their genitals. For the Europeans, wearing clothes was not a matter of choice but a sign of civility, and the issue was not one of obscenity but of a lack of the necessary understanding of decent behaviour. Technically the Africans were not naked, but they were undressed. In Europe, material was directly related to status, as is made plain in sumptuary laws; European travellers commenting on an African's 'undressed' appearance were attempting to locate the Africans within a value system based on European clothing. Once in Europe, Africans wore European clothing, but because they were mainly slaves and nearly always poor, they were very often badly and sparsely clad, unless they worked at European courts.

There are many reports by observers of the practice of circumcision[8] in Africa, and it may have been yet another point of difference between some Africans and some Europeans. In Europe, Christians were not circumcised but Jewish men were, so circumcised black Africans may have found themselves typecast as 'the enemy'. Furthermore, the practice of circumcision also had the added disadvantage of also being associated with Islam. However, a few

---

[8] For example, Wolof women apparently were not circumcised whereas Ethiopian women apparently were. Cesare Vecellio, *Degli habiti antichi et moderni di diversi parte del mondo* (Venice, 1590), p. 488, describes female genital mutilation in Arabia in his section on 'mori neri dell'Africa'.

observors did note that circumcision could be a result of custom rather than religious observance. For instance, Duarte Pacheco Pereira, writing in the first decade of the sixteenth century of the peoples between the Rio Grande and Sierra Leone, specifically stated that some black groups practised circumcision even though they were not Muslims.[9]

Other stereotypes relating to appearance grew up in connection with African practices of personal adornment. Various black Africans had face and body markings when sold or captured and taken to Europe, and others wore ear-rings, armlets, chains, anklets and collars in Europe, as they had in Africa. Whereas in certain societies in sub-Saharan Africa the meanings of these markings and adornments had been clear, and utterly unrelated to criminal or slave status, once in Europe these scars, tattoos and accessories took on other significances. Europeans proved unable or unwilling to distinguish between different types of face and body marking, between decoration, scars earned in battle and punitive disfigurement for crimes. The scars of the black Portuguese court fool, João de Sá Panasco, 'honourably' earned in battle against the Spanish, were turned into a badge of dishonour by being compared to brands on the faces of slaves.[10] The extent of the branding of slaves has not been investigated in many parts of Europe, although there is excellent comparative material for Spain,[11] but markings on the skin of black Africans were another of their distinctive features (which some North Africans may have shared). Pacheco Pereira observed it amongst the Edo of Benin and in the Congo.[12] Alvise da Mosto described the women in Senegambia 'who delight in their youth to work designs upon their flesh with the point of a needle, either on their breasts, arms, or necks. They appear like those designs of silk that are often made on handkerchiefs: they are made with fire, so that they never disappear'.[13] An English report of pouncing, but only

[9] Duarte Pacheco Pereira, *Esmeraldo de situ orbis*, ed. and trans. George H. T. Kimble (London, 1937), pp. 93–4, 96–7.

[10] A. C. de C. M. Saunders, 'The life and humour of João de Sá Panasco, o negro, former slave, court jester and gentleman of the Portuguese royal household (fl. 1524–1567)', in F. W. Hodcroft, D. G. Pattison, R. D. F. Pring-Mill, R. W. Truman, eds., *Medieval and Renaissance Studies on Spain and Portugal in Honour of P. E. Russell* (Oxford, 1981), pp. 180–91 at 185 and *Ditos Portugueses Dignos de Memória*, ed. José H. Saraiva (Lisbon [1979]), pp. 379 (no. 1054) and 146 (no. 378).

[11] Alessandro Stella, '"Herrado en el rostro con una S y un clavo": l'homme-animal dans l'Espagne des XVe–XVIIIe siècles', in Henri Bresc, ed., *Figures de l'esclave au Moyen-Age et dans le monde moderne* (Paris, 1996), pp. 147–63.

[12] Pereira, *Esmeraldo de situ orbis*, pp. 127, 144.

[13] *The Voyages of Cadamosto and Other Documents on Western Afrcia in the Second Half of the Fifteenth Century*, ed. G. R. Crone (London, 1937), p. 70, and John William Blake, ed., *Europeans in West Africa, 1450–1560*, 2 vols. (London, 1942), II, p. 343.

on men, appeared in Richard Eden's account of John Lok's voyage to Mina in 1554–5.[14]

Certain slaves undoubtedly were already ritually scarred or marked on their face when they arrived, for example, in Italy. Some Italian slaves were also branded either upon arrival to mark them as their owners' property or as punishment for 'criminal' acts after their arrival. For instance, in Venice there is evidence that female slaves were beaten and branded for thefts and illicit affairs, and branded on the forehead for attempts to flee their owners.[15] Fugitive slaves in Genoa were likewise branded, but on the cheek.[16] Slave status made such 'crimes' unavoidable, and resulted in a stereotype of black criminality. To the detriment of the black Africans' reputation, anyone with body marks was labelled a criminal, as any white person with these marks could only have acquired them as a result of a brush with the law or as a result of an armed dispute. Once again, African cultural practices led directly to prejudice against black Africans in the European context, and to the stereotype of a black African criminal. These markings, whether acquired in Africa or in Europe, were permanent, and they are often cited in Italian documents (for example) as distinguishing features. For example, two documents from the end of the sixteenth century in Venice also attest to the marking or branding (the exact expression is 'marked with fire') of black African slaves in multiple places, above the breast, on the shoulder and chest, beneath an eye.[17]

In Renaissance images of black Africans in Europe, Africans (even though usually slaves and servants) are often depicted wearing beautiful and expensive jewellery. The black king in scenes of the Adoration of the Magi was nearly always lavishly decked with jewellery, but these scenes did not represent reality as no black African Kings came to Europe during this period.[18] One reason for the preponderance of other bejewelled Africans is that a large proportion of black African images come from courtly settings, where the

[14] Richard Eden's account of John Lok's voyage originally appeared in Richard Hakluyt, *The Principal Navigations, Voyages, Traffiques and Discoveries of the English Nation*, IV, p. 62, and was reprinted in Blake, ed., *Europeans in West Africa*; the reference to pouncing in Blake is at II, p. 343.

[15] B. Cecchetti, 'La donna nel medioevo a Venezia', *Archivio veneto*, 31 (1886), pp. 33–69 and 307–49, at 327 and 328.

[16] Salvatore Bongi, 'Le schiave orientali in Italia', *Nuova antologia di scienze, lettere ed arti*, 2 (1866), pp. 215–46 at 241.

[17] Alberto Tenenti, 'Gli schiavi di Venezia alla fine del Cinquecento', *Rivista storica italiana*, 67 (1955), pp. 52–69 at 65 ('segnata . . . con fuoco') and 68.

[18] See Paul H. D. Kaplan, 'Ruler, saint and servant: blacks in European art to 1520', Ph.D. dissertation, 1983, Boston University, 2 vols. with continuous pagination, p. 124 (Filippino Lippi's black king with gold ear-rings).

Africans would have been clothed and adorned to show off the status of their masters. However, white slaves and servants, although similarly clothed, do not wear similar jewellery (and in particular are not so associated with gold and pearl-drop ear-rings), so there must have been additional reasons. The gold jewellery worn by black Africans in Africa was much remarked upon by travelling Europeans. For example, the narrator of Diogo Gomes' voyage to West Africa of 1456 or 1457 observed that the nobles of King Bormelli wore gold ornaments in their nostrils and ears.[19] The association between gold jewellery and Africans seems to have persisted in the visual record even in the very changed circumstances of black African slavery in Europe, probably because iconographically these African slaves and servants were being used simultaneously as markers of the richness of the continent of Africa, and as embodiments of their inferiority in a European context. No documentary evidence exists for the ownership by people of black African descent of gold jewellery in Renaissance Italy, nor even of records in account books of purchases of gold accessories made on behalf of black Africans by their 'owners' (entries are common for expensive clothing, for example), so the visual and the documentary evidence are contradictory. In some places in Italy, such as Ferrara, Jewish girls aged ten and over had to wear an ear-ring as a distinguishing feature. The Franciscan preacher Giacomo della Marca claimed in a fifteenth-century Advent sermon that ear-rings are jewels 'that Jewish women wear in place of circumcision, so that they can be distinguished from other women'.[20] It was extremely unfortunate that yet again an integral part of the cultural appearance of many black Africans – the wearing of gold ear-rings – could cause them to be linked in a negative fashion with the Jews. Interestingly, the practice of wearing ear-rings crossed over and became fashionable among the European host communities in the first half of the sixteenth century. The Venetian diarist Marin Sanuto recorded his displeasure in December 1525 upon seeing the daughter of a relative who 'according to the custom of *more* (female Moors or black Africans)' had pierced her ears and was wearing large pearl-drop ear-rings set in gold.[21]

The consequences of the changeover in usage of armlets, chains, anklets and collars from gold ornaments used by black Africans in Africa to markers of bondage and slavery in Europe were even more devastating. European travellers often noted these ornaments on African peoples. Richard Eden wrote

[19] *The Voyages of Cadamosto*, p. 95.

[20] Diane Owen Hughes, 'Distinguishing signs: ear-rings, Jews and Franciscan rhetoric in the Italian Renaissance city', *Past and Present*, 112 (1986), pp. 3–59 at 22–4.

[21] Marin Sanuto, *I diarii*, ed. R. Fulin *et al.*, 58 vols. (Venice, 1879–1903), XL, pp. 425–6.

in his account of John Lok's voyage to Mina in 1554–5: 'And albeit they goe in maner all naked, yet are many of them, and especially their women, in maner laden with collars, bracelets, hoopes and chaines, either of gold, copper, or ivory . . . Some weare also on their legges great shackles of bright copper which they thinke to bee no lesse comely.'[22] The frequency with which black slaves in Europe were forced to wear these objects of oppression is not yet clear, but there are glimpses of their use in images and texts. For example, the medal maker Christoph Weiditz from Strasbourg compiled a costume book in the 1520s and 1530s in which he recorded aspects of social life in Spain and the Netherlands. White and black slaves – the former described as galley slaves and the latter loading water onto ships – appear wearing slave anklets or foot-irons (the black slaves also wear ear-rings) and, in a further image, a black slave from Castile carries a wine-skin, with anklets on both ankles and a heavy chain linking one anklet to his waist (fig. 1).[23] In the inscription accompanying the image of the wine carrier, it is explained that the chain signifies that the wearer has already attempted an escape.[24] The 1565 written blazon and the late sixteenth-century sketch of the slave-trader John Hawkins' crest (fig. 2) catch the moment of the blurring of the image of the black African with an armlet, and the bound captive. The blazon describes how Hawkins 'in token of his victorie against the Moores' was assigned upon his helm 'a demy Moore in his proper color, bounde in a corde as bonde and captive, with anneletts on his armes and eares goulde'.[25] In fact, the later sketch shows neither obvious cord nor any ear-rings, but it does show a black African wearing gold armlets.[26] In Europe, these armlets became merely another sign of slave status. The crossover from the African collar to the European slave collar may have followed a similar trajectory, but other than the fact that these too, like ear-rings, at a certain point became fashionable accessories for wealthy whites, very little is known.

Many more stereotypes evolved in Renaissance Europe in connection with perceptions of black African behaviour and the black African character. Lack of appreciation of the rules of civility and civilisation produced the insidious

---

[22] Blake, ed., *Europeans in West Africa*, II, p. 343.

[23] Theodor Hampe, *Das Trachtenbuch des Christoph Weiditz von seinen Reisen nach Spanien (1529) und den Niederlanden (1531/32)* (Berlin and Leipzig, 1927), plates XLVII, LXIII, LXIV, LXV and LXVI.

[24] Hampe, *Das Trachtenbuch*, p. 85.

[25] London, College of Arms, MS ICB 101, f. 109. See W. H. Smyth, 'On certain passages in the life of Sir John Hawkins, temp. Elizabeth', *Archaeologia: or Miscellaneous Tracts relating to Antiquity published by the Society of Antiquaries*, 33 (1849), pp. 195–208 at 205–6.

[26] London, College of Arms, Miscellaneous Grants I, fol. 148.

FIG. 1. Christoph Weiditz, *Black Slave with a Wineskin in Castile*, in *Das Trachtenbuch*, 1529 (paper, 15 × 19.8/20 cm, Nuremberg, Germanisches Nationalmuseum).

stereotype of 'the laughing black', carefree because too stupid to understand the misery of his or her situation. In a description of Portugal written anonymously (but attributed to the Italian military engineer Baccio da Filicaia)[27] in

---

[27] Carmen Radulet, 'An outsider's inside view of sixteenth-century Portugal', *Portuguese Studies*, 13 (1997), pp. 152–8 at 153.

F I G . 2 . *Sketch of the Slave-trader John Hawkins' Crest*, late sixteenth-century (paper, London, College of Arms, Miscellaneous Grants 1, fol. 148).

Tuscan in 1578–80, the Portuguese were characterised as gloomy and melancholic people who did not dare to laugh, whereas their black African slaves were depicted as happy and carefree: 'the slaves are always happy, they do nothing but laugh'.[28] In general, this particular freedom from constraint, instead of being perceived as a positive characteristic, reinforced European views of black Africans as 'savages' who had not reaped the benefits of civilisation and who were naturally suited to slavery. Erasmus' condemnation of pleasurable or immoderate laughter in his treatise *De civilitate morum pueritium* (*On Good Manners for Boys*) of 1530 ridiculed many unrestrained types of laughter as foolish, stupid, insane or wildly impolite, and he dismissed laughing with an open mouth as 'a canine habit'.[29] It is easy to see from this how people of black African descent would have been penalised on account of their ignorance of the rules of civilisation. Another view of black hilarity sees their laughter as

[28] A. H. de Oliveira Marques, 'Uma descrição de Portugal em 1578–80', in A. H. de Oliveira Marques, *Portugal Quinhentista (Ensaios)* (Lisbon, 1987), pp. 127–245 at 241: 'i schiavi sempre sono alegri, ne fanno mai che ridere'.

[29] *Collected Works of Erasmus* (Toronto, Buffalo and London, 1974–), 86 vols. so far, xv, pp. 273–89 at 276 (*On Good Manners for Boys*, ed. and trans. Brian McGregor).

'natural', and their actions[30] and their speech as naturally comic,[31] just like the actions and speech of young children.

Black Africans were also stereotyped as lazy and irresponsible. Most slave owners characterised their slaves as lazy, but even within this framework black Africans seem to have been regarded as lazier than other types of slave. This stereotype may have been related to the European belief that Africa was an Edenic land of plenty whose inhabitants did not have to work; thus when transported to Europe, they continued to do as little work as possible. Giovanni di Buonagrazia, who accompanied Vasco da Gama's second expedition of 1502–3, describes black Africans on the West coast of Africa as 'very lazy people, not working men, their only subject of study being thought'.[32] Buonagrazia was not, however, referring to the civilised Renaissance pursuit of idle leisure that led to cultivation of the mind, but to an uncivilised and unproductive avoidance of the hard work of manual labour, tantamount in his eyes to neglect of duty. This stereotype of black laziness is to be found in European sources already in the second half of the fifteenth century. The sons and heirs of Matteo di Giovanni di Marcho Strozzi of Florence declared in their tax return of 1480 amongst their possessions 'one black female slave aged 18 or 20 for domestic work who works badly and is of little worth; she is lazy as are all black females'.[33]

Other traits or characteristics associated with black Africans were propensities towards drunkenness and criminality, both linked, as usual, to an absence of understanding of the rules of civilised or European behaviour and to a lack of self-discipline (although there were plenty of white Renaissance Europeans who drank and committed criminal acts). Pacheco Pereira remarked that the inhabitants of the Wolof kingdom 'are very great thieves and liars, [and] great drunkards',[34] and once again, African behaviour was perceived to be continued in Europe. Drunkenness in Europe was a problem of public order because it usually took place in squares. In sixteenth-century Spain there was a formula ('he is not a drunk, a thief or a runaway') used in documents relating to slaves,

---

[30] Johan Verberckemoes, *Laughter, Jestbooks and Society in the Spanish Netherlands* (Basingstoke, 1999), pp. 44–5.

[31] Frida Weber de Kurlat, 'Sobre el negro como tipo cómico en el teatro español del siglo XVI', *Romance Philology*, 17 (1963–4), pp. 380–91.

[32] Joan-Pau Rubiés, 'Giovanni di Buonagrazia's letter to his father concerning his participation in the second expedition of Vasco da Gama', *Mare liberum*, 16 (1998), pp. 87–112 at 107 (my translation).

[33] Florence, Archivio di stato, Catasto 1011, 300r: 'una schiava nera di 18/o/20 per servigio di chasa la quale serve male ed è da pocho, è lenti chome sono tutte le nere'.

[34] Pereira, *Esmeraldo de situ orbis*, p. 80.

indicating that these were their most common 'faults'.[35] Many unhappy black Africans must have made the most of the ready availability of cheap alcohol and have taken refuge in the oblivion of drink. For example, the black fool at the Portuguese court, João de Sá Panasco, allegedly took to drink in his old age as (amongst other troubles) many years of dealing wittily with jibes at his status (his mother was a slave) and skin colour took a cumulative toll.[36] One of the sayings directed at Panasco joked precisely that he shared other slaves' proclivity to theft.[37] Research has not yet revealed whether this stereo-typing resulted in black Africans appearing disproportionately in relation to their numbers in the civil and criminal records (although often masters would have 'dealt' with their slaves' supposed thefts themselves rather than taking them to court), but an anonymous painting of Lisbon dated to 1560–80 of the scene around the Chafariz d'el-Rei (the king's fountain) in the Alfama[38] (fig. 3) includes a detail of a black African which appears to represent him being 'arrested' and led away by two constables (fig. 4). This genre painting is highly unusual as it centres on black life and activity; it was probably painted by someone from Northern Europe, for whom this represented a particularly 'exotic' and unfamiliar world. The vignette shows two constables, wearing dis-tinctive red hats with white feathers, marked on their left-hand sleeve at the shoulder with a gold badge of office, dragging away an unwilling and appre-hensive black male, who may be bleeding from a wound to his face or head.

Black Africans were additionally and routinely stereotyped as sexually promiscuous, because for Europeans a lack of civilisation signified wanton sex. The rules governing sexual behaviour in Catholic, patriarchal, hierarchical fifteenth- and sixteenth-century Europe were complicated, and left all female slaves in particular at a great disadvantage. Observation of and contact with Africans on the African continent resulted in Europeans categorising black Africans as libidinous, incapable of restraint and sexually uncontrolled. The fact of Muslim polygamy (although many black Africans were not Muslim) was probably sufficient for this categorisation to take place. Additionally, men were accused of holding women and children in common,[39] or fathers or

---

[35] Aurelia Martín Casares, *La esclavitud en la Granada del siglo XVI: género, raza y religión* (Granada, 2000), p. 397.

[36] Saunders, 'The life and humour', p. 190.

[37] Saunders, 'The life and humour', p. 185, and *Ditos Portugueses*, ed. Saraiva, pp. 51–2 (no. 100).

[38] On this painting, see *Os Negros em Portugal – Secs. xv a xix* (exhibition catalogue), Mosteiro de Belém (Lisbon, 1999), pp. 104–7.

[39] Leo Africanus, *The History and Description of Africa and of the Notable Things Therein Contained, Done into English in the Year 1600, by John Pory, and now Edited with an Introduction and Notes by Dr. Robert Brown*, 3 vols. (London, 1896), III, p. 833.

FIG. 3. Anonymous, *Chafariz d'el-Rei in the Alfama District, Lisbon*, c. 1560–80 (oil on panel, 93 × 163 cm, Lisbon, private collection).

FIG. 4. Anonymous, *Chafariz d'el-Rei in the Alfama District, Lisbon* (detail of black African being arrested), *c.* 1560–80 (oil on panel, 93 × 163 cm, Lisbon, private collection).

brothers of having sex with their daughters or sisters,[40] just like animals that did not recognise relationships of affinity. Once in Europe, black African slaves were at the mercy of the sexual advances of their masters, but the fiction was still maintained that it was the black Africans whose sexuality was uncontrollable. Sometimes less prejudiced observers, such as Conte Giulio Landi, who wrote a description of Madeira and dedicated it to Pope Clement VII,

[40] *The Voyages of Cadamosto*, p. 89.

cast the phenomenon of black sexuality in other terms. In it, Landi related that white Madeirans and Portuguese fell wildly in love with black women and preferred them to their wives, and that also some free white women had sex with black males. He recounted a story of a young merchant he had known in Évora, who was enamoured of a black female slave, even though he had a very beautiful wife, but the wife did not mind, as she was occupied sexually with a black male slave.[41] If this story is to be believed, for Europeans black sexuality was freer, less repressed and more exciting than white sexuality. In general, however, Europeans considered black African sexual promiscuity was both a consequence of a life without boundaries and an example of superior physical prowess.

The third area of stereotyping occurred in conjunction with occupation. Black Africans in Europe were routinely found in only a small range of skilled occupations; the vast majority carried out unskilled, menial work. Their slave status, language difficulties, non-literacy, extreme poverty and a perceived lack of civility, compounded by general European cultural prejudice, all contributed to this limited employment. Skills in the small range of skilled occupations where black Africans could be found had probably been acquired in their home countries, although there were many others, especially artistic ones (for example, ivory-carving, jewellery-making and basket-weaving), whose practitioners were not given the opportunity to exploit or 'reinvent' them once in Europe. Skilled African artisans formed a small but significant settled grouping in various parts of Europe, and they were in a markedly different position to unskilled slaves.

Physical prowess was one of the few accomplishments of black Africans that was valued, and Africans were employed in Europe in a range of physical activities, both of a military and a non-military bent. Martial skills would have found favour in Renaissance Europe, where it was believed that a gentleman should possess the 'manly' virtues manifested by skill at arms.[42] In terms of martial arts, it seems likely that the young black African recorded by Nicolaus Lankmann of Falkenstein at the festivities in Lisbon to mark the wedding of the emperor Frederick III to Leonor of Portugal in 1451, who had been given by the Duke of Seville to the Carinthian knight Christoph Ungenad, was, like his new master, skilled in the use of the lance, as he is mentioned in the

---

[41] *La descrittione de l'isola de la Madera già scritta nela lingua latina dal molto ill. Signor Conte Giulio Landi, et hora tradotta dal latino ne la nostra materna lingua, dal reverendo M. Alamanio Fini* (Piacenza, 1574), p. 41.

[42] See Sydney Anglo, *The Martial Arts of Renaissance Europe* (New Haven and London, 2000), to gain an idea of the range of martial possibilities.

context of a joust.[43] African horsemanship was elsewhere acknowledged as a skill in its own right. João de Barros reported that at the celebrations in Lisbon following the baptism of prince 'Bemoim' (as he was called by the Portuguese) from Senegambia in 1487, Wolof horsemen who had accompanied him gave stunning displays of their virtuosity.[44] The link between black Africans and horses continued in the next century. For example, in a list of employees at the Medici court in 1553, one entry reads: 'Grazzico of Africa, called il Moretto (the little Moor), horseman, page to the knight Prospero'.[45]

Black Africans were also skilled at swordplay of various sorts, and were often allowed to continue working or encouraged to work in this area, so that Africans were often associated with displays of swordsmanship. Gaspar Frutuoso in the Azores in the 1580s encountered a black African head of a fencing school known as Master Pedro, working for the soldier Captain Francisco Dias.[46] Jörg Breu the Younger illustrated a duel with sickles in c. 1560 for Paulus Hector Mair's *Fechtbuch*, in which the opponents were a black and a white combatant, extravagantly dressed in red and green doublet and hose, with the black combatant additionally wearing a large gold ear-ring (fig. 5). The physiognomies of both, shown in profile, were exaggerated in order to emphasise contrast and difference, so contrasting hair, noses and lips confront each other in an image that otherwise is almost perfectly balanced. People of African descent also found employment as soldiers in various armies (for instance, there was a black captain in the 1520s or 1530s involved in a court case in Treviso, who may have been fighting with the imperial troops), or even just as bodyguards (a good example is Bastião/Bastiano, the black African slave brought from Portugal to Italy in the household of the young Cardinal Jaime of Portugal, sold after Jaime's death to the Portuguese bishop of Silves, Álvaro Afonso, and later ordered to stand guard over his former master's tomb in the church of S. Miniato al Monte outside Florence),[47] where their physical powers and presence could be utilised to good effect.

---

[43] *Leonor de Portugal Imperatriz da Alemanha, Diário de Viagem do Embaixador Nicolau Lanckman de Valkenstein*, ed. Aires A. Nascimento, with the collaboration of Maria João Branco and Maria de Lurdes Rosa (Lisbon, 1992), p. 40.

[44] João de Barros, *Ásia de Joam de Barros* (Lisbon, 1552), fol. 32r.

[45] Cosimo Conti, *La prima reggia di Cosimo I de' Medici nel palazzo già della Signoria di Firenze descritta ed illustrata* (Florence, 1893), 'Ruolo degli stipendiati della corte Medicea nell'anno 1553', p. 271, from Florence, Archivio di stato, Depositeria, Salariati, reg. 393, fol. 139r.

[46] Gaspar Frutuoso, *Livro Sexto das Saudades da Terra* (Ponta Delgada, 1963), p. 158. Mestre Pedro's relationship to Francisco Dias is not clear: the exact wording is: 'un seu negro'.

[47] Frederick Hartt, Gino Corti and Clarence Kennedy, *The Chapel of the Cardinal of Portugal, 1434–1459, at San Miniato in Florence* (Philadelphia, 1964), pp. 42, 56 and 160.

FIG. 5. Jörg Breu the Younger, *A Duel with Two Sickles, c.* 1560 (in Paulus Hector Mair's *Fechtbuch,* Cod, icon. 393, vol. VI, fol. 227r, plate 3, Munich, Bayerische Staatsbibliothek).

Black Africans were employed in other pastimes involving physical prowess (or enhanced physicality), for example, as wrestlers,[48] swimming instructors[49] and divers. One such diver, referred to in 1548 High Court of Admiralty records in London as Jacobus (Jacopo) Fraunces (Francesco?), was the slave of Pier-paolo Corsi, a Venetian who was part of the Italian colony in Southampton.[50] In testimony of 8 February 1548, Jacopo asserted that he had lived with Corsi for about two years, and before that in the island of Guinea ('Gynney') where he was born, and that he was twenty or so years old.[51] Jacopo was one of a

[48] Paolo Giovio, *Elogia,* on Ippolito de' Medici, pp. 307ff, quoted in Jacob Burckhardt, *The Civilization of the Renaissance in Italy,* trans. and ed. S. G. C. Middlemore (London, Bombay and Sydney, 1929), p. 291.

[49] Hans Werner Debrunner, *Presence and Prestige: Africans in Europe. A History of Africans in Europe before 1918* (Basel, 1979), p. 22.

[50] Alwyn Ruddock, *Italian Merchants and Shipping in Southampton, 1270–1600* (Southampton, 1951), pp. 129 and 253.

[51] London, National Archives, High Court of Admiralty 13, vol. 93, fol. 203v: 'Jacques Frauncys famulus ut asseruit Petri Paulo cum quo habitavit circiter duos annos et antea in insula de Gynney ubi natus est etate xxti annorum aut circiter'.

team of divers employed in salvage operations along the south coast of England. Another witness, a sailor from Venice, described Jacopo as 'a morisco borne where they are not christenyd' and argued that Jacopo's testimony should not be accepted because he was a slave in a Christian country.[52] This witness showed cognisance of Roman law (which pertained across much of the Italian peninsula) that stated a slave's testimony was inadmissible except under torture,[53] but he also seemed to be concerned that non-Christians should be allowed to give evidence. The same witness revealed that Corsi had put Jacopo up for sale in Southampton but that no one had bought him.[54]

A further cluster of skilled occupations 'permitted' to black Africans in Renaissance Europe centred on music. As music[55] and dance were central components of European Renaissance culture, African aptitude and proficiency in these areas was highly prized. European records constantly testify to the belief in black Africans' innate sense of rhythm, but also to the stereotype of black Africans unable to control their urges to make music, sing and dance, thus turning something very positive into something more negative, linked yet again to black African lack of civilisation and self-control. From the mid-fifteenth century onwards, documentary and visual sources chart the employment (in particular) of black drummers and black trumpeters, mainly (but not solely) at Renaissance courts, where they were in great demand at public and private celebrations and entertainments. The stereotype of the black African as entertainer, as someone who could usefully be employed to 'entertain' or amuse, is important here. Contemporary European descriptions of West Africa and Ethiopia had stressed the role of music across African societies. Alvise da Mosto in the 1450s described the women in Senegambia as 'ready to sing and dance', concluding however that 'their dances are very different from ours'.[56] Francisco Álvares listed the musical instruments in use in Ethiopia in the 1520s: he named (but he would have been approximating some African instruments to ones that were known to him in Europe) trumpets,

[52] London, National Archives, High Court of Admiralty 13, vol. 93, fols. 275v–276r: 'he beleavythe that no credite nor faithe ought to be geven to his [Jacopo's] sayenge as in other strange christiane cuntryes hit ys to no suche slave geven'.

[53] W. W. Buckland, *The Roman Law of Slavery: The Condition of the Slave in Private Law from Augustus to Justinian* (Cambridge, 1908), pp. 86–8.

[54] London, National Archives, High Court of Admiralty 13, vol. 93, fol. 275v, and Ruddock, *Italian Merchants*, p. 129.

[55] See, e.g., *Il libro del cortegiano del Conte Baldessar Castiglione*, ed. Vittorio Cian (Florence, 1967), p. 121: 'esser la musica non solamente ornamento ma necessaria al cortegiano'.

[56] *The Voyages of Cadamosto*, pp. 29–33, 50.

F I G . 6. The Master of Frankfurt, *The Archers' Festival in the Garden of their Guild*
(detail of black pipe and tabor player), *c.* 1493 (oil on wood, 170 × 142 cm,
Antwerp, Koninklijk Museum voor Schone Kunsten, Inv. 529).

drums, tambourines, cymbals, flutes and the *masēnqo*, a single-string bowed
lute.[57]

African drummers are commonplace in European art from this period in
a variety of situations. A black African drummer appears in a painting of

---

[57] Francisco Álvares, *Do Preste Joam das Indias: Verdadera Informaçam das Terras do Preste Joam* (Lisbon,
1540), fol. 136r.

c. 1493 by the Netherlandish artist known as the Master of Frankfurt entitled *The Archers' Festival in the Garden of their Guild,* now in the Koninklijk Museum voor Schone Kunsten in Antwerp (fig. 6).[58] The high-cheek-boned African plays an elongated, reeded instrument known as the long pipe at the same time as playing a tabor, holding the drumstick between the index and middle finger of his right hand. He wears extremely fine clothes (for example, the sleeve on his right side is eye-catchingly flamboyant, ending above the elbow with at least seven long ribbons) in white, gold and red, in contrast to most of the other people in the painting who wear darker colours. The painting appears to represent a variety of archers belonging to separate guilds, but the fête seems to have been sponsored by the guild of St Sebastian. The African drummer musician is positioned next to one of two professional fools included in the painting (this one has a fingered horn stuck suggestively in the front of his belt), and both the fools (who are known to have been central to the guild's ceremonial life) and the drummer musician indicate the festive nature of the event. Christoph Weiditz's costume book of the 1520s and 1530s included a representation of a black African drummer (fig. 7) with the textual legend: 'Thus ride the army drummers in Spain when the emperor rides into a city'.[59] The drummer is finely dressed in white and violet cloth-of-gold and silver livery, with a large gold ear-ring in his right ear, wearing a blue hat and a white feather. He has both hands free to play a pair of tubular or kettledrums slung over the mule on which he is riding. This drummer of African descent employed by the imperial army found a niche for himself that allowed him to use his skills in ways that were acceptable to his European masters. There are also textual references to African drummers in Europe: a black African drummer ('taubronar') and choreographer devised a dance with twelve performers in black and white costumes for the Shrove Tuesday festivities in 1505 at the Scottish court in Edinburgh.[60] References to King

---

[58] On this picture, see *Le siècle de Bruegel: la peinture en Belgique au XVIe siècle* (Brussels, 1963), pp. 172–3 and fig. 9; Stephen H. Goddard, 'The Master of Frankfurt and his shop', Ph.D. dissertation, University of Iowa, 1983, pp. 40–2, 70–6, 311–21, figs. 1–15; and Erik Vandamme *et al., Koninklijk Museum voor Schone Kunsten – Antwerpen, Departement Oude Meesters. Catalogus Schilderkunst Oude Meesters* (Antwerp, 1988), p. 493. In none of these is the figure of the black African pipe and tabor player discussed.

[59] Hampe, *Das Trachtenbuch*, plate 10 and p. 78.

[60] See Peter Fryer, *Staying Power: The History of Black People in Britain* (London, 1984), p. 2, and Paul Edwards, 'The early African presence in the British Isles', in Jagdish S. Gundara and Ian Duffield, eds., *Essays on the History of Blacks in Britain: From Roman Times to the Mid-Twentieth Century* (Aldershot, 1992), pp. 9–29 at 18; they both use Sir James Balfour Paul, ed., *The Accounts of the Lord High Treasurer of Scotland* (Edinburgh, 1902), II, p. 477.

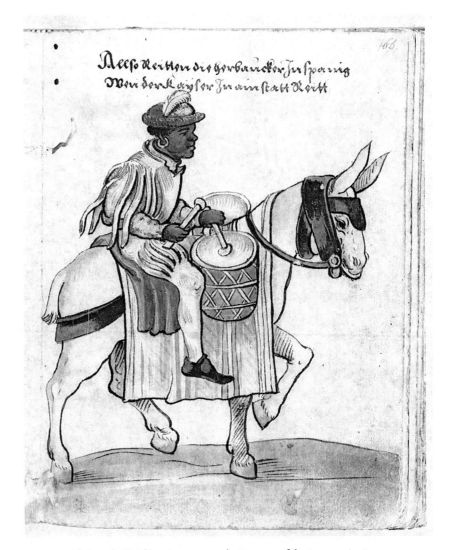

FIG. 7. Christoph Weiditz, *Drummer at the Entrance of the Emperor*, in *Das Trachtenbuch*, 1529 (paper, 15 × 19.8/20 cm, Nuremberg, Germanisches Nationalmuseum).

James IV's payment of expenses for this drummer (he paid at one point for his drum to be (re)painted) are scattered throughout the accounts of the Lord High Treasurer of Scotland.[61]

---

[61] For precise references to the 1902 edition of the accounts, see Fryer, *Staying Power*, pp. 2–3 and 460, and Edwards, 'The early African presence', pp. 17–18 and 26–7.

African trumpeters are also a very visible presence in many European countries during the Renaissance. They had been employed in this capacity in
previous centuries at courts in Spain and Italy,[62] and during the Renaissance
the practice spread. So in 1470 the treasury of the Neapolitan court recorded
a payment for 'a black slave called Martino', who was purchased to be the
trumpeter on board the royal ship *Barcha*.[63] The thirty-year-old Abdul from
Meknès, a 'moro negro' or black Moor, was described as a trumpeter in a
1555 list of galley slaves belonging to Cosimo I de' Medici.[64] Visual representations reinforce this presence. For instance, the African referred to as 'John
Blanke, the black trumpet', who may have come to England in the entourage
of Catherine of Aragon in 1501, and a record of whose monthly wages in 1507
is still extant,[65] appears twice in the Great Tournament Roll of Westminster of
1511.[66] In both representations, he stands out not only on account of his skin
colour, but additionally on account of his head-gear; whereas his white fellow
trumpeters are bare-headed with shoulder-length hair, John Blanke's hair is
hidden out of sight in a multicoloured hat: brown latticed with yellow in the
first image and green with a linear design of gold in the second (fig. 8).[67] In
all other respects, he is dressed in an identical fashion to his fellows, but on
account of his skill with his trumpet he must have been allowed this minor
deviance in dress, which obviously was vital to his cultural identity. This is a
very rare case of a black African in Renaissance Europe in a court setting not
wearing standardised court attire. All the trumpets have a double curve and
are hung with the royal quarterings, fringed in white and green. When other
instruments and possibilities for music-making were lacking, black Africans
fell back on the lowly tambourine. In Palermo, a 1440 edict specifically forbade black Africans from carrying tambourines or small drums, in addition
to other more immediately dangerous objects such as arms, knives and sticks,

[62] See Jean Devisse and Michel Mollat, *L'image du noir dans l'art occidental*, II, *Des premiers siècles chrétiens aux 'Grandes Découvertes'*, 2, *Les Africains dans l'ordonnance chrétienne du monde (XIVe–XVIe siècle)*, (Fribourg, 1979), p. 195.
[63] Nicola Barone, 'Le cedole di tesoreria dell'Archivio di stato di Napoli dall'anno 1460 al 1504', *Archivio storico per le province napoletane*, 9 (1884), pp. 5–34, 205–48, 387–429, 601–37, 10 (1885), pp. 5–47 at 9 (1884), p. 228. See also Charles Verlinden, *L'esclavage dans l'Europe médiévale*, I: *Péninsule ibérique – France* (Bruges, 1955), II: *Italie, colonies italiennes du Levant, Levant latin, Empire byzantin* (Ghent, 1977), II, p. 324.
[64] Florence, Archivio di stato, Mediceo del principato 627, fol. 54r.
[65] Sydney Anglo, 'The court festivals of Henry VII: a study based upon the account books of John Heron, treasurer of the chamber', *Bulletin of the John Rylands Library*, 43 (1960), pp. 12–45 at 42.
[66] Sydney Anglo, ed., *The Great Tournament Roll of Westminster*, 2 vols. (Oxford, 1968), I (text) and II (facsimile); II: plate III, membranes 3–5, and plate XVIII, membranes 28–9.
[67] Anglo, ed., *The Great Tournament Roll*, I, pp. 85 and 98.

FIG. 8. *John Blanke, the Black Trumpet,* Great Tournament Roll of Westminster, 1511 (membrane 28, vellum, whole roll: 59 ft 6 inches, width 14¾ inches, London, College of Arms).

presumably because of the subversive and collectively enticing effect of their rhythms.[68] In the anonymous 1560–80 painting of the Chafariz d'el-Rei in Lisbon, two Africans are moving to the sound of a tambourine even in the confines of a small boat in the harbour.

African dances, as well as continuing the stereotypes of black African physicality and lack of control, had a further (and more unusual) ingredient: they were valued precisely because they differed from European dances. Dancing, although strictly regulated at the higher echelons of society, had an integral place in public and private Renaissance festivities,[69] and learning how to

[68] Henri Bresc, *Un monde méditerranéen: économie et société en Sicile, 1300–1450,* 2 vols. (Rome and Palermo, 1986), II, p. 450.

[69] Barbara Sparti, 'Dancing in fifteenth-century Italian society', in Guglielmo Ebreo of Pesaro, *De pratica seu arte tripudii* (*On the Practice or Art of Dancing*) (Oxford, 1993), pp. 47–61.

dance was part of the education of both Renaissance gentlemen and gentle-women.[70] Usually cultural difference was not at all appreciated, but African dances appealed to Europeans for their seemingly wild and exotic nature, and in fact several seem to have crossed over (like ear-rings and gold acces-sories) and become fashionable amongst certain sections of European society. For example, black Africans probably introduced popular dances such as the *guineo*, *ye-ye* and *zarambeque* to Spain.[71] African love of dancing, in what-ever form, is a constant source of comment in the fifteenth and sixteenth centuries. Gabriel Tetzel, who accompanied the Bohemian Leo of Rožmitál on his travels through Europe in the 1460s, attests to displays of African dancing in Braga in Northern Portugal.[72] When Philip II of Spain was in Lisbon (after Spain's annexation of Portugal), he wrote to his daughters in June 1582 that he had gone to the window to watch black Africans dancing in the streets.[73] Although Madrid had a black population, Lisbon's was far more numerous and therefore noteworthy. In the 1560–80 painting of the Chafariz d'el-Rei in the Alfama District of Lisbon, many black Africans or people of African descent can be seen dancing, including possibly an African/European couple of a black man and a white woman (fig. 9). Yet allowing that people of African descent were good at certain physical activities also led to a negative stereotype, as they were prized for their physical rather than their intellectual or human qualities. Pursuits involving intellectual skills are, on the contrary, only very infrequently mentioned in connection with black Africans, although in the mid-fifteenth century the duke of Orléans paid a black African from Lombardy to play him at chess.[74]

The stereotyping of sub-Saharan Africans on the basis of appearance and character/behaviour as inferior, uncivilised and beyond the pale of Renais-sance society, and their pigeonholing in occupations related to physical prowess and entertainment, resulted not only in their exclusion from much of mainstream European life, but also in their denigration. Many African cultural practices were misunderstood and recast in a negative light. European lan-guages and literacy presented yet more difficulties. Not only did new arrivals

[70] *Il libro del cortegiano*, ed. Cian, e.g. pp. 154–5.

[71] Ruth Pike, 'Sevillian society in the sixteenth century: slaves and freedmen', *Hispanic American Historical Review*, 47 (1967), pp. 344–59 at 349, and Emilio Cotarelo y Mori, *Colección de entremeses, loas, bailes, jácaras y mojigangas desde fines del siglo XVI á mediados del XVIII*, 2 vols. (Madrid, 1911), I, pp. ccl–ccli, ccxxxiii–cclxxiii.

[72] Gabriel Tetzel, *Des böhmischen Herrn Leo's von Rožmital Ritter-, Hof- und Pilger-Reise durch die Abendlande, 1465–67* (Stuttgart, 1844), p. 178.

[73] Fernando Bouza, ed., *Cartas de Felipe II a sus hijas* (Madrid, 1998), p. 86.

[74] This is cited in Kaplan, 'Ruler, saint and servant', p. 596.

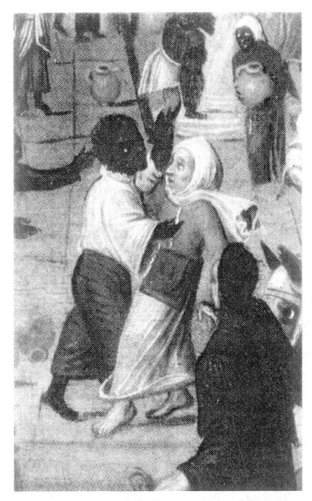

FIG. 9. Anonymous, *Chafariz d'el-Rei in the Alfama District, Lisbon* (detail of African/European couple dancing), *c.* 1560–80 (oil on panel, 93 × 163 cm, Lisbon, private collection).

from Africa have to learn the vernacular of the country to which they were taken, but the language of the educated in Renaissance Europe was Latin, which presented further difficulties. Without access to education, the vast majority of Africans remained non-literate, both in the vernaculars and in Latin. Even people who appear at a superficial glance to have escaped the negative effects of stereotyping, upon closer inspection can be seen to have been trapped within them. At one level, João de Sá Panasco, a black court fool in Lisbon, pursued a successful career in the extremely specialised and erudite cultural world of European humour; at another, his black skin and ex-slave status merely allowed him to be the butt of a further series of jokes. Instead of overturning the stereotype, he became an embodiment of it, a black entertainer par excellence, whose birth and body attracted constant attention, overshadowing his clever use of language. Even when awarded the prestigious and exclusive Order of Santiago, this only produced a cruel joke likening the small red cross on the otherwise black habit of the Order (when worn by Panasco) to a dying ember in a brazier.[75]

But if European reactions to enslaved or poor black Africans in Europe were prescribed by the prevailing stereotypes of them, reactions to high-ranking regal or noble ambassadors from sub-Saharan Africa were more complicated and contradictory. In the first place, these people were free, wealthy and powerful, and came to Europe of their own volition. Second, a belief in and acceptance of the natural order of hierarchy, which expressed itself structurally in kingdoms in Africa as in Europe, was shared by sub-Saharan African cultures and European cultures, and consequently for many Europeans, black African kings and ambassadors appeared to deserve respect. Notions of hierarchy and royalty were so ingrained in Europe that those classified as African princes or members of royal families received greatly superior treatment to non-royals, even if not always treatment equal to European royalty, and not always the same treatment as earlier princely ambassadors.[76] Individuals in these positions still encountered a wall of beliefs about themselves, but acknowledgement of their positions may sometimes have mitigated the harmful effect of the stereotypes. The force of the stereotypes and the contradictions inherent in the juxtaposition of the concept of black African with the notions of freedom, power, status, wealth and civilisation were responsible for uneven responses. At times, their status was not enough to protect them from insult: for example, in 1514 a Congolese ambassador to Portugal complained that he had been insulted by the royal stableman, who offered him an inferior mount and refused to show him due respect.[77]

Peter Russell has analysed the descriptions in two Portuguese chronicles, one by Rui de Pina (c. 1450–1522) and one by João de Barros (1496–1570), of

---

[75] *Ditos Portugueses*, ed. Saraiva, p. 152 (no. 402).

[76] See Ivana Elbl, 'Prestige considerations and the changing interest of the Portuguese crown in sub-Saharan Atlantic Africa, 1444–1580', *Portuguese Studies Review*, 10 (2003), pp. 15–36 at 30–1.

[77] António Brásio, ed., *Monumenta missionaria Africana, África Ocidental (1471–1531)* (Lisbon, 1952), pp. 349–50, cited in P. E. Russell, 'White kings on black kings: Rui de Pina and the problem of black African sovereignty', in P. E. Russell, *Portugal, Spain and the African Atlantic, 1340–1490: Chivalry and Crusade from John of Gaunt to Henry the Navigator* (Aldershot, 1995), chapter 16, pp. 151–63 at 163 and n. 15.

the visit of Prince 'Bemoim' in 1488 to King João II in Lisbon;[78] they provide an excellent textual example of the contradictory response to powerful and important sub-Saharan Africans. Pina was present at Bemoim's visit; Barros had various sources for it. King João II responded to the arrival of Bemoim, his relatives and his retinue by issuing them with European clothing suitable to their rank (to transform them outwardly into Europeans), and by allocating servants to them (to make their status clear). Pina praised Bemoim's impressive appearance and – rather surprisingly, as he had to speak through an interpreter – his oratory (considered one of the most fundamental Renaissance skills), thereby signalling that he had passed the test of entry to the Renaissance 'club'. But Pina revealed his inner struggle to categorise Bemoim when he wrote that 'he did not seem a black barbarian but a Greek prince brought up in Athens'.[79] For Pina, the colour of Bemoim's skin confusingly marked him as a barbarian while his oratorical skill induced classical comparisons. João de Barros reworded this sentiment and toned it down somewhat, but the message was similar.[80]

To counterbalance the textual rendering, I will end with a visual example of what happened to the usual stereotypes of black Africans when the person in question outwardly conformed to Renaissance European expectations of nobility. It is surely relevant that the subject was not required to speak. The identity of the black African represented in the half-length painting by Jan Mostaert entitled *Portrait of a Moor* (fig. 10) of *c.* 1525–30 is not known, but certain assumptions and deductions can be made. Mostaert (fl. *c.* 1475–1555/6)[81] lived most of his life in Haarlem but was also 'honorary painter' at the court of the regent of the Netherlands, Margaret of Austria (d. 1530), whose residence was in Malines,[82] so it is likely the black Renaissance 'gentleman' was attached to or visiting the Habsburg court in the Netherlands. The painting is on panel, and panel paintings had a monetary value and were commissioned, so this portrait was probably commissioned either by the subject or by the person

---

[78] Russell, 'White kings on black kings', pp. 151–63.

[79] Rui de Pina, *Crónica de El-Rei D. João II*, ed. Alberto Martins de Carvalho (Coimbra, 1950), p. 92: 'non pareciam de negro bárbaro, mas de príncipe grego criado en Athenas'.

[80] Barros, *Ásia*, fol. 31v. Earlier (fol. 30v) Barros had remarked that Bemoim had appeared not as a 'principe barbaro . . . mas como podia ser hum dos senhores da Europa'.

[81] On Mostaert, see Max J. Friedländer, *Early Netherlandish Painting from Van Eyck to Bruegel* (London, 1956), pp. 111–18; Max J. Friedländer, *Early Netherlandish Painting*, 14 vols. in 16 tomes (Leiden, 1967–76), x (*Lucas van Leyden and Other Dutch Masters of his Time*), pp. 11–23; and the entry by James Snyder in *The Dictionary of Art*, ed. Jane Turner, 34 vols. (London, 1996), XXII, pp. 199–201.

[82] See Karel van Mander, *The Lives of the Illustrious Netherlandish and German Painters*, ed. Hessel Miedema, 6 vols. (Doornspijk, 1994–9), I, pp. 174–5, and III, p. 196 and 204.

FIG. 10. Jan Mostaert's *Portrait of a Moor*, c.1525–30 (oil on panel, 30.7 × 21.2 cm).
Reproduced by permission of the Rijksmuseum, Amsterdam.

whose court it was. The black African gazes calmly out to his right; his face is composed and his eyes are steady. He has a moustache and longish beard (accepted as a sign of status and/or virility in both Africa[83] and Europe[84]), but significantly he does not have an ear-ring. In every important respect except skin colour, this portrait represents the very essence of a Renaissance gentleman or prince, and it turns the notion of black African stereotypes on its head.

This man demands to be judged by European rather than African standards, and proclaims his identity in European rather than African terms. He is not a slave, he has no body markings, and he wears no gold jewellery or pearl earrings. He is not laughing, looks anything but lazy, drunken or criminal, appears no more or less sexual than a white European ambassador or courtier, and is not represented in a typically 'black African' occupation. He wears expensive Spanish sixteenth-century costume – a white undershirt, a red over-garment and a black waistcoat – which was standard dress across Europe, but it is the powerful red colour of his clothes, and the quality of his accoutrements, that mark him out and proclaim his nobility and status. On his head he has an orange-red hat with a hat badge, on his hands he wears exquisite, rare cream gloves made of kid leather with their own tassel[85] (gloves like this were fitted and made to order, and were only worn by the nobility and aristocracy), and his sword is tucked into a belt with an elaborate beaded and jewelled purse. The purse, known as a *faldriquera* or *fartiquera*, was special – a type of gold embroidery on leather or velvet studded with pearls – and it contained a *fleur de lys*, connecting its wearer to the French royal house. The sword hilt is of blackened iron, and is of a type (with a pair of quillons each with a finger-ring) fashionable from about 1465 to about 1510.[86] The hat badge announces that the subject has visited the shrine of the pilgrimage church at Our Lady of Halle outside Brussels (not very far from Malines); the fact that it is crafted in gold indicates that he was an important, rather than a casual, visitor.[87]

---

[83] Both Pina, *Crónica*, p. 91, and Barros, *Ásia*, fol. 31v comment on Prince Bemoim's beard.

[84] See Loren Partridge and Randolph Starn, *A Renaissance Likeness: Art and Culture in Raphael's Julius II* (Berkeley, Los Angeles and London, 1980), pp. 44–6, 124–5, and Will Fisher, 'The Renaissance beard: masculinity in early modern England', *Renaissance Quarterly*, 54 (2001), pp. 155–87.

[85] For a comparable pair of gloves with a thinner tassel in a painting of 1508, see Ruth Matilda Anderson, *Hispanic Costume, 1480–1530* (New York, 1979), pp. 84 (fig. 212) and 85.

[86] A. V. B. Norman, *The Rapier and Small-Sword, 1460–1820* (London and Melbourne, 1980), type 15, pp. 78–80. The pommel is more difficult to categorise: see pommels 16, 18 and 49, pp. 245–7 and 261–2.

[87] Yvonne Hackenbroch, *Enseignes: Renaissance Hat Jewels* (Florence, 1996), pp. 239 and 245, and fig. 237.

Even the man's slightly swaggering pose, with his left hand turned back on itself at his left hip, betrays his Renaissance (in this case Italian) origins, giving him a superior edge. The stance of the sitter, and the style of these clothes and accessories (from four separate European countries or areas), are as much a testament to this black African's triumphant assimilation of European Renaissance norms as they are of a Habsburg pan-European culture.

This portrait of a 'noble' or ennobled black 'gentleman' in European court dress at least indicates that a few black Africans could, by 'going native' in Renaissance Europe, escape from the very pervasive stereotypes associated with them, but it is an altogether exceptional image, whose whole point may have been its exceptionality. It is not possible to know what the sitter thought about this portrait, but it might be useful to speculate upon two very different plausible interpretations of the intention of the painter, commissioner or sitter in creating this representation of a sub-Saharan African. Was the African here being used as the equivalent of a painted doll, dressed up in European finery for effect, to pun in a visual manner on a stereotype by combining it with its opposite? Had the African as a visitor been lent or given these clothes and accessories – ambassadors from outside Europe were routinely given European clothing when they arrived at royal or papal courts such as Lisbon[88] or the Vatican – and the painter seen in the mixture of messages a captivating jumble of cultural contradictions that he could put to good artistic use? Or was this black African a long-term courtier, born or brought up in Europe, and this image a genuine attempt to record a moment when Renaissance Europe and black Africa came together, and the possibility of forging a black European identity was glimpsed?

It is paradoxical that in order for a definition of whiteness to crystallise in Europe, it may have been necessary for Renaissance Europeans to encounter black Africans in the flesh. The timing of this encounter appears to have had seriously detrimental consequences for black Africans, who were categorised and stereotyped in opposition to Renaissance standards and ideals. But for those rare Africans and people of African descent of a certain status able to avoid these stereotypes and willing to assimilate to Renaissance culture, another possibility may have existed: the positing of a black European identity.

[88] See, e.g., Brásio, ed., *Monumenta missionaria*, pp. 150–1 and 326–7; Russell, 'White kings', p. 157; and Elbl, 'Prestige considerations', p. 31.

CHAPTER TWO

The image of Africa and the iconography of lip-plated Africans in Pierre Desceliers's World Map of 1550

JEAN MICHEL MASSING

Jean Ango (*c.* 1480–1557) was one of the most powerful shipowners in France in the second quarter of the sixteenth century. His boats sailed the seas from the Canadian coast to Sumatra, taking their share of the spice trade by defying the Treaty of Tordesillas (1494) and its division of the newly discovered world into two trade areas, respectively controlled by Spain and by Portugal. Official French policy was to respect the monopolies but Ango backed free trade and, as a privateer, his ships fought Spanish and Portuguese galleons, often returning to Dieppe with rich spoils. He was instrumental in encouraging Giovanni da Verrazzano's attempts in 1523 to find a northern route to China along the North American coast, looking for an opening into the Pacific. Ango's fortune was immense and his two residences, in Dieppe itself and in Varengeville, a few miles away, were substantial and full of treasures.[1] The latter is built around a central courtyard; the façade of the house, which has an open loggia, boasts a large frieze, which includes medallions with heads of Africans.[2] Still more remarkable, however, is the large frieze in Ango's private oratory, a fine Renaissance structure, in the second ambulatory chapel north of the choir of the church of Saint-Jacques in Dieppe (fig. 11); from right to left, it shows native Americans, Guineans, South and East Africans, and the triumphal procession of the Indian King of Cochin.[3] As a model the carver has evidently used the large series of woodcuts representing people from far-away countries by Hans Burgkmair (1508 and 1511) – or, more

---

[1] For his house in Varengeville see the appendix to J. M. Massing, 'La mappemonde de Pierre Desceliers', in H. Oursel and J. Fritsch, eds., *Henri II et les arts* (Paris, 2003), pp. 262–5, with further references. There is no up-to-date study of Ango's house in Dieppe.

[2] For these medallions, L. Vitet, *Histoire des anciennes villes de France. Haute-Normandie. Dieppe*, 2 vols. (Paris, 1833), II, pp. 117 and 430; Vitet, *Histoire de Dieppe* (Paris, 1844), p. 459; P.-J. Féret, *Histoire des bains de Dieppe* (Dieppe, 1855), p. 98.

[3] J. M. Massing, 'Hans Burgkmair's depiction of native Africans', *RES Anthropology and Aesthetics*, 27 (1995), pp. 39–40, fig. 1; with bibliography (p. 39, n. 2; to be completed with Gaffarel, 'Jean Ango', *Bulletin de la Société normande de géographie*, 11 (1889), pp. 262–4). For good photographs of the frieze, M. Mollat du Jourdin and Jacques Habert, *Giovanni et Girolamo Verrazano, navigateurs de François 1er* (Paris, 1982), pp. 148–9, fig. 42.

Bas relief du Trésor de S.t Jacques at Dieppe

Echelle de 9 centimetres pour metre

FIG. 11. Amédée Féret and Charles Mauduit, *Frieze in the Church of St Jacques in Dieppe* (from L. Vitet, *Histoire des anciennes villes de France. Haute-Normandie. Dieppe*, 2 vols. (Paris 1833), II, engr. after p. 112).

precisely, Georg Glockendon's copy of it (published in 1511 and apparently again in 1541). The prints illustrate Balthasar Springer's account of his travels to India (1505–6), on ships chartered by German merchants, to join Francisco de Almeida's expedition to India.[4] Burgkmair certainly knew Springer's writings, but he also seems to have used visual evidence. Some details, especially the costume of the so–called Hottentots, show a clear awareness of South African native dress not specified in Springer's account; this is even more evident in the case of Burgkmair's triumphal procession of the King of Cochin, especially in the costume, the facial characteristics and the hairstyle of the protagonists. Such careful observation is rare in the first quarter of the sixteenth century. Dürer shared Burgkmair's (unusual) interest in the newly discovered countries, their inhabitants, and indeed their dress and their material culture – be it a feather cloak, a mosaic shield or a club.[5] These Northerners recorded the objects with great care and, in their drawings, often managed to capture the characteristics of the inhabitants with discernment and subtlety, whether Africans, Indians or Americans, whereas others, especially Italians, looked for aesthetic solutions and were relatively blind to the rich variety of non-European people. Of course, one would like to know more about the account of newly discovered lands in Guinea and the drawings of Africans sent by Alfonso d'Este to his sister Isabella on 9 April 1491,[6] but Italian material of this type is rare, especially if compared to the surviving material from Northern Europe. For example, in a document dated 19 July 1505, Binot de Gonneville, a ship's captain from Honfleur, mentions he has seen on his voyage to South–East Asia 'numerous animals, birds, fish and other singular things unknown to Christendom' which were drawn (*pourtrayé* and *dessigné* are his

---

[4] For these prints and their influence, Massing, 'Hans Burgkmair', pp. 39–51 (pp. 38–39, nos. 4–6 for a bibliography of the prints).

[5] For Burgkmair's drawings of black youths wearing native American artefacts, see J. M. Massing, in J. A. Levenson, ed., *Circa 1492: Art in the Age of Exploration*, exhibition catalogue, Washington, DC, National Gallery of Art, 12 October 1991–12 January 1992 (New Haven and London, 1991), p. 571, no. and fig. 405, with further references. For Dürer's interest in the newly discovered countries, J. M. Massing, 'The quest for the exotic: Albrecht Dürer in the Netherlands' and 'Early European images of America: the ethnographic approach', both in Levenson, ed., *Circa 1492*, pp. 115–19 and 514–20 (see also pp. 288–9, nos. and figs. 192–3 and 300–1, nos. and figs. 206–8).

[6] For this document, A. Luzio and R. Renier, 'La coltura e le relazioni letterarie di Isabella d'Este Gonzaga', *Giornale storico della letteratura italiana* 33 (1899), p. 38. A. Luzio, *L'Archivio Gonzaga di Mantova*, 2 vols. in I, II, ed. A. Luzio (Verona, 1922), p. 64; C. Giglio and E. Lodolini, *Guida delle fonti per la storia dell'Africa a Sud del Sahara esistenti in Italia*, I (*Guide des sources de l'histoire de l'Afrique*, 5) (Zug, 1973), p. 422.

words) by Maître Nicolas Lefebvre, a man of learning who had asked to join the party.[7]

In Dieppe, around Ango, there was a special interest in the far-off lands, as reflected in its art and its cartography. Dieppe was a major centre for the latter, the most famous map makers being Jean Rotz, Nicolas Desliens, Pierre Desceliers and Guillaume Le Testu.[8] Not much is known about Desceliers's life.[9] In a document of 1537 he is mentioned as Pierre Desceliers, priest, living in Arques, a small market town near Dieppe.[10] A more informative source is Georges Fournier, who, in the second edition of his *Hydrographie* (1663), mentions priests from Arques, who were excellent geographers, of which one was named Desceliers.[11] The cartographer is also mentioned in *Les antiquités et chroniques de la ville de Dieppe* written, c. 1682, by David Asseline, who claimed that Desceliers was the first to have drawn sea charts in France and that he was such a talented geographer and astronomer that he was able to make a world map with, in its centre, a projection of all the parts of the world.[12] More than a hundred years later, in 1785, Charles Desmarquets added that

[7] 'Forces bestes, oyseaux, poissons et autres choses singulieres, inconnües en Chrestienté',
J. Paulmier de Courtonne, *Mémoires touchant l'etablissement d'une mission chrestienne dans le troisieme monde, autrement appelé, la Terre Australe, Meridionale, Antartique et inconnue* (Paris, 1663), pp. 14–15; for this reference, and the document mentioned above, n. 6, see also Massing, 'Hans Burgkmair', p. 47, nos. 28–9 with further references.

[8] For an overall account, R. Hervé, 'Dieppe, Kartographen von', *Lexikon zur Geschichte der Kartographie*, 2 vols. (Vienna, 1986), I, pp. 173–4. Also A. Anthiaume, *Cartes marines, constructions navales, voyages de découverte chez les Normands, 1500–1650*, 2 vols. (Paris, 1916). A list of maps is found in R. Hervé, *Découverte fortuite de l'Australie et de la Nouvelle-Zélande par des navigateurs portugais et espagnols entre 1521 et 1528* (Paris, 1982), pp. 10–11. For an important study of one of the maps and its imagery, *The Maps and Text of the Boke of Idrography presented by Jean Rotz to Henry VIII now in the British Museum*, ed. H. Wallis (Oxford, 1981).

[9] No study of Desceliers takes into consideration the totality of the sources; for an account, with bibliography, see Massing, 'La mappemonde de Pierre Desceliers', in H. Oursel and J. Fritsch eds., *Henri II et les arts* (Paris, 2003), pp. 251–3.

[10] 'Pierre Deschelliers, prêtre, demeurant à Arcques', C. de Robillard de Beaurepaire, 'Recherches sur les établissements d'instruction publique et la population dans l'ancien diocèse de Rouen', *Mémoires de la Société des antiquaires de Normandie*, 28 (1871), p. 330.

[11] 'Certains Prestres d'Arcques, Bourg prés de Diepe, qui estoient excellents Geographes, dont l'un se nommoit des Celiers', G. Fournier, *Hydrographie contenant la theorie et la practique de toutes les parties de la navigation* (Paris, 1643), p. 647.

[12] 'Pour ce qui est des cartes marines, je dyrai . . . que le sieur Pierre des Cheliers, prestre à Arques, a eu la gloire d'avoir esté le premier qui en a fait en France. Aussi estoit-il un si habile géographe et astronome, qu'il fit une sphère plate au milieu de laquelle on voioit un globe qui représentoit toutes les parties du monde', D. Asseline, *Les Antiquités et chroniques de la ville de Dieppe*, ed. M. Hardy *et al.*, 2 vols. (Dieppe, 1874), II, pp. 325–6.

Desceliers had devised a celestial and a terrestrial map, the latter with Asia more or less identical to its real shape.[13]

Three world maps (mappaemundi) by Desceliers are known to scholars, one of them only in reproduction:

1 The World Map of 1546, Manchester, John Rylands Library.[14] This map is traditionally said to be by him, although there are serious doubts, which I share, about the attribution.
2 The World Map of 1550, London, British Library (fig. 12).[15]
3 The World Map of 1553, formerly Library of Graf Hans Wilczek (destroyed).[16]

Another world map, dated 1542, is listed in the inventory of the *guardaroba* of Cardinal Luigi d'Este in 1579.[17]

The second of these mappaemundi is large (135 × 215 cm) and has a cartouche with information stating that it was done in Arques by Pierre Desceliers, in the year 1550.

FAICTE A ARQUES
PAR PIERRES DESCELLIERS
P[RES]B[IT]RE : L AN : 1550

It also carries the arms of France – it was probably devised for King Henri II – as well as those of Anne de Montmorency, Connétable de France and Claude d'Annebaut, Admiral de France.[18] The map, on four large pieces of parchment, is certainly one of the most richly illuminated pictures of the

[13] C. Desmarquets, *Mémoires chronologiques pour servir à l'histoire de Dieppe*, 2 vols. (Paris, 1785), II, pp. 1–2. For the texts mentioned in nos. 11–14, see also Massing, 'La mappemonde', pp. 251–2 and nos. 7–10, for further information.

[14] C. H. Coote, *Autotype Facsimiles of Three Mappemondes, 2: The Mappemonde by Desceliers of 1546* (Bibl. Lind., French MS No. 15) ([Aberdeen], 1898), pp. 10–15, pls. B1–B15. For a critical review of this publication, H. Harrisse, 'The Dieppe World Maps', *Göttingische Gelehrte Anzeigen*, 161 (1899), pp. 437–9. Wallis, *The Maps*, p. 39, was the first to have reservations about the attribution.

[15] C. H. Coote, *Autotype Facsimiles of Three Mappemondes, 3: The Mappemonde of Desceliers of 1550* (BM Add. MS 5413) ([Aberdeen], 1898), pp. 16–8, pls. C1–C16. More recently Massing, 'La mappemonde', pp. 251–62 and 265–8 (p. 265, n. 4, for bibliography).

[16] E. Oberhummer, *Die Weltkarte des Pierre Desceliers von 1553* (Vienna, 1924), introduction.

[17] G. Campori, 'Notizie dei miniatori dei principi Estensi', *Atti e Memorie delle RR. Deputazioni di storia patria per le provincie modenesi e parmensi*, 6 (1872), p. 38; G. Gruyer, *L'art ferrarais à l'époque des princes d'Este*, 2 vols. (Paris, 1897), 2, p. 450; L. V. Delisle, 'Le cartographe dieppois Pierre Desceliers', *Journal des savants*, 1902, p. 674; E. Müntz, 'Les miniatures françaises dans les bibliothèques italiennes', *La Bibliofilia*, 4 (1903), p. 234.

[18] For maps owned by Anne de Montmorency, L. Mirot, 'L'hôtel et les collections du connétable de Montmorency', *Bibliothèque de l'Ecole des Chartes*, 79 (1918), pp. 387–8, and 80 (1919), p. 191.

FIG. 12. Pierre Desceliers, *World Map*, 1550 (London, British Library).

world made in the sixteenth century. Like the Catalan Atlas of 1375, Desceliers's map was consulted flat on a table and viewed from both sides, as the
text and the illustrations of the top half are shown upside down.[19] The map
in fact combines the precision of sea charts – especially for the Mediterranean
and the Black Sea – with the conventions of world maps.[20] Thus, in the
case of Africa, the coastal areas are defined with great precision, even if the
configuration of the continent – especially its eastern half – is not clearly
understood. The World Map of 1550 was never used for navigation (Admiral
Claude d'Annebaut, incidentally, never went to sea); its aim was rather to show
the king the known world, with the most recent French 'discoveries'. French
ambitions in Canada are expressed by a text mentioning the explorations by
Jacques Cartier and later by Jean François de la Roque, Seigneur de Roberval
(1542–3).[21] Roberval, interestingly, set sail from Honfleur and was backed by
investors from Normandy. Although the place names on Desceliers's map have
often been gallicised, the Dieppe cartographer used Portuguese models, such as
the famous world map by Sebastian Cabot (1544).[22] Desceliers must have also
known another map, such as the Carta Marina of Laurent Fries (1525),[23] which
used, with modifications, the Carta Marina of Martin Waldseemüller of 1516.[24]
This sort of model may have encouraged him to enrich his own world map
with illustrations and twenty-two vignettes containing geographical information. It would also explain why the northern coastline of Africa is defined with
great accuracy, as is the whole periphery of the Mediterranean. Africa's western
coast was slowly charted, beginning with Dinis Dias, who in 1445 reached the

[19] For this map, H.-C. Freiesleben, *Der katalanische Weltatlas vom Jahre 1375* (Stuttgart, 1977);
G. Grosjean, *Mappa mundi. Der katalanische Weltatlas vom Jahre 1375* (Zurich, 1977). See also J. M.
Massing, 'Observations and beliefs: the world of the Catalan Atlas', in Levenson, *Circa 1492*,
pp. 27–33 and 120–1, no. and fig. 1.

[20] M. Mollat du Jourdin and Monique de la Roncière, *Sea Charts of the Early Explorers: Thirteenth to
Seventeenth Century* (New York, 1984); T. Campbell, 'Portolan charts of the late thirteenth century
to 1500', in J. B. Harley and D. Woodward eds., *The History of Cartography*, 1: *Cartography in
Prehistoric, Ancient and Medieval Europe and the Mediterranean* (Chicago and London, 1987).

[21] H. Harrisse, *Jean et Sébastien Cabot* (Paris, 1882), pp. 229–31. For these travels, W. P. Cumming,
R. A. Skelton and D. B. Quinn, *The Discovery of North America* (London, 1971), pp. 147–54.

[22] R. Hervé, *Mappemonde de Sébastien Cabot . . . 1544* (Paris, 1968). R. W. Shirley, *The Mapping of the
World: Early Printed World Maps, 1472–1700* (London, 1993), pp. 92–3, no. 81, ill. p. 91.

[23] For the different editions, L. Fries, *Carta marina universalis 1530* (Munich, 1926); M. Petrzilka, *Die
Karten des Laurent Fries von 1530 und 1531 und ihre Vorlage, die 'Carta Marina' aus dem Jahre 1516 von
Martin Waldseemüller* (Zurich, 1970); L. Fries, *Carta Marina. Faksimile – Ausgabe einschliesslich der
'Uslegung'* (Unterschneidheim, 1972); see also Shirley, *The Mapping*, p. 60, no. 56 and 66–3, pl. 53.

[24] J. Fischer and Franz Ritter von Wieser, *Die älteste Karte mit dem Namen Amerika aus dem Jahre 1507
und die Carta Marina aus dem Jahre 1516 des M. Waldseemüller (Ilacomilus)* (Innsbruck and London,
1903), esp. pp. 19–23 and 29–35, pls. 14–26; also Shirley, *The Mapping*, pp. 46–9, no. 42, pl. 43.

mouth of the river Senegal and Cape Verde and was able to sail back, against currents and wind, to report on his discoveries. Later work was undertaken by Bartolomeu Dias, who rounded the Cape of Good Hope in 1487–8,[25] showing – as is clearly indicated in Henricus Martellus's World Map of c. 1489 – that the continent could be circumnavigated.[26] The exploration of the African coast was furthered by Vasco de Gama, who connected the Mediterranean and Atlantic trade world with the Indian Ocean (1497–8) by reaching the east coast of Africa, stopping at the Arab harbours of Quelimane, Mozambique, Mombasa and Malindi before sailing, with the help of an Omani pilot and the monsoon, to Calicut in India.

Although the coastal areas thus became charted, for nearly three centuries Europeans had little knowledge of the interior of the continent, except for a very few specific areas.[27] There was of course the Sahara desert, but Islamic North Africa was likewise inaccessible to Europeans, the ports and their trade being basically closed to Christians. The Nile led to the swamps of Sudan and to the Ethiopian highlands, an effective barrier for the exploration of the heart of the continent. Seen from the sea, the country was inhospitable, unhealthy and dangerous, in some cases impenetrable, as the rivers, including the Senegal, the Niger, the Congo, the Limpopo and the Zambezi, did not allow easy access to the hinterland. Cartographers, when they did not leave a void, filled Africa with animals and images of its inhabitants, along with reported native kingdoms, elaborate systems of rivers and lakes, and a large number of towns all placed more or less at random. The famous Catalan Atlas of 1375 showed only a few cities south of the Atlas mountains. The Sahara was depicted with a lake in its centre, in accordance with medieval convention.

[25] For a good summary, *Prince Henry the Navigator and Portuguese Maritime Enterprise*, exhibition catalogue, London, British Museum, September–October 1960 (London, 1960) pp. 16–17. For the larger image, Peter Russell, *Prince Henry 'The Navigator': A Life* (New Haven, 2000). On Bartolomeu Dias and his time, see vol. II of the *Congresso Internacional Bartolomeu Dias e a Sua Época: Actas*, 5 vols. (Oporto, 1989).

[26] Massing, in Levenson, *Circa 1492*, p. 230, no. and fig. 129, with further references.

[27] For the cartography of Africa, C. de la Roncière, *La découverte de l' Afrique au moyen-âge. Cartographes et explorateurs*, 2 vols. (Mémoires de la Société royale de Géographie d'Egypte, 5–6), (Cairo, 1925); Y. Kamal, *Monumenta cartografica Africae et Aegypti*, 5 vols. (Leiden, 1926–53); A. Kammerer, *La Mer Rouge, l'Abyssinie et l'Arabie depuis l'Antiquité. Essai d'histoire et de géographie historique*, 3 vols. (Mémoires de la Société royale de Géographie d'Egypte, 15–17), (Cairo, 1929–52); E. Klemp, *Africa auf Karten des 12. bis 18. Jahrhunderts* (Leipzig, 1967); R. V. Tooley, *Collector's Guide to Maps of the African Continent and Southern Africa* (London, 1969); O. I. Norwich and P. Kolbe, *Norwich's Maps of Africa. An Illustrated and Annotated Carto-Bibliography* (Norwich, VT, 1997).

As was often the case in maps of the period, the cartographer compensated for the dearth of geographical information by including notes on the land and its main features.[28] Well into the sixteenth century, certain areas of Africa were still identified by their kings, as it was assumed that the continent was mainly occupied by centralised monarchies.[29] On the Catalan Atlas, Africa was also defined by a black man with a camel and a turreted elephant. Camels were first used for the trans-Saharan trade sometime between the second and fifth century AD, after being introduced from Arabia. Thanks to their famous capacity to travel long distances without water, they had completely transformed African trade, opening sub-Saharan areas to Islam.[30] The elephant, which is indeed found south of the Sahara, became one of its symbols: as the text of the Catalan Atlas puts it, Africa is the land of ivory 'on account of the large numbers of elephants that live there'.[31] Elephants are the most frequently found animals on sixteenth- and seventeenth-century maps, then camels and lions. Ostriches somehow lost their medieval popularity, but were still more frequently shown than monkeys, rhinoceroses and crocodiles, not to mention the more fantastic dragons.[32] Such images were used less to symbolise than to hide the lack of knowledge. Jonathan Swift aptly put it in 1733:

So Geographers in Afric-Maps
With Savage-Pictures fill their Gaps;
And o'er unhabitable Downs
Place Elephants for want of Towns.[33]

On the Caverio map of c. 1505, the man leading the elephant which is positioned in Southern Africa is not shown as black; on the other hand, the Miller Atlas wrongly blackens American Indians.[34] Africans, in fact, are often shown on maps as white in complexion, an illustration of the confusion in terminology regarding Moors – basically non-Ottoman Muslims – and the inhabitants

---

[28] W. E. Washburn, 'Representation of unknown lands in fourteenth-, fifteenth- and sixteenth-century cartography', *Revista de Universidade de Coimbra*, 24 (1971), pp. 305–22.

[29] W. George, *Animals and Maps* (London, 1969).

[30] R. W. Bulliet, *The Camel and the Wheel* (Cambridge, MA, 1975), esp. pp. 7–27 and 111–40; P. D. Curtin, *Cross-Cultural Trade in World History* (Cambridge, 1984), p. 21.

[31] Grosjean, *Mappa mundi*, p. 54, for example; for the elephant, George, *Animals*, pp. 42–3.

[32] For this conclusion, George, *Animals*, p. 146.

[33] J. Swift, *On Poetry: A Rapsody* (London, 1733), p. 12; see for example George, *Animals*, p. 21.

[34] E. L. Stevenson, *Marine World Chart of Nicolo de Caverio Januensis, 1502 (circa) . . . with Facsimile* (New York, 1908); Mollat du Jourdin and La Roncière, *Sea Charts*, pp. 216–17, pl. 29. For the Miller Atlas, *idem*, pp. 221–2, pl. 34 and S. Colin, *Das Bild des Indianers im 16. Jahrhundert* (Idstein, 1988), pp. 298–300, no. K4.

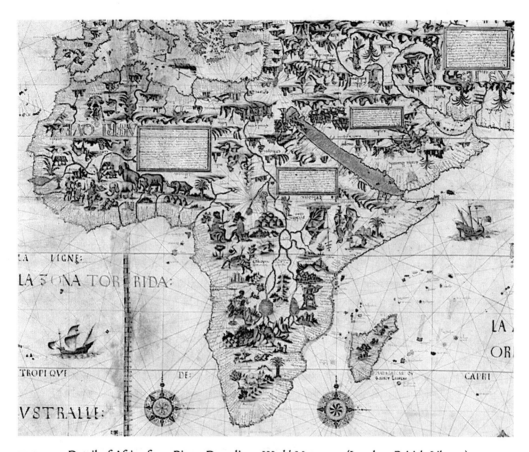

FIG. 13. Detail of Africa from Pierre Desceliers, *World Map*, 1550 (London, British Library).

of Africa in general. It also reflects the general vagueness of knowledge of far-away countries, in periods when terms like Calicut were used to define the newly discovered world.

In his 1550 world map, Desceliers added vignettes with texts referring specifically to Africa, Ethiopia, Madagascar and their inhabitants (fig. 13). The text on Africa provides general information.[35] It mentions that the Nile flows

[35] On Desceliers's maps, see Anthiaume, *Cartes marines*, I, esp. pp. 354–415. The text is the following: 'Affrique a de la partye dorient le fleuve du nil et aux aultres parties totalemment enclose de la mer et la est plus large. La partie plus prochaine de leuroppe est la plus habitee plus fertile et meilleure. Mais la plus grande partie est deserte raison des sablons, bestes cruelles situation et intemperance du ciel du premier temps sans seigne. Les vagabonds vivans bestiallemment dherbes et fruictz darbres. Jusques au temps dhercules lequel leur feist petites maisons du boys des navires dont ilz passerent en libye. En ce pays y a vignes si grosses que les

in an easterly direction, and that the continent is otherwise surrounded by seas. The area closest to Europe is relatively fertile and rich, though a large part is unpopulated because of the sand, the dangerous animals and the inclement climate. The people there are nomadic and live like wild beasts, on plants and fruits – at any rate, we are told, until the time of Hercules, who built them little houses from the wood of ships which came from the Libyan coast. Geographical information is clearly mixed with natural history and mythology. Desceliers comments on the vine which grows so well that a man could not encircle the trunks with his arms, as well as on the multifarious animals found in Africa: lions, elephants, camels, leopards, lynxes, dromedaries, buffaloes, apes, giraffes, rhinoceroses, panthers, horned asses, also hyenas, porcupines, jackals, storks, wild cocks (*pigardes*) and ostriches. The 'snakes' found there include dragons, crocodiles, basilisks and asps. Ethiopia, we learn, is divided into two parts. The country is flat and desolate (*morneuse*), and in its eastern part deserted.[36] Some of its numerous inhabitants have monstrous faces. Those who live in the east are Christians; those in the west, who are called Moors, are Muslims. Gold mines, cinnamon and precious stones are found at Meroe. Not far from there lives Prester John, who rules over sixty-two kings.

The definition of the coast follows the characteristics of portolan charts, insisting on coastal information with important cities and trade posts often symbolised by little images. Though various rivers flow into the sea, their course is largely limited to the coastal areas, including the Congo; the map-maker also showed the Niger prominently, but also traditionally, as (wrongly) flowing westwards. The Nile crosses Africa from south to north, originating in the so-called Mountains of the Moon: there, different streams fill two symmetrically opposed lakes, from which the Nile flows northwards. Here the cartographer has followed Ptolemy – or a later interpolation to his text.[37] On the map, swamps and an area where cinnamon grows separate the two lakes. In

hommes ne pourroient totalemment embrasser le tronc dont les raisins ont une couldee de long. Les bestes sont lyons, elefans, cameaulx, leopardz, unces(?), dromedares, buffles, singes, camaleopardz, rinocerons, pantheres, asnes, cornus, aultres bestes nomées en langue latine Rhises, hyenas, histrices, thoas, ciconias, pigardes et austruces. Les serpents sont dragons, cocodiles, basilicz, aspicz, ceraftas et aultres.'

[36] 'Ilz sontz ethipies cest assavoir ceste ter dasie dicte indie et celle daffrique laquelle est morneuse et plaine de sablons et vers orient deserte. est moult peuplée. Les aulcuns de monstreuse face et ont 2 messions (?) lan. Les aulcuns orientaulx congnoissent Jhesucrist, les occidentaulx mahumet qui sont dictz maures. A meroe ya minieres dor, canelle et Pierre precieuses. Et pres dicy preside presbitre Jehan, sur soixante deulx roys.' For the animals shown on the map, see J. B. Lloyd, *African Animals in Renaissance Literature and Art* (Oxford, 1971), pp. 19–23, pl. 12.

[37] W. G. L. Randles, 'South-east Africa as shown on selected printed maps of the sixteenth century', *Imago Mundi*, 13 (1956), esp. pp. 75–7. For the empire of Monomotapa, see his

the Nilotic swamps of Nubia, between Abyssinia and the kingdom of Meroe (both shown as large islands on the Nile), are seen monstrous inhabitants: headless men with faces on their chests, the Blemmyae (*Collopedes*) and people with multiple arms (here called *Soboride*), well-known figures from medieval cartography and of white complexion.[38] The so-called monstrous races, from the ends of the world, were first mentioned by Greek authors, but it is Pliny who gave them a prominence and a wide diffusion throughout the Middle Ages. In the sixteenth century their reality was certainly challenged by some, but not so effectively as to obliterate their memory.

On the 1550 map the various little scenes shown in the interior of the continent often follow the text of the map, in other cases they reflect information available to the cartographer. The Red Sea is not merely crossed here, as in the Catalan Atlas, by a line suggesting the passage of Moses and the Jewish people (Exodus 14: 21–2), but that episode is illustrated at the conventionally accepted spot.[39] A few flat-roofed houses stand for the towns in Ethiopia, while Prester John (*Prebstre Jhan*) is seen enthroned, with a papal tiara and a triple cross. He is white, like two of his subjects shown in front of him. The idea that there was a fabulously powerful ruler living somewhere in the east originated in a letter supposedly written by him, around 1165, and addressed to the pope and two unidentified lay rulers of Christendom. This potential ally against the Muslims was originally meant to live somewhere in Asia; Marco Polo, among others, searched for him throughout Central Asia. His kingdom was later located in East Africa – first, seemingly in 1306 – and as a result he was conflated with the king of Ethiopia.[40] South of Prester John appears the king of Kilwa (*Roy de quiolla*) dark brown in complexion, enthroned, crowned and holding a sceptre. He is dressed in a pseudo-Roman costume with a cape over his shoulders. On the other side of the Nile, the Congo is symbolised

'South-east Africa and the empire of Monomotapa as shown on selected printed maps of the sixteenth century', *Centro de Estudos Históricos Ultramarinos. Studia*, 2 (July 1958), pp. 103–63.

[38] See e.g. R. Wittkower, *Allegory and the Migration of Symbols* (London, 1977), pp. 45–74 (see also pp. 76–92 and 93–6); J. B. Friedman, *The Monstrous Races in Medieval Art and Thought* (Cambridge, MA and London, 1981). For the Blemmyae and the people with many arms, S. Zajadacz-Hastenrath, 'Fabelwesen', in *Reallexikon zur deutschen Kunstgeschichte*, 6 (Munich, 1973), cols. 748–53 and 788–9.

[39] For the Red Sea in the Catalan Atlas, for example Grosjean, *Mappa mundi*, p. 76 and Massing, 'Observations and beliefs', p. 29.

[40] For Prester John on maps of Asia, I. Hallberg, *L'extrême-Orient dans la littérature et la cartographie de l'Occident des XIIIe, XIVe et XVe siècles* (Göteborg, 1907), pp. 281–5. For Prester John in Africa, R. Silverberg, *The Realm of Prester John* (New York, 1972), pp. 163–92; for his presence on African maps, Kamal, *Monumenta*, IV. 4, p. 1476, but also Jeremy Lawrance, 'The Middle Indies: Damião de Góis on Prester John and the Ethiopians', *Renaissance Studies*, 6 (1992), pp. 306–24.

FIG. 14. Detail of Africans with enlarged lips from Pierre Desceliers, *World Map*, 1550 (London, British Library).

by its ruler (*Roy de manicongo*) dressed in a similar manner with a crown and a sceptre. North of him, and north of the Congo river, is found Western Ethiopia (*Ethiopie interiore*). There, two natives are digging for gold, one of them with a pickaxe.[41] Above them, the artist has depicted a pair who could certainly qualify as 'aulcuns de monstreuse face'. They are sitting opposite each other, probably in the act of bartering (fig. 14); one of them, who carries a club, hands a gold nugget to a companion who holds some flowers. They both are clearly African, of black complexion. One of them has curly hair, and the other long hair falling on his shoulders. In addition to these characteristics, they have enlarged lips, a clear allusion to a well-known practice in various parts of Africa.

In the map, Western Africa is divided into two parts by the river Niger. In the northern half the illuminator – who was most probably Desceliers himself – has shown the king of Fez as a Mediterranean ruler, while an ostrich and a camel respectively mark the Libyan and Mauritanian deserts. South of the Atlas mountains appears the king of Nubia on the east as well

---

[41] Digging for gold and precious stones is also shown in the Far East (with the following text: 'En ce pays y a 4 roys au bas dune haulte montaigne on trouve rubys: et ung grand fleuve y a hiacinthes, saphirs, topasses et aultres clou de giroffle et canelle') and in Java, to stress the richness of the newly discovered countries and, probably, to induce Henri II to develop maritime trade.

as a lion and a camel in the country of the Garamantes. Here, as elsewhere, the labels identifying the different parts of Africa have been added without precise knowledge, except that the cartographer knew which one was closest to the Nile and had a faint idea about their interrelations. He has also included exotic plants in sub-Saharan Africa – they are mentioned, after all, at length in travel accounts – as well as huts to allude to habitations. Some of them simply have four posts covered with a thatched roof, the others are round and made of branches. Not far from Guinea (*Guinee*) can be seen the king of Organa (*Urbana*), a black-bearded ruler, with his subjects; one of them kneels in front of him in a gesture of submission, a traditional formula used to allude to African despotism.[42] North of Elmina castle, finally, are three elephants and a rhinoceros, standard symbols for the black continent.

As far as the African interior is concerned, Pierre Desceliers's World Map of 1550 is certainly one of the most lavish artistic achievements in sixteenth-century cartography. The artist was nicely eclectic in his borrowings from cartographic convention. He certainly also knew the world map devised by Sebastian Münster found in the *Novus orbis regionum ac insularum . . . libellus,* first published in Basel in 1532, although he did not follow its definition of the world (fig. 15). Hans Holbein's woocut (*Typus cosmographicus universalis*) shows the picture of the world on an oval projection, with angels rotating it around its axis with a crank.[43] At the four corners, the artist has represented outlandish people, as well as animals and plants from far-off lands respectively representative of Africa, Asia, Arabia and America.[44] For Africa, Holbein represented a man shooting an elephant, which is trampling his companion. The illustration refers to a passage in Alvise da Mosto (Cadamosto)'s account of his exploration of the west coast of Africa and the Cape Verde islands (1455–6), a text found in Münster's compilation. Cadamosto wrote that 'an elephant is an animal that does not attack man unless man attacks him', which is the case

---

[42] Similar information was conveyed by a number of writers, such as Alvise da Mosto (or Cadamosto). His text was first published in *Paesi novamente retrovati* (Vicenza, Henrico Vicentino, 1507), sig. E4v–F1r; for the translation, Alvise Cadamosto, *The Voyages of Cadamosto and Other Documents on Western Africa in the Second Half of the Fifteenth Century*, trans. and ed. G. R. Crone (London, 1937), pp. 39–40.

[43] Sebastian Münster, *Novus orbis regionum ac insularum veteribus incognitarum . . . libellus* (Basel, 1532). For this map, see *The World Encompassed: An Exhibition of the History of Maps*, exhibition catalogue, Baltimore, Baltimore Museum of Art, 7 October–23 November 1952 (Baltimore, MD, 1952), no. 65; F. Hieronymus, *Basler Buchillustration 1500–1545* (Oberrheinische Buchillustration, 2), exhibition catalogue, Basel, Universitätsbibliothek, 31 March–30 June 1984 (Basel, 1984), pp. 519–21, no. 450, fig. pp. 688–9; H. Wolff, *America. Das frühe Bild der Neuen Welt*, exhibition catalogue, Munich, Bayerische Staatsbibliothek, 10 April–27 June 1992 (Munich, 1992), pp. 70–1, no. 86, ill.

[44] For a study of the image of America, *Das Bild des Indianers*, pp. 198–9, no. B.29, fig. 11.

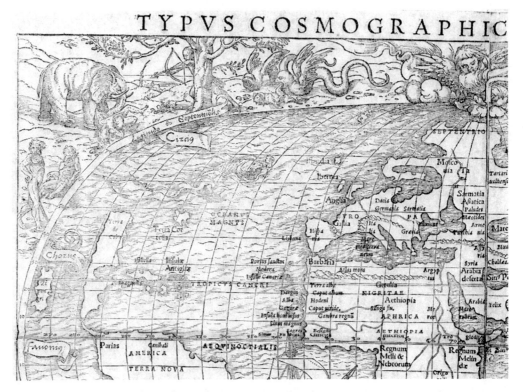

FIG. 15. Hans Holbein, *Typus cosmographicus universalis*, in Sebastian Münster, *Novus orbis regionum ac insulanm veteribus incognitanm . . . libellus* (Basel, 1532), illustration referring to Africa.

here. He also wrote that 'the method of the elephant in attacking a man is to overtake him and deal him so strong an upward blow with his long trunk of a snout . . . that the man falls to the ground'.[45] Holbein's dependence on Cadamosto's text is confirmed by the addition of two dragons so large that they can 'swallow a goat whole, without tearing it to pieces'.[46] The two men with lip-plates nearby are a reference to Cadamosto's account of some Africans who dealt in salt with the Emperor of Melli: 'they were very black in colour, with well-formed bodies. Their lower lip, more than a span in width, hung down, huge and red, over the breast, displaying the inner part glistening like blood'. The upper lip, however, was normal: 'This form of the lips displayed the gums and teeth, the latter, they said, being bigger than their own: they

---

[45] *Paesi*, sig. F4r and Cadamosto, *The Voyages*, p. 47.

[46] *Paesi*, sig. F3r and Cadamosto, *The Voyages*, p. 44; see Hieronymus, *Basler Buchillustration*, p. 520, for this link.

FIG. 16. *African with Lip-plate*, post-card (Paris, n.d.).

had two large teeth on each side, and large black eyes. Their appearance is terrifying, and the gums exude blood, as do the lips'.[47]

The African (actually Senegalese) quoted by Cadamosto must have been quite familiar with the use of lip-plates or labrets (fig. 16). Small holes are

---

[47] *Paesi*, sig. C4v and Cadamosto, *The Voyages*, p. 24; see also p. 22, no. 1. Cadamosto is the source of the accounts found in C. Lycosthenes (Wolfhardt), *Prodigiorum ac ostentorum chronicon* (Basel, 1557), pp. 7–8 and U. Aldrovandi, *Monstrorum historia* (Bologna, 1642), pp. 8–9, both with woodcuts (for which see also Zajadacz-Hastenrath, 'Fabelwesen', cols. 791 and, for the latter, 787, fig. 33b).

made in the lips during infancy and small wood or ivory splints inserted, until
the lower lip is able to hold the full-sized discs.[48] This mutilation is found in
various parts of Africa, among the Lobi, the Saro women of Southern Chad,
the Fali of Cameroon, the Guma people in Sudan and Ethiopia as well as the
Makonde in Tanzania.[49] For Europeans – and this includes cartographers –
Africans with lip-plates must have recalled reports of a monstrous race with
a lip that protruded so much that it was used to protect them from the sun.
In his *Natural History*, Pliny the Elder records this in Ethiopia. According to
Pliny, 'It is certainly reported that . . . there are tribes of people . . . that have
no upper lip and others no tongues. Also one section has the mouth closed'.
Strabo, in his *Geography*, mentions that among the people living in Ethiopia
are Amycteres ('people without noses'), who eat everything, including raw
meat, and live but a short time: they also have the upper lip protruding much
more than the lower.[50] It is Isidore of Seville, however, who first mentions
people who have the lower lip so extended that they use it to cover their
faces from the rays of the sun while sleeping.[51] It was from Isidore that the
type became popular, being found, for example, in the *De universo* by Rabanus
Maurus and the *Speculum historiale* by Vincent of Beauvais, not to mention
some versions of Mandeville's *Travels*.[52] A varied collection of fabulous races
is found in a page of a Solinus manuscript in the British Library, which dates
from the second half of the twelfth century: in the second row of figures, the
first from the left is of our type shown as a standing nude man, seen in profile
and with his legs crossed, his lower lip rising in front of his face. People with
extended lips are also found among the *Marvels of the East*, a type of manuscript

---

[48] For such a lip-plate, see J. Mack, in *Africa: The Art of a Continent*, ed. T. Phillips, exhibition
catalogue, London, Royal Academy of Arts, 4 October 1995–21 January 1996 (London, Munich
and New York, 1995), p. 138, no. 2.19.

[49] See note 48. Also H. Johnston, R. Lydekker *et al.*, *The Living Races of Mankind*, 2 vols. (London,
[1905, 1906]), II, p. 418; W. Hutchinson, ed., *Customs of the World. A Popular Account of the Customs,
Rites and Ceremonies of Men and Women of All Countries*, 2 vols. (London, [1912–14]), II, p. 797;
H. H. Ploss, M. Bartels and P. Bartels, *Woman: An Historical, Gynaecological and Anthropological
Compendium* (London, 1935), I, pp. 246–7 and 250–1, figs. 213–15. There is no overall, historical
assessment of the use of lip-plates.

[50] Pliny, *Natural History*, 6, 35, 187; Strabo, *Geography*, 15, 1, 57; Friedman, *The Monstrous Races*,
pp. 9–10, 57 and 124. Most useful is Zajadacz-Hastenrath, 'Fabelwesen', cols. 791–2.

[51] Isidore of Seville, *Etymologiae*, 11, 3, 18: 'Aliae labro subteriori adeo prominenti, ut in solis
ardoribus totam ex eo faciem contegant dormientes'.

[52] Rabanus Maurus, *De universo*, 7, 7; Vincent of Beauvais, *Speculum Historiale*, 1, 92; John
Mandeville, *Travels*. Texts and translations by M. Letts, 2 vols. (London, 1953), II, pp. 142 and
344. For further and later references, Zajadacz-Hastenrath, 'Fabelwesen', cols. 791–2.

specifically devoted to that topic; a twelfth-century manuscript in Oxford has an image of a man reclining and pulling his large lower lip over his face to protect it from the sun, while the accompanying text includes Isidore of Seville's description.[53] People with extended lips are also found in bestiaries: for example, in the Sion College Bestiary, a manuscript from North-West France produced *c.* 1277 which came, via the Ludwig collection, to the J. Paul Getty Museum (fig. 17). On fol. 117v, a man shown in profile needs his two hands to support his lips, of enormous size, while the text next to him mentions its purported 'traditional' use – to protect the face from the sun – as stressed in another inscription nearby.[54] Another bestiary of the thirteenth century links the fabulous creatures to the text of Psalm 139: 10, 'The mischief of their lips will cover them',[55] while the compendium of moral stories known as *Gesta Romanorum* gives a rather unexpected reading: such people are symbols of the Just, who protect themselves from the temptations of the world.[56] In maps, people with large lower lips are generally associated with the unexplored parts of the world, especially in Africa. Some maps in the *Polychronicon* of Ranulf Higden (died 1363) record people who protect their face with their large lips against the rays of the sun,[57] while an inscription on the Walsperger map, drawn some 100 years later (1448), still mentions such people with

[53] Oxford, Bodleian Library, MS 614, fol. 50v: 'Monstruose quoque gentium scribuntur facies, labro subteriori adeo prominenti ut in solis ardoribus totam ex eo faciem contegant dormientes'. See M. R. James, *Marvels of the East: A Full Reproduction of the Three Known Copies, With Introduction* (Oxford, 1929), pp. 23–4, no. 47, p. 62, no. 47, pl. (Bodl. 614, fol. 50ᵇ); also Zajadacz-Hastenrath, 'Fabelwesen', col. 789, fig. 34. For the Solinus manuscript of the second half of the twelfth century (London, British Library, MS Harley 2799, fol. 243v) see H. Swarzenski, *Monuments of Romanesque Art: The Art of Church Treasures in North-Western Europe* (London, 1954), p. 74, pl. 189, fig. 431; see also Zajadacz-Hastenrath, 'Fabelwesen', cols. 741 and 740, fig. 2.

[54] Malibu, J. Paul Getty Museum, MS Ludwig, xv 4, fol. 117v: for this manuscript, A. von Euw and J. M. Plotzek, *Die Handschriften der Sammlung Ludwig*, 4 vols. (Cologne, 1979–85), IV, pp. 188–206, no. xv 4, figs. 89–116; for fol. 117v (with the inscription: 'Gens labro prominenti unde sibi faciem contra solis ardorem tegunt'), p. 193 and fig. 107; for the wider context of such monstrous races, pp. 200–2, with much information.

[55] G. C. Druce, 'Some abnormal and composite human forms in English church architecture', *Archaeological Journal*, 72 (1915), p. 150.

[56] *Gesta Romanorum*, ed. H. Oesterley (Berlin, 1872), p. 575: 'Tales designant justos, qui habent inferius scilicet ad mundum magnum labium considerationis, attendentes mundi vanitatem detractionis et mendacii; tamen per labium custodie protegant totam faciem i.e. totam vitam per jugem meditationem ne in peccatis dormiant'.

[57] K. Miller, *Mappaemundi. Die ältesten Weltkarten*, 6 vols. (Stuttgart, 1895–8), III, p. 105: 'Gens ista obumbrat faciem cum labro prominente contra solis ardorem'. See also D. Woodward, 'Medieval Mappaemundi', in Harley and Woodward, eds., *The History of Cartography*, esp. pp. 312–13.

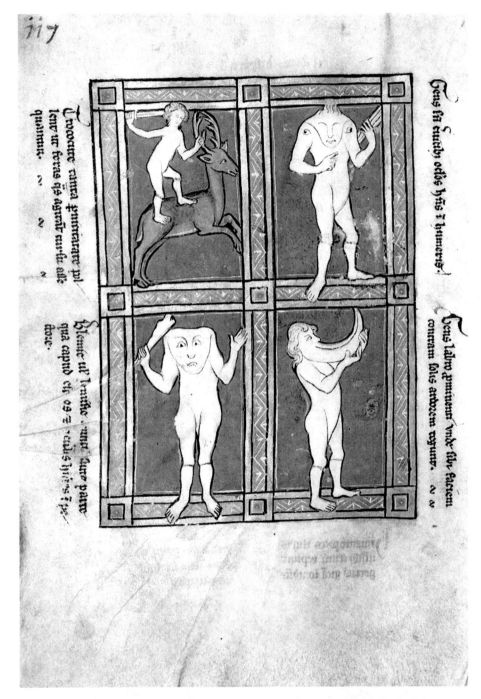

FIG. 17. *Fabulous Beings*, Syon College Bestiary, *c.* 1277 (Los Angeles, The J. Paul Getty Museum, MS Ludwig, XV 4, fol. 117v).

enormous lips.[58] One of the earliest surviving illustrations in cartography seems to be a small figure in a famous thirteenth-century world map in a British Museum psalter; there can be seen, among other oddities, a man with a lower lip stretching out in front of his face.[59] The Hereford map makes the topic much clearer: a sitting man points to the sun above him, and his face is in profile, with the elongated lower lip clearly extending in front of his face.[60]

Desceliers's and Holbein's Africans are more directly based on late medieval images of these fabulous people with large, drooping lower lips. For example, a page of the famous *Nuremberg Chronicle* published by Hartmann Schedel in 1493 (fig. 18) shows a number of such outlandish creatures: one of them sits on the floor, pointing to some plant he is plucking. He has a broad, almost circular lower lip, while the relevant text recalls Isidore's version of the face-covering device.[61] For his vignette of the gold bartering scene, however, Desceliers used a woodcut from a Strasbourg edition of Ptolemy's *Geography* first published in 1522, and again three years later (fig. 19).[62] This is confirmed by the fact that Desceliers's text on Africa is based on the same edition. In the Ptolemy atlases, the imagery of the woodcut is not linked to any text; it shows two nude men, with large falling lower lips, sitting in a rocky landscape. As in Desceliers's map, one of them, with a club, shows a gold nugget to his companion, probably exchanging it for a flowering plant, alluding to the notion that such people have no idea of the true value of things.

---

[58] Miller, *Mappaemundi*, III, p. 148: 'Hy habent labia maxima'. For the Walsperger map, Woodward, 'Medieval Mappaemundi', pp. 316–17, 325, 327, 358 and pl. 21.

[59] Miller, *Mappaemundi*, III, p. 42 and II, 1895, pl. 1. For this map, Woodward, 'Medieval Mappaemundi', pp. 327–8, 331, 333, 340, 348, ill. p. 350, fig. 18.63. On the destroyed Ebstorf map (c. 1235), the lips are grown together, and so elongated that they curve around the head, their end being held in the left hand by the outlandish figure; Miller, *Mappaemundi*, V, p. 60, no. 5: 'Gens que habet ora concreta labioque promoventi ut contra solis radios se tegat.' See also E. Sommerbrodt, *Die Ebstorfer Weltkarte . . . Herbei ein Atlas von 25 Tafeln in Lichtdruck* (Hannover, 1891), p. 68, no. 16 and pl. 23; see also Zajadacz-Hastenrath, 'Fabelwesen', col. 742, fig. 3 and Woodward, 'Medieval Mappaemundi', pp. 291, 307, and 309–10, ill. p. 351, fig. 18.65, for further references.

[60] Miller, *Mappaemundi*, IV, p. 38: 'Gens labro prominenti, unde sibi faciem obumbrans ad solem'. On the Hereford map, see Harley and Woodward, eds., *The History of Cartography*, s.v. 'Hereford map' (p. 331, table 18.5 for a list of the main semi-mythical races found on Mappaemundi).

[61] H. Schedel, *Liber cronicarum* (Nuremberg, 1493), fol. XIIr: 'Item homines habentes labium inferius. Ita magnum ut totam faciem contegant labio dormientes.' See also C. Kappler, *Monstres, démons et merveilles à la fin du Moyen Age* (Paris, 1980), p. 125, fig. 18.

[62] C. Ptolemy, *Opus Geographiae noviter castigatum & emaculatum* (Strasbourg, 1522) and *Geographicae enarrationis libri octo Bilibaldo Pirkeymhero interprete* (Strasbourg, 1525), neither paginated (the woodcut illustrates Tabula II Africae).

FIG. 18. *Man with Elongated Lower Lip*, in Hartman Schedel, *Liber cronicarum* (Nuremberg, 1493), fol. xiiv.

In Desceliers's time, Africa certainly had trading potential for the nations of Europe, but the inhospitality of the land and the high level of mortality of Europeans in Africa meant that few attempted to stay. The European presence was centred on a few trade castles with a meagre garrison of Europeans. The interior was mysterious, supposedly full of riches, as is seen from the gold diggers and the gold bartering scene. The Africans themselves were imagined as being led by very powerful potentates – with Prester John predominant – while Southern and Western Africa was dominated by other rulers, either pagan or Muslim. Wild and fantastic animals cohabited with strange-looking people, perhaps Blemmyae, these mythical people who, according to Pliny, live in the deserts of Libya and lack heads and necks, but have their faces on their chests; there also could be found the strange lip-plated Africans. In Greek and Roman times a faint knowledge of the remotest people may have

FIG. 19. *Africans with Elongated Lips,* in Claudius Ptolemy, *Opus Geographicae* (Strasbourg, 1525), n. p. (woodcut illustrating *Tabula II Africae*).

prompted the definition of the Amyctyrae,[63] who at the time of the European explorations were given a new actuality when the first lip-plated people were recorded by Cadamosto in 1455–6. Still, without visual evidence in front of them, artists could only adapt traditional formulae to match literary evidence, and were unable to reflect the realities of Africa more realistically.

[63] For this phenomenon, E. S. McCartney, 'Modern analogues to ancient tales of monstrous races', *Classical Philology*, 36 (1941), pp. 390–4; also Friedman, *The Monstous Races*, p. 24.

CHAPTER THREE

Black Africans in Renaissance Spanish literature

JEREMY LAWRANCE

In the century following the first sale of African slaves on Portuguese soil in 1444, Spain acquired perhaps the largest black population in Renaissance Europe. Before the end of the fifteenth century, black freedmen founded their own confraternities in Valencia, Barcelona, and Seville; in 1475 the black and mulatto community of Seville had its own judge in the person of Isabella I of Castile's black usher Juan de Valladolid, a hospital, and its chapel under the advocation of the Ethiopian saints Elesbán and Efigenia.[1] At the height of the trade in the 1550s, Spanish traders were importing up to 2,000 black Africans annually through the Casa dos Escravos in Lisbon. It has been estimated that in the mid-sixteenth century Spanish slaves numbered perhaps 100,000, distributed chiefly in the south and in cities; in the Seville census of 1565 they accounted for 7.4 per cent of the population.[2] By 1599 importation of slaves to Spain was rapidly dwindling, but a German visitor to Ayamonte in Andalusia was amazed by its many 'black and half-caste women from the Indies [*sic*] and the island of São Tomé, so beautiful and amorous that the townsmen often marry them'.[3]

[1] Vicente Graullera Sanz, *La esclavitud en Valencia en los siglos XVI y XVII* (Valencia, 1978), pp. 160–6, and Alfonso Franco Silva, *La esclavitud en Sevilla y su tierra a fines de la Edad Media* (Seville, 1979), pp. 222–3; Diego Ortiz de Zúñiga, *Annales eclesiasticos y seculares de la muy noble y muy leal ciudad de Sevilla* (Madrid, 1677), Lib. 12, Año 1474, §10, 373–4; Ruth Pike, 'Sevillian society in the sixteenth century: slaves and freedmen', *Hispanic American Historical Review*, 47 (1967), pp. 344–59 at 345–6. Elesbaas (Kalēb Ellā-Aṣbeḥa, emperor of Aksum c. 514–c. 530) and the martyr Iphigeneia (apocryphal, Martyrdom of St Matthew) are not in the Roman calendar, though the latter is still revered in the black townships of San Luis de Canete in Peru, where her feast (21 September) is celebrated by banqueting on stray cats, formerly a staple of slave diet.

[2] Aurelia Martín Casares, *La esclavitud en la Granada del siglo XVI: género, raza y religión* (Granada, 2000), pp. 91–138, which updates Antonio Domínguez Ortiz, 'La esclavitud en Castilla durante la Edad Moderna', in *Estudios de historia social de España*, ed. C. Viñas y Mey, 5 vols. (Madrid, 1949–60), II (1952), pp. 367–428 at 376–84, and Charles Verlinden, *L'esclavage dans l'Europe médiévale*, I: *Péninsule ibérique – France* (Bruges, 1955), pp. 615–32, 835–46.

[3] Diego (Jakob) Cuelbis, 'Thesoro chorográphico de las Españas' (Madrid, Biblioteca Nacional, MS 18472), quoted in Domínguez Ortiz, 'La esclavitud en Castilla', p. 380, n. 22. In the early 1900s English tourists in nearby Niebla were still struck by the number of mulattos to be seen there: Bernard and Ellen M. Whishaw, *Arabic Spain: Sidelights on Her History and Art* (London, 1912),

The social presence of these black Africans was amply reflected in Spanish literature – the psychological impact of slavery, much less so.[4] Black characters in fiction, like the arresting black faces which gaze out from paintings by Velázquez and Murillo, usually stood silently in the background. Even when they were not mute, Golden Age representations of them were subject to a familiar battery of exaggerations, fears, and subliminal desires, like the absurd claim that Seville had become a 'chequer-board' where black threatened to match white in numbers. The cultural origins of prejudice lay in the ancient and medieval belief in physiognomy, the notion that the body is a scientific index of character. It seemed logical to deduce that 'the strange, ugly, deformed Antipodean peoples of Africa, [. . .] so contrary to us in form and figure', would show equally deformed behaviour: 'with no speech other than bestial grunts, [they] share women like beasts without religion or law, go naked, and never work' (Bartholomaeus Anglicus, De proprietatibus rerum, xv, 52). Blackness was seen as a mark of Noah's curse on the descendants of Ham (Genesis 9: 22–27), and hence as a justification for enslavement.[5] No amount of contact with real Africans could displace such ideas – on the contrary, slavery itself became the most important factor in reinforcing the ethnic stereotype. Hieronymus Münzer's account of a sale of Canarian Guanches in Valencia in 1494, after the Spanish conquest of Tenerife, shows how the humiliations of being stripped for the market block could be read, paradoxically, as further proof of barbarous culture:

In a certain house I saw for sale men and women with their infants and children [. . .] The people are not black but brown, like Berbers, the women shapely, strong-limbed and rather tall; but they are bestial in their manners, for up to now they lived with no religion and were all idolaters. [. . .] They all entered naked, but now they use clothes like us. What an achievement of careful training, to make these animals in men's bodies both human and tame! [. . .] Before the king of Spain's victory they were like beasts, but now religion has made them quite docile; [. . .] I saw many slaves in chains and fetters put to the hardest labour, sawing logs and so on.[6]

---

p. 129, quoted in C. G. Woodson, 'Attitudes of the Iberian Peninsula', *Journal of Negro History*, 20 (1935), pp. 190–243 at 199–200.

[4] The literature is critically surveyed in Baltasar Fra Molinero, *La imagen de los negros en el teatro del Siglo de Oro* (Madrid, 1995).

[5] William McKee Evans, 'From the land of Canaan to the land of Guinea: the strange odyssey of the "Sons of Ham"', *American Historical Review*, 85 (1980), pp. 15–43.

[6] Ludwig Pfandl, ed., 'Itinerarium hispanicum Hieronymi Monetarii 1494–1495', *Revue hispanique*, 48 (1920), pp. 1–179, 679, 'De hominibus schlavis venalibus', pp. 23–4 (an early example of 'Slav', then synonymous with white slaves, being used of the new category of *esclavos negros*).

The last sentence, which strangely overlooks chains and fetters in order to attribute the slaves' useful labour to the civilising effect of clothes, reminds us of the psychotic aversion to displays of the body which characterised Renaissance society, in which costume was the highly-regulated public sign of every moral, social and economic definition of the self. Images of Africans, whether in erudite ethnology or popular caricature, constantly retraced a vicious circle in which the insidious link between body and culture identified black nudity as an allegory of unbridled lechery, giving rise to an image of Africans as noisy, feckless children of nature prone to unrestrained physicality. Stanley Elkins called this the 'sambo stereotype', an iconography which dehumanizes slaves as chattels while sexualising them as bed-mates.[7]

The outlook which read the black physique as a token of animal spirits and lack of moral inhibition was reflected in a growing fashion for *bailes de negros* or dances introduced by slaves, which in their original form involved the titillations of semi-nudity. The *canario, guineo,* and later the exotic *gurumbé, chanchamele, ye-ye, zarambeque* and Angolan *paracumbé,* became bywords for lascivious vulgarity, and this in turn provided the commonest image of black Africans in burlesque and satire.[8] The first extant lyric for such a dance, Fernão da Silveira's *ratorta* for the wedding of Joana of Portugal to Enrique IV of Castile in Córdoba in 1455 in which a king of Sierra Leone has his people dance for the princess, is written in pidgin Portuguese, an imitation of slave creole (*fala de preto, habla de negros*) that inscribes the alienation and marginality of black physiognomy in a risibly infantile language.[9] This artificial dialect soon acquired a conventional spelling and morphology, serving to exaggerate its degrading comic stigma even when performed (as was usually the case) by black slaves.[10]

Peter Russell points out that the earliest Spanish example of *habla de negros* works in a more subversive way. *Verses to Black Men and Women,* printed in

---

[7] Evans, 'From the land of Canaan', pp. 19–21, on the 'scandalous paradox' of promoting slaves to the master's bed, and p. 22 and n.18 on the 'sambo' complex ('docile but irresponsible, loyal but lazy, humble but chronically given to lying and stealing, his behavior full of infantile silliness and his talk inflated with childish exaggeration'). Elkins referred to North America, but Evans adduces many cogent medieval examples from Arabic and other sources.

[8] Emilio Cotarelo y Mori ed., *Colección de entremeses, loas, bailes, jácaras y mojigangas desde fines del siglo XVI a mediados del XVIII,* 2 vols. (Madrid, 1911), I, pp. cxciv, ccxx, cclxv, cclxxi–cclxxii.

[9] *Coudel-moor por breve de ũa mourisca ratorta,* 'A mim rei de negro estar Serra Lioa', in *Cancioneiro Geral de Garcia de Resende,* ed. Aida Fernanda Dias, 6 vols. (Lisboa, 1990–2003), §44, I, pp. 194–5.

[10] On the nexus of *habla de negros, bailes de negros,* and the 'sambo stereotype' see Fra Molinero, *La imagen de los negros,* pp. 19–53.

a broadside of penny ballads written by Rodrigo de Reinosa c. 1500–10, belongs to the late-medieval genre of the flyting or scolding-match.[11] The poem portrays an exchange of abuse and lewd innuendo between the freed-man Jorge and the slave Kumba. It shows a striking interest in the African background of Seville slaves, with touches of realism ranging from Kumba's Senegambian name to the outlandish African lexical items that distinguish their language from conventional *habla de negros*.[12] There is verisimilitude, too, in the way that the pair cling to scraps of status. Jorge calls himself a 'good black' because he serves a bishop and has a freedman's letter of manumission (*ahorría*) to give him 'class' (*porte*); offering to cohabit with Kumba despite her snub nose, he boasts, 'if be in Jolof, me live at court' (vv. 53–58, 71–72). Kumba rejects him because she has a promise from another guardian, her 'brother-in-law' Grisolmo who gives her sweets (a 'white louse', according to Jorge, 55); at mass she sits near her mistress, the wife of the *corregidor* (36–37, 46–49, 65, 79). But the real point of the flyting is Jorge and Kumba's trading of insults about their homelands, as announced in the refrain (1–2):

She begins: Jolof Mandinga gives vexation to you, mister cockroachy black catamite.
He replies: Your land Guinea be an insult to you, madam cockroachy black whore.

The debate is not elevated; it centres on disgusting culinary habits and vulgar expletives. Kumba accuses the starveling Wolof of eating dung-beetles, dogs' heads, lizards and roast flies, and of shitting fleas; Jorge indignantly replies that they feast on couscous, whereas Guinea is a land of 'rotten lousy people' who eat 'rotten fish'.[13]

The only note we might call cultural is Kumba's simple-hearted pride in such sweet Guinean ditties as the barbarous *undul* or *mangana*, and Jorge's

---

[11] *Comiençan unas coplas a los negros y negras* (probably Burgos, c. 1520), fols. 1–2, edited in the Appendix. See P. E. Russell, 'Towards an interpretation of Rodrigo de Reinosa's *poesía negra*', in R. O. Jones, ed., *Studies in Spanish Literature of the Golden Age Presented to Edward M. Wilson* (London, 1973), pp. 225–45; page references are to the revised Spanish translation, 'La *poesía negra* de Rodrigo de Reinosa', in P. E. Russell, *Temas de 'La Celestina'* (Barcelona, 1978), pp. 377–406.

[12] See the notes on *taybo alcuzcuz*, line 13; *caranga, gaúl, carpanga* 19–21; *undul, maagana* 23–24; *choque-choque* 27; *chur-chur, bucamande, garango gur-gur* 61–63; *fongon* 37; and Frida Weber de Kurlat, 'Sobre el negro como tipo cómico en el teatro español del siglo XVI', *Romance Philology*, 17 (1963–4), pp. 380–91; Russell, 'La *poesía negra*', pp. 379–85, 388–94, 396–40.

[13] Russell, 'La *poesía negra*', p. 396 points out that 'Gelofe Mandinga' confuses two ethnic groups, Wolof and Mandinka, and concludes that Reinosa's African references are purely literary. However, only Kumba pairs the names (v.1); Jorge says he is 'from Mandinga' (12, 40) but would be a king 'if he was in Jolof' (54). The African identities are, at any rate, intended to sound authentic.

bragging about his skill at the lewd *guineo*. These references to song and dance are metaphors for another activity, *choki-choki* (26–31 and nn. 11–13); they do nothing to lessen the studied violence of the poem's language, its concentration on the degrading itches of belly and genitals. For Russell the poem is a parody designed to mock slaves 'by means of scabrous and often surrealistic caricature, presenting them as filthy in their habits and Black Africa as a barbaric region' ('La *poesía negra*', p. 385). Yet Reinosa's Africans seem more human than most speakers of *habla de negros*. Flytings demand a carnival emphasis on the repulsive earthiness of the body; what is significant, from the point of view of the author's psychology, is that Jorge and Kumba's appetites and pretensions are indistinguishable from those of whites ('La *poesía negra*', p. 399). If there is disgust, it is because these black subjects act as displaced metaphors of guilty self-loathing.

A more overtly dissident representation occurs in another broadside, the anonymous *Verses of How a Lady Begs a Black Slave to Sing to Her* (c. 1520).[14] The song's thirty-five quatrains are a *glosa* or amplification in matching metre and rhyme of a pre-existing poem, 'Sing little Jorge, sing, he no want sing', which was quoted a century later as 'an old ballad for hushing children' (see n. 2 on vv.1–7). The point of any *glosa* lies in the wit with which it turns the original to unexpected ends. Here an innocent nursery rhyme ('Sing, Jorge, by your true love, and see what I give you, a shackle for your foot and another for your neck') becomes a *requiebro*, or seduction, involving a dangerous reversal of social roles: 'the slave lets himself be persuaded and at last the mistress, surrendering to his attraction, offers him her body'. The poem is a variant of the traditional folk-song of the lady who tries to seduce an unresponsive rustic.[15] Its satire is directed not against the slave but against his mistress, and there is no *habla de negros* except in the refrain *No quere canta*. Instead, the lady's desire to have the slave scratch her 'itch' (43–46, 104–05) makes her speak

---

[14] *Coplas de cómo una dama ruega a un negro que cante* (probably Seville: Cromberger, c. 1520?), fols. 1–2v, edited in the Appendix, below. See Russell, 'La *poesía negra*', pp. 385–8, 399–400; Baltasar Fra Molinero, 'La formación del estereotipo del negro en las letras hispanas: el caso de tres coplas en pliegos sueltos', *Romance Languages Annual*, 3 (1991), pp. 438–43. John M. Hill, 'Notes for the bibliography of Rodrigo de Reynosa', *Hispanic Review*, 14 (1946), pp. 1–21 at 18 and José M. Cabrales Arteaga, ed., *La poesía de Rodrigo de Reinosa: estudio y edición* (Santander, 1980), pp. 184–90, attribute the poem to Reinosa, but this is rebutted by Russell, 'La *poesía negra*', p. 386.

[15] Oral and early printed versions are collected in *La dama y el pastor: romance, villancico, glosas*, ed. Diego Catalán *et al.*, 2 vols. (Madrid, 1977–8). The husband's absence on campaign (175–6) is a common motif, as is the bumpkin's preference for food over sex (85–101): cf. Margit Frenk Alatorre, ed., *Lírica española de tipo popular: Edad Media y Renacimiento* (2nd edn, Madrid, 1977), p. 582, 'Di pastor, ¿quiéreste casar? | Más querría pan', and the Chilean version in Ramón Menéndez Pidal, *Los romances de América y otros estudios* (Buenos Aires, 1939), pp. 32–4.

coarsely, whereas Jorge is not merely correct, but witty. Punning on *cativo*
('slave' and 'captive of love', a traditional courtly conceit), he laments that
his heart is too heavy to sing (8–11, 18–21); the mask slips when he begins
to boast of grinding like a miller (53–56, 63–66) or romping up and down
with the throat of a maestro (158–66), but even here there are no explicitly
improper words. The lady concedes that, cruel as Jorge's teasing has been (78,
126), 'though bay in colour you have white manners' (169–71).[16]

Despite its salacious comedy, the poem portrays the transaction between
the two protagonists with some care. Jorge at first plays the awkward novice,
but once confident that the lady is desperate, hints that she could get what she
wants by giving him his freedom (38–41) and treating him better – perhaps
with something to wet his whistle (86); finally, he goads her with the boast of
an outstanding operatic performance. By contrast, the lady first poses as a minx
(don't be intimidated by these fine gloves, 13–16; you don't know women, but
I could teach you, 23–26; I shall be lying on a perfumed bed where heavenly
pleasures await, 43–51), but soon falls to begging, talking of sad longings that
she would surrender everything to assuage (58–61), plaintively asking what it
is he does not like about her (68–71), and worrying that even if she gives all it
will not satisfy (155–56). The crux of the poem comes in the lady's long central
speech, which breaks the staccato rhythm of question and answer (88–142).
She offers the bribe of a feast – ominously for the husband, a capon – and
then her own enslavement and Jorge's freedom (108–16; at this moment the
refrain changes from 'he no want sing' to 'now he want sing', 112). In return
for the little pleasure of a 'song', she promises to be a chattel at his beck and
call (118–19); he is now the noble (121), by his own gods (?) let him not be a
cruel master (128–31 and n.15 on *buja hamel*).

The lady's desperate plight seems affecting, but this is anachronistic;
sixteenth-century readers would have laughed with scorn at her adulterous
desire for a black man. They would have been more disturbed by the poem's
representation of the slave. The poem plays on stereotypes about the rampant
virility of the African male, figured in the *pliego*'s crude woodcut by Jorge
pointing at his bulging cod-piece (fig. 20). Though deriving from the old
physiognomical concepts, the image was unsettling. Relations between white
masters and black women were condoned, but sex between white women

---

[16] Jorge mimics the diction of courtly love (*cativo, más muerto que vivo, esquivo, cuitado, lastimado, pena,*
ventura, merecer, gloria, puro amor verdadero, crueza; and, with special irony, *servir*, 83; *libertar mi*
pena, 146), whereas the lady uses the only African lexical item ('buja hamel' 130) and some
vulgarities which, though fashionable in the early days of print, are the reverse of courtly ('my
heart is yours from arse to throat', 91; 'pox on you, rascal', 168).

FIG. 20. Woodcut from the broadside *Coplas de como una dama ruega a un negro que cante en manera de requiebro* (Seville, Cromberger, *c.* 1520?), fol. 1.

and black slaves was taboo.[17] Where the threat of black male sexuality arises in other texts the outcome is predictable. In the play *Prodigy of Ethiopia*, for example, a white *dama* evades marriage to an Ethiopian at the cost of cutting off her own hand; in Andrés de Claramonte's *The Black Gallant in Flanders*, despite sleeping in the same billet as the black hero, she deflates his ardour by disguising herself as a boy. Fra Molinero interprets both scenes as metaphors of castration.[18]

Verses of How a Lady Begs a Black Slave to Sing to Her refuses to use ploys such as these to contain the shock of revealing Jorge as an object of desire. It records the unresolved tension between stereotypical images of black Africans and unexpected recognitions. The seventeenth-century paremiographer Gonzalo Correas recorded a proverb that expressed a similarly ambivalent anagnorisis: 'Though black, we are people'.[19] Of another, 'Black with white teeth, white with rotten teeth', he commented:

---

[17] In practice black freedmen occasionally married white women, but such cases were confined to the poorest and most abject classes (Martín Casares, *La esclavitud en Granada*, pp. 255–8, 363–5), with the famous exception of the Neo-Latin poet Juan Latino's love-match with Ana de Carleval, dramatized in Diego Jiménez de Enciso's play *Juan Latino* (Fra Molinero, *La imagen de los negros*, pp. 125–62).

[18] Fra Molinero, *La imagen de los negros*, pp. 55–76, 177–82 at 181.

[19] *Vocabulario de refranes y frases proverbiales* (1627), ed. Louis Combet (Bordeaux, 1967), p. 33: '"Aunke somo negro, onbre somo, alma tenemo" [in *habla de negros*]; . . . against those who disdain to associate with or admit others'. Sebastián de Cobarruvias Orozco, *Tesoro de la lengua castellana o española* (Madrid, 1611), fol. 562: '*Aunque negros, gente somos*, no one should be despised, however humble or low'.

Words of the black, who prides himself on his white teeth and mocks whites for having worse teeth blackened by decay. It implies that there is no one so abject as not to have something to be proud of, nor anyone so fortunate as not to have some spot or defect to embarrass him.[20]

In the compass of a century, the fantastic medieval *imaginaire* of Africans had been overlaid by experience of domestic slaves, but this only drove the sense of difference into murkier levels of the subconscious. *The Black Gallant in Flanders* (before 1634) tells the true story of Juan de Mérida, a freedman who won a captain's commission and a patent of nobility by an act of heroism in the war against William I of Orange (1533–84); the hero is allowed to defend himself eloquently against the racist prejudice of soldiers in his company, but the defence rings hollow – Juan's argument is that he always wanted to be white.[21] Meanwhile, the obligatory *gracioso* or buffoon is a slave who speaks *habla de negros*, thus serving to preserve intact the ethnic stereotype even as the play overtly enacts the proposition that a black man can be as worthy as a white. Equally double-edged is Francisco de Quevedo's portrayal of a black petition for emancipation in *Fortune in Her Wits, or the Hour of All Men* (c. 1634–35); the arguments move the modern reader as eminently reasonable, but Quevedo reveals a contrary intent, which is to satirise slaves (and incidentally Jews) for their delusion in failing to recognise the inferiority of their race.[22]

Cervantes's portrayal of the black slaves Luis and Guiomar in his short story *The Jealous Extremaduran* (between 1602 and 1613) shows, however,

---

[20] Correas, *Vocabulario de refranes*, pp. 229–30, 'Negro de blanco dentón, i blanco de negixón'. The saying reflected a popular trope; the earliest grammar of Spanish illustrated the figure of synecdoche with the example of 'the Guinean: *blanco los dientes, se enfria los pies* ('white teeth, gets cold feet')' (Antonio de Nebrija, *Gramática de la lengua castellana*, Salamanca, 1492, fol. 50v), while Francisco de Quevedo, *La hora de todos y la fortuna con seso*, ed. Jean Bourg, Pierre Dupont, and Pierre Geneste (Madrid, 1987), p. 316, wrote of black women's 'shady beauty' as a kind of dusk in which 'the whiteness of their teeth, pinpointed by the dark and glittering with laughter, imitates the jewels of the night'.

[21] *La gran comedia de el valiente negro en Flandes*, in *Dramáticos contemporáneos a Lope de Vega*, ed. Ramón de Mesonero Romanos, Biblioteca de autores españoles, 43 (Madrid, 1857), pp. 491–509. Juan's defence of negritude broke no new ground; see Alva V. Ebersole, '"Black is beautiful" in seventeenth-century Spain', *Romance Notes*, 12 (1971), pp. 387–91; it mirrors a proverb in Íñigo López de Mendoza (attrib.), *Refranes que dizen las viejas tras el huego* (Sevilla, 1508), fols. A7: 'It was bad fairies that made me black, for I was white' ('Hadas malas me fizieron negra, que yo blanca era').

[22] *La hora de todos y la fortuna con seso*, XXXVII, pp. 313–18. The image of black beauty quoted in n. 20 above is an example of the razor-edge ambivalence of this text; from one point of view the conceit is beautiful, from another it might be taken as derisory. Quevedo permits no such doubts in the grotesque and unpleasant ballad *Black Wedding* in his *Obras completas*, I: *Poesía original*, ed. José Manuel Blecua (Barcelona, 1963), §698, 819–21.

that such ambivalences could be productive. Both the slaves are represented
with characteristics of the sambo stereotype, including *habla de negros*, yet
Cervantes – who himself spent several years as a slave in North Africa –
evinces our sympathy for them and takes pains to specify that they and their
fellow slaves were rewarded with freedom by their dying master, despite their
part in the seduction of his young wife.[23] An even more striking ambiguity
lies at the heart of the best-known representation of a black slave in Spanish
literature, a brief passage in the proto-picaresque *Life of Lazarillo de Tormes and
of his Misfortunes and Adversities* (1554). The scene again confronts the taboo
of sex between a white woman and a black man – a topic so disturbing that
it was censored from one North American edition.[24] The first-person narrator is a working-class orphan who tells the disreputable tale of his rise –
his own word – to the position of town-crier and pimp to a prebendary of
Toledo cathedral. Despite his boasts, Lázaro ends as he began, by living off
the immoral earnings of a woman. When he was eight years old his widowed
mother took up as keeper of a student chop-house and part-time launder-
woman – often euphemisms for prostitution – in Salamanca. There she fell
in with some stable-boys of a nearby patrician, one of whom was 'a dark
man' ('un hombre moreno') – that is, a black slave.[25] Soon Zayd was a regular
visitor:

[23] *Novela del celoso extremeño*, in Miguel de Cervantes, *Novelas ejemplares*, ed. Juan Bautista
Avalle-Arce, 3 vols. (Madrid, 1982), II, pp. 173–221 at 220; the sentence on the manumission of
the slaves is omitted in the corresponding passage of the Porras MS version of the story,
pp. 223–63 at 263.

[24] The fact is noted by Velaurez B. Spratlin, 'The negro in Spanish literature', *Journal of Negro
History*, 19 (1934), pp. 60–71 at 63.

[25] *Lazarillo de Tormes*, ed. Francisco Rico, 2nd edn with bibliography by Bienvenido C. Morros
(Madrid, 1986), pp. 16–20 at 16, n. 14. *Diccionario de autoridades* (repr. of Real Academia
Española, *Diccionario de la lengua castellana*, Madrid, 1726–39), 6 vols. in 3 (Madrid, 1984), IV,
607, explains *moreno*: 'name for a dark-skinned black man, as a euphemism for the proper word
negro'; David Rowland (1586), for whom blackness was evidently a comic motif, translates
moreno as 'Black moor', and *negrito* as 'young blackamoor', adding extra references, e.g. 'vía a mi
madre y a mí blancos y a él no' ('perceiving that my mother and I were white and his father
black as jet'); 'mi hermanico' ('my little black brother'): *The Life of Lazarillo de Tormes*, tr. David
Rowland, ed. Keith Whitlock (Warminster, 2000), pp. 56–61. Thomas Roscoe (1832), with the
more nervous sensibilities of imperial Britain, goes to the opposite extreme, excising all
reference to blackness: *moreno* becomes 'a man of colour rather than of character or fortune' [sic],
the passage on the *negrito* is rendered 'One unpleasantness [sic] attended this intimacy, which was
that my mother presented me with a little brother, very pretty, though of a darkish complexion
[sic]': *The Life and Adventures of Lazarillo de Tormes, Translated from the Spanish of Don Diego Hurtado
de Mendoza. – The Life and Adventures of Guzmán d'Alfarache; or, The Spanish Rogue, by Mateo Alemán*,
tr. Thomas Roscoe, 2 vols. (London, 1881), I, pp. 1–80 at 10–12.

During the day he would come to the door on the pretext of buying eggs, and came into the house. At first I was upset by him and frightened at the sight of his colour and ugly face [Rowland: 'black uncomely visage']; but once I saw that his arrival improved our meals, I began to love him better.

The 'good round cantles of bread', offcuts of meat, and winter firewood which Zayd brought to Antona Pérez were stolen from his master. Lázaro continues:

And so, as both lodging and intimacy continued, my mother came to present me with a very pretty little black boy [negrito], whom I dandled on my knee and helped to wrap up warm. And I remember that once, as my black stepfather ['el negro de mi padrastro'] was playing with the little boy, when the child saw me and my mother white and him not, he ran from him to my mother in fear and, pointing his finger at him, said: 'Mother, bogeyman! [coco]' He laughingly replied, 'Son of a whore!' I, though very young, noticed my little brother's remark and said to myself, 'How many people there must be in the world who shun others because they cannot see themselves!'[26]

Christ's parable of the hypocrites who see the mote in their brother's eye but not the beam in their own (Matthew 7: 1–5, Luke 6: 39–44) is indeed an unlikely aside to have occurred to an eight-year-old. Its point is to turn the tables on white society, of course, but more important is its elision of any stereotyped comment on black thieving and carnality – an ellipsis which extends to the sequel, when Zayd's pilfering to support his family is found out. The story drily records how the 'poor stepfather' ('el triste de mi padrastro, lastimado Zaide') was whipped and larded, the mother given a hundred lashes and forbidden from seeing her partner again. The sententious adult Lázaro cannot refrain from another comment:

Let us not be surprised at a clergyman or friar, the one for stealing from the poor-box and the other from the monastery for their women parishioners and for help with the same again, when love encouraged a poor slave to this.[27]

---

[26] Coco, 'bogey man, bugbear', lit. 'coconut'; Cobarruvias, Tesoro, fol. 218–18v: 'the little face made by the three holes [in a coconut], which look like eyes and a mouth; hence we commonly say coco for the face a monkey makes when it is angry and hoots ko ko . . . . In children's language, any frightening figure, and none more so than those seen in the dark or of black colour; from כוש, Kush, proper name of Ham who reigned in Ethiopia, the land of the black people.' Vulgar hideputa was often affectionate (Lazarillo, ed. Rico, pp. 17–18, n. 26; Rowland: 'Whoreson, art thou afraid of thy father?'), but here the expletive is pointedly accurate. The whole passage is omitted by Roscoe.

[27] 'Help with the same again' ('ayuda de otro tanto') is 'with their bastards (as Zayd did for his)', or a pun on devotas 'women churchgoers/devotees' ('their fair and devout believers', Roscoe) and de botas 'of wineskins' (Lazarillo, ed. Rico, p. 19, n. 34); Rowland gives a cowardly paraphrase ('Let

The order of this comparison is crucial: 'don't blame priests if a slave does it' is a very different proposition from 'don't blame a slave if priests do it'. If the lovesick Zayd sets the standard by which to forgive other delinquencies, Lázaro must take it for granted that priests usually behave less morally than black slaves – a supposition amply borne out in the remainder of his story. Furthermore, this is the text's only mention of *amor*, or love. The thief Zayd, it turns out, is the single character in the story who possesses – and is punished for – the quality of charity.[28] It is not enough, therefore, to make the point that *Lazarillo de Tormes* evades racist comment without resorting to the 'sambo stereotype'. The author does something more significant, suggesting that the health of society may be actively improved by confronting its own bugbears in the mirror of its constructed representations of the ethnic minorities in its midst.[29]

Appendix: Texts of *poesía negra*

1. *Comiençan unas coplas a los negros y negras, y de cómo se motejavan en Sevilla un negro de Gelofe Mandinga contra una negra de Guinea; a él llamavan Jorge, y a ella Comba; y cómo él la requería de amores y ella dezía que tenía otro enamorado que llamavan Grisolmo. Cántanse al tono de 'La niña quando bayléys'. Hechas por Rodrigo de Reynosa* ([Burgos: Juan de Junta, c. 1520]), fols. 1–2.[30]

us never therefore marvel more at those which steal from the poor, nor yet at them which convey from the houses they serve, to present therewith whom they love in hope to attain thereby their desired pleasure, seeing that love was able to encourage this poor bondman or slave to do thus much as I have said, or rather more', *Life of Lazarillo*, p. 59 and n. 11). Antona's lashes (*centenario*) were the penalty for women caught in relations with non-Christians, Zayd's 'larding' (*pringamiento*, melting hot fat on welts after whipping) a standard punishment for slaves (*Lazarillo*, ed. Rico, p. 20, nn. 35–6; cf. Henrique da Mota, *Cancioneiro Geral de Resende*, §797, IV, p. 164: 'Congolese bitch [*perra de Manicongo*], I'll use a rasher of bacon on that back of yours!', vv. 37–40; 'you wants lard me, me die! [vós a mim quero pingar | mim morrer]', vv. 53–4).

28 I owe this point to my colleague Esther Gómez Sierra, in a forthcoming article which persuasively interprets the Zayd episode as the book's centre of gravity.

29 I thank Jon Beasley-Murray and Juan Carlos Bayo for comments on the argument and text; Rebeca Sanmartín, Anthony Lappin, and Catherine Davies for material; and Aurelia Martín Casares for the generous gift of her book. A version of this chapter was given at the Mediterranean XXIV Conference (Castellammare di Stabia, 2002), for which I am grateful to my friend Professor Norman Holub.

30 From the facsimile in Vicente Castañeda and Amalio Huarte, eds., *Nueva colección de pliegos sueltos* (Madrid, 1933), pp. 131–8 at 131–3, with modern punctuation. Previously printed in *Rodrigo de Reinosa: selección y estudio*, ed. José María de Cossío (Santander, 1950), pp. 111–15; Rodrigo de Reynosa, *Coplas*, ed. María Inés Chamorro Fernández (Madrid, 1970), pp. 111–15; *La poesía de Rodrigo de Reinosa*, ed. Cabrales Arteaga, 97–100. The metre is *arte mayor*, with the usual

Comiença ella:	Gelofe Mandinga te da gran tormento,
	don puto negro caravayento.[31]
Responde él:	Tu terra Guinea a vós dar lo afrenta,[32]
	doña puta negra caravayenta.
Dize ella:	A mí llamar[33] Comba de terra Guinea, 5
	y en la mi terra comer buen cangrejo;
	y allá en Gelofe do tu terra sea
	comer con gran hambre caravaju vejo,
	cabeça de can, lagartu vermejo,
	por do tú andar muy muyto fambrento, 10
	don puto negro caravayento.
Responde él:	A mí llamar Jorge, Mandinga es mi terra;
	comer muyto farto taybo alcuzcuz.[34]

wrenching of stress ('doñá pŭtă négra', etc.); see Weber de Kurlat, 'Sobre el negro', p. 387 and n. 20.

[31] **puto**: 'rent-boy', passive partner in a homosexual relationship (*Diccionario de autoridades*, v, p. 443: 'El hombre que comete el pecado nefando, Lat. *cinædus, catamitá*', citing Quevedo on 'pecados de atrás'). **caravayento**: 'scaraboid, cockroach-like', i.e. black, < *cárabo, escarabajo* 'scarab, dung-beetle' (cf. *carávaju vejo* 8, *carávajo preto* 67–8; Cobarruvias, *Tesoro*, fols. 362v–363, s.v. *escaravajo*, 'vil animalejo [. . .] Para dezir que algún hombre o mujer es negro y de ruín talle, dezimos que es un escaravajo'). On the aphaeresis of *es-* see Weber de Kurlat, 'Sobre el negro', p. 390 and n. 28.

[32] **terra**: undiphthongized, like *vejo* 8, *fambrento* 10, *tambén* 24, *vostro* 29, *arrepenta* 31, *parente* 41, *bon(a)* 47, 49, *mel* 49, *forte* 57, *casamento* 65, *corpo* 67, *quera* 68. Such Lusisms are characteristic of *habla de negros*; cf. *lagartu* 9, *muyto* 10, 13, etc., *falar* 14, *deitar, ollo* 22, *demo* 33, *grassa* 'graça' 34, *enbora* 35, *branco* 55, *preto* 67 (see Weber de Kurlat, 'Sobre el negro', pp. 387–8 and n. 28). **lo afrenta**: for *el afrenta* (Hayward Keniston, *The Syntax of Castilian Prose: The Sixteenth Century* (Chicago, 1937), §18.123, 218), by way of Portuguese *o* (cf. *lo corpo* 67; *do, de o* 22, 33).

[33] **a mí llamar**: 'yo [me] llamo'. *(A) mí, (a) tí/vós* + infinitive = 1st/2nd person finite verb; cf. Fernão da Silveira, *Cancioneiro Geral de Resende*, §44, I, 194, v.1 'A mim rei de negro estar Serra Lioa', 5 'querer a mim logo ver-vos'; Henrique da Mota, ibid. §797, IV, 162–68, vv. 43–44 'mim andar augua jardim, | a mim nunca sar roim'; 52 'vós pipo nunca tapar'); see *mí te fazer* 17, *saber mí cantar* 23, *a mí saber bailar* 26, *vós querer* 30, *a mí andar* 54 (the same forms as object pronouns: *a vós dar* 3, *dar a mí* 48, *querer ti matar* 37). Standard *yo/me, tú/te* also occur in this construction (*tú andar* 10, *yo ser* 40; note reduplicated *a mí tener yo* 46, *dar a ti vós* 47, and imperative *andar vós y vete* 61), and, in a few cases, in standard syntax (*yo te juro* 16, *yo juro a Yos* 31, *me apostemo* 35, *yo . . . saibo* 42).

[34] **taybo**: Arabic *ṭayyib*, 'good', cf. 40, 44, 50; *Cancioneiro Geral de Resende*, §44, I, 194, v. 9 'gente meu taibo'; Weber de Kurlat, 'Sobre el negro', p. 388, n. 24. **alcuzcuz**: millet couscous is a staple in Senegambia (Mandinka *futoo, ñoo, sereŋo*), but the word is Arabic; Cossío remarks that Reinosa 'distingue perfectamente las distintas procedencias de uno y otro negro, y creo que es tomado del natural el que él presuma de comer *alcuzcuz*, como *mandingo* influenciado aún por costumbres moras, en oposición a la mayor incivilidad de la negra, plenamente caracterizada de Guinea' (*Rodrigo de Reinosa*, p. lxxvii).

¿Por qué falar ý su puta negra <perra>,[35]
y aver en tu terra pescado marfuz?[36]   15
Yo te juro a Yos y a eta que cruz
que mí te fazer saltar la pimenta,[37]
   doña puta negra caravayenta.

Responde ella: Aver en tu terra muy muyta caranga,
tener en tu terra muy muyto gaúl   20
comer en tu terra muy muyto carpanga[38]
deytar muyta pulga por ollo do cul;
saber mí cantar el dulce undul,
maagana tambén quando me contento,[39]
   don puto negro caravayento.   25

---

[35] **su puta negra perra:** hypermetric; 'perra' looks like an interpolation to correct the irregular
rhyme *terra/negra.* The line remains difficult: 'why talk of this [*ý* adverbial], you black whore [*su*
2nd-person], when there is rotten fish in your country?' (cf. Mota, *Cancioneiro Geral de Resende*,
§797, IV, 164, vv. 44–5 'a mim nunca sar roim, | porque bradar?').

[36] **marfuz:** 'rotten, trashy' < Arabic *marfūḍ* 'rejected' (*rafaḍa* 'discard'), attested in Old Spanish
(Juan Ruiz, *Libro de buen amor*, 119d; and cf. *rafez* 'cheap, vulgar' < *rafīḍ*); see below, 'marfuza' 43
(contrasted with *tayba*, paired with *pioyenta*), 50, 57, 61; Weber de Kurlat, 'Sobre el negro', p. 388,
nn. 25–6.

[37] **Yos:** repeated in 31; from Portuguese *Deus*, 'God' or some African divinity (cf. Asian-English
pidgin *joss* 'pagan idol', *joss-house* 'temple', *joss-stick* 'incense'). **eta que cruz:** *esta cruz*, with loss
of implosive -*s* (Frida Weber de Kurlat, 'El tipo cómico de negro en el teatro prelopesco:
fonética', *Filología*, 8 (1962), pp. 139–68 at 164) and redundant *que.* **mí te fazer saltar la
pimenta:** prob. 'I'll make you jump, (you) black peppercorn!' (cf. Correas, *Vocabulario de refranes*,
229 '*Negra es la ke kema*; entiéndese: la pimienta. *Negra es la pimienta, i kómenla los hidalgos*').

[38] **caranga:** prob. Mandinka *karankoo* 'louse, flea'; cf. 'Andarvos de aý, caranga pioyento' 38,' Tomá
para vós, garango gur-gur' 63; cf. Honduran *caranga* 'flea', standard *carángano, cáncano.* Note that
caranga is here feminine, but *garango, carpanga*, and *caranga* in 38 all take masculine modifiers.
gaúl, carpanga: unpleasant foodstuffs? These may be African-sounding nonce-words (cf. n. 53,
below).

[39] **undul, maagana:** *bailes de negros. Undul* occurs nowhere else; Russell, 'La *poesía negra*', p. 389,
connects it with *ondular* 'undulate [the body]', but on p. 392 and n. 25 notes that the rhyme in -*ul*
may imitate a Wolof suffix. *Ma(n)gana* is mentioned in the refrain of a second poem by Reinosa
in the same broadside, *Otras suyas a los mismos negros; hanse de cantar al tono de guineo*, 'Mangana
mangana, | no tener vino ni chucaracana' (fol. A2v; Castañeda and Huarte, *Nueva colección de
pliegos sueltos*, p. 134; Reynosa, *Coplas*, ed. Chamorro, pp. 117–18); it is perhaps cognate with
Bantu *makana* 'pole' (Russell, 'La *poesía negra*', p. 389 and n. 16), though J. Corominas, *Diccionario
crítico-etimológico de la lengua castellana*, 4 vols. (Berne, 1954), III, 188b, s.v. *magaña* (cf. III, 167–8
and n. 2, s.v. *macana*) proposes an Arabic etymon. Despite Reinosa's *mangana* being 'sung to the
tune of the *guineo*' – by all accounts a merry dance (see n. 40, below) – Luís de Camões quoted a
Castilian verse which sounds more like an early form of blues ('com triste som | lhe cantaram a
mangana'), *Carta*, IV, in *Obras completas*, ed. Hernâni Cidade, 5 vols. (Lisboa, 1946–7), III,
pp. 259–64 at 262.

Responde él: A mí saber bien baylar el guineo,[40]

se querer comigo fazer choque-choque[41]

y con un bezul dos vezes arreo,

en vostro bezer allá se me troque;[42]

si vós querer que a terr[a o]s derroque,[43]   30

yo juro a Yos que no se arrepenta,

doña puta negra caravayenta.

Dize ella: ¡Jesu Jesú, garaos de o demo![44]

No tener tú grassa, vós muyto falar;

yd muyto enbora, que ya me apostemo.[45]   35

[40] **guineo:** Cobarruvias, *Tesoro*, fol. 457v, 'cierta dança de movimientos prestos y apresurados; pudo ser fuesse traýda de Guinea y que la dançassen primero los negros . . . puede ser nombre griego del verbo κινεω, *moveo, incitor*, por la agilidad y presteza de la dança'. See Cotarelo, *Colección de entremeses*, i, pp. cxciv, ccl-ccli.

[41] **se querer:** *se*, Lusism for *si* (cf. *si vós querer fazer* 30); the wrenched stress in *quérer comígo* recurs in the next line and in *te quérer fazér* 69, and so perhaps imitates a black usage. **choque-choque:** 'intercourse', cf. 58; Weber de Kurlat, 'Sobre el negro', p. 391 and n. 30. *Voyage d'Eustache Delafosse à la côte de Guinée, au Portugal et en Espagne (1479–1481)*, ed. Denis Escudier (Paris, 1992): 'le jeu d'amours on y dict [at Elmina in Ghana] *chocque chocque*' (29); 'une jeune garce . . . me vint sievyr me demandant sy je vouloye chocque chocque, et se va commenchier a oster ses braies pensant que la voulsisse tribouller' (30). Perhaps onomatopeic Portuguese sailors' slang (Russell, 'La poesía negra', p. 391 and n. 23), but note Mandinka *coki* 'join', *cokoo* 'game'.

[42] **con un bezul ∼ troque:** meaning obscure, doubtless obscene. **bezul:** prob. a cross between *bezudo* 'thick-lipped' (synecdoche for 'black': Cobarruvias, *Tesoro*, fol. 136, s.v. *bezo*, 'el labio quando es gruesso como el de los negros . . . los que escriven de fisonomía dizen que los que tienen los tales labios gruessos . . . son escarnecedores y maldizientes') and *bozal* 'newly enslaved black African' (< *bozo* 'halter'); cf. Miguel de Cervantes, *La entretenida*, pp. 607–8, 'cual si fuera guineo bezudo y bozal esclavo', in *Teatro completo*, ed. Florencio Sevilla Arroyo and Antonio Rey Hazas (Barcelona, 1987), pp. 543–630 at 561. Other possibilities are suggested by *Diccionario de autoridades*, i, 602, s.v. bezudo 'Gruesso de labios . . . Por analogía se extiende à las cosas inanimadas, que à semejanza tienen las extremidades sacadas hácia afuera à modo de labios, como las heridas, carnosidades, monédas, &c.'; male or female pudenda? **dos vezes arreo:** 'twice in a row'; *Diccionario de autoridades*, i, 410, s.v. arreo 'sucesivamente, sin interrupción ní intermissión . . . Voz baxa'. **bezer:** surely not, *pace* Chamorro (Reynosa, *Coplas*, p. 136), the rare *bezar* 'bezoar-stone' (calculus from the stomach of the oryx, prized as a medicinal antidote). Perhaps an apocope (cf. *cul* 22) of *vecero* 'client (lit. one who takes turn)' or *becerro* 'calf', *se me troque* being a solecism for *me trueque*, 'let me turn myself into your customer or your young bull'.

[43] **a terra os:** the *pliego* reads *a terro vos*, which is hypermetric and ungrammatical; Cossío emends *a terra vos*, but scansion requires *a térr'ŏs dĕrróque* (for *os* at this date cf. *garaos* 33, despite *andarvos* 38). Jorge's offer to wrestle Kumba on her back is straightforward, but to do so 'on the ground' without the amenities of bedding implies an extra dimension of animal wantonness.

[44] **Jesu Jesú:** loss of implosive *-s* is typical of *habla de negros* (cf. *eta* 16; Weber de Kurlat, 'El tipo cómico de negro . . . fonética', p. 161). **garaos de o demo:** Luso-African pidgin for *guardaos del demonio*, 'look out for the devil!', i.e. Jorge (on the loss of the dental in the cluster -rd- see Weber de Kurlat, 'El tipo cómico de negro . . . fonética', p. 164 and n. 73).

[45] **me apostemo:** < *postema* 'sore, boil'; i.e. 'you make me come out in a rash [of anger]'.

No ver[m]e[46] Grisolmo con vós aquí estar;
dar a ti fongon,[47] querer ti matar.
Andarvos de aý, caranga pioyento,
    don puto negro caravayento.

Responde él: Yo ser de Mandinga y estar negro taybo,[48]   40
y estar garrapata vostro parente;
y vostro lenguaje yo muyto ben saybo,[49]
[. . .]
ser terra Guinea de marfuza gente,
no estar tayba mas muyto pioyenta,
    doña puta negra caravayenta.   45

Responde ella: A mí tener yo un otro guardián
que dar a ti vós bon fongon barel,
que dar a mí muyto pedaso de pan
y bona melchocha y turron de mel;[50]
estar vós marfuz y estar taybo él,   50
y vós estar negro muy gusarapento,
    don puto negro caravayento.

Responde él: Estar yo buen negro de obispo criado,
y ser de Gelofe a mí andar en corte;[51]
estar piojo branco vostro cuñado,   55
tener yo alhoría con que me dé porte;

---

[46] **verme:** the *pliego* reads *verte*. Emendation is necessary, not because of the mixed level of address in *te-vós* (typical, e.g. 3, 34, *a ti vós* 47) but because one cannot be seen with oneself.

[47] **fongon:** from the context, 'a beating' (perhaps an African word, but note thieves' cant *fuñar* 'fight'); clearly paroxytone (cf. *bon fóngon barél* 47), despite Chamorro's unconvincing guess, '*Fongón:* puede significar flojo, abandonado, sucio' (Reynosa, *Coplas*, p. 139).

[48] **yo ser de Mandinga y estar negro taybo:** for the typical confusion of *ser/estar* cf. *do tu terra sea* 7, and 50–1, 53, 55, 57, 64, 78, below. For the boast, cf. Correas, *Vocabulario de refranes*, p. 569 and n. 4: '*Rrei de Mandinga, o de Zape:* burla de un rreiezuelo i su chiko rreino, i de presuntuosos. "Mandinga" se dize por menosprezio, apodando, i es provinzia en Ginea'. Quevedo uses *mandinga* as a parodic adjective for 'black, dark' (*Obras completas*, 1: *Poesía original*, §875, 1341); the Spanish Academy records modern regional usages as 'layabout' (Murcia), 'devil' (rural America).

[49] **saybo:** for *sé* 'I know', a solecistic analogical derivation from *saber* typical of infantile speech, in this case based on Portuguese *saiba* (Cossío's conjecture *sabo* and Chamorro's *faibo* are unnecessary). The next line rhyming in *-ente* is missing.

[50] **pedaso, melchocha:** for *pedaço, melcocha*, typical phonetic confusions (Weber de Kurlat, 'El tipo cómico de negro . . . fonética', pp. 161–2). For *muyto, bona, mel* see n. 32, above; *turron,* wrenched stress for *turrón.* In the preceding line, the rhyme-word *barel* is probably Spanish Gypsy cant (*caló*) rather than *habla de negros* (*barí(l)* 'big, thumping'; for *fongon* see n. 47, above).

[51] **y ser de Gelofe, a mí andar:** conditional (standard: 'de estar yo en Gelofe, andaría'). For this presumptuous boast see the proverb quoted from Correas in n. 48, above.

yo no estar marfuz, estar hombre forte;
fazer choque choque en vós me consenta,
   doña puta negra caravayenta.

Responde ella: †Guala nunca herrar le le†[52]   60

Andar vós y vete marfuz a chur-chur,
andar en bon ora vós bucamande.
Tomá para vós garango gur-gur,[53]
vós estar bellaco muy muyto tahur;
Grisolmo me dar fe de casamento,   65
   don puto negro caravayento.

Responde él: Caravajo preto lo corpo te coma,

caravajo preto te quera comer!
Si vós tabanique te querer fazer[54]
y dexar a Grisolmo, por vuestro me toma;   70
aunque tener vós la nariz roma,
mi amo tener muy muyta renta,
   doña puta negra caravayenta.

[52] **Guala ∼ le le:** the *pliego*'s reading is hypometric by as much as a hemistich (if scanned 'gualá nunc' errárle'), and lacks a rhyme with *bucamande*. *Gualá, le* is perhaps Arabic *wa-llāh, lā* 'by Allāh, no!' (cf. *le gualá* Juan Ruiz, *Libro de buen amor*, 1510d); Russell, 'La *poesía negra*', 392 suggests an imitation of the Wolof suffix *-le*. No convincing emendation is possible; *nunca herrarle* or *herrar-l'é* may be from *errar* 'I will never cheat on him [i.e. Grisolmo]', or *herrar* (aspirate *h-*) 'Never! I will brand you [i.e. Jorge, *le* for second-person] with an iron', that is, return you from freedman to slave.

[53] The *pliego* prints these unknown African insults as **achur chur, bucamande, garango gur gur** (for *garango* 'louse' cf. n. 38, above). Russell, 'La *poesía negra*', p. 391 suggests the *-ur* rhymes 'parody the phonology of some West African language'. Modern editors print metrically impossible *Bucamandé*; for Weber de Kurlat 'Sobre el negro', p. 389, it is an African toponym, Cossío conjectures *bu(s)ca mandé*, 'look for Mande [in Africa?]'.

[54] **tabanique te:** Cossío and Chamorro conjecture *tabaniquete* (without proposing a meaning), but the *pliego*'s reading gives a better caesura. At all events, neither *tabanique* nor *tabaniquete* is recorded, and both terminations are very rare. The word could be a malapropism for *tabanico*, diminutive of *tábano* 'gad-fly' (if Kumba is willing to jump horses, as it were), or *tabique* 'partition wall' (if she will share both men), or *tabanque* 'potter's wheel' (if she will spin from one to the other; but this word is not attested until much later). The most likely solution seems to be *tabanco* 'tripe-stall' (*Diccionario de autoridades*, VI, 202 'tienda que se pone en las calles, donde venden de comer para los pobres, y gente de servicio'; in thieves' cant or *germanía*, 'low tavern, brothel'). Luis de Usoz y Río, ed., *Cancionero de obras de burlas provocantes a risa* ('Madrid', i.e. London, 1842) found this word in burlesque poetry, though he coyly refused to elucidate ('vozes como *tabanco, trincadero*, &c. que se hallan también en este cancionero, omití, porque facilmente se adivina su significación', in his 'Glosario', pp. 249–55, at 249); we need not insist on an obscene sense if we take 'te' not as reflexive, but as indirect object ('if you want to make (for) yourself a tripe-stall', i.e. set up a small business as a freedwoman).

Ella, y concluye: Comer en tu terra muyta moxca assada,[55]
                        muyto cangreju assar assador,   75
                        cigarra en caçuela con leche quajada,
                        assar en parrilla moxquito mayor;
                        y[o] estar crïada del carrajador,[56]
                        con mi ama en missa me assento,
                            don puto negro caravayento.   80

2. *Coplas de como una dama ruega a un negro que cante en manera de requiebro, y como*
   el negro se dexa rogar; en fin la señora vencida de su gracia le offrece su persona. Con
   unas coplas de Antón vaquerizo de Morana (s.l.: s.n., s.a. [Seville: Cromberger,
   c. 1520]), fols. 1–2v.[57]

                        Canta, Jorgico, canta.
                            No quere canta.
                        Canta, Jorge, por tu fe
                        y verás que te daré
                        una argolla para el pie   5
                        y otra para la garganta
                            No quere *canta.*[58]

[55] **moxca:** for *mosca.* Palatalization of -s was typical of *morisco* dialect; only Reinosa and two other
early authors use it in *habla de negros* (Weber de Kurlat, 'El tipo cómico de negro . . . fonética',
p. 162; 'Sobre el negro', p. 391, n. 30).

[56] **yo estar:** the pliego reads *y estar,* the emendation is necessary for the sense (scan *yó 'star crï-áda*).
The first hemistich of the next line is hypometric and should probably read *y con mi ama*; a visual
confusion by the compositor of two lines beginning with *y* would account for both errors.
carrajador: i.e. *corregidor,* with typical vowel equivocation (Paul Teyssier, *La langue de Gil Vicente*
(Paris, 1959), p. 247; Weber de Kurlat, 'El tipo cómico de negro . . . fonética', pp. 141–2), but also
a comic echo of the vulgar expletive *carajo,* 'membrum virile'.

[57] From the facsimile in Antonio Rodríguez-Moñino, *Los pliegos poéticos de la colección del Marqués de*
Morbecq: siglo XVI (Madrid, 1962), pp. 46–8, 157–60; previously published by Usoz in the
'Adiciones' to his *Cancionero de obras de burlas,* pp. 214–20 (see 'Advertencias prévias, del Editor',
i–xlii, at xxxiv 'El diálogo de Jorjico, esclavo Morisco sin duda; muestra en lo que se entretenian
várias de las *románticas* damas, y matronas, cuyos maridos estaban en la Tierra Santa') with
variants and a different distribution of speakers that may derive from a lost *pliego*
(Rodríguez-Moñino, pp. 46–7). It is a *villancico* in *arte menor* (octosyllables), the refrain being a
couplet of seven + five-syllable lines.

[58] **argolla:** 'torque, collar'; Cobarruvias, *Tesoro,* fols. 86v-87, s.v. *argolla,* 'círculo de hierro o de oro
que tráyan al cuello; y oy día se traen los de hierro los esclavos por afrenta y custodia, los de oro
la gente noble por honra y adorno . . . . Pocos años ha que las señoras los usavan [i.e. de oro] en
España con el nombre de argollas, hechas de troços con mucha pedrería; las de los esclavos
siempre se usaron. Dize un cantarcillo viejo con que acallavan los niños: "Canta, Jorgico, . . . "
[quoting vv.1–7].' In the lullaby *argolla* meant 'necklace', playing on the metaphor of love as

JORGICO:	¿Cómo cantaré, señora,	
	pues que mi coraçón llora	
	y en vós tal crueldad mora[59]	10
	que me aborrece y espanta?	
	No quere canta.	
LA SEÑORA:	Canta, Jorge, no t'espantes	
	y sirve mejor que d'antes;	
	c'anque ves que traygo guantes,	15
	a quien Dios qu[i]ere, levanta.[60]	
	No quere canta.	
JORGICO:	No puedo cantar cativo,	
	que soy más muerto que bivo	
	de vuestro amor tan esquivo:	20
	si os hablo, hazéysos santa.	
	No quere canta.	
LA SEÑORA:	Jorgico, no desesperes,	
	mal conoces las mugeres;	
	quando bien las conocieres	25
	tu passión no será tanta.	
	No quere canta.	
JORGICO:	¿Cómo cantaré, cuytado,	
	viéndome tan lastimado	
	y de vós tan apartado	30
	que de pensallo me espanta?	
	No quere canta.	
LA SEÑORA:	Canta, Jorge, por tu vida,	
	que ya me tienes vencida	
	pues me ves apercebida	35

servitude. The *glosa* takes it as 'shackle' (114–16) and gives *cantar* a traditional obscene sense;
cf. *Floresta de poesías eróticas del Siglo de Oro con su vocabulario al cabo por orden del a.b.c*, ed. Pierre
Alzieu, Robert Jammes, and Yvan Lissorgues (Toulouse, 1975), §91 'Cabras hay en el mal lugar',
pp. 168–70, vv. 9–16: 'el señor beneficiado | viene a enseñarme a cantar; | . . . Yo llevo, marido,
el bajo ['bass line'], | y el ciego lleva el tenor ['top line'], | y está puesto el facistor ['music stand']
| en la cámara de abajo'. See Russell,' *La poesía negra*', pp. 386–7; and n. 75, below.

[59] **en vós tal crueldad mora:** in the sentimental sense (*la belle dame sans merci*), but Jorge's
metaphors also allude to his real status. Hierarchy in levels of address is maintained throughout:
he uses respectful *vós, señora*; she, familiar *tú* and first name.

[60] **c'anque:** i.e. *que* or *ca aunque*; the *pliego* reads *cã que*, Usoz *aunque*, cf. *anque* 61 (*aun que* 156, 170).
traygo: Usoz's archaic *trayo*, if from another witness, would be better (*lectio difficilior*). **quiere:**
Usoz; the *pliego* reads *quere* (confusion with the next line).

y tener voluntad tanta.
　　No quere canta.

JORGICO:　　Dezís que soys ya vencida
y que estáys apercebida;
dad, señora, la salida,[61]　　　　　　　　　　　40
pues tenéys libertad tanta.
　　No quere canta.

LA SEÑORA:　　Jorge, ven a mi posada
y hallarme-ás acostada
en la cama perfumada　　　　　　　　　　　45
y meterte-ás so la manta.
　　No quere canta.
Jorgico, ten me creýdo
que si cumples tal partido
tú mejores el vestido　　　　　　　　　　　50
gozando de gloria tanta.
　　No quere canta.

JORGICO:　　Yo siempre fui vallestero
y en mi tierra molinero;[62]
tiro y muelo tan certero　　　　　　　　　　55
que quien me gusta se espanta.
　　No quere canta.

LA SEÑORA:　　Jorgico, si bien cantares
quitándome los pesares
haré quanto tú mandares,　　　　　　　　　60
anque ves perfeción tanta.
　　No quere canta.

JORGICO:　　Tengo en moler tal tino
y ando tan bien el camino
que jamás no desatino　　　　　　　　　　65

---

[61] **dad la salida:** Cobarruvias, *Tesoro*, fol. *19v, s.v. *salida*, 'dar salida a una cosa, dar escusa', but Jorge may mean 'give me freedom' (cf. tenéys libertad 41, and 113–16); *Diccionario de autoridades* VI, 23, s.v. salida, 'Se toma tambien por el fin ò término de algun negocio, ù dependencia . . . despacharse ò venderse las cosas'.

[62] **vallestero, molinero:** bowmen shooting and millers grinding gave rise to many *double entendres* in popular poetry; see *Floresta de poesías eróticas*, ed. Alzieu, Jammes, and Lissorgues, §48, 72–3; §80, 141–4; §81, 148, n. 59; J. G. Cummins, ed., *The Spanish Traditional Lyric* (Oxford, 1977), pp. 87–9.

de Medina a Salamanca.[63]
No quere canta.

LA SEÑORA: Canta, Jorge, por tu vida,
¿por qué m'as aborrecida?
Agora que m'as vencida,   70
¿qué es la causa que te espanta?
No quere canta.
No me espanta tu figura,
que mi pena m'asegura;
mas no es mía la ventura   75
ni merezco gloria tanta.
No quere canta.
Jorge, no seas grossero
pues que ves quánto te quiero;
con puro amor verdadero   80
en mí tu vista se planta.
No quere canta.

JORGICO: En el tiempo que he servido
nunca me avéys conocido;
de cantar sin ser querido   85
tengo seca la garganta.
No quere canta.

LA SEÑORA: Yo creo qu'estás sin seso
o qu'estás de amor compreso;
tienes mi coraçón preso   90
desd'el culo a la garganta.
No quere canta.
Jorge, si vienes aýna
mataréte una gallina[64]
y sorberás la cozina   95
que te ablande la garganta.
No quere canta.

---

[63] **de Medina a Salamanca:** this straightforward journey provides no challenge to an expert at 'finding the way'; and what has it to do with grinding? Doubtless there is some obscene *double entendre*, unless it be that the irregular rhyme *salamanca, canta* points to a pun on *so la manta* (cf. 106).

[64] **mataréte:** Usoz reads archaic *matarte he*.

Jorge, ante de acostar[65]
te daré bien a cenar
de un capón que tengo assar[66]   100
con un razimo de planta.
    No quere canta.
Jorgico, con tu canción
detrás aquel pavellón
matarm'ás la comezón   105
cubiertos con una manta.
    No quere canta.
Jorge, de que ayas cantado,[67]
si de mí fueres pagado
quedaré a tu mandado   110
con una voluntad tanta.
    Ya quere canta.
Canta, Jorge, por tu fe,
y luego te quitaré
el hierro que traes al pie   115
y la argolla a la garganta.[68]
    No quere canta.
Si plazer q[ui]eres hazerme[69]
y a tu servicio tenerme,
esto quieras concederme   120

[65] **ante:** Usoz reads *antes*, but for *ante de* see Keniston, *Syntax of Castilian Prose*, §37.79, 539, and 'Index of Spanish words', s.v. *ante*, 712.

[66] **assar:** i.e. *a assar*, a common crasis (Cabrales wrongly reads *assaz*).

[67] **de que:** 'after' (Keniston, *Syntax of Castilian Prose*, §29.811, 404; cf. *de que* + indicative 'since' §28.56, 360, or conditional, §28.45, 356). Future subj. *fueres* in the next line was still standard in unfulfilled conditional sentences (Keniston §32.9, 444–5); Cabrales wrongly reads *fueses*.

[68] **a la garganta:** cf. vv. 4–6; Usoz reads '*de* la garganta' (the italics are not explained). In reality, of course, masters did not normally manumit slaves, and especially not if they wanted them as sexual partners; they might let them buy a *carta de ahorría*, like the Jorge of the first poem, or dispose for them to be freed after their own death (Martín Casares, *La esclavitud en Granada*, pp. 435–55). Miguel de Cervantes Saavedra, *El ingenioso hidalgo don Quijote de la Mancha*, ed. Luis Andrés Murillo, 2 vols. (Madrid, 1978), II, xxiv, p. 229 comments: 'they discharge and set at liberty their *negros* when they are old and past service, and, turning them out of doors with the title of free men, make them slaves to hunger, from which nothing but death can free them' – on which the translator Thomas Shelton (1620) exclaimed, 'He describes the right subtill and cruell nature of his damned Countrymen'.

[69] **quieres:** the *pliego* reads *qeres*, Usoz *quieres*; cf. abbreviated *quies*, 123. Usoz attributes this stanza to Jorge instead of the lady, as a plausible riposte to her promise of manumission, but the use of the *tú* form of address makes this impossible (see n. 59, above).

pues es tu nobleza tanta.
      No quere canta.
Canta si quies sin demora
y ternásme por señora,
que tu cantar me namora,   125
y la tu crueza me espanta.[70]
      No quere canta.
Canta, no seas cruel;
si no, guárdate de aquel
que dizen Buja Hamel[71]   130
que a tu linaje espanta.
      No quere canta.
Canta si quieres cantar
aquel cantar singular
que dezías nel olivar[72]   135
quando plantavas la planta.
      No quere canta.
Canta, yo te lo suplico,
aquel nuevo cantarico
que dizen 'del romerico'   140
que mis días adelanta.[73]
      No quere canta.

JORGICO: Señora, yo cantaré,
mas primero me veré
con vós allí donde sé   145
libertar mi pena tanta.
      No quere canta.
Y allí veréys mi cantar

---

[70] **y la tu crueza:** Usoz omits *y*, but *crueza* can be scanned as two syllables. Possessive article in *la tu* was by then archaic, it perhaps imitates the diction of courtly love lyric.

[71] **buja hamel:** unknown. This word which inspires fear in Jorge's race (*linaje*) is perhaps the name (*Abū Jammāl?*) of a slave-dealer or galley-overseer, a personification of the whip (cf. Wolof *buja* 'beat'; Mandinka *busa* 'whip (v.)', *busoo* 'whip (n.)', *busaraŋo* 'stick'), or an African goblin (Russell, 'La *poesía negra*', p. 403, n. 11, 'expresión árabe para aludir a la superstición negra'; Fra Molinero, 'La formación del estereotipo', pp. 441–2: 'lo sobrenatural').

[72] **nel:** the *pliego* reads *enel* (hypermetric); Usoz *n'el*.

[73] **que dizen del romerico:** the 'new song' of *The Little Pilgrim* was perhaps Juan del Encina's popular *villancico* 'Romerico, tú que vienes' (*Poesía lírica y cancionero musical*, ed. R. O. Jones and Carolyn R. Lee (Madrid, 1975), §128, 241–3); for the significance of the reference to pilgrimage see n. 77. **mis días adelanta:** 'makes my days pass quicker'.

tan perfeto y singular
que no lo pueda tachar   150
ambrilla que lo levanta.[74]
   No quere canta.

LA SEÑORA: Jorgico, pierde cuydado
que según m'as namorado
esto y más haré de grado   155
aunque sepa quedar manca.
   No quere canta.

JORGICO: Señora, no ayáys temor,
que yo soy tal cantador
que quando pierdo el tenor   160
lo cobro con mi garganta.
   No quere canta.
Sé cantar con mil primores
tiples, contras y tenores,
que más de veynte cantores   165
me cobdician la garganta.[75]
   No quere canta.

LA SEÑORA: Landre te mate, malino,
que con tus dichos me fino,
que aunque de color mohíno[76]   170
la plática tienes blanca.
   No quere canta.

---

[74] **ambrilla:** dimin. of *hambre* 'little hunger' is unclear, Usoz's *Mambrilla* more so; perhaps an error for *(h)embrilla*, 'little female (pejor.)'. **lo:** Usoz's reading; the *pliego* prints *los*.

[75] **me cobdician la garganta:** the lady knows exactly what Jorge means by trilling up and down with his throat ('con tus dichos me fino' 165); the *double entendre* was traditional, cf. n. 58, or the woman's lament to a drooping lover, 'Dormidito estás caracol', in *Floresta de poesías eróticas*, ed. Alzieu, Jammes, and Lissorgues, §88, vv. 23–30 'De un punto muy entonado, | caracol, te me has caído: | dabas en mi sostenido ['you were bumping me hard and long' or 'sounding in E-sharp'] | y ya das en fa bemolado ['F-flat']; | pues la clave te he mostrado, | canta con más compostura; | si la clave es de natura ['natural', of musical key; or 'of the genitals'], | ¿para qué es tanto bemol?' (161–3).

[76] **mohíno:** 'down in the mouth' (< *mofar, mo(f)ín* 'grimace'), hence 'black-faced, bay (horse)'; *Diccionario de autoridades*, IV, 588, s.v. *mohino*, 'el macho, ò la mula hijo de caballo y burra, . . . que regularmente tienen el hocico negro, señal de maliciosas ò falsas'. A deliberate euphemism; the lady cannot bring herself to call Jorge *negro*. Leaving aside the poem's title and the unspecific reference to *linaje* in 131, this is the only allusion to his colour (Russell, 'La *poesía negra*', p. 403, n. 11).

FIN: Porque cantas tan donoso,
deste mi cuerpo gracioso
te sirve mientra mi esposo   175
viene dela Tierra Santa.[77]
    Ya quere canta.

[77] **Tierra Santa:** the cuckold's absence at war was a traditional motif in folk-songs about adulterous wives, but Palestine had long since become a destination for tourists and pilgrims (see n. 17), not crusaders; cf. Fadrique Enríquez de Ribera's trip in Juan del Encina's *Trivagia, o viaje a Jerusalem* (Roma, 1521), in his *Obras completas*, ed. Ana María Rambaldo, 2 vols. (Madrid, 1978), II, pp. 187–270.

CHAPTER FOUR

Washing the Ethiopian white: conceptualising black skin in Renaissance England

ANU KORHONEN

The proverb of my title, 'to wash an Ethiopian white is to labour in vain', was repeated so frequently in Renaissance English texts that it was understandable even when either half of the sentence was omitted. It was often coupled with biblical references to how leopards cannot change their spots or blackamoors their skin, and unwashable Ethiopians even appeared in tavern signs. The impossibility of 'whitening' black Africans became a paradigm for all that was useless, impossible and irrational. But why did Ethiopians need to be 'washed white'? In this chapter, I shall look at what black skin meant to white Englishmen of the sixteenth and early seventeenth centuries.

Even in England, people at this time were faced with a growing number of individuals who looked 'different' from local norms.[1] What did people actually see when they encountered darker-skinned individuals, either real people, or textual and visual representations of black Africans? This is a question both of discourse and of visual logic, of the interplay of knowledge, imagination and experience. The topic could be approached from many angles, but here my main interest lies in conceptions of beauty and deformity, and with what

---

[1] Although black Africans were by no means a common sight in Renaissance England, it seems that their number has been underestimated and that African appearance must have been much more familiar than has been thought. See Eldred Jones, *Othello's Countrymen: The African in English Renaissance Drama* (London, 1965), pp. 12–13; Ruth Cowhig, 'Blacks in English Renaissance drama and the role of Shakespeare's Othello', in David Dabydeen, ed., *The Black Presence in English Literature* (Manchester, 1985), pp. 5–7. On the lack of firsthand accounts of Africa and Africans, see Kim F. Hall, *Things of Darkness: Economies of Race and Gender in Early Modern England* (Ithaca and London, 1995), p. 11. English travellers had visited African coasts regularly since the mid-sixteenth century, but compared with many continental countries, this is quite late. It is notable, however, that the African slave trade started almost as early as the first English visits to Africa. For accounts of the early English slave trade, see Sir John Hawkins's three voyages in Richard Hakluyt, *Principal Navigations, Voiages and Discoveries of the English Nation* (London, 1589) and especially Richard Hawkins, *Declaration of the Troublesome Voyadge of Sir John Hawkins to Guynea and the West Indies* (Amsterdam, 1569/1973), sig. A2v–A4; but cf. Richard Jobson, *The Golden Trade* (London, 1623), pp. 88–9 and Emily C. Bartels, 'Othello and Africa: postcolonialism reconsidered', *The William and Mary Quarterly*, 54:1, 1997, pp. 59–61. Drama and literature scholars have been much more interested in representations of people of African origin in England than historians, who are only now starting to trace historical records for 'real' black Africans.

looking at early modern appearance can tell us of the cultural evaluations involved in judgements of skin colour.

In English literary sources, descriptions of and allusions to Africa and its inhabitants are numerous but brief: often they are stereotypical and copied from earlier sources, and sometimes they are completely fanciful and untrue. The fact that African skin was 'black' was mentioned without fail, but usually only in passing, almost mechanically, as a fact that was already well known. Travellers to African coasts, for example, wrote down dutifully that the people they encountered had black skin and recounted other bodily features considered typical of Africans, but rarely paid closer attention to these details.[2] Portrayals of African skin, like African practices, were however loaded with wonder and could induce unease. Black skin was thus both an African commonplace and a strange variation on the norm of white beauty the travellers carried in their interpretative arsenal of the human body.

For the English, sub-Saharan Africa, known as 'the Land of Negroes', was a mysterious continent inhabited by unknown peoples whose main bodily characteristic was the colour of their skin. When these people were brought to England – and a few of them were on some sixteenth-century voyages – they retained their mysterious quality, embodying the legends and fanciful stories familiar from Mandeville's *Travels* and other early travel narratives.[3] At first glance, it may seem difficult to discern a cohesive logic in the brief and sometimes strange allusions in Renaissance texts, but examined more closely, certain interpretative schemes emerge clearly. These include deformity, monstrosity and the overwhelming mystery of black skin, but skin colour was also directly related to the rampant sexuality and the lack of reason and sense which European writers assumed to be true of black Africans.[4] The enigmatic nature of black skin was central to the construction of black 'otherness', and, by implication, therefore, to white identity as well. In the cultural moment when the concept of race had not yet emerged as a labelling device, skin colour could act to define the borders of civility and barbarism.

. . .

[2] See for example Richard Eden's description of Africa, Thomas Wyndham's journey to Benin and Guinea, John Lok's and William Towerson's travels to Guinea, in Richard Hakluyt, *The Principal Navigations, Voiages and Discoveries of the English Nation*, 3 vols. (London, 1599–1600), II. 2, pp. 10, 12, 19–21, 25, 30–31, 39; Jobson, *The Golden Trade*, pp. 27–30.

[3] On the importance of Mandeville's *Travels* in constructing African 'otherness', and on bringing black Africans to England, see Jones, *Othello's Countrymen*, pp. 5–6, 12–13.

[4] See also Marjo Kaartinen, 'Toinen – vieras. Näkökulmia kolonialistisen toiseuden tutkimukseen', in Kari Immonen and Maarit Leskelä-Kärki, eds., *Kulttuurihistoria. Näkökulmia tutkimukseen* (Turku, 2001), p. 391.

In early modern thinking, a desire for order and for a clear relationship between the human 'inner' character and 'outer' appearance was a typical feature. An emerging national English culture was envisioned as a system of orderly hierarchical relationships, where every thing and person had its proper, divinely ordained place. The principle of natural order also entailed the assumption that inner human characteristics were mirrored on the outside, and what was seen on the surface of the body was a reflection both of the inner being and of its cultural niche. Outward appearance could never be wholly separated from the soul and human nature, although some significant exceptions to this rule were also recognised.

Individual bodies characterised by black skin were interpreted through this schema. It is hardly an exaggeration to say that in the English Renaissance black skin was equated with ugliness, or, rather, with deformity. African appearance, both skin colour and the facial features seen as specific to people of African origin, were used to oppose stereotypical images of beauty and ugliness. 'Fair' meant both beautiful and light-skinned. 'Foul' was of course the opposite of 'fair', but it was also associated with the opposite of 'blondness', as dark or black. As Kim Hall has noted, 'black' was often not so much the opposite of 'white' as of 'beautiful' or 'fair'.[5] This of course entails seeing 'white as beautiful' and its necessary opposite 'black as deformed' or ugly. It is a peculiarity of the English language that the same word was used for beauty and blondness – in many other European languages these two are much more clearly differentiated.

In a mid-sixteenth-century conduct book, for example, it is asserted that a silent and chaste woman was always fair, even if she looked like an Ethiopian.[6] A century later, in 1653, Thomas Hall could sentence vain women who constantly combed and curled their hair or wore wigs to a suitable punishment: they should be burned for their sins and forced to scorch their skin in the sun until they acquired the 'hue of the Black-moores'.[7] The punishment for sin was to be burnt in hell-fire; the African sun could be imagined as its earthly equivalent. The whiteness and 'naturall fairenesse of mans skinne' could also be found in Africa – but not on men; it was epitomised in ivory, as Robert Gainsh mentioned in his description of elephants.[8]

Whiteness, then, represented the 'origin'; blackness meant variation and deviation. White Englishmen believed that they quite literally carried the

[5] Hall, *Things of Darkness*, p. 9.
[6] Thomas Becon, *The Iewel of Ioye* (London, 1553), sig. I7–I7v.
[7] Thomas Hall, *The Loathsomnesse of Long Haire* (London, 1653), p. 123.
[8] Gainsh in Hakluyt, *Principal Navigations* (1589), p. 94.

image of God in their bodies and faces, whereas black Africans, whose bodies lacked the clear, pure, white, physical reflection of the divine presence, were seen in terms of sin and alienation from God. In English texts, it is taken for granted that all people wanted to be white. Black skin was a mark of a curse, an affliction, a weakness and a stain.[9]

To understand the Renaissance idea of beauty, two elements are essential: the premise that bodily attractiveness consists in the harmonious proportions of all body parts and features; and the Petrarchist conventions of seeing, enumerating and describing those body parts as linked together by a sweeping gaze that travels over the (female) body. Pure and shining whiteness was the primary quality in the woman deemed fair by the Petrarchist gaze; but if the very canvas where beauty was to be discerned was too dark, the light and harmony of beauty could not be reached.[10] Such foulness was not, however, merely a question of aesthetic judgement. In a late sixteenth-century book discussing human intelligence, a rationale is presented based on Aristotelian and Galenic conceptions of geography and medicine, again linking the inner with the outer: people of extremely hot and dry complexions were foul and deformed. Africans living under the scorching sun could serve as convenient examples, and vice versa – the bodies of beautiful people were neither too hot nor too black.[11]

The idea that beauty is constructed by harmony was especially important when looking at the face: ideally, all the facial features needed to be in perfect balance in terms of their shape and size. The vision of foulness embodied by African appearance, on the other hand, included the stereotypes of thick lips, flat nose and black curly hair. All of these were considered foul not only in themselves, but also in combination; in fact they further highlighted the in any case unquestioned ugliness of black Africans.[12] In poetry, where Petrarchan

---

[9] See for example Joseph Hall, *Salomons Diuine Arts* (London, 1609), pp. 4–5; William Baldwin, *The Canticles or Balades of Solomon* (London, 1598), sig. A3v–A4; Antonio Brucioli, *A Commentary upon the Canticle of Canticles* (London, 1623), sig. B3–B4; Henry Ainsworth, *Solomons Song of Songs* (London, 1623), sig. C1v.

[10] For the Petrarchist gaze on beauty, see Nancy Vickers, 'Diana described: scattered women and scattered rhyme', *Critical Inquiry*, 8 (1981), pp. 265–79; see also Linda Woodbridge, 'Black and white and red all over: the sonnet mistress among the Ndembu', *Renaissance Quarterly*, 40:2 (1987), pp. 247–97.

[11] Juan de Dios Huarte, *The Examination of Mens Wits* (London, 1594), p. 281.

[12] Duarte Lopez, *A Report of the Kingdome of Congo* (London, 1597), pp. 71–86; Samuel Purchas, *Purchas his Pilgrimage* (London, 1614), pp. 649, 688–9; John Bulwer, *Anthropometamorphosis* (London, 1650), pp. 81–91. In the English translation of Lopez there are various woodcuts representing black Africans, but in these images it is difficult to discern any relation to how

ideals of whiteness as beauty, and darker skin as its opposite, were most influential, the nose, lips and hair were focuses of particular attention. Conversely,
in the popular genre of the mock encomium, ugliness and deformity were
evoked through the same facial scheme. For example, in the cruelly satiric
poem by the Scottish courtier William Dunbar, called 'Of ane blak-moir', the
'beautiful' black woman is likened to apes and cats on the basis of her facial
features.[13]

These tropes seem to be an enduring feature of the representation and
understanding of blackness, and they continue to occur all through the early
modern period. According to John Bulwer, a mid-seventeenth-century natu-
ralist, the flat nose of the Tartars, Chinese and Ethiopians was 'native to an
Ape' and could 'never become a man's Face'.[14] These typical features were
also portrayed, and used as local colour, in English court masques in which
white courtiers played black characters.[15] The act of perceiving black skin thus
always presupposed at least an implicit evaluation of beauty, and the inherent
cultural value of whiteness. In everyday life, blackness was of course primarily
visual: the 'racialising' gaze directed at black Africans was a process of giving
meaning to perception and direct observation, to the sight of blackness. This
was a cognitive, interpretative process. Seeing is never neutral. Even when the
sources purport to be simple statements of the fact of blackness, we as historians need to read into that statement its unuttered cultural context before any
kind of understanding of the past is possible.[16]

In this case, the context dictated that black skin could only be discussed
through its explicit foulness, both in a physical and in a metaphorical sense.
This assumption gave Renaissance writers, always delighting in paradox, the
possibility of playing with diametrically opposed interpretations, as Dunbar
does in his poem. The lady – some have suggested it may have been Elen More,
a real African presence at the Scottish court – both was and emphatically was
not beautiful. If, and when, black skin was given positive meanings, these

people of African origin were depicted or understood in texts. Bulwer, on the other hand, notes
that Africans tended to regard these features, so despised by Europeans, as particularly beautiful.
Despite its apparent relativity, this notion is hardly very friendly: soon afterwards Bulwer
describes these women as enjoying 'the statute beauty of our swine'.

[13] William Dunbar, *The Poems of William Dunbar* (London, 1970), p. 66. For parallels to Dunbar's
portraying blackness through mocking praise, see for example the ballad 'A Peerelesse Paragon',
in *The Roxburghe Ballads*, ed. W. M. Chappell (Hertford, 1873–4), II, pp. 301–4; and Richard
Brathwait, *Ar't Asleep Husband?* (London, 1640), pp. 319–21.

[14] Bulwer, *Anthropometamorphosis*, p. 86.   [15] Jones, *Othello's Countrymen*, p. 123.

[16] See Jeffrey Jerome Cohen, 'On Saracen enjoyment: some fantasies of race in late medieval France
and England', *The Journal of Medieval and Early Modern Studies*, 31:1 (2001), p. 116.

meanings necessarily embodied cultural negotiation, since interpreting black as foul was the primary mode of thinking. In the blazon system of beauty, skin colour was conceived of as an absolute quality, something insurmountable and overpowering. Through the satirical blazon, black women entered a field of laughter and sexuality, a potent mixture often used to contextualise black skin. There is of course a difference between the imaginary colour scheme of human skin envisioned by early modern Europeans, forcing a clear dichotomy of black and white, and the visual experiences of real encounters, where black became an approximation, a simplified abstract term bringing together a variety of skin hues, none of which was actually black. Although there were some writers who displayed an awareness that the degree of blackness varied from African to African, this was of little interest to the majority of early modern writers. In popular culture, blackness was fictionalised into a highly abstract but simply observable bodily category. Proverbs, sayings, biblical quotations and many passing remarks in Renaissance texts all come together to construct blackness as an absolute, without differences or degrees, juxtaposed with a whiteness similarly simplified and categorised.

Black skin was perceived as a spectacle produced by this opposition, particularly when it was coupled with something white, be it white skin or white clothes, or with something precious and beautiful, such as gold, silver or jewels. Creating the dichotomy between black and white was essential to judging black as black, the conceptual and 'racial' black, not just a darker hue. 'A blacke face with a white garment, is like a flye drowned in a spooneful of milke', wrote the printer and publisher Nicholas Ling.[17]

This dichotomy could then be used, for example, in proverbs and sayings, where black was simply black: it could not be washed white, purified, or redeemed.[18] No other part of human appearance could wipe away the stamp

---

[17] Nicholas Ling, *Politeuphuia* (London, 1597), fol. 28v.

[18] Stephen Gosson, *The Ephemerides of Phialo* (London, 1586), fol. 62–62v; Arthur Dent, *The Plaine Mans Path-way to Heaven* (London, 1601/1974), p. 156; Maurice Palmer Tilley, *A Dictionary of the Proverbs in England in the Sixteenth and Seventeenth Centuries* (Ann Arbor, 1966), p. 31. According to Carolyn Prager, the proverb was used in 17 works in the field of Renaissance drama, not to mention the countless times it appears in other forms of writing. However, Prager believes that during the sixteenth century, the trope changed from 'a reference that is essentially racially neutral to one that is ethnically charged'. It seems to me that the proverb was never racially neutral, although its negative connotations seem to have grown stronger. Carolyn Prager, '"If I be Devil": English Renaissance response to the proverbial and ecumenical Ethiopian', *Journal of Medieval and Renaissance Studies*, 17:2 (1987), pp. 258, 264. On the overwhelmingly negative English view of Africans, see Alden T. Vaughan and Virginia Mason Vaughan, 'Before Othello: Elizabethan representations of sub-Saharan Africans', *The William and Mary Quarterly*, 54:1 (1997), pp. 29, 42–44.

of blackness. Black Africans were warned not to believe themselves white merely because they had white teeth.[19] Thus for white English people black skin generated a whole range of negative qualities and suspicious attitudes.

Black skin looked exotic and erotic, and it produced mixed pleasures of the senses, where delight combined with horror and desire with distaste. One of the prominent associations, frequently made in connection with black skin and black Africans more generally, was immoderate sexuality and bodiliness. Let us now look at how sexuality was skin deep. The trope of unruly African sexuality already appears in the 1555 translation of Johannes Boemus, *The Fardle of Facions*, but the link to skin was not yet clearly spelled out. Later, in John Pory's translation of Leo Africanus' *A Geographical Historie of Africa*, published in 1600, Africans were described as more prone to sexual transgressions and excesses than any other 'nation' in the world.[20] English writers adopted this idea without questioning it, albeit somewhat slowly. However, even in earlier comments where the connection between black skin and sexuality is weaker, references to African, or black, sexuality often derive directly from judgements and perceptions of skin colour, particularly in the case of women.

For English men and women, looking at or imaging black African men, the connection between sexuality and skin was more obscure. Men's sexuality, of course, was generally contextualised not so much on the basis of their appearance as on their physical prowess, so the surface of the body acquired a different emphasis. This does not mean that male black skin was free of sexual loading – the English sources being examined here reflect male attitudes much more than they do female, and we have very little access to English women's constructions of sexuality in general, let alone the sexuality of black Africans.

It is not difficult to find examples of black women – and their black skin – portrayed as predominantly sexual. I will start from a later example, Richard Brome's mid-seventeenth-century play *The English Moor, or The Mock Marriage*, and then hope to show that to some extent his interpretations can be read backwards into the sixteenth century. When the protagonist of Brome's play

---

[19] See George Pettie, *A Petite Pallace, of Pettie His Pleasure* (London, 1578), p. 66; Dent, *Plaine Mans Path-way*, p. 44.

[20] Johannes Boemus, *The Fardle of Facions* (London, 1555), sig. E8, F1, F6, F8v; Leo Africanus, *A Geographical Historie of Africa* (London, 1600/1969), pp. 37–8, 284–5. On similar ideas in medieval European culture, see Thomas Hahn, 'The difference the Middle Ages makes: color and race before the modern world', *The Journal of Medieval and Early Modern Studies*, 31:1 (2001), pp. 23–5.

paints his white wife's face black, she is automatically interpreted as someone offering sexual favours. Her husband's lustful friends start groping her in corners and cracking jokes about her barbary buttocks.[21] Black skin denoted both access and enticement. In the early seventeenth century, when court performers were fascinated with portraying black characters, the 'curtizan-like' apparel and shocking lechery of court ladies appearing in Ben Jonson's *Masque of Beauty* prompted Dudley Carleton to cry out in moral outrage.[22] Here, too, appearing in a black mask was enough to call forth the sexual connotations of African women. William Dunbar proceeded directly from describing his black woman's outward appearance to her sexual availability: the thick-lipped lady, shining like a barrel of tar in her sumptuous clothes, incited a lusty knight to fight mightily on the battlefield and then end up in her passionate embraces. This love, presented in an overtly physical way, satisfied the knight so deeply that he longed for no other comfort.[23]

Sometimes black skin was imagined as a mask or a veil that hid an original white person, as in John Weever's erotic epigram 'In Byrrham'.[24] Black skin could be compared to paint, and painting a face could be described as 'murdering beauty'.[25] Although early modern Englishmen understood black skin as a real feature, it was conceptualised as a corrupted version of the original skin God intended man to have and which they themselves sported on their bodies. Thus black skin had meaning only in connection with white skin, and white skin, on the other hand, retained its beauty by being compared to dark and black.

Although painted and blackened skin on the stage is not the same thing as real African skin, and satiric poetry cannot be read as direct evidence of everyday behaviour, the attitudes reflected in these examples reveal how close the connection was between perceiving black skin and experiencing sexual desire. In Brome's scene, the men groping the blackened woman are portrayed as believing her to be African, not just painted as such. Their fictitious reactions are not so distant from Carleton's outrage, and Dunbar's desire (although cloaked in layers of courtly Petrarchism, playful distaste and mocking praise) is still intimately connected to and indeed born out of her appearance. They

---

[21] Richard Brome, *The English Moor, or The Mock-Marriage* (London, 1659), pp. 60–1.
[22] For Carleton's comments see Jones, *Othello's Countrymen*, p. 33; Hall, *Things of Darkness*, p. 130; Mary Floyd-Wilson, 'Temperature, temperance, and racial difference in Ben Jonson's *The Masque of Blackness*', *English Literary Renaissance*, 28:2 (1998), p. 195.
[23] Dunbar, *Poems*, pp. 66–7.
[24] John Weever, *Epigrammes in the Oldest Cut and Newest Fashion* (London, 1599/1911), p. 56.
[25] Brome, *The English Moor*, p. 37.

all fix their gaze on the spectacle of black skin, and see it first and foremost as sexual.

But how does this coupling of skin and sexuality work in terms of beauty and ugliness? There is a connection between beauty and lust, a key conceptual union affecting the lives of white English women, and also relevant to how black African women were perceived. Renaissance theorists of emotion believed that 'beauty' in women produced 'love' in men who saw them (and vice versa, with some gendered differences).[26] Thus, emotion was a reaction to some outward stimulus, perceived through the human senses. Love was an affect which a white male felt when looking at a beautiful white female. So where, in this scheme, does blackness take us?

In white women, true beauty was conceptually linked with virtue, although some forms of beauty – especially cosmetically enhanced, 'painted' beauty – could also point towards immorality and vanity. The line between virtuous and depraved beauty was very thin indeed, and it was placed within the realms of sexuality. In terms of affect, a clear difference between white and black appearance emerges. White beauty invited love, an emotion that was intellectually turned into admiration and Platonic adoration, where sexuality also received a transformed interpretation as a cult of controlled passion. Black deformity, on the other hand, aroused the corresponding emotion, but without the exalting power of beauty – not love, then, but lust. And this is where the sexual availability of black women obtained its rationale: the African origin of black women testified *ipso facto* to their sexual corruption, and the colour of their skin appeared as deformity, without the power of white skin to elevate and produce sublime emotions. Seeing foul blackness produced an impure passion, a sinful, denigrating, demonising lust. This kind of ugliness is of course something entirely different from how we think of ugliness in our everyday language. Foulness was deformity, the opposite of beauty, but beauty itself was felt as something producing sublime affects and experiences. Everything that led away from God and virtue, on the other hand, was foul and deformed.

As almost all our Renaissance sources were written through the male gaze, it is self-evident that the black woman appears as doubly 'other' – firstly as a woman, and secondly as a black African. When the object of this desiring gaze was powerfully sexualised in seventeenth-century texts, we are faced

---

[26] Baldassare Castiglione, *The Book of the Courtier* (London, 1561/1974), pp. 303–4; William Painter, *The Palace of Pleasure* (London, 1566), fol. 29; John Northbrooke, *Spiritus est vicarius Christi* (London, 1579), p. 123; Annibale Romei, *The Courtiers Academie* (London, 1598), p. 6.

with the dilemma of white male sexuality: how was one to treat lust, which was understood as always shameful and wrong, and which became even more problematic in relation to black women?[27] The Christian patriarchal model of manhood, and the experience of white superiority, demanded a self-control that incorporated the conceptual prerequisites for maintaining the power of the father and the master. Man was to control woman, and white was to control black. Neither of these objects seemed totally within reach, however, and furthermore, sometimes man could not even control himself when he saw a black woman. In this context, perceiving black women as others rationalises both fear and desire: while they are presented as objects of sexual desire, they are also conceptualised as other, inferior beings, whose lot was to be overpowered and controlled. Black sexuality was twice as great a threat as white sexuality, which itself was difficult enough to handle.

On the other hand, in unions between black men and white women in English Renaissance literature, which are in fact depicted more often than the other way around, sexuality is also always an issue. Here, not surprisingly, given the problematic nature of female sexuality, sinful connotations encircle the white woman as well.[28] In drama, the desire black Africans were shown to feel towards white European women usually ended in disaster, because these relationships seem to be more about lust for power than about sexuality. Black African characters are portrayed as engaging in illicit relationships, often with socially superior women, in order to climb up the social ladder. The women, on the other hand, allowed themselves to be overcome by their animal lusts and were destroyed, whereas the men, even if they succeeded in acquiring an influential position with all the adjoining honour, power and wealth, were shown to resent and envy whiteness and the unquestioned cultural superiority it entailed. Indeed, it was often envy and jealousy that spiralled them towards their inevitable ruin: dark-skinned social climbers, such as Eleazar in *Lust's Dominion* or Aaron in *Titus Andronicus*, became pitiless tyrants, and grew increasingly isolated both socially and psychologically. Black desire for power is often accompanied by an internalised realisation of marginality, and black inferiority. Thus, even here, the visual marker of black skin is linked,

[27] Hall, *Things of Darkness*, p. 205; Joyce E. Chaplin, *Subject Matter. Technology, the Body, and Science on the Anglo-American Frontier, 1500–1676* (Cambridge, MA, 1991), pp. 191–3; for discourses on sexual otherness relating to pleasures of the imagination, and more specifically literary pleasures, see Cohen, 'On Saracen enjoyment', pp. 124–5.

[28] Lynda E. Boose, '"The getting of a lawful race": Racial discourse in early modern England and the unrepresentable black woman', in Margo Hendricks and Patricia Parker, eds., *Women, 'Race', and Writing in the Early Modern Period* (London and New York, 1994), p. 42.

through the experience of inferiority it is supposed to produce, to a cultural judgement that makes black Africans incapable of adjusting to white society.

One might want to see here a white recognition of the impossibility of the cultural niche apportioned to black Africans, but rarely is there any hint of compassion in scenes of black Africans rising above their status: the God-given social hierarchies of English society did not allow for black self-assertiveness or unruliness. The white writers and audiences of these plays clearly could not consider the possibility that a black character might seriously see himself as equal with his white surroundings.[29] Divine order dictated that black Africans could only be in power, legitimately, among their own marginal societies, in Africa.

After all this, it is perhaps somewhat surprising that in non-fictional sources, marriages between Africans and Europeans were not unheard-of, nor even particularly awe-inspiring. The travel writer George Best, although not famous for friendly attitudes towards black Africans, mentions a marriage between an Ethiopian 'blacke as a cole' living in London and an English white woman, and focuses not on the marriage itself but on the question of why their child had black skin.[30] Anthony Copley, on the other hand, published in his jest book an anecdote that played upon the idea of black subjectivity: a blackamoor king was disappointed in his courting of a French white lady when the lady said that she could not love a deformed face such as his. The king concluded that the woman was at fault: her base mind was such a dirty and deformed mirror that his beauty could not be portrayed in it.[31] Examples like these are not, however, very typical.

As the protagonist in one of the best-known Renaissance plays, Shakespeare's *Othello*, is a noble and valorous Moorish knight who has succeeded in securing the love of a beautiful white lady and acquiring a powerful position in the European social system, it could be argued that marriages between Africans and Europeans on stage are a good starting point for examining more positive attitudes towards black Africans. Othello's white wife Desdemona

---

[29] But see Bartels, 'Othello and Africa', pp. 61–64.

[30] George Best in Hakluyt, *Principal Navigations* (1599–1600), III, pp. 51–2. There are, of course, contrary examples as well: in Heywood's play *The Fair Maid of the West*, Bess Bridges, the character embodying white purity who strays from the path of virtue, meets the Moorish king Mullisheg, and their kiss is shown on the stage. The sexual antics of the corrupt Moor, and the loose morals of the lily-white lady allowing herself to be seduced, cause the white male viewers moments of horror, but in the end Bess is saved by a decent marriage. See Jean E. Howard, 'An English lass amid the Moors', in Margo Hendricks and Patricia Parker, eds., *Women, 'Race', and Writing*, pp. 116–17.

[31] Anthony Copley, *Wits, Fits, and Fancies* (London, 1614), p. 13.

appears as a 'prize' for his 'mental whiteness', his understanding of the codes of white male honour. But Othello's rashness, irrationality, gullibility, jealousy and violence can hardly be taken as evidence of nobleness of character – although this blunt formulation moves out of the early modern mindset into a modern, gendered framework.[32] Even if these characteristics are not presented as being caused by his dark skin, they certainly combine in a typical inner conflict of imagined black success stories. In cases like this, we should think in terms of a juxtaposition: black skin against white soul. Othello is black but noble, just as the bride of the *Song of Songs* is black but beautiful. Black skin by no means excluded other characteristics and qualities; instead, playing with contraries, opposites and paradoxes was the early modern way of discussing dichotomies. Black skin could not be changed into white, and it could not be overlooked; it was not something that could be set aside as having no particular meaning. Othello's good characteristics were surprising and noteworthy exactly because he was black; his blackness set them in high relief. The colour of his skin, then, is actually very meaningful, and not just a coincidence. His 'white' nobility does not show through his black skin, but against it.

If black Africans were usually judged on the basis of their physical attributes alone, it is no surprise that English writers describe them as violent as well. Descriptions of Africa construct the trope of violence by presenting black Africans as a band of robbers or warriors, courageous barbarians. Cannibalism and other terrifying practices are commonly mentioned. The frightening 'look' of Africans was an important part of creating this image: the warlike 'tribe' of Giachas or Agagi, for example, was always described in terms of their 'dreadful and devilish' sight, deformed facial features and glowing white eyes, contrasting with the extreme blackness of their skin.[33]

The idea of unreasonable violence was also associated with Africans living in England or Europe. A very good example of this is a ballad called 'A Lamentable Ballad of the Tragical End of a Gallant Lord and Virtuous Lady', where the black African servant of a noble white family is driven to violence by his master's unjust treatment. He imprisons the whole family except the master, tortures all of them, rapes the lady, then kills the children and their mother in a locked tower of their moated castle, in full sight of all the townspeople. The nobleman dies of horror upon seeing this, and finally the black servant

---

[32] For Othello's character linking with Renaissance popular conceptions of people of colour, and these conceptions forming the basic vocabulary of colonialist discourses, see Ania Loomba, *Gender, Race, Renaissance Drama* (Delhi, 1989), pp. 49–52.

[33] Leo Africanus, *A Geographical Historie*, p. 31; Bulwer, *Anthropometamorphosis*, p. 70.

also hurls himself down from a tower window and meets his maker.[34] That the murderer is black is not fortuitous. The protagonist of the ballad is a 'heathenish and blood-thirsty Blackamoor', who does not shy away from violence of any kind, be it sexual or directed at innocent children, who has no respect for social hierarchy or order, and who feels no pity or human emotion towards any of his 'family'. Heathenish cruelty combined with black skin did not sound all that strange to Renaissance readers. The black servant of the ballad is turned into a demon, a personification of evil. It is clear that this visual imagery carried inside it pure fear of the unknown, but the horror evoked by blackness also had an extensive Christian background.

Demonisation of black skin was helped by a long and powerful Christian tradition of depicting demons and the devil himself as black. Their dark skin was both comic and horrifying; it embodied vice, sin and terror.[35] Sin was black, virtue was white; the body was black, the soul was white.[36] In many texts of the Renaissance, black Africans are actually referred to as 'devils', and the link between blackness, vice and sin is graphically emphasized.[37] On the stage, this tradition can already be found in medieval mystery plays, where Lucifer and his fallen angels turn black as a visible sign of their sin against God.[38] Again, the familiar images of blackness were so powerful that the text could evoke them even without much actual description.

Beauty and deformity in Renaissance thinking were also intimately connected to reason and intelligence. Like all creatures driven by their bodily lusts, black Africans were thought of as foolish or lacking understanding. In terms of outward appearance, there was one European conceptual tradition

---

[34] 'A Lamentable Ballad of the Tragical End of a Gallant Lord and Virtuous Lady Together with the Untimely Death of their two Children, Wickedly performed by a heathenish and blood-thirsty Blackamoor, their servant, The like of which Cruelty and Murder was never before heard of', in Chappell, *The Roxburghe Ballads*, II, pp. 49–55.

[35] See Dorothy Hoogland Verkerk, 'Black servant, black demon: color ideology in the Ashburnham Pentateuch', *The Journal of Medieval and Early Modern Studies*, 31:1 (2001), pp. 60–4. This interpretation was enhanced by the connection which English travellers constructed between black skin and ignorance of the Christian message. See Hall, *Things of Darkness*, p. 103.

[36] This idea was often presented in the commentaries of the *Song of Songs*, when the bride calling herself black was explained as symbolizing people living in sin, and her inner whiteness as reflecting the brightness of the redeemed soul and the salvation offered by the church. Baldwin, *The Canticles*, sig. A3v; Brucioli, *A Commentary*, sig. B2v–B3v; Ainsworth, *Solomons Song of Songs*, sig. B4v–C1; see also Paul Edwards, 'The early African presence in the British Isles', in Jagdish S. Gundara and Ian Duffield eds., *Essays on the History of Blacks in Britain* (Aldershot, 1992), p. 14.

[37] See for example Christopher Marlowe/Thomas Dekker, *Lust's Dominion* (London, 1657), sig. B5, C8v, C9v, D11, E4v, E6v, etc.; Bulwer, *Anthropometamorphosis*, p. 108.

[38] Anthony Gerard Barthelemy, *Black Face, Maligned Race* (Baton Rouge and London, 1987), pp. 3–4.

that offered a very handy framework for the link between lack of intellect and black skin: physiognomy. This collection of pseudo-scientific categorizing principles based on outward appearance was designed to make sense of European faces and bodies, but if we look closely at how physiognomy approached bodily features, it soon becomes clear how well suited the ideology was to interpreting black appearance as inferior. For example, in the physiognomical system, thick lips and large noses, traditionally ascribed to Africans, signified stupidity.[39] Even if physiognomy says nothing of black skin, it deals out social judgements on skin hues that belonged to those not completely white – and by extension, noting how stridently black skin was determined as deformity, we might infer a connection here too. If someone familiar with physiognomy wanted to use the system to interpret black skin, it allowed him to do so. I do not want to give the impression that any of the guidelines for physiognomical interpretation actually talked about black Africans; they did not. What I want to show is that most of the intellectual systems at the disposal of white Renaissance Englishmen guided them to deem black skin inferior to their own, and to give it meanings far beyond its actual bodily manifestations. The same conceptual arsenal could be drawn upon in everyday interpretative processes as well, when looking at actual black Africans. The white gaze that viewed black skin, through the awareness that white skin was more beautiful, was not just dichotomising, it was always also hierarchising.

So far, we have hardly touched on what English Renaissance writers thought black skin actually was. Skin colour here has been linked, connected and tied to something, it has appeared in connection with something, it has been read through something else. This is because Renaissance English authors hardly ever describe the appearance of black skin in a direct way. Black was black, a fact of life, not something to be taken apart in a rigorous visual or aesthetic exercise. On the other hand, a form of knowledge that definitely was of acute importance to these writers, particularly those of a more scientific persuasion, was the cause for black skin. This fact alone reveals how forceful was the idea of whiteness as origin. There was never any need to explain how white skin came about, but an explanation continually had to be sought for black skin.

[39] *The Gouernaunce of Prynces* (London, 1898), pp. 233–5; Bartholomeus Cocles, *Le compendion et brief enseignement de physiognomie et chiromancie* (Paris, 1550), sig. B4–B4v; Joannes Indagine, *Chiromantia*, (London, 1558), sig. H2–H4v; see also Juliana Schiesari, 'The face of domestication: physiognomy, gender politics, and humanism's others', in Margo Hendricks and Patricia Parker, eds., *Women, 'Race', and Writing*, pp. 61–2.

In the English context, three main theories were discussed, and all were found
wanting.

The climatic theory supposed that the sun parched the skin of those living in
the far south black, but since the skin colour of Europeans living in Africa did
not darken in the same way, and Africans living in Europe did not gradually
acquire a beautiful white skin, and, furthermore, since Africans were of many
shades, this theory was found seriously lacking. It is, however, an interesting
interpretation, because it does not assume skin colour to be an absolute.
Rather, it sees colour as a continuum, a series of differences.[40] If we think of
Renaissance beauty theories, we can actually find a somewhat similar attitude:
the blacker the skin, the uglier the person. Neither blackness nor ugliness is
absolute, however; instead, there is a continuum of different variations from
the norm of whiteness. And, curiously enough, for people of a certain hue,
those of the same colour were said to seem the most attractive.[41] Even if these
reflections sound more like astonishment and mockery than acknowledging
and respecting ethnic difference, they still reveal beauty or ugliness of skin
colour as more multifaceted than usual. In fact, climatic theory can be seen
as logically leading to a questioning of the simple interplay of skin colour,
morals and human value prevalent at the time.

The gaping holes in the climatic theory invited attempts to explain black
skin though heredity. George Best wondered why the child of a mixed marriage
was black, even when the family lived in England. Could there be a hereditary
reason for black skin? Discussions of generation were very different before
the age of genes, and the most important element in these early discussions

[40] Mary Floyd-Wilson contends that the somewhat marginal geographical status of England and,
in terms of climatic theory, the extreme (even unhealthy) whiteness of its inhabitants compelled
English writers to challenge the theory and prefer the binary opposition of white and black. See
Floyd-Wilson, 'Temperature, temperance, and racial difference', pp. 185–6. Lynda Boose, also
discussing the geographical isolation of England, interestingly notes that of all 'European'
countries, England was 'the most unfamiliar with Africans' because of its marginal location on
the world map: Boose, ' "The getting of a lawful race" ', p. 36. As a Finnish/Nordic historian, I
am of course well placed to point out the ethnocentricity of Boose's critical perspective, too:
even during the Renaissance, Europe did not end at the south coast of the Baltic Sea, and
England's isolation was always relative.

[41] Tommaso Buoni, *Problemes of Beautie and All Humane Affections* (London, 1606), p. 26. Other early
modern writers also pointed out that ugliness of black skin was relative and culturally variable:
where 'we' see whiteness as beauty, Moors, for example, could esteem darker hues – and
pygmies did not mind short people. See for example Juan Luis Vives, *The Passions of the Soul*
(Lewiston, NY and Lampeter, 1990), p. 113; Anthony Gibson, *A Womans Woorth* (London, 1599),
fol. 57–57v; Thomas Browne, *Pseudodoxia Epidemica* (London, 1646), pp. 332–3. Thomas Hahn
has found the same idea in medieval sources as well, see Hahn, 'The difference the Middle Ages
makes', pp. 18–19.

was the role of the mother and her imagination. If during the moment of conception she happened to be thinking of or seeing something potent or distressing, this could have repercussions for the unborn child. Pregnancy was a time fraught with dangers of this kind. Black women, naturally, were thinking of their black husbands – hence their black children. But even white women married to white men could thus conceive black children, if they fixed their imagination on a vision of a black man at the wrong moment. In this way, black skin could be thought of as a 'mutation', appearing at some point during human history through mere error and the activity of a woman's imagination.[42]

Another theory debated during the Renaissance revolved around the curse of Ham, son of Noah, but this theory too was recognised as problematic, because of the many discrepancies and conflicts in the story.[43] Still, George Best, for example, while explaining the curse, called blackness 'a spectacle of disobedience', an indelible visual stain of sin, meant to be seen by all.[44] No matter how emphatically the curse of Ham was denied, it was still repeated all through the seventeenth century, and whether people believed in the curse or not, the association of blackness with lechery, lust and disobedience stuck. Since the early modern mind was always collecting knowledge by combining it, we can see how the popular image of the black African was formed by piling one association of sin on top of another, resulting in a 'bricolage' of devilish and sinful images. But that is all it was: an amalgam of suspicions and assumptions, not a proper theory – or so early modern natural philosophers thought.

All in all, we could say Renaissance England lacked a theory to explain black skin and, consequently, the cultural niche appropriate for black Africans. This was considered a serious problem, and while various writers called for more

[42] Thomas Lupton, *A Thousand Notable Things* (London, 1579), pp. 156–7; Purchas, *Pilgrimage*, p. 655; Browne, *Pseudodoxia Epidemica*, pp. 327–8; Bulwer, *Anthropometamorphosis*, p. 253; see also Chaplin, *Subject Matter*, pp. 138–41. In a literary form this motif is presented in the Ethiopian romance of Heliodorus and its later versions, see *Heliodorus, An Æthiopian Historie* (London, 1569), fol. 52v–53; William Lisle, *The Faire Æthiopian* (London, 1631), p. 182.

[43] The problems of the curse of Ham have been multiplied by Benjamin Braude's revealing article on how the geographical notions familiar to us as Noachic theory are fragmentary and inconsistent, and often anachronistically put together. In the Renaissance, there was no clear idea of the global continental division so familiar to us, and the division of lands between Noah's sons was itself a much debated and incoherent fantasy. What we have here is indeed 'a process of unnatural selection', as Braude describes it! Benjamin Braude, 'The sons of Noah and the construction of ethnic and geographical identities in the medieval and early modern periods', *The William and Mary Quarterly*, 54:1 (1997), 103–42.

[44] Best in Hakluyt, *Principal Navigations* (1599–1600), III, p. 52.

detailed analyses of the topic, it became an ongoing quest for knowledge.[45] As Kim Hall has argued, the theoretical vacuum emphasised the mystery not only of the origins of black skin, but of black Africans in general.[46] And the recognition of this theoretical vacuum is one of the crucial moments of producing racial difference.

The whole point of explaining black skin was to fix whiteness as the origin and the norm, and therefore beautiful, and blackness as a corrupted, deformed, and re-formed variant. Thus any explanation for skin colour points to the hierarchical relationship between different types of skin, reaffirming the connection between whiteness and goodness, and reasserting the power relations whereby white was always controlling black. This is why skin colour could not be discussed neutrally, and why black African inferiority could be condensed through bodily markers. Were it not for the enormous cultural potency of beauty (or appearance more generally) in the Renaissance, this would not mean much, but beauty and deformity were central social signifiers for women in particular (but also for men), both in categorising appearance and in judging the place of others.

We have seen that skin colour, although a theory or category of 'race' had not yet emerged, was a mark of status in many ways. Renaissance English culture was one of visual marking, in which skin colour was itself a category – an identity-marking, morally-defining, 'otherness'-creating category, in many ways analogically functioning like the later category of race. I would argue that the visual and aesthetic category of blackness/whiteness was the grid that contained or led to theological, moral, geographical and other normative judgements, which also in turn took part in constructing that particular category of otherness.

And yet there is a twist. The colour of one's skin was a fact that could be used to categorize people and assign them their place. But it was not strong enough to act as the stable cultural marker demanded by the weight of its associations and meanings. After all, skin colour was only a bodily fact, and the body was changing, transient and temporal. Consequently, the meanings of blackness were floating on the mortal surface; they were without philosophical and scientific fixity. More stable theoretical underpinnings were needed, ostensibly to 'explain' racial difference, but also to fix the meanings of black skin to something more ideologically and historically viable than the

---

[45] See for example Hartwell in Lopez, *A Report*, p. 188.
[46] Hall, *Things of Darkness*, p. 42; for a similar situation in early America, see Chaplin, *Subject Matter*, pp. 52, 139, 160.

body's outer boundary. Uncertainty about the origins of black skin did not mean uncertainty as to its current meanings, but a quest for validating those meanings from a philosophical and scientific standpoint. When, later, the idea of race emerged, truths located on the body's surface could be transposed into biology, and visual experience could be justified and stabilised into scientific notions and categories. This is a process of abstraction, but also of stabilisation of everyday experience.

Skin colour was perhaps not 'the most defining feature for constructing Otherness'[47] in Renaissance England (as Lynda Boose has suggested), but in the encounter between white English and black Africans, it was certainly exceedingly powerful. Joyce Green MacDonald has rightly pointed out that being black was not just about skin colour, but about a vast array of meanings that constructed racial thinking even before the concept of race was born. To MacDonald, skin colour 'as the chief determinant of race is a modern rather than a Renaissance phenomenon'.[48] Yet black skin occurs everywhere in early modern constructions of Africans, and I feel it is necessary to look at what was read into skin colour in general, and in this case, black skin. I would argue that black skin, as a visible and observable sign, was already the principle that allowed the various meanings ascribed to Africa and Africans to be gathered together. Black skin came to embody much of the interpretative apparatus that Europeans engaged in when looking at and understanding Africans; but, as a bodily and transient signifier, skin was not powerful enough to contain these meanings when contacts with Africa and Africans became ever more frequent.

Whichever way we look at it, we are still facing an ethnography created and appropriated by white Europeans, a narrative constructing the black African as emphatically 'other'. But what we should recognise is that there are different ways of theorizing and even describing that 'other'. Looking at early modern discourses distances blackness from the idea of 'scientific race' or 'racism', but at the same time it shows how previous European constructions of difference disturbingly point in a similar direction. Perhaps it is still useful to lay one's finger on the *different* kinds of fictions we create, in order to tear down the fictions of race, or deconstruct the construction of race altogether.

What this should tell us is that we do not need the concept of race to harbour the kinds of prejudices which race entails. The same prejudices can be fixed in other forms of difference and in other intellectual categories. And

---

[47] This formulation comes from Lynda Boose's question on whether skin colour should in fact be focused on as the most important 'racializing' factor in Renaissance England. See Boose, '"The getting of a lawful race"', pp. 35–6.

[48] Joyce Green MacDonald, *Women and Race in Early Modern Texts* (Cambridge, 2002), p. 44.

this partly explains the tenacity of the fictions of race: cultural categories are too devious and multifaceted for us even to grasp in everyday life, let alone simply to do away with. This is one of my main points. But while we can see that doing away with the concept of race does not necessarily allow us more freedom if we continue to be burdened with its intellectual content, considering Renaissance beliefs also shows us that race is a cultural, historical concept, born out of the needs of a specific period in time to define the 'other' that needed containing. It is not a universal, and its scientific value is easily questioned, if the meanings attached to it could be explained at an earlier time through other cultural categories. However tenacious, it is still simply a fiction.

CHAPTER FIVE

Black Africans in Portugal during Cleynaerts's visit (1533–1538)

JORGE FONSECA

Between 1533 and 1538 Portugal was home to an exotic visitor from Northern Europe – the Flemish humanist, Nicholas Cleynaerts. Cleynaerts was a professor in Louvain, Paris and Salamanca, a classical scholar, an Arabist, and the author of some famous grammars. A judicial dispute about an ecclesiastical position in his home town of Diest led him to abandon Brabant and move to Spain, where he became a successful teacher of Latin and Greek in Salamanca. André de Resende, a Portuguese friend from Louvain, was sent there as an emissary of King João III, to find and invite him to Portugal with the promise of a good salary. His role was to teach Latin to Prince Henrique, the king's twenty-one-year-old brother.

The Portuguese court during this period was based at Évora, in the south.[1] The king, greatly involved in cultural renewal, surrounded himself with men of learning, both Portuguese and foreign. Cleynaerts was to live in close proximity with some members of this chosen group. But although he was the recipient of regal hospitality and enjoyed a tranquil and stimulating lifestyle, this did not prevent him from making critical comments about the society in which he found himself, in his personal correspondence with friends at home. His comments refer not only to the country in general but to the social environment of Évora in particular, as well as to Lisbon, the largest city of the kingdom, which he certainly visited, and to Braga, where he established himself during the last two years of his stay, in order to accompany his young pupil, who had been nominated as administrator of the diocese. His correspondents included Latomus, a theologian in Louvain and an antagonist of Luther, who had been his teacher; Polites, a humanist with links to various university centres; and Vaseo, also from Louvain.

One of the features of Portuguese society that impressed Cleynaerts, and that was mentioned by him in the letters he sent to his compatriots, was the existence of black Africans – above all slaves – who were so abundant

---

[1] João José Alves Dias, ed., *Portugal do Renascimento à Crise Dinástica* (Lisbon, 1998), p. 725; Joaquim Romero Magalhães, 'O Enquadramento do Espaço Nacional', in José Mattoso, ed., *História de Portugal* (Lisbon, 1993), p. 54.

that he was led to believe that in Lisbon, for example, 'slaves outnumber free Portuguese'.[2] The attitude of the inhabitants towards this social group gave rise to observations that are revealing of the mental attitude of the author himself with regard to black Africans, slaves and the institution of slavery. The letters that contain these observations have been known to historians for some time, and have been published. Since for the past few years I have been carrying out research on slaves in Portugal, I shall try to compare Cleynaerts's impressions with the results of my investigations to see how far they exaggerate reality (which they certainly do, as was usual in accounts of this type). I will also comment in a critical manner on Cleynaerts's own ideas. For this analysis I will use the editions of the letters by Alphonse Roersch and Manuel Gonçalves Cerejeira.[3] The passages in Cleynaerts's letters about black Africans and slavery concern themselves with the following issues: first, the number of slaves and black Africans in the country; second, their place in the economy and in society; and third, Cleynaerts's position in relation to black Africans and to slavery.

As for the first point, the humanist's observations are very emphatic: 'There are slaves everywhere . . . Portugal is full of this kind of person';[4] 'I had hardly set foot in Évora and I felt as though I had been transported to a city in hell; I came across black people everywhere';[5] and the statement mentioned above: 'I believe that in Lisbon male and female slaves outnumber free Portuguese.'[6]

These impressions are similar to others that are also well known. Garcia de Resende, poet and courtier, at about the same time revealed his preoccupation with the number of slaves entering the country: 'We see in the Kingdom / so many slaves grow / and the natives go / That, if this is so, there will be more / of them, than of us, in my opinion.'[7] Also an anonymous sixteenth-century Italian declared during a visit to Portugal: 'There are such numbers of slaves

---

[2] *Correspondance de Nicolas Clénard*, ed. Alphonse Roersch, 3 vols. (Brussels, 1940–1), I, p. 54: 'quo genere hominum tam est referta Lusitania, ut credam Ulyssipone plures esse huiusmodi servos, et servas, quam sint liberi Lusitani.'

[3] *Correspondance*, ed. Roersch and Manuel Gonçalves Cerejeira, *O Renascimento em Portugal: Clenardo e a Sociedade Portuguesa* (Coimbra, 1974).

[4] *Correspondance*, ed. Roersch, I, p. 54: 'Mancipiorum plena sunt omnia . . . quo genere hominum tam est referta Lusitania.'

[5] *Correspondance*, ed. Roersch, I, p. 57: 'Verum ubi primum ingressus sum Eboram, putabam me venisse in civitatem aliquam Cacodaemonum: tot ubique occurrebant Aethiopes.'

[6] *Correspondance*, ed. Roersch, I, p. 54: 'ut credam Ulyssipone plures esse huiusmodi servos, et servas, quam sint liberi Lusitani.'

[7] Garcia de Resende, 'Miscelânea', *Livro das Obras de Garcia de Resende*, ed. Evelina Verdelho (Lisbon, 1994), p. 572: 'Vemos no Reino meter / Tantos cativos crescer / E irem-se os naturais / Que, se assim for, serão mais / Eles que nós, a meu ver.'

that the cities resemble games of chess, with equal numbers of white and black people.'[8]

Many of these comments were, of course, caricatures, and reflected the surprise felt by visitors from countries where there were very few black Africans, who were struck by their black skin contrasting with the white skin of the majority of the population.[9] Many of the black Africans, slaves and freedmen, were to be seen frequently on the public roads, at the service of their masters in small businesses and in workshops, and were very visible. The impression was increased by the exuberance of their behaviour, because they were, apparently, happier and more extrovert than the local people. The anonymous author said of them: 'while the Portuguese are always sad and melancholic . . . the slaves are always happy, they do nothing but laugh, sing, dance and get drunk publicly in all the town squares'.[10]

But what was actually happening? Through studies of the South of Portugal – the region of the country in which Cleynaerts lived most of the time, and to which most of his descriptions relate – based on baptismal records, I have come to the view that in the sixteenth century slaves represented approximately 6–7 per cent of the total population, and in the Évora region about 5 per cent. In very few localities (except for the Algarve[11]) did their presence exceed 10 per cent of the population. According to the testimony of Cristóvão Rodrigues de Oliveira,[12] 10 per cent of the inhabitants of Lisbon were slaves. The black population was more numerous than this, because it included many freed people and their descendants.[13] Cleynaerts must have mistaken many

---

[8] 'Uma descrição de Portugal em 1578–80', ed. A. H. de Oliveira Marques, in A. H. de Oliveira Marques, *Portugal Quinhentista (Ensaios)* (Lisbon, 1987), p. 240: 'i schiavi . . . sono in tanto numero, che le città paiono giuochi da scacchi tanti bianchi come neri'.

[9] The Italian writer's surprise is all the more remarkable because he was from a country where, unlike Flanders, slaves had been common since the late Middle Ages, and were mainly used for domestic labour: Jacques Heers, *Escravos e Servidão Doméstica na Idade Média* (Lisbon, 1983), pp. 94–6; Iris Origo, *The Merchant of Prato* (London, 1957), pp. 189–96. However, large numbers of black slaves were not common. But Garcia de Resende was also shocked by the growth of the number of slaves, and he was living in a country where they had always existed! It was only a question of numbers.

[10] Oliveira Marques, 'Uma descrição', p. 240: 'che si come i Portoghesi per gravità van sempre mesti et malenconici . . . i schiavi sempre sono alegri, ne fanno altro mai che ridere, cantare, ballare, et ebriacarsi publicamente sopra tutte le piazze'.

[11] Jorge Fonseca, *Escravos no Sul de Portugal: Séculos XVI–XVII* (Lisbon, 2002), pp. 10–17.

[12] Cristóvão Rodrigues de Oliveira, *Lisboa em 1551: Sumário em que Brevemente se Contêm Algumas Coisas . . . que há na Cidade de Lisboa* (Lisbon, 1987), p. 101.

[13] According to Saunders' indications the freed population was about 2 per cent in Lisbon and Évora: A. C. de C. M. Saunders, *A Social History of Black Slaves and Freedmen in Portugal, 1441–1555* (Cambridge, 1982), pp. 55 and 57.

free black people for slaves, but all the same his exaggeration is obvious. Even in Lisbon, the largest centre of slavery, the number of black Africans never surpassed that of white people, or even equalled them, and certainly not in Évora. In Braga and in the north in general there were even fewer, judging by the results obtained by Saunders,[14] who found only a modest presence of slaves and black Africans in this region.

The same is true of Cleynaerts's statement that in almost every house there were female slaves: 'It is difficult to find a house where there is not at least one female slave.'[15] My research revealed that only a wealthy minority of the population – nobles, a good part of the clergy, civil servants, the more prosperous businessmen and owners of workshops and large-scale farmers – possessed slaves. That minority consisted of fewer people than there were slaves. The humanist's remark referred simply to the houses of people of his social milieu, the only one with which as an unsociable priest, dedicated to learning and teaching, he became acquainted during his stay.

As for the second issue, the use of slaves by their owners and their relationship with the free community, Cleynaerts's testimony seems closer to reality. The picture he paints of the lives of slaves who worked in domestic service appears correct. In describing their tasks, he affirms: 'She [the female slave] is the one who goes to the market to buy the necessary things, who washes the clothes, sweeps the house, carries water and deals with the rubbish at the appropriate time: in short, she's a slave, who apart from her appearance is no different from a beast of burden.'[16]

The data show that owners generally gave slaves the more common domestic chores, but gave them to male and female slaves alike.[17] It is common to find references to black male cooks[18] or sweepers.[19] The same goes for the carrying of water from the fountain and the washing of clothes. In Lisbon, at the Chafariz d'el Rei (the king's fountain), there were separate water-outlets for

[14] Saunders, *A Social History*, p. 53.

[15] *Correspondance*, ed. Roersch, I, p. 54: 'Aegre reperias domum, quae non saltem ancillulam huius generis teneat'.

[16] *Correspondance*, ed. Roersch, I, p. 54: 'Ea foris emit quocumque opus est, lavat vestes, verrit pavimentum, fert aquam, effert suo tempore faeces domesticas et humanas, et breviter servam agit, et praeter figuram nihil differt a brutis iumentis.'

[17] Évora, Arquivo Distrital, Câmara de Évora, no. 207, fol. 66v.; Gil Vicente, 'Farsa dos Almocreves', in *Copilaçam de Todalas Obras de Gil Vicente*, ed. Maria Leonor Carvalhão Buescu, 2 vols. (Lisbon, 1984), II, p. 498; José Augusto Alegria, *História da Capela e Colégio dos Santos Reis de Vila Viçosa* (Lisbon, 1983), p. 324.

[18] Évora, Biblioteca Pública, Cód. CXI/1–6; D. António Caetano de Sousa, *Provas da História Genealógica da Casa Real Portuguesa*, 6 vols. (Lisbon, 1935–49), VI, pp. 185 and 197; Évora, Arquivo Distrital, Fundo notarial, Évora, Liv. 210, fol. 121.

[19] Évora, Biblioteca Pública, Cód. CXI/1–6.

people of African descent, free or slaves, of either sex, and for white women, so as to avoid disorder.[20] But almost any kind of work, in all sectors of the economy, could be given to slaves, especially heavier duties, as the choice was entirely up to the owner.

In people's homes, male slaves frequently worked in the stables, and outside the house they often transported goods and minded animals. Cardinal Henrique (who was one of Cleynaerts' students), had seven 'stable slaves'.[21] D. António, Prior of Crato, who later disputed the kingdom with Philip II of Castille, brought from Tangiers, in North Africa, where he had been governor, a Moor named António Luís, whom 'he had in his stable'.[22] In 1558, D. Joana de Sousa from Estremoz gave her muleteer António his freedom and also the beasts he was working with.[23] In 1568 a slave who was a muleteer was arrested in Nisa. He 'had gone with his master's she-mules, which were being taken along with forbidden goods to Castile.'[24]

Others were found working in the agricultural sector, tending cornfields and vineyards. A slave from Alcochete had been attacked by two other men when he was 'watching over the cornfield he had sown'.[25] João, who belonged to a woman from Mora, used to spend his time working on his mistress's vineyards before she decided to free him.[26]

Many black African slaves worked in retail businesses and in workshops around the cities and towns, either directly for their masters, or else on their own account, giving their masters a proportion of their earnings. Eva, who belonged to a goldsmith from Évora, had been selling bread in the city for many years, making him 50 *reais* a day. With her earnings, in 1583 she was able to pay for her own freedom and the freedom of one of her sons, and she also bought a female slave.[27] Jorge Carvalho, from Almada, had a slave shoemaker, who ran away in 1580.[28] There are examples of barbers, carpenters, wax-chandlers, tanners and other workmen; in the Algarve, black slaves were used extensively on oil-presses.[29]

[20] *Os Negros em Portugal – Séculos XV a XIX* (Lisbon, 1999), p. 105.

[21] Évora, Biblioteca Pública, Cód. cxi/1–6.

[22] Setúbal, Arquivo Distrital, Fundo notarial, Almada, Liv. 1/4, fol. 86.

[23] Évora, Arquivo Distrital, Misericórdia de Évora, Liv. 1781–25.10.1558.

[24] Pedro de Azevedo, 'Os Ciganos em Portugal nos Séculos XVI e XVII', *Archivo Historico Portuguez*, 7 (1909), p. 50.

[25] Setúbal, Arquivo Distrital, Fundo notarial, Alcochete, Liv. 4/10, fol. 102v.

[26] Évora, Arquivo Distrital, Fundo notarial, Mora, Liv. 11, fol. 49.

[27] Évora, Arquivo Distrital, Fundo notarial, Évora, Liv. 140, fol. 140v.

[28] Setúbal, Arquivo Distrital, Fundo notarial, Almada, Liv. 2/8, fol. 46.

[29] Manuel Viegas Guerreiro and Joaquim Romero Magalhães, *Duas Descrições do Algarve no Século XVI* (Lisbon, 1983), pp. 116–17.

The anonymous sixteenth-century author previously mentioned stated: 'All of them work with horses and are used as porters, farmers and sailors'.[30] The duke of Bragança, D. Teodósio I, possessed thirty-six slaves, corresponding to 11 per cent of the total number of people who worked for him, among them twenty stable boys, four who worked in the kitchen and pantry, and ten who played *charamelas*, wind instruments used in both religious and secular ceremonies at the duke's court.[31]

Slave labour was so generalised that, according to Cleynaerts, 'all services were carried out by black or Moorish slaves',[32] which led to idleness among the Portuguese and the decline of free labour. Faced with competition from slaves, who were abundant and cheap, wage-earning workers would have greater difficulty in maintaining themselves, both materially and socially, because of the contempt associated with the manual labour performed mostly by slaves. We know that, even so, free labour was much more expensive than slave labour, which meant that a slave whose owner allowed him to practise a trade on his own account could, after a few years, obtain a sum corresponding to his value and buy his freedom.[33] This was a consequence of the greater productivity of wage-earning labour. It led Cleynaerts to complain that he could not find a maidservant to take care of his house, even when he offered a quarter of his salary, and after having acquired three slaves.[34]

An issue raised in a letter to his friend Latomus was the 'free' behaviour permitted to the female slaves and the consequences that resulted, that is the production of new slaves and consequent increase in the owners' patrimony: 'It seems to me that they raise them like someone who raises pigeons'.[35] The study of a number of individual cases permits the conclusion that Cleynaerts's comment was well founded. A merchant from Montemor-o-Novo, a town near Évora, baptised eleven new slaves in twenty-one years, from 1562 to 1582, five

[30] Oliveira Marques, 'Uma descrição', p. 141.
[31] Túlio Espanca, 'Visitas de Embaixadores Célebres, Reis, Príncipes e Arcebispos a Évora nos Séculos XV–XVIII', *A Cidade de Évora*, 27–8 (1952), p. 159; Lisbon, Biblioteca Nacional, Cód. 1544 ('Memórias da Casa de Bragança'), fol. 195v.; Caetano de Sousa, *Provas da História Genealógica*, IV, p. 185; Jorge Fonseca, 'Escravos em Vila Viçosa', *Callipole*, 5–6 (1997–8), p. 30. Also the municipalities hired slaves to play drums and dance in the processions they organised, as at Montemor-o-Novo in 1518 and 1569. Montemor-o-Novo, Arquivo Histórico Municipal, A 1 D 4, fols. 46 and 48; A 1 D 9, fol. 19v.
[32] *Correspondance*, ed. Roersch, I, p. 54: 'Aethiopes et Mauri captivi omnia obeunt munia.'
[33] Fonseca, *Escravos no Sul de Portugal*, pp. 75–6.
[34] *Correspondance*, ed. Roersch, I, p. 54: 'Etiam si quartam census mei partem largiar, non assequar mulierculam quae more nostrate mihi curet familiam, aut rem domesticam.'
[35] *Correspondance*, ed. Roersch, I, p. 54: 'quidam etiam non exiguum quaestum faciunt e vernis natis, ut mihi tanquam columbas alere videantur.'

born of Inês, four of Guiomar and two of other slaves.[36] To a canon, from Évora, were born six new slaves in eight years, from 1585 to 1592, three of the same mother.[37] A farmer from the same city sent seven small slaves to be baptised in nine years.[38]

These slaves were almost always born to an unknown father. When the fathers are known, we find them to be both slaves and free men, white and black, servants, shepherds and artisans, but also 'honourable' men and even priests.[39] But they were rarely born in wedlock, because masters obstructed marriage as it reduced the availability of slaves. Sometimes the fathers of the newly born were the masters themselves, an occurrence which was most certainly much more frequent than the documents recount.

Our humanist did not refrain from telling his friend that 'far from [the owners] being offended by the slaves' immorality, they are glad of the stallions, because the fruit follows the womb's condition; and does not belong to that neighbour priest nor to some African slave.'[40] The allusion to intimacy between priests and female slaves, which Cleynaerts must have known very well because it occurred in his own social environment, refers to a common fact at the time accepted even by the royal Ordinances, which regulated it under the heading 'Of the priests' mistresses and those of other religious'. Complaints were only admitted against priests if they offended in an evident and manifest manner, by having children of these slaves, acknowledging them as such and baptising them.[41]

Against his will, Cleynaerts ended up having to acquire three young black slaves to serve him: Miguel, fifteen years old, António, aged twelve and Sebastião, a child of nine years. He used them in the kitchen and to wait at his table and for all other domestic chores. In his opinion, he did not need all of them for the work that had to be done, keeping them on, as he affirms ironically, to give them a literary career. He taught them Latin while they waited at his table or during his walks with them through the fields that surrounded Évora.[42] When he went to Braga he took them with him, using them as teaching aids in the public classes that he gave to the people of the city,

---

[36] Évora, Arquivo Distrital, Fundo paroquial, Montemor-o-Novo, Vila, Liv. 2 and 3 Baptismos.

[37] Évora, Arquivo Distrital, Fundo paroquial, Évora, Sé, Liv. 9–11, 1585–92.

[38] Évora, Arquivo Distrital, Fundo paroquial, S. Miguel de Machede, Liv. 1, 1581–90.

[39] Jorge Fonseca, *Os Escravos em Évora no Século XVI* (Évora, 1997), pp. 86–8.

[40] *Correspondance*, ed. Roersch, I, p. 54: 'et adeo non offendi ancillae concubitu, ut etiam admissariis equis gaudeant, et partus ventri cedat, non vicino sacerdoti, aut nescio cui Aethiopi et captivo.'

[41] *Ordenações Manuelinas (1521)*, Livro v, Tít. xxvi, § 2 (Lisbon, 1984), p. 83.

[42] *Correspondance*, ed. Roersch, I, p. 110.

during which he made them talk amongst themselves in Latin. These classes were attended by slaves as well as all other types of people.[43]

What do we know about the experience of teaching slaves the rudiments of learning? Obviously, very little. Some knew how to read and write, because their masters wanted to prepare them to become self-reliant when the time came to release them;[44] others signed the deeds of manumission that emancipated them.[45] In one such case, the slave signed but the female owner who freed him did not, because she was illiterate.[46] However, these are rare events and almost always related to slaves owned by masters of a certain cultural level, members of the church and the higher nobility. And what of the teaching of Latin? Did many others try it besides Cleynaerts? For instance, did his friend André de Resende, also a promoter of the language, an archaeologist and humanist, and the owner of Fernando, whom he freed and to whom he left houses and money in his will, and Máximo, whom he 'never managed to befriend'?[47] Or doctor Pedro Margalho, a theologian from Salamanca and Paris, teacher of Princes Afonso and Duarte, who in 1555 ordered the arrest of a runaway slave?[48] Or the poet Garcia de Resende, who was the owner of various slaves?[49] We shall probably never know.

However, this belief in the intellectual capacity of the black slaves was imbued, on Cleynaerts's part, with contempt and racism. Let us start by going back to the master's reaction when arriving in Portugal: 'I had hardly set foot in Évora and I felt as though I had been transported to a city in hell; I came across black people everywhere, for whom I have such a detestation that they alone would be sufficient to make me leave.'[50] And further on he admits to Latomus: 'Until now I still haven't had to deal with those slaves. I only have a servant who is a compatriot of ours.'[51] This attitude of exacerbated ethnocentrism followed immediately by repulsion for human beings who were physically and culturally different from Europeans was not much found among the Portuguese, who

---

[43] *Correspondance*, ed. Roersch, 1, pp. 236–7.

[44] Setúbal, Arquivo Distrital, Fundo notarial, Palmela, Liv. 9/1, fol. 80 – 2.10.1604.

[45] Évora, Arquivo Distrital, Fundo notarial, Évora, Liv. 43, fol. 88v. – 3.3.1566.

[46] Évora, Arquivo Distrital, Fundo notarial, Évora, Liv. 451, fol. 13 – 25.11.1604.

[47] Évora, Biblioteca Pública, Arm. x, no. 1, 26.

[48] Évora, Arquivo Distrital, Fundo notarial, Évora, Liv. 169, fol. 51 – 9.7.1555.

[49] António Bartolomeu Gromicho, 'O Testamento de Garcia de Resende', *A Cidade de Évora*, 13–14 (1947), pp. 3–23.

[50] *Correspondance*, ed. Roersch, 1, p. 57: 'Verum ubi primum ingressus sum Eboram, putabam me venisse in civitatem aliquam Cacodaemonum: tot ubique occurrebant Aethiopes, quos ego sic detestor ut vel soli queant me hinc depellere.'

[51] *Correspondance*, ed. Roersch, 1, p. 57: 'Nihil itaque hactenus mihi fuit negotii cum istis mancipiis. Unum habeo ministrum nostratem.'

in their own country were more used to contact with Africans than were Northern Europeans. The intellectual from Brabant, arriving from a country where black Africans were few in number, felt surprised and shocked at the quantity of black people he found. Thus the exaggerated reaction. But it did not end there. The way in which he classified black Africans, even the ones with whom he dealt on a day-to-day basis, shows an unmasked contempt, although mitigated by kindness. He refers to the three black Africans he has at home as 'monkeys', with which he amuses himself by teaching them to speak Latin.[52] One of them, whom he nicknamed 'Dento' (Toothy), he describes as 'so well armed with teeth' that he is able to lift up his master, and he commented 'not even a dog has greater pleasure in gnawing bones'.[53] Another he called 'Nigrinus' (Little black boy) and the youngest he called 'Carbo' (Charcoal), a name suggested by his friend Resende.[54] When during his stay in Braga he taught Latin to students of all ages, he showed off the three black Africans, making them speak in Latin, which surprised the audience. To amuse his pupils, he also made them jump, run, pull faces and imitate horses.[55]

From this it is possible to conclude that Cleynaerts's observations in his letters about black Africans and slaves in Portugal show a contrast between two European societies, the Flemish and the Portuguese. They also express his condemnation of slavery, not because of the injustice towards the slaves, about which he does not seem the least bit concerned – contrary to what would happen a few years later, with some of the principal figures from the University in Évora, such as Luís de Molina[56] – but because it encouraged the idleness and moral depravity of the Portuguese, vices that he never ceased to criticise. As for the veracity of his accounts, they exaggerate reality most of the time, but this can be attributed to the desire to make his narrative more interesting.

---

[52] *Correspondance*, ed. Roersch, I, p. 111: 'Cum studere non libet, his me oblecto tanquam simiis.'

[53] *Correspondance*, ed. Roersch, I, p. 110: 'Natu maximus Michael est Dento, annos XV, adeo pulchre dentatus, ut me cum universis ducatis, facillime dentibus in sublime tollat, nec minus gaudet rodendis ossibus quam canes.'

[54] *Correspondance*, ed. Roersch, I, p. 110.

[55] *Correspondance*, ed. Roersch, I, pp. 236–7: ' "Heus Dento", inquam, "salta". Mox unum atque alterum edebat saltum, ridentibus spectatoribus. "Tu Nigrine, repe nobis per pavimentum". Sine mora, quadrupedem agebat, magis etiam in cachinnos soluti quotquot aderant. Carbo iussus currere, cursum statim expediebat. Sic et alia multa non tam voce docebam quam gestu, ut per iocum vocabula puerorum animos subirent . . . Si quem conspicerem insigni naso, ridendo et contrectando naso, fungebar docentis officio, et obiter emungebat Dento nares.'

[56] António Manuel Hespanha, 'Luís de Molina e a Escravização dos Negros', *Análise Social*, 35 (2001), pp. 957–8.

PART TWO

Real and symbolic black Africans at court

CHAPTER SIX

Isabella d'Este and black African women

PAUL H. D. KAPLAN

This chapter seeks to make the case that Isabella d'Este, Marchioness of Mantua, and Andrea Mantegna, the pre-eminent artist at her court, together generated a new and influential female version of an already venerable iconographic type: the black African attendant to a white European protagonist. This colour-coded model of subordination was already important in the Middle Ages, and it is, sadly, still visible in Western culture. Fundamental shifts in the meaning of such black and white pairings, however, took place in the decades just before and just after 1500.[1] What Isabella and Mantegna's interaction produced was a new role, initially humble but later occasionally more distinguished, for black women in European art. The new appearance of women and girls amongst images of black Africans attending to powerful whites was undoubtedly prompted by current changes in aristocratic practice, endorsed though not invented by Isabella, which made female black court servants as fashionable as male ones. The continuity between elite social practice, public pageantry, and the imagery of elite art will be a recurring theme in what follows, but the goal is not to reduce the significance of the black presence in any one of these areas to a mere and momentary vagary of aristocratic fashion. To that end I shall stress the ways in which Isabella as well as her relatives and agents might have associated black servants with aspects of the profound geopolitical changes underway during her lifetime.

The image around which my case will be built is one of the most widely known of all Renaissance drawings, Mantegna's *Judith and her maidservant with the head of Holofernes* (fig. 21) now in the Uffizi.[2] This exceptionally beautiful

---

[1] See the author's 'Ruler, saint and servant: blacks in European art to 1520', Ph.D. dissertation, Boston University, 1983, chapters 1, 3, 8, and 11; Paul H. D. Kaplan, 'Titian's Laura Dianti and the origins of the motif of the black page in portraiture', *Antichità Viva*, 21: 1 (1982), pp. 11–18, and 21: 4 (1982), pp. 10–8; Paul H. D. Kaplan, 'Sicily, Venice and the East: Titian's Fabricius Salvaresius with a black page', in *Europa und die Kunst des Islam: 15. bis 18. Jahrhundert* (Akten des 25. internationalen Kongresses für Kunstgeschichte, 5) (Vienna, 1985), pp. 127–36.

[2] Inv. 404: E. Anna Maria Petrioli Tofani and Anna Forlani Tempesti, *I grandi disegni italiani degli Uffizi di Firenze* (Milan, n.d.), cat. 18 with colour plate; Ronald Lightbown, *Mantegna* (Berkeley, 1986), p. 484, cat. 188, fig. 15; Yael Even, 'Mantegna's Uffizi *Judith*: the masculinization of the female hero', *Konsthistorisk Tidskrift*, 61 (1992), pp. 8–20.

FIG. 21. Andrea Mantegna, *Judith and her maidservant with the head of Holofernes*, February 1491/1492 (ink on paper, 38.8 × 25.8 cm, Florence, Uffizi).

sheet, measuring 38.8 × 25.8 cm and executed in ink, is a finished work of art in its own right, and is inscribed at the right with an elegantly lettered signature (ANDREAS MANTINIA) and date (MCCCCLXXXXI FEBR – that is to say February 1492, using the modern style). Despite its fame, the drawing is not often discussed in terms of its content, and few scholars have remarked on the African figure within it.[3] Mantegna's black maidservant, however, appears to be the first black African servant to Judith in European art, and indeed in European culture, since neither in the Bible nor in any other textual source (at least, before 1492) is Judith's faithful attendant described as African. From which earlier traditions was the figure derived, and what prompted her creation at this particular time and place?

Afro-European attendants began to become popular and indeed conspicuous components of European patrician retinues during the era of the Hohenstaufen emperors, and the social use of such servants was quickly translated into visual images.[4] The point of displaying dark-skinned servants was to suggest the potentially universal reach of imperial power. Frederick II (d. 1250) associated himself so closely with African court servants that an impostor, claiming to be the emperor in the 1280s, used Africans handing out treasure to buttress his fraudulent identity. An illumination of this bizarre scene (fig. 22), from 1476, testifies to the long-lasting impact of Hohenstaufen political iconography, and the first appearance of African retainers in an image of the story of the Magi is also connected to Hohenstaufen public pageantry.[5] Other European rulers and nobles (for example, Charles IV of Luxembourg, the Carrara of Padua, and Jean de Berry) began to appropriate this imagery as well, though they were not always able to find living African servants.[6]

Jean de Berry did acquire an African retainer, a gift from the court of Aragon. From the late thirteenth-century Aragonese sovereigns, claiming to be the legitimate heirs of Frederick II, both put heads of black Africans on their

[3] But see Jean Devisse and Michel Mollat, *The Image of the Black in Western Art*, II, *From the Early Christian Era to the 'Age of Discovery'*, part 2, *Africans in the Christian Ordinance of the World (Fourteenth to the Sixteenth Century)* (New York, 1979), pp. 188–90, fig. 191; and Jaynie Anderson, *Judith* (Paris, 1997), p. 43. In the present essay the term 'African' is used as an abbreviated synonym for black African.

[4] Paul H. D. Kaplan, 'Black Africans in Hohenstaufen iconography', *Gesta*, 26 (1987), pp. 29–36.

[5] From Clemens Specker's 'Chronik' in Bern, Burgerbibliothek, Cod. A45, p. 143; see Kaplan, 'Black Africans', p. 34. On black attendants of the Magi, first appearing in Nicola Pisano's Siena pulpit, see Paul H. D. Kaplan, *The Rise of the Black Magus in Western Art* (Ann Arbor, 1985), pp. 7–11; Joachim Poeschke, *Die Sieneser Domkanzel des Nicola Pisano* (Berlin, 1973), pp. 16–20.

[6] Kaplan, 'Ruler, saint and servant', p. 115 (Carrara); Kaplan, *Black Magus*, pp. 57–8 (Jean de Berry), pp. 75–84 (Charles IV), p. 93 (Carrara).

FIG. 22. *The False Frederick II and his African Retainers*, from Clement Specker's 'Chronik', 1476 (Bern, Burgerbibliothek, Cod A45, p. 143).

escutcheon and kept black servants at court.[7] By the middle of the fifteenth century the most active aristocratic employers of black servants were probably the Aragonese kings of Naples, who had an ample supply of African slaves in Southern Italy and Sicily. Close diplomatic and dynastic ties to North Italian princes like the Sforza, the Gonzaga, and certainly the d'Este probably led to the dissemination of this court-centred practice in the Po valley: Isabella's mother and aunt were Aragonese princesses from Naples, her uncle Borso visited Naples twice in the 1440s, and her father Ercole lived there from 1445 to 1448. Alfonso I of Naples not only kept black retainers but also went to some trouble to make diplomatic contact with the Emperor of Ethiopia, then identified by Europeans with the legendary and powerful Prester John.[8] In the Po valley, documentary evidence concerning black court servants is (so far) relatively scarce until late in the 1400s, but the bold placement of Africans in three great mid-century Mantuan and Ferrarese fresco cycles are clear markers of their presence.

[7] Kaplan, *Black Magus*, pp. 15, 73, fig. 35; Kaplan, 'Ruler, saint and servant', pp. 433–53; Devisse and Mollat, *Image of the Black*, pp. 11–3, 259, n. 26, fig. 6.

[8] Kaplan, *Black Magus*, p. 103; Kaplan, 'Ruler, saint and servant', pp. 598–614; Charles Verlinden, 'L'esclavage dans le royaume de Naples à la fin du moyen âge et la participation des marchands espagnols à la traite', *Anuario de historia economica y social*, 1 (1968), pp. 345–401 at 346, 379–85, 393; Charles Verlinden, 'Schiavitù ed economia nel Mezzogiorno agli inizi dell'età moderna', *Annali del Mezzogiorno*, 3 (1983), pp. 11–38 at 16–20, 29–30, 35.

FIG. 23. Andrea Mantegna, detail from *oculus* of the Camera Picta, *c.* 1465–1474 (fresco, Mantua, Palazzo Ducale).

In the earliest of these, Pisanello's *c.* 1447–8 illustration of an Arthurian epic in the Palazzo Ducale in Mantua, the youthful black figure's role is hard to determine – he may be a squire rather than a knight.[9] In the two later cycles of *c.* 1470, black characters wait on members of the contemporary courtly elite, without any reference to fiction or the historical past. At the Palazzo Schifanoia in Ferrara, Francesco del Cossa shows Duke Borso d'Este approached by an older black man whose subordination is expressed by his bent knees and lower physical placement; this African reappears in two other segments of the cycle.[10] Andrea Mantegna, in the frescoed ceiling of the Camera Picta in Mantua (fig. 23), paints a dark face looking down as that of

[9] Devisse and Mollat, *Image of the Black*, p. 116, figs. 120–1; Joanna Woods-Marsden, *The Gonzaga of Mantua and Pisanello's Arthurian Frescoes* (Princeton, 1988), pls. 13, 72.

[10] In the months March, May and July; Ranieri Varese, ed., *Atlante di Schifanoia* (Modena, 1989), pp. 331, 337, 343, 450, 453, 458, no. 9.

the adjoining Gonzaga princess looks up.[11] Most writers have identified this figure as female, though it is hard to be certain as the body is not represented. If, however, this character was intended to be a woman, then it is one of the earliest explicit images of a black maidservant to a living European aristocrat. Isabella d'Este would have seen this image almost instantly upon her arrival in Mantua as a new bride in 1490; the Schifanoia fresco she would of course have grown up with.

The Sforza court in Milan was also deeply attracted to black servants and their visual depiction. By the 1490s Lodovico 'il moro', many of his courtiers, and also his political allies, used actual and fictive black servants as emblems of the duke's nickname.[12] The Sforza had close relations with the Gonzaga and the d'Este, and while the internal dynamics at each court were surely distinct, the vogue for black retainers was consciously shared by the three great families.

In Milan, as elsewhere in Italy and Western Europe before 1492, images of African men are vastly more common than images of African women; but women are not entirely absent. The most powerful such figures (the Queen of Sheba in particular) tend to appear early (from the late twelfth to the fourteenth century) and then fade from view.[13] These representations of women rarely include, beyond brown skin, any other physiognomic signifier of African identity – such as characteristic treatments of hair, lips and nose – though these elements appear early and often in depictions of black men.[14] This hesitation in showing physiognomic markers of ethnicity is perhaps still visible in Mantegna's *oculus* from the Camera Picta (fig. 23).

Mantegna indeed had considerable experience in the depiction of black Africans in the four decades of his successful career which preceded Isabella's arrival in Mantua, and he is a notable figure in the European representation of black Africans even excluding his authorship of the *Judith* drawing and images derived from it. In addition to the Camera Picta fresco (finished by 1474), Mantegna painted an *Adoration of the Magi* (fig. 24) with both a black Magus and a group of African retainers.[15] This panel, from *c.* 1464, is in fact the

[11] Rodolfo Signorini, *Opvs hoc tenve: La Camera Dipinta di Andrea Mantegna* (Mantua, 1985), pp. 230, 234, 240–1; Devisse and Mollat, *Image of the Black*, pp. 190–2.

[12] Kaplan, 'Titian's Laura Dianti', 21: 1, p. 12; Kaplan, 'Ruler, saint and servant', pp. 602–4; Devisse and Mollat, *Image of the Black*, pp. 186–8.

[13] Kaplan, *Black Magus*, pp. 9, 37–42.

[14] For an exception (*c.* 1440), see John Plummer, *The Hours of Catherine of Cleves* (New York, n.d.), p. 85.

[15] Lightbown, *Mantegna*, pp. 86–91, 411–3, cat. 14.

FIG. 24. Andrea Mantegna, *Adoration of the Magi*, c. 1464 (tempera on panel, 77 × 75 cm, Florence, Uffizi).

first influential instance of a black African Magus in Italian art, borrowing from an iconography developed and popularised in Czech and above all German lands between 1350 and 1450, and then adopted by artists from other European regions.[16] As this *Adoration* was surely a Gonzaga commission, it confirms that an attentiveness to black Africans was already part of Mantuan cultural life in the 1460s.

[16] Kaplan, *Black Magus*, pp. 115–16, and more generally chapters 4–5.

Mantegna's earliest surviving image of an African, on the other hand, is of a sharply different type. In his frescoes for the Ovetari Chapel in the church of the Eremitani in Padua, from the early 1450s, a turbaned African man stands just behind the brutal executioner of St James.[17] In Iberia James was the celebrated defender of Christians against Muslims, and in later centuries the saint's Muslim enemies were sometimes denoted by a black figure.[18] Here, however, the imagery is more probably based on a centuries-old European habit of associating black Africans with executioners.[19] Mantegna, then, knew the pejorative as well as the more laudatory aspects of the European iconographic tradition with regard to black Africans.

Did Mantegna, before Isabella's first encounter with him, have as much experience in rendering the story of Judith as he clearly had with figures of Africans? This turns out to be a difficult question to settle. Judith, like Esther, had her triumphant tale told in an eponymous book of the Old Testament. Her name is understood to signify 'Jewish woman' and the account of her daring but carefully planned defeat of the Assyrian general Holofernes reads as a classic instance of the pious underdog who conquers a powerful foe, similar in its outlines to David's victory over Goliath. It is the most forceful and unambiguous story of female heroism in the Bible, and although Judith uses her beauty to get Holofernes's attention and to lull his suspicions, her killing of him is physically direct and indicative of her bodily as well as intellectual and spiritual power.[20]

The Book of Judith was well known to medieval theologians, who allegorised her virtues, but as a subject in the visual arts Judith is largely confined to manuscript illumination until the end of the Middle Ages.[21] Guariento painted a monumental and forceful *Judith* for the Carrara palace in Padua in the 1350s, not really matched until the completion in the 1450s of Donatello's amazing and harrowing bronze sculpture, presumed to have been made for

[17] Now largely destroyed; Lightbown, *Mantegna*, pp. 50–1, 398, cat. 1, pl. 15.

[18] For example, in G. B. Tiepolo's painting now in Budapest; Massimo Gemin and Filippo Pedrocco, *Giambattista Tiepolo* (Venice, 1993), pp. 416–7, cat. 403.

[19] Kaplan, 'Ruler, saint and servant', pp. 188–98; Jean Devisse with Jean Marie Courtès, *The Image of the Black in Western Art*, II, *From the Early Christian Era to the 'Age of Discovery'*, part 1, *From the Demonic Threat to the Incarnation of Sainthood* (New York, 1979), pp. 72–80.

[20] Anderson, Judith; Jane Davidson Reid, 'The true Judith', *Art Journal*, 28 (1969), pp. 376–84; Elena Ciletti, 'Patriarchal ideology in the Renaissance iconography of Judith', in Marilyn Migiel and Juliana Schiesari, eds., *Refiguring Women: Perspectives on Gender and the Italian Renaissance* (Ithaca, 1991), pp. 35–70.

[21] Anderson, Judith, pp. 13–21; Luisa Tognoli Bardin, 'La Giuditta biblica nelle arti figurative: una ricerca', *Arte cristiana*, 83 (1995), pp. 219–26; Adelheid Straten, *Das Judith-Thema in Deutschland im 16. Jahrhundert* (Munich, 1983), pp. 130–46.

the Medici palace.[22] Neither of these works were intended to be seen in a sacred setting, and the overtly politicised content of these images – that foreign enemies would never prevail against the chosen people of an Italian city-state – eventually made the subject a relatively common one, first in later Quattrocento Florence, and then even more distinctively in early Cinquecento Venice.[23] In Venice Judith came to adorn the bases of the flagpoles in Piazza San Marco and an exterior wall of the Fondaco dei Tedeschi at Rialto.[24] The Florentines were more ambivalent about whether Judith was suitable as a public image of state ideology; after eight years in front of the Palazzo Vecchio, in 1503 Donatello's bronze was judged a troubling challenge to patriarchal authority and moved to a less conspicuous site.[25]

Mantegna, who grew up in Padua and visited Florence in 1466, is likely to have known both Guariento's and Donatello's *Judiths*, and perhaps several others besides. Mantegna may have painted a *Judith* early on; the Medici inventory of 1512, recording Lorenzo il Magnifico's collection at his death in 1492, lists 'a little panel in a casket, painted with a Judith with the head of Holofernes and a maidservant, work of Andrea Squarcione [i.e., Mantegna, described with the surname of his former teacher and adoptive parent], 25 florins'.[26] It is possible that this panel, not securely identified with any object known today, was produced during the five months between the execution of the drawing and Lorenzo's death, but several small images of the story of Judith by Botticelli usually dated to the years around 1470 seem to show the impact of Mantegna's style.[27] The link is not only stylistic: both Mantegna's lost work and Botticelli's pictures are unusual in having shown

[22] Francesca Flores d'Arcais, *Guariento* (Venice, 1965), figs. 83–4; Volker Herzner, 'Die 'Judith' der Medici,' *Zeitschrift für Kunstgeschichte*, 43 (1980), pp. 139–80; Sarah Blake McHam, 'Donatello's bronze *David* and *Judith* as metaphors of Medici rule in Florence', *Art Bulletin*, 83 (2001), pp. 32–47.

[23] Anderson, *Judith*, pp. 21–6; McHam, 'Donatello's bronze *David* and *Judith*'; Yael Even, 'The Loggia dei Lanzi: a showcase of female subjugation', *Woman's Art Journal*, 12 (1991), pp. 10–14.

[24] David Rosand, 'Venetia figurata: the iconography of a myth', in David Rosand ed., *Interpretazioni veneziane. Studi di storia dell'arte in onore di Michelangelo Muraro* (Venice, 1984), pp. 177–96 at 194, n. 11; Serena Romano, 'Giuditta e il Fondaco dei Tedeschi', in *Giorgione e la cultura veneta tra '400 e '500. Mito, allegoria, analisi iconologica* (Rome, 1981), pp. 113–25.

[25] Ciletti, 'Patriarchal ideology', pp. 58, 68.

[26] 'Una tavoletta in una chasetta dipintovi su una Giudetta chon la testa d'Oloferno e una serva, opera d'Andrea Squarcione, f. 25', Eugène Müntz, *Les collections des Médicis au XVe siècle* (Paris, 1888), pp. 54, 78.

[27] Florence, Uffizi, and Cincinnati, Art Museum; Ronald Lightbown, *Sandro Botticelli*, 2 vols. (Berkeley, 1978), I, pls. 4–7, II, pp. 21–2, cats. B5–B6; Ronald Lightbrown, *Sandro Botticelli. Life and Work* (New York, 1989), pp. 32–7, pls. 8–10; Sergio Bettini, *Botticelli* (Bergamo, 1942), p. 18.

Judith's maidservant, a figure who had previously appeared almost exclusively in manuscript illuminations. Botticelli's maidservant is not a black African, though her complexion is a little darker than the pale Judith's.

A close reading of the biblical text reveals some remarkable facts about this maidservant. (Beginning around 1500, she is sometimes called 'Abra' in texts, a misunderstanding of the term – abra – used to describe her as a female slave or servant in the Vulgate.[28]) Judith is a widow whose husband Manasseh has bequeathed her, among other riches, many servants. The maidservant accompanies Judith on her bold excursion, assists her in fooling Holofernes, and hides the severed head in her food bag so they can carry it off. Finally, at the end of the book (16:28), the now aged and respected Judith 'made her handmaid free,' clarifying the maid's initial status as a slave.[29] The growing numbers of African slaves in Europe by the 1490s, and the striking preponderance of women among them, are surely two of the factors which prompted Mantegna to depict, evidently for the first time, the maidservant in the Uffizi drawing as a black African.[30]

There was, however, an even more immediate cause for Mantegna's novel decision. Though no documentary proof exists, much circumstantial evidence suggests that the drawing was intended to evoke Isabella d'Este and one of her several black African maidservants. Isabella's fascination with black child servants is extensively documented.[31] On 1 May 1491 Isabella asked Giorgio Brognolo, her agent in Venice, to procure a young black girl ('una moreta') between the ages of one-and-a-half and four, and twice in early June reminded him of the request, emphasising that the girl should be 'as black as possible'. A letter of 14 June reveals that Isabella already had a considerably older African girl: 'We couldn't be more pleased with our black girl even if she were blacker, because from being at first a little disdainful she has now become pleasing in words and acts, and we think she'll make the best buffoon in the world.'

---

[28] *Biblia Sacra*, ed. Alberto Colunga and Laurentio Turrado (4th edn., Madrid, 1965): *abra* used in 8:32, 10:2, 10:5, 16:28 ('dimisit abram suam liberam'); she is also called *puella* (13:5) and *ancilla* (13:11). The word is originally Greek, and can also mean concubine; see s.v., 'abra' in J. F. Niermeyer, *Mediae Latinitatis lexicon minus* (Leiden, 1976), and G. A. Saalfeld, *De Bibliorum sacrorum vulgatae editionis graecitate* (Quedlinburg, 1891). Anderson (p. 14) notes the name but is confused (like several earlier scholars) about its origin; the *c.* 1470 woodcut she illustrates (fig. 1) appears to use the word properly as a synonym for servant. Though *abra* might suggest a similarity to 'Africa', there is no Early Modern text known to me which describes or implies that 'Abra' is black, nor do I know of an image of the African maidservant inscribed with the name.

[29] Douay-Rheims version.   [30] See the essay by Sergio Tognetti in this volume.

[31] Alessandro Luzio and Rodolfo Renier, 'Buffoni, schiavi e nani alla corte dei Gonzaga ai tempi d'Isabella d'Este', *Nuova Antologia*, 19 (1891), pp. 112–46, 140–5; Kaplan, 'Titian's Laura Dianti', 21: 1, pp. 14–15.

This same note was a reply to Isabella's sister-in-law Anna Sforza, living in Ferrara, who had written to Isabella of how she (Anna) had invited her own very young black maidservant to share her bed, because the girl was so ill.

Brognolo, who had spent some years in Naples[32] and must have been familiar with the courtly preference for black servants, reported in late June that he had located a four-year-old black girl, not really for sale but rather the daughter of a free African gondolier and his black wife. (The numerous black gondoliers of Venice were highlighted in Sanuto's 1493 guidebook, and depicted in several paintings by Carpaccio of 1494–5.[33]) But Brognolo then had to reveal the bad news that Isabella's mother Eleonora d'Aragona, in Ferrara, had scooped her by inviting the entire family to enter Eleonora's service. After being thwarted in this peculiar bidding war, Isabella quickly obtained from a Venetian orphanage a two-year-old black girl, and then opened negotiations for a black boy who was a slave in a Venetian patrician household. In 1497 Isabella purchased an enslaved little black girl for her sister Chiara.

Not just the acquisition of these African children, but also the elaborate nature of Isabella's efforts to procure them, mark her as one of the more obsessed devotees of this fashion for human accessories. While Isabella's relatives at other Italian courts were also captivated by this custom, she seems to have been the only woman in Mantua with such servants. Perhaps she never felt she had enough of them, but through the medium of art Mantegna was able to increase their numbers. In any case, given that the Uffizi drawing is dated to February of 1492, just a few months after Isabella's intense attempts to secure more African girls, it is hard to imagine that the work was designed to please anyone but her.

There is another kind of evidence that the drawing was made for Isabella. Its high finish, fancy signature and date mark the sheet as a completed work of art meant to pass out of the artist's possession. It could have been a commissioned work, but it may also have been a gift meant to curry favour with a prospective patron. In either case, Isabella is by far the most likely patron involved. In 1491–2 Mantegna, then in late middle age, was trying to establish a cooperative and fruitful relationship with the new young *marchesa*, who was already a demanding and discerning consumer of art in all forms. Isabella soon wanted

[32] Clifford M. Brown and Anna Maria Lorenzoni, 'Isabella d'Este e Giorgio Brognolo nell'anno 1496', *Atti e Memorie della Academia Virgiliana di Mantova*, n.s., 41 (1973), pp. 97–122 at 98.

[33] Marino Sanuto, *De origine, situ et magistratibus urbis Venetae ovver la città di Venetia* (1493–1530), ed. A. Caracciolo Aricò (Milan, 1980), pp. 21–2; Kaplan, 'Titian's Laura Dianti', 21: 1, pp. 13–4. The Carpaccio paintings are *The Miracle of the True Cross* (Venice, Accademia) and *Heron Hunt in the Lagoon* (Los Angeles, Getty Museum), each with two black rowers.

her portrait painted by Mantegna, but she was never to be satisfied by his results in this genre.[34] Either Mantegna, or Isabella, or both, realized that he could better fulfil her desires through narrative compositions dominated by idealised and powerful women who symbolised Isabella's virtues rather than resembling her physical self. Mantegna's *Pallas expelling the vices*, made for Isabella's *studiolo* in *c.* 1499–1502, is the best-known example of this approach.[35] But the Uffizi drawing already points in this direction: the strong but elegant heroine is hardly a recognisable portrait of the seventeen-year-old Isabella, but she certainly embodies Isabella's aspirations. Holofernes's courtiers say of Judith (11:19): 'There is not such another woman upon earth in look, in beauty, and in sense of words' – and such an encomium reflected Isabella's own self-regard.

Neither in Isabella's native Ferrara nor in her adoptive city of Mantua did Judith become an artistic emblem of public patriotism, as happened in Florence and Venice. Isabella rather saw in the story, it would appear, a sort of proto-feminist assertion that strength (literally or metaphorically) was not incommensurate with beauty and elegance. Indeed, later Renaissance consorts such as Eleonora of Toledo and Bianca Cappello also used Judith as an emblem of their virtues.[36] More immediately, the 1489 nuptials of Maddalena Gonzaga, soon to be the sister-in-law of Isabella, included the performance by the Jews of Pesaro of the drama of Judith and Holofernes; a black African, or someone made up to look like one, was part of the spectacle, but did not serve as Judith's attendant.[37]

We now need to consider more deeply the relationship between the two women in the Uffizi drawing as it might have been understood in the 1490s. This relationship is marked by a curious mixture of subordination and alliance. The black girl is subordinate in scale and age, and her position is literally marginalised while Judith occupies the centre of the sheet. The servant's face appears in the more informal three-quarter pose, while Judith is shown rather formally in profile. The African's clothes in part tend to mask the shape of her body, and her rumpled leggings are unfashionable; Judith's dress and slipping cloak are elegant and reveal her handsome physique. Judith grasps the sword,

[34] Lightbown, *Mantegna*, pp. 86–8; Jennifer Fletcher, 'Isabella d'Este, patron and collector', in David Chambers and Jane Martineau, eds., *Splendours of the Gonzaga* (London, 1981), pp. 50–64.

[35] Paris, Louvre; Jane Martineau, ed., *Andrea Mantegna* (New York, 1992), pp. 427–30, cat. 136.

[36] Eleonora had a favourite hatband depicting Judith; Bruce Edelstein, 'Bronzino in the service of Cosimo I de' Medici and Eleonora di Toledo, together and apart', presentation at the Annual Meeting of the College Art Association, Boston, 1996. Capello was given Botticelli's *Judith* now in the Uffizi in 1575; Lightbown, *Sandro Botticelli*, ii, p. 21.

[37] Guido Mondovi, ed., *Per le fauste nozze Rimini – Todesco – Assagioli 9 Settembre 1883* (Mantua, 1883), pp. 6, 9–11. The black figure was apparently part of Holofernes's retinue.

while the servant holds only the bag for the severed head. Skin colour is not, surprisingly, a part of the drawing's oppositions; like Albrecht Dürer (fig. 36), Mantegna realized that in the graphic conventions of Renaissance drawing, so dependent on chiaroscuro, it would be difficult to convey literally dark skin. The facial features of the two figures are nevertheless very distinct, and the maid's ear-ring, along with the treatment of her nose, lips and hair, conveys her African identity. (It is as if Mantegna has inverted the earlier standards in the European depiction of African women: moving from an emphasis on colour and an avoidance of physiognomic markers of difference – still the norm in his earlier fresco in the Camera Picta (fig. 23) – to an emphasis on facial features and an avoidance of colour.[38]) Yet despite all these contrasts, the two women are indeed allied, by their opposition to the Assyrians, and by their collective female triumph over an ostensibly more powerful male. Their poses and gestures have a consonance which confirms the biblical text's account of their trusting relationship.[39]

Contemporary viewers of the drawing, including Mantegna and Isabella themselves, would have seen in it echoes of traditional tropes. The maidservant brings the bag forward a little like an African attendant might hand a precious gift forward to a Magus adoring Christ, though here the 'gift' is the severed head.[40] The aforementioned connection of black Africans with scenes of execution would also have come to mind. Isabella, though perhaps not Mantegna, would have known of the notorious assassination of one of her Sforza cousins in 1476 (illustrated in a *c.* 1505 woodcut) (fig. 25) in which a black man played a notable role; here, as in the Uffizi drawing, the African figure is virtuous, a Sforza military servant loyally exacting revenge on an assassin.[41]

What else would Isabella have brought to the perception of Mantegna's drawing? So much has been written about Isabella's shopping mania and her micromanaging of artists (as if these were not also traits of male aristocrats) that

---

[38] See this volume, p. 130.

[39] Anderson, *Judith*, p. 43, suggests that conflict defines the women's relationship, a view I cannot share.

[40] See for example Nicolas Solana, fig. 18 in Kaplan, *Black Magus*.

[41] Lorenzo dalla Rota, *Lamento del Duca Galeazzo duca de Milano elqual fu morto da Iovaneandrea da lampognano* (Florence, Bernardo Zucchetta for Piero Pacini, 1505) is said to be the first appearance of the woodcut, later copied in at least two undated Venetian editions; Prince d'Essling, *Les livres à figures vénitiens*, 3 parts in 5 vols. (Florence, 1907–15), part 2, vol. II, 603–5, cats. 2473–74. From a 1616 Venetian edition (*Lamento de l'Illustrissimo Sig. Galeazzo Duca di Milano*), fol. 2r: 'Vn Moro mio Staffier corendo fune/adosso Zuan Andrea qual era morto,/& degli vn colpo che'l fe cascar giune.' An earlier 'good' armed black African is found at Chartres, as the guard told by Solomon to cut the child in two; Devisse with Courtès, *Image of the Black*, pl. 30.

FIG. 25. *Assassination of Giangalezzo Sforza*, from Lorenzo dalla Rota, *Lamento del Duca Galeazzo* (Florence, 1505) (woodcut, 10.2 × 8 cm).

one hardly thinks of her as interested in the major political trends and shifts of her day.[42] But, of course, she was. Isabella d'Este was probably named after her royal second cousin Isabella of Castile, who had been crowned queen in 1474, the year of the d'Este princess's birth; and this must have given the Italian Isabella a more vivid interest in Spanish voyages and conquests.[43] In the spring of 1491, just before the flurry of letters concerning Isabella's search for black servants, two significant events took place. Back in Ferrara, on the Thursday before Easter, Isabella's father Ercole d'Este began the practice, maintained for at least seven years, of washing the feet of six to eight 'religiosi indiani', most likely Ethiopian monks on their way to Rome as pilgrims.[44] On 9 April 1491, Isabella received letters from her brother Alfonso describing an island

[42] For a fairer view, see Rose Marie San Juan, 'The court lady's dilemma: Isabella d'Este and art collecting in the Renaissance', *Oxford Art Journal*, 14: 1 (1991), pp. 67–78.

[43] Queen Isabella was also interested in black slaves in the 1470s; Peter Russell, '*Veni, vidi, vici*: some fifteenth-century eyewitness accounts of travel in the African Atlantic before 1492', *Historical Research*, 66 (1993), pp. 115–28 at 120.

[44] Werner Gundersheimer, ed., *Art and Life at the Court of Ercole I d'Este: The 'De triumphis religionis' of Giovanni Sabadino degli Arienti* (Geneva, 1972), pp. 90–4.

recently discovered off the Guinea coast, as well as 'drawings with pictures of the new generation found there, including the people, their dress, horses and spice trees'.[45] In 1497 the Venetian government, having received a 'black king' from the Canary Islands sent by Ferdinand and Isabella, nearly decided to send him as a gift to the Mantuan court.[46] In 1499, even as yet another black servant was acquired by her, Isabella received letters concerning the recent Portuguese voyage around Africa to India.[47] Beginning in 1493 Isabella began to collect information about the Western hemisphere, and acquired a globe delineating the new Spanish discoveries in 1514.[48] Isabella's curiosity about extra-European lands and peoples was reignited in 1522. In that year she again acquired an adolescent black maidservant, and welcomed to the Mantuan court Antonio Pigafetta, a Vicentine who was the principal survivor of Magellan's circumnavigatory expedition.[49] Isabella's interest in the peoples and places Europeans now had access to was not unique among Italian elites; her father, husband and brother were curious as well.[50] And it was not merely an idle curiosity. Italian navigators and slave-traders were deeply involved in these voyages, and Italian princes must have envied (and even contemplated, despite their lack of resources) the mercantile and colonial expeditions of the Atlantic powers.[51] For Isabella and her relations in Milan and Ferrara, the vogue for black court servants referred not only to the traditions of earlier elites but also to contemporary aspirations to participate in European expansion.

When Mantegna completed the Uffizi *Judith* in February of 1492, he may not have been thinking of such geopolitical matters – though the departure of Columbus's voyage later in the year reminds us that such things were in the air. But the rapid multiplication of images of Judith with an African maidservant, first by Mantegna and then by others, indicates that the new character had a surprising resonance for Isabella and her contemporaries. A delicate monochrome painting in distemper by Mantegna (fig. 26), now in

---

[45] The drawings are lost; Alessandro Luzio and Rodolfo Renier, 'La coltura e le relazioni letterarie di Isabella d'Este Gonzaga', *Giornale storico della letteratura italiana*, 33 (1899), pp. 1–62 at 38.

[46] Guglielmo Berchet, ed., *Fonti italiane per la scoperta del Nuovo Mondo*, 2 vols. (Rome, 1892), I, pp. 41–2.

[47] Luzio and Renier, 'Buffoni, schiavi e nani', p. 144; Luzio and Renier, 'La coltura', pp. 38–9.

[48] Luzio and Renier, 'La coltura', pp. 37–8.

[49] Luzio and Renier, 'La coltura', p. 39; Luzio and Renier, 'Buffoni, schiavi e nani', p. 145.

[50] Berchet, ed., *Fonti italiane*, pp. 141–6, 150, 165; Luzio and Renier, 'La coltura', pp. 38–9.

[51] For example, a letter about the da Gama expedition known to Isabella and her relatives was written by Bartolomeo Marchionni, a noted Italian slave-merchant in Lisbon; Carlo Giglio and Elio Lodolini, *Guida delle fonti per la storia dell'Africa a Sud del Sahara esistenti in Italia* (Zug, 1973–4), p. 421.

FIG. 26. Andrea Mantegna, *Judith, c.* 1495–1500 (distemper on linen, mounted on millboard, 48.1 × 36.7 cm, Dublin, National Gallery of Ireland).

Dublin, was important in the dissemination of the figure.[52] The Dublin picture is dated, by style, to *c.* 1495–1500, and evidently formed a pair with an image of Samson and Delilah; both works imitate relief carving in stone. It has recently been plausibly suggested that this pair of pictures was made for Isabella, as emblems of female virtue and vice.[53] The composition is simpler than the Uffizi drawing, and the figures are less vivid. The maidservant is still clearly an African, but older, more careworn, and less compelling than in the drawing. Another monochrome of *Judith* by Mantegna (fig. 27), now in Montreal, from *c.* 1500–5, imitates bronze, but here the maidservant's simplified features make her ethnicity uncertain.[54] In the eighteenth century this work was in a Gonzaga collection, but nothing is known of its commission.

Three drawings, now in Washington, DC (fig. 28), Chatsworth, and Rotterdam, are regarded as copies after the same lost original by Mantegna, and the early date (1482) inscribed on one of them is mistrusted by scholars, who prefer the 1490s.[55] The composition is similar but not identical to the Uffizi drawing; the maidservant is certainly African, and the relationship between the women is close. These copies again look like finished works of art, not preparatory sketches, and the lost original is presumed to have had the same character. This composition was used, with little alteration, by Girolamo Mocetto for an engraving of *c.* 1500–5 (fig. 29), which served to make the black maidservant still more widely known.[56] The print's influence is visible, for instance, in a small bronze plaquette by Andrea Briosco, where the African identity of the servant is still clear.[57]

There are a few other Mantegnesque images of Judith in which the maidservant is white; the most famous of these is a small painting in the National Gallery in Washington, DC. The latest attribution here, however, is to Giulio Campagnola, a Paduan artist much influenced by Mantegna but whose patrons

---

[52] National Gallery of Ireland, 48.1 × 36.7 cm; Martineau, *Andrea Mantegna*, pp. 403–5 (entry by Keith Christiansen), cat. 129.

[53] Martineau, *Andrea Mantegna*, pp. 403–5.

[54] Museum of Fine Arts, 65.3 × 31.4 cm; Martineau, *Andrea Mantegna*, pp. 411–13, cat. 133.

[55] Washington, DC, National Gallery of Art, 34.7 × 20.2 cm; Lightbown, *Mantegna*, p. 474, cat. 156. Chatsworth, Duke of Devonshire (inscribed 1482), 36.8 × 24.5 cm; Martineau, *Andrea Mantegna*, pp. 441–2, cat. 143. Rotterdam, Boymans – Van Beuningen Museum, inv. 1.488, 34 × 23.2 cm; A. E. Popham, *Italian Drawings Exhibited at the Royal Academy, Burlington House, London, 1930* (London, 1931), p. 43, cat. 156, pl. 135. See also Paola Barocchi, ed., *Il giardino di San Marco: maestri e compagni del giovane Michelangelo* (Florence, 1992), p. 41.

[56] 30.9 × 20.9 cm; Jay Levenson, Konrad Oberhuber and Jacquelyn Sheehan, *Early Italian Engravings from the National Gallery of Art* (Washington, DC, 1973), pp. 386–9, cat. 148.

[57] 10.4 × 7.8 cm; Davide Banzato and Franca Pellegrini, *Bronzi e placchette dei Musei Civici di Padova* (Padua, 1989), pp. 51–2, cat. 23. Many copies survive.

FIG. 27. Andrea Mantegna, *Judith*, c. 1500–5 (tempera and gold on linen,
65 × 31 cm, Montreal, Museum of Fine Art).

FIG. 28. After Andrea Mantegna, *Judith*, 1490s (ink and black chalk on paper, laid on canvas, 34.8 × 20.2 cm, Washington, DC, National Gallery of Art).

FIG. 29. Andrea Mocetto after Andrea Mantegna, *Judith*, c. 1500–5 (engraving, 30.9 × 20.9 cm).

were mostly from the Veneto and Ferrara.[58] Mantegna himself seems to have stuck with his iconographic innovation and taken pride in it. The frescoed decorations of Mantegna's own funerary chapel in Mantua, planned by the master but completed by his heirs after 1506, include a small monochrome depiction of *Judith* with her African servant (fig. 30).[59] Mantegna would perhaps have been pleased that Vasari's famous collection of drawings included yet another of his Judiths with a black maidservant. In 1568 Vasari wrote that 'in our album is . . . a drawing by the hand of Andrea finished with chiaroscuro, in which is a Judith, who puts the head of Holofernes in the pocket of her black slave ('d'una sua schiava Mora').' While this work was once identified with the Uffizi drawing, Vasari's technical specifications do not match, and the Uffizi work shows no sign of having been mounted in the way Vasari preferred.[60] It may be that the lost model for the Washington, DC (fig. 28), Chatsworth and Rotterdam copies was the work owned by Vasari, since in this composition it is easier to mistake the food bag for a large pocket of the servant's clothing.[61]

How many of these images belonged to Isabella is hard to say, but she may have sought out another *Judith* with a black servant after Mantegna's death. An early, c. 1510–12 painting by Correggio (fig. 31), now in Strasbourg, matches an item in the Gonzaga inventories of 1627: a Correggio *Judith*, 'mezza figura, finta da notte'.[62] Correggio spent several years at the Mantuan court, and later executed important works for Isabella's *studiolo*, one of which we shall turn

---

[58] 30.1 × 18.1 cm; Martineau, *Andrea Mantegna*, pp. 435–6, cat. 140 (after *c*. 1490, Pietro Guindaleri?); David Alan Brown, 'Mantegna's Judiths', presentation at 1993 conference, 'Italian art in public and private collections; new attributions/new iconography', Fordham University, New York City (*c*. 1497–9, Campagnola); for another view, see Barocchi, *Il giardino*, pp. 40–2, cat. 4. On the other Mantegnesque images of Judith with maids who are not African, see: Martineau, *Andrea Mantegna*, pp. 437–8, cat. 141 ('Premier engraver', *c*. 1497–1500), pp. 439–41, cat. 142 (drawing, Chatsworth, inscribed date of 1472 suspect), pp. 443–4, cat. 144 (engraving by Giovanni Antonio da Brescia, *c*. 1506–7). For textual traces of images of Judith attributed to Mantegna – probably now lost – see Lightbown, *Mantegna*, p. 466 (cat. 99 and cat. 101), p. 468 (cat. 121), p. 469 (cat. 138).

[59] Lightbown, *Mantegna*, pp. 250, 452–3, cat. 58, pl. 157.

[60] Lightbown, *Mantegna*, p. 484, with the full passage from Vasari (1568, p. 491); Lightbown and E. Tietze-Conrat (*Mantegna: Paintings Drawings Engravings* (London, 1955), p. 204) argue against linking Vasari's work and the Uffizi drawing, as proposed by Bernard Berenson, *The Study and Criticism of Italian Art. Second Series* (London, 1902), pp. 50, 56–7.

[61] Alternatively, Vasari's drawing might have been a cruder version of the Uffizi image now in the Louvre (31 × 23.5 cm), which has been trimmed for mounting; Licia Ragghianti Collobi, *Il libro de' disegni del Vasari* (Florence, 1974), p. 84; on other secondary copies of the Uffizi drawing (British Museum, Ashmolean, Munich, formerly Leipzig), see K. T. Parker, *Catalogue of the Collection of Drawings in the Ashmolean Museum*, 3 vols. (Oxford, 1938–80), II, pp. 16–7, cat. 23.

[62] Musée des Beaux-Arts, 20 × 27 cm; Cecil Gould, *The Paintings of Correggio* (Ithaca, 1976), pp. 33, 273; David Ekserdjian, *Correggio* (New Haven, 1997), pp. 35–7; both authors note close links to Mantegna's Uffizi *Judith*.

FIG. 30. Andrea Mantegna and heirs, *Judith*, after 1506 (fresco, Mantua, Duomo, funerary chapel of Andrea Mantegna).

to shortly. Outside of Mantua, other major artists began to receive requests for images of Judith from private patrons (Giorgione produced several) and the iconography of the African maidservant gradually made headway, finally appearing in works by Titian and Veronese.[63] The black servant never became completely normative in depictions of Judith, but I would estimate that in

---

[63] Harold Wethey, *The Paintings of Titian*, 3 vols. (London, 1969–75), I, p. 95, cat. 44, pl. 193, Detroit, Institute of Arts, *c.* 1570; Terisio Pignatti and Filippo Pedrocco, *Veronese*, 2 vols. (Milan, 1995), II, p. 422, cat. 313, London, L. Koetser Gallery; pp. 422–4, cat. 314, Genoa, Palazzo Rosso; pp. 424–8, cat. 318, Vienna, Kunsthistorisches Museum.

FIG. 31. Correggio, *Judith*, *c.* 1510–12 (oil on panel, 20 × 27 cm, Strasbourg, Musée des Beaux-Arts).

Cinquecento painting there are more images of black women in this role than in any other, and there are later examples as well.[64]

---

[64] See for example the paintings by Johann Liss and Agostino Carracci; Anderson, *Judith*, pls. 42, 50; and Mattia Preti, in Margarita Stocker, ed., *Judith: Sexual Warior, Women and Power in Western Culture* (New Haven, 1998), pl. 136.

F I G . 3 2 . Andrea Mantegna, *Adoration of the Magi, c.* 1497–1500 (distemper on linen, 48.5 × 65.6 cm, Los Angeles, The J. Paul Getty Museum).

To return to Mantua and the Gonzaga: the impression may have been given that Isabella was the only person at court who favored black retainers and their representation in works of art, and this is hardly true. Her husband, the Marquis Francesco, employed male black Africans – in 1493 he sent an African military aide to deliver some sonnets to Isabella – and by the very end of the massive project of Mantegna's *Triumphs of Caesar* in 1494, a black musician and a black soldier had been added to the elaborate compositions. The African identity of the soldier, at least, represented a change from the preparatory drawings, and thus may signal an intervention by Francesco to have his aide portrayed.[65] A few years later (*c.* 1497–1500) Mantegna painted his second *Adoration of the Magi* (fig. 32), a smaller distemper version with half-length

[65] Luzio and Renier, 'Buffoni, schiavi e nani', p. 144; Martineau, *Andrea Mantegna*, pp. 357–8, cat. 108, and pp. 369–70, cat. 114 (entries by Charles Hope).

figures, with another prominent black Wise Man; this was probably destined for one or the other of the ruling couple.[66]

For a decade or two there are fewer Mantuan images with black characters, but around 1520 two further depictions of dark-skinned women appear. The Palazzo d'Arco, once known as the Palazzo Imperiale but of uncertain ownership at this time, was decorated with an elaborate cycle of astrological subjects by the painter Giovanni Maria Falconetto. The segment dedicated to Leo (July) is dominated by an image of the Diana of Ephesus (fig. 33), a deity whose face was sometimes represented with dark stone in ancient sculpture, but hardly ever so shown during the Renaissance. Falconetto's Diana has a dark face, but also dark hands, feet and breasts; the treatment of lips and nose suggest an African physiognomy; and of the set of eight tiny putti who nurse from her multiple breasts, four are dark-skinned and four are white. There is nothing else like this in Renaissance art, and the emphasis on brown skin and African features can only be the result of the Mantuan context and, at least indirectly, Isabella's interests. The most plausible candidate for the role of patron is Benedetto Tosabezzi, a retired diplomat and intimate of the Gonzaga rulers.[67]

In 1522 Isabella once more acquired a young black woman. According to a friend, this one was 'recently captured . . . apparently 16 or 17 years old and very pretty . . . very well made. She has a beautiful face, except that her lower lip is thick.'[68] Soon after, the recently widowed Isabella moved within the Palazzo Ducale and therefore recast the painted decoration of her famous *studiolo*. Between 1523 and 1530 Isabella commissioned Correggio to execute a pair of allegories for the new *studiolo*. Unlike the male-oriented erotic mythologies Correggio was then executing for her son Federigo, Isabella's pictures present a world of strong and virtuous women. The most ascendant female character is Minerva, in the canvas usually called *The allegory of virtue* (fig. 34); she is very much Mantegna's Judith translated into the idiom of the High Renaissance – strong, smart and exquisite.[69] At the left is a woman

[66] Los Angeles, Getty Museum; Martineau, *Andrea Mantegna*, pp. 237–8, cat. 56; Dawson Carr, *Andrea Mantegna: The Adoration of the Magi* (Los Angeles, 1997).

[67] Giuseppe Amadei *et al.*, *Il Palazzo d'Arco in Mantova* (Mantua, 1980), pp. 86–95, colour pl. on 78; Rodolfo Signorini, *Lo zodiaco di Palazzo d'Arco in Mantova* (3rd edn, Mantua, 1989), pp. 20–1; Hermann Thiersch, *Artemis Ephesia. Eine archäologische Untersuchung. Teil I. Katalog der erhaltenen Denkmäler* (Berlin, 1935), p. 94.

[68] Luzio and Renier, 'Buffoni, schiavi e nani', p. 145.

[69] Paris, Louvre; Peter Porçal, 'Le allegorie del Correggio per lo studiolo di Isabella d'Este a Mantova', *Mitteilungen des Kunsthistorischen Institutes in Florenz*, 28 (1984), pp. 225–76 at 244, 252; Egon Verheyen, *The Paintings in the 'Studiolo' of Isabella d'Este at Mantua* (New York, 1971), pp. 57–9; Ekserdjian, *Correggio*, pp. 274–5 (including details on a version in Rome).

FIG. 33. Giovanni Maria Falconetto, *Leo (July)*, c. 1520 (fresco, approx. 300 × 150 cm, Mantua, Palazzo d'Arco).

FIG. 34. Correggio, *Allegory of Virtue, c.* 1523–1530 (tempera on canvas, 149 × 88 cm, Paris, Louvre).

FIG. 35. Titian, *Laura Dianti and her Page*, c. 1523 (oil on canvas, 119 × 93 cm, Switzerland, private collection).

symbolizing the cardinal virtues. To the right, once more subsidiary (to the goddess) in scale, posture and marginal position, is a woman whose dark skin is rarely noted by scholars. Unlike Judith's maidservant in the Uffizi drawing, this woman is highly idealised and quite beautiful by European Renaissance standards. She holds a pair of dividers, instruments of measurement, over a

FIG. 36. Albrecht Dürer, *Portrait of Katherina*, 1521 (silverpoint, 20 × 14 cm, Florence, Uffizi).

globe so vaguely painted that one cannot be sure whether it is the terrestrial or the celestial sphere – perhaps it is both – and gestures toward the earth and the sky in the background. She embodies knowledge of, and implicitly power over, the world and the cosmos, and thanks to Isabella's preferences and interests, Correggio has constructed an image (paradoxical to the modern viewer, at least) in which a woman of colour represents at once European expansionism and the peoples whose subjugation accompanied it.

Mantegna's and Correggio's use of subordinated dark-skinned women were to have an influence on a number of late Renaissance artists; Titian's 1559

Diana and Actaeon contains one of the best-known examples.[70] Other Gonzaga patrons also perpetuated the tradition of representing black figures. Isabella's son Ercole commissioned two tapestries including depictions of Africans (a black Ceres with a cornucopia, and a black putto).[71] Even in the seventeenth century this tradition endured, in the form of a haunting stone bust of a black man now in the Sala dei Fiumi in the Palazzo Ducale of Mantua.[72] But few of these later Gonzaga works seem connected to contemporary developments in the life of Africans and Afro-Europeans. For that one would have to look at Titian's *c.* 1523 portrait of Laura Dianti (fig. 35).[73] Dianti was the mistress of Isabella's brother Alfonso, Duke of Ferrara, and both the duke and his lover used black court servants. Titian's picture is indebted to Mantegna's images of Judith, but the black attendant has become male and shrunk in age and stature. The boy is now truly no more than an accessory, though a very beautiful one, who can no longer collaborate but only gaze awestruck at his great lady. The power relationships established by the European enslavement of ever larger numbers of black Africans become clearer here than in Mantegna's or Correggio's works. Finally, for the most truthful European depiction of a black maidservant, one must return to the drawing collections of the Uffizi, which contains Dürer's famous silverpoint *Portrait of Katherina* (fig. 36), of 1521.[74] If the viewer is ever in danger of being seduced by the fantasy of loyal and eager servitude that Mantegna's drawing promotes, a look at the lonely, melancholy, and dignified slave of the Portuguese factor in Antwerp should effectively break the spell.

[70] Marie Tanner, 'Chance and coincidence in Titian's *Diana and Actaeon*', *Art Bulletin*, 56 (1974), pp. 535–50, with references to other relevant images of black women, including a *Three Fates* (Rome, Palazzo Barberini) attributed to Sodoma or (more recently) Marco Bigio; Fiorella Sricchia Santoro, ed., *Da Sodoma a Marco Pino: pittori a Siena nella prima metà del Cinquecento* (Siena, 1988), p. 140, fig. 84. Note also the black maidservant in Sodoma's *Alexander and Roxane* in the Villa Farnesina; Andrée Hayum, *Giovanni Antonio Bazzi – 'Il Sodoma'* (New York, 1976), cat. 20, pp. 164–77, fig. 42.

[71] Clifford Brown and Guy Delmarcel, with Anna Maria Lorenzoni, *Tapestries for the Courts of Federico II, Ercole, and Ferrante Gonzaga, 1522–1563* (Seattle, 1996), pp. 148–51, fig. 30 (workshop of Jan van Tieghem after Raphael, Mantua, Palazzo Ducale, before 1557), and p. 174, fig. 79 (*Playing putti*, workshop of Nicholas Karcher after Giulio Romano, Milan, Museo Poldi Pezzoli, 1540–5).

[72] Giancarlo Malacarne, *Il Palazzo Ducale di Mantova* (Mantua, 1996), p. 58.

[73] Switzerland, private collection; Kaplan, 'Titian's *Laura Dianti*'.

[74] Friedrich Winkler, *Die Zeichnungen Albrecht Dürers*, 4 vols. (Berlin, 1936–9), IV, p. 40, cat. 818.

CHAPTER SEVEN

Images of empire: slaves in the Lisbon household and court of Catherine of Austria

ANNEMARIE JORDAN

Although A. C. de C. M. Saunders presents a very detailed social history of black Africans in Portugal from 1441 to 1555, the pages dedicated to slaves at the Portuguese court in the Renaissance are brief.[1] Slaves from the Portuguese colonies – first North African Moors and black West Africans, and subsequently Amerindians (Tupi) from Brazil[2] – played an important role as an essential labour force and as exotic components at court, greatly altering day-to-day life, culture and ceremonial. A large number of slaves (mostly women and children) were acquired for the households of the urban palaces of Lisbon (for example, the Paço da Ribeira) and the secondary royal residence in Évora, as well as the rural palaces of Sintra, Almeirim, Paços da Serra and the Paços da Ribeira (in Muge),[3] where they were employed as domestics, primarily as housekeepers,[4] pages or servants in the royal apothecaries, kitchens, gardens and stables.[5] This chapter will not only survey royal slaves at

---

[1] See A. C. de C. M. Saunders, *A Social History of Black Slaves and Freedmen in Portugal, 1441–1555* (Cambridge, 1982). Also *ibid.*, 'The legacy of black slavery in Renaissance Portugal,' *Camões Center Quarterly*, 4: 1 and 2 (1992), pp. 14–19.

[2] Since the discovery of Brazil in 1500, Indian slaves were sent back to Portugal on an average of twenty-four a year. The quantity of Amerindians at court was relatively small as they proved to be inadequate slaves, often melancholic, who starved themselves to death. See John Hemming, *Red Gold: The Conquest of the Brazilian Indians* (London, revised edn, 1995), p. 37; Saunders, *A Social History*, pp. 180–1.

[3] Annemarie Jordan, 'Portuguese royal collections (1505–1580): a bibliographic and documentary survey', M.A. thesis, George Washington University, 1985, pp. 6–29. The court migrated seasonally, in the summer months residing at Sintra and in the winter at Almeirim. Certain slaves lived permanently at these residences, tending the royal herds and the palace kitchen gardens, such as the orange groves at Sintra. Compare with Saunders, *A Social History*, p. 80.

[4] *Varredeiros* (or *varredores*), placed in charge of housekeeping and maintenance duties, were young men responsible for sweeping the corridors, halls and rooms of royal residences.

[5] It should be noted that the majority of documents concerning slaves consulted in the Lisbon archive (Instituto dos Arquivos Nacionais/Torre do Tombo, hereafter IAN/TT) relate primarily to slaves in the queen's household, so my discussion centres on Catherine of Austria. IAN/TT, Núcleo Antigo 792 (hereafter NA 792), an account book of Catherine of Austria's treasurer, Diogo Çalema, contains numerous references to the queen's acquisition and clothing of black African and Amerindian slaves between 1539 and 1545. For extant documents concerning

court during the sixteenth century, but also demonstrate how their presence influenced the manner in which Portuguese monarchs, in particular the queen, Catherine of Austria (1507–78), constructed a public image of themselves as rulers of empire. Catherine's self-fashioning was part of a deliberate approach undertaken to offer her subjects and court a fitting image of a queen consort, who wielded political power and influence over far-flung domains filled with exotic peoples, flora and fauna.[6]

Portugal was one of the first European societies where slaves were commonplace, and where owning black Africans became a sign of social prestige and distinction. Slaves with special skills were especially appreciated and sought out by Portuguese royalty, aristocrats and rich patricians, and by 1552 many affluent households owned at least one slave for domestic duties as this illustration attributed to António de Holanda shows (fig. 37).[7] Renaissance Portuguese society favoured white Moorish slaves because they were considered beautiful; however, as Muslims they were considered to be untrustworthy.[8] Black Africans were deemed ugly but faithful, while mulattos were especially liked because they were more Caucasian in appearance, and Christian.[9] In possessing and employing slaves, Portuguese nobles and rich patricians followed

João III's black slaves – e.g. António, engaged in the king's kitchen, Francisco, who worked as a *varredor* in the Casas da India and Mina, and those in his stables, including Duarte (a white slave) and António (a black African) – see IAN/TT, Corpo Chronológico (hereafter CC) 1, maço 52, doc. 101 (28 Mar. 1534); CC 1, maço 55, doc. 82 (18 June 1535); CC 1, maço 56, doc. 138 (22 Jan. 1536); CC 1, maço 56, doc. 163 (26 Feb. 1536). The exact number of black slaves owned by the Crown remains uncertain as related documents do not always identify servants as slaves, and it must be assumed that many more slaves were black than has been previously presumed. See also Saunders, *A Social History*, p. 80; Isabel Ribeiro Mendes, 'O 'Deve' e o 'Haver' da Casa da Rainha D. Catarina (1525–1557)', *Arquivos do Centro Cultural Português*, 28 (1990), pp. 191–6.

[6] Cf. Karen C. C. Dalton, 'Art for the sake of dynasty: the black emperor in the Drake Jewel and Elizabethan imperial imagery', in Peter Erickson and Clark Hulse, eds., *Early Modern Visual Culture: Representation, Race, and Empire in Renaissance England* (Philadelphia, 2000), pp. 178–214. During the 1450s, black Africans were used for political purposes at the Lisbon court, and included in public ceremonies and fêtes in order to impress foreign dignitaries and diplomats with regard to the extension and power of the Portuguese king in West Africa. See Peter Russell, *Prince Henry 'the Navigator': A Life* (New Haven, 2001), p. 259, n. 38.

[7] In early fifteenth-century Europe, black African domestic servants were seen as exotic household luxuries for the rich; however, when Portugal later imported quantities of African slaves, even modest urban households could afford one: Russell, *Prince Henry*, p. 253.

[8] Saunders, 'The legacy', pp. 18–19.

[9] Saunders, *A Social History*, pp. 174–5. Black Africans were generally thought to make better slaves because they were capable of sustained hard physical labour, and they therefore fetched better prices. Their colour also made them more conspicuous in a white society and therefore less likely to attempt escape. Eanes Gomes de Zurara thought black slaves, obtained south of the River Senegal, were preferred in Portugal because they were easier to convert than Muslim slaves (black or white) from North Africa: Russell, *Prince Henry*, p. 253.

FIG. 37. Attributed to António de Holanda, *Scene with a Black Slave in the Household of a Wealthy Patrician*, Book of Hours of King D. Manuel, 1517–38 (parchment, 14 × 11 cm, Lisbon, Museu Nacional de Arte Antiga, inv. no. 14 Ilum., fol. 5v).

the example set by the king and his court. Favoured individuals at court also possessed slaves, as did the musician, Diogo de Madrill, who owned a black slave from Benin, baptised and given his surname: Pedro de Madrill.[10] By 1552, the majority of slaves in Portugal were black: some 32,000 in a national population of 1,000,000, with black Africans forming about 10 per cent of the total inhabitants of Lisbon, Évora[11] and other towns in the Alentejo and Algarve. Prices for slaves in the early decades of the sixteenth century started at 15,000 *reais* each, tripling by mid-century to 45,000 to 50,000 each and later stabilising at between 15,000 and 30,000 *reais* by the 1570s.[12]

One of the first gifts King João III (ruled 1521–57) presented to his new bride, Catherine, in 1526, shortly after her arrival at the Portuguese court, was

[10] Saunders, *A Social History*, p. 201. See John Vogt, 'The Lisbon Slave House and African trade, 1486–1521,' *Proceedings of the American Philosophical Society*, 117: 1 (1973), p. 12, n. 69, for a discussion of how gifts of prime slaves to the king's entourage, including musicians, drained the revenues of the Lisbon slave house.

[11] Jorge Fonseca, *Escravos em Évora no Século XVI* (Évora, 1997).

[12] Saunders, *A Social History*, p. 27.

FIG. 38. Attributed to Cristovão de Figueiredo and Garcia Fernandes, *The Santa Auta Retable: The Encounter of Prince Conan and St Ursula* (detail with black musicians), 1522–5 (oil on panel, 66.8 × 71.2 cm, Lisbon, Museu Nacional de Arte Antiga, inv. no. 1462 A–B Pint).

a black pastry chef and confectioner by the name of Domingos de Frorença (Florence?).[13] His talents, and those of others like him, such as Manuel, the queen's black cook,[14] were highly esteemed, as later documents confirm, since sweets and other delicacies of the queen's table were relished throughout her reign.[15] Slaves with musical and dance abilities were recruited for court fêtes, entertainments, royal entries and for duties in the royal chapel.[16] A panel of *c.* 1522–5, attributed to Cristóvão de Figueiredo and Garcia Fernandes from *The Santa Auta Retable*, which probably celebrates the marriage of Catherine to João III in 1525, shows six black musicians in realistic detail (fig. 38).

[13] IAN/TT, CC 1, maço 33, doc. 108 (7 March 1526). It cannot be determined whether this slave had originated from Florence, Italy. Black Africans engaged as cooks were quite common in Renaissance Portugal.

[14] IAN/TT, CC 1, maço 58, doc. 58 (15 March 1537).

[15] Annemarie Jordan, 'Queen of the seas and overseas: Dining at the table of Catherine of Austria, Queen of Portugal', in *European Royal Tables – International Symposium Acts* (Lisbon, 1996), pp. 14–43.

[16] *Danças mouriscas*, or Moorish dances, were very popular at the Lisbon court. See Annemarie Jordan Gschwend, 'Os Produtos Exóticos da Carreira da India e o Papel da Corte Portuguesa na sua Difusão', in *Nossa Senhora dos Mártires: A Última Viagem* (exhibition catalogue) (Lisbon, 1998), pp. 122–141 at 127–8.

This early sixteenth-century image is the first representation of a black wind ensemble in Europe, and all the instruments in it have been identified.[17] King João III had a black chaplain and singer called D. Afonso who also played the organ.[18]

From the beginning of her reign, Catherine became actively engaged in the acquisition of slaves to maintain and run her household, and the courts of her children and ladies,[19] and as the years passed she would show increasing concern for the welfare and well-being of slaves in her employ. By order of the king, a number of slaves were granted to the queen as part of her annual income from the customs houses, Casa da Índia[20] and Casa da Mina,[21] as well as the Casa dos Escravos, the Lisbon slave house situated directly adjacent to the royal palace on the Lisbon waterfront, the heart and hub of the overseas trade.[22] The majority of Lisbon's black population, many belonging to the crown, served as labourers and porters for the maritime traffic centred there. An anonymous view of the Lisbon waterfront near the Alfama district, supposedly executed between 1560 and 1580 (fig. 3),[23] depicts a wide cross-section of its black population engaged in a variety of jobs and duties, from water-bearers working at the king's fountain (the Chafariz d'el-Rei) to private servants in livery attending to the daily errands of their masters and mistresses.[24] A freed black, prominently shown in the foreground, mounted on a horse, wears a

---

[17] Saunders, *A Social History*, p. 106 and fig. 5.

[18] *Ditos Portugueses Dignos de Memória*, ed. José H. Saraiva (Lisbon, [1979]), p. 443 (no. 1263).

[19] IAN/TT, CC I, maço 58, doc. 58 (15 March 1537) for the slave Francisco: 'que serve as damas'.

[20] IAN/TT, CC I, maço 49, doc. 115 (30 Sept. 1532): 'que el Rei meu señor me mandou dar na casa da Imdia.' Annemarie Jordan, 'The development of Catherine of Austria's collection in the Queen's household: its character and cost', Ph.D. dissertation, Brown University, 1994, p. 55, nos. 56–8.

[21] IAN/TT, CC I, maço 51, doc. 113 (21 Sept. 1533): 'tres escravas novas que se chamam huaa felipa e a outra maria e a outra caterina que recebeo de martim mendez thezoureiro da casa da mjna'. IAN/TT, NA 792, fol. 241 (19 May 1541): 'hua peça por nome de framcisquo que Reçebeo de gaspar tibaao tesoureiro da casa da mina e o entregou a Joham de larez Resposteiro de camas para servir varredeiro' and fol. 245 (29 Dec. 1540) for two other males (António and João) also sent by Bras Correo, treasurer of the Casa da Mina, to João de Larez.

[22] Vogt, 'The Lisbon Slave House', pp. 1–16. For two young female black Africans described as 'smart' (*pretas ladinhas*) who Catherine received from Pero Alvarez, *recebedor* of the Lisbon slave house in 1543, see IAN/TT, NA 792, fol. 14v. *Ladino* was a word used for a foreigner who spoke Portuguese well.

[23] *Os Negros em Portugal – Sécs. XV a XVI*, (Lisbon, 2000), pp. 104–7. The dating of this picture remains problematic as a noblewoman depicted in a tower window wears a dress fashionable in the 1530s and 1540s.

[24] A thorough discussion is in Saunders, *A Social History*, pp. 62–88. By 1620, 400 black women in Lisbon were firmly positioned in their assigned roles as either domestic servants or as sellers of produce and fish at market places. See Nicolau de Oliveira, *Livro das Grandezas de Lisboa*, preface by Francisco Santana (Lisbon, 1991), p. 573.

FIG. 39. Anonymous, *Chafariz d'el-Rei in the Alfama District, Lisbon* (detail with black cavalier), *c.* 1560–80 (oil on panel, 93 × 163 cm, Lisbon, private collection).

cape bearing the red cross of the Order of Santiago (fig. 39), underscoring how some freed slaves reached prominent social positions.

João de Sá Panasco,[25] a black African considered one of the most spirited men of João III's court, was one such case.[26] He began his career as a court jester entertaining João III and Catherine of Austria with his witty jokes and parodies, and was later appointed gentleman (*cavaleiro*)[27] of the royal household and the

[25] A. C. de C. M. Saunders, 'The life and humour of João de Sá Panasco, o negro, former slave, court jester and gentleman of the Portuguese royal household (fl. 1524–1567)', in F. W. Hodcroft *et al.*, eds., *Mediaeval and Renaissance Studies on Spain and Portugal in Honour of P. E. Russell* (Oxford, 1981), pp. 180–91.

[26] Conde de Sabugosa, *Bobos na Corte*, preface by Ayres d'Ornellas (Lisbon, 1924); *Anedotas Portuguesas e Memórias Biográficas da Corte Quinhentista. Istorias e Ditos Galantes que Sucederão e se Disserão no Paço*, ed. Christopher Lund (Coimbra, 1980), pp. 115–17; Saunders, *A Social History*, p. 199, n. 98. It seems that three black Africans were admitted as knights in the Order of Santiago during the sixteenth century: in 1550 Luís Peres, *fidalgo* and Lord Chamberlain of the household of the King of Congo; in 1579, D. Pedro da Silva, *homen preto* and *cavaleiro fidalgo*, who was an ambassador of the king of Angola; and, probably, Panasco. See Francis A. Dutra, 'A hard-fought struggle for recognition: Manuel Gonçalves Doria, first Afro-Brazilian to become a Knight of Santiago,' *The Americas*, 56 (1 July 1990), pp. 93–4, nos. 13–14.

[27] The records are not clear about Panasco's appointment, although a 1547 document describes him as: 'Joam de saa, homen preto caval[ey]ro de minha casa'.

king's valet (*moço fidalgo*). Both as courtier and entertainer, Panasco was always present at the royal table. In 1535, he accompanied the king's brother, Infante D. Luis (1506–55), on the Emperor Charles V's military campaign in North Africa, and at a later date was awarded the habit of the Order of Santiago, like the mounted black cavalier illustrated here, for his services to the crown.[28] Despite these honours, court chroniclers record that Panasco was stigmatized by his colour and discriminated against by his white peers, growing bitter in old age and taking to drink.[29] Thus, for a former slave, freedom and a career at court were not always a guarantee for betterment of social status, even though there was some degree of fluidity, with black Africans enjoying various gradations of freedom. This was a court that treated black slaves and lower-class free whites in much the same way.

Slaves in Catherine's household were well treated and employed in positions of trust. Young women and children were generally preferred over males, who were given the posts of sweepers/cleaners (*varredeiros*) or positions in the queen's stables.[30] Many of Catherine's slaves were purchased directly by the queen from West Africa, as in 1550, when she acquired six male and four female 'pieces' or *peças*,[31] as they were called in contemporary account books, from Cristóvão de Rosales, the captain of the Portuguese factory at Arguim,[32] in present-day Senegal, for a total of 150,000 *reais*.[33] The fact that Catherine, when buying her own slaves, resorted to acquiring them from their source,

[28] Francis A. Dutra posits Panasco entered the order between 1550 and 1557, the year of João III's death. After 1551, Pope Julius III conceded *in perpetuam* the Grand-Mastership of the Santiago order to the Crown during the reign of João III, who established a royal council with judicial powers to administer the order's affairs. At this juncture, new rules and religious intolerance were introduced, forbidding the admission of people with 'tainted' blood or of non-noble origins.

[29] Saunders, *A Social History*, pp. 82–3.

[30] Clothes for the queen's 5 *varredeiros* were purchased in 1531. See IAN/TT (CC 1, maço 47, doc. 72). In 1533 for 2 males (CC 1, maço 51, doc. 98); for 5 males in 1533 (CC 1, maço 51, doc. 99); for 3 males in 1537 (CC 1, maço 58, doc. 58); for 3 males in 1550 (CC 1, maço 85, doc. 97); for 3 males in 1553 (CC 1, maço 90, doc. 9); for 4 males in 1554 (CC 1, maço 93, doc. 74); for 3 males in 1555 (CC 1, maço 95, doc. 63).

[31] A *peça* normally represented one healthy, male slave in his prime. Older men, boys, women and children were usually broken up into groups regardless of family relationships to make up the equivalent of one *peça*. This grouping could be made up of two to three individuals: Russell, *Prince Henry*, p. 398, n. 7. However, in the document under discussion, a *peça* can be either male or female.

[32] The slaving factory at Arguim was established in the late 1440s, and was ratified by Pope Nicholas V's bull, *Romanus pontifex*, in 1455. IAN/TT, NA 792, fol. 245 (20 Dec. 1540) for 6 females slaves (Giomar, Felipa, 2 Catarinas, 2 Annas) sent from Arguim to Catherine by Francisco de Naao.

[33] IAN/TT, CC 1, maço 85, doc. 118 (26 Dec. 1550). All four women cited in this document were christened Maria, five of the men António and one Fernando. During the reign of João III and Catherine of Austria, many black Africans were baptised João and Catarina.

reflects that she was price conscious and well informed about the better rates in Africa. Other male slaves, used to sweep the palace (for example, Pedro and Bastião), were procured by the king for his wife in the marketplace of Évora (Alentejo), when the court temporarily resided there from 1531 to 1538, after a devastating earthquake and the outbreak of plague in Lisbon.[34] Yet others were obtained from private individuals.[35]

The queen acquired three female Amerindian slaves, possibly Tupi (cf. fig. 40), from Brazil in 1537, and she supplied them with the necessary clothes and bedding soon after their arrival at court.[36] Two male Amerindians in the queen's service, Duarte Frois and Bastião, are also recorded in her documents. Frois began his court career in 1537.[37] He must have been a favourite of the queen, since he was granted a sum of money in 1556,[38] and he appears to have received an education at Catherine's court. In 1544 he was apprenticed to João Diaz, who was selected to teach him goldsmith work.[39] As the document in fig. 41 proves, Duarte was able to sign his own name. We are confronted here with the first signature of a Brazilian (Tupi) Indian ever recorded in the Renaissance. The second Brazilian Indian, Bastião, was engaged for a number of years in the queen's dispensary (*botica*),[40]

[34] IAN/TT, CC 1, maço 59, doc. 51 (27 Aug. 1537): 'que el Rey meu señor mandou comprar na praça desta cidade de Évora'. During the Évora years, other slaves were acquired in Lisbon, afterwards brought to the Alentejo by the *guarda reposte* responsible for the queen's wardrobe and slaves. See IAN/TT, CC 1, maço 51, doc. 98 (22 Oct. 1533): 'huu deles amtonio e o outro bastiam que ora trouxe de Lix [a] [Lisbon] balltasar cornejo'.

[35] IAN/TT, NA 792, fol. 195 (8 Dec. 1543): 'que despendeo em compra de hun escravo por nome de Gaspar Ladinho que foy de dona ana pereira o quall emtregou a baltasar cornejo para serviço da guarda reposte'.

[36] IAN/TT, CC 1, maço 58, doc. 96 (26 May 1537): 'pera as tres escravas Imdias que ora vieram'. IAN/TT, NA 792, fol. 204v (10 Jan. 1544): 'a dona Joana camareira mor para vestido de hua escrava Imdia da Rainha Nossa Semhora'. See IAN/TT, NA 792 for references regarding Joana Lopez, a female Amerindian slave, in the queen's household.

[37] IAN/TT, CC 1, maço 58, doc. 58 (15 March 1537): 'a duarte Indio que lavra'. *Lavra* here implies Duarte worked well with his hands and had artistic talents.

[38] IAN/TT, CC 1, maço 100, doc. 69 (9 Jan. 1557): 'a duarte froes Imdio dous mil rs de que lhe faço merçe'.

[39] IAN/TT, NA 792, fol. 209: '200 reais que no dito deu a joão diaz por Imsinar a duarte a fazer canotilho embraçado [a chain of twisted gold or silver loops]'. Also NA 792, fol. 161: '5,611 reais que despemdeo por mandado verball em çertas cousas do serviço da dita Senhora que servião para o ofiçio que sua Alteza mamdou emsinar a duarte Imdio seu escravo'. There is evidence that in 1544 Duarte was held in detention, perhaps as some sort of disciplinary measure: IAN/TT, NA 792, fol. 207: '350 reais que no dito tempo despemdeo na prisam de duarte Imdio escravo de Sua Alteza'.

[40] IAN/TT, CC 1, maço 90, doc. 9 (8 May 1553); CC 1, maço 88, doc. 74 (28 July 1552); CC 1, maço 90, doc. 104 (28 July 1553); CC 1, maço 93, doc. 120 (5 Oct. 1554); CC 1, maço 97, doc. 10 (5 Nov. 1555).

FIG. 40. Vasco Fernandes and Francisco Henriques (?), *The Adoration of the Magi* (detail of Tupi Indian), 1502–6 (oil on panel, 103.2 × 79 cm, Viseu, Museu de Grão Vasco, inv. 2145).

FIG. 41. Mandate signed by Catherine of Austria for clothes given to Duarte Frois for his work (detail with his signature), 1 February 1552 (Instituto dos Arquivos Nacionais/Torre do Tombo, Lisbon, Corpo Chronológico 1, maço 87, doc. 78).

in what was truly a position of trust, perhaps because he possessed shamanic, healing powers learned in Brazil.[41] Over the years, Bastião too was granted clothes and favours by the queen, but in 1557 he was relieved of his position in the *botica*, possibly for reasons of health, and sent to live at her summer residence at Xabregas, conceivably in some form of retirement.[42] Bastião was replaced by another slave, Simão, who was probably a black African.[43] Six female slaves (at least one of whom was definitely a black African in 1543)[44] and one Amerindian worked in the queen's dispensary, one of the most important sections of her household, as it supplied the kitchen and wardrobe with all the necessary spices for cooking and other uses. In addition, as the Lisbon court in the Renaissance was a superstitious one,[45] the dispensary was used to make potions of all kinds from exotic resins, gums and plants, which were

[41] I am grateful to Paul Kaplan for this suggestion.
[42] IAN/TT, CC II, maço 246, doc. 14 (13 Jan. 1557): 'Bastião que servya na Botiqua que mandey entreguar a amtonio alvarez almoxarife dos paços de enxabregas pera laa servir'.
[43] See IAN/TT, CC I, maço 97, doc. 77 (15 Feb. 1556).
[44] Saunders, *A Social History*, p. 82, n. 95. Also IAN/TT, NA 792, fol. 188v, no. 671 (13 July 1543) for 3 *cruzados* paid to the black slave (*negra*) who worked in the dispensary.
[45] See Jo Castle, 'Amulets and protection: pomanders', *Bulletin of the Society of Renaissance Studies* 27, 2 (May 2000), pp. 12–18.

ingested for protection against diseases and fevers.[46] Although the queen had often previously employed black African slaves as cooks in her kitchens or as dispensers in her pharmacies, and must therefore have trusted them not to harm her, the mood later seems to have changed, because in 1565 an edict was passed whereby slaves working in royal dispensaries and pharmacies were no longer allowed to handle medicines.[47]

There are indications, although this cannot be entirely confirmed, that not only Indians but also black Africans at Catherine's court were educated, some learning to read and write like Duarte Frois. In 1494, when the German physician, Hieronymus Münzer, visited Portugal, he noted that black Africans were obliged to become Christian, and to learn to read and write Latin.[48] Pero Fernandez, who worked as the queen's sweeper for many years,[49] was equally able to sign his name, as the document in fig. 42 confirms.[50] He too was well liked and given gifts of money, and was entrusted with the highly important task of informing the queen of the contents of cargoes on ships arriving from India.[51] Obviously the queen's confidence in this slave prompted her to rely upon him rather than a white household official. However, not all of Catherine's slaves were literate, and there is some doubt whether all of her black African slaves even spoke Portuguese; one of her housekeepers was nicknamed Jorge Bocall, *boçal* or *negro boçal*, indicating a black African who could only speak an African language.[52] Young female slaves, on the other hand, were given some formal training and education (religious and otherwise), and several were sent by the queen to learn sewing and needlework at convents near Lisbon and Évora, so their acquired skills could be applied in the queen's service. Madanella and Agueda, who later worked in the queen's wardrobe, lived at the Franciscan Convent of Nossa Senhora da Esperança de Boa Vista

[46] Jordan, 'The development', p. 382; Jordan, 'Os productos exóticos', pp. 135–7. Catherine had a regular supply of ginger, nutmeg, musk, benzoin, bezoar stones and other medicinal drugs sent to her from India each year.

[47] Saunders, *A Social History*, p. 82.

[48] Hieronymus Münzer, *Itinerário do Dr. Jerónimo Münzer (Extractos)*, trans. Basílio de Vasconcelos (*O Lusitano*, 80 (Coimbra, 1931)), pp. 51–6. Some black Africans did refuse baptism and can be identified in records by their African names: Russell, *Prince Henry*, p. 255.

[49] See Jordan, 'The development', pp. 102–5. IAN/TT, CC 1, maço 85, doc. 97 (15 March 1551); CC 1, maço 92, doc. 152 (11 June 1554); CC 1, maço 95, doc. 63 (11 May 1555); CC 1, maço 98, doc. 96 (20 June 1556); CC 1, maço 99, doc. 10 (17 July 1556); CC 1, maço 101, doc. 12 (4 April 1557).

[50] This is not the case with receipts for other slaves in Catherine's employ, where it is evident that they were illiterate and could not sign their own name.

[51] IAN/TT, CC 1, maço 92, doc. 95 (17 April 1554): 'dey a pero fernandez homen preto dous cruzados por portaria de aleixo de Moraes polas novas que trouxe dos naos da India'.

[52] Saunders, *A Social History*, p. 99. IAN/TT, CC 1, maço 51, doc. 99 (26 Oct. 1533).

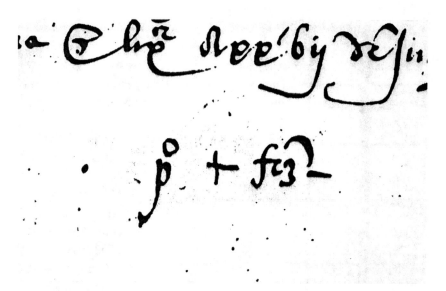

FIG. 42. Mandate signed by Catherine of Austria for clothes given to Pero Fernandes for his work as housekeeper (detail with his signature), 20 June 1556 (Instituto dos Arquivos Nacionais/Torre do Tombo, Lisbon, Corpo Chronológico I, maço 98, doc. 96).

in Lisbon[53] for one year.[54] Another young slave girl was sent to the Bernadine (a Cistercian order) convent in Almoster near Santarém in 1544, to be trained in a similar fashion.[55] In 1549, the abbess of the Convento de Jesus,[56] in Viana do Alentejo (Évora), addressed a pleading letter to Catherine. She writes to

[53] This convent, first known as Nossa Senhora da Piedade da Boa Vista, dedicated to the Virgin of Compassion, was founded in 1530 by Isabel de Mendanha as a religious order for aristocratic women. It later took the name Nossa Senhora da Esperança, from a confraternity of sailors and navigators established there. Joana d'Eça, the former maid of honor of Catherine of Austria, rebuilt the convent in the mid-sixteenth century, establishing a Franciscan order with eighty nuns, to which Catherine was especially devoted. See Júlio de Castilho, *A Ribeira de Lisboa*, 5 vols. (4th edn, Lisbon, 1981), IV, pp. 143–4.

[54] IAN/TT, CC I, maço 91, doc. 51 (21 Nov. 1553): 'minhas escravas que estão apremdemdo a lavrar no mosteiro de nosa señora da esperamça de boa vista sete mil rs de tempo de hun anno que começara do primeiro dia deste mes'. Also IAN/TT, CC I, maço 97, doc. 10 (5 Nov. 1555); CC I, maço 97, doc. 77 (15 Feb. 1556), citing Madanella working in the queen's wardrobe.

[55] IAN/TT, NA 792, fol. 202v (20 May 1544): 'duzentos reais que deu a maria pirez madre em almoster para vestido e provimento de hua nigrinha que crya por mandado da dita Senhora'.

[56] This convent, no longer extant, was founded in 1548 for noble widows and unmarried women, and patronized in the sixteenth century by members of the Portuguese royal house, especially Isabel of Bragança, Catherine of Austria's sister-in-law. The community of sixty nuns followed the Augustinian Rule, and was subsequently the first and only religious community for women in Portugal to be integrated into the Hieronymite order.

say a ward in her charge, a young female slave, was sick, and unable to return immediately to the queen's service (see Appendix). In addition, she begs the queen's forgiveness for the slave's lack of skill, explaining that her nuns had done their best to train her to sew, but as poor, humble women themselves (with little means and food) they could do no better. Although the girl worked slowly, the abbess wrote, she did her job thoroughly. Thus she was content to return her charge to court, with the hope that the queen would make a generous donation for these services rendered. Such activities demonstrate Catherine's close involvement in the daily lives of her slaves, and, moreover, that specialized training was much in demand at court.

Slaves became the personal property of the queen, and those designated for her household were placed under the direct control of the courtier (*guarda reposte*) responsible for her wardrobe[57] and tapestries.[58] From the wardrobe, slaves were sent as needed to work in other sectors of the queen's household.[59] Documents reveal at least three female and five male slaves were employed in the queen's wardrobe at any given time between 1535 and 1552, while two others were assigned to her personal quarters. Two male slaves (João and Fernandes) worked as housekeepers for the queen's valet of the bedchamber.[60] Five female slaves – Violante, Margarida, Justa, Maria and Francisco – served the queen's ladies at different periods (cf. fig. 43).[61] During Catherine's reign between nineteen and twenty-three female slaves a year were placed under

---

[57] Slaves at other European courts were similarly placed under the control of the wardrobe. Cf. Alan Ryder, *The Kingdom of Naples under Alfonso the Magnanimous: The Making of a Modern State* (Oxford, 1976), p. 77.

[58] During most of Catherine's reign, this post was filled by Baltasar Cornejo, also the queen's goldsmith, and who had purchased the office of tapestry keeper: Jordan, 'The development', pp. 59–60, n. 76.

[59] IAN/TT, NA 792, fol. 194v, no. 721 (5 Nov. 1543) for monies given to Gonçalo Casquo, valet of the bedchamber, for clothes he purchased for the slave, Francisco, the queen's *varredor*, 'que ele tem en seu poder' and fol. 205 (18 June 1544), for clothes given to three slaves under Casquo's care: Bastião, Pero and António.

[60] IAN/TT, CC I, maço 49, doc. 69 (14 Aug. 1532); CC I, maço 54, doc. 41 (2 Jan. 1535): 'das escravas que servem demtro da minha casa'; CC I, maço 56, doc. 31 (11 Sept. 1535): 'de vestir a tres escravas que servem na minha guarda Reposte'; CC I, maço 58, doc. 18 (11 Dec. 1536); CC I, maço 87, doc. 88 (8 Feb. 1552): 'vestiaria que ham daver dous escravos meus que serve na dito Reposte'. Also IAN/TT, NA 792, fol. 167v, no. 522 (16 Mar. 1542) for clothes bought for António, Diogo and Duarte, slaves employed in the *guarda reposte*.

[61] IAN/TT, CC I, maço 47, doc. 85 (29 Oct. 1531): 'violante e margarida que serve as damas'; CC I, maço 83, doc. 74 (28 July 1552): 'Justa que serve as damas'; CC I, maço 90, doc. 104 (28 July 1553): 'Justa e marya que serve as damas'; CC I, maço 58, doc. 58 (15 Mar. 1537); CC I, maço 97, doc. 77 (15 Feb. 1556): 'francisco que serve na limpesa das damas que tem henrique velho reposteiro em seu poder'. Also CC I, maço 88, doc. 138 (3 Oct. 1552) for clothes bought for the latter slave, Francisco.

FIG. 43. Garcia Fernandes and Jorge Leal, *The Birth of the Virgin* (detail with a black lady's servant), early sixteenth century (oil on panel, 136 × 81 cm, Lisbon, Coll. António Trindade).

the control of the queen's chief maid-of-honour (*camareira mor*), Joana d'Eça[62] engaged in the Lisbon royal palace either as the queen's laundresses, or as servants in her pharmacy or her privy chamber (*retrete*).[63] The female slaves responsible for the laundry were even granted their own slave, a child by the name of Caterina, to assist them.[64] Catherine's daughter, Princess Maria of Portugal (1527–45), the future wife of Philip II of Spain, also had personal slaves, Maria and Catarina, to serve her.[65] Ines Pirez, who may have been a black African, worked as a nurse for the queen's aristocratic ladies,[66] while another black African, Maria, lived at the rural palace of the Paços da Serra, as a servant for the shepherds responsible for the supply of meat and milk for the queen's table.[67] One of Catherine's former slaves, a manumitted North African muslim (*mourisco forro*), João de Beja, held an important position in the queen's stables, no doubt because of his skills in horsemanship.[68] Other black slaves also worked in the queen's stables: António, Fernando, António 'grande' and António 'pequeno', all of whom were under the control of her Master of Horse (*estribeiro mor*). Black stable boys often accompanied their mistress on the queen's peregrinations between royal palaces, as attendants in her entourage. A procession in a miniature from the workshop of Simon Bening shows one such black attendant with an aristocratic hunting party (fig. 44). On average, Catherine's household numbered between 220 and 250 employees and servants per annum, of whom approximately 10 per cent were North African, sub-Saharan black and Amerindian slaves.[69]

   As documents corroborate, female slaves who personally attended the queen and her female court were highly regarded and treated almost as if they were

[62] IAN/TT, CC I, maço 53, doc. 106 (18 Mar. 1550): 'pera a vestearia que ham daver dezanove escravas'. CC I, maço 100, doc. 4 (24 Nov. 1556) for clothes bought for twenty-three slaves.

[63] IAN/TT, CC I, maço 83, doc. 74 (28 July 1552); CC I, maço 90, doc. 104 (28 July 1553); CC I, maço 97, doc. 10 (5 Nov. 1555): 'luisa que serve no Retrete'; CC I, maço 97, doc. 77 (15 Feb. 1556): 'escravas que servem no paço', and IAN/TT, NA 792, fols. 95–6 (19 Sept. 1538).

[64] IAN/TT, CC I, maço 83, doc. 74 (28 July 1552): 'cateryna escrava que as serve'; CC I, maço 90, doc. 104 (28 July 1553): 'a negrinha que as serve'; CC I, maço 97, doc. 10 (5 Nov. 1555): 'catheryna que serve as moças do lavor'.

[65] IAN/TT, CC I, maço 47, doc. 85 (29 Oct. 1531): 'caterina e maria que servem a princesa'.

[66] IAN/TT, CC I, maço 53, doc. 78 (12 Aug. 1534); CC I, maço 97, doc. 10 (5 Nov. 1555).

[67] Saunders, *A Social History*, p. 80. IAN/TT, CC I, maço 88, doc. 112 (13 Sept. 1552): 'maria preta que myguel cabrera trouxe dos paços da serra que servya aos pastores das bacas e cabres de S. Al.'

[68] Saunders, *A Social History*, p. 82. IAN/TT, CC I, maço 73, doc. 60 (1 Mar. 1543); CC I, maço 87, doc. 86 (7 Feb. 1552) and CC I, maço 97, doc. 127 (20 Mar. 1556).

[69] Jordan, 'The development', p. 56. Also IAN/TT, NA 792, fol. 204 (5 Mar. 1544) for clothes Catherine's maid-of-honour, Joana d'Eça, purchased for three white slaves: Axaa, Fátima and Marião.

FIG. 44. Workshop of Simon Bening, *Scene of an Aristocratic Hunting Party including a Black Attendant*, Month of May, Book of Hours of Infante Ferdinand, 1530–4 (parchment, 13.3 × 9.8 cm, Lisbon, Museu Nacional de Arte Antiga, inv. no. 13 Ilum.).

freed maids of honour.[70] They were granted rich, brightly coloured clothes and shoes, besides several changes of clothing. One document underscores how slave women were often dressed in the finest of materials imported from India: exotic textiles for exotic women that reflected the elevated status of their princely and aristocratic mistresses.[71] Maria de Loronha, a black slave who served the queen's ladies, had an outfit consisting of a straw hat (*sombreiro*), a blue cape, a petticoat made of Rouen cloth from Paris, a skirt made of beige Perpignan cloth and a black doublet sewn by the queen's tailor, Fernão Ruiz.[72] In 1554 a laundress, Margarida da Esperança, was given 4,000 *reais* for a skirt made with a coarse fabric referred to as *arbim despada*.[73] The clothes given to male servants were more sombre, often black, a colour considered at the Iberian courts to represent elegance and magnificence.[74]

Not only did Catherine spend a great deal of money clothing her slaves, she also generously provided them with beds, blankets, bedding and other necessary accessories, such as wooden chests to store their belongings.[75] She helped one black woman, Isabel Ribeiro, buy her wedding bed after her marriage to Baltasar Beloso.[76] These beds and pallets were costly, with mattresses made of wool or cloth (fustian), and equipped with assorted sheets and blankets. The Amerindian, Duarte, received such a bed in 1554, with a large Rouen wool mattress, Brabant sheets, a blanket made in the Alentejo and a pallet.[77] Beds

---

[70] Saunders, *A Social History*, p. 82. IAN/TT, NA 792, fol. 194v, no. 722 (14 Dec. 1543) for clothes, to the value of 300 *reais* each, bought for the following female slaves; Margarida de Taide, Genevra do Rio, Joana da Gama, Isabel Botelha, Ana Vaz, Isabel, Margarida da Silva, Apolonia and Isabel Gonçalvez. Even children of Catherine's female slaves were provided with clothes: IAN/TT, CC I, maço 96, doc. 147 (24 Oct. 1555): 'dous myll reais que dey a camarejra mor para cueyros (swaddling clothes) dos nygrynhos filhos de isabell escrava de sua Alteza'.

[71] IAN/TT, CC I, maço 88, doc. 112 (13 Sept. 1552): for clothes given to Maria, the slave of the Paços da Serra, who received among other items, leather shoes and two coifs for her hair imported from India (made from *pano da India*), perhaps white cotton from Cambay. Also IAN/TT, NA 792, fol. 61 for an Indian cloth head-dress made for an Amerindian slave.

[72] IAN/TT, CC I, maço 93, doc. 26 (24 July 1554). See Saunders, *A Social History*, p. 95, n. 37.

[73] IAN/TT, CC I, maço 94, doc. 13 (14 Nov. 1554). This is a large sum to spend on a single skirt. See also CC I, maço 88, doc. 74 (28 July 1552); CC I, maço 90, doc. 104 (28 July 1553); CC I, maço 97, doc. 10 (5 Nov. 1555); CC I, maço 97, doc. 77 (15 Feb. 1556) for references to Margarida as laundress.

[74] IAN/TT, CC I, maço 47, doc. 72 (13 Sept. 1531).

[75] IAN/TT, CC I, maço 54, doc. 39 (2 Jan. 1535) for two beds for her new slaves (*escravas novas*), Joana and Ana; CC I, maço 54, doc. 41 (2 Jan. 1535); CC I, maço 58, doc. 96 (26 May 1537); CC I, maço 93, doc. 120 (3 Oct. 1554).

[76] IAN/TT, CC I, maço 86, doc. 17 (8 Feb. 1551).

[77] Saunders, *A Social History*, p. 96, ns. 48–9. IAN/TT, CC I, maço 54, doc. 39 (2 Jan. 1535); CC I, maço 54, doc. 41 (2 Jan. 1535); CC I, maço 93, doc. 120 (3 Oct. 1554).

were at a premium in this age; even at court, several people often shared the same bed.

Catherine's concern for her slaves extended beyond their welfare. She troubled herself with their emancipation, manumitting several in her lifetime, and promising manumission to all in her employ at the time of her death in a codicil to her last will and testament.[78] The queen's generosity was not just limited to gifts of money,[79] clothes or beds: in 1554 one freed black woman, Margarida da Silva, formerly in Catherine's dispensary,[80] was given money by the queen in order to buy herself a house in Lisbon.[81] Two other women, who had worked as the queen's laundresses for many years, probably since their childhood, Clemencia de Santa Maria and Catarina da Cruz, were manumitted in 1554. Related documents describe them as orphans (without families and dowries), who were sent by Catherine to Brazil, probably the town of Salvador da Bahia, to be married, much in the same way white Portuguese orphans were shipped to Goa to marry and begin new lives.[82] Before their departure, the queen made sure Catarina and Clemencia were regally outfitted with a trousseau of clothes and accessories amounting to 71,711 *reais*. This mandate, seven folios in length, describes in detail the items needed for their new households: rich clothes made from Perpignan, Parisian Rouen and *arbim despada* cloth, yellow cloaks, capes made from black London cloth with gold braid, scarlet satin petticoats and doublets, Holland cloth shirts, leather shoes, cork shoes (*chapins*), belts, needles, mirrors, brushes, combs, scissors, brass basins, leather and wooden chests, wool

---

[78] *Gavetas do Torre do Tombo*, ed. A da Silva Rego, 12 vols. (Lisbon, 1960–77), VI, p. 33: 'Item he minha vontade e mando que todas as minhas escravas fiquem livres e forras como ja as tenho libertado'. This was not always the case with former Portuguese queens. Maria, Manuel I's second wife and Catherine's aunt, only manumitted her female slaves if they chose to marry or take religious vows, conceding these slaves a grant of 20,000 *reais* each. Those who refused were obliged to enter the households of her daughters as slaves. See *Gavetas do Torre do Tombo*, VI, p. 107 and Saunders, *A Social History*, p. 140, n. 38.

[79] In 1544 Catherine gave 400 *reais* to an unnamed black African from the Congo, possibly a servant or a member of D. Henrique's entourage, who was visiting the Lisbon court: IAN/TT, NA 792, fol. 206. See n. 86 below.

[80] IAN/TT, CC I, maço 90, doc. 104 (28 July 1553).

[81] IAN/TT, CC I, maço 93, doc. 134 (11 Oct. 1554): 'a marguarjda da silva que foy minha escrava dez mil rs que lha faço merçe para ajuda de tomar sua casa'.

[82] IAN/TT, CC I, maço 97, doc. 72 (6 Feb. 1556): 'he verdade que caterjna da cruz e clemencia mandou sua alteza ao brazil pera laa as casarem'. Saunders, *A Social History*, p. 82, n. 97 suggests Catarina and Clemencia were white or mulatta, which made them more attractive and marriageable. Their colour cannot be precisely ascertained, but I posit they were black or mulatta. See also Timothy Coates, 'State-sponsored female colonization in the *Estado da India*', *Santa Barbara Portuguese Studies*, 2 (1995), pp. 40–56.

mattresses, Brabant sheets, pillows and pillowcases made of Brittany cloth, blankets, assorted towels, napkins, knives, folding tables, water basins, assorted pewter vessels, copper candlesticks and snuffing scissors. What became of their New World adventure and whether they established themselves well is not known.

From Catherine's charitable deeds, it can be deduced that she had a social conscience. When slaves fell sick or were wounded she provided medical attention, paying her personal physicians large fees to treat them, as the case of her housekeeper, João, who suffered a serious head injury at the palace at Almeirim in 1552 and was treated by the queen's surgeon, Mestre Luís.[83] Even Catherine's preoccupation with Brazilian natives, far from the Lisbon court, is recorded. In 1562 she wrote to the town council of Salvador, urging the governor Mem da Sá and his officials to aid the Jesuits in their conversion of the Indians, and 'treat the heathen who become Christian well, and not vex them nor take their lands'.[84] Catherine was motivated both by her deep religiosity and by a great sense of duty towards her subjects during her regency of Portugal between 1557 and 1562.

The spiritual welfare of the slaves in her household, as well as in her empire, was another of Catherine's priorities. Dom Henrique, described as a nephew of the King of Congo, came to visit the Lisbon court in 1544. When he returned to Africa, Catherine sent a bishop, João Baptista,[85] along with him, paying for new clothes for Henrique.[86] In 1556 the queen outfitted her Moorish slave, Diogo Carvalho, who worked as a *varredor*, with clothes and a bed when she sent him to sent to study Christian doctrine at the College of Orphans

---

[83] Saunders, *A Social History*, p. 109, n. 132. IAN/TT, CC I, maço 89, doc. 27 (30 Nov. 1552): 'pague a mestre luis soherjião que curou Joam escravo varredeiro mil rs que lha mando dar pela cura que lhe fez em almeirjm estando forrado da cabeça'.

[84] Hemming, *Red Gold*, p. 148.

[85] On the tenure of this Dominican bishop, see Conrad Eubel *et al.*, *Hierarchia catholica medii aevi*, 8 vols., 2nd edn (Padua, 1913–78), III, pp. 227, 332 and 345.

[86] In 1490 the first missionaries came to sub-Saharan Africa at the request of King Nzinga of Congo (also known as Manicongo), who was baptised. His son Afonso (born Nzinga Mbemba) was sent to Portugal to study and amazed the Lisbon court with his intelligence and intense piety. Afonso's son, Henrique, became the first black African bishop, but the Henrique mentioned here is a different relative: IAN/TT, NA 792, fol. 207 (5 April 1544): '800 reais de merçe a dom Amrique sobrinho delRey de comgro [Congo] que foy para o dito Reino com o bispo dom Joham bautista para hun vestido por mandado.' For a discussion of the value of the clothing given to black African envoys arriving at the Portuguese court in the early sixteenth century (and the differential between these and clothes given to white envoys or to earlier black African envoys), see Ivana Elbl, 'Prestige considerations and the changing interest of the Portuguese crown in sub-Saharan Atlantic Africa, 1444–1580', *Portuguese Studies Review*, 10 (2003), pp. 15–36 at 31.

in Lisbon.[87] Another Moor by the name of Martinho was ordered to learn doctrine at the Convent da Trindade in Lisbon, near the Misericórdia, while a Moorish female slave, Catarina d'Eça, resided at Catherine's hunting palace at Almeirim for two months, taking religious instruction before being baptised upon the queen's orders.[88]

Although Catherine appeared to have been clement towards her slaves and the native peoples under her rule, she also did not hesitate to treat them as commodities, disposing of them as she wished as exclusive, expensive and exotic gifts to members of her family and court.[89] When Baltasar Cornejo, the keeper of the queen's wardrobe, retired from this post in 1551, Catherine presented him with the slave Francisco who had formerly worked under him.[90] Her favourite ladies were also given female slaves: Dona Guiomar de Coutinha was given Isabel; Jerónima went to Joana Vasquez; and her favorite, Mécia de Andrade, was rewarded with Luçia, a small girl, in 1555.[91] Two other slaves, both named Maria, were presented to Joana d'Eça and a courtier, Boiça, in 1556.[92] When Catherine's daughter, Maria, married in 1543, Catherine supplied her with twelve slaves (black Africans, white Muslims, mulattos and Amerindians), for her new household in Spain.[93] In 1554 Maria's son and heir, Infante Carlos, was sent three male slaves from the Lisbon court by his grandmother, Catherine.[94] After his early death in 1568, two of these slaves

---

[87] IAN/TT, CC 1, maço 100, doc. 36 (20 Dec. 1556). Catalogued in Jordan, 'The development', pp. 359–60, cat. 117. The latter school was an orphanage placed under the direction of the Santa Casa da Misericórdia in Lisbon. Founded by Catherine, the Colégio dos Meninos Órfãos was well-endowed by the queen with funds to support thirty orphaned boys, who were taught Latin and music. See Coates, 'Female colonization', pp. 42–4.

[88] Until 1571 the Inquisition was installed in this convent. See Isabel Mendes Drumond Braga, 'A Vivência de uma Religiosidade Diferente: os Mouriscos Portugueses entre a Cruz e o Crescente', *Piedade Popular* (Lisbon, 1999), pp. 118–9.

[89] IAN/TT, NA 792, fol. 200 (19 April 1544) for 300 *reais* given to João de Prestar for clothing a slave who resided in his house; a slave he had received from the queen.

[90] IAN/TT, CC 1, maço 93, doc. 138 (12 Oct. 1554): 'mandavos que deys a baltesar cornejo que foy meu guarda Reposte huu escravo per nome francisco que servya em minha Reposte de que faço merçe ao dito baltesar cornejo avendo Respeito ao servicjo que me fez no officio de guarda Reposte que me ora alargou'.

[91] CC 1, maço 95, doc. 20 (15 Mar. 1555).   [92] CC 1, maço 97, doc. 72 (6 Feb. 1556).

[93] Archivo General de Simancas (hereafter AGS), Casa y Sitios Reales, leg. 73, 1545, unfoliated: 'el dicho dia se despacho otra para catalina fernandez esclava de color negra, beatriz esclava de Tunez, mencia diaz de color negra, catalina correa de color negra, antonia de la silva de color de yndia (Brazil), catalina lois de color blanca, maria de la cruz de color blanca, francisca de castro de color blanca, elena mourisca de color lora, antonio esclavo de color negro, francisco de color negro, juana pirez esclava de color morena que quedo con la duquesa de alba'.

[94] IAN/TT, CC 1, maço 88, doc. 67 (20 July 1553).

were manumitted and sent to train in the workshop of the court jeweler and lapidary, Jacopo da Trezzo, as stipulated in the prince's testament, but what became of their careers is not documented.[95] Catherine purchased clothes in 1541 for a female slave (who may have been black) sent to Brussels as a gift for her sister, Mary of Hungary (1505–58), regent of the Netherlands.[96] News of Catherine's gifts of slaves circulated at court: one mother superior of an unnamed convent, Maria da Silva, wrote supplicating Catherine in the name of God to send her two female slaves, because having recently built a convent, the nuns were no longer financially able to pay servants' wages.[97] Whether these nuns were granted this favour is not known.

For Portuguese monarchs and for Catherine of Austria, who had amassed by the mid-sixteenth century an extensive collection of wild animals, exotica, naturalia, luxury commodities and export wares from Africa, Asia, China and Japan,[98] the slaves at her court also functioned as visual symbols of her power, literally representing the various frontiers of her rule. Nowhere in Renaissance Portugal is the image of the black African as a symbol of empire

---

[95] In Carlos' 1564 testament, two black slaves, Diego de San Pedro and Juan Carlos, doubtless the slaves Catherine sent, were granted their freedom after his death. In 1571 Philip II reconfirmed their manumission. In 1568, however, it is recorded Jacopo da Trezzo received 3,080 *reales* for feeding and clothing these slaves, when they worked and lived in his atelier in 1564 and in 1565, indicating that they were apprenticed there before their manumission. See *Colección de documentos ineditos para la historia de España*, 24 (1854), pp. 515–50; Jean Babelon, *Jacopo da Trezzo et la construction de l'Escurial. Essai sur les arts à la cour de Philippe II* (Paris, 1922), p. 36. For Carlos' household accounts of 1564 and 1568 see AGS, Contaduría Mayor de Cuentas (CMC), 1ª época, leg. 1031 and CMC, 1ª época, leg. 1070.

[96] IAN/TT, NA 792, fol. 147: '300 reais que no ditto dia despemdeo para vestir hua escrava que ha dita Senhora [Catherine] mandou a sua Irmãa.'

[97] IAN/TT, Cartas Missivas, maço 3, doc. 13, fol. 4, 6 April 15?? (illegible date). Also cited in Saunders, *A Social History*, p. 67, n. 17. In 1543 João III donated 4 slaves (2 men and 2 women) to the monastery of Nossa Senhora da Assunção in Faro, which was patronized by Catherine of Austria. See IAN/TT, NA 792, fol. 195 (26 Oct. 1543) for the clothes Catherine purchased for these same slaves.

[98] Annemarie Jordan Gschwend, 'In the tradition of princely collections: curiosities and exotica in the Kunstkammer of Catherine of Austria', *Bulletin of the Society for Renaissance Studies*, 13 (October 1995), pp. 1–9; Almudena Pérez de Tudela and Annemarie Jordan Gschwend, 'Luxury goods for royal collectors: exotica, princely gifts and rare animals exchanged between the Iberian courts and Central Europe in the Renaissance (1560–1612)', in *Exotica. Portugals Entdeckungen im Spiegel fürstlicher Kunst- und Wunderkammern der Renaissance. Die Beiträge des am 19. und 20. Mai 2000 vom Kunsthistorischen Museum Wien veranstalteten Symposiums*, ed. Helmut Trnek and Sabine Haag. *Jahrbuch des Kunsthistorischen Museums Wien*, 3 (Mainz, 2001), pp. 1–127; and Annemarie Jordan Gschwend and Almudena Pérez de Tudela, 'Exotica Habsburgica. La casa de Austria y las colecciones exóticas en el Renacimiento temprano', in *Oriente en palacio. Tesoros asiáticos en las colecciones reales españolas* (Madrid, 2003), pp. 27–44.

better reinforced than in the court portrait of Catherine's daughter-in-law, Juana of Austria (1535–73), painted in Lisbon in 1553 by Cristóvão de Morais (fig. 45).[99] This work was the queen's personal commission, with all the visual components carefully assembled to reflect her majesty and that of her court.

From the extant documentation it is possible to piece together a great deal of information and so reach several conclusions. The small page to the left of the princess, is, in reality, a female child, her gender specified in Juana's 1574 inventory, where this portrait is carefully recorded.[100] Another document confirms that the girl was a wedding gift from her husband, Prince João, shortly after her arrival at the Lisbon court,[101] while other documents identify the various pieces of jewelry the princess wears as presents Catherine and João III gave her in December 1552.[102] An unpublished inventory of Juana's dowry, drawn up two months later in Lisbon, on 23 February 1553, helps to pinpoint the painting's date of execution: the portrait was painted between 31 December 1552 and 23 June 1553, before Juana's eighteenth birthday.[103] If

[99] Annemarie Jordan, *Retrato de Corte em Portugal. O Legado de Antonio Moro (1552–1572)* (Lisbon, 1994), pp. 105–15, fig. 5. Morais trained not only in Portugal, but also in Flanders, and is documented to have spoken fluent Flemish. See Joaquim Oliveira Caetano, 'O Que Janus Via. Rumos e Cenários da Pintura Portuguesa (1535–1570)', M.A. thesis, Universidade Nova, Lisbon, 1996, pp. 44–5.

[100] Cristóbal Peréz Pastor, 'Inventarios de los bienes que quedaron por fin y muerte de Doña Juana, Princesa de Portugal, Infanta de Castilla, 1573', *Memorias de la Real Academia Española*, 9 (1914), p. 362, no. 40: 'Un medio retrato de la dicha Serenísima Princesa, Nuestra Señora, de pincel, en lienzo, en un marco de madera sin molduras, con la mano en la cabeza de una negrilla'. For more on this portrait and others of Juana of Austria, see Annemarie Jordan, 'Los retratos de Juana de Austria posteriores a 1554: la imagen de una princesa de Portugal, une regente de España y una jesuita', *Reales sitios*, 151 (2002), pp. 42–65.

[101] IAN/TT, Cartas Missivas, maço 3, doc. 16: 'querja fazer merçe a Sua mulher da escrava que lhe pede'.

[102] An unpublished letter written on 30 December 1552 by Luis de Sarmiento, the Castilian ambassador in Portugal, confirms these gifts. See AGS, Estado (Portugal) leg. 375, fol. 86: 'el serenissimo rrei le dio um muy hermoso joyel de un rrubi muy grande y un diamante colgado del una perla muy gruesa y la serenissima rreina le dio una cruz de diamantes y una sarta muy gruesa de perlas'.

[103] Juana's inventory does not cite these jewels since they were not items brought with her from Spain. The inscription: AETATIS. SVE. 17. confirms that the portrait was executed before June 1553. Lorne Campbell, *Renaissance Portraits: European Portrait-Painting in the 14th, 15th and 16th Centuries* (New Haven, 1990), p. 135, fig. 159, posits another date of execution (between 1552 and 1553), assuming Juana was born in 1537. He attributes the portrait to a follower of Anthonis Mor, negating the Morais attribution, but does not propose a possible painter. Mor had left the Lisbon court before Juana's arrival, where this portrait, without question, was painted. See Campbell's controversial commentary and unsubstantiated views regarding this and other conclusions published in 1994, in his review in *Journal of the History of Collections*, 8, 2 (1996), pp. 223–4.

FIG. 45. Cristóvão de Morais, *Portrait of Juana de Austria with her Black Slave Girl*, 1553 (oil on canvas, 99 × 81 cm, Brussels, Musées Royaux des Beaux Arts de Belgique, inv. no. 1296).

painted after April 1553, Juana may already have been pregnant with her son, Sebastião, the future king of Portugal.

The colour symbolism of black contrasted with white is quite explicit. Black was the favorite colour worn at the Iberian courts, and Renaissance royalty married in black. Juana wore a black velvet and satin dress for her 1552 entry into Lisbon, probably the same costume as shown in the Morais paint-ing.[104] Black, the colour of elegance and splendour, coupled with the black slave, serves to heighten the pale skin and beauty of the princess.[105] Slaves in Renaissance portraits were added as visual foils to help emphasize the princely, aristocratic rank of the sitter; this notion is reinforced by Juana's emphatic ges-ture of placing her hand on the child's head. This is the first time a black slave is shown juxtaposed with a royal sitter in a Portuguese court portrait.[106]

Other visual elements underscore the imaging of empire. Juana holds in her left hand an Oriental folding fan, one imported from the Ryukyu islands in the Japanese archipelago, which became an exotic dress accessory adopted at the Lisbon court long before it was in vogue at other European courts.[107] A particular fan made of painted paper with lacquered guard ends, a type supposedly first brought to Portugal in late 1552 by the first Japanese convert, represents Asia, the eastern half of the Portuguese empire, while the black slave girl, as Africa, represents the western half.

This portrait was expressly commissioned to commemorate the dynastic union of the Avis and Habsburg royal houses, raised to a more symbolic level with the imminent birth of Juana's child as heir to these respective empires. The column in the background alludes to the twin columns of Hercules in

---

[104] Jordan, *Retrato de Corte*, p. 112 n. 38. The princess donated this costume to the Madre de Deus convent in Lisbon before she returned to Spain in May 1554.

[105] Pierre de Bourdeille suggested that an excellent painter should execute the portrait of a beautiful lady by placing next to her an old hag, a black slave or a hideous dwarf so that their ugliness or blackness could give greater lustre and brilliance to the lady's great fairness and beauty: Campbell, *Renaissance Portraits*, p. 134.

[106] For other images of black Africans in Portuguese art consult Paul H. D. Kaplan, 'Titian's *Laura Dianti* and the origins of the motif of the black page in portraiture', *Antichità viva*, 21: 1 (1982), pp. 11–18, and 21: 4 (1982), pp. 10–18; Paul H. D. Kaplan, 'Sicily, Venice and the East: Titian's *Fabricius Salvaresius with a black page*', in *Europa und die Kunst des Islam: 15. bis 18.Jahrhundert* (Akten des 25. internationalen Kongresses für Kunstgeschichte, 5) (Vienna, 1985), pp. 127–36; and Jean Morisse and Michel Mollat, *L'Image du Noir dans l'Art Occidental*, vol. II: *Des premiers siècles chrétiens aux "Grandes Decouvertes"* Part 2: *Les Africans dans l'ordonnance chrétienne du monde (XIVe–XVIe siècle)* (Fribourg, 1979), pp. 192–6.

[107] Annemarie Jordan, 'Exotic Renaissance accessories: Japanese, Indian and Sinhalese fans at the courts of Portugal and Spain', *Apollo*, 150, 453 (Nov. 1999), pp. 25–35, and Annemarie Jordan Gschwend, 'Los primeros abanicos orientales de los Habsburgos', in *Oriente en palacio. Tesoros asiáticos en las colecciones reales españolas* (Madrid, 2003), pp. 267–71.

the device of Juana's father, Emperor Charles V: 'Non Plus Ultra', his empire extending beyond the pillars of Hercules, the known boundaries of the ancient world. Catherine of Austria, aware of the different ideologies of empire shared by the Iberian courts, closely supervised this commission, dictating the manner in which Juana, as the future queen of Portugal, should be represented. This portrait was intended as a pendant to one of Prince João, painted by Anthonis Mor at the Almeirim palace the year before.[108]

Catherine of Austria was conscious of her extraordinary situation. By means of the precious cargoes brought to Lisbon, she was brought into close contact with distant worlds and peoples separated from her by geographical distance. Her frequent gifts of slaves and other exclusive exotica to her family, ladies and favourites were intended as demonstrations of the opulence, exoticism and splendour of her cosmopolitan court. Catherine enjoyed a position that few female consorts shared at this time. In terms of royal imaging, the queen took full advantage in promoting herself, her family and court through her slaves and her collecting, both of which represented external symbols of her power and rule, and reaffirmed her social status and position as Queen of Portugal.

Appendix

IAN/TT, Corpo Chronológico 1, maço 83, doc. 12 (1549)

Letter from the abbess of the convent of Viana do Alentejo to Catherine of Austria, concerning a small slave girl sent there by the queen, in 1549, to be educated in religion and sewing, for which the abbess solicited a generous grant of money.

pello procurador desta casa per que os dyas pasados escrevy a V. A. e llevou ho pemteador que a sua escravynha fez/soube que mandava V. A. que lha llevasem e fose em companhya da mulher de dyogo llopez/he por aese tempo a escravynha estar doemte/não me atrevy mandalla nem bollyr com ella/aguora em comp“rymento do mandado de V. A. amando/per personas que ha ham de llevar com tamto Resguoardo e acatamento como cousa de V. A./escreveo a ysabell da myzquyta que lha vaa apresemtar e alleve per sua persona/V. A. nos perdoe por amor de Jhu xpo os defallecymentos que achar em seu ymsyno/por que como Rellygyosas symprez emceRadas nestas paredes não sabemos ymsynar se não a quyllo que usamos/e no llavrar e quoser/suas forças e despusyçam não puderão cheguar a mais/por ser muito doemtya e fraqua/llavra e quose de vaguar maas faz tudo muito bem feyto/e com muito

[108] Jordan, *Retrato de Corte*, pp. 53–62, fig. 4.

llympeza como V. A. llaa podera ver/nosos desejos foram sempre e sam muuy gramdes para nysto e em tudo servyr a V. A./maas as forças sam muuy pouquas e de pobres Rellygyosas/e en como pastora dellas e que suas neçesydades e mynguoas temporais me quaRegam e dam muita descomsollaçam/peço a V. A. por amor de noso Señor se llembre desta casa e de nosa gramde pobreza a quoall per esa escravynha podera saber como de que estava amtre nos e vyo ho que umanamento padeçemos e como a quella que em sy he e tam zellosa do acreçentamento muito e emparo da Rellygyam/nos faça allguma merce para ajuda do sostemtarmos esta em que estam emparadas oytemta Rellygyosas fydallgas e desemparadas que com muita vertude e pacyencya sofrem os mais dos dyas comerem hua Raçam de pão e hun pouquo de calldo sem azeyte/e todas muuy contynua muito pedymos e pedyremos ao Señor deus por muito acreçememtamento da vyda saude e Reall estado de V. A. e dell Rey noso señor e prynçepe seu filho como esta portador sabera dyzer e com tamto fervor esta llembrança temos per a real estado de vosa alteza.

   da abbadessa de vyana

CHAPTER EIGHT

Christoph Jamnitzer's 'Moor's Head': a late Renaissance drinking vessel

LORENZ SEELIG

In 1996 a little-known work of art came to light unexpectedly: the 'Moor's Head' by the Nuremberg goldsmith Christoph Jamnitzer (figs. 46–8).[1] This splendid object, which since at least 1811 had been in the private collection of the Kings of Saxony – first in Lichtenburg castle near Torgau and later in Moritzburg castle near Dresden – was buried in the forest of Moritzburg in the spring of 1945 when the Red Army was approaching the city. It was only in 1996 that the 'Moor's Head' was discovered and dug up by two young treasure-hunters.[2] In December 1999 it was sold at Sotheby's in London[3] and in the following year acquired by the Bayerisches Nationalmuseum in Munich.[4]

The 'Moor's Head', 52 cm (*c*. 20 inches) high, embossed in partially gilt silver, is supported by a large foot with pointed lobes and etched ornaments in 'mauresque' (Moorish) style. The head itself nearly seems to balance on a hexagonal stem framed by filigree-like scroll-brackets. The obliquely cut neck is embossed on its underside with an armorial device: a bird of prey with wings spread, charged across his breast with a fess holding three crescent moons.

[1] A. Pabst, 'Weitere Werke des Christoph Jamnitzer', *Kunstgewerbeblatt*, 1 (1885), pp. 129–30, ill.; M. Rosenberg, *Jamnitzer. Alle erhaltenen Goldschmiedearbeiten. Verlorene Werke. Handzeichnungen* (Frankfurt am Main, 1920), no. 65, plate 65; E. Kris and O. v. Falke, 'Beiträge zu den Werken Christoph und Hans Jamnitzers', *Jahrbuch der Preußischen Kunstsammlungen*, 47 (1926), p. 189, n. 4, p. 192, fig. 8; O. v. Falke, 'Aus dem Jamnitzerkreis', *Pantheon*, 19 (1937), p. 13, fig. 3; I. O'Dell-Franke, 'Zu Zeichnungen von Christoph Jamnitzer', *Niederdeutsche Beiträge zur Kunstgeschichte*, 22 (1983), p. 96; see the exhibition catalogue *Der Mohrenkopfpokal von Christoph Jamnitzer*, ed. R. Eikelmann, Munich, Bayerisches Nationalmuseum (Munich, 2002); especially L. Seelig, '"Ein Willkomme in der Form eines Mohrenkopfes von Silber getriebener Arbeit". Der wiederentdeckte Mohrenkopfpokal Christoph Jamnitzers aus dem späten 16. Jahrhundert', *ibid.*, pp. 19–123 (the catalogue was published after the manuscript of this contribution had been completed).

[2] *Der Schatz der Wettiner. Die Moritzburger Funde. Dokumente. Fundbericht. Katalog, Dresden, Residenzschloß* (Leipzig, 1997), exhibition catalogue, pp. 39–41, no. 4, ill.

[3] Sale catalogue, *The Moritzburg Treasure*, Sotheby's, London, 17 December 1999, lot 24.

[4] *Bayerisches Nationalmuseum. Handbuch der kunst- und kulturgeschichtlichen Sammlungen*, ed. R. Eikelmann (Munich, 2000), pp. 156–7, ill.

FIG. 46. Christoph Jamnitzer, *Moor's Head*, Nuremberg, *c.* 1600 (silver, rock crystal, Munich, Bayerisches Nationalmuseum).

The graceful head, growing out of the elongated neck, shows the features of a young African with full lips, a short broad nose and tightly curled hair. The intense gaze of the large eyes and the slightly open lips make the youthful face highly expressive. The subtle modelling, especially of the cheeks and the lips, is remarkable. The Moor wears a head-band chased with eight letter Ts. The head is crowned by a high volute and a plumed head-dress set with rock crystals foiled in green, red and blue. A large drop ear-ring made of shell hangs on the right ear; that on the left ear is lost. The 'Moor's Head' is also a

F I G. 47. Christoph Jamnitzer, *Moor's Head*, Nuremberg, *c.* 1600 (silver, rock crystal. Munich, Bayerisches Nationalmuseum).

drinking vessel: the upper part of the head can be taken off, like a cover (with the head-dress as handle). By that means, it was possible to drink either from the cover or from the head itself (the most probable option).

After the 1996 excavation the 'Moor's Head' was cleaned and restored twice, once in London and once in Munich. Today, traces of a black opaque paint, perhaps from the nineteenth century, are still to be seen. Originally, there was probably a translucent black lacquer combined with red on the lips and white on the eyes. Thus the 'Moor's Head' was characterised by strong

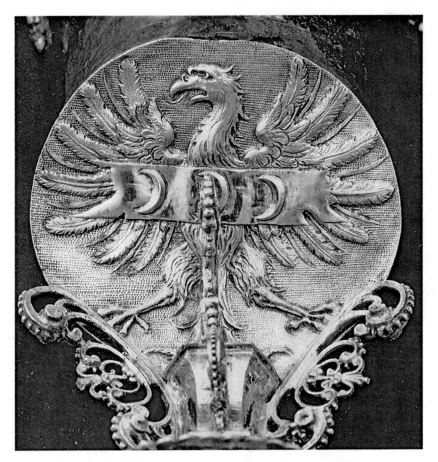

FIG. 48. Christoph Jamnitzer, *Moor's Head*, Nuremberg, *c.* 1600 (silver, rock crystal, Munich, Bayerisches Nationalmuseum).

colour effects enhanced by the gilt base and head-band, and the foiled rock crystals of the head-dress.

Jamnitzer's 'Moor's Head' is a heraldic work of art representing the armorial bearings of the Florentine patrician family, the Pucci, whose coat of arms is a Moor's head with a head-band charged with three Ts.[5] (These were interpreted in the seventeenth century as 'Tempore Tempora Tempera';[6] originally

[5] P. Litta, *Famiglie celebri italiane*, series I, 7 vols., series II, 2 vols. (Milan, 1819–83), 1st series, v, s. v. Pucci di Firenze, plate I; J. B. Rietstap, *Armorial général*, 2 vols. (Gouda, 1884–7), II, p. 496; G. B. di Crollalanza, *Dizionario storico-blasonico delle famiglie nobili e notabili italiane estinte e fiorenti*, 3 vols. (Pisa, 1886–1890), II, p. 303.

[6] F. Baldinucci, *Notizie dei professori del disegno da Cimabue in qua*, ed. F. Ranalli, 5 vols. (Florence, 1845–7), III, p. 293 (life of Giovanni Caccini); cf. J. Dielitz, *Die Wahl- und Denksprüche, Feldgeschreie, Losungen, Schlacht- und Volksrufe* (Frankfurt am Main, 1887), p. 323.

there were three hammers [*martelli*], because the Pucci originated from the carpenters' guild.) The coat of arms of the Pucci is often found in Florence and Tuscany, for instance at the Palazzo Pretorio in Poppi[7] where members of the Pucci family, especially in the seventeenth century, often held the position of *vicario*, representing the grand duke.[8] Their coat of arms can also be seen in important works of art which belonged to them, for instance in the paintings representing the story of Nastagio degli Onesti by Sandro Botticelli and his workshop from 1482–3, today in the Prado in Madrid and in a private collection,[9] or on the maiolica service made for a member of the Pucci family *c.* 1532–3 in Urbino.[10] Certainly the most striking example that can be compared with Jamnitzer's 'Moor's Head' is the figure of a Moor bearing the coat of arms of the Pucci painted by Giovanni Mannozzi, known as Giovanni da San Giovanni, in the first third of the seventeenth century for the Palazzo Pucci in Florence, and today in the Uffizi (fig. 49).[11] The fresco shows 'una figura d'un moro sedente' ('a figure of a seated moor'),[12] wearing a head-band distinctly decorated with T motifs; furthermore, the Moor is accompanied with the motto of the Pucci: 'candida praecordia', 'white at heart'.[13]

The relief on the underside of the neck of Jamnitzer's 'Moor's Head' (fig. 48) also bears a coat of arms, probably that of the Florentine patrician family, the Strozzi. Their coat of arms is a fess with three crescent moons.[14] But how should the bird of prey be interpreted? In my opinion it is not an eagle

[7] J. Devisse and M. Mollat, *L'Image du noir dans l'art occidental*, II, *Des premiers siècles chrétiens aux 'Grandes Découvertes'*, part 2, *Les Africains dans l'ordonnance chrétienne du monde (XIVe–XVIe siècle)* (Fribourg, 1979), p. 210, fig. 218.

[8] F. Pagnini, *Il castello medievale dei Conti Guidi oggi Palazzo Pretorio di Poppi* (Arezzo, 1896), p. 90ff. (list of vicars); G. Cappelletto, *Storia di famiglie. Matrimonio, biografie famigliari e identità locale in una comunità dell'Italia centrale: Poppi dal XVIII al XIX secolo* (Venice, 1996), pp. 30–1.

[9] R. Lightbown, *Sandro Botticelli*, 2 vols. (London, 1978), I: pp. 21, 69–70, ills. 28A–C, II: pp. 47–51, nos. B35–38; D. Thiébaut, *Botticelli* (Cologne, 1992), pp. 78–9, ills. 1–4.

[10] J. Triolo, 'Il servizio Pucci (1532–1533), di Francesco Xanto Avelli. Un catalogo', *Faenza*, 74 (1988), pp. 32–44, 228–84; J. Rasmussen, *The Robert Lehman Collection*, X, *Italian Majolica* (New York/Princeton, 1989), pp. 132–40, nos. 77–80; J. Triolo, 'L'Urbs e l'Imperatore: a proposal for the interpretation of the Pucci Service by Xanto Avelli', *Italian Renaissance Pottery: Papers Written in Association with a Colloquium at the British Museum*, ed. T. Wilson (London, 1991), pp. 36–45; J. E. Poole, *Italian Maiolica and Incised Slipware in the Fitzwilliam Museum* (Cambridge, 1995), pp. 338–42, nos. 391–2; *Le Dressoir du Prince. Services d'apparat à la Renaissance, Château d'Écouen, Musée de la Renaissance* (Paris, 1995), exhibition catalogue, pp. 42–5, nos. 9–13.

[11] A. Banti, *Giovanni da San Giovanni, pittore della contraddizione* (Florence, 1977), pp. 39, 73, no. 55, fig. 99. I am very grateful to Elizabeth McGrath for having drawn my attention to this fresco.

[12] Baldinucci, *Notizie*, III, p. 293.   [13] Dielitz, *Die Wahl- und Denksprüche*, p. 38.

[14] Siebmacher's *Großes Wappenbuch*, reprint, 35 vols. (Neustadt an der Aisch, 1972–86), V, *Die Wappen der europäischen Fürsten*, p. 254, plate 361; Rietstap, *Armorial général*, II, p. 858; Crollalanza, *Dizionario*, II, pp. 567–8.

FIG. 49. *Young Moor representing the Pucci Coat of Arms*, Giovanni da San Giovanni, called Mannozzi, Florence, first half of the seventeenth century (fresco, Florence, Galleria degli Uffizi).

FIG. 50. Niccolò Fiorentino or workshop, *Portrait Medal of Filippo Strozzi* (reverse and obverse), Florence, *c.* 1489 (bronze, Berlin, Staatliche Museen zu Berlin Preußischer Kulturbesitz, Münzkabinett).

but a falcon, which in heraldry is not usually distinguished from the eagle. From the fifteenth century onwards the falcon, one of the favourite devices of the Strozzi, was added to their coat of arms. The combination of the two motifs, the falcon and the three crescent moons, is particularly obvious in the portrait medal of Filippo Strozzi,[15] produced in the style of Niccolò Fiorentino (fig. 50). It was probably made *c.* 1489 on the occasion of the laying of the foundation stone of Palazzo Strozzi in Florence. The reverse of the medal features a moulting falcon above an escutcheon with the three crescent moons. The tradition continued in a remarkable way, for a century later, in 1593, the motif of the falcon – but without the crescent moons – was taken up in a portrait medal of Alessandro Strozzi (fig. 51),[16] and combined with the motto: EXPETO (that is: 'expecto', I expect, I wait for). A few years later the embossed relief of Jamnitzer's 'Moor's Head' combined the falcon

[15] G. Pampaloni, *Palazzo Strozzi* (Rome, 1963), p. 9, plate XLV, a–b; H. Nickel, 'Two falcon devices of the Strozzi: an attempt at interpretation', *Metropolitan Museum Journal*, 9 (1974), p. 231; *The Currency of Fame: Portrait Medals of the Renaissance*, ed. S. K. Scher, New York, Frick Collection (London/New York, 1994), exhibition catalogue, pp. 134–5, no. 44, ill. (G. Pollard); W. Koeppe, 'French and Italian Renaissance furniture at The Metropolitan Museum of Art. Notes on a survey', *Apollo*, 138, no. 388 (new series) (June 1994), pp. 28–9, fig. 10. For a thorough discussion of the heraldic motifs of the Strozzi especially in the fifteenth century, cf. J. Russell Sale, *Filippino Lippi's Strozzi Chapel in Santa Maria Novella*, Ph.D. dissertation, University of Pennsylvania, 1976 (New York/London 1979), pp. 83–99.

[16] L. Börner, *Bestandskataloge des Münzkabinetts Berlin. Die italienischen Medaillen der Renaissance und des Barock (1450–1750)* (Berlin, 1997), p. 168, no. 730; G. Toderi and F. Vannel, *Le medaglie italiane del XVI secolo*, 3 vols. (Florence, 2000), II, p. 565, no. 1718, III, fig. 1718.

FIG. 51. *Portrait Medal of Alessandro Strozzi* (obverse and reverse), Florence, 1593 (bronze, Berlin, Staatliche Museen zu Berlin Preußischer Kulturbesitz, Münzkabinett).

with the three crescent moons by placing them directly onto the breast of the bird (however not in a fess, but in a scroll).

What is the explanation for the combination of Strozzi and Pucci coats of arms in the 'Moor's Head'? Until now it had been assumed that this magnificent ceremonial cup and centre-piece was made on the occasion of the wedding of Filippo Strozzi and Maria Pucci in 1615,[17] as a sumptuous gift from the Strozzi to the Pucci. However, current research by a study group at the Germanisches Nationalmuseum in Nuremberg, which is preparing a systematic study of Nuremberg goldsmiths' work, shows that the Nuremberg hallmark on the 'Moor's Head' is not that of *c.* 1615 but that of the end of the sixteenth century[18] (it can be more precisely dated to between 1594 and 1602). The visual style of the 'Moor's Head' corresponds to this earlier date; the drinking vessel is closer to the earlier works of Christoph Jamnitzer than to the later ones, which are more advanced stylistically.

So the question arises again of the identities of both the patron and the recipient of the 'Moor's Head'. The meaning of the heraldic relief on the underside of the neck is not immediately clear, but it seems to allude to the customer or patron who puts his device in a less visible place on a work of art (comparable to signatures of artists on the neck section of medals or on the rear-side of busts). In my opinion, two stepbrothers may be patrons

---

[17] Pabst, 'Weitere Werke', pp. 129–30; *The Moritzburg Treasure*, p. 56.

[18] R. Schürer, 'Markenzeichen. Nürnberger Beschaumarken zur Zeit Christoph Jamnitzer', *Der Mohrenkopfpokal*, ed. R. Eikelmann, pp. 125–33.

of the 'Moor's Head': Alessandro Strozzi (whose portrait medal has already been mentioned) and his stepbrother Roberto, the most prominent members of the Strozzi family in Florence at the end of the sixteenth century. In 1592–3 they jointly began the construction of the Palazzo Nonfinito in the via del Proconsolo in Florence,[19] designed by Bernardo Buontalenti, with its rich decorative sculpture that particularly features Strozzi motifs.

How did the commission for the 'Moor's Head' cup reach Christoph Jamnitzer from Florence? The answer may be that there was a middleman residing in a German-speaking area. Roberto Strozzi corresponded regularly with a cousin, Cosimo Strozzi, who served around 1600 as commander of the city of Pest in Hungary and in the first decade of the seventeenth century as a military officer in Prague (after 1605 he became Venetian governor in Candia or Crete[20]). As Christoph Jamnitzer had close relations with the court of Emperor Rudolph II and travelled perhaps twice to Prague, it is possible that Cosimo Strozzi, who was in imperial service, conveyed the commission for the 'Moor's Head' from Florence to Christoph Jamnitzer – but this is only a hypothesis.

The question of the recipient of this considerable gift is also unresolved. Probably the 'Moor's Head' was a present to the Pucci family. Around 1600 the most prominent members of the family were two brothers, also named Alessandro and Roberto, both extremely wealthy and important patrons of the church of Santissima Annunziata, not far from Palazzo Pucci. Between 1599 and 1601 the brothers had constructed the monumental portico of Santissima Annunziata in Florence, which forms an impressive backdrop to Piazza Santissima Annunziata.[21] Roberto Pucci also financed the paving of the square where in 1608 the bronze equestrian monument of Grand-Duke Ferdinando I was erected.[22] The Latin dedication by the two Pucci brothers on the frieze of the portico is framed on both sides by the coat of arms of the Pucci family; the black Moor's head contrasts effectively with the white escutcheon. There are similar shields above the two lateral doors in the portico, and even the pavement is decorated with a Moor's head executed in marble intarsia. Thus, the coat of arms of the Pucci family is omnipresent here.

[19] I. Bigazzi, *Il Palazzo Nonfinito* (Bologna, 1977), passim.

[20] Litta, *Famiglie celebri*, 1st series, VI, s. v. Strozzi di Firenze, 1839, plate XII; Bigazzi, *Il Palazzo Nonfinito*, pp. 77–8, 134, note 353; F. Vannel and G. Toderi, *La medaglia barocca in Toscana* (Florence, 1987), p. 112, at no. 180.

[21] M. C. Fabbri, 'La sistemazione seicentesca dell'Oratorio di San Sebastiano nella Santissima Annunziata', *Rivista d'arte*, 44 (1992), pp. 71–152.

[22] Fabbri, 'La sistemazione', p. 84; D. Erben, 'Die Reiterdenkmäler der Medici in Florenz und ihre politische Bedeutung', *Mitteilungen des Kunsthistorischen Institutes in Florenz*, 40 (1996), p. 332.

After the death of his brother Alessandro in 1601, Roberto continued the work, in particular by redecorating the family chapel, the Oratorio di San Sebastiano, in Santissima Annunziata, between 1604 and 1608. The chapel, sumptuously adorned with polychrome marble, included the cenotaphs of three Pucci cardinals of the sixteenth century, and thereby became a monument to the fame of the Pucci dynasty. As Roberto Pucci was the last male member of the older branch of the Pucci family, he obviously intended to emphasise the importance of his ancestors as well as his own personal rank. After his death in 1612 the family trust of the Pucci, with its enormous fortune, devolved upon the younger branch.[23] For that reason it can be presumed that the 'Moor's Head' may have belonged to Alessandro and/or Roberto Pucci who both stressed the importance of the family and its coat of arms. (They had an additional link to the Strozzi brothers through their choice of the same sculptor, Giovanni Battista Caccini). However, in the inventories of silver belonging to the Pucci family from the eighteenth century onwards the 'Moor's Head' is not listed;[24] and even today in the Florentine Pucci family there exists no oral tradition that this exceptional work of art was kept in their palace.

The question of origin remains unresolved. But it is clear that Christoph Jamnitzer's 'Moor's Head' belongs to the category of heraldic drinking vessels, known in German-speaking areas since the late Middle Ages. Sixteenth-century examples are especially outstanding, above all in Nuremberg.[25] Particularly remarkable is a drinking vessel today in the Museum für Kunst und Gewerbe in Hamburg worked by the Nuremberg goldsmith Paulus Tullner c. 1564.[26] It is in the shape of a lion holding a pot (in Southern German *Hafen*) for oil (in German *Öl*) in its paws; consequently, the lion represents the coat of arms of the Nuremberg family Oelhafen. Further important examples have been preserved amongst the treasure of the Teutonic Order in Vienna. One instance is the so-called 'Bobenhausen'scher Willkomm', the Bobenhausen Welcome Cup[27] (also worked by Paulus Tullner c. 1572), in the shape of a

[23] Litta, *Famiglie celebri*, 1st series, v, s. v. Pucci di Firenze, plates vi–vii; R. Ciabani *et al.*, *Le famiglie di Firenze*, 3 vols. (Florence, 1982–92), iii, p. 184.

[24] Florence, Archivio privato della famiglia Pucci, Miscellanea, filza 18. I am especially grateful to Marchese Puccio Pucci and Marchese Giannozzo Pucci for permission to work in the archives and for generous help during my research.

[25] I. O'Dell-Franke and A. Szilágyi, 'Jost Amman und Hans Petzolt. Zeichnungsvorlagen für Goldschmiedewerke', *Jahrbuch der Kunsthistorischen Sammlungen in Wien*, 79 (1983), p. 103.

[26] *Wenzel Jamnitzer und die Nürnberger Goldschmiedekunst, 1500–1700*, Nuremberg, Germanisches Nationalmuseum (Munich, 1985), exhibition catalogue, pp. 236–7, no. 40, ill. (K. Pechstein).

[27] *Wenzel Jamnitzer*, p. 237, no. 41, ill. (B. Demel).

fox holding a goose in its mouth, which represents the coat of arms of the Grand Master of the Teutonic Order, Heinrich von Bobenhausen. However, apart from Christoph Jamnitzer's 'Moor's Head', there are no known heraldic drinking vessels in the shape of heads dating from the sixteenth century.

But other traditions of head-shaped drinking vessels exist – beyond the field of heraldry – which are much more complex. There is at least in German a close linguistic connection between heads and drinking vessels. In medieval German the word *Kopf* (head) also means drinking vessel, because of its round spherical form.[28] Without doubt, the double sense of the word *Kopf* goes back to the archaic period when it was the practice to drink from human skulls.[29] Astonishingly, in sacred rituals this custom was retained until the late eighteenth century. As early as the sixth century, there are testimonies to the practice of drinking from the skulls of saints.[30] This was a kind of pious remembrance of the sacred dead (in German *Minnetrinken*[31]), and in addition a manifestation of the hope that healing forces were transferred from the saint to the true believer. Particularly in Southern Germany there are several significant examples of this custom. For instance, in the former Benedictine Abbey of Ebersberg, at the feast of Saint Sebastian, wine was presented to the faithful in a silver mounted cup which was said to be the cranium of the saint;[32] the cup even has a silver foot, added in the seventeenth century, on which it can stand.[33] There is an even more striking example in the former Augustinian canons' church of Au am Inn where the relic of the head of Saint Vitalis is mounted with silver and precious stones (fig. 52).[34] The cranium of

---

[28] H. Kohlhaussen, 'Der Doppelmaserbecher auf der Veste Coburg und seine Verwandten', *Jahrbuch der Coburger Landesstiftung* (1959), pp. 109–10; I. Richter, *Das Kopfgefäß. Zur Typologie einer Gefäßform*, M.A. thesis, University of Cologne, 1967 (Cologne, 1967), pp. 84, 99, n. 161.

[29] R. Andree, 'Menschenschädel als Trinkgefäße', *Zeitschrift des Vereins für Volkskunde*, 22 (1912), pp. 1–33.

[30] Kohlhaussen, 'Der Doppelmaserbecher', p. 110.

[31] G. Schreiber, *Deutsche Weingeschichte. Der Wein in Volksleben, Kult und Wirtschaft* (Cologne, 1980) (Werken und Wohnen, Volkskundliche Untersuchungen im Rheinland, 13), pp. 375–87; R. W. Sänger, *Die Greifenklaue der Domherren zu Speyer aus der Kunstkammer der Markgrafen von Baden* (Berlin/Karlsruhe, 2001) (Patrimonia, 206), pp. 16–18.

[32] Andree, 'Menschenschädel', pp. 1–10, fig. 1, 3; R. Rückert, 'Zur Form der byzantinischen Reliquiare', *Münchner Jahrbuch der bildenden Kunst*, 3rd series, 8 (1957), p. 29; E. Krausen, 'Die Pflege religiös-volksfrommen Brauchtums bei Benediktinern und Zisterziensern in Süddeutschland und Österreich', *Studien und Mitteilungen zur Geschichte des Benediktiner-Ordens und seiner Zweige*, 83 (1972), pp. 276, 288–9; Schreiber, *Deutsche Weingeschichte*, pp. 316–7, 382.

[33] Rückert, 'Zur Form', p. 29, fig. 15.

[34] *Die Kunstdenkmale des Königreiches Bayern, 1, Oberbayern*, part 2 (Munich, 1902), pp. 1907, 1933–1934, fig. on p. 1933; Rückert, 'Zur Form', p. 29; Krausen, 'Die Pflege', p. 277.

FIG. 52. *Head Relic of Saint Vitalis*, 1517 (bone with silver mounts, Au am Inn, parish church).

the head is sawn off so that it forms a bowl that could be used for drinking sacred wine in remembrance of the saint. In form and function this example is a remarkable parallel to Jamnitzer's 'Moor's Head'.

Outside the ecclesiastical sphere, these vessels obviously are regarded in a negative light. For instance, in the extensive literature of the sixteenth century criticising the excessive consumption of alcohol, mention is made of a number of curious, profane drinking vessels that are considered signs of moral decadence.[35] These Renaissance treatises single out cups in the shape of fools' heads,[36] and several such drinking vessels still exist today.[37] The most remarkable specimen is the fool's head cup belonging to the Gesellschaft zum Distelzwang in Bern in Switzerland (on loan to the Bernisches Historisches Museum) worked by a goldsmith from Überlingen on Lake Constance c. 1570.[38] This item is a tumbler in the literal sense: if the bowl is filled with wine it has to be fully drained before being placed back on its steady supporting base. Inevitably, this results in an increased consumption of alcohol. In this special case, the silver cover with the fool's face becomes a kind of mirror in which the drinker recognises himself. It seems, then, that in Renaissance Europe there was a certain reluctance to drink from vessels in the shape of human heads, and the practice was restricted to cups representing human beings who did not correspond to contemporary norms, for instance fools or even Moors.

In the sixteenth century antiquarians and collectors knew about ancient vessels in the shape of heads, especially made of bronze. There is, for example, an Etruscan wine jug in the form of a young man's head, from the third quarter of the fourth century, today in the Staatliche Antikensammlungen in Munich,

[35] A. von Saldern, *German Enameled Glass. The Edwin J. Beinecke Collection and Related Pieces* (New York, 1965), pp. 27–8; K. Pechstein, 'Von Trinkgeräten und Trinksitten. Von der Kindstaufe zum Kaufvertrag: Pokale als Protokolle des Ereignisses', *Das Schatzhaus der deutschen Geschichte. Das Germanische Nationalmuseum*, ed. R. Poertner (Düsseldorf/Vienna, 1982), pp. 402–4; D. Heikamp, *Studien zur mediceischen Glaskunst. Archivalien, Entwurfszeichnungen, Gläser und Scherben* (Florence, 1986) (Mitteilungen des Kunsthistorischen Institutes in Florenz, 30, nos. 1–2), pp. 25–9; L. Seelig, 'Kunst und Kultur des Trinkens. Ein Kemptener Silberbecher der Renaissance als Spiegelbild bürgerlicher Tafelsitten', *Allgäuer Geschichtsfreund*, 98 (1998), p. 22.

[36] See especially J. Mat(t)hesius, *Sarepta oder Bergpostill sampt der Jochimßthalischen kurtzen Chronicken* (ed. Nuremberg, 1564), p. CCLXXIII; E. Kris, *Goldschmiedearbeiten des Mittelalters, der Renaissance und des Barock*, part 1: *Arbeiten in Gold und Silber* (Vienna, 1932) (Publikationen aus den Kunsthistorischen Sammlungen in Wien, v), p. 31.

[37] R. Fritz, *Die Gefäße aus Kokosnuß in Mitteleuropa, 1250–1800* (Mainz, 1983), pp. 58, 101–2, nos. 78–80, plates 41, 42a–b.

[38] R. L. Wyss, *Handwerkskunst in Gold und Silber. Das Silbergeschirr der bernischen Zünfte, Gesellschaften und burgerlichen [sic] Vereinigungen* (Bern, 1996), pp. 55–6, no. 1, fig. on p. 55.

FIG. 53. Workshop of Andrea Riccio, oil lamp, Padua, *c.* 1500 (bronze, Munich, Bayerisches Nationalmuseum).

which is said to come from the *Kunstkammer* (art cabinet) of Duke Albrecht V of Bavaria established in the 1560s.[39] Ceramic examples are much more frequently preserved, though these seem not to have been known in sixteenth-century Europe.[40] There are numerous specimens from Greek and Etruscan workshops – drinking vessels as cups and pouring vessels as jugs – featuring black Africans, especially Ethiopians.[41] The Africans, who were believed

[39] S. Haynes, *Etruscan Bronzes* (London, 1985), pp. 95, 300, at no. 149; *The Etruscans*, ed. M. Torelli, Venice, Palazzo Grassi (Milan, 2001), exhibition catalogue, p. 611, no. 227, ill. (F. W. Hamdorf).

[40] Richter, *Das Kopfgefäß*, passim.

[41] Richter, *Das Kopfgefäß*, pp. 38–9, 41–2, 45; F. M. Snowden, Jr, *Blacks in Antiquity: Ethiopians in the Graeco-Roman Experience* (Cambridge MA, 1970), especially pp. 24, 27; J. Vercoutter, J. Leclant, F. M. Snowden and J. Desanges, *L'Image du noir dans l'art occidental*, I: *Des Pharaons à la chute de l'Empire romain* (Fribourg, 1976), figs. 153–4, 159–60, 178–80, 193, 199, 208–11, 216–7; for examples in Karlsruhe and Munich see 'Badisches Landesmuseum. Neuerwerbungen 1973', *Jahrbuch der Staatlichen Kunstsammlungen in Baden-Württemberg*, 11 (1974), pp. 184–8, figs. 5–6;

to live in countries of permanent sunshine, represented the pleasures of a blissful life. However, as part of a vessel, they adopted a functional character, in correspondence with their social rank as slaves in ancient society.

Antiquity can be seen to play an important part once again if Jamnitzer's 'Moor's Head' is compared to other sculptural representations of black Africans.[42] The earliest Renaissance objects to be discussed here are also utensils: bronze lamps made in Northern Italy, especially in Padua about 1500, based with more or less variety on Roman models (fig. 53). These lamps take the form of black African[43] (or often satyr[44]) heads with an open mouth and a protruding tongue to hold the wick. As in antique prototypes, the Africans are represented as servants and in a particularly disfiguring and distorted manner.

Probably the earliest sculptural representation of a black African outside a functional context, and not portrayed as a prisoner or a slave (fig. 54),[45] is the bronze statuette of the so-called black Venus, created *c.* 1580, perhaps in the Netherlands after a North Italian model (fig. 55).[46] In accordance with tendencies in mannerist poetry – represented, for instance, in a sonnet by Giambattista Marino[47] – the black African woman is linked to the attribute of beauty, thus becoming a 'black Venus'. The erotic appeal of the unusually

Badisches Landesmuseum. Bildkatalog. 400 ausgewählte Werke aus den Schausammlungen (Karlsruhe, 1976), no. 71; 'Staatliche Antikensammlungen. Neuerwerbungen', *Münchner Jahrbuch der bildenden Kunst*, 3rd series, 46 (1995), pp. 195–6, figs. 10–11 (F. W. Hamdorf).

[42] Cf. the survey by M. Kopplin, '"Du bist schwarz, doch du bist schön". Zum Bildnis des Mohren in der Kunst des 16. bis 18. Jahrhunderts', *Kunst und Antiquitäten*, 6 (1987), pp. 36–45.

[43] K. Pechstein, *Bronzen und Plaketten vom ausgehenden 15. Jahrhundert bis zur Mitte des 17. Jahrhunderts* (Berlin, 1968) (Staatliche Museen Preußischer Kulturbesitz, Kataloge des Kunstgewerbemuseums Berlin, III), no. 76; *Die Beschwörung des Kosmos*, Duisburg, Wilhelm Lehmbruck-Museum (Duisburg, 1994), exhibition catalogue, pp. 219–20, nos. 94–5; this copy undoubtedly displays black African features.

[44] H. R. Weihrauch, *Die Bildwerke in Bronze und in anderen Metallen* (Munich, 1956) (Bayerisches Nationalmuseum München, Kataloge, XIII, 5), p. 67, no. 90, ill.

[45] See the bronze statuette of a seated black slave kept in chains, made in Northern Italy in the first half of the sixteenth century: L. Planiscig, *Die Bronzeplastiken. Statuetten, Reliefs, Geräte und Plaketten* (Vienna, 1924) (Kunsthistorisches Museum in Wien, Publikationen aus den Sammlungen für Plastik und Kunstgewerbe, 4), p. 13, no. 15, ill; L. Planiscig, 'Der "Zwerg auf der Schnecke" als Repräsentant einer bisher unbeachteten naturalistischen Richtung des venezianischen Cinquecento', *Jahrbuch der Kunsthistorischen Sammlungen in Wien*, new series 13 (1944), p. 249, fig. 220; *Genuß & Kunst. Kaffee, Tee, Schokolade, Tabak, Cola, Schloß Schallaburg* (Innsbruck, 1994), exhibition catalogue, p. 324, no. 19.1.3, ill.

[46] M. Bückling, *Die Negervenus* (Frankfurt am Main, 1991); *Von allen Seiten schön. Bronzen der Renaissance und des Barock*, ed. V. Krahn, Berlin, Staatliche Museen zu Berlin – Preußischer Kulturbesitz, Skulpturensammlung/Altes Museum (Heidelberg, 1995), exhibition catalogue, pp. 324–6, no. 98, pp. 108–13, nos. E 14–E 18.

[47] Bückling, *Die Negervenus*, pp. 53–5.

FIG. 54. *Black Prisoner*, Northern Italy, first half of the sixteenth century (bronze, Vienna, Kunsthistorisches Museum).

FIG. 55. *Black Venus*, Flanders or France, late sixteenth century (bronze, Vienna, Kunsthistorisches Museum).

FIG. 56. *Head of a Black African*, Flanders, second third of the seventeenth century (bronze, Brunswick, Herzog Anton Ulrich-Museum).

slim elongated body in elegant attitude contrasts with the peculiarly reserved, indifferent expression of the face of the woman who contemplates her features in a mirror (lost in the particularly fine copy in the Kunsthistorisches Museum in Vienna). When these bronze statuettes made their appearance, princely art cabinets also contained contemporary products of African cultures, especially ivory trumpets, salt-cellars and spoons, which, however, were kept separately from the bronzes of the beautiful Africans.[48]

[48] Cf. *Exotica. Portugals Entdeckungen im Spiegel fürstlicher Kunst- und Wunderkammern der Renaissance*, ed. W. Seipel, Vienna, Kunsthistorisches Museum (Milan/Vienna, 2000), exhibition catalogue, pp. 126–40, nos. 33–52.

In the second quarter of the seventeenth century, a new wave of representations of black Africans in sculpture inspired by the art of Rubens and van
Dyck appeared.[49] The most important example is the bronze head of a black
African in the Herzog Anton Ulrich-Museum in Brunswick (fig. 56),[50] the
work of a Flemish sculptor of the second third of the seventeenth century.
With remarkable sensitivity the artist succeeds in depicting the impressive
skull with its strongly bulging forehead, the full cheeks and the short curled
hair as well as the full lips and the broad nose. All these elements are integrated
in a remarkable overall sculptural scheme. It may be noted that the bronze in
Brunswick – probably the earliest individual representation of a black African
in Northern European sculpture – is not a bust but only a head with a short
strong neck.

About twenty years earlier, between 1615 and 1624, the Florentine sculptor
Pietro Tacca executed the famous 'Quattro Mori' surrounding the pedestal of
the monument of Grand-Duke Ferdinando I in Livorno.[51] In 1607 Tacca had
studied the Turkish and African pirates kept as galley slaves in the so-called
'bagno' in the town and had made wax models of them. One of the four huge
slaves on the pedestal of the monument has features that identify him as a
black African (fig. 57).[52] Unlike his companions, he is already resigned and
has accepted his fate, hanging his head with a sad expression. Pietro Tacca's
bronze of the young black African – together with the three other prisoners –
is one of the rare examples of late Renaissance and early Baroque sculpture
where a political programme can be perceived. The slaves on the monument of
Grand-Duke Ferdinando form a sharp contrast to the more generalising conceit
of the four prisoners – including an obviously black African slave (fig. 58) –
representing the four Ages of Life, which were placed on the pedestal of the
equestrian monument of Henri IV at the Pont-Neuf in Paris, begun by Pietro

[49] A wooden statuette of an African woman in the Bayerisches Nationalmuseum in Munich,
published as 'Flemish, about 1630–1640' (T. Müller, 'Original und Nachbildung', Pantheon, 20
[1962], pp. 208–12), is no longer considered an authentic work of the seventeenth century, as
Dr. Peter Volk kindly informed me.

[50] H. R. Weihrauch, 'Ein Bronzekopf aus dem Rubenskreis', Pantheon, 33 (1975), pp. 121–4;
U. Berger and V. Krahn, Bronzen der Renaissance und des Barock. Katalog der Sammlung. Herzog
Anton Ulrich-Museum Braunschweig (Brunswick, 1994), p. 184, no. 144, ill.

[51] H. Keutner, 'Über die Entstehung und die Formen des Standbildes im Cinquecento', Münchner
Jahrbuch der bildenden Kunst, 3rd series, 7 (1956), pp. 158–9, n. 71, fig. 19; J. Pope-Hennessy, Italian
High Renaissance and Baroque Sculpture, 3 vols. (London, 1963), text vol., p. 64, fig. 60, cat. vol.,
pp. 92–3, ill. vol., plate 96; K. Watson, Pietro Tacca: Successor to Giovanni Bologna (New
York/London, 1983), p. 210; M. Tommasi, Pietro Tacca, ed. M. Gregori (Pisa, 1995), pp. 53–62,
plates 12–28; Erben, 'Die Reiterdenkmäler', p. 332, fig. 29.

[52] Tommasi, Pietro Tacca, plates 12–15, 18, 21, 23, 28.

FIG. 57. Pietro Tacca, *Black African Slave* on the pedestal of the monument of Grand-Duke Ferdinando I of Tuscany, 1615–23/4 (bronze, Livorno, Piazza della Darsena).

FIG. 58. Pietro Francavilla and Francesco Bordoni, *Black African Slave*, Paris, *c.* 1614–18 (bronze, Paris, Musée du Louvre).

FIG. 59. Nicolas Cordier, *Head of a Black African*, Rome, *c.* 1610 (polychrome marble, Dresden, Staatliche Kunstsammlungen, Skulpturensammlung).

Francavilla shortly before 1614 and completed after his death by his son-in-law, Francesco Bordone, in 1618.[53] The monument of Ferdinando I in Livorno illustrates the victory of the Grand-Dukes of Tuscany over the North African pirates, who were a permanent threat to the navigation and commerce of the

[53] Cf. L. Seelig, *Studien zu Martin van den Bogart, gen. Desjardins (1637–1694)*, Ph.D. dissertation, Munich 1973 (Altendorf, 1980), pp. 53–5; J.-R. Gaborit, *Le Louvre. La sculpture européenne* (London/Paris, 1994), fig. p. 51; C. Avery, article 'Pietro Francavilla', *The Dictionary of Art*, 34 vols. (London, 1996), XI, pp. 502–3, with bibl.; G. Bresc-Bautier, I. Leroy-Jay Lemaistre and G. Scherf, *Musée du Louvre. Département des Sculptures du Moyen-Age, de la Renaissance et des Temps Modernes. Sculpture française, II, Renaissance et Temps Modernes*, 2 vols. (Paris, 1998), I, pp. 382–3, ill.

Mediterranean as well as to the coasts of Tuscany.[54] In 1562 Cosimo I had tried to intensify the fight against the pirates by founding the military Order of Santo Stefano with its special mission to support the Tuscan galley fleet. Roberto Pucci, patron of Santissima Annunziata, was a commander, a *balì*, of the Order of Santo Stefano. Thus officially he was a committed adversary of both North Africans and black Africans in the service of the pirates, even though in his coat of arms he had an attractive representation of a Moor.

Besides the sculptures in bronze, there are also outstanding marble sculptures, especially in polychrome material, which can be compared with Jamnitzer's 'Moor's Head'. Nicolas Cordier, a sculptor from Lorraine active in Rome from about 1593 to 1612, after restoring some ancient polychrome sculptures,[55] transferred their colour scheme to works of his own[56] – for instance to the bust of a young black African in Dresden (fig. 59).[57] The head itself is completely worked in black marble (*bigio morato*), and only the eyeballs are accentuated by white marble. Furthermore, there is a subtle differentiation of the surface: that of the skin is highly polished and shining, that of the voluminous coiffure is intentionally matt. In addition, the Dresden head is characterised by its immediate, spontaneous expression: the head is slightly turned to the left, the gaze is raised, the lips are slightly opened. In particular, the highly sculptural modelling of the flesh lends the decorative bust its lively appearance.

Equally remarkable is the portrait bust of the ambassador of the Kingdom of the Congo to the papacy, Antonio Emanuele Funta, known as Nigrita, sculpted by Francesco Caporale in Rome in 1608 (fig. 60), immediately after the death of the black African prince. The bust was only placed on his tomb in the baptistery of Santa Maria Maggiore in Rome in 1629.[58] It is the earliest known sculpted portrait of a black African historic personality in Europe,

---

[54] G. Guarnieri, *I Cavalieri di Santo Stefano nella storia della marina italiana (1562–1859)* (3rd edn, Pisa, 1960), passim; R. Burr Litchfield, *Emergence of a Bureaucracy: The Florentine Patricians, 1530–1790* (Princeton, 1986), pp. 29, 33–4, 37; Erben, 'Die Reiterdenkmäler', pp. 337–8.

[55] For antique polychrome sculpture see R. M. Schneider, *Bunte Barbaren: Orientalenstatuen aus farbigem Marmor in der römischen Repräsentationskunst* (Worms, 1986); R. M. Schneider, 'Coloured marble: the splendour and power of imperial Rome', *Apollo*, 154, new series, no. 473 (July 2001), pp. 3–10.

[56] S. Pressouyre, *Nicolas Cordier: Recherches sur la sculpture à Rome autour de 1600* (Rome, 1984) (Collection de l'École Française de Rome, 73), p. 413, no. 20, figs. 194–5; Schneider, *Bunte Barbaren*, pp. 215–7, nos. BK 12–6, plates 42–4.

[57] *Verborgene Schätze der Skulpturensammlung*, Dresden, Staatliche Kunstsammlungen (Dresden, 1992), exhibition catalogue, p. 48, no. 30, fig. on p. 20 (I. Raumschüssel).

[58] E. Bassani and W. B. Fagg, *Africa and the Renaissance: Art in Ivory* (Munich/New York, 1988), pp. 216, 218, fig. 295; A. Bacchi, *Scultura del '600 a Roma* (Milano, 1996), p. 782, fig. 271; for the

FIG. 60. Francesco Caporale, *Bust of Antonio Emanuele Funta, called Nigrita*, Rome, 1608 (polychrome marble, Rome, Santa Maria Maggiore).

executed in black marble directly from the death mask. The noble image of Nigrita is underscored by his voluminous 'all'antica' cloak while the attribute of the quiver refers to the African origin of the deceased ambassador.

These works by Nicolas Cordier and Francesco Caporale prove that the preference for polychrome sculptures culminated around 1600. This is equally true for precious works of art, especially cameos worked in agate or onyx and often mounted in gold and enamel settings. Frequently, brilliant cameo cutters chose the picturesque motif of black men and women who – cut in

commission of the bust cf. article 'Francesco Caporale', *Dizionario biografico degli Italiani*, 58 vols. so far (Rome, 1960–), XVIII, pp. 671–2.

FIG. 61. Miseroni workshop, *Cameo with Black Diana*, Milan, last quarter of the sixteenth century; Andreas Osenbruck, mounts, Prague, *c.* 1610 (jasper, gold, enamel, diamonds, Vienna, Kunsthistorisches Museum).

brown or black relief – make an effective contrast with the white background (fig. 61)[59] (significantly the mounting of a Renaissance cameo representing a

---

[59] See e.g. two cameos from the Milanese workshop of the Miseroni in the Kunsthistorisches Museum in Vienna: the cameo of the so-called black Venus mounted by Jan Vermeyen (*Prag um 1600*, Essen, Villa Hügel [Freren, 1988], exhibition catalogue, p. 474, no. 349, colour plate 76/3 [R. Distelberger]), and the cameo of a black Diana mounted by Andreas Osenbruck (*Prag um 1600*, II, Vienna, Kunsthistorisches Museum [Freren, 1988], exhibition catalogue, p. 239, no. 715, colour plate 28/2 [R. Distelberger]); for this group see also *Princely Magnificence: Court Jewels of*

Moor, preserved in the Cabinet des Médailles of the Bibliothèque Nationale in Paris, bears the inscription: 'E PER TAL VARIAR NATVRA E BELA'[60]: 'By reason of this variety nature is beautiful'). The opulence of the dress and the jewellery of the Moors shown in such cameos gives visual form to the traditional notion of a 'rich' Africa. The belief owes its existence to reports of the treasures of gold, silver and ivory to be found, especially on the coast of West Africa.[61] It is for this reason that pearl ear-rings, which form such a contrast to black skin and which appear in the cameos as well as in Jamnitzer's 'Moor's Head', are essential attributes of black Africans in European art.[62]

After this discussion of representations of black Africans in sculpture and jewellery, it is time to return to Christoph Jamnitzer's 'Moor's Head'. In comparison with the bronze sculpture in Brunswick, the Nuremberg goldsmith accentuates the general structure of the head. The skull, seen from the front, nearly forms an oval, an impression also conveyed by the very short curls of hair that have no proper volume. The dominance of the oval form is strengthened additionally by the head-band with its more or less abstract T-motifs. Details like the bow-like eyebrows – above the strongly spherical eyes – also pick up the oval shape of the skull. And even the ears are like a graphic ornament, in the shape of a C. At the same time, the sculptural rendering of the lips, for instance, is of astonishing sensitivity in its tender, smooth modelling.

On the whole, the silver-gilt head is conceived as an autonomous entity. Unlike the Brunswick bronze, with its irregularly formed neck, the neck of Jamnitzer's 'Moor's Head' has a nearly geometrical shape which is formed with razor-sharp precision and exact artistic calculation. Obviously the artist was anxious to accentuate the more or less abstract construction of the head and at

the Renaissance, London, Victoria and Albert Museum (London, 1980), exhibition catalogue, p. 70, no. 70 (A. Somers Cocks).

[60] E. Babelon, Catalogue des camées antiques et modernes de la Bibliothèque Nationale (Paris, 1897), no. 596; A. Somers Cocks and Charles Truman, The Thyssen-Bornemisza Collection. Renaissance Jewels, Gold Boxes and Objets de Vertu (London, 1984), pp. 68–9, no. 2.

[61] S. Poeschel, Studien zur Ikonographie der Erdteile in der Kunst des 16.–18. Jahrhunderts (Munich, 1985), pp. 181–2.

[62] For the motif of the ear-ring worn by black Africans cf. L. Schmidt, Der Männerohrring in Volksschmuck und Volksglaube mit besonderer Berücksichtigung Österreichs (Vienna, 1947), pp. 23–33 and P. H. D. Kaplan, 'The earliest images of Othello', Shakespeare Quarterly, 39, 2 (summer 1988), p. 182. Members of marginal social groups are often marked by ear-rings and ear-pearls; cf. Aufs Ohr geschaut. Ohrringe aus Stadt und Land vom Klassizismus bis zur neuen Jugendkultur, Berlin, Museum für Deutsche Volkskunde, Staatliche Museen Preußischer Kulturbesitz (Berlin, 1989), exhibition catalogue, pp. 11–12, 79–82 and the chapter by Kate Lowe in this volume.

the same time to stress the beautiful features of the face, giving them a calm and subdued aura, in contrast to the psychological understanding of the black slave portrayed by Pietro Tacca. However, when necessary, Christoph Jamnitzer could give his Moors spontaneous expressions and violent movements, as can be seen in the mahout of his Berlin fountain in the shape of an African elephant.[63]

Jamnitzer's 'Moor's Head' is given its unmistakable appearance by two characteristic elements: the head-band and the head-dress. The head-band tied at the neck – an important feature of numerous representations of Moors – is an ancient symbol of rule (similar to the diadem) which was adopted in the Middle Ages,[64] for instance on the head of Emperor Frederick I (Barbarossa) from about 1160 at Cappenberg in Westphalia.[65] In the course of the fourteenth century, at least in Germany, the king's head with the band was transformed into the image of the Moor with the head-band, especially in heraldry.[66] Often the head-band became a rather picturesque motif. Christoph Jamnitzer, however, gives to the especially broad and taut band the appearance of a diadem adorned with the linear T-letters (which may also allude to the traditional sign in the shape of a tau inscribed on the forehead of the blessed who – according to Ezekiel 9: 4 ff. – are saved on the Day of Judgement[67]). That is why the 'Moor's Head' by Christoph Jamnitzer has such a severe, and at the same time noble, form.

In contrast to the head-band, the head-dress in the shape of feathers is not a traditional element in European depictions of Moors. In the iconography of the four continents, the feather dress usually belongs to the Americas and not to Africa[68] (the Indians in the engravings in the *Historia Americae* published

[63] K. Pechstein, *Goldschmiedewerke der Renaissance* (Berlin, 1971) (Staatliche Museen Preußischer Kulturbesitz, Kataloge des Kunstgewerbemuseums Berlin, v), no. 102, ill.

[64] L. Veit, 'Der Königskopf mit der Stirnbinde auf Münzen und Siegeln der Stauferzeit und des ausgehenden Mittelalters. Ein Herrschaftszeichen und heraldisches Symbol', *Anzeiger des Germanischen Nationalmuseums* (1976), pp. 22–30.

[65] H. Grundmann, *Der Cappenberger Barbarossakopf und die Anfänge des Stiftes Cappenberg* (Cologne/ Graz, 1959), pp. 63–4; Veit, 'Der Königskopf', pp. 22, 28; B. Falk, 'Bildnisreliquiare. Zur Entstehung und Entwicklung der metallenen Kopf-, Büsten- und Halbfigurenreliquiare im Mittelalter', *Aachener Kunstblätter*, 59 (1991–3), pp. 171–5, no. 30, figs. 79–81.

[66] Veit, 'Der Königskopf', p. 25.

[67] Article 'Tau', *Lexikon für Theologie und Kirche*, 3rd edn, 11 vols. (Freiburg im Breisgau/Basel/ Rome/Vienna, 1993–2001), xi, cols. 1275–6 (with lit.). I am very grateful to Elizabeth McGrath for this suggestion concerning the link to the tau sign.

[68] Article 'Erdteile', *Reallexikon zur deutschen Kunstgeschichte*, 9 vols. (Stuttgart 1937-Munich 2001, to be continued), v, cols. 1174–5; Poeschel, *Studien*, pp. 187–190.

by Theodor de Bry in 1591[69] wear head-ornaments which are astonishingly similar to that of Jamnitzer's 'Moor's Head'). However, in late Renaissance and early baroque festivities or theatrical performances, personifications of Africa as well as Africans often wear comparable feather ornaments,[70] which are a synonym for exotic origin or exotic appearance.

But Jamnitzer's 'Moor's Head' does not have a naturalistically conceived feather head-dress. On the contrary, the head-dress is transformed into a highly stylised jewel which shows striking parallels to ornaments for hats, the so-called *aigrettes* of *c.* 1600.[71] These *aigrettes* shape the feathers into abstract forms that are typically accentuated by rows of densely set precious stones. This can be compared with an *aigrette* in the museum in Bern, made *c.* 1600 in Southern Germany, lavishly enamelled and set with rubies.[72] Like the head-dress of Jamnitzer's 'Moor's Head', it is strictly symmetrical.

Finally, it is useful to consider the general form of Jamnitzer's 'Moor's Head'. This is not a bust in the narrow sense but a head on an elongated neck. Such a shape is almost without parallel in Renaissance sculpture as usually there is at least a kind of base representing the upper part of the chest. A comparison may be made with ancient bronze heads, or imitations of them, intended to be set on a marble bust or statue and which sometimes have a neck cut in a

---

[69] H. Nickel, 'The graphic sources for the Moor with the emerald cluster', *Metropolitan Museum Journal*, 15 (1980), pp. 207–8, fig. 9.

[70] See the feather aprons of the black actors in the pageant celebrated on the occasion of the Kolowrat marriage in Innsbruck in 1580 (E. Scheicher, 'Ein Fest am Hofe Erzherzog Ferdinands II.', *Jahrbuch der Kunsthistorischen Sammlungen in Wien*, 77 [1981], p. 131, fig. 86, p. 143, fig. 101) or (for an English example) the feather head-dress in the design by Inigo Jones from 1605 for the figurine of 'Niger's Daughter' in Ben Jonson's play *The Masque of Blackness* (E. Jones, *Othello's Countrymen: The African in English Renaissance Drama* [London, 1965], pp. 27, 32–3, plate 2; *Christian IV and Europe*, Copenhagen, Rosenborg Castle, Nationalmuseet, Statens Museum for Kunst, etc. [Copenhagen, 1988], exhibition catalogue, p. 144, no. 521, colour plate XXXI on p. 577) or the feather head-dress of Johann Friedrich Duke of Württemberg as Moor in the ballet performed on the occasion of the baptismal festivities which took place in Stuttgart in 1616 (M. Firla, *Exotisch – höfisch – bürgerlich. Afrikaner in Württemberg vom 15. bis 19. Jahrhundert*, Stuttgart, Hauptstaatsarchiv Stuttgart [Stuttgart, 2001], exhibition catalogue, pp. 30–1, no. Nr. 2.6a, ill.).

[71] Y. Hackenbroch, *Renaissance Jewellery* (Munich/New York, 1979), pp. 189–93; H. Tait, *Catalogue of the Waddesdon Bequest in the British Museum*, I: *The Jewels* (London, 1986), pp. 91–6, figs. 81–2, plate VIIA, pp. 277–8, fig. 252; B. Januszkiewicz, *Klejnoty i stroje ksiazat Pomorza Zachodniego XVI–XVII wieku* (Warsaw, 1995), p. 41, no. 3, fig. pp. 41–2; Y. Hackenbroch, *Enseignes* (Florence, 1996), pp. 184–5.

[72] F. Deuchler, 'Eine süddeutsche Hutagraffe um 1600', *Jahrbuch des Bernischen Historischen Museums*, 49–50 (1959–60), pp. 82–90.

similar way.[73] There is, however, an essential difference: the neck of Jamnitzer's 'Moor's Head' is not open on the underside or the rearside but closed with the armorial relief. Because of this gesture towards classical bronzes – or bronzes in classical style – the 'Moor's Head' has an especially noble character. At the same time this head, conceived so clearly and strictly, is integrated into the composition of a drinking vessel and rests on a gothicising base.

After the examination of so many motifs, it is worthwhile to ask a very important question in the context of the present book: did the sculptor and goldsmith Christoph Jamnitzer shape this head of a black African youth on a living model? During his presumed stay in Italy he would have been able to encounter many black Africans, especially in the large centres, at the seaports and in the courts. In Nuremberg (in spite of its commercial relations, especially with West Africa[74]) there were only occasionally a few black Africans, as for instance the mahout announced in a broadsheet of 1629 with a woodcut illustration of the African with his elephant.[75] But even supposing that Christoph Jamnitzer had seen black Africans (in Italy, Nuremberg or elsewhere), he was not aiming at a realistic portrait of an individual. On the contrary, it was his intention to create an ideal image in which distinct features of black Africans are inserted, but which achieves its serene dignity especially through the motif of the diadem-like head-band, a feature which in this particularly severe form, distinguished by the geometric T-letters, has no parallels in earlier representations of black Africans. Though primarily created as a drinking vessel, Jamnitzer's 'Moor's Head' transcends the purpose of a functional utensil and becomes a sculptural work of art with a fascinating charisma – appropriately for the coat of arms of one of the noblest families of Renaissance Florence.

In an article officially published in 2002, although not printed until 2004, Jørgen Hein has drawn attention to an important document in the State Archives in Copenhagen ('Der Mohrenkopfpokal von Christoph Jamnitzer. Provenienz, Deutung und Kontext', *Münchner Jahrbuch der bildenden Kunst*, 3rd series, 53 [2002], p. 163–174). An inventory of Lichtenburg Castle in 1642

---

[73] Cf. G. Lahusen and E. Formigli, *Römische Bildnisse aus Bronze. Kunst und Technik* (Munich, 2001), especially nos. 40, 63, 101, 109, 114, 173, 188, 190, ill.

[74] Jakob Strieder, 'Deutscher Metallwarenexport nach Westafrika im 16. Jahrhundert', *Das reiche Augsburg. Ausgewählte Aufsätze Jakob Strieders zur Augsburger und süddeutschen Wirtschaftsgeschichte des 15. und 16. Jahrhunderts* (Munich, 1938), pp. 160–3; P. Martin, *Schwarze Teufel, edle Mohren. Afrikaner in Geschichte und Bewußtsein der Deutschen* (Hamburg, 1993), pp. 51, 396–7, n. 80.

[75] Martin, *Schwarze Teufel*, p. 62, fig. p. 60.

proves that the 'Moor's Head' was part of the estate of the Danish princess Hedwig (1581–1641), the widow of the prince-elector Christian II of Saxony (reigning 1591–1611). For that reason it is possible that the 'Moor's Head' was made for the wedding of Christian II and Hedwig celebrated in Dresden in 1602. Perhaps the 'Moor's Head' cup was one of the prizes at the tournament organized on the occasion of the wedding.

PART THREE

The practicalities of enslavement and emancipation

The trade in black African slaves in fifteenth-century Florence

SERGIO TOGNETTI

This chapter will elucidate some aspects of the trade in black African slaves in fifteenth-century Florence. Slavery in the late Middle Ages, at least in its main features, is a well-known phenomenon as a consequence of Charles Verlinden's major work on Mediterranean Europe.[1] Among the important Italian cities involved in the slave trade, Genoa and Venice have received the greatest attention from scholars, and therefore have generated the most historiography. They were among the most populous urban centres on the continent, with port structures and economic ambitions focused principally on international trade. The two cities could also count on strong and powerful merchant colonies in the basins of the Aegean and Black Seas. Merchants from Genoa and Venice had been trading in slaves in Khios, Laiazzo, Pera, Caffa, Tana and Famagusta since the second half of the thirteenth century, although the growth of the slave trade received a significant boost in the decades after the Black Death.[2] Genoese and Venetian merchants, being so deeply rooted in these emporia in the Levant, had far greater possibilities than other Europeans or Italians of forging contacts with non-Christian peoples. The indispensable condition permitting men or women to be reduced to slavery, and in a similar fashion to any other goods that were an object of regular market transactions, was precisely that the individuals in question were not

---

[1] C. Verlinden, *L'Esclavage dans l'Europe médiévale*, I: *Péninsule Iberique – France* (Bruges, 1955); II: *Italie, colonies italiennes du Levant, Levant latin, Empire byzantin* (Ghent, 1977).

[2] Beyond the works included in the previous footnote, see for example C. Verlinden, 'Le recrutement des esclaves à Venise aux XIVe et XVe siècles', *Bulletin de l'Institut Historique Belge de Rome*, 39 (1968), pp. 83–202; D. Gioffré, *Il mercato degli schiavi a Genova nel secolo XV* (Genoa, 1971); J. Heers, *Esclaves et domestiques au Moyen Age dans le monde méditerranéen* (Paris, 1981); G. Pistarino, 'Tratta di schiavi da Genova in Toscana nel secolo XV', in *Studi di storia economica toscana nel Medioevo e nel Rinascimento in memoria di Federigo Melis* (Pisa, 1987), pp. 285–304; M. Balard, 'Esclavage en Crimée et sources fiscales génoises au XVe siècle', in H. Bresc, ed., *Figures de l'esclave au Moyen-Age et dans le monde moderne* (Paris and Montreal, 1996), pp. 77–87. A wide and updated bibliography on this subject is included in F. Panero, *Schiavi, servi e villani nell'Italia medievale* (Turin, 2000), pp. 341–57, 361–9 and in the monographic issue of *Quaderni storici*, 107: 2 (2001) ('La schiavitù nel Mediterraneo').

Christian.[3] However, the prohibitions sanctioned by canon law, and by its civil counterpart receptive to religious norms, still did not manage to stop some Christians from being reduced to slavery. The numerous studies on the slave trade have in fact clarified that the great mass of people brought to Italian cities from emporia in the Levant were Tartars, Circassians, Russians and other unbaptised Slavs or Saracens, although a small number were Greeks, Christian Orthodox Slavs and Rumanians, Albanians and Armenians.

The privileged position occupied by the Genoese and Venetians in the trade in human beings is also documented by a few statistical data relating to the density of slaves in some Italian cities, which is deducible from reliable fiscal sources. In the Florentine *catasto* of 1427, there are only 360 female slaves (the vast majority of the total number were female), or less than 1 per cent of the whole Florentine population, estimated at about 37,000 inhabitants.[4] In the Pisan catasto of 1428–9, out of a population of 7,400 inhabitants, slaves (55 women and 3 men) once again constituted less than 1 per cent.[5] In Genoa, on the other hand, data taken from indirect taxes on possession of slaves in the first decades of the fifteenth century indicates at a conservative estimate more than 2,000 slaves, or 4 to 5 per cent of the inhabitants.[6] In the 1380s and 1390s, the presence of slaves in Genoa had reached the exceptionally high figure of 4,000 or even 5,000 people.[7]

As far as the slave trade in Italy in the fourteenth and fifteenth centuries is concerned, certain fundamental aspects are clear; some relate to its persistence over time, while others can be linked to modifications connected to the variation in economic trends in Mediterranean trade. In the towns of North and Central Italy, that is in the communes, slaves were exclusively female: the urban elites bought adolescent girls and female children chiefly but not solely for domestic duties. It is very rare to find slaves employed in manual labour connected to the work of artisans or in farming, although more frequently they were used as nurses or wet-nurses. The highest prices were paid for young women aged between fifteen and twenty-five years old: long life expectancy and increased attraction played a determining role for male buyers. Most of the slaves bought during the fourteenth century for the main cities in North

---

[3] In Florence a fundamental law about this was enacted in 1364: see I. Origo, 'The domestic enemy: the eastern slaves in Tuscany in the fourteenth and fifteenth centuries', *Speculum*, 30 (1955), pp. 321–66 at 324–5.

[4] C. Klapisch-Zuber, 'Women servants in Florence (fourteenth and fifteenth centuries)', in B. Hanawalt, ed., *Women and Work in Preindustrial Europe* (Bloomington, 1986), pp. 56–80 at 69.

[5] B. Casini, *Aspetti della vita economica e sociale di Pisa dal catasto del 1428–1429* (Pisa, 1965), pp. 18–19.

[6] Gioffré, *Il mercato degli schiavi*, pp. 68–9.   [7] *Ibid.*, p. 80.

and Central Italy were Tartars and Circassians, whereas in the fifteenth century Russians formed the majority, at least until the fall of Constantinople and the dismantlement of the Genoese trading colonies on the Black Sea. In the second half of the fifteenth century, with the drastic and unexpected rupture of the previous sources of supply, a much reduced flow of slaves was concerned in particular with Moors, Berbers and black Africans. At the beginning of the sixteenth century, the slave trade in Italy, in terms of its organisation and the structures within which it had operated since the thirteenth century, was in a phase of critical and general decline.

This brief outline also applies in part to the south of Italy, with some important differences.[8] Geographical proximity to the coast of Africa and thus to caliphates and emirates inhabited by non-Christian peoples, towards whom there existed an attitude of more or less permanent hostility, led to a higher quota of Saracen slaves than elsewhere on the peninsula. Obviously too this quota of Moor and Saracen slaves allowed for a considerable number of males captured during acts of open war or piracy. Second, above all in the predominantly rural regions in Southern Italy, the presence of male slaves employed to carry out agricultural duties became more accentuated in the passage from the fourteenth to the fifteenth centuries, when the demographic vacuum caused by repeated epidemics of plague reached its negative apex. In a sort of anticipation of the colonial slavery of modern times, the majority of slaves present in Southern Italy in the second half of the fifteenth century were males working on the land, with by then a net preponderance of black Africans. Charles Verlinden himself stated that 'slavery in Sicily at the end of the fifteenth century was, above all, black slavery'.[9]

The slave trade in black Africans consequently spread during the fifteenth century, replacing the oriental slave trade, which declined after the military conquests of the Ottomans in the basins of the Black and Aegean Seas, and in the Balkans. At the same time, the commercial routes of this trade changed. Until the 1440s, black slaves were sold to Italians and other Europeans by Arab merchants operating in the cities on the Mediterranean coast of Africa. After the voyages combining exploration, trade and plunder by the Portuguese (and also Italian) sailors, under the patronage and financial sponsorship of Prince

---

[8] See C. Verlinden, 'L'esclavage en Sicile au bas moyen âge', *Bulletin de l'Institut Historique Belge de Rome*, 35 (1963), pp. 13–113; C. Verlinden, 'L'esclavage dans le royaume de Naples à la fin du moyen âge et la participation des marchands espagnols à la traite', *Anuario de historia económica y social*, 1 (1968), pp. 345–401; H. Bresc, *Un Monde méditerranéen: économie et société en Sicile, 1300–1450* (Rome and Palermo, 1986), pp. 439–75.

[9] Verlinden, *L'esclavage en Sicile*, p. 91.

Henry of Portugal, known as 'the Navigator', black Africans reduced to slavery from the coastal areas of Senegal and Guinea started to flow into the ports of the Algarve and into Lisbon itself.[10] Florentine sources from the 1460s and 1470s describe these new slaves as 'teste nere venute da Lisbona' ('black heads from Lisbon'). The great Florentine merchant-bankers were also drawn to participate in this potential source of profit. Here the account books of the Cambini bank, an important Florentine mercantile and banking firm, provide some interesting points of departure in the attempt to define the slave trade in black Africans between Portugal and Tuscany at the end of the Middle Ages more clearly.[11]

The Cambini bank, active between 1420 and 1482 (the year of its bankruptcy), has left 79 extant account books, preserved in the Estranei *fondo* of the Archive of the Ospedale degli Innocenti in Florence. Among these, the most useful for this chapter are the ledgers ('libri mastri') and the record books (*ricordanze*). The business strategy and economic geography around which the activity of the bank gravitated for decades foresaw its regular presence in some commercial centres considered of strategic importance, regardless of variations in circumstances and profit margins. One of the fixed points of the commercial and financial interests of the Cambini had always been Lisbon. In the Portuguese capital, some Florentine merchants of high status operated on behalf of the bank, both as agents and as partners (*accomandatari*). They are documented many times in Portuguese archives: Bartolomeo di Iacopo di ser Vanni, Giovanni di Bernardo Guidetti and Bartolomeo di Domenico Marchionni are the most famous. It is through these Florentine businessmen who were resident in Lisbon that the Cambini bank began to take an interest in the slave trade in black Africans and to promote their import into Tuscany at the beginning of the 1460s. In fact, at this date the coasts of West Africa were being scoured by numerous naval expeditions supported by Prince Henry 'the Navigator'. In the course of the 1450s, the merchant navigators Alvise Ca' da Mosto (Venetian) and Antoniotto Usodimare (Genoese) had taken part in the voyages of exploration, culminating in the 'discovery' of the Cape Verde Islands, while many Portuguese voyagers had searched the landing places of

---

[10] C. Verlinden, 'Les débuts de la traite portugaise en Afrique (1433–1448)', in *Miscellanea medievalia in memoriam Jan Frederik Niermeyer* (Groningen, 1967), pp. 365–77; B. W. Diffie and G. D. Winius, *Foundations of the Portuguese Empire, 1415–1580* (Minneapolis, 1977), pp. 74–95.

[11] For the history of the business and of the family, see S. Tognetti, *Il banco Cambini. Affari e mercati di una compagnia mercantile-bancaria nella Firenze del XV secolo* (Florence, 1999).

Senegal and Guinea.[12] The slave trade in black Africans constituted one of the most macroscopic consequences of European raids on sub-Saharan Africa.

The first documented example in the Cambini account books of the dispatch of black African slaves from Lisbon to Tuscany dates from 1461. In July of that year, a Portuguese ship called the *Santa Maria di Nazarette* docked in Livorno with a cargo of multiple and heterogeneous merchandise, including amongst much else untreated leather from Ireland and Portugal, silk from Iberia, cochineal from Sintra and three black female slaves. They had been embarked in Lisbon by a trusted partner and business agent of the Cambini, Giovanni Guidetti, who also sent to Florence a meticulous statement of accounts.[13] The poor slaves had been acquired in Lisbon between the end of May and the beginning of June and their clothing must have been absolutely minimal, as Guidetti wrote that because they were naked, he had been compelled to spend 300 reals on each for clothes, as well as 600 reals for food. The names of the young women (Isabell, Barbera and Marta) are a clear testimony to the fact that they had been baptized, and the same account book reports straightforwardly that 'non sono christiane . . . ma l'abbiamo batezate a parole' ('They are not Christians . . . but we have informally baptised them with words'). The purchase price paid in Lisbon in Portuguese reals shows a palpable hierarchy of values corresponding to variation in one physical norm: Isabell, though black, was defined as 'più biancha' ('whiter') and she was worth 8,500 reals; Barbera had cost 7,500 reals; and Marta, described as 'ben nera' ('quite black'), only 6,500 reals. Therefore a darker skin brought about an effective depreciation in value, a fact that correlates exactly with the price structure of the contemporary market for slaves in Genoa.[14] These slaves were destined for domestic chores: Isabell had been bought directly to satisfy the household requirements of the Cambini; Barbera had been purchased on behalf of Giovanni degli Albizzi, a member of an important Florentine patrician family; and Marta had been acquired on behalf of Ridolfo di ser Gabriello, a Florentine merchant resident in Pisa, who was an agent of the Cambini for their business affairs in Pisa and Livorno. Adding together all the costs and expenses sustained between the acquisition in Lisbon and the arrival of the ship at Livorno, the slave of the Cambini family cost 9,351 reals, the equivalent of 46.15 *fiorini di suggello*, a sum that would exceed 50 florins

---

[12] Diffie and Winius, *Alle origini*, pp. 123–41.

[13] Florence, Archivio dell'Ospedale degli Innocenti (hereafter AOIF), Estranei, 250, fol. 79; 233, fol. 33r.

[14] Gioffré, *Il mercato degli schiavi*, pp. 127, 140–1.

with the addition of the expenses for the journey from Livorno to Florence.[15] The value of the slave therefore was considerable, comparable to the annual salary of a qualified craftsman such as a master-mason,[16] or to the production cost of a standard piece of the finest quality woollen cloth manufactured in the Florentine district of S. Martino and made with precious English wool.[17] At any rate, in the income-tax return presented by the Cambini brothers for the catasto of 1469, Isabell had been replaced by another black African slave, aged twenty-four, called Giovanna, whose value was estimated at 31 *fiorini di suggello*.[18]

At the end of 1464 Giovanni Guidetti sent three more black African slaves through the Cambini bank's account. The caravel called the *Santo Spirito* that docked in Livorno in January 1465, chartered by the Portuguese João Afonso, brought three women all destined for Florentine buyers. Unfortunately, in only one instance does the account book record the name of the buyer and the sum paid for the purchase: the Florentines Piero and Giuliano di Francesco Salviati paid 36.18 *fiorini di suggello* 'per una testa nera ebbono da noi . . . per loro in chasa' ('For a black head they received from us . . . for their own domestic use').[19] In September of the same year, another black female slave acquired and sent by Giovanni Guidetti arrived in Livorno on the whaling-ship *Dispensiero*, chartered by a Portuguese business man whose name has been Tuscanised into 'Luigi Stefani' by the Florentine book-keeper. This time the consignee of the slave is known: Stefano Mucini, a member of a Florentine family with strong interests in the trade between Tuscany and Portugal.[20]

In 1467 three more black African female slaves arrived in Livorno on a sailing-ship from Lisbon. Giovanni Guidetti dispatched them through his own account; he wanted to sell the slaves in Pisa and Florence, using the Cambini bank as broker. The whale-boat the *Santa Maria Nunziata*, chartered once again by a Portuguese merchant and ship-fitter, Lopo Iannis, docked at Livorno in August. One slave called Barbera was sold to the Florentine Benedetto di ser Francesco Guardi for 51.14 *fiorini di suggello*; the other two, a woman and a baby girl, were sold in Pisa to the Florentine merchant Niccolò

[15] AOIF, Estranei, 223, fol. 35v.

[16] R. A. Goldthwaite, *The Building of Renaissance Florence* (Baltimore, MD, 1980), pp. 437–8.

[17] S. Tognetti, 'Uno scambio diseguale. Aspetti dei rapporti commerciali tra Firenze e Napoli nella seconda metà del Quattrocento', *Archivio storico italiano*, 158 (2000), pp. 461–90 at 482. The measure of a Florentine cloth or *panno* was 13 *canne* = m. 30.42.

[18] Florence, Archivio di Stato (hereafter ASF), Catasto, 923, fols. 634r–636v. The partners of the bank until April 1462 were the brothers Francesco and Carlo di Niccolò Cambini; from that date until 1481, the brothers Francesco and Bernardo di Niccolò were partners instead.

[19] AOIF, Estranei, 251, fol. 68; 227, fol. 105r.   [20] AOIF, Estranei, 227, fol. 130r.

di Paradiso Mazzinghi for the combined price of 42.10 *fiorini di suggello*.[21] In June 1470 the whaling-ship belonging to one Portuguese, João Sodré, and fitted by another called 'Andrea Pieris', docked in Livorno with a black African slave. The woman had been bought in Lisbon for 8,500 reals by Piero Ghinetti, a new partner and agent of the bank, and she was reserved for the Cambini family.[22]

The examples specified until now clearly refer to an entirely occasional trade, limited to the satisfaction of a moderate request for slaves destined for domestic service in the houses of rich Florentine merchant-bankers. The paltry volume of transactions shows the marginal character of the slave trade in the business strategy of the Cambini bank. A partial exception to this is constituted by the large-scale operation organised by Giovanni Guidetti who, in 1474, made two more substantial shipments of female slaves from Lisbon to Tuscany.[23] In January 1474, the Portuguese ship the *Santa Maria Nunziata*, chartered by Bartolomeu Afonso, arrived in Livorno with 26 slaves (25 women and 1 man); and in April, the ship *Santa Maria di Grazia*, also equipped by a Portuguese called 'Piero Ferrandi', disembarked 9 female slaves in Livorno. Some of the women who were the objects of the trade were defined as having white skin, others as having black skin; for the remainder of the women, and for the man, the Cambini account books give no further details. A doubt remains over which ethnic group can be linked to adjectives such as '*bianca*' or '*alba*' ('white'), given that the slaves were coming from Lisbon; maybe these terms indicate Saracens or Berbers, or whoever could be differentiated by skin colour from the women captured in sub-Saharan Africa.

At least in terms of the Florentine slave trade in the second half of the fifteenth century, this was a transaction of a certain financial substance. Between the hiring of the ship, the port operations, the costs of land transport, the taxes, the expenses of clothing some of the almost naked slaves and the price of commercial and financial brokerage, Giovanni Guidetti's current account at the Cambini bank was debited 140 large florins. The sales were delayed until 1476, making the wait for the proceeds a long one. The bank in Florence and its agents in Pisa and Naples sold 25 black and white slaves on behalf of Guidetti, crediting him with net proceeds of 1,071 large florins; the male slave and the other women were consigned to Lena Vettori, Guidetti's wife, who lived in Florence. For two of these slaves, the final result of the trade, but not the sum of the yield, is known; the bank could not be involved in financial

---

[21] AOIF, Estranei, 252, fol. 179; 229, fols. 122–5.   [22] AOIF, Estranei, 254, fol. 112.
[23] AOIF, Estranei, 259, fol. 99; 260, fol. 31; 235, fols. 31v–32r.

transactions that were not its responsibility. Summaries of the transactions documented in the bank's account books are shown in the Appendix to this chapter.[24]

The sample is sufficiently detailed to hazard some general observations. First, it underlines the overwhelming preponderance of females, a phenomenon that confirms what was said at the beginning about slavery in the large towns in North and Central Italy. When the colour of the skin is specified, it is quite clear that slaves with white skin were much more desirable than those with black skin. The difference in price is very marked, to the point where some white women reached the price of 60 large florins (the equivalent of 72 *fiorini di suggello*), a rather prohibitive sum in relation to the economic use of owning such expensive slaves. Just to give again an idea of the real value of these slaves, Antonio di Zanobi di ser Martino and Co., who were silk merchants and manufacturers, purchased a white slave by exchanging her for a piece of black velvet 30 *braccia* long and two widths of pile high ('a due altezze di pelo').[25] It is probable that the acquisition of a slave by a rich merchant was a response to pressures of prestige or in some cases to straightforward sexual interest rather than being fuelled by calculations of savings relating to domestic personnel. Nor should it be forgotten that in the fifteenth century some Florentine institutions dealing with foundlings, such as the Ospedale di San Gallo or the Ospedale degli Innocenti, brought up a significant number of children born to slaves (between 14 per cent and 30 per cent of registered foundlings) whose fathers can be more or less openly identified with members of the rich Florentine merchant class.[26]

The majority of commercial transactions concerned precisely members of the mercantile and entrepreneurial circles of the city, as can be deduced from the surnames of the buyers. These included people of a certain importance, like Bernardo, the son of the humanist Giannozzo Manetti, and Francesco Sassetti, the general manager of the Medici bank. Two transactions concerned Lucca

---

[24] For a better understanding of the data, remember that the large florin became a money of account in 1471, replacing the old *fiorino di suggello*, compared to which it enjoyed a fixed premium of 20 per cent. Any comparison with the amounts cited previously must therefore take into account that after 1471 100 large florins were the equivalent of 120 *fiorini di suggello*. See on this R. A. Goldthwaite and G. Mandich, *Studi sulla moneta fiorentina (secoli XIII–XVI)* (Florence, 1994), pp. 29–73.

[25] AOIF, Estranei, 235, fol. 217r. A Florentine *braccio* corresponds to 58.5 cm.

[26] Origo, 'The domestic enemy', pp. 346–7; Klapisch-Zuber, 'Women servants', pp. 70–1; R. C. Trexler, 'The foundlings of Florence, 1395–1455', in R. C. Trexler, *The Children of Renaissance Florence* (reprinted Asheville, NC, 1998), pp. 7–34 at 22–4, 27 (originally printed in *History of Childhood Quarterly*, 1: 2 (1973), pp. 259–89).

and two more concerned Pisa. In Lucca the buyers came from the most elevated level of society.[27] In the case of Pisa, the purchases were made by a leather merchant and tanner (*cuoiaio*) and a shoemaker (*calzolaio*), or an entrepreneur and an artisan from the most important industry of the city (leather tanning and manufacture).[28] Finally, two transactions concerned Naples, through the brokerage of important merchant-banking firms like those belonging respectively to Filippo and Lorenzo Strozzi, and to Tommaso Ginori.[29] The buyers were the Count of Fondi and a certain Girolamo Liperotto Falconi who, according to the Cambini account books, seems to have been an official of the Neapolitan mint.

Considering the size of the turnover and the number of slaves as objects of sale, this operation is the only commercial one that can be considered a real trade, aiming to fulfil a not altogether occasional request for slaves. Other more limited cases can, however, be found in the Cambini account books in the second half of 1470s. The Portuguese ship the *Santa Maria Nunziata*, docking in Livorno on 23 September 1478, brought two black African female slaves belonging to Bartolomeo Marchionni, a Florentine merchant-banker resident in Lisbon. One of the slaves was described as 'di nazione nera d'età d'anni XVI in circha chiamata Luza' ('of black race, about sixteen years old, called Luza').[30] The girl was sold in Florence to two brothers, Chiaro and Pellegrino di Francesco da Casavecchia;[31] at that time, Pellegrino was one of the clerks of the Cambini bank and his not so negligible annual salary

---

[27] Giovanni Guidiccioni was at the time one of the most important merchant and silk manufacturers in Lucca, whereas messer Iacopo da Ghivizzano was a member of the inner circle of the Lucchese ruling class. On them, see S. Polica, 'Le famiglie del ceto dirigente lucchese dalla caduta di Paolo Guinigi alla fine del Quattrocento', in *I ceti dirigenti nella Toscana del Quattrocento* (Florence, 10–11.XII.1982 and 2–3.XII.1983) (Florence, 1987), pp. 353–84; M. E. Bratchel, *Lucca, 1430–1494: The Reconstruction of an Italian City-Republic* (Oxford, 1995), *ad indicem*.

[28] S. Tognetti, 'Attività industriali e commercio di manufatti nelle città toscane del tardo Medioevo (1250 c.–1530 c.)', *Archivio storico italiano*, 159 (2001), pp. 423–79 at 454–6; and see the articles by L. Galoppini, M. Tangheroni and S. Tognetti in S. Gensini, ed., *Il cuoio e le pelli in Toscana: produzione e mercato nel tardo medioevo e nell'età moderna* (San Miniato, 21–22.II.1998) (Pisa, 1999).

[29] On Filippo Strozzi the elder's business affairs there is a vast bibliography; see at least R. A. Goldthwaite, *Private Wealth in Renaissance Florence. A Study of Four Families* (Princeton, 1968), pp. 52–73; *Il giornale del banco Strozzi di Napoli (1473)*, ed. A. Leone (Naples, 1981); M. Del Treppo, 'Aspetti dell'attività bancaria a Napoli nel '400', in *Aspetti della vita economica medievale* (Florence, Prato and Pistoia, 10–14.III.1984) (Florence, 1985), pp. 557–601; M. Del Treppo, 'Il re e il banchiere. Strumenti e processi di razionalizzazione dello stato aragonese di Napoli', in G. Rossetti, ed., *Spazio, società, potere nell'Italia dei comuni* (Naples, 1986), pp. 229–304. On Tommaso Ginori's business affairs, see M. Cassandro, 'Affari e uomini d'affari fiorentini a Napoli sotto Ferrante I d'Aragona (1472–1495)', in *Studi di storia economica toscana nel Medioevo e nel Rinascimento in memoria di Federigo Melis* (Pisa, 1987), pp. 103–23.

[30] AOIF, Estranei, 237, fol. 152.   [31] *Ibid.*, fol. 187.

amounted to 50 large florins.[32] Since the slave cost 40 large florins, once again it is permissible to doubt the strictly economic benefit of owning this type of servant. The second slave, called Margherita, was not sold in Florence. She was initially kept for a month in the house of Leonardo di Francesco Ringhiadori, another clerk of the Cambini bank.[33] Then, after having a bubo treated by a barber, Margherita was sent back to Pisa where she was exchanged for some cloth unloaded in Livorno from Venetian galleys on their regular return from Aigues-Mortes.[34]

The owner of the two slaves, Bartolomeo Marchionni, was at the time partner and agent of the Cambini in the Portuguese capital. Belonging to a family of Florentine apothecaries who had a shop overlooking Brunelleschi's basilica of San Lorenzo, he had become an apprentice at the Cambini bank when he was about fifteen. Sent to Lisbon at the beginning of 1470s, he would become, in the space of a few years, one of the most important businessmen in Portugal, taking an interest in an impressive variety of commercial and financial transactions. Becoming a naturalised Portuguese in 1482, at the beginning of the sixteenth century he also participated in the financing of the voyages of 'discovery' and trade led by captains of the Portuguese navy of the calibre of Pedro Álvares Cabral and Afonso de Albuquerque, realising fabulous profits.[35] Among the manifold occupations in which he was involved, the slave trade in black Africans was not a matter of second rank – rather the contrary. Almost thirty years ago, Virginia Rau described Marchionni as one of the first slave-traders in Renaissance Europe. In the three years from 1493 to 1495, the registers of Casa dos Escravos in Lisbon record 1,648 slaves belonging to Marchionni, and between 1489 and 1503 he would send 1,866 black African slaves from Lisbon to the kingdom of Valencia.[36] These data are illuminating on two counts. In the first place, it is evident that the new geographical 'discoveries' had opened up new prospects of gain for the great international merchants: unfortunately, among them was also the racialised slave trade in sub-Saharan Africans. Nevertheless, at the same time, it is easy to see that this trade in human beings did not find very propitious terrain in the urban society of Renaissance Italy. Marchionni, who traded in hundreds of slaves each year, made only sporadic and very limited shipments to his native country,

---

[32] Tognetti, *Il banco Cambini*, p. 353.   [33] *Ibid.*

[34] AOIF, Estranei, 240, fol. 169v; 237, fol. 171; 236, fol. 66v.

[35] Tognetti, *Il banco Cambini*, pp. 287, 294–8.

[36] V. Rau, 'Notes sur la traite portugaise à la fin du XVe siècle et le Florentin Bartolomeo di Domenico Marchionni', *Bulletin de l'Institut Historique Belge de Rome*, 44 (1974), pp. 535–43; see also Verlinden, *L'esclavage dans l'Europe*, 1, pp. 625–8.

preferring to concentrate on markets where there were, in embryonic form, what were to become colonial types of cultivation (first and foremost, the cultivation of sugar cane). The possession of black African slaves in Florence was due in large part to mainly non-economic motives, such as notions of social prestige and the fascination of the exotic.

Genuine revitalisation of slavery in the Grand-Duchy of Tuscany, as in other states of modern Italy, would only take place between the sixteenth and the eighteenth centuries, when hard labour and galley-slaves were introduced into the Mediterranean navies.[37]

Appendix

Female slaves sold through the Cambini bank in Florence on behalf of Giovanni Guidetti in Lisbon (1474–1476)

Buyers	Place of delivery	Other middlemen	Physical description	Returns in large f.
Paolo di Giovanni di Zanobi	Florence	Giovanni Portinari & Co. (goldbeaters)	Black	35
Francesco di ser Antonio Parigi	Florence	Zanobi Girolami & Co.	White	60
Messer Iacopo da Ghivizzano	Lucca	Giuliano Cambini in Pisa and Giovanni Guidiccioni (Lucchese merchant)	White	60
Giovanni Guidiccioni Lucchese (merchant)	Lucca	Giuliano Cambini in Pisa	White	58
Bernardo di Giannozzo Manetti	Florence	–	Black	45
Tommaso di Francesco Ginori	Florence	–	White	63
Francesco di Tommaso Sassetti	Florence	–	Not specified	50
Giovanni di Corrado Berardi	Florence	Berardo di Corrado Berardi	Not specified	56
Giorgio di Niccolò Ugolini	Florence	Niccolò Ugolini & Co. (woollen merchants and manufacturers)	Not specified	54
Giovanni di Rineri Grisi (leather merchant and tanner)	Pisa	Giuliano Cambini in Pisa	Not specified	42

(cont.)

[37] F. Angiolini, 'Slaves and slavery in early modern Tuscany (1500–1700)', *Italian History and Culture*, 3 (1997), pp. 67–86.

(*cont.*)

Buyers	Place of delivery	Other middlemen	Physical description	Returns in large f.
Guido di ser Giovanni Guiducci	Florence	–	Not specified	40
Iacopo di Francesco Lottieri	Florence	–	Not specified	40
Bartolomeo di Giuliano Zati	Florence	Giuliano Cambini in Pisa	Not specified	60
Giovan Gualberto del Giocondo	Florence	–	Not specified	55
Iacopo di Alessio Lapaccini	Florence	–	Black	43
Felice di Deo del Beccuto	Florence	–	Not specified	53
Roba di Mino Squarcialupi	Florence	–	Not specified	40
Bartolomeo di Andrea Cambini	Florence	–	White	50
Girolamo Liperotto Falconi	Naples	Strozzi and Ginori companies of Naples	Black, 10 years old	32[a]
Count of Fondi	Naples	Strozzi and Ginori companies of Naples	White, 10 years old	40[b]
Morello (shoemaker)	Pisa	Gabriello di Ridolfo in Pisa	Black	40
Gino di Francesco Ginori	Florence	Giuliano Cambini in Pisa	White	50
Lena (wife of Giovanni degli Albizzi)	Florence	–	Black	25
Paolo Mini (silk merchant and manufacturer)	Florence	–	Not specified	60
Antonio di Zanobi di ser Martino & Co. (silk merchants and manufacturers)	Florence	–	White	60
Torrigiano Torrigiani	Florence	Lena Guidetti	Not specified	?
Niccolò di Ugolino Martelli	Florence	Lena Guidetti	White	?

[a] This is net of the expenses for transport, the indirect taxes and the cost of mediation in Naples.
[b] See the preceding footnote.

CHAPTER TEN

'La Casa dels Negres': black African solidarity in late medieval Valencia

DEBRA BLUMENTHAL

The relationship between the Valencian stonemason Francesch Martinez and his black female slave had always been a stormy one. Frustrated with his inability to control his slave, Martinez – also known as Francesch the 'hot-tempered' – admitted that he frequently resorted to beating her in his attempts to get her to provide him with better service.[1] Indeed, Martinez confessed that in his most recent clash with the slave, had bystanders not intervened, he 'would have caused her great harm'. As it was, he had still hit Ursola hard enough on the head to warrant emergency medical attention.[2] Seeking 'to protect himself from further inconveniences', Francesch's first impulse had been to try and unload the slave on some unsuspecting buyer. Francesch relatively quickly found an interested party, but as soon as the potential buyer

---

[1] Although no laws explicitly limiting the power of masters and mistresses to discipline their slaves can be found in the kingdom's law code (the *Furs de Valencia*), in 1452 a female slave named Joliana filed charges of 'cruelty' (*sevicia*) against her master, an innkeeper in the city's red-light district ('hostaler del bordell'). Valencia, Archivo del Reino (hereafter ARV), Justicia Criminal 102, Cedes M. 4, 14 July 1452. Unfortunately, the exact nature of this 'cruelty' was not specified, nor was I able to encounter any further details concerning this case. The fact that a slave's charges of 'cruelty' were granted a hearing before the criminal court, however, suggests that although, according to the letter of the law, masters and mistresses could mistreat their slaves with relative impunity, other factors – in this instance, perhaps community norms of behaviour – prevented them from doing so.

[2] ARV, Gobernación 2348, M. 7, fol. 2r: 'E dix que en veritat sta que per quant ell dit testimoni no podia haver bona servitut de la dita Ursola moltes veguades li convenia batre la en tant que darrerament la naffra en lo cap que si no la y haguessen levada estava preparat de fer li hun gran dan de la qual naffra la guarri mestre Johan de Tensa cirurgia qu'es creya que morria.'

Although there was no statute requiring masters and mistresses to provide their slaves with medical treatment, community norms – in combination, no doubt, with economic interest – seem to have dictated that masters and mistresses looked after their slaves' physical welfare. According to the kingdom's legal code, if a third party provided medical treatment or material sustenance to a slave in the absence of his/her master, the master (and/or mistress) was obliged to compensate them for it. Failure to do so was interpreted as a forfeiture of the rights of ownership. *Furs de València*, ed. G. Colon and A. Garcia, 8 vols. (Barcelona, 1974), II, p. 202. For a case in which a physician sued a slave's mistress for her failure to pay an outstanding medical bill of 125 *reals*, see ARV, Gobernación 2279, M. 11, fols. 44r–45v (1450).

learned of the severity of Ursola's head injury, the deal fell through.[3] Finding himself right back where he started, confronted with the prospect of taking this unruly – and now gravely ill – female slave back into his household, Francesch, on the advice of some unnamed individuals, decided to 'let her go to the house of the black Africans ['la casa dels negres']'. For there, they reasoned, under the supervision of its 'housemother' (mad[r]astra), Ursola would be both 'cured (guarria) and cheered (se allegraria – for which, read pacified)'.[4]

This rather intriguing reference to a 'casa dels negres' – a place where, in the latter half of the fifteenth century, a black African slave woman could go to seek charitable assistance as well as receive medical attention – raises several tantalising questions regarding the position of black Africans in late medieval Iberian societies. When, how and why was this 'casa dels negres' founded, and what function did it serve for the burgeoning community of black Africans, both free[d] and slave, in fifteenth-century Valencia?

Most scholars studying the institution of slavery in medieval Iberia have tended to examine it within the context of Muslim–Christian relations.[5] And yet a striking feature of the slave population in fifteenth-century Valencia was its ethnic, as well as religious, diversity. In addition to prizes of war seized in corsair activity against Muslim Granada and North Africa, the male and female slaves available for purchase in Valencia's markets included Greeks, Russians, Tartars, Circassians, and, increasingly, black Africans. Indeed, by the fifteenth century, having eclipsed Barcelona as the Crown of Aragon's principal port and most populous city, Valencia had established itself as a major hub in the revitalised slave trade of the later Middle Ages. While in the fourteenth century, 'white' slaves brought from eastern Mediterranean ports supplemented the steady stream of Muslim captives, towards the latter

---

[3] ARV, Gobernación 2348, M. 7, fol. 2r.   [4] ARV, Gobernación 2348, M. 7, fol. 2r.

[5] See Manuel Ruzafa García, 'La esclavitud en la Valencia bajomedieval: mudéjares y musulmanes', in Maria Teresa Ferrer i Mallol and Josefina Mutgé i Vives, eds., De L'Esclavitud a la Llibertat. Esclaus i Lliberts a L'Edat Mitjana (Barcelona, 2000), pp. 471–91; Olivia Remie Constable, 'Muslim slavery and Mediterranean slavery: the medieval slave trade as an aspect of Muslim-Christian relations', in S. L. Waugh and P. Diehl, eds., Christendom and its Discontents (Cambridge, 1996), pp. 264–84; Mark D. Meyerson, 'Slavery and the social order: Mudejars and Christians in the Kingdom of Valencia', Medieval Encounters, 1:1 (1995), pp. 144–73. For more recent work examining the experiences of black African slaves and freedmen in the late medieval Crown of Aragon, see the contributions of Teresa Vinyoles i Vidal, 'Integració de les llibertes a la societat Barcelonina baixmedieval', and Fabiana Plazolles Guillén, 'Trayectorias sociales de los libertos musulmanes y negroafricanos en la Barcelona tardomedieval', in Mallol and Vives, eds., De L'Esclavitud a la Llibertat, pp. 593–613.

half of the fifteenth century, with the colonisation of the Canary Islands and the beginning of Portuguese exploration of the coast of West Africa, vessels arriving in Valencia's port (*grau*) transported cargoes of Canarian and black African slaves, marking the shift from a Mediterranean to an Atlantic-centered slave trade.

In contrast with the experiences of eastern Orthodox[6] and Muslim slaves, it has been noted that these black slaves imported from sub-Saharan Africa likely 'endured far greater alienation and disorientation' upon their arrival in Valencia. Mark Meyerson has observed that while Muslim captives could readily be assimilated into the local free Muslim community, black Africans 'could not enter a community resembling that from which they had been uprooted; nor were conditions propitious for recreating one in Valencia'.[7] Nevertheless, while the local support network available to black Africans was certainly limited in comparison to that available to Granadan and Maghriban Muslims, there is evidence that, by the end of the fifteenth century, free and slave members of the city's growing black African community had forged bonds of solidarity and were acting cooperatively. Most notably, this chapter will be examining the activities of a 'black' confraternity, founded in Valencia in 1472 that, among other things, collected alms and negotiated contracts of manumission on behalf of their black African fellows in captivity. Although this confraternity's efforts were hardly on the same scale as those of the kingdom's sizable free Muslim population,[8] much less those of the Christian redemptionist orders such as the Mercedarians and Trinitarians,[9] in the process

---

[6] Jacques Heers has argued that Greek, Russian, Tartar and Circassian slaves were almost seamlessly absorbed into the local population. After converting to Roman Catholicism and assimilating the language and customs of their masters, most were freed and many intermarried with freeborn members of their new communities. Jacques Heers, *Esclaves et domestiques au moyen-age dans le monde méditerranéen* (Paris, 1981).

[7] Mark Meyerson, 'Slavery and solidarity: Mudejars and foreign Muslim captives in the Kingdom of Valencia', *Medieval Encounters*, 2:3 (1996), pp. 308–9.

[8] See Meyerson, 'Slavery and solidarity'; Francisco Javier Marzal Palacios, 'El ciclo de la esclavitud sarracena en la Valencia bajomedieval: esclavización, rescate y vuelta a casa de los esclavos de Cherchell (1409–25)', in Mallol and Vives, eds., *De L'Esclavitud a la Llibertat*, pp. 493–509; and Andrés Díaz Borrás, 'Los redentores Valencianos de cautivos sarracenos durante el siglo XV', in Mallol and Vives, eds., *De L'Esclavitud a la Llibertat*, pp. 511–26.

[9] See James Brodman, *Ransoming Captives in Crusader Spain: The Order of Merced on the Christian–Islamic Frontier* (Philadelphia, 1980) and Ellen Friedman, *Spanish Captives in North Africa in the Early Modern Age* (Madison, 1983). For the efforts of royal and municipal institutions to redeem Christian captives, see Maria Teresa Ferrer i Mallol, 'Els redemptors de captius: mostolafs, eixees o alfaquecs (segles XII–XIII)', *Medievalia*, 9 (1990), pp. 85–106; Maria Teresa Ferrer i

of securing the liberation of a lucky few, they helped endow the city's black African community – both freed and slave – with a sense of corporate identity.

In his examination of the efforts of the local free Muslim community to redeem 'foreign' (Granadan and North African) co-religionists from captivity, Meyerson convincingly argues that redemptionist activity strengthened feelings of Muslim solidarity. The exertions of these Valencian Mudejars thus not only 'had a significant impact on the material circumstances of individual slaves and masters,' but also played a substantial role in shaping 'collective and individual mentalities, Muslim and Christian, slave and free'.[10] It is in the context of considering the position of black Africans in fifteenth-century Valencian society – their comparative integration or marginalisation – that I wish to examine the redemptionist activities of this 'confraternity of black Africans'. Whereas Meyerson has held up this confraternity as a symbol of the relative lack of vitality and autonomy of the black African community in comparison with the Muslim,[11] I will consider here how it both reflected and fostered feelings of black African solidarity.

After discussing the evidence available concerning the composition and size of the black African population in fifteenth-century Valencia, I will outline what we know about the circumstances surrounding the establishment of this confraternity. In particular, I will be examining a document issued by the Crown in 1472, confirming and ratifying statutes contained in the confraternity's charter of foundation. The bulk of the chapter, however, will be devoted to an analysis of two court cases filed by two different black African women, both of whom were demanding recognition of their freed status on the grounds that they had been redeemed through the efforts of the confraternity. The transcripts of these court cases provide us with some precious details concerning its activities – who its members were; how they selected the individual beneficiaries of their acts of charity; and, finally, how they assembled the necessary funds to redeem their black African fellows from captivity. In conclusion, after examining the nature and extent of the confraternity's activities, I will turn to a discussion of how masters and mistresses reacted to them and consider

Mallol, 'La redempcio de captius a la corona catalano-aragonesa (segle XIV),' *Anuario de estudios medievales*, 15 (1985), pp. 237–97; Andrés Díaz Borrás, 'Notas sobre los primeros tiempos de la atención valenciana a la redención de cautivos cristianos (1323–1399)', *Estudis Castellonencs*, 3 (1986), pp. 337–54; Juan Torres Fontes, 'La hermandad de moros y cristianos para el rescate de cautivos', in *Actas del I simposio internacional de Mudejarismo* (Madrid-Teruel, 1981), pp. 499–508.
[10] Meyerson, 'Slavery and solidarity', pp. 308–9.
[11] Meyerson downplays the significance of the confraternity's foundation as an expression of black African identity, arguing that, in forming it, they were simply 'emulating the institutions and rituals of their former masters'. Meyerson, 'Slavery and solidarity', p. 308.

what impact such expressions of black African solidarity had on contemporary perceptions of black Africans and on intercultural relations in Valencia.

Although the exact size of the black African population during this period is difficult to establish, it is fair to say that black Africans were a conspicuous minority of the city of Valencia's overall population – according to varied estimates, numbering some 70,000 inhabitants.[12] However, it would seem that they comprised a considerably more significant proportion of the city's slave population. My research in the city's notarial records indicates that, by the latter half of the fifteenth century, black Africans constituted at least 40 per cent of the slaves purchased and sold both in public auctions and private sales between households.[13] Prior to their sale, all captives entering the kingdom of Valencia first had to be presented before Crown officials so that the legitimacy of their enslavement could be confirmed and a 20 per cent tax assessed on their sale price (the *quinto*). Between 1445 and 1516, Vicenta Cortes and A. Teixeira da Mota have documented the arrival of some 6,740 black African slaves in the port of Valencia. Although the first reference to a black African slave in the account books of the Mestre Racional does not appear until 1447, Teixeira da Mota found that, by 1460, black African 'captives' were outnumbering *moros*. In 1461, the Mestre Racional assessed 70 *negres*, as opposed to 5 *moros*; in 1462, 83 *negres*, as opposed to 17 *moros*; and, in 1469, 1470 and 1471, 55, 54, and 72 *negres*, respectively, as opposed to 15, 8, and 5 *moros*. By the last decade of the fifteenth century, black Africans arrived in shiploads of between 100 and 200 men, women and children.[14] The most active slave trader during this period was Cesare de' Barchi, a Florentine merchant operating on behalf of a fellow Florentine, Bartolomeo Marchionni, based in Lisbon. Between 1489 and 1497, de' Barchi alone (on Marchionni's behalf) transported over 2,000 black African slaves to Valencia.[15]

[12] Antoni Furió, *Història del País Valencià* (Valencia, 1995), p. 189. Augustín Rubio Vela, 'Sobre la población de Valencia en el cuatrocientos (Nota demográfica)', in *Boletín de la sociedad castellonense de cultura*, 56 (1980), pp. 158–70.

[13] This figure is based on my analysis of a random sample of 252 slave sales dating from between 1470 and 1480 preserved in notarial registers found in the ARV and Valencia, Archivo de Protocolos del Patriarca. See the second chapter of my doctoral dissertation, Debra G. Blumenthal, 'Implements of labor, instruments of honor: Muslim, eastern and black African slaves in fifteenth-century Valencia', Ph.D., Department of History, University of Toronto, 2000.

[14] See Vicenta Cortes, *La esclavitud en Valencia durante el reinado de los Reyes Católicos (1479–1516)* (Valencia, 1964), A. Teixeira da Mota, 'Entrée d'esclaves noirs à Valence (1445–82): le remplacement de la voie saharienne par la voie Atlantique', *Revue française d'histoire d'Outre-Mer*, 66 (1979), nos. 242–3, pp. 195–210, and P. E. H. Hair, 'Black African slaves at Valencia, 1482–1516: an onomastic inquiry', *History in Africa*, 7 (1980), pp. 119–39.

[15] Cortes, *La esclavitud*, p. 76.

Since these records provide us with only the vaguest descriptions, the geographical provenance of these black African slaves is equally difficult to ascertain. Even in those rare instances when specific geographical or topographical details were supplied, P. E. H. Hair has pointed out that they 'were often employed . . . in a loose or inaccurate sense.' The imperfect 'hearing and recording by the Valencian clerk' (or, moreover, 'the modern editor'), further compounds the difficulty of determining the exact geographical origin of slaves arriving in the port of Valencia during the latter half of the fifteenth century. The most common provenance given for a black African slave during this period was 'de Jalof,' which Hair reasons was employed 'in a general sense, to indicate slaves drawn from the wide region also occasionally known as "Cabo Verde", that is, the coast of (modern) Senegal and its immediate hinterland.' In Hair's view the term was relatively accurate inasmuch as 'this was the first area to be reached and exploited by the Portuguese, a trade beginning in the 1440's'.[16] Although some of the black slaves offered for sale in Valencia during this period had reached peninsular Europe via the trans-Saharan slave trade (obtained in North Africa or elsewhere in the Iberian peninsula), so that they could have spent the greater part, if not all, of their lives outside of black Africa, the bulk seem to have come more or less directly from there, by way of Lisbon. Hence, they were often described by Valencian Christians as 'muy bozal', or 'very bush'.[17]

Nevertheless, the examination of civil and criminal court records from this period reveals that these black Africans quickly became acquainted with the customs and practices of their masters, learning their language as well as their laws. Indeed, they were as adept as their eastern Orthodox and Muslim counterparts in turning the kingdom of Valencia's legal code to their best advantage, negotiating the terms of their contracts of manumission and even taking their masters and mistresses to court, protesting that their legitimate claim to freedom had been violated according to the dictates of Valencian law.

Indicative of the growing strength and stature of the city's black African community, on 3 November 1472, some forty[18] black freedmen appeared in the

---

[16] Hair, 'Black African slaves', pp. 119–22.

[17] For an example, see ARV, Bailia 194, fols. 150r–151r (26 September 1494).

[18] The foundation charter does not give us a firm number for its membership in 1472. Rather, it vacillates, granting privileges to an unnamed group of black freedmen, 'los quals son en nombre de trenta set fins en quaranta'. Miguel Gual Camarena, 'Una confradia de negros libertos en el siglo XV', *Estudios de Edad Media de la Corona de Aragon*, 5 (1952), pp. 457–66. The instrument of the confraternity's foundations, transcribed in the aforementioned article, can be found in Barcelona, Archivo de la Corona de Aragon, Reg. 3512, fols. 217–18 (Diversorum Locumtenencie ii).

Royal Palace in the city of Valencia seeking crown approval for the foundation of a confraternity ('elemosinam, confratriam sive consorcium') dedicated to the Virgin Mary, 'Our Lady of Grace', and under the supervision of the local Augustinian convent. Though clearly functioning prior to this date,[19] the confraternity sought the extension as well as the confirmation of its privileges from the future Ferdinand the Catholic, at that time acting as the lieutenant general of the Crown of Aragon. The charter relates how, for several years now, a group of black freedmen had gathered annually to express their devotion to the 'Virgin Mary of Grace'. Each year, they had had a candle made and, after 'assembling all together, carried it with great devotion' to the chapel dedicated to her in the Augustinian convent. Inasmuch as they now wished to 'increase their merits' by expanding their activities in the service of God and the Virgin Mary, they were requesting the Crown's sanction. The document specifies that they did not think that they would be able to do this 'comfortably' (comodament) without first securing 'your royal majesty's approval'. In a document that was transcribed and published some fifty years ago by Miguel Gual Camarena, this group of black freedmen was granted the following rights and privileges: the right to meet whenever and however many times they wished without needing a special permit,[20] to purchase a house where they could hold their meetings,[21] to have a royal standard made which they, 'alongside other guilds', would carry in public acts and processions, as well as display in the window of the confraternity's house,[22] to elect annually four stewards (maiorals) to oversee the confraternity's administration,[23] to appoint an ombudsman (sindich) to represent the confraternity's interests before royal and municipal officials,[24] and, finally, to issue new ordinances and/or collect dues whenever circumstances required it.[25]

Besides spelling out the details of the confraternity's administration, however, the charter offers some clues regarding the social as well as religious aspirations of these black Africans in founding this confraternity. According to the language of the charter itself, these black men, 'having been transformed

---

[19] The charter acknowledges that these black freedman 'ab licencia e auctoridat del portant veus de governador han acostumat congregarse tots anys, los quals per servey honor e gloria de nostre senyor Deu e de la sacratissima Verge Maria, mare sua, ordenaven cascuns anys fer un ciri e aquells tots congregats, ab molta devocio portaven a la capella de la Verge Maria de Gracia del monestir del benaventurat Sent Agosti.' Gual Camarena, 'Una confradia', pp. 465–6.

[20] It is important to note, however, that while Ferdinand confirmed the confraternity's right to assemble without a special permit, he nevertheless insisted that the size and the timing of their assemblies be in accordance with the dictates laid down in the kingdom's legal code, the Furs de Valencia. Gual Camarena, 'Una confradia', p. 464.

[21] Gual Camarena, 'Una confradia', p. 465.   [22] Ibid.   [23] Ibid.   [24] Ibid.   [25] Ibid.

from slaves into free men,' had decided to found their confraternity not only as an expression of their devotion and desire 'to serve, honour, and glorify our Lord God and the most holy Virgin Mary', but also, in addition, out of a zeal to perform acts of charity.[26] Prominent among the statutes regulating the confraternity's activities is one affirming a commitment to aid 'any one of their brothers . . . who otherwise would not be able to live or sustain their lives'.[27] Since there are no ordinances specifying the requirements and/or the procedures for joining it, it is somewhat unclear how membership in this black African collective was defined. Was it only black 'freedmen' who were to be considered 'brothers'? Or could black African slaves, too, figure among its members?

The privileges extended to this initial group of black freedmen ('negres liberts') would be passed down to subsequent generations. The charter confirmed that the Crown granted these rights 'as much to you who are here now as to all of those who will be in your aforementioned brotherhood or confraternity in the future'.[28] In the absence of membership lists and/or any other documentation that might shed light on the subject, the identities of those who came to enjoy these privileges and/or benefit from this foundation's charity remains lamentably obscure. In what follows, I will be examining two court cases that reveal the identities of some of the members of this 'black' confraternity as well as the intended beneficiaries of their admittedly limited resources.

Given the date (1478) and context of the aforementioned reference to the 'house of the black Africans,' the 'casa dels negres' was, in all likelihood, the house which this group of black freedmen sought Ferdinand's permission to purchase some six years previously as a place to 'hold their meetings and conduct the confraternity's business'.[29] While Ursola's master seems to have sent her to the 'casa dels negres' primarily out of a feeling of exasperation

---

[26] Gual Camarena, 'Una confradia', p. 464: 'Ea propter cum vos homines nigri ex servis liberi facti cupiatis elemosinam et confratriam sive consorcium habere, iuxta Sacre Scripture eloquium que inter nos unanimam dilectionem et caritatem habere ac caritatis opera docet exercere.'

[27] Gual Camarena, 'Una confradia', p. 465: 'Item que si per necessitat de malaltia o per pobresa o miserabilitat, algu dels dits confrares sera posat en necessitat que altrament no puxa viure e sostentar la sua vida, que aquells tals sian ajudats e sostenguts per los dits confrares de tot lo que hauran mester e per lur sostentacio.'

[28] Gual Camarena, 'Una confradia', p. 466: 'Tam pro vobis qui nunch estis quam pro illis omnibus qui erunt de iamdicta elemosina vestra sive confratria in futurum'.

[29] Gual Camarena, 'Una confradia', p. 465: 'Item que los dits confrares e maiorals tinguen facultat poder comprar e tenir una casa en la present ciutat de Valencia, en la qual aquells se puxen ajustar e congregar per fer e tractar los negocis e actes de la dita confraria.'

and a desire to keep the unruly slave out of his household, there is also a suggestion made here that she was being sent there to receive medical treatment. Hence, it would seem that the 'casa dels negres' was more than a 'clubhouse'. It also functioned as a hospice, a place where the poor and miserable among the city's ever-growing black African community could come to receive charitable assistance, be it food, shelter, medical treatment, or even the funds with which they could purchase their freedom.

In the following discussion of two lawsuits filed by black African slave women demanding their liberty, it will become clear how the 'casa dels negres' also seems to have served as the hub of the black African community's redemptionist activities. The redemption of their fellow black Africans in captivity seems to have figured prominently among the confraternity's charitable activities.[30] Indeed, shortly after Ursola had been sent to the 'casa dels negres' – a woman, the so-called *mad[r]astra* or housemother of the 'casa dels negres' – appeared on Francesch's doorstep, beseeching him to grant the black female her liberty in exchange for payment of a redemption fee of forty *lliures*. While Francesch would later testify that he had only grudgingly agreed to the terms of this redemption agreement – doing so only 'so that he would not be forced to beat her again due to the disturbances that she [otherwise] would have continued to cause him'[31] – at least on paper it would seem that Francesch had achieved the best of all possible solutions. Not only would the payment of the redemption fee fully compensate him for the slave's initial purchase price, but also, until she paid the forty *lliures* off in full, Ursola was obliged to continue providing him with service. Moreover, Francesch had achieved all this without having to accept the unruly slave back into his household. Throughout this entire period, Ursola would remain in the protective custody of the 'casa dels negres'.

While, at least initially, Ursola seems to have honoured this agreement, 'coming to his [Francesch's] household two or three times to make bread', very soon thereafter, Ursola simply stopped showing up. After Ursola failed to show up to work a few times, Francesch related how he sent his wife after

---

[30] For further examples indicating that redeeming captives and lending aid to prisoners were charitable activities commonly performed by confraternities during this period, see Maureen Flynn, *Sacred Charity: Confraternities and Social Welfare in Spain, 1400–1700* (Ithaca, 1989), pp. 62–4; Christopher Black, *Italian Confraternities in the Sixteenth Century* (Cambridge, 1989), pp. 73, 217–23, 260; and Nicholas Terpstra, ed., *The Politics of Ritual Kinship: Confraternities and Social Order in Early Modern Italy* (Cambridge, 2000), pp. 25–6, 213–14, 218.

[31] ARV, Gobernación 2348, M. 7, fol. 2r: 'E ell dit responent per que no hagues a tornar a batre la per los desordes de aquella poria venir en algun inconvenient dix que era content. E axis partiren.'

her, demanding that, in accordance with their agreement, she come to his household to make bread. Perhaps even more defiant now that she was no longer living under her master's roof, Ursola reportedly refused, responding that 'this did not seem satisfactory to her. She was unwilling to give him both money and service.'[32] Hardly disposed to allow this black female slave to name her own terms, Francesch sent his apprentices ('seus jovens') over to the 'house of the blacks' with orders to seize Ursola and have her incarcerated in the municipal prison. Once again, however, Francesch was confronted by a group of black Africans who quickly appeared on his doorstep to intercede on Ursola's behalf. They urged him to give the black female another chance to earn her freedom, imploring Francesch to accept the already agreed upon redemption price of forty *lliures*. Now, however, in recognition of the fact that Ursola was no longer willing to provide him with service in the interim during which the redemption fee was being assembled, they offered, in compromise, to pay her ransom off in slightly larger installments of twenty-five *solidos* per month.[33]

Seventeen years later, in 1495, the nobleman Bernat Sorrell was similarly asked by 'some black freedmen' to accept a redemption fee for his black female slave named Johana.[34] Like Francesch, Bernat had been experiencing difficulties in controlling his slave. Feeling that he had been 'poorly repaid' in his investment, Bernat contracted the services of a broker, 'wishing to deliver himself' of the unruly slave by selling her to a new owner. Despite this broker's best efforts, however, a willing buyer could not be found, for 'wherever they went, the slave presented herself so poorly that no one wanted to buy her'. Frustrated with Johana's impudence, Bernat had her imprisoned and reportedly had decided to book Johana passage on a ship to Ibiza where

[32] ARV, Gobernación 2348, M. 7, fol. 2r: 'E sequis de la dita Ursola en virtud de la dita concordia vench a pastar a la casa de ell dit responent dos o tres veguades. E com no haguessen en casa dell dit responent pastar trametiha la muller del dit responent per aquella demanant la que vingues a pastar. E aquella respos que no li venia be car no li volia donar dines e fahena.'

[33] ARV, Gobernación 2348, M. 7, fol. 2r: 'E ell dit responent vehent que no era volguda venir segons promes havia trames dels seus jovens e feu la portar a la preso ab cor de sperar li comprador e vendre la puix aquella no li atenyia lo que promes li havia. E tenint la presa fonch pregat per negres e alguns altres que la dona a capleuta ab fermances. E que si volia que ella li daria les quaranta lliures empero que no hagues a pastar e que les dites quaranta lliures paguaria ves cascun mes vint e cinch solidos e que ja tenia quaranta solidos que'ls hi donaria.'

[34] ARV, Gobernación 2410, M. 15, fol. 26r (219r): 'en dies passats la dita Johana stant sclava del dit mossen Sorell per cert guarts al dit mossen Sorell benvisos aquella fos posada en la preso e a part alguns negres franchs de la present ciutat menesaren e tractaren ab lo dit mossen Sorell de rescatar e enfranquir la dita Johana e axi fon concordat entre aquells e axi es ver.'

he could get rid of her once and for all. Before he had a chance to do so, however, 'the black men who beg alms in the city in order to redeem black slaves' interceded on her behalf.[35]

The intervention of this group of black men was not fortuitous. The broker later testified that almost immediately upon taking custody of the slave, Johana had urged him continually 'not to look for a buyer or a new owner for her because she could not and would not serve anyone'. Rather, Johana had boasted, 'she had sought out and secured the assistance of some black friends and relatives of hers in the city who would redeem her'.[36]

When first solicited by a group of black Africans, the nobleman had been sceptical. Bernat testified that he did not think that they could raise enough money, reportedly telling them that Johana 'was worth a lot of money to him and that he did not think that they could pay what she was worth to him'. It was only after several meetings that he was convinced, and set Johana's redemption fee (*rescat*) at thirty-six *lliures*.[37] Such wariness indicates that contemporaries did not regard black Africans as having many resources at their disposal, which begs the questions, who were the members of this black African confraternity, and how did they assemble the requisite funds?

---

[35] Testimony of the nobleman Bernat Sorell: 'sta en veritat que en l'any LXXXXV poch mes o menys volent se desexir ell dit testimoni de la dita Johana negra sclava que tunch era de ell dit testimoni e per tenir ell dit testimoni mal grat de aquella dona carrech a mestre Miquel corredor que li cercas algun comprador. E axi de fet lo dit corredor pres la dita sclava e porta aquella per Valencia e sabent la dita sclava que ell dit testimoni la volia vendre lla hon anava donava tan mala raho de si mateixa que nengun no la volia comprar. E stant axi ell dit testimoni feu metre la dita sclava en la preso per mal encorra que per del que aquella feya e dellibera de trametre la ab una barca en Ayviça per vendre la. E en aço dix lo dit corredor a ell dit testimoni que huns negres qui acaptaven per Valencia per a rescatar catius negres li havien parlats dihent que si ell dit testimoni si posava en la raho ells la rescataren.' ARV, Gobernación 2411, M. 22, fol. 5r (54r).

[36] Testimony of the broker (*corredor de orella*), Miquel Ramon: 'fonch lliurada la dita Johana negra per lo magnifich mossen Bernat Sorell cavaller per obs de vendre aquella . . . essent la dita Johana negra en poder de ell dit testimoni aquella dix a ell dit testimoni que no li çerquas comprador ni amo per que ella no poria servir ni serviria a nenguna persona pero que ella treballaria e procuraria ab alguns negres amichs e parents de aquella de la present ciutat que la rescatarien.' ARV, Gobernación 2411, M. 22, fol. 6r–v (55r–v).

[37] ARV, Gobernación 2411, M. 22, fol. 5r (54r): 'Al qual dix ell dit testimoni que la dita sclava li stava en gran preu e que no creya la y pagassen segons lo que valia per que sola y pagaven be que ell dit testimoni la'ls vendria e lliuraria. E apres de esser se afrontas los dits negres ab ell dit testimoni present lo dit corredor diverses vegades concordaren que per lo rescat de la dita sclava li donarien XXXVI lliures. E axi fonch content ell dit testimoni.'

Four black men are mentioned in the trial transcript as the negotiators of Johana's redemption. Interestingly enough, they were not all freedmen. Two of the four, in fact, were slaves. In addition to a mattress-maker (*matalafer*) named Johan Monpalau, the former slave of the nobleman Jofre de Monpalau, and a black porter (*traginer*) and freedman named Johan Moliner, were Pedro (now deceased) and Anthoni, both slaves belonging to noble masters.[38] Free and slave, all four were described as members of the 'confraternity of the blacks' and all four participated, ostensibly on equal footing, in the negotiation of Johana's ransom. Indeed, the testimony of witnesses reveals that slaves were not only members of the 'confraternity of the blacks', but could also serve as its elected officials. The notary who drew up Johana's redemption agreement reveals, in passing, that the confraternity's *baci* or alms collection box was managed by the aforementioned Pedro, a slave belonging to the nobleman Pallars.[39] In securing Johana's redemption, black African slaves and freedmen living in the city of Valencia worked together, pooling their resources in an attempt to protect a member of their reinvented and reconstituted community from another separation and exile.

Yet what at first glance seems to constitute impressive evidence of the strength and cohesion of the black African community in fifteenth-century Valencia must be kept in perspective. Closer examination of these cases exposes the many limits on the confraternity of the black Africans' powers and capabilities. Despite the confraternity's best efforts, the black African females effectively were at the mercy of their masters and, when that failed, the Valencian court system, to implement their redemptions. First and foremost, masters had to agree to accept payment of a ransom. Appealing to the 'benevolence'

[38] Testimony of the broker Miquel Ramon: 'E recordas ell dit testimoni que los negres qui menejaven lo dit rescat se nomenen la hu Johan lo traginer e l'alter Johan lo matalafer de mossen Monpalau e l'altre Anthoni catiu del dit mossen Anthoni Johan.' ARV, Gobernación 2411, M. 22, fol. 6v (55v). See also the testimony of Joan Monpalau, 'matalafer negre olim sclau del magnifich mossen Jofre de Monpalau cavaller habitador de Valencia': 'en veritat sta que tres anys ha poch mes o menys ell dit testimoni ensemps ab dos altres negres nomenats la hu Johan Moliner e l'alter nomenat Pedro lo qual dit Pedro es ja mort e passat de la present vida en l'altra anaren a pregar axi ço de fet pregaren al magnifich mossen Anthoni Johan cavaller que per amor de Anthoni negre catiu de aquell volgues ajudar a fer compliment al rescat de la dita Johana negra.' ARV, Gobernación 2411, M. 22, fol. 4r (53r).

[39] Testimony of the notary acting as Bernat Sorell's procurator, Miquel Gari: 'com hun negre del noble mossen Pallars e altre negre de mossen Anthoni Johan treballaven que lo magnifich mossen Sorell vene als dits negres la dita Johana per obs de enfranquir aquella de les caritats del baci que aquells tenien lo qual dit baci regia lo dit negre del dit noble mossen Pallars.' ARV, Gobernación 2411, M. 22, fol. 9v (58v).

of their masters, slaves, in conjunction with members of the 'confraternity of the blacks', had taken great pains to convince masters to give them the opportunity to purchase their liberty. And yet, even after this first hurdle had been surmounted, there was still the issue of whether masters would, in actual practice, respect and abide by the terms of the redemption agreement. Indeed, in the first example, while Ursola and her black African benefactors argued that Francesch, by accepting payment of the first installment of her 'ransom' (*rescat*), had agreed to the terms of the redemption agreement, Francesch would later argue that he had only accepted the sum in pledge (*comenda*), and that this in no way bound him to allow Ursola to purchase her freedom.[40] Hence, in glaring contravention of what members of the black African community considered a legally binding contractual agreement, Francesch had turned around and sold Ursola to a new master. While in his defense Francesch, somewhat implausibly, emphasised his slave's agency, reselling her 'with her co-operation and complicity', in the 'demanda de libertat' she filed before the kingdom's governor, Ursola, in contrast, affirmed her extreme vulnerability. Not only had her master ignored her legitimate claim to liberty, but he had also decided to have her packed off 'secretly in the night' and sold on the island of Ibiza. In Ursola's eyes, this was the worst possible fate, for she would be cut off from all of her friends and supporters – in particular, one surmises, from those who had come to her assistance from the 'casa dels negres'. Indeed, Ursola maintained, this was precisely the reason why her master had decided to send her there. Once in Ibiza, she explained, 'nobody would ever learn anything about the promise of liberty that had already been granted to her.'[41]

In the second case, though the confraternity of the blacks successfully purchased Johana's redemption, the black female's freed status would later be contested. Despite the fact that she had been living for the past five years unhindered and undisturbed as a 'freedwoman . . . maintain[ing] her own household, work[ing] for her own sustenance . . . exercising all those acts

[40] Francesch insisted that he received certain sums of money from Ursola (and, presumably, from the members of the black African confraternity), but only *en comenda*. Francesch claimed that this in no way obliged him to grant her her freedom and that he had never agreed to the renegotiated terms of the contract of manumission. ARV, Gobernación 2348, M. 7, fols. 2v, 36r.

[41] ARV, Gobernación 2348, M. 7, fol. 1r: 'Item diu que lo dit en Builaygua apres alguns dies no curant e oblidant se la dita concordia contra tota raho e justicia secretament una nit pres aquella dita Ursola e mes aquella en poder de hun qui dien Segarra al qual se diu la havia venuda e aquell la s'en porta la volta de Puçol dient la portava a enbarquar la en mar per portar la a Yviça e aqui vendre la e transportar la en manera que may s'en sabes res in francam libertatis ja per ell atorgada a la dita Ursola. E axi es ver.'

which persons freed from servitude are accustomed to perform, and being regarded and reputed as such by everyone who knows her in the present city',[42] a nobleman named Anthoni Johan was now claiming her as his slave. How could this happen? On what grounds could Johana's freed status be contested five years after the fact? The story of Johana's redemption and the subsequent dispute concerning her freed status highlights the significant constraints on the black African confraternity's charitable activities in fifteenth-century Valencia.

Relative to the free Muslim population to which local and foreign Muslim slaves had access, the freed black African community, in terms of both size and collective wealth at its disposal, was tiny. The resources to underwrite the confraternity's charitable activities seem to have come from membership dues (*taches*) as well as monies collected by members of the confraternity who begged for alms throughout the city.[43] Nevertheless, in their efforts to assemble the funds necessary to purchase Johana's freedom, the members of the confraternity of the blacks found themselves some ten *lliures* short of the required thirty-six *lliures* redemption fee. The agent contracted to broker the transaction noted how, shortly after the terms of payment had been set, the black Africans began having some difficulties raising the required sum of money. He testified, 'some differences had arisen' such that 'those with whom he had negotiated the terms of the slave's redemption were not bringing anything into effect'. While the original four black men continually assured him that they would get him the money 'very soon', they ultimately were forced to appeal to an outside source.[44]

---

[42] Testimony of Johana 'negra liberta pobre e miserable persona serventa en dies passats del magnifich mossen Bernat Sorell cavaller': 'com ella dita proposant ha pus de cinch anys fos sclava del dit mossen Sorell e la confraria dels negres de la present ciutat ha ja rescat e libertat aquella de poder del dit mossen Sorell . . . de forma que per tot lo dit temps de cinch anys fins al dia de huy aquella continuament ha tengut la casa e feta fahena per sustenacio sua stant e possessio de persona liberta e exercint tots aquells actes que persones libertes de servitut acostumen exercir e per tal es tenguda e reputada en la present ciutat entre los conexents aquella.' ARV, Gobernación 2410, M. 15, fol. 7r (200r).

[43] See, for instance, the testimony of a broker describing the members of the confraternity of the blacks as 'huns negres qui acaptaven per Valencia per a rescatar catius negres.' ARV, Gobernación 2411, M. 22, fol. 5r (54r). See also the relevant clause in the charter of foundation for the 'cofradía de los negros libertos' empowering members to 'fer tacha e taches entre aquells, segons les sera ben vist.' Gual Camarena, 'Una confradia', p. 465.

[44] Testimony of the broker Miquel Ramon: 'sta en veritat que emisa[n]t se ell dit testimoni ab los dits negres a los quals menejava e contractava del rescat de la dita Johana negra per que'l possaven per noves e no portaven res a effecte a los quals li avia concordat ell dit testimoni que per lo rescat de la dita Johana negra donassen al dit mossen Bernat Sorell XXVI lliures aquells

The key figure behind the confraternity's efforts to secure Johana's redemption was a black male slave named Anthoni Johan, the namesake of his master, the nobleman Anthoni Johan. All accounts describe him as being wildly infatuated with Johana, some testifying that he was the father of Johana's daughter, others describing Anthoni as Johana's husband.[45] Bernat's decision to send Johana off to the island of Ibiza might account for Anthoni's 'great passion' to secure her liberation, especially when he himself remained a slave. Thus, in an attempt to keep his family together, Anthoni had mobilised the members of his confraternity. When their efforts to raise Johana's redemption fee fell short, however, Anthoni turned to the only remaining resource at his disposal, his master, beseeching him to provide the remaining funds necessary to purchase her freedom.[46]

While witnesses testifying on Johana's behalf unanimously confirmed that Anthoni's master donated ten *lliures* towards Johana's redemption 'out of charity' and/or love for his black male slave Anthoni,[47] the nobleman himself

digueren a ell dit testimoni que nos envias que de ora en ora staren per haver diners e que molt pres li donaris les dites XXXVI lliures.' ARV, Gobernación 2411, M. 22, fol. 6v (55v).

[45] ARV, Gobernación 2410, M. 15, fol. 26r (219r): 'que en lo mene per de concordia de rescat entrevingue hun negre appellat Anthoni sclau qui es del dit mossen Anthoni lo qual li era marit o enamorat de la dita Johana per lo qual causa tenia gran passio que la dita Johana fos enfranquida que los dits negres in seguint lo dit concert de rescatar la dita Johana ensemps ab lo dit Anthoni Johan acaptaren lo preu concordat per lo rescat de la dita Johana.'

[46] ARV, Gobernación 2410, M. 15, fol. 26r (219r): 'que los dits negres in seguint lo dit concert de rescatar la dita Johana ensemps ab lo dit Anthoni Johan acaptaren lo preu concordat per lo rescat de la dita Johana de la qual preu sols restava X lliures a compliment del dit rescat. . . . que lo dit Anthoni Johan per lo desig que tenia que la dita Johana fos franqua prega molt al dit mossen Anthoni Johan volgues fer compliment al dit rescat.'

[47] According to Johana's advocate, 'quant lo dit mossen Anthoni Johan dona per rescat les dites X lliures dix que aquelles donava per caritat e per sguart de seu negre.' ARV, Gobernación 2410, M. 15, fol. 26v (219v). Likewise in another document submitted on Johana's behalf it was affirmed that at the time of the monetary transfer, the nobleman Anthoni Johan 'dix e fonch hoit dir tals paraules aquestes deu lliures done pero per amor de meu negre per traure'l de mal.' ARV, Gobernación 2411, M. 22, fol. 1v (50v). Joan Monpalau, the 'matalafer negre' testified that, in response to the members of the confraternity of the blacks' pleas for assistance, the nobleman Anthoni Johan 'dix e respos que era content per amor del dit Anthoni ajudar al dit rescat de la dita Johana fins en X lliures'. ARV, Gobernación 2411, M. 22, fol. 4r (53r). Johana's former master, the nobleman Bernat Sorell testified that when he went to the silk exchange (*lonja*) in order to collect Johana's redemption fee, he encountered the nobleman Anthoni Johan astride his mule and in the company of the two black men with whom his broker had negotiated the redemption price. 'E stant axi dix lo dit mossen Anthoni Johan tals o semblants paraules en effecte si es deu lliures pague yo per fer plaher al meu negre.' ARV, Gobernación 2411, M. 22, fol. 5r (54r). The broker Miquel Ramon likewise testified that when he drew up the contract of manumission, the nobleman Anthoni Johan had said 'tals o semblants paraules en effecte aquestes X lliures done per fer plaher al meu negre.' ARV, Gobernación 2411, M. 22, fol. 6v (55v). Finally, the notary

would later claim that he had purchased the black female as his slave. Five
years later, producing a contract of sale stating that he had paid twenty-five
lliures for her, Anthoni insisted that he was Johana's master and that it was
completely within his rights to put her up for sale.[48] This case reveals not
only the extreme vulnerability of freed slaves, but also the limited resources
of the black African community. Dependent on a master's 'charity' to secure
the remaining ten *lliures* necessary to procure a slave's enfranchisement, the
only mechanism available to the members of 'the confraternity of the blacks'
to provide surety for the loan was to have a 'fictitious' contract of sale drawn
up, asserting that the nobleman, Anthoni Johan, had purchased Johana for
twenty-five *lliures*. The members of the black confraternity had, in effect,
pledged Johana's own person as a security for the loan necessary to purchase
her freedom.

Inasmuch as both of these black females won access to the governor's court
to plead their cases, they were remarkably fortunate. Indeed, in both instances,
the governor ruled in their favour. In a sentence issued on 25 May 1478, the
governor ordered Francesch to accept payment of the redemption fee negotiated on Ursola's behalf by the members of the 'casa dels negres'.[49] Likewise,

---

Miquel Gari testified that 'feta la dita carta de venda los predits mossen Johan e mossen Sorell ell
dit testimoni e hun corredor e lo predit negre Anthoni del dit mossen Anthoni Johan anaren a la
taula del contrast de la dita ciutat per posar lo preu de la dita cativa e essent en la dita taula del
contrast per posar la dita moneda lo dit mossen Anthoni Johan e mossen Sorell ell dit testimoni
e los dits negres dix lo dit mossen Anthoni que per amor del dit son negre hi posava e o
bestrahia en lo dit preu o rescat X lliures del seu.' ARV, Gobernación 2411, M. 22, fol. 10r (59r).

[48] Johana's advocate, however, maintained that the contract of sale was a 'fictitious' document,
drawn up solely for the purposes of securing the loan ('per seguretat de la bestret de les dites X
lliures . . . fos fet contracte de compra e venda'). For the testimony of the nobleman Anthoni
Johan, see ARV, Gobernación 2410, M. 15, fol. 32v (225v). See also the governor's ruling, note 50.

[49] The governor, however, still asked Ursola to provide guarantors who would stand surety for her,
ensuring her compliance with the terms of her contract of manumission. Unfortunately there is
no record of who these guarantors were nor whether they were her benefactors from the 'casa
dels negres'. Moreover, if Ursola failed to live up the terms of the agreement, Francesch was
entitled to reclaim her as his slave. 'E lo dit spectable comte governador . . . pronuncia sentencia
e declara en e per la forma seguent. E actenent que per merits del present proces e alias
clarament consta e apar del pacte fet e concordat entre lo dit mestre Francesch Martinez alias
Builaygua e la dita Ursola sclava de aquell ço es que la dita sclava hagues a donar e paguar
quaranta lliures al dit en Francesch Builaygua ço es vint cinch solidos a la fi de cascu mes tant e
cant longuament fins que les dites quaranta lliures fossen pagades en axi que paguades les dites
quaranta lliures la dita Ursola sclava fos franqua e delliures de tota servitut. Per tant e alias
pronuncia sentencia e declara que lo dit en Builaygua sia tengut de servar lo dit pacte a la dita
Ursola ara spressament entes e declarat que la dita Ursola sis tenguda donar sufficient e ydonea
fermança de tenir a dret la persona sua. En axi que si los dites terminis no paguarava les dites

thirteen years later, the governor affirmed Johana's freed status, ordering the nobleman Anthoni Johan, 'under great penalties', not to disturb or molest Johana in any way.[50] Admittedly, these black African females had been forced to turn to the kingdom's justice system to secure their freedom. Nevertheless, this ought not to undermine completely the achievements of 'the confraternity of the blacks'. Although Ursola and Johana ultimately had to call upon Crown officials to uphold the contracts of manumission it had negotiated on their behalf, their stories are testaments to how this confraternity provided hope, solace, and a sense of corporate identity to the black African community.

The impact this black confraternity had on contemporary perceptions of black Africans and on intercultural relations in Valencia is something that bears further examination. At this stage in my investigation, all I can really offer here are some preliminary observations based on extant references to the 'confraternity of the blacks' in various chronicles and the individual reactions of the aforementioned slave owners to the efforts of the confraternity to ransom their slaves. Despite the growing number of black Africans living in the Iberian peninsula, the statements of contemporary chroniclers suggest that, well into the sixteenth century, black Africans continued to be regarded by some as somewhat strange and disturbing creatures. In his account of the events of Alfonso the Magnanimous's reign, Alfonso's chaplain, Melchior Miralles, related how, in 1472 – the same year the royal charter confirming the rights and privileges of the 'confraternity of the blacks' was issued – two black African drummers astride mules had led a procession celebrating

quaranta lliures lo dit en Francesch Builaygua puxa repetir e retenir aquella dita Ursola axi com a sclava propria del dit en Francesch Builaygua.' ARV, Gobernación 2348, M. 7, fol. 36r–v.

[50] He did, however, recognise Anthoni Johan's right to pursue the recovery of the ten *lliures* he 'lent' to Johana to pay her redemption fee. The governor's sentence was issued on 5 March 1501. 'Entrant en lo dit petitori per la dita Joana negra se diu e allega que lo dit contracte es ficte e simulat e que no es stat fet sino per alguns sguarts altres e no que la veritat fos aquella que lo dit mossen Anthoni Johan hagues comprada a ella dita Johana sino per quant volent quitar la confraria dels negres a ella dita Joana per hun sclau negre del dit mossen Anthoni fonch pregat lo dit mossen Anthoni Johan volgues bestraure les dites X lliures e per seguretat de la bestret de les dites X lliures fonch fet e pactat fos fet contracte de compra e venda. . . . Per tal e alter pronuncia sentencia e declara la dita requesta per la dita Johana posada axi en respecte del possessio com del petitori procehir e haver loch de justicia declarant aquella dita Johana esser libera e franca e immune e nexa et vinculo conjuncte potestatis. Salvant empero dret al dit mossen Anthoni Johan a la exactio de les dites deu lliures perdes de la dita Johana bestretes per lo dit mossen Anthoni Johan per fer compliment al rescat o delliurament de aquella.' ARV, Gobernación 2411, M. 22, fol. 13r–v (62r–v).

the arrival of the bishop of Sigüenza to Valencia. Melchior found the drumming so strange and alarming that, he exclaimed, 'it seemed as if the world was about to end'. In 1599, the anonymous chronicler of the celebration of Philip III's nuptials was similarly impressed by the appearance of a group of 'richly attired' black Africans performing a dance 'en tono de Guinea'.[51] It is in a context in which black Africans were regarded as exotic 'others' that we ought to evaluate contemporary reactions to the confraternity of blacks and their participation in civic processions.

In the confraternity's foundation charter, it is suggested that one of the reasons why this group of black Africans wished to establish a confraternity formally was that they were anxious to participate 'alongside other guilds' in royal and civic celebrations. The relevant statute reads, 'said black Africans beseech your royal majesty' for permission to design and make their own standard

so that whenever it should happen that it becomes necessary to celebrate some special occasion or solemnity in the service of your royal highness, as in the case of the celebration that was made [during the time of the Catalan Revolt] in honor of the glorious and felicitous recovery of your city of Barcelona, they can walk alongside the other offices and make merry as they look forward to with great anticipation that they would be able to do when the most serene and illustrious princess of Castile and Leon and queen of Sicily, your wife [Isabel], enters this kingdom.[52]

Thus, in 1580, 'the confraternity of black Africans, with its banner', marched at the head of a procession celebrating Philip II's recovery from an illness. Likewise, in 1586, 'la confraria dels negres' participated in the procession welcoming Philip II to the city.[53]

Although the participation of this black African confraternity in civic processions might be seen as evidence of the religious and social assimilation of

---

[51] Cited in Vicente Graullera Sanz, 'Los negros en Valencia en el siglo XVI', *Estudios jurídicos en homenaje al Profesor Santa Cruz Teijeiro*, 2 vols. (Valencia, 1974), I, p. 394.

[52] Gual Camarena, 'Una confradia', p. 465: 'Item, senyor, suppliquen los dits negres a vostra real maiestat que sia de vostra merce atorgarlos que puxan tenir e fer hun standart real, assi que quant occorrera ques haia de fer alguna festa o solempnitat per servey de vostra real senyoria, axi com es stada la festa que es stada feta per aquesta gloriosa e felicissima reduccio de la vostra ciutat de Barchinona, puxen anar ensemps ab los altres officis e fer alegries, les quals speren ab molt desig se faran quant la serenissima e illustrissima senyhora princesa de Castella e Leo e reyna de Sicilia, muller vostra, entrara en aquest Regne.'

[53] Cited in Gual Camarena, 'Una confradia,' p. 463. See *Llibre de Memories de Diversos Sucesos e Fets Memorables e de Coses Senyalades de la Ciutat e Regne de Valencia (1308–1644)*, ed. Salvador Carreres Zacares, 2 vols. (Valencia, 1935), II, pp. 919 and 984.

black Africans, further analysis of these accounts suggests that, from the perspective of their white Valencian Christian contemporaries, significant barriers
impeded their complete integration. For example, although the confraternity
of the blacks was the first group to render homage to the king on the occasion
of Philip II's entry into the city in 1586, closer reading of this account reveals
that they had taken a distinct route through the city in order to get there. After
noting how they had marched 'along a different pathway, outside the order of
the procession', the anonymous chronicler insists, somewhat unconvincingly,
that 'they were not gazed upon any less than the others . . . for on that day
they had made themselves look very gallant'.[54]

The reactions of individual masters to the 'confraternity of the blacks'
seem to have varied according to their assessment of how its activities might
impact on them. When it suited their interests, masters were receptive to –
and, occasionally, even financially supportive of – its efforts to redeem fellow black Africans from captivity. While Bernat Sorrell may have been sceptical initially of their activities, once it became clear that he could profit
from them, he acceded to their offer to purchase Ursola's freedom. Although
later he would deny it, Anthoni Johan had, according to the testimony of
several witnesses, contributed his own money towards Johana's redemption. One ought not to read too much into such actions, however. They
do not appear to have been motivated by feelings of Christian empathy for
the plight of black African slaves, much less reflective of abolitionist sen-
timents. Fear and self-interest seem to have played a larger role in determining their response. As Anthoni Johan himself testified, the only reason
why he had co-operated with the confraternity of the blacks' efforts to
'release' Johana from the control of her present master, Bernat Sorell, was
to secure the happiness, hence continued good service, of his own black
male slave. Moreover, one could argue that the only reason why Francesch
and Bernat co-operated with the confraternity's efforts was because they
had exhausted all other possibilities for gaining profit from their slaves.
Anxious to preserve household harmony and unable to find their slaves

---

[54] 'La confraria dels negres yxqué també en aquesta jornada, ab sa bandera nova que per a dit
effecte havien fet, ab una dau en aquella pintada la Mare de Deu, sots invocació de la
Misericordia y venguda del Spirit Sanct, los quals aixi mateix anaren a fer obediencia a sa
magestat, primer que les banderes del dit officis y per altre camí fora del orde de la processió los
quals no feren menys mirats que los demés que acompanyaren les altres banderes, per ço que
pera dita jornada se havien fet molts galants.' Cited in Gual Camarena, 'Una confradia,' p. 463.
See *Llibre de Memories de Diversos Sucesos*, ed. Carreres Zacares, II, p. 984.

a new buyer, they accepted offers of a redemption fee strictly as a last resort.

It bears emphasis that when the black Africans in question first broached the topic of redeeming slaves from captivity, they had approached masters from a position of extreme dependence – as slaves and freedmen appealing to a master's lordly beneficence. In this context, masters do not seem to have felt threatened by such group activity. A master's reaction to, and portrayal of, black African solidarity changed dramatically, however, once he was dragged before the court of the governor to answer charges of fraud and unlawful detainment. In both of the court cases discussed above, the master responded by trying to undermine the members of the black African confraternity's credibility, insinuating that they were engaging in illicit sexual activities. The mason Francesch Martinez, for instance, likened the 'casa dels negres' to a glorified brothel. In his defense against charges that he had reneged on a promise to allow members of the confraternity to redeem his black female slave from captivity, Francesch insisted that, in the end, 'for many reasons', he had decided to decline their offer. Most notably, Francesch explained, he was concerned that, in order to raise the necessary funds, Ursola would be forced into prostitution.[55] Rather than retaining custody of his slave out of greed or for selfish motives, Francesch maintained that he was acting out of a paternalistic concern for Ursola's welfare.[56]

The nobleman Anthoni Johan similarly defended himself against charges of greed and faithlessness by linking black Africans with illicit sexuality. Rather than purchasing Johana for his own personal profit, Anthoni Johan insisted that his only motive had been to control his black male slave's libido. Johana's advocate himself admitted that Anthoni Johan's slave was 'so enamoured with said Johana that on several different occasions he had fought with other black men over her'. In one incident, the slave had received a serious knife wound to the head.[57] The nobleman thus insisted that he purchased Johana 'solely

---

[55] ARV, Gobernación 2348, M. 7, fol. 2v: 'E ell dit responent es estat tots temps en si mateix de acord de no fer ho per molts esguarts. Primerament que les gents li donarien carrech que la sua negra hagues estar a guany e que dels dines del guany se hagues a quitar. E huy en dia lo delliber dell dit responent es no pendre les dites quaranta lliures sino tenir la per cativa.'.

[56] For her part, Ursola insisted that she could pay back her redemption price 'honestly' by working as a salaried domestic or a washerwoman: 'que la dita Ursola per guanyar los dits vint e cinch solidos pogues anar hon se volgues a guanyar ves a soldada guanyant ab alguna persona o a fer bugades vel alter honestament'. ARV, Gobernación 2348, M. 7, fol. 1r.

[57] ARV, Gobernación 2411, M. 22, fol. 1v (50v): 'Item diu ut prius que lo dit Anthoni Johan negre stava tan enamorat de la dita Johana que diverses vegades per causa de aquella havia hagut

out of fear [for his slave's well-being], so that his black male slave, who was insane with desire for this black female, would not be killed one night!'[58] Several other witnesses made reference to this black female slave's powerful charms, presenting the sexual promiscuity of black Africans as a significant threat to public order. After noting how the slave named Anthoni had been injured in a fight with other black males over Johana, Stephania, the wife of a carpenter, testified that while Johana was living 'as a freedwoman' in the house she rented from her, she had seen how the nobleman Anthoni Johan had been forced, on more than one occasion, to send his squire to Johana's household in pursuit of his black male slaves. Each time the squire came to her house, Stephania recalled, the squire would complain, 'That whorish black woman! She has corrupted and driven crazy all the black men!'[59]

Although these charges betray contemporary prejudice about the 'natural' libidinousness of slaves and, in particular, the natural libidinousness of black African and mulatto slaves, in the end, such insinuations were not enough to discredit these black African females' claims to freedom, nor the activities of the confraternity of the blacks. As noted above, both black African females won confirmation of their freed status in the court of the governor and the testimony of witnesses reflects acceptance, if not respect, for the efforts of 'the confraternity of the blacks'. The prison warden (carceller) Jacme Marti testified that while Johana was detained in the city prison (preso comuna), he observed how many black people came to visit her, telling her that they wanted to redeem her from the power of her master. Only a short time afterwards, he continued, he had heard that these black men had been successful, redeeming the slave from her master's custody, 'although he could not say for what price'.[60]

questions ab altres negres e hun dia li havien donat una gran coltellada en lo cap per la qual vingue a punt de morir e per aquesta occasio lo dit mossen Anthoni Johan donas les dites X lliures.'

[58] Testimony of Anthoni Johan, cavaller: 'que lo dit negre catiu de ell dit responent stava molt destorbat ab la dita Joana negra cativa de ell dit responent. E prega a ell dit responent que la compres. E axi ell dit responent per por que una nit no li matassen lo dit negre compra la dita Johana.' ARV, Gobernación 2410, M. 15, fol. 32r (225r).

[59] Testimony of Stephania, the wife of the carpenter Gaspar Pugeriol: 'E dix ella dita testimoni no saber res sobre lo dit capitol . . . salvo que venint hun scuder del dit mossen Anthoni Johan a casa de la dita Johana negra per cerquar los negres catius del dit mossen Anthoni Johan li hoya dir diverses vegades ella dita testimoni tals o semblants paraules en effecte aquesta bagassa de negra sean tots los negres destorbats e perduts.' ARV, Gobernación 2411, M. 22, fol. 7r (56r).

[60] Testimony of Jacme Marti, 'carceller de la preso comuna de la present ciutat': 'que pot haver quatre o cinch anys poch mes o menys lo dit mossen Bernat Sorell feu metre en la dita preso la

The Muslim community of Valencia was larger and richer and of higher standing than the black African one. Accordingly, black African slaves were much more dependent than Muslims on the beneficence of their masters and the kingdom's justice system to win their freedom. Though of perhaps limited importance in terms of the number of black African slaves redeemed, the charitable activities of this 'confraternity of the blacks' nevertheless represent a concerted effort on the part of black Africans in fifteenth-century Valencian society to reverse the realities of natal alienation and subjugation, to re-establish their communities and, once founded, to preserve them from threats of division and disintegration.

dita Johana negra e essent aquella en la dita preso venien alli molts negres a parlar ab aquella dihent que la volien quitar e rescatar de poder del dit son amo. E poch temps apres hoy dir ell dit testimoni que los dits negres la li avien rescatada empero no poria dir ell dit testimoni per quant prech ni per quant no.' ARV, Gobernación 2411, M. 22, fol. 5v (54v).

CHAPTER ELEVEN

Free and freed black Africans in Granada in the time of the Spanish Renaissance

AURELIA MARTÍN CASARES

1   Black Africans, the Renaissance and Spain[1]

The Renaissance spirit is associated with progress and renewal, humanism and arts. Almost no black Africans took part in this movement in Spain with the important exception of Juan Latino, the sixteenth-century professor of Latin at the University of Granada[2] who achieved fame through his literary works.[3] Being black was otherwise synonymous with slavery for the people of fifteenth- and sixteenth-century Spain. Even though slavery is opposed to the spirit of the Renaissance, enslavement was common at the time. Aristotle, the so called 'prince of philosophers', was one of the main theorists to develop the idea that some people were naturally born to be slaves, and his theory was in full force during the Renaissance. Thus the relationship between slavery and the optimism about the human condition inherent in Renaissance ideas was one of contradiction.

My intention is to compare the lives and social perceptions of black Africans who were emancipated with those who remained slaves. I will analyse the change that took place from the moment they were set free and present several examples of social promotion of black Africans in Spanish Renaissance society. I have based my research primarily on historical sources (notarial, ecclesiastical, court, etc.) from different archives, complemented by the study of literary sources. But it must be understood that the freedom experienced by this handful of people was exceptional and has nothing to do with what we understand by freedom today.

---

[1] I would like to thank Una Flett and James Dahlgren for their help with the translation of this text.

[2] Francisco Bermúdez de Pedraza, *Historia eclesiástica de Granada* (Granada, 1639). I have used a modern edition (Granada, 1989), p. 260: 'Estudió Artes y fue maestro en ellas y quiso estudiar Medicina, y disuadióle un amigo discreto no fuese el negro médico. Aplicóse a leer gramática y tuvo la cátedra desta universidad.'

[3] I have dealt briefly with this interesting character from a historical point of view in my book *La esclavitud en la Granada del siglo XVI: género, raza y religión* (Granada, 2000).

Before developing the subject, I would like to pay some attention to terminology. What are we talking about when using the word 'black'? The Castilian[4]
word *negro* (black) could be used to describe people from very different cultures, religions and nations. The following seven groups of people could be
described or referred to as *negros* in early modern documents:

1) Sub-Saharan people from different ethnic groups speaking different native
   languages, mainly from the area called 'Guinea'[5] but also from the Congo
   and Angola. They could be Muslims (since Islam had entered the area),
   Christians (since there were also Christian missions there) or animists
   (keeping their traditional religion). They constituted the largest group
   of black Africans, most of them slaves;
2) North African Muslims (freed or slaves) of sub-Saharan origin who spoke
   Arabic;
3) People with sub-Saharan ancestors born in Spain or Portugal, baptised and
   Castilian-speaking;
4) Moriscos (Spanish Muslims converted by force to Christianity, either free
   or enslaved) with sub-Saharan blood;
5) People from the Canary Islands who had dark skin and were in most cases
   slaves;
6) Hindus or Tamils from India brought by Portuguese slave merchants;
7) African Americans brought to Spain by their Spanish owners living in the
   Americas.

It is obvious that the word *negro* refers exclusively to the colour of the skin
and has a strong biological reference. The common characteristic of these
groups of people is that they had sub-Saharan ancestors. But the word 'black'
suggests a uniform origin even if the cultural, religious and geographical
references of the groups of people mentioned are very heterogeneous. And
even with regard to those coming from sub-Saharan Africa, it has to be
emphasised that there were as many internal differences in 'black' Africa as
in 'white' Europe. Classification of people on racial categories, such as skin
colour, aims to biologise social-economical differences since racial categories
are perceived as 'natural'. Oppositions such as black/white give the impression
that it is the race (or skin colour) that marks the difference between people and
their economic conditions. A correlation between poverty and dark skin was a
clear equation for any Spaniard at the time. My belief is that their inferior social

---

[4] Castilian was the word used for the Spanish language of that epoch.
[5] In the sixteenth century, the Spanish and Portuguese gave the name Guinea to a vast territory
corresponding to Western sub-Saharan Africa. Sometimes black Africans were also called *guineos*.

condition clearly informs the stereotypes of moral and intellectual inferiority in black Africans found in sixteenth- and seventeenth-century Spanish literature. The social stigmatisation of black Africans was greater than that of other groups sold as slaves in Spain (such as Arabs) since what was taken into account was not culture or religion but the colour of their skin.

But after reading the documents, it becomes clear that descriptions of colour are arbitrary, inconsistent and sometimes even contradictory ('clear black', 'almost black', 'dark black', 'very dark black', etc.) since there is no such thing as 'pure black' or 'pure white'. Descriptions of skin colour depend on subjective perception through comparing groups. The words 'black' or 'white' are reductionist terms with the goal of using racial categories to maintain social hierarchies.

Although many contemporary authors use the word 'black'[6] to describe people who have sub-Saharan ancestors, authors such as Orlando Patterson would clearly disagree with the use of this term. He writes: 'I refuse to call any Euro-American or Caucasian person "white" and I view with the deepest suspicion any Euro-American who insists on calling Afro-Americans "blacks" '.[7] Patterson prefers to use a geographical-cultural category rather than a racial one, but the reason he argues for his choice is not the 'biological essentialism' of the word 'black', but the negative meanings associated with the word 'black' in dictionary definitions and therefore in American mentalities.

This article is devoted to the study of 'people with sub-Saharan ancestors' living in Spain during the sixteenth century, but I have consciously chosen to use the term 'black Africans' to refer to them[8] because it makes for easier reading and, more significantly, I believe that using politically correct terminology is not as important as the approach to the subject and the ideology it conveys.

2 Muslims, Christians and their black slaves: fourteenth to sixteenth centuries

The Muslim entry into the Iberian peninsula in 711 and their presence until the sixteenth century makes Spain an interesting nation in the European context.

[6] Angela Davis, 'The meaning of emancipation according to black women', in Angela Davis, *Women, Race and Class* (London, 1982).

[7] Orlando Patterson, *Rituals of Blood: Consequences of Slavery in Two American Centuries* (New York, 1998), p. 22.

[8] I have to say that in my book, *La esclavitud en la Granada* (mentioned above), I hardly use the word 'black' since chapters are based on geographical origins of enslaved people, and this schema lets me use geographical categories to describe groups of slaves such as *subsaharianos* (sub-Saharan) or *norteafricanos* (North African), etc.

Slavery was a normal institution in Islamic Spain for this entire period. Most of the slaves were black Africans coming from the trans-Saharan slave trade.[9] During the slow Christian expansion, traditionally called the Reconquest (*reconquista*), the battles between Christians and Muslims resulted in the taking of many prisoners who were enslaved by both sides.

By the fifteenth century, Spain had been conquered by the Christians except for the Kingdom of Granada, a large Muslim territory formed by today's provinces of Granada, Málaga and Almería (basically the south-east part of Andalusia). The Kingdom of Granada was ruled by Muslims until 1492 and once conquered by the Christians, the majority of the population remained Muslim. In 1505, twelve years after the victory of Ferdinand and Isabella, all the Spanish Muslims[10] were forced to convert and were called 'Moriscos'.

The Moriscos became subjects of the Catholic Crown and as such had the right to own slaves. Black Africans were used as slaves by everyone, especially by the Moriscos who preferred them to North African Arabs, as Moriscos were themselves descendants of Arabs and Berbers. Christians purchased either white Arab or black African slaves depending on market conditions. The number of slaves (whatever their origin) in sixteenth-century Spain varied significantly from south to north. In most Andalusian cities they added up to 10 per cent of the total population in urban areas (in some periods even more) but as we travel north their presence diminishes to 2–3 per cent.[11] The Christians of the inland cities of Seville[12] and Córdoba[13] purchased a significant number of black slaves from Portuguese[14] slave merchants. On the other hand, the inhabitants of Mediterranean coastal cities, such as Málaga or Almería,[15] could more easily buy or capture white Arab slaves due to the proximity of North Africa. In any case, the Mediterranean trade also provided

---

[9] Arabs called them *abid* (literally, slaves) or *sudan* (literally, black Africans, but synonymous with slaves).

[10] Apart from the Kingdom of Granada, several areas in Christian territory still remained populated by free Muslims, such as parts of the regions of Valencia, Aragón, Extremadura and Castilla-La Mancha.

[11] Alessandro Stella, *Histoires d'esclaves dans la péninsule ibérique* (Paris, 2000), pp. 76–7.

[12] Alexis Bernard, 'Les esclaves à Seville au XVIIe siècle', Ph.D. dissertation, Université de Lyon II, 1998.

[13] Albert Ndamba Kabongo, 'Les esclaves à Cordue au debut du XVIIe siècle (1600–1621)', Ph.D. dissertation, Université de Toulouse Le Mirail, 1975.

[14] A. C. de C. M. Saunders, *A Social History of Black Slaves and Freedmen in Portugal, 1441–1551* (Cambridge, 1982).

[15] Bernard Vincent, 'L'esclavage en milieu rural espagnol au XVIIe siècle: l'example de la région d'Almería', in Henri Bresc, ed., *Figures de l'esclave au Moyen Âge et dans le monde moderne* (Paris, 1996), pp. 165–76.

black slaves coming from the traditional trans-Saharan slave routes, as Bernard Vincent has explained.[16]

Due to several Morisco rebellions, the Crown took away the privilege of Morisco slave ownership in 1560[17] and forced them to sell their slaves to Christian neighbours or set them free. Francisco Nuñez Muley, a noble Morisco, in a last desperate attempt to defend the Morisco right to own slaves, argued that black Africans from Guinea were the lowest kind of people and so Moriscos should be able to keep them.[18] However, the law was duly passed, and 1560 marks the first liberation of a small group of black slaves.[19] Most of the liberated black Africans lived in the mountains of the Alpujarra or in the Morisco quarter of Granada. There are still several streets in the Albaicín named after the black Africans, such as the Callejón de los negros (alley of the black Africans), the Placeta de los negros (square of the black Africans) and the Barranco de los negros (ravine of the black Africans). For the rest of the sixteenth century, slaves were mainly the property of Christians, and only the wealthy, assimilated Moriscos who had proved their Christianity had permission from the Crown to keep, buy and sell slaves.

Most sub-Saharan slaves brought to Spain as children or adolescents learnt to speak Castilian very quickly. Those who had just arrived and could not speak Castilian were called *bozales*, those who spoke fluent Castilian were called *ladinos*, and finally those who were learning and spoke a little Castilian were called 'half *ladino*' or 'half *bozal*'. On the other hand, many black Africans owned by Moriscos spoke fluent Arabic and knew only a few words of Castilian. Allusions to the so-called 'half language' of black Africans are common in literature, black characters generally changing –l– for –r– and –r– for –g– when speaking Castilian.

Most black Africans and mulattos had Spanish names since baptism was the rule for all, even for those who were owned by Moriscos.[20] Only a few kept

---

[16] Bernard Vincent, 'Les noirs à Oran aux XVIe et XVIIe siècles', in Berta Ares Queija and Alessandro Stella, eds., *Negros, mulatos, zambaigos: derroteros Africanos en los mundos ibéricos* (Seville, 2000), pp. 59–66.

[17] The law was passed by the Cortes de Toledo in 1560 and reiterated in the *Nueva Recopilación de Leyes del Reino* in 1566.

[18] 'Tampoco hay inconveniente en que los naturales de este reino tengan negros. ¿Estas gentes no han de tener servicio?. . . . ¿Qué gente hay en el mundo más vil y baja que los negros de Guinea?', in Luis de Mármol Carvajal, *Rebelión y castigo de los Moriscos* (orig. 1600, Málaga, 1991), p. 71.

[19] Individual slaves had been freed previously, but not groups.

[20] On the question of syncretism and religious identity, see: Aurelia Martín Casares, 'Cristianos, musulmanes y animistas: identidades religiosas y sincretismo cultural', in Ares Queija and Stella, eds., *Negros, mulatos, zambaigos*, pp. 207–21.

their African names for a long period. The surname was generally that of the owners, whether they were Christians or Moriscos. As most slaves belonged to several owners during their lives, their surnames changed according to their master's. Freed slaves generally kept the surname of their last owner. The rule was not always strictly applied as some took the name of the village where they lived,[21] or were given nicknames such as 'Ramicos' (Small bouquet).[22] I came across the case of a black slave called Juan Blanco[23] (John White), which may be a joke in bad taste since his owner's surname was not Blanco.

3   Freedom and the possibilities of integration for black Africans

The status of an emancipated slave was not the same as that of a free born person in early modern Spain. Emancipated slaves were fatally stigmatised by their past. Analysing numerous documents, phrases such as: 'slave who belonged to', or 'who is free and was a slave', or 'recently freed from slavery', etc., make clear the insistence of emphasising their slave past and distinguishing them from those who had been born free.[24]

This generalized attitude denigrating emancipated slaves, whatever their origin, became accentuated in the case of black Africans because the dominating ideology made black and slave synonymous. This was clearly portrayed in the testament of a widow, dated 1566, who wills her estate to two black heirs (brother and sister), emphasising: 'The colour of their faces gives rise to the suspicion that they are slaves, but I say and declare that they are not, and that they have never been but free people'.[25] It is interesting to note that her statement was necessary precisely because slaves did not have the right of inheritance. It is evident that the association between dark skin and slavery was an integral part of the mentality of the time. Thus, freed black Africans were doubly handicapped in comparison with other freed people with regard to social integration.

---

[21] Granada, Archivo de Protocolos del Colegio Notarial, Legajo 145, fol. 14r (1565): 'Sebastian de Lojuela, de color negro, vecino del lugar de Lojuela, jurisdicción de la ciudad de Almuñecar'.

[22] Ramicos was one of the two slaves who accompanied Don Juan de Guzmán, the Duke of Medina Sidonia, one of the principal nobles of Castile. Ramicos may be a reference to some kind of skin mark. Granada, Archivo Municipal, Cabina 504, Legajo 793, pieza 13, fols. 40v–43v: 'Inventario de todos los bienes, villas y heredamientos de Don Juan de Guzmán, Duque de Medina Sidonia, hecho en la ciudad de Sevilla donde vivió y murió, 1507'.

[23] Juan Blanco was acused of having stolen a piece of silk cloth and an embroidered handkerchief. Granada, Archivo de la Alhambra, Legajo 78–1–12 (1562).

[24] Granada, Archivo de Protocolos del Colegio Notarial, Legajo 150, fol. 496v: 'Pedro Macarruf, moreno, esclavo que fue de Lorenzo Macarruf'. Examples such as this can be found in notarial documents relating to freed black slaves in most of the public and private archives of Spain.

[25] Granada, Archivo de Protocolos del Colegio Notarial, Legajo 150, fol. 68 (1566).

Moreover, the majority of slaveowners did not liberate their slaves gratuitously but rather only after the payment of a redemption fee. Relatives and friends were generally those who paid the fee,[26] and slaves who came from distant places, such as sub-Saharan Africa, had fewer possibilities of being freed. In Granada there were two main black and mulatto confraternities (Nuestra Señora de la Encarnación y Paciencia de Cristo in the church of San Justo y Pastor and San Benito de Palermo in the church of Santa Escolástica, located in the centre of the Christian city), both very poor, although they did manage to help slaves obtain their freedom.[27] In some cases, when slaves were manumitted without payment, it is reasonable to assume that they were bastard children of their owner. White masters sexually abusing their female slaves was unfortunately quite common. Bastard offspring born under the slaveowner's roof, and freed later when they reached the prime of life, often received financial support or land which sugests the paternal and emotional connection.[28] But in most cases, bastard children remained a secret and were never freed.

Of course, most black Africans were not born in Spain but arrived as adolescents or adults. Many came by Atlantic trade, transported either by Canary Island or Portuguese merchants.[29] Others arrived by the Mediterranean trade routes, connecting with trans-Saharan routes, finally crossing the straits by boat. Many were used as galley slaves of the Muslims, others simply

---

[26] This is, for example, the case of Pedro, whose mother was also a slave, but who once freed scraped together enough money to pay the redemption fee of her son who was thirteen when freed in 1563. 'Y es hijo de Ana Hernández, que asi mesmo fue mi esclava, y al presente es libre, que nos convenimos me pagase 80 ducados por el rescate del dicho Pedro y ella me los ha pagado' ('And he is the son of Ana Hernández, who was also my slave, and now she is free, and she agreed to pay me 80 ducats for the redemption of Pedro and she has already paid me'). Granada, Archivo de Protocolos del Colegio Notarial, Legajo 198 (1563). Another example is the case of Isabel and her two daugthers, Luisa and María, the three of them enslaved during the Morisco revolt and liberated in 1573 by Francisco Pérez, husband of Isabel and father of the two girls, who paid 100 ducats as redemption fee. Granada, Archivo de Protocolos del Colegio Notarial, Legajo 191, unfoliated (1573).

[27] Martín Casares, *La esclavitud en la Granada*, p. 422.

[28] Granada, Archivo de Protocolos del Colegio Notarial, Legajo 212, fol. 156 (1564): 'Y Luis Brío, tejedor de terciopelo, dice que es padre de la dicha Micaela y así lo tengo entendido y me ha rrogado liberte a la dicha Micaela y para la ayuda a las costas que yo he hecho en la crianza della me ha ofrecido y quiere dar 12 ducados' ('And Luis Brio, velvet weaver, says that he is the father of Micaela, and I have heard so, and he begged me to free Micaela and for helping with the expenses I incurred in bringing her up, he offered and wants to give me 12 ducats').

[29] A black slave from Senegal called Francisco said that he was brought to Cádiz by the Portuguese merchant who captured him. Granada, Archivo de la Alhambra, Legajo 101–47 (1566). The first Portuguese settlements in the area called Guinea date from 1444 and 1446 and many Portuguese slave traders sold slaves in Spain.

arrived as free servants. A few, interestingly, freed (for various reasons) by their Arab owners, went on to join the bands of pirates which raided the Iberian coast.[30]

The Mediterranean sea was a very busy, chaotic place. Apart from the normal business of fishing, there were primarily three activities in which black Africans were involved: first, Arabs (with their black galley slaves) came to Spain to plunder and capture Christians; second, Spaniards (with their black galley slaves) plundered North Africa and captured black and white Muslims; third, black and white Moriscos left Spain with their black slaves looking for a better life in Muslim countries. In some cases, these Moriscos found new careers as spies or guides for pirates due to their excellent knowledge of the Iberian coast. Some, becoming pirates themselves, used their black slaves to help fight, plunder and capture Christians. The trip by boat from Tetuán (in Morocco) to Castel de Ferro (in Granada) lasted one day and one night.[31] Curiously, it is the same maritime route used today by sub-Saharan Africans and Arabs attempting to enter Spain illegally – the cause of so many of the recent tragic news stories.

In some official documents, black Africans are to be found escaping to the Spanish coast from Muslim vessels in order to avoid the hard life of a galley slave. Others simply got lost on shore during pirate raids. Black Africans unable to prove their free status were in deep trouble. The Spanish were very concerned to prevent spying along the coast. When black Africans could not speak Castilian, which was very frequently the case, the Spanish authorities usually found a translator during the interrogation.[32] If the authorities were unconvinced, it was a one-way street back into slavery.

These 'escaped' or 'lost' black Africans understood that the only road to freedom was to declare their desire to convert to Christianity. And some genuinely did want to convert, as they had suffered terrible treatment under their Muslim owners. There were many instances during the subsequent inter-rogation (which sometimes involved torture on the rack) when the Spanish lawyer provided for the suspect successfully defended the position of 'religious

---

[30] Granada, Archivo de la Alhambra, Legajo 100–47 (1561).   [31] *Ibid.*

[32] Haxa, a slave from the north of Africa who spoke good Castilian, was the interpreter in several cases in Granada. For example, she was the interpreter in the trial in which freedom was granted to a black man called Suzma found lost on the coast of Granada and put in jail where he was dying of hunger. The text says: 'Llevando consigo una esclava que se llama Haxa para que interpretase porque la lengua berberisca es cerrada' ('Taking with them a slave called Haxa to interpret because the Berber language is hard to understand'). Granada, Archivo de la Alhambra, Legajo 100–6 (1553).

refugee'. However, an unsuccessful defence usually meant being sold back into slavery (the money going to the Crown) or working as a galley slave, the very life they were trying to escape.

When a slave escaped from his/her master, it was not easy to hide. Most cities in early modern Spain were small enough for everyone to know each other. Any new arrival would be noticed sooner or later, and the fact of being black made him/her even more conspicuous. Black Africans who did not have documentation proving their free status or who could not be identified by other citizens were usually sold again as slaves.

On the other hand, black Africans from different ethnic or tribal backgrounds living in the same town tended to help each other, even if this represented a grave danger for the people helping the runaway. Additionally, black confraternities played an important unifying role for black Africans of different cultures as well as offering solidarity.

Most freed black Africans who went back to Africa, as well as escaping slaves, left their possessions in Spain. The few goods they had were confiscated and sold in public auctions (the money going to the Crown), as in the case of the following family of freed black Africans. In 1556, Melchor,[33] his mother and his brothers abandoned the few possessions they had: a woollen cloak, two pillows of dyed burlap, a blanket, a mattress (half wool and half floss silk), another mattress (half wool and half tow), six tow baskets (one of them full of wool), a piece of orange cloth, four plates and four bowls, a green pot, two pitchers, one earthenware pitcher, three rush mats, a wool comb and two heddles for weaving. Most of their goods were old and some were broken, but everything was sold at public auction, proclaimed by the town crier in front of the entire village. The sale amounted to an insignificant 1.326 *maravedís* for the Crown. Like Melchor and his family, most freed black Africans were poor and lived from hand to mouth.

4 How to survive as a freed black African in Castilian society

Most freed black Africans had miserable jobs involving hard physical labour for which they received little recognition and even less money. Others still less fortunate were forced to beg or rely on charity.

Analysing first the employment of black Africans in urban areas, we find a significant percentage caring for horses and mules, animals of fundamental importance at this time. For example, in 1507, the Duke of Medina Sidonia

---

[33] Granada, Archivo de la Alhambra, Legajo 62–19 (1556).

had seven black slaves working in the stables (where they also slept).[34] We also find examples of stableworkers in literature, as in the novel[35] written by María de Zayas (1590–1661) at the begining of the seventeenth century. A lady who was the lover of her black free servant visited him every night in the stables where he worked, his room being so small that only one single bed would fit in it.

Freed black men were stableworkers and also worked as unskilled labourers: hod carriers, builders, diggers, pavers, etc. Employers and labourers found each other in the public squares of the cities. Francisco Xailyn is a good example of a freed black African who earned his living through hard labour. At eight or nine years old, he was captured in Senegal[36] by Portuguese merchants and then sold to a Spanish Morisco who liberated him in 1566. Once freed, he found employment as a labourer.[37]

Freed black Africans were also esparto workers, smelters and casters in foundries, carriers and vendors of water (common in Andalusia), and of firewood, bakers or butchers. Commonly at this time, butchers often also served as public executioners.[38]

In some cases, although rarely, old owners put their freed slaves to learn a craft with a master craftsman. This is the case of Juan, who was freed at the age of seventeen and put to work with a tailor to learn the trade in 1539.[39] As his owner was a priest and his mother a slave, one might imagine that Juan was the son of the priest. Regarding black Africans working as apprentices in workshops, it is interesting to note that guild legislation[40] expressly mentioned that neither slaves nor freed people could learn any craft, and that master

---

[34] Granada, Archivo Municipal, Cabina 504, Legajo 793, pieza 13, fols. 40v–43v (1507): 'Inventario de todos los bienes, villas y heredamientos de Don Juan de Guzmán, duque de Medina Sidonia, hecho en la ciudad de Sevilla donde vivió y murió'.

[35] María de Zayas, 'El prevenido engañado', in *Novelas amorosas y ejemplares compuestas por Doña María de Zayas y Sotomayor* (Madrid: 2000), first published in Zaragoza in 1637.

[36] He was said to be a *jolof* from the ethnic group of Wolofs in Senegal.

[37] He was freed at the age of thirty. 'Se anduvo alquilando en esta ciudad en la plaza de la Alhacaba ganando de comer por su trabajo' ('He rented himself as a labourer in this city in the square of Alhacaba earning his food with his work'). Granada, Archivo de la Alhambra, Legajo 101–47 (1566).

[38] In 1714, folowing this old tradition, the mayor of the town of Lorca was officially reprimanded because he used the slave of a widow as a public executioner. The document states he was wrong to have done so since there were so many slaves whose owners were butchers: 'Habiendo tantos esclavos de los carniceros debería haberse servido de ellos'. Granada, Archivo de la Chancillería, Legajo 513, Cabina 2.566, pieza 25 (1714).

[39] Granada, Archivo de Protocolos del Colegio Notarial, Legajo 44 (1539).

[40] As in the case of the 'Ordenanzas' of Seville and Granada, sixteenth-century local legislation kept in the Archivo Municipal of Seville and the Archivo Municipal of Granada.

craftsmen who dared to take slave or freed men as apprentices would be punished with a fine payable in *maravedís*. The purpose was obviously to stop any possibility of competition within the craft, but the fact that the law existed means that slaves and freed people did work as craftsmen.

Since women were excluded from most officially recognised paid jobs, they had no other choice but to get married and work in the home as housewives. Some masters gave their female slaves a few goods as dowry (generally old used goods) when freeing them so that they could more easily find a husband, but most owners were strongly opposed to the marriage of their female slaves, especially if the suitor was a free man who would pay his wife's redemption fee sooner or later. Most freed and slave women became economically dependent on their husbands once they were married. And most married couples were the same skin colour, which does not necessarily mean of the same origin.[41] There was 'colour endogamy', meaning that a black man or woman would generally marry another black person no matter whether he/she was born in Senegal, Morocco or Cartagena de Indias. Then as now, taboos on interracial marriage worked to keep ethnic groups in their place.

Some freed black women worked in taverns and inns.[42] Black women also earned their living working as sorceresses – making love filters, finding lost objects, curing illnesses with herbal remedies, etc.[43] A good proportion of them were tried and condemned by the Spanish Inquisition, although witch hunts, torture and terrorising were not as extreme in Spain (except for isolated cases in the north) as in Northern Europe.[44]

[41] Esperanza de Orozco, a North African 'black' slave, married in 1581 a 'black' man from Portuguese India called Francisco Mejía. Granada, Archivo de la Curia Episcopal, Legajo 1579–1585. I have analysed more than forty dossiers ('Expedientes matrimoniales'), preserved in the Archivo de la Curia Episcopal de Granada, of marriages that took place in the city during the sixteenth and early seventeenth centuries. The dossiers form one of the most interesting sources for the study of slavery, though they have not previously been used for this purpose. They each consist of twenty to forty pages, describing many details of the lives of the couples concerned. I have to say that the ecclesiastical archives of Spain are in very bad condition due to the general neglect of the Catholic Church.

[42] Inés, a black girl of eighteen, worked in the Mesón del agua with the widow who owned the inn, Granada, Archivo de Protocolos del Colegio Notarial, Legajo 150, fol. 607 (1566). The number of taverns and inns in Granada was very high since the city housed the litigants who came to the Chancery, the only one in the south of Spain. For example, in the central disctrict of Santa María there were twenty-four inns, four taverns and one house that offered a bed. Simancas, Archivo General, Censo de Granada de 1561, fol. 117v.

[43] Aurelia Martín Casares, 'La hechicería en la Andalucía Moderna ¿una forma de poder de las mujeres?', in Mary Nash and María José de la Pascua, eds., *Pautas históricas de sociabilidad femenina: Rituales y modelos de representación* (Cadiz, 1999), pp. 101–12.

[44] Brian P. Levack, *The Witch-Hunt in Early Modern Europe* (London, 1995).

In rural areas, some black women and men worked as farmers on their own land or by hiring themselves out to work. Other black Africans living in the countryside had small plots of land with mulberry trees, sugar cane or vines. For example, Sebastian de Lojuela, a black farmer, bought six fields of sugar cane in 1565 with his savings.[45] Likewise, Alonso Calderón,[46] a freed black African who had been a slave of Francisco Calderón, had a plot of arable land with eight or nine mulberry trees and some vines. Sometimes they bought trees on other people's land and took care of them, gathering the fruit and selling it in the public markets. Some black Africans used to gather wild chestnuts to sell and mulberry leaves for raising silkworms.[47] Women also owned pieces of land and worked in the countryside.[48]

When work did not bring in enough to make a living, they sometimes stole fruit. In fact, some black boys ended up in jail after being caught stealing fruit or vegetables. A young black man called Juan was accused of climbing over the walls of a fruit garden to steal from it.[49] The owner of the orchard personally saw him and when he tried to stop him, the boy responded with threats and stones. In some cases thieves were condemned to be whipped in the street or banished from the place for a period of two to four years.[50]

Although the great majority of black Africans lived as I have described, there were a few black people who enjoyed a certain social renown in early modern Spain. The most famous case is Juan Latino, the black professor of Latin who wrote several books and who died in 1590. Francisco Henríquez de Jorquera, author of the *Anales de Granada*, describes him as 'one of the most eminent black people the world has ever known'.[51] He was born a slave,

---

[45] Granada, Archivo de Protocolos del Colegio Notarial, Legajo 145, fol. 14r (1565).

[46] Granada, Archivo de la Alhambra, Legajo 101–19 (1566).

[47] A black man called Francisco, who arrived in Spain in 1521 at the age of nine and was freed in 1543, earned his living by selling mulberry leaves for raising silkworms and by working in the vineyards. He was said to be a very good worker. Granada, Archivo de la Alhambra, Legajo 137–15 (1543).

[48] Many freed women such as Costanza Firiha, who had been the slave of a Morisco, worked in the countryside. Once freed she bought a small plot of land for her own use, with vines and two olive trees. Granada, Archivo de Protocolos del Colegio Notarial, Legajo 150, fol. 120r (1566).

[49] Granada, Archivo de la Alhambra, Legajo 223–145 (1573).

[50] On 4 February 1562 a black man was sentenced to 100 lashes in the street around the district of the Alhambra where he lived. Subsequently he was banished from Granada for four years. He had been accused of robbery of goods of an estimated value of six ducats but had no money to pay for them. Granada, Archivo de la Alhambra, Legajo 78-1-16 (1562).

[51] Francisco Henriquez de Jorquera, *Anales de Granada. Descripción del Reino y su ciudad. Crónica de la Reconquista (1482–1492). Sucesos de los años 1588 a 1646.* I have used the latest edition published by the University of Granada in 1987, II, p. 533.

but later freed and brought up in the houses of the Duke of Sessa. It is quite possible that the duke was his father because most documents state clearly that the duke was very fond of him. Juan Latino married a white woman and they had a daughter. In his later years he went blind, perhaps through devoting so much time to reading by candlelight. Even when blind he used to walk through the streets with his pupils reading Horace or Virgil. He was buried at the church of Santa Ana, a church located in the centre of the Christian city, where he lived, near the high altar where his name is engraved on a white marble slab.[52] He was a good friend of the archbishop of Granada and they frequently had lunch together. Francisco Bermúdez de Pedraza, author of the *Historia eclesiástica de Granada* of 1639, makes reference to the following exchange, which apparently took place between them. The archbishop asked Juan Latino: 'Master, what would have become of us if we had not studied?', to which Juan Latino replied wittily: 'Your Grace would be a brutish day labourer and I would be brushing down horses'.[53] It is worth noting that both men considered their studies to have been the basis of their social position, though their success was probably more related to the fact of having wealthy parents or protectors.

Another black person who escaped slavery was a Dominican priest Cristóbal de Meneses, of whom almost nothing is known except that he was said to be a good priest and preacher.[54] A third is the Licenciado Ortíz, who was a lawyer of the Royal Court. He was the son of a black woman and a knight of a military order. He lived with his mother and took care of her, but he did not want to hear a word about his father. When asked why he hated his father, he answered with the following paradox: 'I owe more to my mother who gave me a good father than to my father who gave me a despicable mother'.[55]

---

[52] Bermúdez de Pedraza, *Historia eclesiástica*, p. 260: 'Cegó de viejo porque vivió noventa años y ciego leía en la Universidad y por las calles con sus pupilos delante, iban leyendo a Horacio o Virgilio, y el maestro explicando. Fue sepultado en la parroquia de la Señora Santa Ana junto a las gradas del Altar mayor se lee su nombre en losa blanca.'

[53] Bermúdez de Pedraza, *Historia eclesiástica*, p. 260: 'Comía con él muchas veces, y una de ellas le dijo el arzobispo: señor, maestro, qué fuera de nosotros si no hubiéramos estudiado? Y respondiole con donaire: Vuestra merced fuera un destripaterrones y yo almohazara caballos.'

[54] Bermúdez de Pedraza, *Historia eclesiástica*, p. 260: 'También fue negro deste tiempo el padre fray Cristóbal de Meneses de la orden de Santo Domingo, fue buen sacerdote y predicador y de graciosa y agradable conversación'.

[55] Bermúdez de Pedraza, *Historia eclesiástica*, p. 260: 'Tenía en casa a la negra de su madre, la regalaba y quería bien, pero a su padre no quería hablar más que de gorra y preguntado por sus amigos la causa, respondió: Debo más a mi madre que me dio tan buen padre que a mi padre que me dio tan ruin madre'.

The embroideress Catalina de Soto is also listed with these three men, all described as 'prodigies', but she is regarded as a sexual object.[56] She was called the 'Queen of Black Africans' and described as a pretty woman with a pleasant face and an attractive body. She was well known for her embroidery and was said to be the first needlewoman of Spain and to have the best hands for embroidery of her time. She also valued trousseaux for white women who were going to marry, as was the custom at the period. The chronicler who informs us of her existence met her when he was a child, and says that he used to follow her because it was so unusual to see a clean, smart black woman with two white women servants following her.[57]

Other cases in which black Africans were promoted to higher social groups may have existed, but they are exceptional and have to be treated and remembered as such. Although it must have been better to be freed, since at least they could not be arbitrarily beaten or punished, most black Africans lived in terrible conditions, whether as slaves (the majority) or free. The word 'Renaissance' had no meaning for most black Africans in early modern Spain and unfortunately still has no meaning for many black immigrants today.

[56] Bermúdez de Pedraza, *Historia eclesíastica*, p. 260: 'Y porque no se queje el femíneo sexo de que no cito sus negros prodigios, sea el cuarto la negra Catalina de Soto, que mereció por sus ilustres partes ser Reina de negras'. ('So that women don't complain that I don't mention female black prodigies, the fourth will be Catalina de Soto, who deserved to be called the Queen of Black Africans')

[57] Franciso Bermúdez de Pedraza, *Historia eclesíastica de Granada*, p. 260: 'Yo la conocí en mi puecia y me iba tras ella pareciéndome gran novedad ver una negra muy aseada y compuesta, con dos criadas blancas detrás de ella'.

CHAPTER TWELVE

Black African slaves and freedmen in Portugal during the Renaissance: creating a new pattern of reality

DIDIER LAHON

The implicit reference in the title of this chapter to the notion of 'anomaly' and to the various ways in which societies react when faced with a fact or event that does not fit naturally into their traditional framework belongs to Mary Douglas.[1] It will be the reference point for this analysis of the presence in Portugal of a black population, made up of both slaves and freedmen, following the revival of the slave trade from the second half of the fifteenth century. It is a fact (or more broadly speaking a 'thing') that does not fit into a given whole or sequence.

Slavery was not unknown in Portugal in the fifteenth century. However, whereas in other Southern European countries, like Spain or Italy, slaves tended to come from the Eastern Mediterranean or from black Africa, slaves in Portugal were mostly Muslim, captured during raids on the North African coast or through privateering in the Mediterranean. The introduction of black Africans into Portugal is thus more a break in anthropological rather than in sociological terms. Although Africa and black Africans were not unknown, they were nonetheless, there as elsewhere, the subject of the most diverse and fanciful myths and of generally pejorative representations reaching back into the Middle Ages and Antiquity. Thus, when Zurara was writing his *Crónica de Guiné* in the 1450s, 'the qualities attributed to the Ethiopians are somewhat unusual and steeped in strangeness'.[2] Describing the first wave of slaves from the Saharan coast arriving in the Algarve in August 1444, Zurara, in a passage that professes to be inspired by Christian charity, does not neglect to point out that these people 'are of the generation of the children of Adam', although then he goes on to say that it 'was a marvellous thing to see that there were among them some who were more or less white, handsome and well set up, others less white, who looked dusky, and others as black as Ethiopians, with faces and bodies so disfigured that it almost seemed to the men who were

---

[1] Mary Douglas, *Purity and Danger: An Analysis of Concepts of Pollution and Taboo* (London, 1966).
[2] François de Medeiros, *L'Occident et l'Afrique (XIIIe–XVe siècle)* (Paris, 1985), p. 191.

watching that they were looking at images of the lower hemisphere'.[3] So here we are presented with a contrast – almost white equates to handsome with a fine physique, while the opposite, black, is frighteningly ugly in face and body. The black African male therefore seems to confirm the aesthetic canon and awake ancestral fears for centuries associated with his colour.[4] Zurara returns to the aesthetic theme when he notes, with regard to a young girl of fourteen, that she 'had well formed limbs and even reasonable presence, given that she was from Guinea'.[5]

Zurara is expressing here one of the constants of the relationship with 'otherness' among peoples who have been involved in the trading of slaves and their use as a source of labour. Slaves are commonly represented as individuals without a social or political existence, onto whom can be grafted somatic features, predominantly that of ugliness, and character traits likening them to animals, such as stupidity, sloth and lust.[6] Zurara shows clearly that they do not fit into a given whole or sequence and so constitute an 'anomaly' according to the definition given by Mary Douglas. And the reactions of an individual or a society to such an anomaly may range between the two poles of positive and negative. A negative reaction is to be unaware of the anomaly, to fail to perceive it or, conversely, to perceive it and condemn it. A positive reaction, on the other hand, would be to confront it deliberately and try to 'create a new pattern of reality in which it [the anomaly] has a place'.[7] This is because all societies confronted by events or ideas that challenge their preconceptions, aberrant or ambiguous forms by the standards of their system, have to face up to them, at the risk of losing the trust they have invested in themselves.

From around 1350, the Iberian peninsula had in fact dealt with the presence of Moors, Jews and New Christians as an anomaly within its social body.[8] The enforced conversions imposed on the Jewish community opened

---

[3] Gomes Eanes de Zurara, *Crónica de Guiné*, ed. José de Bragança (2nd edn, Oporto, 1973), ch. 25, p. 122: 'são da geração dos filhos de Adão' and 'era uma maravilhosa cousa de ver, que entre eles havia alguns de razoada brancura, fremosos e apostos; outros menos brancos, que queriam semelhar pardos; outros tão negros como etiopes, tão desafeiçoados assim na cara como nos corpos, que quasi parecia, aos homens que os esguardavam, que viam as imagens do hemisfério mais baixo'.

[4] Medeiros, *L'Occident et l'Afrique*, chs. 8 and 9.

[5] Zurara, *Crónica de Guiné*, ch. 87, pp. 366–7: 'na qual havia assaz boa apostura de membros, e ainda presença razoada segundo Guiné'.

[6] Zurara, *Crónica de Guiné*, ch. 26, p. 126.   [7] Douglas, *Purity and Danger*, p. 38.

[8] Albert A. Sicroff, *Los estatutos de limpieza de sangre – controversias entre los siglos XV y XVII* (Madrid, 1985). For Portugal, despite its anti-Semitic character, see the work by Lúcio de Azevedo, *História dos Cristãos-Novos Portugueses* (Lisbon, 3rd edn, 1989).

up the way to suspicions of crypto-Judaism and later, after 1450, to the adoption of laws on racial purity which became widespread during the sixteenth century. Compared with Spain, however, issues of racial purity in Portugal did not emerge with the same degree of intensity until later, after the decree of expulsion of 1496, followed in 1497 by a resolution preventing inquiries into the religious behaviour of converts for twenty years. This privilege was confirmed ten years later and then given a sixteen-year extension in 1512. In the meantime, outbursts of hatred claimed several thousand victims from among the community of New Christians.

In 1515, however, the king asked the pope to introduce the Inquisition into Portugal. But it was not until October 1536, under King João III, that it was finally established. Both in Spain and Portugal, the Church and the Crown were for a long time opposed to all discrimination between Old and New Christians.[9]

It was in this context, of the peninsula asserting its religious and political identity in the face of communities which had recently been forcibly converted, that Portugal had to deal with two new intimately linked cultural and ideological challenges – the process of the 'discoveries' and the introduction into its territory of a heathen (sometimes Muslim) African population reduced to slavery in the name of Christianity. Time and again, Zurara, in his style so often a 'bigot verging on hypocrital',[10] gives us the key to the official ideology: 'although their bodies were to some degree enslaved, this was a small matter in comparison with their souls, which would eternally enjoy true freedom', or even: 'When they arrived in Portugal and were given prepared food, which had been prepared and cooked, and clothing for their bodies, their bellies began to swell and for a while they fell ill, until they were cured by the nature of the land. But some were of such a complexion that they could not endure it and they died, but as Christians'.[11]

---

[9] In Portugal two decrees, in 1505 and 1524, prohibited this distinction which was finally proscribed in 1773.

[10] Luis Felipe Thomaz, *Le Portugal et l'Afrique au XVe siècle: les débuts de l'expansion* (IICT, separate series n. 221) (Lisbon, 1989), p. 52.

[11] Zurara, *Crónica de Guiné*, ch. 14, p. 80: 'que posto que os seus corpos estivessem em alguma sujeição, isto era pequena cousa em comparação das suas almas, que eternalmente haviam de possuir verdadeira soltura'; and ch. 26, p. 126: 'E logo que começavam de vir a esta terra e lhes davam os mantimentos artificiaes e as coberturas para os corpos, começavam de lhe crecer os ventros, e por tempos eram enfermos, até que se reformavam com a natureza da terra, onde alguns deles eram assim compreicionados que o não podiam suportar e morriam, empero Cristãos'.

This long introduction is necessary in order to analyse the changes in attitude of Portuguese society between 1450 and 1600 to the new challenge presented by the influx of non-Christian African slaves.

An understanding of the ideology during the second half of the fifteenth century is once again provided by the *Crónica de Guiné*. However, it should be added that this chronicle was used by several authors in the first half of the sixteenth century, including Valentim Fernandes, João de Barros and finally by Bartolomé de Las Casas in his *Historia de las Indias*. The influence of this text, completed in 1453, thus extends beyond its own time. Indeed it is more than just a traditional chronicle. Of course it glorifies and justifies the enterprise of the 'discoveries', laying emphasis in turn on the spiritual and economic advantages these brought to Portugal. But as regards the newly conquered populations, especially those already present or who would be brought to the metropolis, Zurara seems paradoxically to blaze a trail for a philosophy that broke right away from the notion of the enemy within and without, represented by the Moors, Jews and New Christians.

It is in this light that the famous description of the arrival of the first slaves at Lagos, often cited as an example of Christian spirit, should be read. Most of chapter XXVI shows the relatively smooth process of assimilation of the slaves, the ease with which they became integrated into society, the kindness and 'great favour' with which they are treated, their rapid manumission, their baptisms and marriages in which the masters 'showed as much reverence as if they had been their children or relatives'.[12] This is an idyllic picture that probably bore little resemblance to reality. But it does show the main idea that the author wishes to convey, which is the immediate obliteration of differences, of 'otherness', the normalisation of the distressing situation of the slaves, their ready acceptance by the population. Thus, Zurara gradually builds up a model of behaviour towards the slaves and tries to 'create a new pattern of reality into which it [the anomaly] has a place',[13] to the point that he does not forget to heap opprobrium on those who did not conform to the new cultural and political order that was to take over.[14]

Thus, while the chronicler portrays these new arrivals in terms of a set of anomalies, both moral and physical, Portuguese society is attributed with the power of rapidly transforming, adapting and absorbing them. Although expressed in terms of assimilation, is Zurara not voicing an ideology of

---

[12] Zurara, *Crónica de Guiné*, ch. 36, p. 126: 'Não faziam menos solanidade que se foram seus filhos ou parentes'.

[13] Douglas, *Purity and Danger*, p. 38.   [14] Zurara, *Crónica de Guiné*, ch. 36, p. 169.

interbreeding, which would result in redemption? Would this not be the model that the first sovereigns attempted to put into practice via the confraternities?

Let us briefly look at the birth of the first black Portuguese confraternity of Nossa Senhora do Rosário (Our Lady of the Rosary), the model for all such brotherhoods that were to spring up in Lisbon and later in the overseas territories. A document dating from the end of the fifteenth century suggests that black confraternity members were already heading a brotherhood at this time, but there is no definite evidence that this was the confraternity of Nossa Senhora do Rosário of the Dominican monastery in Lisbon. However, in 1505, there were black slaves and freedmen belonging to this institution, which welcomed members from all levels of society regardless of status and wealth. In so doing, it was applying its own statutes which preached the widest possible ecumenicalism and encouraged the bringing together of all social classes and their communion in Christian brotherhood. Whether this was manifested in terms of social solidarity is another matter.[15] This equality before God could be summed up by the phrase 'my brother, my slave'. Be that as it may, at the start of the sixteenth century, the Dominican confraternity of Nossa Senhora do Rosário was, in ethnic terms, a mixed brotherhood, which in 1513 elected black members to its governing body.

In 1518, the Crown granted them their first financial privilege – 500 *reis* for each caravel returning from the Fort at Mina. Over the next few years – between 1518 and 1526 – they obtained the privilege of 'demanding and requiring the freeing and manumission of any black man or woman who is a member of the brotherhood'.[16] Further privileges gradually strengthened the financial footing of the black confraternity members; for example, in 1549 they obtained permission to receive and collect alms throughout the capital. However, as early as 1540–1550 the first split between black and white members occurred. Cristóvão Rodrigues de Oliveira notes in 1551 that the Dominican confraternity of Nossa Senhora do Rosário in Lisbon is split in

---

[15] F. de Almeida was of the view that in Portugal 'os escravos eram em geral tratados com benignidade; e deviam êles sentir o orgulho da personalidade, ao menos quando nos actos religiosos e perante Deus se vissem iguais a seus senhores', as 'nos escravos viu sempre a igreja homens criados por Deus e remidos pelo sangue precioso de Jesus Cristo ... mas não deixou de providenciar que ao escravo fôsse garantida a assistência espiritual, pela instrução na doutrina e pelo sacramento, em ordem à salvação eterna. Desta assistência resultavam para o escravo reais vantagens na ordem social.' See Pedro de Azevedo, 'Os Escravos em Portugal de 1580 a 1816', *Miscelânea Científica e Literária Dedicada ao Doutor J. Leite de Vasconcellos*, I (1934), pp. 458–85 at 482–3.

[16] 'Demãndar e obrigar a ljberdade e allforria de quaesquer pretos e pretas que forem confrades', António Brásio, ed., *Monumenta missionaria Africana*, vol. I, 1st series, doc. 143, pp. 472–4.

two: 'In this monastery there are seven brotherhoods: the brotherhood of Jesus, governed by nobles and principal citizens, the brotherhood of Nossa Senhora do Rosário, which is divided into two sections, one for honourable persons, and the other for free and enslaved blacks in Lisbon'.[17] Already, equality between the members of the institution was no longer of interest. At this time, 10 per cent of the 100,000 inhabitants of the capital would be slaves, for the most part black.

In the period leading up to this split, the black African wing, with royal support, lost its connection with the body which supervised its finances and no longer had to be accountable to it for the alms or monies collected. Finally, in 1565, the split and the separation were officially recognised. The black wing drew up its own statutes under the guarantee and supervision of the Crown. From then on, all black confraternities in Lisbon wishing the same privileges had to have their statutes – compromissos – confirmed by the royal authorities. Also from this time on, whether in Lisbon or the rest of the country, a distinction was always made in writing between the two confraternities of Nossa Senhora do Rosário, using the formula dos brancos (of the whites) or dos pretos (of the blacks). Nevertheless, the conflict did not stop with the access to full autonomy that was sanctioned by the statutes of 1565. It was to develop over several decades and involve several Generals of the Order of the Dominicans and two popes. It was only resolved at the start of the seventeenth century, and ended with the defeat of the Dominican confraternity of Nossa Senhora do Rosário dos pretos and its disappearance in 1646.

Little is known about what initially caused the disagreement between the black and white members of the confraternity. However the documentation suggests that it essentially concerned the privilege whereby masters were compelled to free their slaves if the redemption fee was paid and the financial arrangements that allowed this operation to take place. We are not so much concerned here with the various legal details and arguments used by the two parties, but rather with the chronology of the conflict[18] and what it revealed.

---

[17] Lisboa em 1551, Sumário (Lisbon, 1987), p. 67: 'Há neste mosteiro sete confrarias: a confraria de Jesus, regida por pessoas nobres e principais cidadãos; e a confraria de Nossa Senhora do Rosário, repartida em duas, uma de pessoas honradas, e outra dos pretos forros e escravos de Lisboa.'

[18] Lisbon, Instituto dos Arquivos Nacionais/Torre do Tombo (hereafter IAN/TT), Conventos Diversos, Livro de S. Domingos, Liv. 30 MSS. This conflict is recounted in a rather confused manner in a series of 8 manuscripts, doubtless copies of originals, inserted among the 450 folios making up Book 30. Twenty-five fols. r and v, mostly undated, in different places in the book, refer to this conflict. On the basis of a number of indicators, the texts can be dated to the last quarter of the sixteenth century, although in places they refer to events before this time.

It was following the recognition of the statutes in 1565, during the regency of Prince Henrique, that the legal battle broke out. However, there is a document that places the first interventions by the high authorities of the Dominican Order no later than 1559. These authorities opposed the co-existence of the two confraternities of Nossa Senhora do Rosário within the same church and, as the black confraternity was considered to be the dissident faction, it was the target.

For their part, the white members, somewhere between 1571 and 1579, drew up a strongly worded indictment of the actions of the black members, in which they also attributed some blame to certain ecclesiastics and officers of the white confraternity: 'In the first place, certain former officers of the brotherhood and priests should bear the blame for their ill-considered zeal. It would have been more to the service of God and Our Lady to bring them into this brotherhood, set them on the right track and instruct them about salvation, and not let them get into their present state. In the brotherhood they could have been saved, like all the people of this city. Instead, they have let some black people form a group, placing a little table at the door of the church, then a larger one further inside, as if it were a brotherhood, as a result of which the present uprising has occurred'.[19] According to the report, an initial letter patent in favour of the white wing 'is in the office of the provincials of this convent without ever having been put into effect',[20] while a second one seems to have had the same fate. Moreover, there would have been no authority or arrangement between the black confraternity and the Dominican fathers, and only the white confraternity had the right to collect alms within Lisbon and its surrounding area. Clearly, the argument is in bad faith, as its authors must have known of the royal privileges granted to the black institution, which amounted to its official recognition. It is an obvious ploy – to deny the official existence of the black branch and disregard the king's interventions.

[19] IAN/TT, Conventos Diversos, Livro de S. Domingos, Liv. 30 MSS, fol. 145: 'E a primeira culpa tiveram alguns oficiais antiguos desta confraria e padres fundados em hum bom zello mal considerado porque muito mais serviço de deos e da Senhora hera recolhelos nesta Irmandade e encaminhalos e insinalhos para se salvarem que não virem ao estado em que estam E nella se podiam salvar como todo o povo desta cidade e não fazerem como fizeram deixando alguns negros irem fazendo hû ajuntamento pondo hûa mezinha a porta da Igreja e depois outra maior e mais dentro a maneiro de confraria por onde se vieram a alevantar de maneira que fazem'.

[20] IAN/TT, Conventos Diversos, Livro de S. Domingos, Liv. 30 MSS, fol. 145: 'A qual comisaon ou breve esta no escritorio dos provinseais deste convento sem nunqua averem dar excequsam'.

As far as the white members were concerned, the black brothers had become intolerable. Their attitude was an affront to the authority of the white members of the confraternity and even to that of white masters generally. Indeed, the text states that 'these barbarians' no longer have any respect for the convent or the good fathers whom they disobey by bringing actions against them and challenging the jurisdiction of the confraternity in the secular courts. Not content with disrupting, alarming and financially exhausting the confraternity through countless legal actions over more than twenty years, they behave in an inappropriate manner during divine service. In addition 'because they are a barbaric and senseless people, [they are] full of ambition and given to stealing and drinking and troubling the slaves in their masters' service, stirring them up and allowing them to bring goods which they have stolen from their masters into their congregations, pretending that the brotherhood has the right to free them. And they do the same to widows. As soon as their husbands are dead their black slaves come to their aforementioned congregations with what they have stolen and involve them in sequestration proceedings and trouble them by removing their slaves from their control'.[21] In other words, during the manumission proceedings instituted by the confraternity, the slaves remained in the hands of the judicial authorities. Widows waiting for the outcome of the process lost not only their power over their slaves but also, more importantly, the income they earned from them.

The text stresses the need to 'extinguish so great a fire',[22] as disorder within the confraternity is jeopardising the devotion to the rosary. The insubordination of its black members is likened in its effects to an epidemic or devastating invasion: 'and thus they lay waste the land with their baseless requests and demands, and they cultivate this vineyard like one who will eat the fruits thereof'.[23]

In other words, these 'barbarians' mutinying against the Church and against the confraternity must, for the good of all, be brought back into the fold;

---

[21] IAN/TT, Conventos Diversos, Livro de S. Domingos, Liv. 30 MSS, fol. 145: 'por ser hýa gente barbara e desa [visados], e cheos de ambicam incrinados a furtar e beber e a inquietarem os cativos do serviso do seus senhores e provocaremnos e consentirem trazerem furtos quem fazem a seus senhores a sua congregaçam para fingirem ser direito da confraria para os forrarem. E o mesmo fazem as viuvas tanto que lhes morrem seus maridos se vem os seus negros a dita congregação com o que lhes tem furtado e as trazem em demandas arrestadas e inquietas tirandolhes os escravos de seus poderes.'

[22] IAN/TT, Conventos Diversos, Livro de S. Domingos, Liv. 30, MSS, fol. 145v: 'deitar agoas a tamanho fogo'.

[23] IAN/TT, Conventos Diversos, Livro de S. Domingos, Liv. 30, MSS, fol. 145v: 'E com isto asolam a terra com peditorio demandas e envensois e grangeam esta vinha como quem lhe come o fruto como elles fazem'.

they must rejoin the confraternity, agree to be confraternity members and nothing else. They would thus be in God's service 'restraining the others from performing many heathen practices and abuses in their festivals, like satyrs in the fashion of their country. On those occasions they do not hear mass or a sermon. Hitherto there has been no one to stop them from doing this, to set them right and prohibit their diabolic inventions,[24] though they could prevent it and ensure that they follow only Christian practice, for it is for this reason that they come here'.[25] Slavery was thus clearly justified by evangelising. However, by emphasising the unorthodox practices of the black brothers, the text betrays, without exaggeration, the lack of effect of religious instruction. The report ends with a proposed approach that would be adopted in 1586 – uniting into a single confraternity or, alternatively, setting up the black confraternity in another of the Order's monasteries. But as this date shows, no decision was taken for several decades and, in the interval, the black confraternity not only pursued its activities, but strengthened its internal organisation with the aid of the privileges granted firstly by King Sebastião and, after his time, by King Henrique.

In 1580, Portugal came under Spanish control and the black confraternity lost its royal support. After 1586 it suffered further attacks and, despite putting up a valiant fight, was expelled from the Dominican monastery. One by one, the renewal of its privileges was refused. In 1591, a papal letter, pinned to the doors of the churches of Lisbon, stated that any rebellion against the white confraternity was regarded as an offence punishable under ecclesiastical and secular law. The following year, Pope Clement VIII confirmed all the measures taken against the black confraternity and by the end of the sixteenth century it had lost most of its privileges. The epilogue was in February 1607 – the Supreme Court granted a request by the judge and white members of the confraternity for the reconsideration 'of the privileges which were formerly conceded to the said brotherhood when it was for black men'.[26] It was not until 1646 that its prerogatives were restored, excepting that of arresting the master for debt without justification.

[24] Here the term denotes the games and festivities of the black African members.
[25] Lisbon, IAN/TT, Conventos Diversos, Livro de S. Domingos, Liv. 30 MSS, fol. 145v: 'tirando os outros de muitas gentilidades e abuzos de que estão uzando em suas festas feitos satiros a seu uzo de suas terras ao modo gentilico sem nellas ouvirem misa nem pregação sem aver ateguora quem os tire diso e encaminha nem defenda suas diabolicas envensois podendolho evitar e defender que o não uzem senão o modo cristam pois para isto vem qua'.
[26] Lisbon, Biblioteca da Ajuda, Letter from Philip II to D. Pedro of Castile, doc. 51-v-71, fol. 85v, dated 22 August 1606: 'dos privilégios que se tinhão concedidos a ditta confreria quando era dos homens pretos'; see also Lisbon, Biblioteca da Ajuda, Livro de Consulta do Desembargo do Paço, 107, doc. 51-VIII-18, n. 312, 10 February 1607.

What conclusions, albeit provisional, should be drawn so far? First, that by encouraging and giving unstinting support to the freeing of slaves, the royal authorities and at least a part of the Church, for reasons that are not entirely clear, opened up a wide breach in the absolute power of the masters. For behind the privilege of liberty lay a challenge to the perpetuation of slavery over several generations. Once the slave had been baptised, married, admitted to a confraternity – in other words educated, assimilated and trained in the principles of the Catholic faith – slavery had fulfilled its mission to 'civilise'. It would therefore be an essential function of the mixed confraternities of Nossa Senhora do Rosário to call for and compel the freeing of slaves deemed sufficiently adapted to Portuguese society. The initial measures in favour of the black confraternity members seemed to be part of a process of at least partial resocialisation of the element of the slave population which had adapted best. The special nature of the treatment of slaves in Portugal in the sixteenth century, which took the discretionary power of release away from the masters, insofar as they could not in theory object to it, means that the treatment of slaves on Portuguese soil takes on a completely different form to all other slave systems of the modern era.

Such an attitude may appear paradoxical and contradictory. It goes against the underlying ideology of all systems of slavery and drives a wedge into the relationship between domination and exploitation. The fact that these prerogatives were never extended to the overseas confraternities during the seventeenth and eighteenth centuries, despite their requests, suggests that they would be regarded as incompatible with the system and socially and economically dangerous for its continuation. It should be stressed that when the privilege of freedom was granted (by 1529), colonial slavery in the Americas was almost non-existent.

This system of privileges is similar to that of Muslim countries where 'sovereigns or the representatives of Islam, in order to affirm public law even in private relations, give legal guarantees to slaves and the right to have recourse to law in certain limited and clearly defined cases'.[27] In both cases, religious ideology created the fiction of the mission of civilisation and redemption to justify the subjection of peoples considered to be barbarians and heathens. Be that as it may, granting a few extra rights to slaves, at a time when the integration of freedmen, still few in number, did not pose a threat to the stability of the system, could be an attempt to put the civilising ideology into practice, to create a new model of slavery, one that was humane and based

[27] C. Meillassoux, *Anthropologie de l'esclavage* (Paris, 1986), pp. 114–15.

on religious values. This idea had already been expressed by Zurara in the
Crónica de Guiné.

Nevertheless at the end of the fifteenth century, in Portugal as at the very
heart of the papacy,[28] the mandatory baptism of slaves introduced in 1454 by
Nicholas V was still not regarded as a priority. Likewise, evangelisation was
of secondary importance. There was as yet no cloak of ideology to justify the
trading and ownership of slaves – that came into existence in the sixteenth
century and continued until the slave trade ceased in Europe in the nineteenth
century.[29]

This is the picture that emerges from a reading of a number of documents
from after 1450 which show that many slaves did not have Christian names, a
fact also mentioned by Saunders writing with reference to the slaves owned
by King João II.[30] The ideological structure did not really take shape until 1513
with the diplomatic campaign waged by King Manuel in Rome intended to
demonstrate 'his egregious piety so that the pope would grant him increased
control over the Church in Portugal and overseas'.[31] In his address to the pope,
the king confesses that he has a heavy conscience about the large number of
black slaves who die without being baptised. He asks for a font to be specially
erected for baptising slaves in the church of Nossa Senhora da Conceição in
Lisbon,[32] so that *all those who wish*[33] to receive the sacrament when they arrive in
the capital can be baptised. He also asks for the captains of slave ships to be able
to baptise slaves who are in danger of dying. In the papal bull *Eximiae devotionis*,
Leo X complies with King Manuel's request and in January 1515[34] confirms
the privileges and instructions granted to the clergy of the church of Nossa
Senhora da Conceição. The terms of renewal of the instructions in 1529, 1537
and 1559 suggest that the actual measures were still limited in their scope.[35]

---

[28] Hubert Deschamps, *Histoire de la traite des noirs de l'antiquité à nos jours* (Paris, 1971).

[29] A text sent to the queen in 1777 complains of the competition from foreigners (English, Dutch,
French) in the Portuguese slave trade in Angola and considers this to be even more serious as it
is inflicting great damage from a religious point of view. In the Academia das Ciências (Lisbon),
Miscelânea Curiosa, Série Vermelha, Discurso demonstrativo sobre a entrada dos escravos no
Para, Maranhão, depois d'extincta a Companhia: resposta ao que esta Representou a esse
respeito à Raynha Nossa Senhora Anno 1777, fols. 21–35.

[30] A. C. de C. M. Saunders, *A Social History of Black Slaves and Freedmen in Portugal, 1441–1555*
(Cambridge, 1982), p. 40, and Azevedo, 'Os Escravos', doc. xv, p. 305.

[31] Saunders, *A Social History*, p. 40.

[32] Saunders, *A Social History*, p. 41; Brásio, ed., *Monumenta missionaria*, 1st series, i, pp. 275–7.

[33] My emphasis.

[34] *Preclara tue celsitudinis* of 10 January 1515, Brásio, ed., *Monumenta missionaria*, 1st series, i,
pp. 328–30.

[35] Brásio, ed., *Monumenta missionaria*, 1st series, ii, pp. 62–3 and 436–8.

This is the background to the law of 1514,[36] obliging masters to have their slaves baptised within three months of their arrival or lose their rights over them to the Crown. Minors under ten years of age had to receive the sacrament within a month; adults and children over ten years retained the right to refuse the sacrament.[37] In this case, the master kept his rights. This option would be confirmed by the Philippine Ordinances, while the period for baptising adults was increased to six months and remained in force up until the nineteenth century.[38]

This law of 1514 is to be seen in the light of a royal decision of 13 November 1515, which has generally been considered from the point of view of public health. The reasons invoked by the sovereign for this legislation would probably have inspired Hieronymus Bosch had he passed through Lisbon. This is because, prior to 1515, particularly 'near the cross that is on the path from St Catherine's Gate to Santos', close by the banks of the Tagus, there was a heap of ordure onto which deceased slaves were thrown 'at the mercy of the ravening dogs'. King Manuel decided to have an enormous pit dug into which the corpses could be placed and quicklime regularly thrown in to speed up the decomposition of the remains.[39] This is the origin of the Poço dos Negros, whose existence is recalled to this day in a Lisbon street name. Presumably, slaves whose bodies were left to rot in locations outside Lisbon, and those thrown into the Poço, were those who disembarked unbaptised from the slave ships and those who, for one reason or another, died as heathens and so could not be buried in consecrated ground. It was, therefore, not usually a sign of cruelty or contempt for the slaves, as baptised slaves were buried in the same way as the poor of their parish, as the parish registers show.

It was probably in a move to remedy this situation rather than to follow the rules imposed by the Council of Trent that in 1568 Prince Henrique, then Archbishop of Lisbon, removed the option of refusing baptism.[40] First a pastoral letter was issued stating that all slaves over seven years of age had to be baptised. Thus anyone who displayed any weakness in their faith was

---

[36] *Ordenações Manuelinas*, liv. IV, tit. XCIX.

[37] On Cape Verde, see Daniel A. Pereira, 'Cabo Verde. Catequização e Baptismo de Escravos (1690–1700)', *Estudos da História de Cabo Verde* (Praia, 1986), pp. 103–50.

[38] *Ordenações Filipinas*, liv. V, tit. XCIX.

[39] Lisbon, Arquivo Histórico da Câmara Municipal, Livro 1° do Provimento da Saúde do Senado, fol. 51; E. Freire de Oliveira, *Elementos para a História do Município de Lisboa*, 17 vols. (Lisbon, 1882), I, p. 509, and José Ramos Tinhorão, *Os Negros em Portugal, Uma Presença Silenciosa* (Lisbon, 1988), p. 222.

[40] The Council of Trent proclaimed 'quem disser que o batismo é de livre uso, ou seja, não necessário à salvação, será anátema'. L. F. de Alencastro, *O Tratado dos Viventes* (São Paulo, 2nd edn, 2000), p. 167.

to be given regular instruction in the catechism and could not receive any of the sacraments until this had been properly completed.[41] The same year, on learning from a survey that most masters prevented their slaves from marrying, the archbishop[42] allowed slaves to marry without regard to the views of their owners,[43] provided that they knew the fundamental precepts of the Christian faith.

Well before this date, in 1547, a Portuguese ecclesiastic had presented a report to the Fathers of the Council of Trent on the deplorable spiritual conditions of the slaves in Lisbon. He wrote that the Moorish and black slaves 'do not have the faith, and are completely ignorant of the Creed, and of the Lord's Prayer, which is a consequence especially of the neglectfulness of prelates, as well as of their masters. They are permitted to have illicit sexual relations, and these sometimes happen between baptised and unbaptised persons, and also between slaves and free people.'[44] These criticisms were echoed in the better-known indictment of the Dominican Fernando Oliveira who, in 1554, condemned masters who 'do not teach their slaves to know and serve God . . . They do not let them hear mass or the gospels, they do not know what lies behind the church door, and they do not keep Sundays and holy days'.[45] In 1587, like his colleagues in Lima, the Jesuit Father Ignácio Martins took the initiative of gathering together the twenty distinct African groups then present in Lisbon and preaching the gospel to them in their own tongues.[46]

Thus, when seen in a broader context, the full significance of the story of the privileges awarded to the mixed Dominican confraternity, followed by the story of the conflict, becomes apparent. The initial decisions led to the almost

---

[41] Fortunato de Almeida, *História da Igreja em Portugal*, 4 vols. (Oporto, 1968), ii, p. 564.

[42] Saunders, *A Social History*, p. 104; 'Constituições Extravagantes do Arcebispado de Lisboa', tit, v, const. i, fols. 9r–v.

[43] Adrian IV, pope from 1154–9, had granted this right to slaves who came under civil law in the *Sete Partidas*: Partida iv, tit. v, lei i.

[44] Franciscus de Conceptione, 'Annotationes in abusus sacramentorum', in *Concilii Tridentini actorum, partis tertiae, volumen secundum*, ed. Theobladus Freudenberger (Freiburg, 1972), pp. 189–90: 'Nec [neophiti servi] virtutem fidei nec symbolum nec dominicam orationem sciunt. Hoc autem cum dominorum patrinorumque negligentia, tum maxime ex praelatorum incuria provenit. Eisdem passim a dominis permittitur concubinatus, et aliquando fidelis cum infideli, nonnumquam liberi cum servo.' See also Alexandre Herculano, *História da Origem e Estabelecimento da Inquisição em Portugal*, 3 vols. (Lisbon, n.d.), iii, pp. 29–30.

[45] Padre Oliveira Fernando, *Arte da Guerra do Mar*, facsimile of the 1555 edn (Lisbon, 1983), chap. iiii, pp. 24–5: 'nam ensinã a seus escravos, como hã de conhecer nem servir a Deos . . . nem os deixão yr ouvir missa nem evangelho, nem sabem a porta da ygreja pera isso, nem goardam domingos nem festas.'

[46] Padre Baltasar Teles, *Cronica da Companhia de Jesu em Portugal* (Lisbon, 1645–7), Part ii, book iv, ch. xxxxviii.

unrestricted freeing of a large number of slaves, provided certain financial conditions were met, and coincided with the diplomatic approaches to the papacy of the period 1510–30. However, the very existence of a conflict shows that this step was fairly quickly challenged, then put a stop to by the slave-owners, who included all social classes. The first manifestation was the conflict in the Dominican confraternity, the various episodes and eventual outcome of which at the start of the seventeenth century clearly reveal the imposed and voluntarist nature of the royal plan and, at the same time, the absence of a broad consensus within society. In spite of the principles the white members of the confraternity repeatedly claimed to have, contemporary accounts and the decisions of the archdiocese in 1568 show that the majority of owners had no interest in their slaves having a close relationship with the Church, and even objected to it. This was even more the case with the confraternity of Nossa Senhora do Rosário, a hotbed of dissent and rebellion against the masters' absolute power.

This institution thus lay at the heart of a major social issue. The precarious situation that was brought to light went beyond the strict framework of the confraternities and took on a much wider social dimension. The conflict within the confraternity of Nossa Senhora do Rosário, followed by the creation of an autonomous black confraternity in 1565, probably confirmed the Crown in its awareness of a split between a minority, but powerful, 'civilising' current, which included several high ecclesiastical authorities, and an opposing current in favour of maintaining the unequivocal master–slave relationship. This latter group was mainly composed of the mass of owners and a growing section of the nobility whose class ideology would increasingly find an expression in the idea of racial purity and the concept of impurity attached to it. Although there is no mention of it in the documents relating to the conflict in the confraternity, one cannot completely reject the theory that the principle of racial purity played some part in the split into two wings – one 'honourable', the other not.

Although the racial purity clause prevented New Christians of Jewish or Moorish origin from entering religious orders from 1550, there was not yet any official policy with regard to black Africans and mulattos. In an article dating from 1994, Maria Emília Madeira Santos examined the question of the legitimation of mulatto children born from illegitimate relationships between masters (noble or otherwise) and their slaves. Taking the example of the islands of Cape Verde and São Tomé in the first half of the sixteenth century, she notes that after a first wave of legitimations: 'The transfer of the phenomenon . . . from the Atlantic islands to continental Portugal was surprisingly rapid and definitive and soon extended to the whole country'. Thus between 1560 and 1577, there were thirteen grants of legitimacy relating to persons from ten different towns and regions in continental Portugal, and in eight out of the thirteen cases the father was a priest. In one case, Isabel Dias, the daughter of a black slave woman and Luís Dias, a knight of the Royal Household, was declared not only to be legitimate but also entitled to inherit her father's fortune. Santos adds, however, that 'the social phenomenon is observable from the 1520s to around 1580 . . . but afterwards becomes unusual'. The cases examined would thus have 'benefitted from the lack of ideas in Portugal about the real situation within families and social groups'.[47] Santos is probably not far wrong when she concludes that 'the new occurrences did not provoke fear or suspicion or aversion, nor did they unleash rejection or hostility. We are in the sixteenth century, a time for every kind of surprise.' Her conclusion is backed up by several other examples. One such is Jerónimo Nunez, 'a free black male', recorded in 1580 as being among the 60 voters and signatories to a decision by the municipality of Braga[48] concerning the acclamation of Philip II of Spain as King of Portugal. Another example is that of Dona Simoa, a wealthy female landowner from São Tomé, a mulatta married to a Portuguese nobleman who, in 1594, having no descendants, left her entire fortune to the Misericórdia. There was also the mulatto, Afonso Álvares, a poet and schoolmaster, who was probably born at the start of the sixteenth century. Finally, although here political attitudes are involved, let us not forget the members of African royal families who came to Lisbon to study during the sixteenth century and who were not all from the Congo.

Proof of the relative absence of out and out prejudice against mulattos or black Africans in the sixteenth century can be found in two iconographic references. One was recently discovered during the restoration of the reredos in the church of the monastery at Belém, painted 1570–2. On one of the panels depicting the crucifixion of Christ, the three Marias are in the background with a male bystander. One of the Marias is black and only her face is visible (fig. 62). This figure 'disappeared' during restoration work in 1673.[49]

[47] Maria Emília Madeira Santos, *Mulatos, sua Legitimação pela Chancelaria Régia no Século XVI* (Lisbon, 1994), pp. 237–46.

[48] A. do Rosario, ed., 'Acordos e Vereações da Câmara de Braga nos Dois Últimos Anos do Senhorio de D. Frei Bartolomeu dos Mártires (1580–1582)', *Bracara Augusta*, 24 (1970), p. 305.

[49] Vitor Serrão, 'O Retábulo-Mor do Mosteiro dos Jerónimos (1570–1572) pelo Pintor Lourenço de Salzedo', in *História e Restauro da Pintura do Mosteiro dos Jerónimos* (Lisbon, 2000), pp. 17–77.

FIG. 62. Lourenço de Salzedo, *Christ carrying the Cross* (original, and now restored, detail of three Marias), one of the scenes from *The Life of Christ* on the high altarpiece in the main chapel of the Mosteiro dos Jerónimos, 1570–2 (oil on canvas, Lisbon, S. Maria de Belém).

The other is a painting of Flemish origin from the last decades of the sixteenth century and represents the Chafariz d'el-Rei – the king's fountain – in Lisbon (see fig. 3). There was a particularly large black and mixed race population around this area, both slaves and freedmen. It was where the professional water carriers and sellers – *aguadeiros* – worked, and slaves from the houses came to fetch water from the largest fountain in the city. Situated close to the banks of the Tagus in one of the bustling merchant and residential areas of the capital, it was frequented by all sectors of the population. In the foreground of this painting[50] depicting nearly two hundred people, more than half of them black, there is a richly dressed black knight, his cloak bearing the cross of the Order of Santiago (see fig. 39).[51] This iconographic reference

[50] *Os Negros em Portugal – Sécs. XV–XIX*, Mosteiro de Belém (Lisbon, 1999), exhibition catalogue, pp. 106–7 and 171–87.

[51] The Moroccan Prince Muley Cheik whose father, an ally of King Sebastião, had been killed in the Battle of Alcacer Kebir in 1578, was made Knight of the Order of Santiago in 1594. A black Muslim, he had been baptised the previous year. The only proof of racial purity required was the absence of 'Jewishness', see E. Martínez López, *Tablero de Ajedrez. Imágenes del negro heroico en la comedia española y en la literatura e iconografía sacra del Brasil esclavista* (Paris, 1998), p. 48, n. 52. See also Anne-Marie Jordan's chapter in this volume, pp. 159–60.

confirms that prejudice against black Africans or mulattos had not at that point reached all sectors of society, in particular one of the most prestigious religious and military orders of the Iberian peninsula.[52]

But the fact cannot be disregarded that black Africans and mulattos who tried to improve their social position were not free from attack in language that already revealed feelings of racial superiority.[53] This manifested itself through the gradual application, coinciding in time roughly with the development of the conflict in its final stages, of the 'racial purity' clause to the 'newly converted' black Africans and mulattos. Thus the question of interbreeding was clearly an issue, in racial terms, from the end of the sixteenth century and particularly at the start of the seventeenth century. Black Africans and mulattos in general, and not only when they were slaves, were dismissed together with Jews and Moors as 'impure races' against which society must protect itself. But during the sixteenth century, the documentation consulted never explicitly mentions racial purity with reference to black Africans.[54] This does not mean that there were no implicit references. Two bishops, of Portalegre and of Cape Verde, expressed anti-slavery views founded on a conservative ideology, which did not however exclude evangelical considerations. They acknowledge the contradictory relationship between catechesis and slavery, despite the legally redeeming effect of baptism allowed to slaves. Basing their argument on the principle of a 'just war', they condemn illicit enslavement which they regard as a grave offence against the holy faith. However their condemnation of the introduction of slavery into the city was primarily on the grounds of the evil influences this brought into traditional society.

In a book published in 1589, Amador Arrais, Bishop of Portalegre, spoke of the serious harm that the introduction of 'foreigners' and slaves had on the employment of the native white inhabitants and poor of the country: 'before this rabble [the slaves] came into the country there were no beggars, though the population was the same as now . . . Poor and rich lived togther, and the rich fed them, and everyone had enough to live on.' And he adds: 'if, moved by Christian charity, the kings wish to make them into Christians, let them be

[52] Martine Lambert-Gorges and Elena Postigo, 'Santiago et la porte fermée: les candidatures malheureuses à l'habit', *Les sociétés fermées dans le monde ibérique (XVI–XVIIIe s.)* (Paris, 1986), pp. 139–68. In Spain, restrictions on access to the Order of Santiago increased from 1580 onwards and were permanently reinforced in the seventeenth century.

[53] Cf. *Ditos Portugueses Dignos de Memória*, ed. José H. Saraiva (Lisbon, [1979]); C. Berardinelli, 'Quatrocentos Anos de Chiado', *Revista da Biblioteca Nacional*, series 2, 6:1 (1991), pp. 7–19.

[54] Where there was an exclusion, for example from a guild, black skin colour was not given as the reason in this period.

taught in their own country, and there let them be preached to and baptized, without expectation of personal gain.'[55] In a letter addressed to the king, Pedro Brandão, bishop of Cape Verde from 1589 to 1594, speaks of the many serious disadvantages resulting from the influx of African slaves into the kingdom – the disruption of economic stability, rising food prices, wheat shortages, poor people without employment as the rich only use slave labour, loss of status of manual trades because they were associated with slavery, 'mixing of blood' which disfigures the kingdom, etc.[56] Here is the notion of defilement that would later be the basis for the application of the racial purity clause to black Africans and mulattos, in trade guilds, in numerous white confraternities and brotherhoods, and in increasingly broad sectors of society. Pedro Brandão's criticisms nevertheless end with a request for the Crown to grant freedom to Christian slaves. This would not be the last attempt doomed to failure.[57]

By the seventeenth century, the ambiguity had disappeared and require-ments of racial purity were explicitly applied to all newly converted popula-tions. In 1622, the masters of the Goldsmiths' guild stated that their trade was 'the purest and requires the greatest purity' which 'it is just and right that black people, mulattos and Indians should not practice, even if free'.[58] In 1627, a knight of the Order of Christ drew up a bill of entailment by testament which excluded from the right of inheritance any individual 'with Moorish, Jewish or mulatto blood, bastards and women married to any of these, or intending to do so'.[59] Some years later, according to the synodal edicts of the Archdiocese of Lisbon dated 1640,[60] no one having 'any Hebrew blood, or any other that

---

[55] Amador Arrais, *Diálogos* (Oporto, 1974), p. 285: 'antes que esta canalha viesse ao Reyno, avendo tanta gente Portugueza como agora, nenhuma mendigava . . . Os pobres vivião com os ricos, & os ricos os sustentavão, & todos tinhão remedio pera a vida'. And he adds 'se movidos de charidade Christã pretendem os Reys fazelos Christãos, nas suas terras os mandem ensinar, là lhe mamdem prègar, là os mandem baptizar, sem pertenção algua de teresse proprio'. On p. 91, taking the opposite view to Seneca (Letter to Lucilio, no. 47), he states with regard to servants and slaves: 'Inda que mil annos tenhamos a hum lobo por cordeyro, nunca faremos cordeyro do lobo'.

[56] Brásio, ed., *Monumenta missionaria*, III, 2nd series, doc. 110, pp. 442–5; Alencastro, *O Tratado dos Viventes*, p. 167.

[57] Richard Gray, 'The papacy and the Atlantic slave trade: Lourenço da Silva, the Capuchins and the decisions of the Holy Office', *Past and Present*, 115 (1987), pp. 52–68.

[58] Freire de Oliveira, *Elementos*, x, pp. 169–71: 'o dito officio é o mais limpo e requer maior limpeza', 'e como taes é justo e razão que não aprendam nem usem do dito officio negros, mulatos, nem indios, posto que forros sejam'.

[59] *Archivo Historico Portuguez*, I (1903), pp. 116–23: 'quem tenha raça de mouro, judeu, ou mulato, nem bastardo algum, ném femea cazada ou se cazar com os taes'.

[60] *Constituições Sinodaes, Lisboa, 1656 (1640)*, liv. I, tit. XII- decreto II, par. I, 'Dos interrogatorios que são necessarios em geral pera as Ordens Sacras, Summarios, e informações de geração, vida e

is impure, or mulatto, or black' could claim the right to enter holy orders.[61] The notion of a tainted nation gradually shifted from the Jews and Muslims towards the newly converted heathen peoples and their mulatto descendants. Was this racial purity clause that once again marked out black Africans and mulattos as an anomaly within society widespread throughout the population, or did it only prevail among the ruling classes and well-off middle classes? Research has not yet provided the answer. But the notion did seem to permeate many sectors of society during the seventeenth and eighteenth centuries.

Despite what we believe to be a cultural and political attempt to reduce or positively control ambiguity in the period up to 1500, the reversal of this trend, albeit gradual, noted from that date onward seems to provide yet further proof that cultural categories were, then as now, public, political, rigid and not easily challenged.[62] Although there was criticism of slavery, this was not aimed primarily at the institution as such, but at its social consequences on the deep-seated identity of the country. It was interbreeding (the emancipated slaves and their free descendants being the principal vectors) rather than slavery that was gradually perceived as an anomaly. This was the reason for introducing a rule of avoidance; and those who did not obey became themselves the victims.

There are still many more points to be studied if we are to understand the mechanisms of this change. It can doubtless be explained by the opposition to the spirit of the Renaissance which, in the second half of the sixteenth century, was spreading rapidly among a section of the high clergy, the nobility and the royal entourage.[63] But the possibility cannot be dismissed that it was heavily influenced by the setbacks and disappointments, over evangelisation and the conversion of the African populations, that characterised the end of the sixteenth and start of the seventeenth centuries.

---

costumes'. Among the impediments are, p. 98: 'Se tem parte de nação Hebrea, ou de outra qualquer infecta, ou de mulato, ou de negro'. Between 1537 and 1588 none of the edicts mentions these restrictions.

[61] At the beginning of the sixteenth century, several family members of the King of Congo were members of the Order of Christ. Educated in Lisbon, they entered holy orders. D. Henrique, D. Afonso's son, was appointed Bishop of Utica, but he never obtained jurisdiction of a diocese.

[62] Douglas, *Purity and Danger*, pp. 38–9.

[63] José Sebastião da Silva Dias, *A Política Cultural da Época de D. João III*, 2 vols. (Coimbra, 1969).

CHAPTER THIRTEEN

The Catholic Church and the pastoral care of black Africans in Renaissance Italy

NELSON H. MINNICH

The history of the Catholic Church's attitudes toward black Africans in Renaissance Italy is a complicated topic, aspects of which have already been studied by scholars. The highest levels within the Church, especially the popes, dealt with black Africans primarily under such headings as ecclesiastical, military and cultural relations with Christian Ethiopia,[1] the evangelisation of pagan black Africa,[2] and the problem of pastoral care for the black slaves imported into Renaissance Italy. Because the first two topics have already

The research on which this chapter is based has been generously supported by a senior scholar grant from the Renaissance Society of America and by a faculty research grant-in-aid award from The Catholic University of America. I am most grateful to Professor Kate Lowe for encouraging me to work on this topic, for assisting me with bibliography, and for making possible my participation in the conference.

[1] See such studies as Salvatore Tedeschi, 'Etiopi e copti al concilio di Firenze', *Annuarium historiae conciliorum*, 21 (1989), pp. 380–97, esp. 383, 391–97; Nelson H. Minnich, 'The Orator of Jerusalem at Lateran V', *Orientalia christiana periodica*, 40 (1974), pp. 364–76, esp. 374–5; Girma Beshah and Merid Wolde Aregay, *The Question of the Union of the Churches in Luso-Ethiopian Relations (1500–1632)* (Lisbon, 1964); Jeremy Lawrance, 'The Middle Indies: Damião de Góis on Prester John and the Ethiopians', *Renaissance Studies*, 6 (1992), pp. 306–24; Philip Caraman, *The Lost Empire: The Story of the Jesuits in Ethiopia 1555–1634* (Notre Dame, 1985); and Mauro da Leonessa, *Santo Stefano Maggiore degli Abissini e le relazioni romano-etiopiche* (Città del Vaticano, 1929).

[2] Alfonso García Gallo, 'Las bulas de Alejandro VI y el ordenamiento jurídico de la expansión portuguesa y castellana en Africa e Indias', *Anuario de historia del derecho español*, 27–8 (1957–8), pp. 765–75; Charles-Martial de Witte, 'Les lettres papales concernant l'expansion portugaise au XVIe siècle', *Neue Zeitschrift für Missionswissenschaft*, 40 (1984), pp. 1–25, 93–125, 194–205; 41 (1985), pp. 41–68, 118–37, 173–87, 271–87; *Monumenta missionaria Africana, Africa Ocidental (1471–1531)*, ed. António Brásio (Lisbon, 1952), pp. 421–2 (the papal brief *Exponi nobis*, dated both 4 May and 12 June 1518, encouraged the training and ordination of native black clergy); Georges Goyau, 'Les débuts de l'apostolat au Congo et dans l'Angola (1482–1590): clergé portugais et apôtres Jésuites. Grandeur et décadence de l'empire chrétien congolais', *Revue d'histoire des Missions*, 7 (1930), pp. 481–514; Teobaldo Filesi, *Le relazioni tra il regno del Congo e la Sede Apostolica nel XVI secolo* (Como, 1968); Teobaldo Filesi and Isidoro de Villapadierna, *La 'missio antiqua' dei cappuccini nel Congo (1645–1835): studio preliminare e guida delle fonti* (Rome, 1978); Hans Werner Debrunner, *Presence and Prestige: Africans in Europe. A History of Africans in Europe before 1918* (Basel, 1979); Teobaldo Filesi, 'Enrico, figlio del re del Congo, primo vescovo dell' Africa nera (1518)', *Euntes Docete*, 19 (1966), pp. 365–85; Charles-Martial de Witte, 'Henri de Congo, évêque titulaire d'Utique (+ c. 1531), d'après les documents romains', *Euntes Docete*, 21 (1968), pp. 587–99; François Bontinck, 'Ndoadidiki Ne-Kinu a Mumemba, premier évêque du Kongo

received some scholarly attention, I shall concentrate on the third, that is less studied and dealt with primarily on the local level. The official Church in Europe seems to have been fundamentally welcoming to black Africans. Their entrance into the Church of Rome was seen as yet another manifestation of the arrival of the Golden Age,[3] as a partial fulfilment of the scriptural injunction that the Gospel be preached to the ends of the earth (Matt. 28: 19), that all people come to the knowledge of the true God (I Tim. 2: 4) – not surprisingly one of the Three Wise Men was depicted in Renaissance art as a black African[4] – and that there be but one flock and one shepherd (John 10: 16).[5]

The Renaissance popes took varying positions on slavery, an institution that was widely accepted in numerous contemporary cultures and one that enjoyed a basis in biblical teachings. In 1425 Martin V (1417–31) threatened with excommunication those who engaged in the slave trade. By his bull *Romanus pontifex* (1455), Nicholas V (1447–55) reaffirmed his earlier concession to the Portuguese king of the right to reduce the enemies of Christ to perpetual servitude, and allowed him to purchase from infidels through legitimate exchange or by a lawful contract of sale black Africans taken into captivity. Calixtus III (1455–8) confirmed this by his bull *Inter caetera quae* (1456), and Alexander VI (1492–1503) by the bull *Eximiae devotionis* (1493) extended to the Spanish monarchs what had been granted to the Portuguese. The popes allowed this slave trade in the hope that it might lead to conversions. Innocent VIII (1484–92) permitted the trading of foodstuffs with the Barbary merchants in exchange for slaves who could then be converted to Christianity. Pius II (1458–64), however, in 1462 condemned black slavery as a *magnum scelus* and ordered bishops to impose ecclesiastical penalties on those who practised it.[6] Paul III (1534–49) in his bull *Sublimis Deus* of 2 June

(c. 1495–c. 1531)', *Revue Africaine de Théologie* [Kinshasa], 3 (1979), pp. 149–69; and François de Medeiros, 'Une structure de domination. La mentalité sous-jacente à la traite négrière et le propos de l'évangélisation au XVIe siècle', *Eglise et histoire de l'église en Afrique. Actes du colloque de Bologne, 22–25 octobre 1988*, ed. Giuseppe Ruggieri (Paris, 1988), pp. 29–40.

[3] John W. O'Malley, 'Fulfillment of the Christian Golden Age under Pope Julius II: text of a discourse of Giles of Viterbo, 1507', *Traditio*, 25 (1969), pp. 265–338, esp. 323, line 127 to 325, line 186.

[4] Peter Mark, *Africans in European Eyes: The Portrayal of Black Africans in Fourteenth- and Fifteenth-Century Europe* (Syracuse, NY, 1974), pp. 48–53; Paul H. D. Kaplan, *The Rise of the Black Magus in Western Art*, Studies in the Fine Arts: Iconography, No. 9 (Ann Arbor, 1985), pp. 103–6 and 115–19 for Italian Renaissance iconography; Richard C. Trexler, *The Journey of the Magi: Meanings in History of a Christian Story* (Princeton, 1997), pp. 102–7.

[5] W. Eugene Shiels, *King and Church: The Rise and Fall of the Patronato Real* (Chicago, 1961), p. 50 (bring all sheep into one fold), p. 55 (divine duty to further the expansion of Christendom).

[6] Antonino Pieruzzi, *Summa theologica*, 4 vols. (Verona, 1740), III, col. 197B (slavery of divine, customary, civil, and canonical law); Shiels, *King and Church*, pp. 52–3, 56, 83; Nicholas V seems

1537 condemned the unjust enslavement of native peoples (he made no dis-tinction between Amerindians and black Africans), excommunicated anyone who enslaved them, and insisted that the only way to convert them was by preaching and good example, and not by severe treatment and forced labour. By his bull *Veritas ipsa* also of 2 June 1537, he forbad absolutely any enslave-ment of Indians. His forthright stand was undermined by his own *motu proprio* of 8 June 1548 allowing the citizens of Rome to hold slaves.[7] Indeed, Cardinal Luigi d'Este (d. 1586) had eighty slaves in his villa at Tivoli outside Rome. When they rose up in rebellion in 1580, he purchased another fifty.[8]

Most black Africans in Renaissance Italy were either slaves or of freed slave origins. The fall of Constantinople in 1453 shut down the flow of slaves to Italy from the Ukraine. Their place was taken principally by Circassians, Turks and Moors. The term *mauro* or *moro* could denote an Arab or Berber, but also an Ethiopian or sub-Saharan black African; it did not necessarily apply only to Muslims. The term *Aethiops* was similarly ambiguous, for in the Renaissance it could denote someone from Ethiopia proper but could also be applied to a person living as far west as present-day Nigeria.[9] The black slaves of Northern and Central Italy seem to have come by way of Genoese traders in Majorca,

to have dispensed the Portuguese king from the prohibition against trading with Saracens found in canon law – see *Corpus juris canonici editio Lipsiensis secunda*, eds. Emil L. Richter and Emil Friedberg, 2 vols. (Leipzig, 1879) [hereafter cited as Friedberg], II, col. 1290 and Antonino, *Summa theologica*, III, 198B; G. Jean-Pierre Tardieu, *L'Église et les noirs au Pérou (XVIe et XVIIe siècles)*, 2 vols. (Lille, 1987), I, pp. 41–4; L. Conti, 'A Igreja Católica e o tráfico negreiro', *O Tráfico de Escravos Negros Sécs. XV–XIX: Documentos de Trabalho e Relatório de Reunião de Peritos Organizada pela UNESCO em Port-au-Prince, Haiti, de 31 de Janeiro a 4 de Fevereiro de 1978*, trans. António Luz Correia (Lisbon, 1979), pp. 335–6; Iris Origo, 'The domestic enemy: the Eastern slaves in Tuscany in the fourteenth and fifteenth centuries', *Speculum*, 30 (1955), pp. 321–66, 323 (Church tolerated slavery as a necessary evil), 328 (Martin V's prohibition), 355 (a black slave musician) – I am grateful to Professor Dennis Romano for the Origo reference; Giovanni Marrone, *La schiavitù nella società siciliana dell'età moderna* (Caltanissetta, 1972), p. 28.

[7] Ludwig von Pastor, *The History of the Popes from the Close of the Middle Ages*, 40 vols., trans. Frederick Ignatius Antrobus *et al.* (St Louis/London, 1923–53), XII, pp. 518–20; a translation of *Sublimis Deus* is to be found in *Readings in Church History*, ed. Colman J. Barry, 2 vols. (Westminster, MD, 1960), II, pp. 625–6; the text of *Veritas ipsa* can be found in *America Pontificia primi saeculi evangelizationis, 1493–1592*, ed. Josef Metzler, 2 vols. (Città del Vaticano, 1991), I, pp. 364–6, no. 84; Comune di Roma, *Registri di bandi editti notificazioni e provvedimenti diversi relativi alla città di Roma ed allo stato pontificio*, I (*Anni 1234–1605*) (Rome, 1920), p. 63, no. 102; *Bando sopra a tenere de li schiavi e schiave in Roma* dated 12 January 1549.

[8] Pasquale Lopez, *Clero eresia e magia nella Napoli del Viceregno* (Naples, 1984), p. 103, n. 148.

[9] Matteo Gaudioso, *La schiavitù domestica in Sicilia dopo i normanni: Legislazione, dottrina, formule* (2nd rev. edn, Catania, 1979), pp. 40, 59; Giovanna Anastasi Mottà, 'La schiavitù a Messina nel primo Cinquecento', *Archivio storico per la Sicilia Orientalia*, 70 (1974), pp. 305–42 at 326; on the term *Aethiops*, see the map of Diego Riberio (Seville 1529) reproduced in the *Encyclopedia of the Renaissance*, ed. Paul F. Grendler, 6 vols. (New York, 1999), I, p. 15; Erasmus described an *Aethiops* as 'quod atro, quod simis naribus' – thus, for Erasmus the two defining characteristics are dead

Spain, and Portugal, or from the Barbary coast. From 1450 to 1550 Southern Italy experienced a large influx of black Africans who came primarily from the slave markets of Tripoli and the Monti Barca region of Western Cyrenaica with its trading centers of Barce and Benghazi, the terminal points of caravan routes that crossed the Sahara from Nubia and the Nile Valley and from the area around Lake Chad and the Niger Valley. The Muslim king of Bornu (in modern-day Northeastern Nigeria) was known for raiding pagan areas to the south to obtain slaves whom he sold to Berber traders.[10] The Spanish capture of Tripoli in 1510 facilitated this flow of black slaves into Italy. Scholars estimate that the slave population of Renaissance Sicily varied between 1 and 3 per cent depending on the times and regions, the Genoese slave population was perhaps 4 to 5 per cent. In the late fifteenth century 83 per cent of the slaves of Naples were black Africans, and they also predominated among the slave population of Messina.[11] They often worked as domestic servants or farm labourers or as rowers on galley ships; but wealthy people also had slaves as a sign of social distinction.

black skin and a flat (literally, 'monkey') nose, two attributes more applicable to a West African, sub-Saharan Black than to an Ethiopian – see *Dialogus Ciceronianus*, ed. Pierre Mesnard [*Opera omnia Desiderii Erasmi Roterdami*, 1–2] (Amsterdam, 1971), pp. 581–710 at 692, lines 13–14.

[10] Origo, 'Domestic Enemy', pp. 330 and 354; Marrone, *Schiavitù*, pp. 13–27, Gaudioso, *Schiavitù domestica*, p. 40–1; Motta, 'Schiavitù a Messina', p. 314; Carmelo Trasselli, *Siciliani fra quattrocento e cinquecento* (Messina, 1981), p. 100 and his 'Considerazioni sulla schiavitù in Sicilia alla fine del Medioevo: Documenti e rassegne', *Clio*, 1 (1972), pp. 67–90 at 86–8; Maurice Aymard, 'De la traite aux chiourmes: la fin de l'esclavage dans la Sicile moderne', *Bulletin de l'Institut Historique Belge de Rome*, fascicule XLIV: *Miscellanea Charles Verlinden* (Rome, 1974), pp. 1–21 at 2; of the 644 slaves listed in the Palermo 1565 census, the colour of 456 is cited and of these 224 were *negri* of whom 112 were described as *negri di Burno* – see Ridolfo Livi, *La schiavitù domestica nei tempi di mezzo e nei moderni: Ricerche storiche di un antropologo* (Padua, 1928), p. 120; on the caravan trade routes, see Fernand Braudel, *The Mediterranean and the Mediterranean World in the Age of Philip II*, trans. Siân Reynolds from the 2nd rev. edn (New York, 1972), I, p. 183, fig. 14 and D. Lange, 'The kingdoms and peoples of Chad', in *General History of Africa*, 8 vols., IV: *Africa from the Twelfth to the Sixteenth Century*, ed. D. T. Niane (Berkeley, CA, 1984), pp. 238–65 at 257 and 259, figs. 10.4 and 10.5, on the king of Bornu's slave raids, p. 250; on Nubian slaves, see J. Devisse and S. Labib, 'Africa in inter-continental relations', in *ibid.*, pp. 635–72 at 651; on *habasha* slaves from Ethiopia, see Taddesse Tamrat, 'The Horn of Africa : The Solomonids in Ethiopia and the states of the Horn of Africa', in *ibid.*, pp. 423–54 at 438. Commercial connections between Bornu under Idris b.' Ali surnamed Katakarmabe (*c.* 1497–1519) and Tripoli under the Spanish were renewed *c.* 1512 and continued under successive regimes – see B. M. Barkindo, 'Kanem-Borno: its relations with the Mediterranean Sea, Bargirmi and other states in the Chad basin', in *General History of Africa*, 8 vols., V: *Africa from the Sixteenth to the Eighteenth Century*, ed. B. A. Ogot (Berkeley, CA, 1992), pp. 492–514 at 496 and 499, map of trade routes on p. 514.

[11] On Tripoli, see Braudel, *Mediterranean*, II, p. 755, and Trasselli, *Siciliani*, pp. 100, 156–7; on the estimates of scholars, see Aymard, 'De la traite', pp. 4–6; on black Africans in Naples, see Devisse and Labib, 'Africa', p. 651; on black Africans in Messina, see Motta, 'Schiavitù a Messina', pp. 313–14; on Genoa, see Steven A. Epstein, *Speaking of Slavery: Color, Ethnicity, and Human Bondage in Italy* (Ithaca and London, 2001), p. xii.

The legal rights enjoyed by slaves in Renaissance Italy varied. In Northern and Central Italy they were treated as mere property. The laws of the kingdoms of Naples and Sicily, most notably the prescriptions of Frederick II of Sicily in 1310, provided legal safeguards, even if local variants also existed. In Sicily slaves were treated like serfs, their liberty limited by obligations to their masters; they enjoyed an attenuated personhood before the law and were not to be treated as animals or mere property. Indeed, slaves themselves could own property, travel about, and even sue their masters in a court of law. Masters were forbidden to kill a slave, to brand them on the face, flagellate them, amputate one of their limbs, castrate or circumcise them, put them into prostitution or rape them, or insult their baptised slaves as *canes renegatos* (cursed dogs).[12] Many slaves, so it would seem, either bought their freedom (usually the price for which they were purchased or their current commercial value) or else were emancipated by their masters out of motives of Christian charity, as a reward for loyal service, or to free their own progeny.[13] Although slavery was accepted as part of medieval society, thoughtful persons saw it as contrary to human dignity, something introduced into human society by sin, and the conditions under which new persons became enslaved were suspected of not conforming to such juridic norms as captives in a just war – an issue raised by a Portuguese theologian at the Council of Trent.[14]

The presence of slaves, most of whom were non-Christian upon their arrival in Italy, presented the Church with problems and opportunities. The Council of Basel in its nineteenth session on 7 September 1434, echoing previous conciliar legislation and responding primarily to conditions in Spain, laid down rules for encouraging the conversion of infidels and Jews. Bishops were to compel them with charity and kindness to attend sermons in their native languages

[12] Origo, 'Domestic Enemy', p. 334; Gaudioso, *Schiavitù domestica*, pp. 65–7; Marrone, *Schiavitù*, pp. 234–6; Trasselli, 'Considerazioni', pp. 71–81; in Genoa, however, a master could rape his slave, see Epstein, *Speaking*, p. 64.

[13] Motta, 'Schiavitù in Messina', pp. 311, 329, 334–6; Trasselli, 'Considerazioni', p. 83; to prevent a diminution of the estate and eliminate any motive for hastening the death of one's master, Genoese law prohibited any manumission by will – see Epstein, *Speaking*, pp. 86–93, 99.

[14] The Portuguese theologian Franciscus a Conceptione, OFM Observ., at a congregation of minor theologians meeting in Bologna in August of 1547, questioned the way black Africans in Portugal had become slaves – *Concilium Tridentinum*, Tomus VI, Volumen II, ed. Theobaldus Freudenberger (Freiburg im Breisgau, 1972), p. 190, lines 17–23; for his other criticisms of the mistreatments of blacks by their masters and the pastoral neglect of their souls by prelates, see *ibid.*, 189, 36 to 190, 30 and 194, 20–4; for the comments of a notary in a 1515 manumission document, see Trasselli, 'Considerazioni', p. 69, n.3; the Jesuit provincial of Naples, Bernardo Colnago, in 1578 claimed that it was wicked and against the law for Christians to be held against their will in servitude – see Rome, Archivum Romanum Societatis Jesu (hereafter ARSJ), Neap. 72, fol. 20r.

that explained Catholic beliefs. Social contacts with Christians were to be minimised, a distinctive garb worn, and they were forbidden to buy Christian religious objects. At the diocesan synods of Palermo in 1586 and 1615, similar legislation was passed to restrict personal interactions between Christians and infidels or pagans (*gentes*) – no distinction was made as to whether they were free or slave, and infidels (that is, Muslims) seem to have been the primary targets. Violations of these provisions brought severe penalties ranging all the way to excommunication for Christians. Infidels were ordered to wear a distinctive white cap. Invoking biblical and patristic teachings against familiar contact with the unclean, the faithful were not to live with them, nor dine with them, nor seek their medical assistance, nor engage in commerce with them. Christians were prohibited in particular from sleeping in the same room or bed with an infidel, especially from engaging in sexual activity with them or marrying them. Christians were not allowed to borrow from them nor use as collateral or sell them objects sacred to Christians such as gold and silver crosses, images of saints, an *Agnus Dei*, or reliquaries. Infidels were to be expelled from church during the celebration of the Mass lest they show contempt or derision for its rites and the Eucharist and disturb the ceremonies. Christians may admit, indeed should invite and even compel with great skill, infidels to hear sermons in the hope that they receive the seed of God's Word.[15]

That the infidels at times resisted efforts to convert them is well documented in the frequently 'edifying' reports of the Jesuits who taught Christian doctrine to all levels of society, but especially to the very ignorant: the poor, sick, prisoners, galley slaves, and rural slaves – such as the black rural slaves near Messina.[16] The Jesuits complained of those who refused to open their ears

---

[15] *Constitutiones illustrissimi et reverendissimi domini Domini Caesaris Marulli Archiepiscopi Panormitani in diocesana synodo promulgatae die xiij Iunij Anno M.D.LXXXVI.* (Palermo, 1587), pp. 18–9 (pars I, caps. x and xi), and p. 129 (pars IV); *Synodus diocesana celebrata ab illustrissimo et reverendissimo domino Domino Ioannettino Doria S. R. E. Cardinale et Archiepiscopo Panormitano, Anno Domini M.DC.XV.* (Palermo, 1615), pp. 18–9 (pars. I, cap. v). This legislation seems to reflect the earlier legislation of Lateran IV (1215) regarding Jews, Lyon II (1274) regarding Saracens, and Basel (1434) regarding Jews and infidels; see *Decrees of the Ecumenical Councils*, 2 vols., ed. Norman P. Tanner *et al.* (Washington, DC, 1990), I, pp. 265–7, 311, 483–5. According to Origo, 'The domestic enemy', p. 334, many cities in Central Italy mandated by statute that slaves be baptised immediately upon arrival. Basel's decree, however, supposes free consent to baptism and requires prior instruction: Tanner, *Decrees*, I, pp. 483–4.

[16] According to the Jesuit Constitutions, rectors of houses and provincials were to write every four months letters regarding 'anything noteworthy and pertaining to edification'; 'only the edifying reports' were to be shared with other Jesuits so that 'each region can learn from the others whatever promotes mutual consolation and edification in our Lord': see Ignatius of Loyola, *The Constitutions of the Society of Jesus*, trans. and ed. George E. Ganss (St. Louis, 1970), pp. 292–3, nos. 673–5; on the Jesuit ministry of teaching Christian doctrine, see John W. O'Malley, *The First*

and hearts to the arguments that showed the errors of Islam, and who were trapped in their Islamic law, which they affirmed was good. Laymen who tried hard but without success to convert their slaves would bring them to the Jesuits.[17]

The Jesuits seem to have been particularly interested in working with black Africans. Perhaps that was related to the enthusiasm St Ignatius had shown for a mission to Ethiopia. The 'Ethiopians' the Jesuits met in Sicily were not noble Christian warriors but poor slaves.[18] Black Africans served by the Jesuits of Messina responded favourably to fathers who would seek out the slaves on their day off by going to the gardens and other places where they gathered to celebrate, and engage them there in discussions and teach them Christian doctrine. Over time the black slaves became so attached to the Jesuits that they not only converted to Christianity and went to confession and attended Mass in their church, but also did nothing without consulting them. When they became upset over being violently mistreated by their masters and thought of flight, they first had recourse to the Jesuits who would intervene on their behalf with their masters. When controversies arose among themselves, black slaves looked to the Jesuits to arbitrate their differences. In a case reported in

Jesuits (Cambridge, MA, 1993), pp. 115–27, 171–4; for their apostolate among slaves in prisons, see the reports from Naples of 1561 (ARSJ, Neap. 193, fols. 30r and 33r) and of 1622 (Neap. 77, fol. 23v), and among the galley slaves of Naples in 1593 (Neap. 72, fol. 69r), reports from among the rural black slaves of Messina in 1569 (Sic. 182, fol. 420v) and 1597 (Sic. 183 1, fol. 165r); on the prominence of Ledesma's *Dottrina Christiana*, see the letter of Francesco Fornare from Catania of 30 November 1569 in which he reported that every Thursday evening for two and a half hours the rector taught from Ledesma's compendium (Sic. 182, fol. 433r).

[17] The slave Thomas, a *mauro* in Palermo of 1553, resisted for eight years the efforts of his master, the Jesuit provincial of Sicily J. Domenech, to convert him: see *Monumenta Historica Societatis Jesu, Litterae Quadrimestres ex universis praeter Indiam et Brasiliam locis in quibus aliqui de Societate Jesu versabantur Romam missae*, 4 vols. (1546–56), II (1552–54) (Madrid, 1895), pp. 419–23; on the slaves who resisted conversion and in particular on the slave Thomaso who initially countered that there was much good in the law of Mohammed, that he did harm to no one, and was confident that God would save him, but later converted, see the report from Naples of 1610 (ARSJ, Neap. 72, fol. 138r–v), on the persistent hostility of two *more* toward the efforts to convert them (*ibid.*, 139r); on a master bringing his resistant slave to the Jesuits to convert, see the report from Messina of 1585 (Sic. 183 1, fol. 73v); and on the hostility of the slave Joseph toward efforts to convert him, see Neap. 193, fol. 177r (1584). See also Sic. 182, fols. 447v (1570), 464r (1574), and 471v (1581).

[18] Mauro da Leonessa, *Santo Stefano*, pp. 230–7; Alfonso de Sandoval, S. J., working among black slaves in colonial Venezuela, noted the Jesuits' traditional zeal for the salvation of 'dark-skinned peoples' – see Ronald J. Morgan, 'Jesuit confessors, African slaves and the practice of confession in seventeenth-century Cartagena', in Katharine Jackson Lualdi and Anne T. Thayer, eds., *Penitence in the Age of Reformations* (Aldershot, 2000), pp. 222–39 at 227–8; and O'Malley, *First Jesuits*, pp. 327–8.

1597, one black slave was about to kill his enemy who was already wounded and lying prostrate on the ground, crying out for mercy. A Jesuit priest ordered his attacker to put down his sword, and the would-be killer complied.[19]

The Jesuits of Naples eventually gave organisational structures to their work among the slaves. A quarter-century earlier in 1577 the new Theatine cardinal-archbishop of Naples, Blessed Paolo Burali (1511–78), had established a confraternity to meet the spiritual needs of the numerous slaves who were either as yet unbaptised or new in the faith. Based in the church of S. Arcangelo a Baiono, led by Scipione Mormile, and composed of many honourable and pious nobles, the confraternity took on the task of instructing these slaves in the Christian faith. A rule prescribed various prayers and spiritual exercises for its members, listed questions that they were to ask catechumens, and counseled them on how they could assist them both before and after baptism. To help the neophytes, Burali had posted throughout the city an edict warning of the spiritual harm that is inflicted on the new Christians by their masters who deal harshly with them, instead of treating them humanely and with Christian charity. Burali was jubilant when in January of 1578 he was able to baptise with his own hands some of the converted slaves. Unfortunately, Burali died a few months later and his confraternity adopted other ministries.[20]

In 1605 the Jesuits founded their own confraternity known as the Epifania del Signore. Located in an oratory in their college, it was dedicated to giving moral assistance to the work of converting slaves. Its members were artisans from each quarter of the city, recruited because of their mature age, fine reputation and good life. Among their numbers were *consoli dell'arte*, the civic officials who headed the artisan guilds. Every Sunday after the midday meal, they would go to the houses of their neighbours who owned unbaptised slaves, and bring these slaves to the oratory of the Jesuit college. Having left the slaves in the care of a Jesuit instructor, the artisans assembled separately and engaged in spiritual exercises typical of other confraternities, ending with a benediction. One of the distinguishing practices, however, was the recitation in the oratory of the *dottrina cristiana*, an exercise in which the newly baptised were welcome to join. When the artisans had finished their prayer service, they returned the slaves to their masters. This confraternity dell'Epifania had its own officials, constitutions, and rules based on much experience in the

---

[19] ARSJ, Sic. 182, fol. 420v (Messina, 1569); Sic. 183 1, fol. 165r (Messina, 1597).

[20] On Burali, see G. DeCaro, 'Burali, Paolo (Scipione)', in *Dizionario biografico degli italiani*, 15 (1972), pp. 370–6; and Lopez, *Clero*, pp. 107–9.

work of converting slaves, especially those who were Muslims, rules that all members engaged in the apostolate were required to read.[21]

The slaves met as a group with a Jesuit scholastic who had spent six years of his youth as a captive of the Turks, and hence knew very well the Turkish or *moresca* tongue. Because Muslims were more accustomed to defend their religion with arms than reasons, he encountered much belligerency when he proceeded to provide arguments that demonstrated the errors of Islam. By letting his listeners mull over his presentations, he gradually weakened their adherence to old beliefs. He then explained to them the teachings of the Christian faith, and urged those who accepted Christ to recommend them-selves to the Blessed Virgin. Five years later in 1610, the Jesuits claimed that no one who had done this had died without receiving baptism, a sacrament administered in Naples to adults in a special ceremony in the cathedral on Epiphany and Pentecost. In those five years the Jesuits reported that sixty slaves had been baptised. The rate of conversions seems to have increased for there were 24 baptisms in 1618, 27 in 1626, 22 in 1627, and 19 in 1630.[22] What percentage of these converts were black Africans rather than Berbers or Turks is not indicated in the records, but one suspects that most were not Africans.

A particularly interesting feature of the conversion stories reported by the Jesuits was the number of times baptism followed the apparition of a saint iden-tified by name who urged conversion to Christianity on someone described as an *afer* or *maurus*. In one story from Messina dated 1598, an eighty-year-old African shepherd was guarding his flock one night when a grave monk appeared to him and urged him to become a Christian. When the African asked, 'Who are you?' the monk responded, 'I am Vincent.' The shepherd then asked if he had come to steal his sheep. At these words the monk dis-appeared. On another occasion, awakened from his sleep, the same shepherd heard a strange voice urging him to convert to Christianity. When he asked the identity of the speaker, he was told that she was Mary who is venerated in the church called Mamertini della grotta. Lighting a torch, he looked around the room but saw no one. He failed to follow the advice of Vincent or Mary until, stricken by misfortune and falsely accused, he fled to God for help. He

---

[21] Lopez, *Riforma Cattolica*, p. 88; ARSJ, Neap. 72, fols. 138r–140v (1610), 167r (1610), 209v (1611). I was unable to consult the two studies of Gennaro Nardi: 'Nuove ricerche sulle istituzioni napoletani a favore degli schiavi. La congregazione degli schiavi dei PP. Gesuiti', *Aspernas: Organo dell'Accademia ecclesiastica napoletana*, 14 (1967), pp. 294–313, and 'Due opere per la conversione degli schiavi a Napoli', *Aspernas: Organo dell'Accademia ecclesiastica napoletana*, 13:2 (1966), pp. 170–205.

[22] ARSJ, Neap. 72, fols. 138r, 140v, and 167r (1610); Lopez, *Riforma Cattolica*, p. 88.

sought out a Jesuit, revealed to him the apparitions and their message, and with ardour replacing sluggishness he undertook instruction and was baptised with much ceremony in the Jesuit church.[23] A *maurus* of Palermo was reportedly 'addicted to Islam' until an image of a distinguished and beautiful Virgin Mary appeared to him while he slept. When he awoke the image disappeared, but then the saints Peter, John the Baptist and Octavius also appeared to him. He was converted and baptised, taking the name of Octavius.[24] According to recent studies, black Africans of this period placed much importance on revelations in the form of dreams, visions and voices. These were seen as messengers from the other world that could lead to and validate a conversion.[25] Their occurrence at night suggests that most, if not all, were in fact dreams in which the slaves' conflict over whether to hold onto the hope of returning someday to their homeland or to adjust to the new society in which they found themselves was resolved by an inner voice telling them to stay and conform to the society by adopting its religion. The Jesuits made them feel welcome by tending on occasion to their physical needs, acting as their advocates, and instructing them in the ways and beliefs of their new religion. These followers of St Ignatius attributed the conversions to God, who predestines some to salvation and whose grace gave force to their words and actions.[26] That some slaves put off until the approach of death the decision to convert may have been due in part to the loss of hope that someday they would return to their homeland and resume the public practice of their old religion, or to their awaiting the total absolution of their sins through baptism and the promised immediate entrance into heaven.

Church officials took measures to insure the seriousness of the conversions, probably in reaction to earlier abuses in this area.[27] In the ecclesiastical province of Sorrento, as the result of a decree of the council of 1584 under Archbishop Giovanni Donzelli, OP, no adult slave or emancipated infidel was allowed to be baptised without prior instruction in all that a Christian should know, on which there was to be a careful examination, and the permission of the bishop was also required.[28] Many other councils in Southern

---

[23] ARSJ, Sic. 183 1, fol. 180v (1598).   [24] ARSJ, Sic. 183 1, fol. 249r–v (1605).

[25] John Thornton, *Africa and Africans in the Making of the Atlantic World, 1400–1680* (Cambridge, 1992), pp. 236–55, esp. 242, 254–5.

[26] ARSJ, Sic. 183 1, fols. 9r and 250r (predestination), and 73v (God giving force).

[27] See Sergio Tognetti in this volume on the pro-forma baptism of black slaves imported into Italy from Portugal.

[28] Giovanni Domenico Mansi *et al.*, eds., *Sacrorum conciliorum amplissima collectio*, 53 vols. (Paris, 1901–27), xxxvi bis, col. 291A (Cap. xxi: De sacramento baptisimi, nr. 14).

Italy demanded a period of reflection both before and after an adult received the sacrament.[29] Although Christian doctrine was beginning to be taught on a regular basis in local parishes, adult converts seem to have been sent to religious houses for instruction.[30] In their reports the Jesuits would at times explicitly assert that those they had instructed went on to practise their faith and live as good Christians. In one colourful account, a seventy-year-old black African from the Messina area had neglected the practice of his faith until frightened by a dream in which deformed 'Ethiopians' stirred a huge kettle placed over the flames. When asked what was in the pot, one of the cooks took out a human head and various bones. On seeing this, the elderly man called in terror on the name of Jesus and exhorted his companions to flee. But he found to his horror that he himself could not escape because one of the cooks held him by his clothing. Crying and trembling, he awoke and went to a Jesuit priest to free himself by confession from the crimes of his whole life. Thereafter he entered upon the Christian way, going to confession and communion on a weekly basis, his terror now turned into joy.[31] Scholars have found little or no evidence for the survival of Islamic or idolatrous cults in Sicily. The vast bulk of the slaves seem to have converted with only about five per cent retaining their old religion, and these may have eventually regained their freedom and returned to their homelands.[32]

[29] Michele Miele, *Die Provinzialkonzilien Süditaliens in der Neuzeit* (Paderborn, 1996), p. 500.

[30] e.g., *Constitutiones . . . Marulli in diocesana synodo M.D. LXXXVI.*, p. 15 (where parents are required to send their children for instruction in the faith to the local church on feast days, and all [not just children] are urged to learn the rudiments of the faith, with the Jesuits in particular being commended for their expertise in this apostolate). For pre-baptismal instruction in religious houses, see the record of seven Turkish brothers being first instructed by the Dominicans in the convent of Santa Maria and three other Turks being instructed in the Jesuit college before their baptism by the vicar-general of Palermo in the convent of Santo Domenico on 21 June 1597, Archivio Storico Diocesano di Palermo (hereafter cited as ASDP), Parrocchia San Giacomo la Marina, anagrafe parrocchiale, MS 70 (1578–79), cc. non numerate. I am grateful to Dottore Giovanni Travagliato, Responsabile di Sala Studio of the ASDP, for his assistance at times in reading the registers.

[31] E.g., ARSJ, Sic. 183 I, fols. 9r (some other Moors were catechised and baptised by ours and live as good Christians – Messina 1581), and 250r (an Ethiopian now leads a good Christian life after a frightening dream of cannibalism – Messina 1605); Neap. 72, fols. 138r (Thomaso perseveres and receives the sacraments), and 138v (Francesco comes to church every day and frequents the sacraments).

[32] While Trasselli, 'Considerazioni', p. 83, n.5 finds no evidence of non-Christian cultic survivals; Aymard, 'De la traite', p. 10 holds that a small minority of 5 per cent retained their old religion; and Motta, 'Schiavitù a Messina', p. 332 cites the case of the slave Mamura marrying the freed Ali according to their law.

That some slaves may have sought baptism in the hope that it would bring about their emancipation is suggested in some sources. At the Neapolitan diocesan synod held under Cardinal Alfonso Carafa, a case was heard on 14 February 1565 brought by the two black Christian slaves Giovanni and Caterina, who asked the cardinal to order their masters to treat them as free and equal persons now that they had been baptised, and either pay them for their services or grant them manumission. Their masters should not be allowed to force fellow Christians to serve them. The synod decided, however, to reject their petition, citing the various provisions of *Distinctio* LIV of Gratian's *Decretum* against ordaining a slave. Baptism does not free one from servitude of the body. While the reception of orders by a bishop or priest would alter one's servile condition, baptism, by itself, did not.[33] Fear that the baptism of his slave would free him seems to have led one master in 1609 to have three of his agents violently attack and try to intimidate his slave on the eve of his baptism as he exited the palace of Giuseppe Pisculo, OFM, bishop of Catanzaro, who had just approved him for baptism.[34]

Church records are full of evidence of the baptism of slaves. Children of slaves were baptised within eight days of birth, irrespective of the religion or wishes of their parents. While the baptising priest carefully recorded the names of the slave mother and her master, no effort was made to identify the father. This contrasted sharply with the records of a free infant, even when illegitimate, whose father was identified or a blank space was left to be filled in later, or an excuse was offered stating that the name was withheld 'honoris causa'.[35] The baptism of adult converts was usually made into a special event.

---

[33] *Acta et decreta synodi neapolitanae* (Naples, 1568), pp. 87–8; Friedberg, I, cols. 206–14. *Capita* xiii–xviii of *Distinctio* LIV did, however, provide for the freeing of a converted slave who belonged to a Jew or infidel (*ibid.*, cols. 211–12). The same policy was incorporated into Sicilian civil law (see Gaudioso, *Schiavitù domestica*, pp. 143–4). In the medieval Latin crusader kingdoms in the Holy Land, the conversion of a Muslim slave to Christianity brought freedom. This policy led to insincere conversions or efforts by masters to prevent conversion. Gregory IX in two letters of 1237 and 1238 addressed to the patriarch of Jerusalem ruled that slaves must be allowed to convert but their conversion would not bring freedom (see Epstein, *Speaking*, pp. 175–6).

[34] Lopez, *Riforma Cattolica*, pp. 270–1, doc. no. 10; in Sicily baptism did not bring freedom if the master was Christian (see Gaudioso, *Schiavitù domestica*, p. 63). But a legal maxim prevailed in twelfth-century Bari 'that no one of the Christian religion should be held as a slave without a legitimate reason, except those born of slaves' (see Epstein, *Speaking*, p. 85).

[35] Civil law in Sicily mandated the baptism of infant slaves no matter what the religion of the parents (see Epstein, *Speaking*, p. 95). The requirement of baptism within eight days is found in the decrees of the synod of Palermo of 1586 (see *Constitutiones . . . Marulli . . . in diocesana synodo*, p. 41); for examples of infant children of slaves being baptised, see ASDP, San Giacomo la

In Naples the archbishop or his substitute administered baptism twice a year at Epiphany and Pentecost. In Palermo the vicar general came to the convent of S. Domenico to administer baptism to some slaves, and a special priest came to the parish of S. Margherita to baptise the freed 'Moor', Elisabetta.[36] The Jesuits went out of their way to make baptism as festive as possible. In Naples they conducted the ceremonies with solemn pomp; the baptised were in white robes, their godparents selected from the highest ranks of Neapolitan aristocracy ('princes and dynasts'), and the church packed with supporters who cried and applauded. In Messina they added the sound of flutes and the sweetest symphony of singers. Once again two noblemen served as godparents, and the newly baptised African was congratulated with the greatest signs of benevolence and humanity by distinguished citizens of Messina and paraded through the city in a four-wheel carriage. In Malta there was music and song, the greatest solemnity in a church full of well-wishers, and the introduction of a *dialoghetto* in which the black slave recited the *dottrina cristiana*. The Jesuits reported that they made their baptismal ceremonies so attractive in order to encourage other slaves to seek baptism.[37] Another possible reason for the public festivities was to encourage Christians, who were subject to

Marina, MS 39 (1549–50), entries for 3 and 20 July 1550, MS 71 (1579–80), fols. 7v (18 September 1579), 57r (12 April 1580), and 69r (4 June 1580); Santa Margherita, MS 4360 (1548–56) entries for 20 November 1548, 24 December 1548, and 18 January 1549; Trasselli, 'Considerazioni', pp. 82–3, n. 51 cites an unpublished study of the baptismal records of San Giacomo la Marina in Palermo for the years 1556–57 according to which 429 infants were free born, 3 of unknown father, 15 illegitimate (parents unmarried), 18 adult slaves, and 17 children of slaves. Aymard reports that slaves are found in the sacramental registers of parishes ('De la traite', p. 3) and that the proportion of slaves to free baptised at S. Giacomo la Marina of Palermo varied between 1 slave for every 5.5 free in 1520–9 to 1 slave for every 49 free in 1570–9 ('De la traite', p. 9). Scholars speculate that masters may frequently have been the fathers of their slaves' children. Sexual relations between a master and his female slave were not punished unless rape or violence was used. Many female slaves, more so than male slaves, were later freed by their masters. There is evidence that even priests had sexual relations with their slaves: see Gaudioso, *Schiavitù domestica*, pp. 68–9 and Marrone, *Schiavitù*, p. 230.

[36] ARSJ, Neap. 77, fol. 3r–v (Cardinal-archbishop of Naples, Ottavio Acquaviva (1605–13), or his substitutes personally baptised in the cathedral on Epiphany and Pentecost); ASDP, San Giacomo la Marina, MS 70 (1578–9), entry for 21 June 1579 (the godparents were Colantonio Spadafora and Dona Joanna Ventimiglia, members of the aristocracy); Santa Margherita, MS 4361, fol. 31v (13 August 1575 with godparents maestro Antonio Lumonacu and Angila La Ziza).

[37] ARSJ, Neap. 72, fol. 50r (Naples 1592), Sic. 182, fol. 464r (Messina 1574: 'per animare gli altri'), Sic. 183 1, fol. 180v (Messina 1598: 'ut hoc exemplum aliis esset incitamentum'), Sic. 183 1, fol. 335r (Malta 1612). On the Southern Italian Jesuits' use of pageantry and props when preaching penance, see Jennifer D. Selwyn, '"Schools of mortification": theatricality and the role of penitential practice in the Jesuits' popular missions', in Lualdi and Thayer, eds., *Penitence in the Age of Reformations*, pp. 201–21. I am grateful to Maureen Miller for this reference.

raids by Muslim corsairs and were engaged at times in formal warfare with Islamic states. The baptisms were mini-victories over Islam and suggested that Christianity would ultimately triumph. The festive celebration of adult baptisms on the Epiphany and Pentecost, holy days that commemorated the spreading of the Christian faith to peoples of distant lands (Matthew 2: 1–12 and Acts 2: 5–12), was not only in keeping with the solemnity of these feast days, but also seemed to indicate that Christ's final commission to make disciples of all nations (Matthew 28: 19) was in fact being carried out.

Evidence that the new converts received the sacraments of penance and communion can be found in the reports of the Jesuits, who made explicit reference to black slaves frequenting the sacraments, a phrase used to denote these two sacraments. The fifteenth-century Dominican archbishop St Antonino had urged masters to provide opportunities for their slaves to hear Mass and sermons and to go to confession and communion at the required times, although masters were not supposed to force them to pray or to receive the sacraments.[38]

That black Africans, whether slave or freed, were married with church ritual, as was required of all Catholics after the implementation of the decree *Tametsi* (1563) of the Council of Trent,[39] is documented in parish registers. Their right to marry, even against the wishes of the masters, was guaranteed by both civil and ecclesiastical law.[40] The registers of Palermo record, for example, that in 1587 Ferdinando Toscaova married Caterina nigra.[41] In Messina there is evidence in 1539 of Violante, the wife of Magnifico Giovan Benedetto Prosimo, who left in her will money to fund a dowry so that her black slave Angela could marry.[42]

Evidence of black Africans' reception of the other sacraments is fragmentary at best. That black Africans also received confirmation and the last rites is likely but not easily documented. While ordination was possible, such factors

[38] E.g., ARSJ, Neap. 72, fol. 138r–v; and Sic. 183 1, fols. 165r (Messina 1597: 'Saepe enim ut se nostrorum maculis abluans aut caelesti pane reficiant ad divinam mensam accursunt'), 250r (Messina 1605: 'singulis hebdommadis utroque sacramento'); 250v (Messina 1605: reports the story of a black African who was so frightened by a dream of cannibals that he went to confession and thereafter practised his Christianity). Pieruzzi, *Summa theologica*, III, cols. 200E, 201D. The decree *Omnis utriusque* (1215) of the Fourth Lateran Council required all Christians of the age of discernment to confess annually and communicate during Eastertide: see Tanner, *Decrees*, I, p. 245.

[39] Tanner, *Decrees*, II, pp. 755–7.

[40] Gaudioso, *Schiavitù domestica*, pp. 83–5, 140–1; Pieruzzi, *Summa theologica*, III, col. 201C.

[41] ASDP, Santa Margherita, MS 4362, fol. 45r (Toscaova on 1 October 1587).

[42] Motta, 'Schiavitù a Messina', p. 328.

as recent conversion, illegitimacy, slave status, and an absence of the necessary education probably all contributed to the apparent lack of black priests in Italy. Leo X's brief, *Exponi nobis*, double-dated 4 May and 12 June 1518, issued in response to the request of King Manuel I of Portugal, dispensed from the impediments of defect of birth and absence of a specific benefice to which to be assigned those Christians from 'Ethiopia, India, and Africa' who had converted from 'Islam and the sects of certain pagans and infidels', who were baptised and sufficiently instructed 'in the cult of the Orthodox faith and in the observance of divine precepts' in the city of Lisbon, who planned to return to their native lands to preach the Word of God and the evangelical discipline, and who sought major orders in order to carry out this task more effectively. Prior to their departure, they were to be ordained by the principal chaplain of the royal chapel, a bishop or archbishop appointed by the king of Portugal, and once ordained they were allowed freely and licitly to celebrate Mass and dispense the sacraments in their native lands, even outside of the stipulated times and parish churches.[43] Except for the case of the Ethiopian monk Abba Pietro Tesfà Sion Malhezò (or Malbazò), originally of the monastery of Debre Libanos in Ethiopia, who was ordained a priest in Rome probably in the 1540s, according to Paolo Giovio, I have yet to find evidence of black Africans being ordained in Renaissance Italy, either to serve the local church in general or its black population in particular, or to go as missionaries to Africa. The Ethiopian priests of the monastery of S. Stefano in Rome clearly celebrated the Mass in their monastery.[44]

That the sacrament of episcopal ordination could be available to black Africans is evident in the case of Ndoadidiki Ne-Kinu a Mumemba, better known by his baptismal name of Henrique (c. 1494–1531), son of Afonso I, the king of the Congo. Having been trained in the humanities and theology at the monastery of Santo Elói in Lisbon, Henrique was to be sent by his father Afonso on an embassy to Julius II in Rome in 1512/13, but the legation never departed, due to the failure of his relative D. Pedro de Sousa to arrive from Africa to accompany him to Italy.[45] King Manuel I petitioned Leo X in 1518 to promote Henrique to the episcopacy so that he could better promote the faith in his native Congo. The pope consulted the cardinals in consistory who objected to Henrique's youth and lack of sufficient learning. The recent Fifth Lateran Council in 1514 had mandated in *Supernae dispositionis arbitrio* a minimum age of twenty-seven, while Henrique in 1518 was twenty-three

---

[43] *Monumenta*, pp. 421–2.   [44] Mauro da Leonessa, *Santo Stefano Maggiore*, p. 198 n.
[45] *Monumenta*, pp. 270–3; de Witte, 'Henri de Congo', p. 589.

or twenty-four. His academic training was apparently insufficient to qualify him for the office of bishop. To overcome these difficulties, Leo X stipulated that Henrique could function only as an administrator and not exercise his episcopal office until he came of canonical age, and that he should have as his advisers men expertly trained in theology and canon law. The pope also dispensed him from the defect of birth. Leo X announced in his letter to Manuel I of 3 May 1518 that he had secured the consent of the cardinals to the appointment of Henrique as bishop. In the consistory of 5 May it was agreed to appoint him titular bishop of Utica in North Africa, without the obligation to reside in that see *in partibus infidelium*, and with faculties to exercise his episcopal functions only in the diocese of Funchal and with the consent of its bishop, who was to provide him with an annual pension of 200 ducats.[46] He was thus an auxiliary bishop under D. Diogo Pinheiro, the bishop of Funchal (1514–26), who properly exercised ordinary jurisdiction over the Congo – indeed, at the time Funchal was the largest diocese in the world, including parts of South America, Africa and Asia. Despite claims that Henrique had visited Rome and was consecrated a bishop there by Leo X, the new bishop-elect received priestly ordination in Portugal by 1 December 1520 and episcopal consecration probably in early 1521, at the hands of the royal chaplain, D. Fernando Coutinho de Vasconcelos e Menseses, bishop of Lamego (1513–40), and of his ordinary, D. Pinheiro. In his letter to Henrique of 22 May 1518, Leo X allowed him to be consecrated bishop once he completed his twenty-sixth year.[47] Having been consecrated, he departed for Africa in 1521 where he functioned as auxiliary bishop in the Congo. Leo X gave as the reason for dispensing him from some of the requirements of canon law the expectation that as a native bishop he would be more effective in promoting the faith among his people.[48] Portuguese kings, exercising their patronage rights over Africa, opposed the appointment of subsequent black bishops,

---

[46] *Monumenta*, pp. 414–7; Tanner, *Decrees*, I, p. 615* ('there can be no dispensation for them to be in charge of churches before their twenty-seventh year of age': Lateran V).

[47] *Monumenta*, p. 419; de Witte, 'Henri de Congo', p. 595 (gives early 1521 as the more probable date); Bontinck, 'Ndoadidiki', p. 163 (holds for ordination by 1 Dec. 1520 and consecration in early 1521); Debrunner, *Presence*, p. 44, no. v (gives 1 Dec. 1520 as the date); among those claiming that Henrique was consecrated in Rome is J. Vansina (based on a contribution by T. Obenga), 'The Kongo kingdom and its neighbours', in Ogot, ed., *Africa from the Sixteenth to the Eighteenth Century*, p. 555.

[48] *Monumenta*, p. 414 ('ut promotionem hanc ad eiusdem fidei nostre propagationem plurimum profuturam speremus') and p. 417 ('ut eidem Genitori tuo gratior et acceptior esse, populis vero Ethiopum salubria christianae fidei documenta prebere, officium praedicationis exercere, et viam quae iter pandit ad gloriam verbo pariter et exemplo, maiori auctoritate et gravitate ostendere, efficacioresque in auditorum animos effectus venerabilius imprimere valeas').

despite the pleas of Congolese kings and their embassies sent to Rome during the Renaissance.[49] While foreigners who worked in the Roman Curia or held high posts were on occasion appointed to Italian sees, no black African was apparently so employed and honoured.

Some evidence exists for black confraternities in Southern Italy. In his survey of the confraternities of Palermo, Antonino Mongitore noted that according to tradition the Senate of Palermo in the early 1570s entrusted to a congregation of Christian slaves the church of S. Maria di Gesù – the confraternity was called S. Maria di Gesù dei negri. At some later unspecified time (but before 1660) when Christian slaves no longer used the church, the Senate granted it to the congregation of mule-drivers. How long the Christian slaves used the church and what they did there is never explained.[50] In Messina a confraternity of black slaves was based in the church of S. Marco by 1584 and held its functions there until sometime in the seventeenth century. From passing comments in a hostile report, it can be determined that the confraternity had its own officials, and its members as a group participated in rituals such as Forty Hours Devotions and a Corpus Christi procession at other churches. They regularly hosted in their own church a religious service for newly elected members of the Senate of Messina. Unfortunately, these black slaves were also the targets of numerous practical jokes. For example, at a Forty Hours ceremony the organist began to play one of their dance tunes as they entered the church. So taken were they by the music that they put down their torches and crosses and began to dance, a sight considered scandalous by some, given the sacred setting. The neighbouring Spanish friars of the SS. Trinità della Redenzione dei Cattivi in the church of S. Filippo accused the black slaves of numerous ridiculous activities, and eventually succeeded in getting the authorities to abolish the slaves' confraternity, destroy its church, and transfer to a chapel in their own church the picture of St Mark, so that the Senate of Messina would now process to the Trinitarians' church.[51]

[49] de Witte, 'Henri de Congo', pp. 597; Debrunner, *Presence*, p. 46.

[50] Antonino Mongitore, *Storia sacra delle chiese di Palermo*, III: *Chiese di unioni, confraternite, e congregazioni di Palermo*, Biblioteca Comunale di Palermo (hereafter cited as BCP), MS Qq E9, pages 62–5 or fols. 45v–47r, esp. 63/46r–65/47r; the surviving contemporary documents of the confraternity of S. Maria di Gesù preserved in the archdiocesan archives do not mention Christian slaves – e.g., ASDP, Registri delle deliberazioni, S. Maria di Gesù, MSS 3134 and 3167; and *Le confraternite dell'arcidiocesi di Palermo: storia e arte*, ed. Maria Concetta Di Natale (Palermo, 1993), p. 300.

[51] Gaetano La Corte-Cailler, 'Burle del secolo XVII agli schiavi in Messina', *Archivio per lo studio delle tradizioni popolari: rivista trimestrale diretta da G. Pitrè e S. Salomone-Marino*, 20 (Palermo, 1901), pp. 202–8.

In Naples, in conjunction with the confraternity of the Epifania del Signore founded to promote the conversion of slaves, the Jesuits also established the confraternity of the Purificazione to help slaves once they had converted. On the urgings of the Jesuit cardinal St Robert Bellarmine, Pope Paul V on 5 November 1605 granted certain indulgences to its members, who numbered twenty-two. They would meet in the oratory of the Jesuit college where they were taught Christian doctrine, how to frequent the sacraments, and devotion to the Blessed Virgin. Among their activities seems to have been helping to convert fellow slaves. Many slaves, neophytes and catechumens who were not formally members of the confraternity, also frequented its meetings. Not only did the Jesuits provide the baptised slaves with their own confraternity so as not to feel abandoned once converted, but they also got the leading confraternity of nobles in Naples to adopt as one of its charitable works the protection of slaves.[52]

That freed black Africans could and did enter religious orders is both suggested and documented in various records. Sicilian civil law, reflecting similar provisions in canon law, provided that a slave needed the consent of his master to become a religious, but that the master could not refuse if offered the price of the slave. If the slave belonged to a Jew, no permission or compensation was required. If he belonged to a church, he received his full freedom on becoming a religious, but reverted to slavery if he abandoned the monastery. That black slaves could seek entrance is suggested by three documents. In Messina the black slave Angela was left money in 1539 to pay for her entrance fee into a convent, should she so choose. The Jesuit provincial of Naples, Giuseppe Fabrizio, reported in 1557 that a talented slave from Africa[53] who was recently baptised had decided to serve God forever in the Jesuit order – whether he was admitted and whether as a lay brother or scholastic I have been unable to determine. According to the 1551 rule of the monastery of S. Stefano Maggiore next to St Peter's Basilica in Rome, someone who had been a captive of Saracens or gentiles but then freed could seek entrance into the monastery provided he was upright, humble, meek, concerned for his soul and willing to obey the prior in all things. Although initially founded under Sixtus IV as a hospice for Ethiopian pilgrims, S. Stefano became a monastery with a community of monks and friars from such Western orders

---

[52] ARSJ, Neap. 72, fols. 111v and 140v; in 1607 there were 13 confraternities with 1,803 members under the direction of the Jesuit college of Naples (*ibid.*, 110r); for examples of slaves helping to convert other slaves, see *ibid.*, 138r (Thomaso) and 139r (Maria); Lopez, *Riforma Cattolica*, p. 87.

[53] ARSJ, Neap. 193, fol. 3v. The report by Father Giuseppe Fabrizio, S. J., describes him as one of the two 'ex Affrica servi . . . qui Afrorum linguam callet'.

as the Benedictines, Franciscans, and Dominicans, whose numbers ranged from thirty-eight prior to the Sack of Rome to six to fourteen thereafter. They were all of black African origin and seem to have come from 'Ethiopia'.[54]

The most famous case of a black African who became a religious is the Franciscan lay brother saint known as Benedetto il moro (c. 1524–89). He was born in Sicily of married Christian parents whose status, and his own status as slave or free, is variously described and argued by scholars.[55] He lacked any formal education.[56] At twenty-one years of age this pious farm worker entered a local Franciscan congregation of hermits, and when this group was suppressed by the Pius IV in 1562, he transferred to the Reformati branch of the Observant Franciscans, spending most of the remainder of his life working in the kitchen and sweeping the floors of the monastery of S. Maria di Gesù, some two miles from Palermo. Both as a hermit and as a friar, he earned a reputation for remarkable humility, asceticism (frequent flagellations, constant fasting on bread and water and vegetables, long nightly vigils), prayer (his body was seen to levitate and become luminous while he prayed),

---

[54] Gaudioso, *Schiavitù domestica*, pp. 139–40; Motta, 'Schiavitù a Messina', p. 328; ARSJ, Neap. 193, fol. 3v (2 January 1557); Epstein, *Speaking*, p. 89; Mauro da Leonessa, *Santo Stefano Maggiore*, pp. 127–32 (Franciscan and Dominican Ethiopians), 177 (Sixtus IV gave Ethiopians the monastery), 188–91 (diverse orders and numbers), 210–11 (1551 rule).

[55] The sources and scholars disagree on the legal status of Benedetto and his parents. That his father Cristoforo was a slave of Vicenzo Manasseri (Manseri) at the time of his legitimate marriage to Diana Larcan, and later freed on the death of his master, was asserted in 1623 by Fra Antonino da Randazco (procurator of his cause) in Rosalia Claudia Giordano, ed., 'Appendice documentaria, trascrizione del manoscritto 3 Qq C36 n. 19 della Biblioteca Comunale di Palermo', in Giovanna Fiume and Marilena Modica, eds., *San Benedetto il moro: santità, agiografia e primi processi di canonizzazione* (Palermo, 1998), p. 125, and repeated by his modern biographer Ludovico Maria Mariani, *San Benedetto da Palermo, il moro Etiope, nato a S. Fratello* (Palermo, 1989), p. 38; that Diana (the family name Larcan was adopted from the slave-holding lords of San Fratello) was also a slave is asserted by Trasselli, 'Considerazioni', p. 81 and Mariani, *San Benedetto*, p. 38; that she was free at the time of her marriage was asserted by Randazco in Giordano, ed., 'Appendice', p. 125; that Benedetto was a slave at birth is strongly suggested by his own repeated statements that he was 'uno scavo negro' – e.g., Randazco in Giordano, ed., 'Appendice', p. 134, by the deposition of 1594 recalling his words – e.g., 'Ordinaria inquisitio', BCP, MS 3 Qq E42, fol. 92r, and by the recorded statement of Girolamo Lanza regarding Benedetto as 'questo schiavotto' in 'Processo del Benedetto di San Fratello [1625]', BCP, MS 3Qq E40, p. 14, see also p. 11bis. That his parents were promised that he would be freed as their first-born son and that he was emancipated at the age of ten, see Pol de Léon Albaret, OFM, 'Benedict the Black', in Malachy Carroll and Pol de Léon Albaret, *Three Studies in Simplicity: Padre Pio, Martin de Porres, Benedict the Black* (Chicago, 1974), p. 148 and Debrunner, *Presence*, p. 47, no. v (1); that he was freed at birth was asserted by Randazco in Giordano, ed., 'Appendice', p. 125 ('nacque franco') and Mariani, *San Benedetto*, p. 39. The date of his birth is variously given as 1524 or 1526 by Mariani, *San Benedetto*, p. 207.

[56] Debrunner, *Presence*, p. 47, no. v (1).

and wonder-working (clairvoyance, cures of fatal illnesses, even resuscitation of the dead).[57] Manifestations of prejudice based on the legal status of his parents and his own skin colour seem to have been the exception, and his patient non-response to two such insults (both delivered by impatient fellow friars who called him 'scavo negro' (black slave) and 'cani perro' (dogs' dog)) was duly noted by his official Franciscan biographer, Antonino da Randaczo, whose narrative repeatedly displays the writer's own prejudices.[58] Benedetto himself, schooled in Franciscan humility, would openly invoke his blackness and slave status as a way to deflect others' admiration for him.[59] Nonetheless, he was elected superior of S. Maria di Gesù in 1578 and 1583 and appointed master of novices by his fellow friars, consulted by the learned men of Palermo on ethical and exegetical questions even though he lacked formal education, and visited at his monastery by people from every level of society who sought his prayers, advice and healing powers.[60] Respect for his sanctity outweighed any possible prejudices. The official Church in Palermo and Rome allowed for the re-internment of his incorrupted body in the sacristy of S. Maria di Gesù in 1592 and, in 1611, its relocation to the church and placement in a costly silver casket donated by King Philip III of Spain. It also honoured him, unofficially at first, with the title of 'Blessed', sponsored four inquests (in 1594–5, 1620, 1625–6, and 1734) to verify his sanctity, and eventually formally beatified and canonised him in 1743 and 1807 respectively, thus according him the highest honours the Church can confer on any of its members.[61]

What kind of picture emerges from the fragmentary evidence here presented? Because the official Church was welcoming to black Africans, the

[57] Mariani, San Benedetto, pp. 24–7, 49, 183–5, 210–11; Randaczo in Giordano, ed., 'Appendice', p. 129.

[58] Randaczo in Giordano, ed., 'Appendice', pp. 125–7 (prejudicial statements: although Benedetto's parents were black, they were of good morals and good Christians and fearful of God; his father Cristoforo was of such good morals as not to be considered a black slave but some respected and virtuous person; the deceitful world could not stain Benedetto because he was of black colour), 132 (insult), 135 (prejudicial statement: Benedetto should be unknown and little esteemed as black), 145 (insults).

[59] Randaczo in Giordano, ed., 'Appendice', pp. 127, 132, 134; 'Ordinaria inquisitio', BCP, MS 3 Qq E42, fol. 92v.

[60] Giuseppe Morabito, 'Benedetto il moro', Bibliotheca Sanctorum, eds. Filippo Caraffa and Giuseppe Morelli, 12 vols. + index (Rome, 1961–87), II, cols. 1103–4, esp. 1104; Cardinal Salvatore Pappalardo, Archbishop of Palermo, S. Benedetto 'il moro': un fiore esotico sbocciato in Sicilia. Lettera dell'arcivescovo nel IV centenario della morte del santo (Palermo, 1989), p. 10; Randaczo in Giordano, ed., 'Appendice', pp. 134, 143–65.

[61] Randaczo in Giordano, ed., 'Appendice', pp. 119–20, 168–70; Giovanna Fiume, 'Il processo "De Cultu" a Fra' Benedetto da San Fratello (1734)', in Giovanna Fiume, ed., Il santo patrono e la città. San Benedetto il moro: culti, devozioni, strategie di età moderna (Venice, 2000), pp. 231–52; Morabito, 'Benedetto il moro', col. 1104.

popes treated with respect the representatives and petitions of the Christian kings of Ethiopia and the Congo, and some popes even tried to prevent the slave trade, while others allowed it in the hope that it might lead to conversions. The hierarchy of the Church actively encouraged the conversion of black slaves in Italy and tried to see that they were provided with proper pastoral care and even protection on occasion. The multiplicity of native African languages and dialects, the relatively small number of black Africans, the assistance of Christian blacks who knew Italian, and the use of Latin in religious services that most Italians themselves did not understand, probably all help to account for the failure of the Church to train its priests in African languages so that more effective pastoral care could have been given. If the popes and bishops, with their humanistic and theological education, were often sympathetic to black Africans, on the local level, especially among the uneducated, prejudice raised its ugly head so that helpless black slaves could be victimised by their owners and become the targets of discriminatory insults and practical jokes, and even a saint was not spared. A mixed picture thus emerges and much more research must be conducted before any firm conclusions can be drawn.

PART FOUR

Black Africans with European identities
and profiles

Race and rulership: Alessandro de' Medici, first Medici duke of Florence, 1529–1537

JOHN BRACKETT

'Hail Alessandro of Colle Vecchio'.[1] This insulting bit of graffiti, scrawled by his enemies on the walls of his lodging in Rome in 1535, was a most unwelcome sight to Alessandro de' Medici, first Medici duke of the city of Florence. Alessandro was arriving in the eternal city to defend himself against charges leveled by Florentine exiles before the Holy Roman Emperor Charles V, that he was a tyrant whose despotic rule had deprived republican Florence of its liberty. The graffito reference was to the duke's birth: his mother was a peasant woman (actually a freed slave, as we will see in later discussion) living in the village of Colle Vecchio, near Rome. Remarkably, it was his mother's peasant status, rather than her Moorish or slave birth, which seems to have stoked the contempt of his critics.[2] Based on Florentine usage of the term 'slave' in the sixteenth century, I will argue that Alessandro's mother was a black African.[3] The libel was directed at her status as a peasant who had previously been a slave, not at her 'race.' Thus, Alessandro was being mocked not as the possessor

---

[1] Benedetto Varchi, *Storia fiorentina*, ed. Gaetano Milanesi, 2 vols. (Florence, 1963), II, p. 442: 'Viva Alessandro da Colle Vecchio'.

[2] According to the *Grande dizionario della lingua italiana*, ed. Salvatore Battaglia, 21 vols. (Turin, 1961–2002), X, *moro* refers to someone born of North African descent. Originally, this meant the specific land of Mauritania. Today in Italy, it is generically used to refer to all dark-skinned Africans, black or brown, or even colloquially to refer to anyone of African descent. The editor supports this meaning with examples of usage from Collenuccio and Ariosto, for the sixteenth century. Also referenced is the famous statue of *I quattro mori* chained at the base of the monument to Grand-Duke Ferdinando I de' Medici at Livorno.

[3] *Ibid.* The term *moro* also, according to Battaglia, refers to black slaves ('servo o schiavo') in the Florentine context of the sixteenth century. Bernardo Segni, *Storie fiorentine*, ed. Glauco Masi, 3 vols. (2nd edn, Livorno, 1830), I, p. 163, refers to Alessandro's mother as 'una schiava.' In Iris Origo, 'The domestic enemy: the Eastern slaves in Tuscany in the fourteenth and fifteenth centuries,' *Speculum*, 30 (1955), pp. 354–5, and in Alberto Tenenti, 'Gli schiavi di Venezia alla fine del cinquecento,' *Rivista storica italiana*, 67 (1955), p. 54, because of their great cost, slaves were few and far between, and were the exotic ornaments of the rich by the sixteenth century. Under the grand dukes, Origo continues, Moorish footmen were kept, as well as the occasional black ('coloured') maid. Language usage reflects the social reality that the few slaves in Italian/Florentine society were Moors, i.e. Berbers or sub-Saharan black Africans ('Ethiopians'), exported from Northern Africa or Spain.

of inferior African blood but as a royal impostor, the offspring of a peasant or ex-slave ruling over a noble city.

Alessandro de' Medici was born at Urbino in 1511 of an illustrious line on his father's side. The identity of his father remains a subject of dispute among historians; to a lesser extent his mother's ethnic origin is also disputed. Nonetheless, he was unexpectedly made Duke of Florence at the age of nineteen in 1529, by virtue of an agreement (the Treaty of Barcelona) between Pope Clement VII and the Emperor Charles V; then murdered in 1537, at the age of twenty-six, in a tyrannicide committed by his enigmatic cousin, Lorenzino de' Medici, assisted by a hired assassin. Given its trajectory, Alessandro's was a short though remarkable life, and a remarkable life-story, told, however, exclusively in a negative key. In the statements of many of his Florentine contemporaries, and in the view of not a few historians of the Renaissance in Florence, this young Italian man, mixed black and white, has been held responsible for the extinction of Florentine 'liberty', author of a tyranny precipitating the city into the 'unspeakably corrupt and degraded existence of the next three hundred years of despotism which followed'.[4]

Attracting my interest is the question: what role, if any, did Alessandro's Moorish heritage play in his selection for rulership, and in the assessment of his reign by contemporaries and later historians? In striking what may seem a dubious note regarding the impact of the duke's Moorishness on his image, I am not attempting to undermine my own article but simply acknowledging the difficulty of interpreting silences concerning what we call his 'race'. In fact, his 'race' is never mentioned (although his physical features are described in a neutral way), even by his greatest enemies, the host of Florentine exiles, forced out of the city by his alleged tyranny, nor even by the man who hated him enough to have killed him, his cousin Lorenzino. Does this mean that his skin colour was meaningless to his contemporaries, without negative

---

[4] T. Adolphus Trollope, *A History of the Commonwealth of Florence*, 4 vols. (London, 1865), IV, p. 553. The myth of Florentine liberty had and has extraordinary lasting power. As Hans Baron argued in *The Crisis of the Early Italian Renaissance* (Princeton, 1966), Florentines themselves first invented an extraordinary link between Florence and Roman liberty in the early fifteenth century, shortly after escaping conquest and subjugation by the 'tyrant' of Milan, Giangaleazzo Maria Visconti. Leonardo Bruni asserted that the foundation of Florence had been accomplished by Roman soldiers from the republican era, Sulla's veterans; thus, Florentines had a commitment to republican liberty in their blood as a people. Donald Weinstein in *Savonarola and Florence: Prophecy and Patriotism in the Renaissance* (Princeton, 1970), and Lorenzo Polizzotto in *The Elect Nation: The Savonarolan Movement in Florence, 1494–1545* (Oxford, 1994), both credit Savonarola with building on this vision of Florentine specialness, adding a religious twist. The myth was particularly alive among British historians in the nineteenth century, as we will see, as it is today among some British and American scholars, in the work of men as distinguished as Nicolai Rubinstein and Marvin Becker.

signification, or that his enemies felt constrained from voicing opinions on that particular subject? Nor was his 'race' mentioned in an overtly negative way by the harshest of his British critics, the nineteenth-century writers T. Adolphus Trollope and G. F. Young. Did men like Young and Trollope, on the other hand, sense that it was unnecessary to attack him directly on those grounds, though they, like the exiles of the time, savaged him in every other way?[5]

Based on a couple of written descriptions of Alessandro authored by contemporaries, and several portraits, it is clear that Alessandro's mother was a Moor, although one Italian author writing during the Fascist period denies this. Historians writing in the sixteenth century state that his father was Lorenzo de' Medici, Duke of Nemours and ruler of Urbino, in direct descent from Lorenzo 'il magnifico' and Cosimo 'il vecchio'. But because the Medici pope Clement VII chose Alessandro as first Duke of Florence over Ippolito de' Medici, Alessandro's cousin, Medicean exiles argued that he was actually Clement's bastard son. Thus there are questions concerning the identities of both his mother and his father. I will argue that his mother was a black African, and that Lorenzo was his father.

Looking first at the written documentation to support both his blackness, and the question of fatherhood, I will then introduce evidence from portraits to prove his African biological heritage.

There is one Italian author, Ugo Romagnoli, writing in *I Medici profili e vicende*, published in 1939 in Bologna, who claimed that Alessandro's mother was not a Moor but was instead 'an eastern woman'.[6] Romagnoli wrote that Alessandro only appeared to have been a mulatto because of his curly hair and olive-tinted skin.[7] Instead, Romagnoli argued that his mother was a peasant woman, white but not an ethnic Italian or a black African, in the service of Alfonsina Orsini, wife of Piero de' Medici, who was living in exile in Rome (1494–1512 being the period of Medici exile, comprising Alessandro's birth in 1511). The woman's name was Simonetta, and she was married to a coachman in the same service. Romagnoli concludes his discussion with the allegation that

---

[5] There is little interest among contemporary historians in either Alessandro or his reign. There is no biography of him, and no study focuses on the significance of the period 1529–37, despite its pivotal importance in the course of Florentine history. His successor, Cosimo I, has attracted much more attention. The 'drama' of the loss of Florentine liberty, followed by the tyrannicide of Lorenzino, was the perfect ending point for histories of the Florentine 'commonwealth' for British republicans like Trollope and Young.

[6] Ugo Romagnoli, *I Medici profili e vicende* (Bologna, 1939, 1944 2nd edn), p. 155: 'una di quelle donne Levantine.' Women from this region were brought to Florence by merchants to serve as their concubines, he states. His clear intention is to repudiate the claim that Alessandro was of African, i.e., inferior blood.

[7] *Ibid.*, p. 156.

Alessandro had his mother poisoned to hide his shameful origins.[8] As to the identity of the father, Romagnoli asserts that it was Clement, not Lorenzo. Providing no footnoted citations, Ugo claims that archival documents, and the contemporary historians Varchi, Segni, and Ammirato, support his conclusions.

As mentioned above, his mother was resident in Colle Vecchio but she had been employed in Urbino.[9] It is also a fact that she was married to a coachman, named Lostensor. The former is attested to by Lorenzino de' Medici,[10] the latter by Simonetta herself.[11] No overt mention was made of Simonetta's ethnic

---

[8] *Ibid.*

[9] It is likely that Alessandro's mother was resident in Colle Vecchio after giving birth to her son, and then being freed by Lorenzo from her service in Urbino.

[10] Lorenzino de' Medici, *Aridosia, Apologia, rime e lettere*, ed. Federico Ravello (Turin, 1921), pp. 213–14. Lorenzino wrote that she was a house servant in Urbino but that she lived in Colle Vecchio, near Rome. The term 'serva di casa' used above to describe Simonetta's status, is alternated in the sources with *schiava*, meaning 'slave.' This causes some confusion as to whether she was a servant or a slave, legally distinct categories. Dennis Romano, *House and Statecraft: Domestic Service in Renaissance Venice, 1400–1600* (Baltimore, 1996), p. xxv, writes that in practice, slaves were virtually indistinguishable from servants: 'They performed the same tasks as other domestics, and when manumitted, they blended imperceptibly into the larger populace.' Franco Angiolini, 'Schiave', in Angela Groppi, ed., *Il lavoro delle donne* (Rome, 1996), p. 106, writes: 'La linea discriminante tra schiave e serve, qualora sia esistita, doveva essere molto sottile'. Thus, the apparent confusion in terms of contemporary writers is actually the result of the nearly identical functionality of female slaves and servants in the households of the wealthy. Given her race, Simonetta was once a slave who was then manumitted, living in Colle Vecchio after her manumission.

[11] L. A. Ferrai, *Lorenzino de' Medici e la società cortigiana del cinquecento* (Milan, 1891), p. 449. In Appendix II, doc. IX, dated 12 Feb. 1529, is a letter from Simonetta to Alessandro asking him for money to support herself, two young children, and her coachman husband, Lostensor. Several interesting questions are raised here. What was the relationship between Simonetta and Lorenzo? According to Iris Origo, 'The domestic enemy,' pp. 344–5, in Roman and Lombard law the status of a slave child followed the mother; the status of a child of a free father and a slave mother was a slave. To avoid this condition, the female slave had to be living with the master as a recognised concubine or a special dispensation was needed for the child to be heir to the father's status. On the other hand, Ridolfo Livi, 'La schiavitù medioevale e la sua influenza sui caratteri antropologici degli italiani,' *Rivista italiana di sociologia*, II (1907), p. 574, states that Florence passed a law ordering that the status of the child of a slave follow the condition of the father but he provides no citation or effective date. Since Lorenzo was not married, was Simonetta his recognized concubine? Was she then freed as Lorenzo took all rights to the child as his heir; then, did Lorenzo arrange her marriage to the footman, Lostensor, himself almost certainly a Moor? Arranged marriages between freed slaves and servants or other dependents were a fairly common practice among the Italian elite (Livi, 'La schiavitù', pp. 573–4). Francesco Datini had a child by a slave woman, whom he took for his heir (his barren wife was in agreement), whom he then set free and married to one of his servants. He then married his child to a wool-merchant of Prato with a dowry of 100 florins. Giovanni Morelli had an uncle who actually married a slave woman after the death of his wife, and had a child by her (Steven A. Epstein, *Speaking of Slavery: Color, Ethnicity and Human Bondage in Italy* (Ithaca and London, 2001), p. 24). The ethnicity of

origin by Lorenzino, Varchi or Segni. The charge that Alessandro had his poor mother poisoned was the work of his enemies among the exiles. In fact, Ferrai, quoting Guicciardini in Ammirato's *Istorie fiorentine*, states that it was the exiles that were responsible for both stories: that Clement was Alessandro's father, and that he had poisoned his mother.[12] They were inventions in a war of words designed to discredit the duke, to make him seem worse than the Roman emperor Nero.

What more can be said of Simonetta's race? Gabrielle Langdon in 'Pontormo and Medici lineages: Maria Salviati, Alessandro, Giulia and Giulio de' Medici', citing the contemporary historian Bernardo Segni on the race of Alessandro's mother, says that Segni accepted what she calls the tradition of Alessandro's mother as a Moorish slave named Simonetta.[13] But Segni wrote of Alessandro's parentage:

Alessandro de' Medici, who was the natural son of Lorenzo, born of a slave woman named Anna (who also had relations with Giulio prior of Capua and then Pope Clement, and also with a coachman who was employed in the house) when they were rebels; it was thus uncertain whose son he was.[14]

Simonetta's husband is indicated by his name, Lostensor, not an Italian name but I have not been able to determine its ethnic origin. Epstein identifies a trend in that male Moorish slaves in Genoa possessed unusual names: Alderacoman, Alonsiho, Ioham, Calem, Hamet, Aspertino, are some examples. Angiolini also tells us that the majority of male slaves in Italy during the sixteenth century were Moors from Iberia, produced by the *reconquista*, as well as Moors and blacks from Northern and Central Africa ('Schiavi,' pp. 92–3). Given the sixteenth-century context and the unusualness of his name, Simonetta's husband was very likely of black African descent as well. Both may have been freed, living in Colle Vecchio – hence their poverty.

[12] Ferrai, *Lorenzino de' Medici*, p. 160.

[13] Gabrielle Langdon, 'Pontormo and Medici lineages: Maria Salviati, Alessandro, Giulia and Giulio de' Medici,' *Racar, revue d'art canadienne*, 19 (1992), p. 36, n. 75.

[14] Segni, *Storie fiorentine*, I, p. 163: 'Alessandro de' Medici, il quale figliuolo naturale di Lorenzo, nato d'una schiava chiamata Anna, la quale avendo avuto ancora che fare con Giulio priore di Capua e poi papa Clemente, ed ancora con un vetturale, che tenevano in casa, quando erano ribelli, era incerto di chi fosse figiuolo.' Segni appears to contradict himself, saying first that Alessandro was the natural son of Lorenzo, then, that because 'Anna' had relations with both a coachman, Lostensor her husband, and Clement, that it was unclear who the father actually was. In fact, this is the same claim made by Lorenzino in his *Apologia* (*Aridosia, Apologia*, pp. 213–14) written about 1539, which serves as his defense in the murder of Alessandro. One charge made against him was that he had not only killed a duke but a relative. He makes the aforementioned claim to demonstrate that Alessandro was not his relative since by Roman Law (he said) the child of a wanton woman (like Simonetta) was always considered the child of her husband (Lostensor). Since Lostensor was very likely of black African descent or possibly a Berber/Arab, it cannot be the case that he was the natural father; that Clement was the father had been discounted by Guicciardini, Alessandro's defender. Segni's source was undoubtedly Lorenzino, Duke Lorenzo having died in 1519, and Simonetta having died sometime after 1529 by whatever cause; he was

While Segni does not say that she was Moorish, the racial identification was bound up in the definition of the word *schiava* (slave), as we have established above. Although he writes that her name was Anna, we can accept that her name was Simonetta, which is how she signs a letter of 1529 to Alessandro.[15] Alessandro was born in Urbino, where Simonetta worked. His mother was resident in Colle Vecchio by at least 1529. Other contemporary writers – Benedetto Varchi, who was commissioned to write a history of Florence by Alessandro's successor Cosimo I, and Jacopo Nardi, the principal spokesperson for the exiles – do not mention her race even indirectly. Nardi does state that Alessandro was too much of a coward to recognise her. Although he does not say why, the reason was certainly her peasant status and wretched poverty.[16] This extreme poverty attests to her free status, occasioning the request for financial help from her son, which is the reason she writes to Alessandro: she did not have enough money to eat, which would hardly have been the case if she were still someone else's slave. Personal freedom has its costs. Riguccio Galluzzi, still a particularly authoritative historian who wrote in the eighteenth century, states only that she was a 'house servant', but to Lorenzo in Urbino, not to Alfonsina's household in Rome.[17] Ferrai stated that Alessandro resembled his mother, 'a beautiful and strong peasant woman from Colle Vecchio'.[18] It is possible that neither Ferrai nor Romagnoli knew of the diffusion of black and North Africans in Italy, especially Sicily and Southern Italy, in urban and rural settings by the sixteenth century. It is almost certain that neither knew anything about the relatively common practice of manumitting slaves of all types, and their absorption into the general populace. We, however, need not be led into accepting their uninformed conclusions about Simonetta's ethnicity.

It is no less difficult to determine with certainty the identity of Alessandro's father, but this is not as important to me as it was to his contemporaries. From my reading of the historians Varchi, Segni, Nardi, Galluzzi, Ferrai, and of Lorenzino, it seems clear that Francesco Guicciardini was correct in identifying this rumour as part of the efforts of the exiles to undermine Alessandro's

the only possible source regarding the circumstances of Alessandro's birth. It is also highly unlikely that Lorenzo would have accepted Alessandro as his child were he not certain that he was the father. There is also the issue of the manumission of both Simonetta and Alessandro, also matters of Roman Law, if son were to be heir to the father (see note 11 above).

[15] Lorenzino de' Medici, *Aridosia, Apologia*, pp. 213–14. Lorenzino wrote that she was a servant in Urbino but that she lived in Colle Vecchio, near Rome. Also, Ferruccio Martini, *Lorenzino de' Medici e il tirannicidio nel rinascimento* (Rome, 1972), p. 38, for a copy of Simonetta's letter.

[16] Jacopo Nardi, *Istorie della città di Firenze*, ed. Lelio Arbib, 2 vols. (Florence, 1838–41), II, p. 39: 'E la madre per la sua viltà no vuol conoscere'.

[17] Riguccio Galluzzi, *Istoria del granducato di Toscana* (Milan, 1974), p. XXXII.

[18] Ferrai, *Lorenzino de' Medici*, p. 71.

legitimacy in the mind of Charles V. Even Lorenzino does not suggest that Clement was the father, writing well after Clement's death in 1534, but creates a spurious scenario that would have been even worse by assigning fatherhood to Lostensor, Simonetta's coachman husband. Ippolito de' Medici, Alessandro's cousin, whom the exiles hoped to install as duke after Alessandro was removed, was apparently unaware of the rumour or simply put no stock in it. He believed that he should have been chosen to rule Florence because he was more closely related to Clement.[19] Most conclusive is the acceptance by Furio Diaz that Lorenzo was Alessandro's father, and that the youth exhibited his father's proud and prepotent personality.[20] The strongest documentary evidence for the position that Clement was the duke's father comes from Mercatti's *Storia cronologica*, which cites a clause from the Barcelona Treaty of 1529, promising Charles V's illegitimate daughter, Margherita, in marriage to Alessandro. There is stated the claim that Alessandro was the natural son of Clement.[21] The origin of this clause is most likely in the perceived importance to Charles of cementing a relationship with the pope; why would he have cared whether Alessandro was descended from the most illustrious branch of the Medici? It was Charles' act that would establish the Medici as hereditary nobility in Florence; previously, they were political and social anomalies, members of the third estate who had somehow come to rule an important city. Clement, on the other hand, was pope! Whatever the truthfulness of this clause – and the weight of evidence favours Lorenzo as father – the more important issue still remains the ethnicity of Alessandro's mother.

There is substantial artistic evidence in several portraits of Alessandro to support the conclusion that his mother was a black African.[22] I will introduce three of these portraits and a tapestry as evidence. Commenting disparagingly on portraits of Alessandro in the Uffizi Gallery in Florence, the English historian G. F. Young (quoting Trollope) wrote:

The portraits of this wretched youth which hang on the walls of the Florentine gallery show the lowness of the type to which his organization belonged. The small, contracted features, the low forehead, and mean expression, are altogether unlike any of the Medici race, in whom, whatever else they might be, there was always manifestation of intellectual power.[23]

[19] Varchi, *Storia fiorentina*, II, pp. 45 and 292–3.
[20] Furio Diaz, *Il granducato di Toscana: I Medici* (Turin, 1976), pp. 38 and 54. Diaz is the most authoritative historian of the grand-ducal state of the Medici.
[21] Trollope, *A History*, IV, pp. 486–7.
[22] For a complete run of portraits of Alessandro, see Karla Langedijk, *The Portraits of the Medici, Fifteenth to Eighteenth Centuries*, 3 vols. (Florence, 1981), I, pp. 221–42.
[23] G. F. Young, *The Medici* (New York, 1923), pp. 497–8. Young was most likely referring to the portrait by Girolamo Macchietti's workshop (fig. 64).

Even though Trollope says not a word about Alessandro's 'race' – not even to mention his skin colour, hair or lips and nose – it is clear that the duke's physical appearance was so repugnant to him that his revulsion spills over into a negative assessment of his character. But such an overt connection need not have been made. In eliding physical characteristics judged to be negative, especially the 'low forehead', with negative character traits associated with certain physical features – Alessandro's lack of intelligence – Trollope and Young show themselves to have been influenced by scientists who believed in physiognomy, that is that particular assemblages of physical features somehow indicated character. In Alessandro's case, the features attributed to him were indicative of the lower-class, criminal 'type' of human being, who could hardly have been a true exponent of the noble Medici. Young and Trollope come close to assigning the young duke to a different race but pull up short of that unimaginable conclusion.

There is little written evidence describing Alessandro's physical appearance to temper what we see in paintings, but what there is lends strong support to the conclusion that portraits of him are accurate and not exaggerations of some kind. The contemporary historian Bernardo Segni wrote that Alessandro was a person who was 'well put together, stocky and strong, with a dark colour, and a wide nose'.[24] Segni was politically active in the city and thus saw Alessandro with his own eyes; his assessment contains no value judgment, though. The modern historian, Ferrai, described him as being 'dark in colour, naturally robust, made stronger by continual exercise'.[25] Scipione Ammirato described him in 1647 as having 'brown skin, fat lips and curly hair'.[26] Proceeding to an examination of the portraits and the tapestry will demonstrate that Alessandro was what we could call today a black man, that is, a man of mixed white and African descent.

One portrait of Alessandro originally believed to have been by Agnolo Bronzino is now thought to have been painted after 1553 in his workshop (fig. 63). This famous bust-like miniature of the duke from the shoulders up shows him in possession of the dark skin, wide nose and curly hair that writers ascribed to him. He clearly appears to have been a mulatto or black by our standards; in fact, it is in this portrait that his Africanity is most apparent. In the portrait of Alessandro by the workshop of Girolamo Macchietti of 1585

[24] Segni, *Storie fiorentine*, II, p. 425: 'persona raccolta, nerbuto, di color nero, e di naso grande'.
[25] Ferrai, *Lorenzino de' Medici*, p. 71. He was 'bruno di carnagione, e di complessione robusta fortificata dai continui esercizi'. Here Ferrai states that Alessandro resembled his mother.
[26] Langdon, 'Pontormo and Medici lineages', p. 36, n. 73: 'color bruno, labbri grossi e capegli crespi'.

ALEX. MED. FLOR.   DVX I. LAVREN. F.

FIG. 63. Workshop of Agnolo Bronzino, *Portrait of Alessandro de' Medici*, after 1553 (oil on tin, 16 × 12.5 cm, Florence, Galleria degli Uffizi, Inv. 1890, no. 857).

(fig. 64), the duke is dressed in light armour that is black in colour and richly trimmed in gold.[27] He is also wearing a black sword in a black scabbard, and a tunic of gold cloth decorated in a black pattern. The dark colouration of his

[27] See Marta Privitera, *Girolamo Macchietti: un pittore dello Studiolo di Francesco I (Firenze 1535–1592)* (Milan/Rome, 1996), pp. 176–8.

FIG. 64. Workshop of Girolamo Macchietti, *Portrait of Duke Alessandro de' Medici*, 1585 (oil on panel, 140 × 116 cm, Florence, Deposito delle Gallerie (Soffittone di Palazzo Pitti), Inv. 1890, no. 2237 (serie Aulica)).

skin (brown) and curly hair are evident, as are his thick lips and wide nose. His expression displays suspiciousness, evidence of a troubled character, which is not surprising given the insecurity of his position in the city. However, in the third portrait, that by Giorgio Vasari of 1534 (fig. 65), Alessandro's African features appear less distinct. It is a real piece of Medici propaganda, showing Alessandro seated in profile turned to his left, wearing a full suit of armour, holding a sceptre, while gazing outwards through a hole in the wall of some enclosed space over the city of Florence in the background. The duke is the protector of his realm in this guise.[28] His facial features are a bit different from those in fig. 63: although his skin is clearly brown, his nose is more aquiline but his hair is still clearly frizzy. Alessandro, in his royal splendour, is still clearly of African heritage. The fourth image is a tapestry of 1573–4, designed by Giovanni Stradano and woven by Benedetto di Michele Squilli, preserved in the Museo Civico of Pisa (fig. 66).[29] A seated Clement VII is depicted selecting Alessandro as Duke of Florence – a kind of secular annunciation. Even in the black and white version included here, the darkness of his skin, in comparison with those around him, is striking as he stands to the left of the seated pope with his hand on his sword. His lips are thick, his nose wide, and his hair is very curly.

Taken together, the written and pictorial evidence are more than sufficient to prove Alessandro's black African descent. At the time the duke was nicknamed 'the Moor' and 'the mule' of the Medici.[30] Both of these nicknames were meant to indicate his bastard status; the latter may have added the dimension of his mulatto status.[31] But did his blackness have any meaning beyond defining his appearance to his contemporaries? To answer this question, we must recognise that Alessandro and his fellow Italians lived in a world where race meant something substantially different than it does today.

Ivan Hannaford, writing in *Race: The History of an Idea in the West*, demonstrates that the word 'race' only entered into general usage in European languages during the sixteenth century. In Italy, 'race' (*razza*) was variously

---

[28] Malcolm Campbell, 'Il ritratto del duca Alessandro de' Medici di Giorgio Vasari: Contesto e significato', in Gian Carlo Garfagnini, ed., *Girogio Vasari tra decorazione ambientale e storiografia artistica* (Florence, 1985), pp. 339–61. Campbell's article discusses the political symbolism of this portrayal of Alessandro.

[29] Matilde Stefanini Sorrentino, *Arazzi medicei a Pisa* (Florence, 1993), pp. 68–70.

[30] Piero Bargellini, *La spendida storia di Firenze dal duca d'Atene a Cosimo I* (Florence, 1964), p. 243.

[31] *Novo vocabolario della lingua italiana secondo l'uso di Firenze*, ed. Emilio Broglio, 4 vols. (Florence, 1870–97), III, under *mulo*. In Florentine usage, *mulo* indicated bastard status.

FIG. 65. Giorgio Vasari, *Alessandro de' Medici*, 1534 (oil on panel, 158 × 115 cm, Florence, Galleria degli Uffizi, Inv. 1890, no. 1563).

FIG. 66. Giovanni Stradano (design), Benedetto di Michele Squilli (execution), *Clement VII selects Alessandro de' Medici as Duke of Florence*, 1573–4 (tapestry, 460 × 670 cm, Pisa, Museo Civico).

defined as: sort, species, race, kind, brood, stock, descent, lineage or pedigree.[32] These terms are a clear indication of an awareness of different categories of human beings with distinct origins. But the modern idea of race based on a genetic inheritance determining unchangeable qualities of character and mental capacity only began to form in the seventeenth century, coming to fruition in the late eighteenth and nineteenth centuries. Hannaford convincingly argues that what distinguished civilised peoples from barbarians or 'ethnics', from the ancient period to the early seventeenth century, was the presence in these societies of a 'public sphere' as a realm of politics where discourse led to decisions affecting the 'state'. Those societies without a public sphere were viewed as trapped in the meaningless realm of private life, the structure of which was determined by the necessities of survival: procreation and family, along with economic activity. Basing his argument on certain texts, beginning with Plato's *Timaeus* and Aristotle's *Politics*, Hannaford states that, conceptually, the idea of the public sphere – open to all well-spoken men of talent and education – limited as it was in its application, nonetheless inhibited the development of the concept of racial differences immutably rooted in Nature. The public sphere allowed men to give meaning to their lives, to become civilised, while barbarians lived only according to the necessities of survival in the natural world. So, by sheer force of character and talent, by education and a clear perception of what was important, any man could overcome his racial \ societal beginnings to become civilised. Even whole societies could change, given the right circumstances.

Another important idea was added in the later Roman period when Christianity had taken hold. In the *City of God*, written in the immediate aftermath of the first barbarian sacking of Rome, the African bishop St Augustine adds the concept of fellowship in Christian faith: by faith in Christ, all men could be members of the 'City of God'.[33] Regardless of the condition of their bodies, all men were rational and mortal as god had made them. So, human beings could voluntarily enter into two sorts of realms where their ethnic differences could be overcome or left behind in the pursuit of achieving entry to superior forms of community, one pagan and one Christian. By the sixteenth century both have been brought together in an uneasy union. Civilised

---

[32] Ivan Hannaford, *Race: The History of an Idea in the West* (Baltimore, 1996). Hannaford's primary goal is to debunk the argument that racism has been a constant in European societies, present from the ancient through the modern period. Those taking that position have misread the works of philosophers such as Plato and Aristotle, and similarly mischaracterised the views of the ancient Greeks more generally on their views of other neighbouring peoples in the Mediterranean.

[33] *Ibid.*, p. 95.

Europeans were bound together through covenants of law and faith. Both 'citizen' and 'subject' were willing partners in the sacrament, combining the political with the religious.[34] Perhaps it was due to the absence of 'nations' in the modern sense that 'civilised' behaviour was conceived of as open to those with the desire, talent and will to acquire it, rather than enclosed by the artificial political boundaries of European nation-states, which conferred civilisation automatically on their inhabitants.[35]

Italy in the sixteenth century was, as were other parts of Europe, little more than a geographical expression. Binding Italians together was a combination of the land, a sense of the Roman past, and Christianity. Otherwise, the Italians were composed of many different peoples: the Florentines were different from the Pisans and the Sienese; all of the inhabitants of the peninsula spoke their own languages or dialects, and directed their allegiances in varying degrees towards their city, town, patron saint, lord or family association. A similar range of differences prevailed among the other peoples of the earth. Among the educated, it was largely the views of the Roman Pliny the Elder (d. 79 BC), expressed in his *Natural Histories*, that held sway. All manner of barbarians and strange creatures – part human, part animal, human but with some parts missing – were to be found, many of the strangest located in Africa below the Sahara. The largely literary opus of the ancients was supplemented (and partly contradicted) by the experience of Italian businessmen/explorers in Africa.[36] According to Machiavelli, there at one time existed African exemplars of *virtù* – Masinissa, Jurgurtha and Hannibal in antiquity.[37] In the Renaissance, such possibilities also existed. All of the negative distinctions existing between the varieties of human beings could be overcome by the individual in possession of the virtues necessary to succeed in the public sphere: talent, wisdom and knowledge, will and courage. These characteristics, cultivated by the humanist programme of study, launched talented men and women into the 'republic of letters', a cosmopolitan world of writers and artists.

Courage and military prowess could provide another route out of the morass of ethnicity. In *Gli Hecatommitti*, a collection of stories written by Giambattista Giraldi Cinzio and published in 1580 in Venice, is a novella entitled, 'Un capitano moro piglia per mogliera una cittadina venetiana' ('A Moorish captain takes a Venetian citizen as wife'), which served as the basis of Shakespeare's

---

[34] *Ibid.*, p. 184.   [35] Norbert Elias, *The Civilizing Process* (New York, 1982).

[36] John B. Friedman, *The Monstrous Races in Medieval Art and Thought* (Cambridge, MA, 1981), pp. 1, 7, 27 and 41. See also, Katherine George, 'The civilized West looks at primitive Africa, 1400–1880', in *Isis*, 49 (1958), pp. 62–72.

[37] Niccolò Machiavelli, *The Art of War*, trans. Elis Farnesworth (New York, 1965), p. xiii.

play, *Othello the Moor of Venice*.[38] I need not recount in detail the story outline of such a well-known piece of literature. In an age of mercenary soldiers and sailors, the Venetian government chooses the Moor to head its Cyprus garrison because of his courage and skill in battle. He marries a young Venetian woman of good family because both are so attracted to the high level of personal virtues present in the other that they overcome the natural differences which otherwise separate Moor from Italian. The Moor's jealousy and murder of his wife reestablished those ethnic differences. The point, though, is that no hard and fast set of qualities puts one group permanently above or below another. Like the Moor of Cinzio's novella, Alessandro's blackness did not diminish his desirability to Italian women, nor did it prevent Charles V from giving his own illegitimate daughter, Margherita, to the duke in marriage.[39]

In Alessandro's case nobility was undoubtedly part of his attraction. Initially, his distinction of birth was a specifically urban and Italian variety; he was in direct descent from the most renowned branch of the Medici family, which ran from Cosimo 'il vecchio' through Lorenzo 'il magnifico'. This seems to me the most likely reason why Clement chose Alessandro as duke in preference to his cousin Ippolito. Establishment of the family as genuine nobility would have to be set firmly in the most illustrious line of the Medici. But for others, like Ippolito and Charles V, it was closeness to the pope, bound in allegiance to the empire, which should have provided the foundation of Medici rule in ducal Florence. Ennoblement brought the conference of certain virtues, recognised even in patrician Florence, some of which lesser persons possessed only in the most unusual cases, but never across the board. These civic virtues, which any prince ought to display, included: Justice, Prudence, Temperance and Magnanimity, along with Fortitude and Peace. Military virtues included Prowess and Courage, and the Christian virtues were Faith, Hope and Charity. That Alessandro possessed these virtues was the message of official image-making designed to counter the negative picture that his enemies passionately constructed of him as the worst of tyrants. No one was more determined to establish the worthiness of Alessandro as prince than his successor Cosimo I, the most successful of the Medici grand-dukes. Cosimo assumed responsibility for raising Alessandro's two illegitimate children (he had no opportunity

---

[38] Giambattista Giraldi Cinzio, *Gli Hecatommitti*, 2 vols. (Venice, 1580), deca terza, novella VII.

[39] Alessandro had two illegitimate children, Giulia and Giulio. The identity of the mother is uncertain. Gabrielle Langdon argues that she was Taddea Malaspina, an attractive young widow, resident for a time in Florence at the Pazzi palace with her sister Ricciarda. Alessandro is known to have spent many evenings at the palace. See Langdon, 'Pontormo and Medici lineages', p. 38, ns. 83 and 87.

FIG. 67. Francesco da Sangallo, *Portrait Medal of Alessandro de' Medici and Cosimo I de' Medici* (obverse and reverse), sixteenth century (bronze, Florence, Museo Nazionale).

of having children by his wife, Margherita), and arranging good marriages for them.[40] He was also determined to avenge Alessandro's murder, finally achieving that goal in Venice in 1548 with the assassination of Lorenzino.

We have already presented examples of this positive image-making in portraits of the duke dressed up in his armour as protector of the city (figs. 64 and 65). While we do not know who commissioned the first portrait, Alessandro himself commissioned the Vasari (fig. 65). To this can be added the medallions struck in the sixteenth century by Francesco da Sangallo, present-ing the opposed images of Alessandro and Cosimo I, Duke and grand-duke (fig. 67). Already by the sixteenth century, of course, ways of propagandisti-cally presenting the civic virtues of Medici rulers had become well-known, having had their beginnings with Lorenzo 'il magnifico'.[41]

[40] Langdon, 'Pontormo and Medici lineages', p. 26. Cosimo never missed a chance to enhance his own status.

[41] Nicolai Rubinstein, 'The formation of the posthumous image of Lorenzo de' Medici', in Edward Cheney and Neil Ritchie, eds., *Oxford, China and Italy* (London, 1984), pp. 94–106. Rubinstein's article reconstructs the careful efforts made by his supporters to create a public, civic image of Lorenzo de' Medici as a great citizen – rich and powerful – who presided over the greatest period of Florence's history. Needless to say it glosses over his less attractive qualities and actions, such as coercing the police to persecute his enemies in the aftermath of the Pazzi conspiracy, dipping into the public treasury to supplement private, family funds, and prowling the city at night chasing women. The construction of this public image of Lorenzo was a first for Florence, Rubinstein writes.

Literature also played its role in orchestrating the creation of Alessandro's official public image, as it had with Lorenzo. In Alessandro Ceccheregli's *Delle azioni e sentenze di Alessandro de' Medici ragionamento*, originally published in 1564, the author clearly intended to present the late duke's image in a way worthy of a prince. In form, Ceccheregli's book was modelled on Boccaccio's *Decameron*.[42] In it, a group of noble friends are gathered together to exchange uplifting stories concerning Alessandro's numerous worthy deeds and utterances while moving in and around Florence. Despite the literary intentions of the author, we cannot simply dismiss these stories as fiction. Piero Bargellini wrote that the young duke extended his justice to everyone, and that he listened willingly to the poor.[43] The aim of these vignettes was to demonstrate that Alessandro had the requisite virtues of a prince, particularly Justice and Magnanimity, which he displayed in defense of poor, helpless women in these stories. A second example of praise literature is a fragment of a sonnet, written to Alessandro by a certain Lisabetta da Cepperello, a Florentine, sometime during the sixteenth century:

New Alessandro and in Italy the only one/Crowned not only with green laurel/But with other leaves of gems and gold/Since even to the heavens you will fly/Because of you will be heard from one pole to the other/The restored fame of our city/And it will pass from Mount Atlas, to the Indus river and Mauretania/Of your exalted deeds the noble host.[44]

Having had the opportunity to examine briefly some of the artefacts that remain of the effort exerted to create a positive image of Alessandro, we pass now to an assessment of his real life deeds.

Through a deal struck between Charles V and Pope Clement VII in 1529, to solidify the allegiance that the papacy would owe to the Holy Roman Empire, the nineteen-year-old Alessandro de' Medici was named Duke of Florence. By 1530–1 with the support, sometimes reluctant, of the best families, he became an absolute prince, and republicanism in the city became a vestige of the turbulent past. The civil strife attached to the republic had finally become too

---

[42] Alessandro Ceccheregli, *Delle azioni e sentenze di Alessandro de' Medici* (Bologna, 1865), originally published in 1564.

[43] Bargellini, *La splendida storia di Firenze*, p. 243.

[44] Angelo de Gubernatis, *Antologia di poetesse italiane del secolo decimosesto* (Florence, 1883): 'Nuovo Alessandro ed in Italia solo/Coronato non pur di verde Lauro/Ma d'altre frondi che di gemme e d'auro/Onde per sino al ciel n'andrate a volo/Per voi s'udra da l'uno a l'altro polo/De nostra citta ristauro/E passar da l/Atlante, a l'Indo e al Mauro/De l'opre eccelse vostre il degno stuolo.' I want to thank Professor Paul H. D. Kaplan for this reference.

much for many patricians to bear in the aftermath of the latest rout of the
Medici from the city in 1527, and the horrors of the siege of 1529–30. Clement
had desired this outcome from the very beginning; but he solicited opinions
about the ultimate form of Florentine government from Medici supporters in
the city. The pope shrewdly wanted the suggestion of royal absolutism to come
from the mouths of Florentines themselves.[45] Francesco Vettori, Machiavelli's
good friend, and Filippo Strozzi were among the most ardent advocates of
this resolution of Florentine political affairs. After consultation with the pope,
Filippo returned to the city from Rome with Clement's blessing to begin
construction of a new Florentine ship of state. Hence, the new government
included a Council of 200, a higher Council of 48, and then four councillors
to advise Alessandro directly.[46]

The immediate impression that most had of Alessandro on his arrival in
the city in 1530, fresh from tutelage at the court of Charles V, was not a
negative one – just the opposite, in fact. The historian Ferrai writes that until
1534 (the year of Clement's death) Alessandro's government was much more
mild and beneficial than many historians give it credit for.[47] And, according
to Bernardo Segni, the young man established himself in the Medici palace,
and set about making friends with many young patrician Florentines. He was
so approachable, in fact, that Clement, aware of the many enemies that the
family had, admonished him to be more reserved and cautious.[48] Alessandro
did take some action against a few of his enemies, confiscating the property
of some, and imprisoning others at his pleasure. At least equally distressing to
Florentines – at least to those who wrote about him – was his licentiousness.
The duke apparently sought many sexual conquests among women of élite
families (married and single), women of the lower classes and, rumour had it,
among the presumed virgins of Florence's many convents,[49] (but Ferrai argues
that there is no hard proof that the duke despoiled the virginity of nuns
in convents). Add to this his arrogant personality – hardly unusual among
patricians or aristocrats – the bad behaviour of his entourage – again, hardly
unusual among men of his class – and any number of costly feasts, and one
could easily conclude that a very poor example was being set at the top. It
is likely that the young man was not paying much attention to governing,
but Lorenzo 'il magnifico' committed exactly the same indiscretions, exiting
the mud with a considerably cleaner image than did Alessandro. Segni wrote

---

[45] Galluzzi, *Istoria del granducato*, pp. xxxvii–viii.   [46] Segni, *Storie fiorentine*, i, p. 361.
[47] Ferrai, *Lorenzino de' Medici*, pp. 127–8.   [48] *Ibid.*, pp. 351–2.   [49] *Ibid.*, p. 160.

that Clement's many written admonishments had no effect on modifying Alessandro's behaviour.

Alessandro quickly became the victim of very bad press due in large part to the decision to narrow the base of government, severely limiting the numbers of remunerative government positions available to be filled by an impoverished patriciate. The result was that a number of these families went into exile, hoping to find a way of toppling the Medici duke from power. Holding government offices had long been one of the defining characteristics of the Florentine elite, conferring honour on those families whose male members had a history of occupying the highest positions. But more was at stake than family honour, since the pay and emoluments that attached to these offices was substantial. In the aftermath of the devastating siege of 1530, many patricians wanted to occupy those offices to remake their wealth.

With the death of Clement in 1534, the efforts of the exiles gained momentum, and Alessandro's actions against Medici enemies gained in ferocity because of his fear and uncertainty, as he was now bereft of his most important benefactor and protector.[50] Construction of the Fortezza da Basso was accelerated, worked on by the poor without pay, yet paid for through taxation of the poor. By this point, Filippo Strozzi had also chosen exile in Venice, where he became a leader in the efforts to unseat Alessandro. Furio Diaz characterises Strozzi as the consummate opportunist, seeking only to protect his own wealth and position. Diaz goes on to say that this same motive extended to all of the exiles, and, we might add, to those who decided to protect themselves, like Francesco Guicciardini, by backing the duke. But it has been the exiles, especially Strozzi, who have been mythologised as defenders of republican liberty against tyranny.[51] These same men had a determinative role in shaping this myth, as we shall see. Alessandro's disappointed cousin, Ippolito, made a cardinal by Clement, let himself become the focal point of exile efforts to convince Charles V to restore liberty in Florence, replacing Alessandro with himself.

In 1535 the exiles, with Ippolito as their masthead, planned to meet Charles V in Naples, as he made his way back from a glorious victory over the Moors in Tunisia. There, they would plead their case that Alessandro had broken his promise to the city and to the emperor to maintain Florence's republican form of government and thus its liberty. Unexpectedly, Ippolito died, immediately setting off speculation that Alessandro had had him poisoned,

[50] Galluzzi, *Istoria del granducato*, p. xxxix.   [51] Diaz, *Il granducato di Toscana*, pp. 61–2.

although it must be emphasised in fairness to the duke, that this was only one of three theories concerning the reason for the cardinal's death then in circulation. Having little choice the exiles pressed ahead with their plan but now without a real alternative to propose to Charles. Francesco Guicciardini was Alessandro's defender before the emperor. Both sides were asked to submit their positions in writing, then they awaited Charles' verdict. But the exiles had lost more than a leader with Ippolito's demise, they had also lost the chance of offering him to the French in their efforts to dislodge the emperor from Italy. With Ippolito's death followed by the reopening of hostilities with France, and Charles' victory in Tunisia, the exiles lost a political option that they could have used to pressure Charles to decide in their favour. The historian Jacopo Nardi was the principal presenter of the exiles' position, as he tells us himself. In a long oration that is the centerpiece of his *Istorie della città di Firenze*, he makes two points against Alessandro. The first is that by doing away with the principal institutions of Florentine government, the *Signoria* and the *gonfaloniere di giustizia*, the duke had violated his agreement with Charles to preserve Florentine liberty, and was therefore a tyrant. His second point is that by a host of behaviours and his dissolute moral condition – his bastard status, his sexual licentiousness, the murders of two men with his own hands, arbitrary and personal use of governmental power – Alessandro was unfit to rule.[52] To these calumnies Francesco Guicciardini responded initially by sidestepping the issue related to morality; then he went on to defend the lawfulness of Alessandro's government by pointing out that liberty did not consist of granting licence to the poor to despoil the wealth of the rich, or in allowing the ignorant to rule over better prepared men.[53] Alessandro had protected the position and prosperity of the city; and his government was defended by a major faction of the traditional elite in the city. Charles took some time in responding, since the exiles' case was not without merit. But his major concern was with his position in Italy *vis-à-vis* the French, towards whom the exiles tended, and thus his concern for the stability of Florence won out. With the promise to Alessandro of his illegitimate daughter in marriage, the duke emerged from this confrontation in a more solid position in the city than before 1536. The next year he was stabbed to death at the hand of his cousin, who then fled to Venice, where he was hailed among the exiles as the 'New Brutus'.[54]

---

[52] Nardi, *Istorie*, II, pp. 39–42.   [53] Diaz, *Il granducato di Toscana*, pp. 61–2.
[54] Romagnoli, *I Medici profili*, pp. 165–77.

A mixture of fact and judgement, as any political history must be, this is the 'story' of Alessandro's brief reign in Florence. While I am not interested in attempting a revisionist interpretation of his rule now, the point has to be made that Alessandro's first decisions were closely guided by Pope Clement, assisted by Medici supporters in Florence. Even after Clement's death, Alessandro was still really only at the head of a faction of Florentines who had traditionally controlled the government.[55] When it came to governance, he followed the lead of others, and he was unlikely to have preferred anything else. Judgments concerning his place in Florentine political history have been unduly influenced by the rhetoric of historians writing at the time – Nardi, Segni, Varchi – either because they were anti-Mediceans (Segni and Nardi), or because they wished, like Varchi, to extol the virtues of his patron Cosimo I in part by denigrating Alessandro, his predecessor. The portrayal of Alessandro's 'just' murder by the 'Tuscan Brutus' is the natural stuff of dramatic narratives, and has been written up as such almost to the present day by influential artists enthralled by the idea of the loss of Florentine *libertas*, combined with the classical role of the hero who seeks to restore liberty by eliminating a tyrant, and the end of the Florentine Renaissance.[56] The deeply intertwined roles of Alessandro and Lorenzino in the 'story' of Florentine liberty, however, no longer attract the attention that they once did among contemporary scholars dismissive even of how the idea once came into acceptance.[57]

Almost like conjoined twins, the stories of Alessandro and Lorenzino de' Medici have been surgically separated by scholars today. After the separation, Alessandro's survival literally and historically has been much briefer and less

[55] Diaz, *Il granducato Toscana*, pp. 61–2.

[56] Ferrai, *Lorenzino de' Medici*, pp. 2–3. Poems were written in Lorenzino's honour immediately after the murder, rhymes were composed, commemorative medals struck, even a statue by Jacopo Sansovino was executed. This story, the tyrannicide of a monster by his cousin, has attracted no less attention since then by writers fascinated by the story of liberty lost in Florence. Lorenzino's *Apologia*, immediately mocked by Medici supporters as a *lamento*, was judged variously in the nineteenth century on its artistic merits as an example of humanist writing in the Cinquecento by several literary critics. His story has been of interest to an international cast of writers including: plays by the English dramatist Robert Merry, *Lorenzo: a tragedy in five acts*, performed at Covent Garden in 1791 (later translated into Spanish), Alfred de Musset, *Lorenzaccio*, Alexandre Dumas (the elder), *Lorenzino: drama en cinq actes et en prose*, and Giovacchino Forzano, *Lorenzino: drama in tre atti e sei quadri*; in a poem by Vittorio Alfieri entitled *L'Etruria vendicata*; a novel by Arvin Upton, *Lorenzino* (New York, 1977); and two newspaper articles by the historian Roberto Ridolfi, published by Roberto Massagni, *Lorenzino, sfinge Medicea* (Florence, 1983).

[57] All of this should qualify the argument that the political ideal of republican liberty in the Italian Renaissance is nothing more than an American invention. See Anthony Molho, 'The Italian Renaissance, Made in the USA', in A. Molho and G. S. Wood, eds., *Imagined Histories: American Historians Interpret the Past* (Princeton, 1998), pp. 263–94.

healthy than his cousin Lorenzino's. Despite the lack of a balanced assessment of his rule – apart from Diaz's brief treatment – negative judgements of Alessandro's reign tell us something important about race in the Italian Renaissance. For Alessandro's contemporaries, there seems to have been no connection made in their writings between blackness and his character. He was a cruel tyrant, a monster and a murderer who did not even know who his own father was, but none of these judgements is derived from his blackness. At least, such a connection is not made in the texts. Despite the existence of a generalised but also occasional denigration of black Africans in Italian society based on skin colour, as discussed by Stephen Epstein in his *Speaking of Slavery: Color, Ethnicity, and Human Bondage in Italy*, racism did not exist intellectually in the same way that it does today. At least a few were able to escape that denigration by entry into the public sphere. In Duke Alessandro's case, the Medici inheritance and the innate qualities of princes and kings, that is issues of rulership, triumphed over issues of 'race'.

CHAPTER FIFTEEN

Juan Latino and his racial difference[1]

BALTASAR FRA-MOLINERO

The Afro-Hispanic poet Juan Latino (1518? – c. 1594) was the author of an epic poem in Latin, *Austrias carmen* (Granada, 1573), dedicated to Don Juan de Austria, Philip II's half-brother and the military star of his day.[2] Juan Latino became a legend in his own time as an example of a rarity, a black person who wrote and, what is more, in Latin. In this chapter I intend to elucidate the circumstances of the composition and the content of this major work, which can be seen as an important aspect of the formation of a Spanish national and ethnic identity during the Renaissance. Juan Latino's is a privileged testimony of the use of the literary, or writerly, as a means to establish an identity against the grain of a society that regarded blackness as meaning both permanent lack of freedom and ultimate lack of dignity, or honour, to use the sixteenth-century expression.

Juan Latino had three reasons for seeking to place himself in the midst of the humanistic discourse of the Renaissance. First, by writing in Latin he wished to affirm his magisterial position in contrast with the slave status of most black Africans – including himself at one point in his life – in Spain at the time. Second, he opened a rhetorical divide between black Christians like him and the African Muslims who had been declared the enemies of the state, his political and religious orthodoxy being demonstrated through the verses of the *Austrias carmen* and other Latin compositions. Juan Latino's third goal was the establishment of the dignity of all black Africans through their association with the biblical Ethiopia. The third proposition opens the door to the unstated corollary that should follow, which is that black Africans should not be considered natural slaves in the Aristotelian sense.

---

[1] I wish to express my gratitude to my colleague Thomas Hayward, for his kind direction in the translation and interpretation of the Latin passages included in this chapter, and also to Professor Charles I. Nero, for his comments on several aspects of black intellectual history.

[2] The first edition of *The Austriad* or *Austrias carmen* appeared at the end of a volume of Latino's Latin verse in celebration of the Royal House of Habsburg, or Austria, as it is known in Spain. Johannes Latinus, *Ad Catholicum pariter et invictissimum Philippum Dei gratia Hispaniarum Regem, de foelicissima serenissimi Ferdinandi Principis nativitate epigrammatum liber* (Granada, 1573; Nendeln-Lichtenstein, 1971). For a modern critical edition, with a Spanish translation, see José A. Sánchez Marín, *La Austríada de Juan Latino* (Granada, 1981).

As a black African and a former slave, Juan Latino used his strong sense of racial identity in the service of the ideal of imperial Christian monarchy represented by Spain in his time. Yet if there was one place in the Spanish empire where political ideology and reality were at odds, that place was Granada, where Juan Latino lived. At the time he wrote *Austrias carmen*, Granada was the scene of the worst civil and ethnic conflict of Philip II's reign. All containment walls had broken in 1568. That year, the Moriscos, as the population of Muslim descent was known, rose in arms against the Christians, who had established their political and economic power after the conquest of the Kingdom of Granada in 1492. The 1568 uprising and subsequent repression, known as the War of the Alpujarras, lasted until 1572. Don Juan de Austria was called to direct the decisive phase of the military campaign that brought about the final defeat of the insurrection.[3]

The Spanish Crown saw the events in Granada as part of a larger conflict in the Mediterranean sea that involved the competition for supremacy between the Spanish monarchy and the Ottoman empire. The recently conquered Kingdom of Granada was in this sense a frontier, attacked by Muslim corsairs – the Turks – and harbouring a population of former Muslims and now nominal Christians who were in a permanent state of discontent. Granada is regarded by literary historians as the birthplace of Spanish Renaissance poetry, and it contains some of the most remarkable Renaissance architecture in Spain. During the sixteenth century, however, it could not easily rid itself of conflict between two religions and two ethnic groups which had been at war with each other since the Middle Ages. The circular palace erected by Charles V in the Alhambra was part of a cultural programme in which Renaissance humanism partook of the crusading spirit of the Spanish *reconquista*, a view of history and politics that was a powerful force in Spanish political discourse. The University of Granada, founded in 1531, was another element that aimed at providing the former Muslim kingdom with a new cultural atmosphere from which the majority population of Moriscos would be excluded for all practical purposes.

The humanistic discourse of Juan Latino's poetry reproduces the tensions and fault lines of an ideal Catholic universalism amidst the realities of political and social exclusion of ethnic and religious groups. Juan Latino's *Austrias*

---

[3] The War of Granada was the subject of some of the best historiography in the Spanish Renaissance. Three contemporary accounts come to mind, Diego Hurtado de Mendoza's *Guerra de Granada*, ed. B. Blanco-González (Madrid, 1970), first published posthumously in Lisbon in 1627, but written in the decade after the end the of the war; Ginés Pérez de Hita's *Guerras civiles de Granada*, Part II (Madrid, 1963), pp. 515–687; and Luis Mármol Carvajal's *Historia del rebelión y castigo de los moriscos del reino de Granada*, ed. Buenaventura Carlos Aribau (Madrid, 1946).

carmen should be understood as a piece of cultural politics in which the author himself had a strong personal stake. An address to King Philip II, *Ad regem Catholicum et invictissimum Philippum elegia*, that Juan Latino published in the same volume as the *Austrias carmen* gives us a clearer image of him, and the way in which he connected his racial identity with the act of writing in Renaissance Spain. In sixteenth-century Spanish the word *negro* denoted both a person of black appearance and a black person who was a slave, without distinction.[4] Therefore, race and slavery become an underlying motivation in Juan Latino's writing. He was black, yet not a slave, and writing became a way to perform his freedom.

When *Austrias carmen* appeared in 1573, the naval victory off the coast of Greece at Lepanto that had taken place less than two years earlier was still being celebrated in Granada. The allied forces of the pope, Venice and Spain had defeated the armada of the Ottoman empire as part of their campaign against Turkish domination of the Eastern Mediterranean, which had extended rapidly towards the west. Months before this triumph, however, Don Juan de Austria had led the military intervention that put down the uprising of the Moriscos. For Juan Latino, writing about Don Juan de Austria in Granada was a significant political move. In fact, Don Juan was responsible not only for the military defeat of the Moriscos – a painful story of massacres and vengeful repression – but moreover he represented the king's new policy. While his father Charles V had attempted a certain moderation and a campaign of assimilation, after the uprising Philip chose a different course. The Morisco population of men, women and children living in the mountainous region of the Alpujarras was enslaved and dispersed. The Alpujarras had been the site of the worst episodes of the war.[5] Of all the rebels that Philip II encountered during his reign, in Spain and abroad, only the Moriscos suffered enslavement as a punishment for their uprising. One has to agree with Aurelia Martín Casares that Islam

---

[4] The double meaning, black/slave, contained in *negro* is revealed by Sancho Panza when he imagines a plan to sell his would-be black vassals of the kingdom of Micomicón as slaves in Spain: '¿Qué se me da a mí que mis vasallos sean negros? ¿Habrá más que cargar con ellos y traerlos a España, donde los podré vender, y donde me los pagaran de contado, de cuyo dinero podré compar algún título?' [What is it to me if my vassals are blacks? What more have I to do than make a cargo of them and carry them to Spain, where I can sell them and get ready money for them, and with it buy some title?]. Miguel de Cervantes Saavedra, *Don Quijote de la Mancha*, ed. Florencio Sevilla Arroyo and Antonio Rey Hazas (Madrid, 1996), part I, p. 369. The English translation is taken from Miguel de Cervantes Saavedra, *The Ingenious Gentleman Don Quixote of La Mancha*, tr. John Ormsby (London, 1885).

[5] Aurelia Martín Casares's study of slavery in sixteenth-century Granada shows how many more women than men were enslaved after the rebellion, especially in the Alpujarras area outside the city: Aurelia Martín Casares, *La esclavitud en la Granada del siglo XVI: género, raza y religión* (Granada, 2000), p. 109.

was the differentiating factor.[6] Juan Latino very clearly took the side of the victors, and he had very good reasons to do so.

The central part of Juan Latino's rhetorical strategy in his praise of the victor of Lepanto is an act of self-referentiality. In writing to the king, he called himself 'Joannes Aethiops christicola', John the Ethiopian, a Christian brought to Spain in his childhood.[7] According to the data gathered by his biographer Antonio Marín Ocete, Juan Latino had been a slave in the house of the Count of Cabra, a member of the powerful Fernández de Córdoba family.[8] Tradition or legend attributes to Juan Latino a strong desire for education, which he would have acquired while accompanying his young master, Don Gonzalo Fernández de Córdoba, the future Duke of Sessa, to his daily grammar classes in Granada. Records from the University of Granada indicate that he obtained a bachelor's degree in 1546, and later a chair in Latin Grammar in 1556. The title page of the 1573 edition states that Juan Latino held the chair of Latin at the University of Granada, but no such chair existed. Juan Latino's position was that of lecturer in Latin at the Cathedral school. However, his position as lecturer made him a member of the University faculty, or *claustro*.[9] His fame and the publication of his epic poem in Latin caught the attention of other writers soon after his death. In the second decade of the seventeenth century, the playwright Diego Ximénez de Enciso echoed Juan Latino's real or invented biography in a play which used his name as its title, *Juan Latino*.[10] The importance of this play should not be underestimated. It is the first testimony in Europe of a white writer reflecting on the life and work of a black one,

---

[6] Martín Casares, *La esclavitud*, p. 176.

[7] 'Haec Ioannes Aethiops, christicola, ex Aethiopia usque infans adventus' from *De translatione corporum regalium* (Granada, 1576). For a discussion of Juan Latino's contested birth place, see Antonio Marín Ocete, *El negro Juan Latino. Ensayo biográfico y crítico* (Granada, 1925), p. 8.

[8] In the *Austrias carmen* he makes reference to the house of his former master, the Duke of Sessa, latinised as 'duces . . . Suessas'. According to Latino, the dukes were fortunate in war but short of money: 'foelicesque duces bello, non aere Suessas' (Latino, *Austrias carmen*, Part 1, l. 411).

[9] Marín Ocete, *El negro*, pp. 21–2.

[10] Diego Ximénez de Enciso, *El encubierto. Juan Latino*, ed. Eduardo Juliá Martínez (Madrid, 1951). The comedy's secondary plot involves the ethnic confrontation between Old Christians and Moriscos on the one hand, and descendants of *converso* Jews and black Africans on the other. The events of the comedy occur during the time of the war in Granada. The leader of the rebellion, Don Fernando de Válor, is the rival of black slave Juan Latino for the same lady, the historical Ana de Carleval, Juan Latino's wife. The gender and racial tensions of the play are accented by the characterisation of Doña Ana de Carleval as a *bachillera*, a young woman with a passion for learning. Juan Latino has to compete for the Latin chair with a character called Villanueva, of *converso* origin. Diego Ximénez de Enciso had *converso* origins too, and it was even alleged that a maternal great-grandmother had been a Moorish slave. See Ruth Pike, 'The converso origins of the Sevillian dramatist Diego Jiménez de Enciso,' *Bulletin of Hispanic Studies*, 67 (1990), p. 131.

even if a white writer whose personal fortune was dependant on the slave trade.[11]

The play is an explanation of the marvellous phenomenon of a black slave who writes in Latin. Ximénez de Enciso chose to deal with the thorny issue of Juan Latino's legal status and make it the centre of a very interesting reflection on freedom and artistic patronage. While Renaissance humanism equated human dignity with literacy and the knowledge of Latin, artistic fame and glory could only be attained through the sponsorship of the powerful and rich. Printing was very expensive, apart from being strictly controlled by the Crown and the Inquisition. In the play, black Juan Latino's freedom is as elusive as that of any writer who needs a Spanish grandee to practise his art without fear. The playwright was part of the political entourage of the Count-Duke of Olivares, both being from Seville, and the fact that he could stage and publish his plays was the result of that patronage. In the play, Juan Latino is a metaphor for writing, considered as a privileged freedom. By presenting him in a scene in which he is seeking the patronage of Don Juan de Austria, Ximénez de Enciso defines Juan Latino as an adornment of the aristocracy, and almost a product of it. In this, the playwright was following Juan Latino's own words. Juan Latino wanted to be considered a great ornament in King Philip II's kingdom of letters. The difference between the playwright and the historical Juan Latino consisted in their different political agendas. Ximénez de Enciso wanted freedom to write, whereas Juan Latino wanted to write in order to be accepted as a free man.

By saying that Juan Latino was born in the city of Baeza, Spain, Ximénez de Enciso was making his character more Spanish and less African, in the sense that the latter term was associated with Islam. The historical Juan Latino, on the other hand, insisted that he had been born on the African continent, which he calls Ethiopia, and not Africa, a term used in the sixteenth century to refer to the northern coast of the continent.[12] Ximénez de Enciso's play

---

[11] Like so many merchants from Seville, the Enciso family was actively involved in the slave trade from Western Africa to Cartagena in the Indies. A document from 1596 now in the Newberry Library of Chicago (Chicago, Newberry Library, Ayer Collection, Spanish America, MS 1111) shows Andrés Ximénez de Enciso, who lived in Cartagena, giving power of attorney to his brothers Diego (the playwright) and Pedro to dispose of their parents' inheritance. Another document in the same library indicates that Pedro Ximénez de Enciso invested in slave ships that made the voyage to Angola 'para comprar esclavos' in 1639 (Chicago, Newberry Library, Ayer Collection, Spanish America, MS 1089).

[12] Ximénez de Enciso was following the opinion of his contemporaries, such as Francisco Bermúdez de Pedraza (*Antiguedad y excelencias de Granada* [Granada, 1608]), who states that Juan Latino was born in 'Berbería', or the coast of North Africa, and that his parents were not free (Marín Ocete, *El negro*, p. 7).

had its own political motivations. He presented the black writer as a model of assimilation in contrast with the descendants of converso Jews and Moriscos. If Latino was writing during the War of Granada, Ximénez de Enciso was living in its aftermath more than thirty years later, during the final expulsion of the Moriscos decreed by Philip III in 1609. Thus the image created of him by later writers does not correspond to the way Juan Latino wrote of himself. Ximénez de Enciso saw in him an example of the assimilated individual, while Juan Latino spoke of himself in terms of difference.

Juan Latino is the only known black humanist of sixteenth-century Spain and one of its most important neo-Latin poets. Black and humanist were contradictory terms then, something Latino was acutely aware of. Henry Louis Gates observes that literacy and writing as a measure of human worth in the European Renaissance were value concepts that were used as an exclusionary argument.[13] Barbarous and pagan people were excluded from true humanity by the mere fact of their lack of letters. This was rehashed Aristotle, and yet the age of European expansionism was putting this and other classical concepts to the test. After the conquest of America, controversy arose when writers such as Garcilaso de la Vega el Inca, or Bernardino de Sahagún, explored the existence of cultures without letters in Inca Peru and Aztec Mexico which could be compared favorably to Greece, Rome, and even early modern Europe. In this examination of other (subjected or subjectable) cultures and nations, eloquence was the litmus test by which black Africans and Amerindians were judged. Tvetzan Todorov has pointed out the importance given to eloquence by pro-Indian humanists in the sixteenth century. The practice of ritual speeches by Aztecs and Incas was seen as proof of the dignity of their civilisation. However, the absence of writing was perceived as a sign of their cultural inferiority and the need to be conquered.[14]

Within the confines of Spain, on the other hand, Renaissance humanists for the most part did not stop to consider the validity of the cultural productions of Jews and Muslims, who had been highly literate for centuries in Spain itself, but who represented enemy religions in Juan Latino's time. The accusation of heresy could be raised quite easily against those who sought to learn Hebrew or Arabic, and the bonfire was used as a weapon to reduce manuscripts in those languages to ashes. Cultural difference in Spain did not curry much favour. Invoking ancient, non-Christian letters in Spain was counter-productive. Being eloquent in the language of orthodoxy – Latin – seemed to Juan Latino the best way to assure his rightful place in the human fold.

[13] Henry Louis Gates, Jr, *The Signifying Monkey: A Theory of African-American Literary Criticism* (New York, 1988), p. 129.
[14] Tzvetan Todorov, *The Conquest of America: The Question of the Other* (New York, 1992), p. 79.

Juan Latino wrote his *Austrias carmen* knowing that the colour of his skin and his former legal status as a slave were going to be as, if not more, relevant than his work as a teacher and scholar. He found it necessary to defend himself against challenges to his desire to write. In his poem *Ad Catholicum et invictissimum regem Philippum elegia*, he asks the king to be allowed to sing the praises of the royal half-brother Don Juan de Austria. The composition serves as a prefatory poem to the longer *Austrias carmen*. Although black, Juan Latino says, he is capable of speaking in humanistic Latin, the most prestigious language of Christian Europe, and he asks permission to do so as a pre-emptive measure. Speaking in the king's presence, or even addressing him, was more a privilege than a right. The possible accusation of inappropriateness was not imaginary, for not everybody had the right to write in sixteenth-century Spain, and printing was a royal privilege that Juan Latino explicitly requests in this poem. The authority to write had to be sought or earned through extra-literary means. Most women, people of Jewish or Muslim descent, and black Africans were excluded from the literary circuits of the time.[15] For individuals in these groups, there was a very small distance between being praised as *Latino* (learned in Latin) and being accused of being *ladino* (sneaky), as Cervantes pointed out in the prefatory verses of the first part of *Don Quijote*:

Pues al cielo no le plu-
que saliese tan ladi-
como el negro Juan Lati-
hablar Latines rehú-
        (*Don Quijote* I: 27)

[Since Heaven did not want me to be as well-spoken as black Juan Latino, I prefer not to speak all that Latin stuff.][16]

---

[15] Lope de Vega drove the point home in his comedy *La dama boba* (II: 1916–24). Nise, a young woman whose fondness for learning and letters renders her ineligible for marriage, is compared to Juan Latino, here regarded as a black slave: 'No era tan blanco en Granada / Juan Latino que la hija / de un Veinticuatro enseñaba / y siendo negro y esclavo, porque fue su madre esclava / del claro duque de Sessa / honor de España y de Italia / se vino a casar con ella / que gramática enseñaba' [And in Granada Juan Latino was not so white, and yet he taught the daughter of a councillor. And being black and a slave, because his mother was also a slave of the famous Duke of Sessa, honoured in Spain and Italy, he ended up marrying her after teaching her grammar]. Lope de Vega, *La dama boba*, ed. Diego Marín (Madrid, 1985), p. 137.

[16] These famous verses in the preface of the first part of *Don Quijote* are written as a form of riddle, in which the last syllable of each line is missing ('versos de cabo roto', or broken-end verses). The reader has to use wit to complete them, and multiple readings therefore can result from the exercise. The complete verses should read: "pues al cielo no le plu[go] / que saliese tan ladi[no] / como el negro Juan Lati[no] / hablar latines rehú[so]."

In Spain and the conquered lands of the Spanish Indies, the word *ladino* was used initially to mark individuals of conquered nations and races who could understand and speak Spanish. *Ladinos* were placed in intermediary positions as translators, but were not necessarily trusted, since to be *ladino* also meant to be cunning and devious. Cervantes was making a joke with deep racial implications when he placed someone gifted by nature as a Latinist on the same plane as a black African. At a time when some vernacular languages were pushing towards the centre in European culture, writing in Latin was not as important as it had been earlier in the Renaissance. The cultural rift was becoming evident. Cervantes went on: 'No me despuntes de agudo' (do not try to be too smart). As a black writer, Juan Latino was always under suspicion, his Latin art being both an issue of admiration and distrust. His person and his knowledge of Latin had to be legitimated at every turn, because his racial difference was constructed on the basis of perceived moral and intellectual inferiority. Latin eloquence, while still revered by many, was becoming the object of derision for a growing mass of literate people in Spain, like Cervantes himself, who read and wrote in Spanish but no longer knew Latin well.

As if anticipating future mockery, Juan Latino pursues a strategy of ironic reversal of cultural roles as he mounts an apologia of his right to speak and write. In the prefatory poem to the *Austrias carmen*, he imagines a situation in which whites do not have the upper hand, and he calls that imaginary locus 'Ethiopia'. Henry Louis Gates exemplified his theory of 'signifyin(g)' – the equivalent of ironic reversal – by referring to the Spanish case of Juan Latino.[17] As Gates points out, Juan Latino establishes a principle of cultural relativity when he states that whites and their ways do not prevail in a culture of black Ethiopians. Years before Montaigne published his essay on the cannibals of Brazil, Juan Latino notes the relation between cultural values and political power:

Quod si nostra tuis facies Rex nigra ministris
displicet, Aethiopum non placet alba viris.
Illic Auroram sordet qui viserit albus.
Suntque duces nigri Rex quoque fuscus adest.
                    (*Ad Catholicum . . . elegia* 10)

---

[17] Gates, *The Signifying Monkey*, p. 90. Gates uses the spelling 'Signifyin(g)' putting the final 'g' between brackets in order to emphasize the non-velar ending of the final 'n' in Black American English vernacular pronunciation, thus calling attention to this rhetorical device in African American culture.

[Because if my black face displeases your ministers, oh king, a white one is not pleasant either among the Ethiopians. Anyone visiting the parts of the East will not be held in esteem if he looks white. Noblemen there are all black, and so is their king.]

Genre, style, language and addressee made *Austrias carmen* and the other Latin poems of the 1573 volume a book almost without readers in its day. It was an academic product, written by a Latin instructor and not meant for the entertainment of a large audience. No translations of the work are known to have been made in Juan Latino's time. But the book was a decidedly political work, because writing it was itself the message.

Juan Latino's protector, Archbishop Pedro Guerrero, had promoted the use of Arabic in the evangelization of the Morisco population in spite of the lack of priests who could speak the language. Establishing a Latin school for Morisco youths was another linguistic measure in the same direction, in his attempt to create a Morisco priesthood. His effort was aimed at staving off the voices that advocated repression, led by the president of the Chancillería, Pedro de Deza, who would succeed him after his death in the archbishopric. In its desire to convert the Morisco population to Christianity, the Church considered it appropriate to encourage male Morisco children and teenagers to learn Latin grammar.[18] The Latinization of the Morisco upper class was seen as the path to assimilation. Archbishop Guerrero saw fit that his protegé Juan Latino would occupy the chair of Latin at Granada cathedral. The member of one subjugated group – black Africans – whose members generally assimilated to the language and religion of the ruling group, Juan Latino was presented as an example to the other group – the Moriscos – whose assimilation was desired by some, rejected by others, and always difficult. Not being white, Latino might gain acceptance from the Moriscos, and not being a Morisco, he was not under suspicion.

There were no plans to include Moriscos in the power structure of the city of Granada after the conquest, and the odds were against the peaceful assimilation of the Moriscos to the Christian majority in Spain. Granada was a society divided by ethnic strife and dominated by a siege mentality. Land ownership was changing hands, and the Moriscos were suffering rapid encroachment on their lands by Old Christian immigrants from outside Granada. To make matters worse, in 1566 Philip II signed a *pragmática* (royal decree) making it

---

[18] Antonio Domínguez Ortiz and Bernard Vincent, *Historia de los moriscos. Vida y tragedia de una minoría* (Madrid, 1979), pp. 98–9.

illegal to dress, speak, dance, sing and conduct several kinds of daily business in the traditional way of the Moriscos.[19] Included in the measures was a prohibition on owning black slaves.[20]

Being a former slave of the Duke of Sessa, and his protegé, Juan Latino knew very well where his allegiance lay. But in 1572 his friendship with Archbishop Guerrero could be seen as impolitic, due to the latter's soft approach to the Moriscos. Also the Duke of Sessa was jealous that Don Juan de Austria was in command of military operations and tried to upstage him on occasion, a fact that the latter resented.[21] Don Juan left Granada at the end of 1570, while the war was still in progress, to lead an expedition against the Ottoman empire. The massacres and massive enslavements of Moriscos started under Don Juan's command and were not over by the time Juan Latino was writing *Austrias carmen*.[22] The composition opens with prayers in Granada both for the distant victory and for the continuing repression:[23]

---

[19] Julio Caro Baroja, *Los moriscos del reino de Granada. Ensayo de historia social* (2nd edn, Madrid, 1976), p. 153. The royal decree was signed by Philip II on 17 November 1566, and it was publicly read in Granada on 1 January 1567, the anniversary of the conquest of the city and kindgom by the Catholic Monarchs in 1492. The famous address by Don Francisco Núñez Muley, a Morisco nobleman, was an immediate response to the decree. Through him, the Moriscos defended their cultural difference, and denounced the efforts of the conquerors and their descendants to exclude their ethnic group and destroy their way of life. The text of the complete address is preserved in manuscript form in Madrid, Biblioteca Nacional, MS 6.176. The first modern edition is by R. Foulché-Delbosc, 'Memoria de Francisco Núñez Muley,' *Bulletin Hispanique* (1899), pp. 205–37. Other modern editions can be found in K. Garrad, 'The original Memorial of Don Francisco Núñez Muley,' *Atlante*, II:4 (1954), pp. 168–226.

[20] Núñez Muley believed that it was necessary to own black slaves in order to preserve the structure of society: 'Should all the Moriscos be the same and carry loads on their backs or the plow?' (Foulché-Delbosc, 'Memoria', p. 231). Mármol Carvajal (*Historia*, p. 164a), Hurtado de Mendoza (*Guerra*, p. 117) and Ximénez de Enciso (*Juan Latino*, p. 215) echo the same words of protest in favour of the right to own black slaves. The Old Christian population alleged that black slave women would help increase the Morisco population. Black Africans living in Granada, according to a Jesuit priest, were more gullible and easy to convert to Islam. See Nigel Griffin, '"Un muro invisible": Moriscos and *cristianos viejos* in Granada,' in F. W. Hodcroft, D. G. Pattison, R. D. F. Pring-Mill and R. W. Truman, eds., *Medieval and Renaissance Studies on Spain and Portugal in Honour of P. E. Russell* (Oxford, 1981), p. 142.

[21] Domínguez Ortiz and Vincent, *Historia*, p. 38.

[22] The slave population of Moriscos in Granada comprised 14 per cent of the total inhabitants of the city, compared to only 2 per cent before the beginning of the conflict. Most of these slaves were women (Martín Casares, *La esclavitud*, p. 115).

[23] Juan Latino's account of the battle of Lepanto in *Austriadis carmen* was written before Fernando de Herrera produced his poem 'A la victoria de Lepanto' (1572), and certainly years before Juan Rufo published his *Austríada* in 1584 (Marín Ocete, *El negro*, p. 46). Juan Latino was the only one of these writers who witnessed the war.

Viderat exactos Mauros Garnata rebelles,
haereticumque malum, manifestae crimina gentis,
extinctumque genus, penitusque ex urbe reuulsum,
supplicium iuste Regem sumpsisse Philippum.
(Austrias Carmen I: 35–8)

[Granada had witnessed the expulsion of the Moors who rebelled / and with them
their evil heresy, the crime of a guilty people. / Their progeny was destroyed, and
quickly expelled from the city. / King Philip justly imposed this punishment.]

The civil war in Granada gave Juan Latino an opportunity to signal his
racial difference from the defeated, many of whom shared his skin colour.[24]
Although he had met Don Juan de Austria and was acquainted with the
highest nobility in Granada, his condition as a person of black descent and
a former slave made his privileged position a tenuous one most of the time.
By calling himself an Ethiopian, Juan Latino proclaimed his black skin in
classical terms but also established his connection with the Christian religion.
His foreignness and blackness indicated his condition of enslavement in the
eyes of his contemporaries, but this would be counterbalanced by his self-
fashioning as someone chosen by destiny to praise a member of the house
of Habsburg. In the prefatory poem dedicated to Philip II he brings together
the need to sing about the new Christian victory and the need for a new
singer:

Res nova vult vatem regibus esse novum
Auribus alme tuis non haec victoria Ponto est
Audita, hic scriptor nec fuit orbe satus,
Aethiopum terris venit qui gesta Latinus
Austriadae mira carminis arte canat.
Is genibus flexis orat te, invicte Philippe,
Cantator fratris possit ut esse tui.
Nam si nobilitant Austriadae bella poetam
Phoenicem Austriadam, quod niger, ille facit.
(Ad Catholicum . . . elegia 9)

[New things want a new poet at the service of kings. / This victory at sea has not
reached / your ears yet, Sire. This writer was not born in these parts of the world / His
name is Latinus, and he came from the lands of Ethiopia / to sing the deeds of Juan

---

[24] One of the early leaders of the rebellion, Farax Aben Farax, was black. The fact is mentioned by
Ginés Pérez de Hita, who gives him the name of El Cañerí (Guerras civiles, p. 606b).

de Austria with the admirable art of poetry. / Unconquered Philip, on his bended knee this singer asks / to be your brother's poet. / If the wars of the Austriad make the poet famous, / the poet's blackness will make Don Juan a phoenix.]

Like so many people in the African diaspora since the early modern age, Juan Latino was a powerful user of the art of naming, as names can create new identities and social relations.[25] By placing the terms 'Aethiopum' and 'Latinus' at opposite ends of the same verse, the poet calls attention to the contrast in the reader's mind between these signifiers of blackness and of knowledge of Latin. Rather than a signifier of whiteness, this black man's Latinity will be about something different. He insists on the power of name association by starting the next verse with the word 'Austriadae', thus linking his blackness and Latinity to the fortune of the Habsburg dynasty. As a poet worthy of a king, Juan Latino plays with the Latin terms 'Phoenicem' and 'Austriadam'. Latino seems to be calling Don Juan de Austria a phoenix and a Phoenician, that is, someone also black, in the sense that Phoenicians were related to the East, where Ethiopia was located in the the geographical imaginary of the humanists.[26] With this play on words, Juan Latino equates the nobility of Don Juan and the Habsburg dynasty with peoples and portents from the East, the lands of the black Africans and of the phoenix. Ovid describes the mythical phoenix as a bird which rises from the ashes of a nest of myrrh and lives not on normal food, but on frankincense. Like the phoenix, Don Juan's military exploits need the glory of poetry. Both Juan Latino and the frankincense are black, and both come from the eastern lands of Ethiopia. The verbal play of words inscribed race as a category with political implications.

Juan Latino proclaims his 'Ethiopianness' against the 'Africanity' of the defeated Moriscos in order to distinguish his former slave condition from the fate the Granada Moriscos were facing. He defends his right to be a poet of kings through a biblical exegesis that gives worth to black Africans as Ethiopians:

Terribilis classis gentes motura Philippi,
Orbi portentum tunc erit Austriades.
Prodigiosa viros turbabit fama poetae
Voluentes fastis haec monumenta tuis.

[25] There is evidence of common naming patterns of persons, music bands, vehicles, churches and stores among black Africans in the US, Puerto Rico, Haiti, Jamaica, and West Africa. See J. A. Dillard, *Black Names* (The Hague, 1976).
[26] Gates, *Signifying Monkey*, p. 90.

Aurora hunc peperit, Reges Arabumque, beatos,
Primitias gentum quos dedit illa Deo.

                    (*Ad Catholicum . . . elegia* 9–10)

[The fleet of Philip will scatter the terrible nation / and then the Austriad will be
an omen for the world. / The marvellous fame of the poet will rouse men / as they
consider these memorials in your chronicles. / Aurora gave birth to the poet, as well
as to the blessed kings of the Arabs, / the first fruits of the nations, whom she has
given to God.]

Juan Latino was marking racial differences from the Moriscos on religious
grounds for many reasons, not the least of them being Philip II's *pragmática* of
1566 barring them from ownership of and trading in black slaves. This latter
fact made the distinction between a black Christian and a black Muslim a vital
one. His former slavery was an accident of fortune, because all men are born
naturally free, following the legal definition contained in the medieval code
of the *Siete Partidas*.[27] Unlike the rebels, whose uprising against the king as
their natural lord deserved punishment, he had done nothing reprehensible
which justified his enslavement; though a slave, he was blameless. Religious
heresy, and not skin colour or a slave raid, should be the only basis for rightful
enslavement, as Juan Latino seems to say without saying it. Although he taught
Latin to the children of the Morisco nobility, Juan Latino did not have any
reason to feel solidarity with them. The 'Garnatae adolescentiae moderator',
as he called himself in some of his Latin epigrams, showed a very clear dislike
for Muslims, for whom he reserves negative epithets enveloped in classical
allusions: 'discinctos Mauros, imbelles temnite Parthos' [do not respect the
loosely-clothed Moors, the cowardly Parthians] (*Austrias carmen* 1: 484). This
apparent lack of racial, as opposed to religious, solidarity was noted by black
intellectuals of the 1930s.[28] Juan Latino wanted to show his difference through
the cultural marker of his humanistic Latinity. The words free and slave appear
in the *Austrias carmen* mixed with derogatory terms used against the Turks. In
one scene, a Christian captain offers freedom to the captive Muslim oarsmen
in the event of a Christian victory:

Prospice Maure, tuae remex en consule uitae,
remigii numerum ni turbas arte maligna,

---

[27] J. A. Doerig, 'La situación de los esclavos a partir de las *Siete Partidas* de Alfonso el Sabio (Estudio
histórico-crítico)', *Folia humanística*, 4: 40 (1966), pp. 337–61.

[28] Velaurez B. Spratlin, *Juan Latino: Slave and Humanist* (New York, 1938), p. 42.

atque fidem nostris seruas ductoribus unam,
uictore Austriada tu liber sorte futurus.

(Austrias carmen I: 376–9)

[Listen, Moorish oarsman, watch out for your life; / if you do not disturb with evil means the course of our navigation / and if you serve our leaders faithfully / upon the victory of the Austriad you will be freed.]

While the Muslim captives may gain their freedom through an act of service to the Catholic cause, Juan Latino bases his own claim to freedom on his self-proclamation as an Ethiopian. His use of biblical Ethiopia as a rhetorical device brings him legitimacy but also primacy over other Christians. In a Spain consumed by the socially exclusive practices of 'limpieza de sangre', (purity of blood), Juan Latino recalls the biblical story of the Ethiopian eunuch who was the disciple of the apostle Philip (Acts 8: 27), thus making Ethiopia the first Christian nation:

Candace regina genus, nigrumque ministrum
vel curru Christo miserat illa suum:
Legerat ille genus non enarrabile Christi,
Austriadae pugnas non canet iste tui?
Obuius Aethiopem Christum docet ore Philippus,
Discipulum Christus mittit ad Aethiopem:
Non temere Aethiopi coelo datus ergo Philippus,
Ne Aethiopi iusta haec forte Philippe neges.
Quid quod et Austriades exactor gentis iniquae
Garnatae vadim viderat esse suum.

(Ad Catholicum . . . elegia 10)

[Queen Candace, who was of the same Ethiopian race, sent her own black servant to Christ in a chariot. If that man read the inexplicable birth of Christ, why should not one of your own men sing the battles of your own Austriad brother? Philip, the disciple, taught Christ's words from his own mouth when he met the Ethiopian. Thus Christ sent a disciple to that Ethiopian. Philip therefore was sent by heaven to an Ethiopian as part of a plan. King Philip, do not deny by an accident this justice to an Ethiopian. Pay attention that even your Austriad brother, the expeller of the unjust race, had noticed that this his poet was from Granada.]

For Juan Latino, the history of the Ethiopian eunuch is the birthright of all black Africans within the Christian fold. He insists on this point later in the poem: 'Si Christus vitae fuscos non despicit autor / Catholicus vatem respice iure tuum.' [If Christ, the source of life, did not look down on dark people, Catholic monarch, treat your poet with justice]. Through a deft use of naming, the words 'Ethiopian' and 'Philip' appear in proximity in two consecutive verses. The contrast drives the point home, because in the first case, 'Non temere Aethiopi coelo datus ergo Philippus' the 'Ethiopian' and 'Philip' are the eunuch and the apostle of the Bible, while in the second case, 'Ne Aethiopi iusta haec forte Philippe neges', the persons concerned are himself and the king. By associating King Philip with his patron saint the apostle Philip, Juan Latino enhances his own position as an Ethiopian in contradistinction to the historical reality of black slavery in Renaissance Spain.

The episode of the Ethiopian eunuch allows Juan Latino to draw attention to his person by establishing a relationship between the act of reading, his racially charged exegesis, and the ineffability of Christ's life, which he as an Ethiopian is destined to explicate. Juan Latino applies the term 'inenarrabile' to the story of Christ, in a textual borrowing from the Vulgate: 'in humilitate iudicium eius sublatum est / generationem eius quis enarrabit / quoniam tolletur de terra vita eius?' [In his humiliation his judgment was taken away: and who shall declare his generation? For his life is taken from the earth] (Acts 8: 33).[29] The passage the Ethiopian eunuch was reading was from the Old Testament (Isa. 53: 7–8). The prophet is talking about someone who suffers humiliation and an unfair trial, someone who will leave this earth. So who will ensure that his family's history will be preserved? The apostle Philip explained to the Ethiopian eunuch that the words referred to Jesus of Nazareth, thus making the act of reading an important part of the process of conversion to Christianity. Only the very knowledgeable could understand the references Juan Latino was including in the words 'legere' and 'inenarrabile'. In Juan Latino's poem the place of the Ethiopian eunuch is now occupied by King Philip, who is reading without understanding. The words from the Old Testament that foretold Christ's humiliation, his unspeakable destiny and death, can be explained by Juan Latino the Ethiopian, who takes the place of the apostle Philip. Juan Latino is an Ethiopian apostle Philip, while the king, being white, is like the Ethiopian who seeks the word of God. But through the term 'inenarrabile', Latino may also be talking about the humiliation of his enslavement and that of other black people like him, which he is not allowed to recount.

---

[29] *Biblia Sacra*, ed. Alberto Colunga and Laurentio Turrado (5th edn, Madrid, 1957). The translation is from the King James Bible.

This complicated play of biblical allusions serves a very carefully planned purpose, but one that cannot be stated openly. Ethiopia does not owe anything to Europe in terms of Christian faith, since the Ethiopians are the first among the Christian peoples. Juan Latino is negating the validity of any religious justification for the enslavement of black Africans. He sees himself rather as a gift sent by heaven to the Spaniards to help propagate the Christian faith in Granada, where it is now needed most. Juan Latino does not need to apologise or thank the Spaniards for his enslavement. He is the gift, like the gifts of the three Magi, and he places the king of Spain under the Christian duty of listening. Like all Ethiopians, he carries the word of God in his mouth.

Juan Latino does not equate his former slave condition to any concept of Christian salvation. He did not share the belief of late eighteenth-century Anglophone black writers that slavery was a fortunate accident – fortunate fall – on the road to Christianity, with Africa being regarded as a dark and pagan land of errors.[30] The fortunate fall doctrine is absent in his discourse. Latino's position is that, as an Ethiopian, he deserves first place among the Christians now involved in a fight for survival against the forces of Islam represented by the Ottoman empire. Without mentioning it, he is resurrecting the medieval legend of Prester John, the Christian emperor of Ethiopia whom Christians wished to reach in order to join forces against the imagined common enemy: Islam.[31] By associating himself with Ethiopia, Juan Latino was in fact denying legitimacy to the discourse that regarded the enslavement of black Africans as 'payment' or 'duty' for their Christian salvation. Being of Ethiopian descent, Latino says, makes him a member of the first Christian nation, older in its Christianity than any *cristiano viejo*, or Old Christian, in Spain. Juan Latino never stated this openly, but he was turning the concept of purity of blood against itself.

The right to sing the praises of Don Juan de Austria should be given to him, he suggests, because he had met the military hero personally in Granada, and he was an Ethiopian, of the race of the first Christians, who should not be a race of slaves in Spain. Juan Latino chooses the Latin word *genus*, which

---

[30] Wilson Jeremiah Moses, *The Wings of Ethiopia. Studies in African-American Life and Letters* (Ames, IA, 1990), pp. 144–5.

[31] The figure of Prester John had lost considerable lustre by the time Latino was writing, especially after the first contacts between the Portuguese and the Abyssinian Empire in the early part of the sixteenth century. A passage in *Viaje de Turquía*, which is a play of words on Prester John and 'Preto John' or 'Black John', is indicative of the derision this medieval story caused in the Spain of the imperial expansion (Jeremy Lawrance, 'The Middle Indies: Damião de Góis on Prester John and the Ethiopians', *Renaissance Studies* 6 (1992), p. 316).

one may translate in English as race, to designate the race of King Philip (the Spaniards), the race of the Turks and all Islamic nations, the race of the Ethiopians, and the race of Christ, a touchy subject in itself, since Jesus was a Jew. *Genus* is an ascription that crosses national origins, skin colour and religions.

Once his Christian Ethiopian right to sing is established, Juan Latino proceeds to show his Latinity in the second part of the prefatory poem: 'Omnia quae Latio scribit sermone Latinus, / versibus et veris, arma ducesque, canit' [In all Latino writes in the Latin language, he sings with true verses about the military leaders and their battles.] The Virgilian 'arma virumque cano' becomes 'arma ducesque cano', but now with a Christian twist. If Aeneas was the victim of an unhappy race that had to leave Troy to found Rome, now a son of Rome, a Catholic prince, has defeated an army of the enemy of the faith, and the old medieval dream is becoming reality. The newborn son of Philip II, Prince Ferdinand, now one year old, may be the conqueror of Jerusalem for Christendom. The final allusion to the Tarpeian crow is one last stroke of Juan Latino's familiarity with classical literature, and a self-deprecating joke.[32] He is black like the crow and he will be singing with loquacious song the exploits of the house of Austria:

Virtute et patrem referens nil linquet inausum,
sub iuga Turcarum mittet et imperium:
Sub te iam Christi reddet pietate sepulchrum,
Regibus et fato debita regna tuis.
Haec tibi certa suo promittit carmine cornix,
Foelix cuncta bene, et prospera, dixit, erunt.
(Ad Catholicum . . . elegia 11)

[With his virtue, and taking after his father, there will be nothing he will not dare. / He will put the Turkish empire under the yoke. / Under your command he will piously bring back Christ's tomb from the enemy, / as well as the rest of the kingdoms that are owed to your dynasty by destiny. This crow promises in his song that all these things will happen, / and he happily says: 'all these things will be well and favourable'.]

---

[32] Bermúdez de Pedraza mentions that the Duke of Sessa used to joke about his slave's Latin abilities by saying 'Rara avis in terra, corvo simillima nigro' which Bermúdez de Pedraza would translate freely as 'My black slave is as rare on this earth as a phoenix', but should be 'a rare bird in these parts, quite like the black raven' (Henry Louis Gates and and Maria Wolff, 'An overview of sources on the life and work of Juan Latino, the "Ethiopian humanist"', *Research in African Literatures*, 29:4 (1998), p. 21).

The poem *Ad Catholicum... elegia* answers the question as to why a black African in Renaissance Spain would write a long epic poem in Latin dedicated to the king's brother before he is asked. Latinity, the medieval concept of *studium*, was for him an ideal of equality that was being denied in modern times by a vernacular slavery based on skin colour. Some of his contemporaries saw it in this way also, as exemplified by the anecdote (see p. 259 above) in which he equated himself to his patron, Archbishop Guerrero of Granada, through their previous lowly station in life and common life-long dedication to the world of letters.[33]

By comparing his lot to that of a white man of humble origins, Juan Latino establishes an ideal equality among classes and racial groups through the humanities that otherwise did not exist in his society. If we are to believe the anecdote, Latinity was supposed to erase differences in social class and race, notwithstanding the fact that, as a black man, he could never aspire to an ecclesiastical position like the archbishop's. Juan Latino knew that his name was always prefaced by others with the word *negro*. His contemporaries referred to him as 'El negro Juan Latino', and here lay the contradiction of his project. By changing his received name (Juan de Sessa, after his former master) to that of his new teaching profession (Juan Latino) he wanted to perform a different racial discourse than the one practised in his time. He believed what postmodern theorists propose today, namely, that race is a series of discursive practices.[34] By speaking Latin, one would be performing a change in the racial discourse of the sixteenth century. Juan Latino, however, could not change the material conditions of black slaves around him solely by reciting Virgilian *loci* with his students through the streets of Granada.[35] The owners of the discourse, the white majority, still chose to use the qualifier *negro* before *Latino*.

Juan Latino persisted in seeking a space to speak while remaining part of the Spanish monarchy, which he believed was a political project inspired by Catholic, universal justice. At the same time he was more than aware that his Christian ideal was challenged by the stark realities of slavery and ethnic conflict, the city of Granada being an example of a world in crisis. For him, his Latinity underlined the difference between being African and being Ethiopian. In the *Austrias carmen* the words African, Moor and Turk are made mutually

[33] Francisco Bermúdez de Pedraza, *Historia eclesiásitica de Granada*, facsimile edn (Granada, 1989), p. 260b.

[34] Jonathan Xavier Inda, 'Performativity, materiality, and the racial body', *Latino Studies Journal*, 11:3 (2000), p. 83.

[35] Bermúdez de Pedraza, *Historia eclesiástica*, p. 260b.

exchangeable. Africa is the northern part of the continent, the space that ever since Roman times has had to be conquered from people who rejected the Pax Romana and its Latinity, now represented by King Philip II of Spain and the Catholic imperial order. Ethiopia, on the other hand, is the promise of Christian universality.

Juan Latino's *magnum opus* ends with an Ethiopian reference in the Bible. There are not many self-referential pasages in the *Austrias carmen*, but Juan Latino reserves the final verses to exalt blackness. The victory of Lepanto under the leadership of Don Juan de Austria is celebrated with a reference to Psalm 67: 32 in the Vulgate (68: 31 in the King James version): 'venient legati ex Aegypto, Aethiopia praeveniet manus eius Deo' [Princes shall come out of Egypt; Ethiopia shall soon stretch out her hands unto God]:

Oceanusque tibi victori brachia tendet
Aethiopesque procul pulsabunt tympana laeti
Victorique sui celebrabunt thura Sabei.
                    (*Austrias carmen* II: 1054–6)

[And the Ocean shall stretch its open arms to you in your victory, / and the Ethiopians far away shall play their drums in joy, / and the Sabeans will burn frankincense constantly in your honour as one of their heroes in battle.]

These same biblical verses would be used later on throughout the English-speaking world by writers of African descent, from the eighteenth century to the present day, as a source of racial pride. But for Juan Latino Ethiopia is not so much a geographical site as a spiritual one, the repository of the first Christian message. Latino's mental map is decidedly medieval in scope, preferring a world centred on Jerusalem and the East to the modern navigational charts of his time that privileged the Atlantic Ocean and its slave routes. The biblical references to the New Testament – for example, to the Magi and the Ethiopian eunuch – authorise him to proclaim the Christian primacy of all black Africans over the rest of the nations and races. Like the Magi, Juan Latino and the Ethiopian race present themselves as willing gifts from God, investing themselves with a Messianic destiny, because God spoke to them first. Juan Latino proclaims his God-given right to speak in the sacred language of Latin. He was the first black intellectual in Europe to construct a discourse of black pride, and more than four hundred years later, the appeal to Ethiopia still resonates.

CHAPTER SIXTEEN

Black Africans versus Jews: religious and racial tension in a Portuguese saint's play

T. F. EARLE

The Portuguese Afonso Álvares is remembered as one of the very few black Africans in sixteenth-century Europe to have achieved literary success. He is thought to be the author of four plays, all of them based on saints' Lives, which were many times reprinted in the early modern period and continued to be popular until the nineteenth century.[1] All four are *autos*; in other words, they are specimens of a typically Portuguese dramatic form, the short verse play, usually with a religious or comic theme or, very often, as in the case of Álvares himself, with both. The *auto* originated in Portugal in the early sixteenth century, not long before Álvares's own literary career began, in the 1530s.

Literary history is full of myths, and Afonso Álvares the black dramatist may be one of them. Authentic information dating from the sixteenth century about the existence of a black writer (or rather one of mixed race) named Afonso Álvares is to be found in an exchange of satirical poems between him and a renegade friar, António Ribeiro Chiado, who, as it happens, was also a dramatist. These poems remained in manuscript for many centuries. Álvares's plays, on the other hand, which were first printed during or shortly after their author's life, contain almost no biographical information about him, apart from brief rubrics about their comissioning by the Augustinian canons of São Vicente de Fora, a large Lisbon church. So Afonso Álvares the dramatist and Afonso Álvares the satirical poet may be two different people. The poems certainly contain some indications that we are dealing with one, not two, Álvares, but neither poet says that the other was a dramatist. Given

---

[1] The plays are *Auto de São Vicente*, edited by I. S. Révah in *Bulletin d'histoire du théâtre portugais*, 2: II (1952), pp. 219–51 (the only modern edition of any of the plays), *Auto de Sant'Iago* and *Auto de Santo António*, early, undated editions reprinted in facsimile by Carolina Micaëlis de Vasconcellos, *Autos portugueses de Gil Vicente y de la escuela vicentina* (Madrid, 1922) and *Auto de Santa Bárbara* (Lisbon, 1668). This last play has not been reprinted in modern times, but there is a nineteenth-century edition made for the popular market (Oporto, 1859). Further bibliographical information in Justino Mendes de Almeida, *Edições Seiscentistas Raríssimas de Literatura Popular* (Oporto, 1940), as well as the standard bibliographies by Barbosa Machado and Inocêncio.

their intense dislike of each other, one would expect some reference, probably abusive, to their literary work.[2]

Still, satirical poet and religious dramatist have been identified as the same person for many centuries. The eighteenth-century bibliographer Barbosa Machado records that Álvares was brought up in the household of the aristocratic Dom Afonso de Portugal, bishop of Évora and member of ducal family of the Braganças, which was close to the Crown itself. There is a tradition that he later became a schoolmaster. After his patron's death in 1522, Álvares went to Lisbon where at some point he attracted the interest of the Augustinian canons. Two of the plays, the *Auto de São Vicente* and the *Auto de Santo António*, can be dated by internal evidence to the terrible year of 1531 in which Lisbon was afflicted by a major earthquake and by the plague.[3]

The exchange of satirical *redondilhas* (a popular verse form, usually of five or seven syllables) between Chiado and Álvares was also prompted by an ecclesiastical commission. Álvares, writing in the name of the guardian of the Franciscan monastery from which Chiado had absconded, criticises him for his low birth and immorality. Chiado replies with a torrent of racial and other abuse, and the exchange continues in this vein for some hundreds of lines.

The poems do not show either writer at his best. However, from them something can be learned about the otherwise very shadowy Álvares. It seems certain, for example, that he was a mulatto. The word, and synonyms like *pardo* or *baço*, appears several times in Chiado's attack on him. His mother is said to have been a black woman who worked in a kitchen or bakery: 'Your mother was at the oven, straight from the bush (*tão boçal*) so that I laugh to think how you put up with living somewhere like that'.[4] Chiado further claims that Álvares had been a slave in Arronches, a town near the border with Spain, and that he had only obtained his freedom through marriage. Marriage and enslavement were usually considered incompatible so this is an

---

[2] There is an edition, mostly reliable, by Alberto Pimentel, 'Querela entre o Chiado e Affonso Alvares' in *Obras do Poeta Chiado* (Lisbon, 1889), pp. 171–216. There is also an earlier edition, *Letreyros Muyto Sentenciosos . . . Feytos por Antonio Chiado* (Lisbon, 1783). The MS, probably written in the sixteenth century, is in Évora, Biblioteca Pública, cxii / 1–37, fols. 396–411. When quoting from it I have resolved abbreviations silently.

[3] See *Auto de São Vicente*, ll. 100–10. In the unpaginated *Auto de Santo António* a Franciscan friar also mentions plague and earthquake as having followed each other: 'E se apressados / fomos com aquelles tremores passados / & tambem agora com peste presente' (And if we were afflicted a while ago by earthquake and now again by plague).

[4] 'Tua mãe esteve em forno / [e] tão boçal que m'estou rindo / como sofres tal sojorno', Évora MS, fol. 409. The word *boçal* (in Spanish, *bozal*) was often used to describe an African not used to European ways.

authentic seeming touch.[5] Yet enslavement in Arronches does not tally well with Barbosa Machado's statement that Álvares was brought up in the bishop's palace in Évora. If the bishop was his father – as he may well have been – he probably would have manumitted the child himself.[6]

It is probably unwise to pursue the biographical details contained in Chiado's satirical attack too far, though the frequency of his references to Álvares's mixed blood suggests that he was in reality a mulatto. Mulattos were afforded a much higher level of tolerance than black Africans, which helps to explain Álvares's social promotion.[7] The most interesting part of the exchange of poems is Álvares's reply to the racial insults which Chiado heaps upon him. The reply, which modern scholars have ignored, despite the information it contains about Álvares's life, seems to confirm Barbosa Machado's belief that the mulatto poet had connections with a noble household. It also shows that Álvares was quite comfortable with his colour: 'My colour does not disfigure my honour or my wit'. Being black, or half-black, is no barrier to nobility: 'If I were judged on the nobility which comes to me from the higher part (da parte superior), you would be as far beneath me as a slave is beneath his master'.[8]

Álvares's confidence may seem surprising. But he would have known that there were members of the court and of the ecclesiastical hierarchy in Portugal who sincerely believed that black people as well as white could be Christians. The chapters by Jordan and Lahon show that these beliefs were not due to any supposed indifference to race on the part of the Portuguese. Rather they were a matter of religious conviction.

It is not only in the lines quoted that Álvares hints that he is nobly born, as will appear shortly. What did he mean by the mysterious words 'da parte superior'? Chiado had covered him and his mother with every kind of opprobrium, but he never says who his father was. Carolina Michaëlis de Vasconcelos lets slip the notion, almost by accident, that his father was the bishop in whose household Álvares was brought up.[9] If that was a slip on her part it was a

---

[5] Évora MS, fol. 409. For the question of slave marriages, see Jorge Fonseca, Escravos no Sul de Portugal, Séculos XVI–XVII (Lisbon, 2002) pp. 159–61.

[6] Fonseca records examples of this practice, Escravos no Sul de Portugal, pp. 151 and 186.

[7] A. C. de C. M. Saunders, A Social History of Black Slaves and Freedmen in Portugal, 1441–1555 (Cambridge, 1982), discusses the place of mulattos in Portuguese society, pp. 172–7.

[8] 'a cór não me desfea / minha honrra e descrição'. 'Que a nobreza que me vem / da parte superior / se disto julguado for / ficas de mim tão aquem / como o servo do señor' (fol. 410 v).

[9] Vasconcellos, Autos portugueses de Gil Vicente, pp. 42 and 46, where she says, without presenting any evidence, that Álvares 'nascera e se criara nos paços do bispo, seu pai' ('he was born and brought up in the palace of his father, the bishop').

most suggestive one. Sexual relationships between slaves and their masters, including masters who were priests or noblemen, were very common.[10] What is more, Dom Afonso de Portugal, grandson of the first Duke of Bragança, was notoriously lax sexually, to the extent that Leo X instigated an investigation of his activities.[11] The bishop had literary interests himself, and among his white children were a poet and compiler of moral axioms and an Erasmian archbishop.[12] Afonso Álvares, schoolmaster and poet, and very probably dramatist also, might have acquired a literary education as well as a Christian name from a noble father.

Nobility of birth, says Álvares, is a guarantee of nobility of soul. He had read this, 'creo que no Dante' (I think in Dante), and draws the conclusion that he is a better man than Chiado, the renegade monk. On Chiado's head are heaped all sorts of religious insults: he is tempted by the serpent, a second Lucifer, a lost sheep and a Judas.[13] The reference to Dante, even if at second hand, and the familiarity with the language of the Bible show that we are dealing with a writer of some learning, convinced of his personal worth despite the racial disadvantage.

There is a clear link between Álvares the poet and Álvares the dramatist in that in both these activities he depended on ecclesiastical patronage. Poems and plays are stylistically akin and are both composed in the traditional *redondilha* metre. They both show evidence of a profoundly interiorized Christian faith. Although the evidence is not one hundred per cent conclusive, it is at least reasonable to assume that the undoubtedly black author of the poems also wrote the four far more interesting and challenging plays.

However, the reading of one of the plays that follows does not depend on the uncertainties of Álvares's biography. The *Auto de São Vicente* would be interesting whoever had written it. It is a play in which there are undoubtedly racial tensions, not necessarily involving Africans, and it is also in its own way an accomplished, if largely forgotten and misunderstood, work of art. If there were two Afonso Álvares an analysis of the play would be only tangential to the theme of this book, though a worthwhile exercise in its own right. But if the two are really one, which is certainly more than 50 per cent probable, then mulatto authorship gives the *auto* a certain piquancy. At the

---

[10] Fonseca, *Escravos no Sul de Portugal*, pp. 149–56.

[11] By the bull *Non absque gravi* of 11 March 1517 which does not, however, go into detail. See *Corpo Diplomático Portuguez*, ed. Luiz Augusto Rebello da Silva and others, 14 vols. (Lisbon, 1862–1910), XI, pp. 147–8.

[12] For the careers of these people, see Dom Francisco de Portugal, 1st Count of Vimioso, *Poesias e Sentenças*, ed. Valeria Tocco (Lisbon, 1999), pp. 11–12.

[13] Évora MS, fol. 410r.

very least it would show how thoroughly the second-generation immigrant had assimilated European religious culture.[14] And its racial tensions would become an example of how minorities tend to distrust each other, rather than the majority which oppresses them both.

Yet in the plays there are no black characters and no references to black Africans, though in the *Auto de Sant'Iago* there is a comically stereotyped Moslem from the Maghreb who speaks bad Portuguese. More interesting than him is the treatment of Jewish characters in the *Auto de São Vicente*. The play is full of disguised references to the New Christians, an example (if Álvares was really a mulatto) of rivalry between two minorities in a predominantly white and Christian society. Hostility between black Africans and Jews certainly existed in sixteenth-century Portugal and has been documented by Maria José Tavares.[15] But many white writers also expressed alarm at the presence in Portugal of a substantial minority of Jews who were believed to practise their religion behind closed doors.

The great crisis in the history of the Jews in Portugal was the sudden expulsion of their Spanish co-religionists by the Catholic monarchs in 1492. The first Portuguese monarch to try to come to grips with the problems raised by the influx of refugees was King Manuel (1495–1521). His policy towards the new arrivals from Spain was tolerant, or at any rate ambiguous, for the ensuing forced conversion was sweetened by a promise that no inquiry would be made into their religious practices for twenty years.[16] However, in 1531 his son King João III obtained from the pope the right to establish an inquisition in Portugal to investigate the faith of the New Christians, and that right, at first secret, was made public in 1536. In the 1530s and 40s writing about the Jewish question changes in character, perhaps in response to the shift in official policy.

Before 1530 Christian writers who mention Jews do so with a violent anti-Semitism which could be seen as a protest against what they considered to be an unregulated social evil. The most famous example is the cruel treatment given to the Jew in Gil Vicente's *Auto da Barca do Inferno* of 1517 or 1518, who is not even allowed to board the devil's boat but has to be towed to hell behind it. In his verse sermon of 1506 he again says that the Jews are incapable of

[14] Saunders, *A Social History of Black Slaves*, pp. 149–50 and 161–2, finds that 'Catholicism offered an attractive channel for the expression of the blacks' religious feelings', unless they had come under the influence of Islam. But few would have had Álvares's intellectual grasp of the faith.

[15] See her *Judaísmo e Inquisição* (Lisbon, 1987), pp. 93–4.

[16] See I. S. Révah, ed., *Diálogo Evangélico sobre os Artigos da Fé conta o Talmud dos Judeus . . . de João de Barros* (Lisbon, 1950), p. xix. In 1512 King Manuel extended the concession for a further sixteen years.

conversion.[17] In the *Cancioneiro Geral* of 1516 Álvaro de Brito Pestana also makes a violent attack on 'subtle Jewish tricks' and on those who retain their old faith while pretending to adhere to the new one.[18]

However, in the 1530s the tone changed. Gil Vicente writes sympathetically about a Jewish family in the *Auto da Lusitânia* (1532),[19] while in his *Auto da Cananeia* (1534) the allegorical character Hebreia accepts with joy the news, brought by the *Lei da Graça* (Law of Grace), that the true Messiah, in other words, Christ, has come.[20] A whole new literature encouraging Jews to convert came into existence, perhaps connected to a shift in the offical view which now recognised that there was in Portugal a substantial population of non-Christians, who would need to be persuaded to change their religious adherence: João de Barros, *Ropica Pnefma* (1532, but finished in 1531),[21] the same author's *Diálogo Evangélico* (1542), and Francisco Machado's *Espelho de Cristãos-Novos e Convertidos*, written in 1541.[22]

The *Auto de São Vicente* should also be seen in this context, as a play which proclaims the rewards of the true faith without being excessively hostile to Judaism. The play was probably written in 1531, a year of earthquake and plague which was certainly a test of a change of attitude. On that occasion Gil Vicente sent a famous letter to the king containing the text of an address he had given to the friars of Santarém, in which he concluded that the earthquake was a natural phenomenon and regretted that it should have been blamed on non-believers.[23] In the address, which is remarkable for its tolerance, he admitted that there might be some in Lisbon who were not Christian but declared that they should be converted, not made the object of expulsion and scandal. It is noteworthy, too, that he tactfully avoids the words 'Jew', 'Marrano' or 'New Christian'.

Álvares' *Auto de São Vicente* also deals with the relationship between natural disaster and religious belief. His play was intended for a mixed audience, of high-ranking ecclesiastics but also ordinary people, and he could not possibly

---

[17] Gil Vicente, *Copilaçam de Todalas Obras*, ed. Maria Leonor Carvalhão Buescu, 2 vols. (Lisbon, 1983), II, p. 625: 'Es por demás pedir al judío / que sea cristiano en su coraçón'. (It is too much to expect of a Jew that he should be a Christian in his heart).

[18] 'Bulras habraicas sotis'. See *Cancioneiro Geral de Garcia de Resende*, ed. Aida Fernanda Dias, 6 vols. (Lisbon, 1990–2003), I, pp. 214–16.

[19] João Nuno Alçada shows how the family's humble position, as tailors, is an indication of their moral worth, in 'Novo significado da presença de *Todo o Mundo* e *Ninguém* no *Auto da Lusitânia*', *Arquivos do Centro Cultural Português*, 21 (1985), pp. 199–271 at 226–7.

[20] Gil Vicente, *Copilaçam*, I, 327.   [21] Révah, *Diálogo Evangélico*, pp. xxvii–xxviii.

[22] There is a modern edition of *Ropica Pnefma* by Révah, 2 vols. (Lisbon, 1983). For Machado, see *The Mirror of the New Christians*, ed. Mildred Evelyn Vieira and Frank Ephraim Talmage (Toronto, 1977).

[23] See Gil Vicente, *Copilaçam*, II, pp. 642–4.

have attempted Gil Vicente's intellectual subtlety. Nevertheless, he avoids the open expression of intolerance. He too does not use the word Jew or any of its synonyms, except in those parts of his play which refer directly to the historical events of the life of Christ. This is all the more remarkable given that nearly every episode in the play contains references one way or another to the New Christians. He may have felt that the work of conversion is better achieved by insinuation than by direct statement, and his conception of the saint's play as essentially festive would naturally also exclude incitement to racial hatred. As one of the characters says, in the introduction to the retelling of the legend: 'And as this is the day of our lord St Vincent, it would be a great mistake if anything untoward was included, apart from peace and joy'.[24]

But Álvares' play is not just the protest of a Christian, black or otherwise, against the Jewish presence. What he achieves in the *Auto de São Vicente*, very skillfully for the most part, is to integrate his concerns about crypto-Judaism with the other features of a typical saint's play: the narrative of a martyrdom, in this case one that took place in the early Christian era, probably in the fourth century; and the satire of contemporary life, in other words, the life of Lisbon in the 1530s.

Literary skill is not something many people would associate with Afonso Álvares. It is worth pausing for a moment to consider why his reputation is so low, because by clearing up some of the misconceptions about him his considerable achievements can be better understood.

Portuguese literary history has a curious tendency to concern itself exclusively with great figures. Undoubtedly the great figure in late medieval drama is Gil Vicente, and other dramatists inevitably suffer by comparison with him. Álvares is classed as an inferior being, a member of the so-called 'school of Gil Vicente' (*escola vicentina*). Even such serious scholars as Carolina Micaëlis de Vasconcellos and I. S. Révah are convinced that Álvares's *autos* are servile imitations of Vicente's.[25] To my mind, however, there is no need to assume any contact between the two writers. In the 1530s they were both at work, but their patrons and their subject matter were different. Vicente was a court dramatist, who only once accepted a commission from an ecclesiastical body, to write the *Auto da Cananeia*,[26] while Álvares worked exclusively for the

[24] 'E porque agora este dia / hé do senhor sam Vicente, / muyto grande erro seria / entrar enconveniente / senam de paz e alegria' (ll. 469–73).
[25] Vasconcellos, *Autos portugueses de Gil Vicente*, pp. 95–6. Révah's most substantial article on the play is 'O "Auto de Sam Vicente" de Afonso Álvares', *O Século*, 1 January 1951, pp. 13 and 19. He repeats his belief that he was a merely derivative writer in *Dicionário das Literaturas Portuguesa, Galega e Brasileira*, ed. Jacinto do Prado Coelho (Oporto, 1960), s.v. Álvares, Afonso.
[26] According to the rubric, it was written at the request of Dona Violante, the abbess of a convent in Odivelas.

Augustinian canons of São Vicente de Fora. All Álvares's *autos* are saint's plays, but Gil Vicente's only contribution to the genre is the incomplete *Auto de São Martinho.*

Modern research emphasizes the need to see Gil Vicente not just as a great originator, but in terms of the European, and especially French, medieval dramatic tradition to which he made a distinctively Portuguese contribution. Through the order which employed him Álvares would also have been aware of foreign drama, and he should be seen as working in parallel with Vicente, not in his shadow.[27]

Another myth which has grown up around Álvares is that he was an exclusively popular and accordingly a simple, ingenuous writer. This misconception probably derives from the printing history of the plays, which continued to appear for centuries after Álvares's death in chapbook editions clearly intended for the popular end of the market. The last such chapbook was printed as late as the mid-nineteenth century. But if Álvares became a devotional writer for an unsophisticated public he did not necessarily begin as one. It is true that his plays, like most medieval plays, are strongly rooted in a particular locality – Lisbon, and especially the church of São Vicente de Fora to the east of the medieval city – and no doubt were performed during civic and religious festivities. In the *Auto de Santo António*, references to ships and the sea suggest that the fishing or sailing community may have been involved in some way in the production. The many comic low-class characters in satirical scenes also suggest that Álvares was writing at least in part for the groundlings.

Medieval society was inclusive, and medieval festivities did not only involve the poor and humble. The social range of the characters of Álvares's plays includes, in the *Auto de São Vicente*, the allegorical figure of Lisbon, described as a 'grande senhora' (l. 408) and, in the hagiographical sections of the plays, bishops and kings as well as the saints themselves. The *autos* were sponsored by the Augustinian canons, and not merely as popular entertainment. They contain plenty to interest a sophisticated ecclesiastical audience, and in the *Auto de Santa Bárbara*, in which there are no comic urban scenes, Álvares showed that he had some humanistic as well as religious learning. In that play at least ten classical deities are mentioned by name, and Álvares also

---

[27] For Gil Vicente and French medieval theatre see the careful exposition in José Augusto Cardoso Bernardes, *Sátira e Lirismo: Modelos de Síntese no Teatro de Gil Vicente* (Coimbra, 1996), pp. 126–40. Luciana Stegagno Picchio, *História do Teatro Português*, trans. Manuel de Lucena (Lisbon, 1964), p. 96, also says that Álvares must have had some contact with European drama independently of Vicente but seems to contradict herself on the next page: 'a influência de Gil Vicente é notória'.

shows knowledge of Zeus's adventures with Alcmena and Danaë and, in the area of Roman history, of the cruel punishment of Manlius Torquatus's son.

But the chief obstacle to the appreciation of Álvares's work is that until very recently, perhaps even as late as the 1980s, the type of drama that he wrote seems to have been almost completely impenetrable to modern scholars. Writing in 1983 about French medieval drama, Alan Knight makes the point that the dichotomies comic/tragic, sacred/profane are simply not applicable to medieval religious playwrights, who were not even aware of them. Yet, if we are to believe Knight, nearly all critics, influenced consciously or unconsciously by classical or neo-classical norms, have used such dichotomies quite anachronistically when attempting to classify the forms of medieval drama.[28] The result has been incomprehension, the privileging of one aspect of a play at the expense of others. This is certainly the case with I. S. Révah. In his 1951 discussion of the *Auto de São Vicente* he writes quite perceptively about the satirical scenes, but can do no more than summarise the religious content of the play, despite the fact that the martyrdom of St Vincent occupies nearly two-thirds of it.

Álvares makes life hard for traditional criticism by writing with equal conviction about events which supposedly took place in his own time but also about other events which he knew happened in the late pagan world of fourth-century Spain. The fact that he was conscious of at least some of the social and political differences between those two very different epochs further stacks the odds against him and makes a just appreciation of his work difficult. Yet it may be that it is possible to find an approach to Álvares which puts his apparent disregard for chronology into perspective. For him, as for other medieval writers, the central fact of human existence is always the Passion of Christ and the redemption of mankind. All human activity, whatever the period in which it occurs, must be seen in relation to that one supreme event. In the face of it historical differences melt away, and the martyrdom of St Vincent, which itself closely mirrors the Passion, is a message of contemporary relevance to the troubled Lisbon of 1531, wracked by natural disasters and threatened by non-Christian intruders.

The first scenes of Álvares's play, which take place in Lisbon, are a setting for the martyrdom or passion narrative which follows, but can also be seen as forming part of that same narrative. In the *auto*, as in French theatrical writing of the same period, there is 'no clear distinction between pure drama . . .

---

[28] Alan E. Knight, *Aspects of Genre in Late Medieval French Drama* (Manchester, 1983), pp. 4–15.

and public ritual act'.[29] The mixture of stage comedy, sacred drama and parts of the most solemn and sacred liturgy in the Church's year make plain the omnipresence in space and time of the Christian story.

The *Auto de São Vicente* opens with a monologue of nearly two hundred lines spoken by the city of Lisbon, personified as a princess who has fallen on hard times. It is a lament for the ruinous state of the city, ravaged by famine, plague and earthquake, and deserted by the best of its inhabitants, who have gone to win new lands for Portugal overseas. God has allowed all these evils to occur, because in the place of the Christian heroes has come a 'torpe semente' (base seed), 'who use much villainy, keep little faith, and do business falsely, because their nature is of this kind'[30]. Lisbon does not say who these evil foreigners are, and a modern reader might perhaps suppose that they were black slaves, like Álvares's own presumed ancestors. However, the association between divine punishment and the presence in the city of foreigners calls to mind Gil Vicente's protests against those who blamed the Jews for what had recently happened in Lisbon.[31] And references later in the play also make it clear that the Jews are the foreigners in question. The monologue ends with a prayer to the Virgin and to St Vincent himself for intercession.

At one level, Lisbon's words are a protest against the social conditions of the day. But there is a religious significance too, because social protest is mediated through a speech redolent with references to the Passion story.

There is a Biblical text, closely linked to the liturgy of the Passion, with which Lisbon's lament has strong associations. The 'Lamentations of Jeremiah' is also a monologue spoken by the personification of a city, Jerusalem, 'she that was great among the nations, and princess among the provinces, how is she become solitary!' (Lamentations, 1.1) Lisbon too was an 'alta princesa' ('high princess', l. 12). Jerusalem has been invaded by the Babylonian foe: 'she hath seen that the heathen entered into her sanctuary, whom thou [God] didst command that they should not enter into thy congregation' (1.10). Lisbon also complains of the presence of the ungodly. Jerusalem's young men are taken captive (1.14), and the people reduced to famine (2.11–2), events which as already noted also have parallels in Álvares's text.

---

[29] *Ibid.*, p. 133.

[30] 'Que usam muyta vileza, / mantendo pouca verdade, / tratando com falsidade, / porque sua natureza / hé desta calidade.' (ll. 151–5)

[31] Silva Terra has published a Spanish poem about the earthquake which also hints that the Jews were responsible but does not name them, in José da Silva Terra, 'De João de Barros a Jerónimo Cardoso: o Terramoto de Lisboa de 1531', *Arquivos do Centro Cultural Português*, 23 (1987), pp. 373–416 at 383–4 and 394.

In the sixteenth century, and for many centuries afterwards, the Lamentations formed an important part of the liturgy of Holy Week, sometimes in musical settings which have become famous. Verses from the Lamentations were said or sung in the services known as *Tenebrae*, which took place on Maundy Thursday, Good Friday and Easter Saturday. In the Coimbra *Officium* of 1576 sections from the Old Testament book are intercut with readings from the Gospels, thus closely associating the sinfulness and sufferings of Jerusalem with sinful humanity, which is redeemed by the Passion of Christ.[32] The city of Lisbon's monologue in the *Auto de São Vicente* seems to belong to the world of the Lamentations while at the same time being a comment on the disasters of 1531 and an explanation of their cause. It is hardly necessary, or appropriate, to apply to Álvares's modest text the full panoply of the four-fold exegesis of the Bible. Nevertheless, it is clear that Lisbon's speech can be understood on a number of levels, which include an anagogical or spiritual one.

The meanings of the speech, then, are varied, but its tone is predominately serious. It is very typical of medieval drama that Álvares should follow it with a farcical scene, easily the liveliest of the play, in which two peasants, Pero Casco and his wife Isabel Vaz, complain about one another and their mistreatment at the hands of petty officialdom.

The change from solemnity to humour should not disguise the fact that the farcical scene is closely related to Lisbon's opening monologue, because it is an exemplification of the evils of which she had complained. Pero and Isabel are peasants who have come to Lisbon to sell some chickens. However, their produce has been confiscated in lieu of duty by one of the *almotacés*, the petty officials who supervised markets and the cleaning of the streets, as well as having a role in what we would now consider to be town planning. It is not just what the Portuguese peasants consider to be an injustice that rankles with them, it is above all that the perpetrator is a foreigner, a Castilian named Talaveira or Talavera.

The Arquivo Histórico da Câmara Municipal de Lisboa still contains a number of incomplete registers of the names of officials, but no Talavera appears as an *almotacé* in the 1530s.[33] Perhaps it was an invented name. It is certainly suggestive, because Talavera is not a Portuguese surname, but the name of a town in Western Spain in which during the Middle Ages there was

---

[32] *Officium hebdomadae sanctae, in die Palmorum, usque ad Sabbatum sanctum inclusive, secundum Romanam Ecclesiam novissime impressum* (Coimbra, 1576), fols. 53v–6, 108–9 and 147–9.

[33] See Lisbon, Arquivo Histórico da Câmara Municipal, Livros de Provimento de Ofícios, docs. 42, 54 and 58 where some *almotacés* of the sixteenth century are named.

an important Jewish community.[34] Tax collection was a traditionally Jewish occupation.

Pero and Isabel's complaints of mistreatment at the hands of a Spanish-speaking official may, therefore, be understood as a protest at the presence in Portugal of crypto-Jews in positions of power. The play's understated nature means that it is not possible to be certain of this. Yet it still remains the case that the farcical scene is an exemplum of the play's opening monologue. Where are the honest Portuguese officials? ask Pero and Isabel. They have disappeared, to be replaced by the crooked-dealing foreigner. The complaints of Lisbon, in her monologue at the beginning of the play, were directed at the same undesirable shift in the composition of the city's population. And the farcical dispute, over some chickens (to which curds are later added, l. 301), reminds the audience of the famine which threatens the once wealthy capital. The scene ends in an impasse, which Lisbon herself is unable to resolve. Instead, she tells the audience to listen attentively to the story of St Vincent which is to follow, a reminder of the play's religious message, that man's sinfulness can only be redeemed by the divine sacrifice.

Peter Brown has uncovered a number of reasons for the popularity of the cult of the martyrs in the early Christian era, most of which seem still to have been compelling in the sixteenth century. Martyrs were 'very special dead' who, despite torture and mutilation, retained their physical integrity on resurrection. Their tombs became places of renewal, and their former humanity a guarantee that they would intercede in heaven for their devotees. They were often shown in the pose of the crucified Christ, and were thus identified with his sufferings, but also with his triumph.[35]

In the *Auto de São Vicente* an angel twice insists on the martyr's resurrection (ll. 921–5 and 1188–98), though the retention of bodily integrity is more a feature of Álvares's other martyrdom play, the *Auto de Santa Bárbara*, than of this one. The martyr's function as intercessor is a feature of Lisbon's monologue, as we have seen. Álvares also lays great stress on the parallels between Vicente's sufferings and those of Christ, in this going beyond his probable source, the *Golden Legend* of Iacopo da Varazze, better known as Jacobo da Voragine.

---

[34] For the history of the Jewish community of Talavera during the Middle Ages and the flight of some of its members to Portugal after 1492, see Juan Blázquez Miguel, *Herejía e heterodoxia en Talavera y su antigua tierra* (Talavera, 1989), pp. 74–82 and 89–90.

[35] Peter Brown, *The Cult of the Saints: Its Rise and Function in Latin Christianity* (London, 1981), pp. 72–80.

One of the misconceptions about Álvares that circulates in handbooks is that he was totally dependent for his information about the lives of the saints on the *Golden Legend*.[36] He must have known the book, which was available to him in Latin, Portuguese and Spanish, but was quite capable of adapting it for his own purposes.[37] In the case of the legend of St Vincent he largely avoided gruesome details of torture, for instance, to concentrate on the spiritual meanings of the saint's martyrdom. He also makes significant alterations to the characters in the story.

The legend of St Vincent is a very simple one.[38] Vincent was a missionary in pagan Spain who was captured, interrogated and martyred by the country's rulers. Álvares departs from tradition by calling Vincent's interrogators pharisees (*fariseus*). They are described as such several times. They also speak Spanish, while Vincent and his companion, a bishop, speak Portuguese. Álvares's emphasis on the Jewishness of the saint's persecutors is anachronistic, because the religion of fourth-century Spain as portrayed in the play is pagan and not in any way Jewish. However, the presence of the Pharisees makes even more apparent the many parallels between the sufferings of St Vincent and those of Christ. Vincent is sent from them to the king, Daciano, as Christ is sent from the Pharisees to Pilate. Vincent is crucified and challenged to get down from the cross (Matthew 27:40–2). As if this was not sufficient, Vincent himself describes Christ's persecution by the Jews and his crucifixion (*Auto de São Vicente*, ll. 805–16) as does the Bishop (ll. 634–44).

The necessary link between the martyrdom of St Vincent and contemporary Portugal is provided by the devil. His long scene shows how evil is always with us. The devil seems to glide effortlessly between St Vincent's time and the sixteenth-century present, because sin, death and judgement are a constant reality. So is the disruptive presence of the Jews. They were responsible for the death of Christ and the death of St Vincent. But the devil also refers to a sixteenth-century preoccupation when he says: 'And against this [the word of Christ] there are those who presume and insist with false and empty arguments that there will come a more holy Messiah who will redeem them'

---

[36] See for example António José Saraiva and Óscar Lopes, *História da Literatura Portuguesa* (4th edn, Oporto, no date) p. 205 and, more recently, *Biblos: Enciclopédia Verbo das Literaturas de Língua Portuguesa* (Lisbon, 1995–), s.v. Álvares.

[37] See Mário Martins, 'O Original em Castelhano do "Flos Sanctorum" de 1513', *Estudos de Cultura Medieval*, 3 vols. (Lisbon and Braga, 1969–83), I, pp. 255–67 at 255–6 for the Portuguese and Spanish versions.

[38] See Iacopo da Varazze, *Legenda aurea*, ed. Giovanni Paolo Maggioni, 2 vols. (Florence, 1998), I, pp. 174–9.

(ll. 1003–8).[39] This, the most explicit mention of the New Christians of the play, is perhaps connected to the visit to Portugal in 1525–6 of the mysterious David Reubeni, who preached the imminent coming of the Messiah.[40] Yet the devil is also obliged reluctantly to confess that the possibility of redemption through the intercession of the saints exists at this and at all other times.

The final scene of the play returns to the legend of St Vincent, and the story of the miraculous discovery and burial of his body. It is an intelligent summing up of all that has passed on stage, bringing together social criticism and religious significance, and once again bridging the gap between the fourth century and the sixteenth. To do this Álvares had to discard most of the popular legendary material that had grown up around the cult of the saint, another proof that he was not simply a dramatist of the people.

St Vincent was one of those saints who refused to stay buried until he was laid in the right grave. The *Golden Legend* gave a start to the tale, which was much embroided in Portugal. The saint's body, miraculously discovered on the promontory in the Algarve which bears his name, was transported to Lisbon in a boat guided by two crows, and reburied there.[41] The story, already current in the early Middle Ages, was completely disregarded by Álvares, who simply has two peasants stumble over the corpse. They are then informed of its identity by an angel, and it is given a solemn reburial.

Undoubtedly one reason why Álvares resisted the temptation to drama-tise the saint's journey to Lisbon was that his relics were kept not in his patrons' church of São Vicente de Fora, despite its dedication, but in the nearby cathedral.[42] But the picturesque details would undoubtedly have obscured the meaning of the final scene of his play.

In it we are back in the comic world of the Portuguese peasants, this time Costança and Gonçalo, described in the rubric as a 'tolo pastor' (idiotic shepherd). Costança complains that her beasts are dying of hunger (ll. 1083–5), a comment which reminds the audience of the tribulations of Lisbon. But the language of the peasants is full of allegory. Gonçalo tells Costança that God has punished her flock for its indiscipline. The animals 'enjoy feeding and grazing

---

[39] 'E contra isto hé presumir / e arguir / com teymas falsas, vazias / dizendo que há-de vir / outro mais sancto Mixias / que os há-de redimir'.

[40] Tavares, *Judaísmo e Inquisição*, p. 122.

[41] Mário Martins, *Peregrinações e Livros de Milagres na nossa Idade Média* (Lisbon, 1957), pp. 41–52 recounts the development of the legend from the period of the Arab domination of the peninsula onwards.

[42] For the not very edifying story of how this came about, see *Crónicas dos Sete Primeiros Reis de Portugal*, ed. Carlos da Silva Tarouca, 3 vols. (Lisbon, 1952–3), I, pp. 104–5.

on forbidden wheat, I mean other people's wheat' (ll. 1100–4).[43] They wander from place to place and die because the sheep have not been separated from the goats (ll. 1115–3). Here are the words of Christ about judgement (Matthew 25:32–3) and also yet further reference to the Jews, identified with the goats through their association with the scapegoat, and even to the quarrel about chickens of the early part of the play.

Very similar language about herself and her tribulations is used by the allegorical character Hebreia in Gil Vicente's *Auto da Cananeia*, written two years later, in 1534. She too is a shepherdess, who complains '[My flock] is always feeding at someone else's table',[44] and, like Álvares's peasants, regrets her animals' tendency to stray, another clear reference to the Jewish diaspora: 'My flock is given to straying, and you will always see them on the move, from one sin to another, and from one captivity to another'.[45]

The peasants' discussion is interrupted by their discovery of the corpse of St Vincent. The scene has obvious connections with the visit of the apostles to the tomb of Christ, the *Visitatio sepulchri* of many medieval plays. An angel tells Gonçalo and Costança to fear not (Matthew 28:5) and to arrange for the saint to have a Christian burial. The play ends with the burial, in an unspecified location.

The scene takes place simultaneously in two widely separated chronological epochs. The peasants are not pagan Spaniards, but Portuguese Christians, so their discovery of the saint's body must have occurred at the time of his transportation to Portugal. However, since Gonçalo and Costança have the preoccupations with famine and death of the sixteenth century, we are once again reminded that the martyrdom of St Vincent, like the passion of Christ which it so closely resembles, is an event of eternal significance.

As often happens in medieval literature, the meaning of the *Auto de São Vicente* is repeated over and over again in the different scenes of the play. It is simply that those who believe in Christ and in the mysteries of his Passion and resurrection will be saved by the intercession of the saints and of the Virgin, and that those who do not will be punished in this world and the next. There is no doubt that Álvares had in mind the New Christian population of Lisbon, but this is a play about conversion, not extermination, as we have seen. In the play he shows considerable resource, and considerable tact, in integrating racial and religious themes.

[43] 'Porque folga de pacer / e comer / sempre o trigo vedado / alheo quero dizer'.
[44] Vicente, *Copilaçam*, 1, p. 326: '[Meu gado] sempre pasce em mesa alheia'.
[45] *Ibid.*: 'Que meu gado é tão erreiro, / que sempre o verás andar / dum pecar em outro pecar / de cativeiro em cativeiro'.

The *Auto de São Vicente*, like Álvares's other plays, is a didactic and confessional work written in response to an ecclesiastical commission. It is not a work of the highest literary quality, but very far from being despicable. Álvares was not as inventive as Gil Vicente, and not as imaginative in his use of language. But he was not naive, nor was he an unlearned writer capable only of addressing a popular audience. If he really was a mulatto, with a black African slave mother, he achieved the considerable intellectual feat of assimilating entirely the religious values of a European society. Perhaps if he had used his talents to rebel against them, rather than to attack another minority group on the grounds of their failure to follow the Christian faith, we would admire him more. But if he had done so, he would almost certainly have been silenced. Instead he survived to produce a body of work which gave much pleasure for three centuries at least. In the injustice and horror of a slave society, he stands out as a beacon of hope.

Bibliography

PRIMARY SOURCES

A. Archival and manuscript sources

Barcelona
Archivo de la Corona de Aragon, Reg. 3512

Bern
Burgerbibliothek, Cod. A45 (Clemens Specker, 'Chronik')

Chicago
Newberry Library, Ayer Collection, Spanish America MS 1111, 1089

Évora
Arquivo Distrital
   Câmara de Évora, no. 207
   Fundo notarial, Évora, Liv. 43, 169, 210, 451
   Fundo notarial, Mora, Liv. 11
   Fundo paroquial, Évora, Sé, Liv. 9–11
   Fundo paroquial, Montemor-o-Novo, Vila, Liv. 2 and 3 Baptismos
   Fundo paroquial, S. Miguel de Machede, Liv. 1
   Misericórdia de Évora, Liv. 1781
Biblioteca Pública
   Arm. x, no. 1, 26
   Cód. cxi/1–6
   cxii/1–37

Florence
Archivio di stato
   Catasto 923, 1011
   Depositeria, Salariati, reg. 393
   Mediceo del principato 627
Archivio dell'Ospedale degli Innocenti, Estranei 223, 227, 229, 235, 236, 237, 240,
   250, 251, 252, 254, 259
Archivio Pucci, Miscellanea, filza 18

Granada
Archivo de la Alhambra, Legajo 62-19; 78-1-12; 78-1-16; 100-6; 100-47; 101-19;
   101-47; 137-15; 223-145

Archivo de la Chancillería, Legajo 513, Cabina 2.566, pieza 25
Archivo de la Curia Episcopal, Legajo 1579–1585
Archivo de Protocolos del Colegio Notarial, Legajo 44, 145, 150, 191, 198, 212
Archivo Municipal, Cabina 504, Legajo 793, pieza 13

Lisbon

Academia das Ciências, Miscelânea Curiosa, Série Vermelha, 'Discurso demonstrativo
    sobre a entrada dos Escravos no Para, Maranhão, depois d'extincta a Companhia:
    resposta ao que esta Representou a esse respeito à Raynha Nossa Senhora Anno
    1777'
Arquivo Histórico da Câmara Municipal, Livros de Provimento de Oficios, doc. 42,
    54 and 58
    Livro 1° do Provimento da Saúde do Senado
Biblioteca da Ajuda
    doc. 51-v-71
    Livro de Consulta do Desembargo do Paço, 107: doc. 51-VIII-18
Biblioteca Nacional, Cód. 1544 ('Memórias da Casa de Bragança')
Instituto dos Arquivos Nacionais/Torre do Tombo
    Cartas Missivas, maço 3, doc. 13; 16
    Conventos Diversos, Livro de S. Domingos, Liv. 30 MSS
    Corpo Chronológico I, maço 33, doc. 108; maço 47, doc.72 and doc. 85; maço 49,
        doc. 69 and 115; maço 51, doc. 98, 99 and 113; maço 52, doc. 101; maço 53, doc.
        78 and 106; maço 54, doc. 39 and 41; maço 55, doc. 82; maço 56, doc. 31, 138
        and 163; maço 58, doc. 18, 58 and 96; maço 59, doc. 51; maço 73, doc. 60; maço
        83, doc. 12 and 74; maço 85, doc. 97 and 118; maço 86, doc. 17; maço 87, doc.
        86 and 88; maço 88, doc. 67, 74, 112 and 138; maço 89, doc. 27; maço 90, doc.
        9 and 104; maço 91, doc. 51; maço 92, doc. 95 and 152; maço 93, doc. 26, 74,
        120, 134 and 138; maço 94, doc. 13; maço 95, doc. 20 and 63; maço 96, doc. 147;
        maço 97, doc. 10, 72, 77 and 127; maço 98, doc. 96; maço 99, doc. 10; maço
        100, doc. 4, 36 and 69; maço 101, doc. 12;
    Corpo Chronológico II, maço 246, doc. 14
    Núcleo Antigo 792

London

British Library, MS Harley 2799
College of Arms
    MS ICB 101
    Miscellaneous Grants 1
National Archives, High Court of Admiralty 13, vol. 93

Madrid

Biblioteca Nacional
    MS 6.176
    MS 18472 (Diego (Jakob) Cuelbis, 'Thesoro chorográphico de las Españas')

Malibu, California
J. Paul Getty Museum, MS Ludwig, xv 4

Montemor-o-Novo
Arquivo Histórico Municipal, A 1 D 4; A 1 D 9

Oxford
Bodleian Library, MS 614

Palermo
Archivio Storico Diocesano di Palermo
   Parrocchia San Giacomo la Marina, MS 39, 70, 71
   Parrocchia Santa Margherita, MS 4360, 4361, 4362
   Registri delle deliberazioni, S. Maria di Gesù, MS 3134, 3167
Biblioteca Comunale
   MS Qq E9, Antonio Mongitore, 'Storia sacra delle chiese di Palermo, III: Chiese di unioni, confraternite e congregazioni di Palermo'
   MS 3Qq E40, 'Processo del Benedetto di San Fratello', and E42, 'Ordinaria inquisitio'

Rome
Archivum Romanum Societatis Jesu, Neap. 72, 77, 193; Sic. 182, 183 I

Setúbal
Arquivo Distrital, Fundo notarial
   Alcochete, Liv. 4/10
   Almada, Liv. 1/4; 2/8
   Palmela, Liv. 9/1

Simancas
Archivo General
   Casa y Sitios Reales, leg. 73
   Censo de Granada de 1561
   Contaduría Mayor de Cuentas, 1ª época, leg. 1031, 1070
   Estado (Portugal), leg. 375

Valencia
Archivo de Protocolos del Patriarcha
Archivo del Reino, Bailia 194
Archivo del Reino, Gobernación 2279, M. 11; 2348, M. 7; 2410, M. 15; 2411, M. 22
Archivo del Reino, Justicia Criminal 102, Cedes M. 4

B. Printed sources

Acta et decreta synodi neapolitanae (Naples, 1568)
Africanus, Leo, *A Geographical Historie of Africa, written in Arabicke and Italian . . . Before which . . . is prefixed a Generall Description of Africa, and . . . a Particular Treatise of*

all the ... Lands ... Undescribed by J. Leo, trans. and collected by J. Pory [London, 1600] (Amsterdam and New York, 1969)

The History and Description of Africa and of the Notable Things Therein Contained, Done into English in the Year 1600, by John Pory, now edited with an Introduction and Notes by Dr. Robert Brown, 3 vols. (London, 1896)

Ainsworth, Henry, *Solomons Song of Songs* (London, 1623)

Aldrovandi, Ulisse, *Monstrorum historia* (Bologna, 1642)

The Letters and Memorials of William Cardinal Allen (1532–1594), ed. by Fathers of the Congregation of the London Oratory (London, 1882)

Álvares, Afonso, *Auto de Santa Bárbara* (Lisbon, 1668; Oporto, 1859)

Auto de Sant'Iago and *Auto de Santo Antonio* (facsimile edn), both in Vasconcellos, Carolina Micaëlis de, *Autos portugueses de Gil Vicente y de la escuela vicentina* (Madrid, 1922)

Auto de São Vicente, ed. I. S. Révah, *Bulletin d'histoire du théâtre portugais*, 2:2 (1952), pp. 219–51

Álvares, Francisco, *Do Preste Joam das Indias: Verdadera Informaçam das Terras do Preste Joam* (Lisbon, 1540)

America Pontificia primi saeculi evangelizationis, 1493–1592, ed. Josef Metzler, 2 vols. (Città del Vaticano, 1991)

Anedotas Portuguesas e Memórias Biográficas da Corte Quinhentista. Istorias e Ditos Galantes que Sucederão e se Disserão no Paço, ed. Christopher Lund (Coimbra, 1980)

Anglo, Sydney (ed.), *The Great Tournament Roll of Westminster*, 2 vols. (Oxford, 1968)

Anon., *Coplas de cómo una dama ruega a un negro que cante* (probably Seville: Cromberger, c. 1520?)

Arrais, Amador, *Diálogos* [1589] (Oporto, 1974)

Baldinucci, Filippo, *Notizie dei professori del disegno da Cimabue in qua*, ed. F. Ranalli, 5 vols. (Florence, 1845–7)

Baldwin, William, *The Canticles or Balades of Salomon* (London, 1549)

Barone, Nicola, 'Le cedole di tesoreria dell'Archivio di stato di Napoli dall'anno 1460 al 1504', *Archivio storico per le province napoletane*, 9 (1884), pp. 5–34, 205–48, 387–429, 601–37; 10 (1885), pp. 5–47

Barros, João de, *Ásia de Joam de Barros* (Lisbon, 1552)

Diálogo Evangélico sobre os Artigos da Fé contra o Talmud dos Judeus ... de João de Barros, ed. I. S. Révah (Lisbon, 1950)

Ropica Pnefma, ed. I. S. Révah, 2 vols. (Lisbon, 1983)

Barry, Colman J. (ed.), *Readings in Church History*, 2 vols. (Westminster, MD, 1960)

Beauvais, Vincent of, *Speculum Historiale*

Becon, Thomas, *The Iewel of Ioye* (London, 1553)

Berchet, Guglielmo (ed.), *Fonti italiane per la scoperta del Nuovo Mondo*, 2 vols. (Rome, 1892)

Bermúdez de Pedraza, Francisco, *Antiguedad y excelencias de Granada* (Granada, 1608)

Historia eclesiástica de Granada [1639], facsimile edition (Granada, 1989)

Biblia Sacra, ed. Alberto Colunga and Laurentio Turrado (4th edn, Madrid, 1965)

Biblia Sacra, ed. Alberto Colunga and Laurentio Turrado (5th edn, Madrid, 1977)

Blake, John William (ed.), *Europeans in West Africa, 1450–1560*, 2 vols. (London, 1942)

Boemus, Johannes, *The Fardle of Facions*, trans. William Waterman (London 1555)

Bouza, Fernando (ed.), *Cartas de Felipe II a sus hijas* (Madrid, 1998)

Brásio, António (ed.), *Monumenta missionaria Africana, Africa Ocidental (1471–1531)* (Lisbon, 1952)

    História do Reino do Congo (MS 8080 da Biblioteca Nacional de Lisboa) (Lisbon, 1969)

Brathwait, Richard, *Ar't Asleep Husband?* (London, 1640)

Brome, Richard, *The English Moor, or The Mock-Marriage* (London, 1659)

Browne, Thomas, *Pseudodoxia Epidemica* (London, 1646)

Brucioli, Antonio, *A Commentary vpon the Canticle of Canticles*, trans. Thomas James (London, 1598)

Bulwer, John, *Anthropometamorphosis* (London, 1650)

Buoni, Tommaso, *Problemes of Beautie and All Humane Affections*, trans. S. L. Gent (London, 1606)

Cabrales Arteaga, José M. (ed.), *La poesía de Rodrigo de Reinosa: estudio y edición* (Santander, 1980)

Cadamosto, Alvise de, *Paesi novamente retrovati* (Vicenza, Henrico Vicentino, 1507)

    The Voyages of Cadamosto and Other Documents on Western Africa in the Second Half of the Fifteenth Century, ed. G. R. Crone (London, 1937)

Camões, Luís de, *Obras completas*, ed. Hernâni Cidade, 5 vols. (Lisbon, 1946–7)

Cancioneiro Geral de Garcia de Resende, ed. Aida Fernanda Dias, 6 vols. (Lisbon, 1990–2003)

Castiglione, Baldassare, *Il libro del cortegiano del Conte Baldessar Castiglione*, ed. Vittorio Cian (Florence, 1967)

    The Book of the Courtier, trans. Sir Thomas Hoby [1561] (London, 1974)

Catalán, Diego *et al.* (eds.), *La dama y el pastor: romance, villancico, glosas*, 2 vols. (Madrid, 1977–8)

Ceccheregli, Alessandro, *Delle azioni e sentenze di Alessandro de' Medici* [1564] (Bologna, 1865)

Cervantes Saavedra, Miguel de, *The Ingenious Gentleman Don Quixote of La Mancha*, trans. John Ormsby (London, 1885)

    El ingenioso hidalgo don Quijote de la Mancha, ed. Luis Andrés Murillo, 2 vols. (Madrid, 1978)

    Novelas ejemplares, ed. Juan Bautista Avalle-Arce, 3 vols. (Madrid, 1982)

    La entretenida, in *Teatro completo*, ed. Florencio Sevilla Arroyo and Antonio Rey Hazas (Barcelona, 1987), pp. 543–630

    Don Quijote de la Mancha, ed. Florencio Sevilla Arroyo and Antonio Rey Hazas (Madrid, 1996)

Chappell, W. M. (ed.), *The Roxburghe Ballads* (Hertford, 1873–4)

Chiado, António Ribeiro, *Letreyros Muyto Sentenciosos . . . Feytos por Antonio Chiado* (Lisbon, 1783)

'Querela entre o Chiado e Affonso Alvares', in *Obras do Poeta Chiado*, ed. Alberto Pimentel (Lisbon, 1889), pp. 171–216

Cinzio, Giambattista Giraldi, *Gli Hecatommitti*, 2 vols. (Venice, 1580)

Claramonte, Andrés de, *La gran comedia de el valiente negro en Flandes*, in *Dramáticos contemporáneos a Lope de Vega*, ed. Ramón de Mesonero Romanos, Biblioteca de autores españoles, 43 (Madrid, 1857), pp. 491–509

Clenardus, Nicholaus, *Correspondance*, ed. Alphonse Roersch, 3 vols. (Brussels, 1940–1)

Cobarruvias Orozco, Sebastián de, *Tesoro de la lengua castellana o española* (Madrid, 1611)

Cocles, Bartholomeus, *Le compendion et brief enseignement de physiognomie et chiromancie* (Paris, 1550)

Colección de documentos ineditos para la historia de España, 24 (1854), pp. 515–50

Comune di Roma, *Registri di bandi editti notificazioni e provvedimenti diversi relativi alla città di Roma ed allo stato pontificio*, 1 (*Anni 1234–1605*) (Rome, 1920)

Conceptione, Franciscus de, 'Annotationes in abusus sacramentorum', in *Concilii Tridentini actorum, partis tertiae, volumen secundum*, ed. Theobaldus Freudenberger (Freiburg, 1972)

Concilium Tridentinum, Tomus VI, Volumen II, ed. Theobaldus Freudenberger (Freiburg im Breisgau, 1972)

Constitutiones illustrissimi et reverendissimi domini Domini Caesaris Marulli Archiepiscopi Panormitani in diocesana synodo promulgatae die xiij Iunij Anno M.D.LXXXVI. (Palermo, 1587)

Coote, C. H., *Autotype Facsimiles of Three Mappemondes, 1: The Harleian, or Anonymous, Mappemonde, circa 1536* (BM, Add. MS 24.065), *2: The Mappemonde by Desceliers of 1546* (Bibl. Lind., French MS No. 15), *3: The Mappemonde of Desceliers of 1550* (BM Add. MS 5413) ([Aberdeen], 1898)

Copley, Anthony, *Wits, Fits, and Fancies* (London, 1614)

Corpo Diplomático Portuguez, ed. Luiz Augusto Rebello da Silva *et al.*, 14 vols. (Lisbon, 1862–1910)

Corpus juris canonici editio Lipsiensis secunda, ed. Emil L. Richter and Emil Friedberg, 2 vols. (Leipzig, 1879)

Correas, Gonzale, *Vocabulario de refranes y frases proverbiales* [1627], ed. Louis Combet (Bordeaux, 1967)

Cotarelo y Mori, Emilio (ed.), *Colección de entremeses, loas, bailes, jácaras y mojigangas desde fines del siglo XVI á mediados del XVIII*, 2 vols. (Madrid, 1911)

Courtonne, Jean Paulmier de, *Mémoires touchant l'etablissement d'une mission chrestienne dans le troisieme monde, autrement appelé, la Terre Australe, Meridionale, Antartique et inconnue* (Paris, 1663)

Crónicas dos Sete Primeiros Reis de Portugal, ed. Carlos da Silva Tarouca, 3 vols. (Lisbon, 1952–3)

Decrees of the Ecumenical Councils, 2 vols., ed. Norman P. Tanner *et al.* (Washington, DC, 1990)

Delafosse, Eustache, *Voyage d'Eustache Delafosse à la côte de Guinée, au Portugal et en Espagne (1479–1481)*, ed. Denis Escudier (Paris, 1992)

Dent, Arthur, *The Plaine Mans Path-way to Heaven* [1601] (London, 1974)

Diccionario de autoridades (repr. of Real Academia Española, *Diccionario de la lengua castellana*, Madrid, 1726–39), 6 vols. (Madrid, 1984)

Dinis, António Joaquim, O. F. M. (ed.), *Monumenta Henricina*, 15 vols. (Coimbra, 1960–74)

Ditos Portugueses Dignos de Memória, ed. José H. Saraiva (Lisbon, [1979])

Dunbar, William, *The Poems of William Dunbar* (London, 1970)

Encina, Juan del, *Trivagia, o viaje a Jerusalem* (Roma, 1521), in Juan del Encina *Obras completas*, ed. Ana María Rambaldo, 2 vols. (Madrid, 1978)

Erasmus, Desiderius, *Dialogus Ciceronianus*, ed. Pierre Mesnard [*Opera omnia Desiderii Erasmi Roterdami*, 1–2] (Amsterdam, 1971), pp. 581–710

Erasmus, Desiderius, *On Good Manners for Boys*, ed. and trans. Brian McGregor, in *Collected Works of Erasmus* (Toronto, Buffalo and London, 1974–), xv, pp. 273–89

Floresta de poesías eróticas del Siglo de Oro con su vocabulario al cabo por orden del a.b.c., ed. Pierre Alzieu, Robert Jammes and Yvan Lissorgues (Toulouse, 1975)

Foulché-Delbosc, R., 'Memoria de Francisco Núñez Muley', *Bulletin Hispanique* (1899), pp. 205–37

Fournier, G., *Hydrographie contenant la theorie et la practique de toutes les parties de la navigation* (Paris, 1643)

Frenk Alatorre, Margit (ed.), *Lírica española de tipo popular: Edad Media y Renacimiento* (2nd edn, Madrid, 1977)

Frutuoso, Gaspar, *Livro Sexto das Saudades da Terra* (Ponta Delgada, 1963)

Furs de València, ed. Germà Colon and Arcadi Garcia, 8 vols. (Barcelona, 1974)

Gavetas do Torre do Tombo, ed. A. da Silva Rego, 12 vols. (Lisbon, 1960–77)

Gesta Romanorum, ed. Hermann Oesterley (Berlin, 1872)

Gibson, Anthony, *A Womans Woorth* (London, 1599)

Giordano, Rosalia Claudia (ed.), 'Appendice documentaria: transcrizione del manoscritto 3 Qq C36 n.19 della Biblioteca Comunale di Palermo', in Giovanna Fiume and Marilena Modica (eds.), *San Benedetto il moro: santità, agiografia e primi processi di canonizzazione* (Palermo, 1998)

Gosson, Stephen, *The Ephemerides of Phialo* (London, 1586)

Gubernatis, Angelo de, *Antologia di poetesse italiane del secolo decimosesto* (Florence, 1883)

Guerreiro, Manuel Viegas and Magalhães, Joaquim Romero, *Duas Descrições do Algarve no Século XVI* (Lisbon, 1983)

Hakluyt, Richard, *The Principal Navigations, Voiages and Discoveries of the English Nation* (London, 1589)

   The Principal Navigations, Voyages, Traffiques and Discoveries of the English Nation . . ., 3 vols. (London, 1599–1600)

Hall, Joseph, *Salomons Diuine Arts* (London, 1609)

Hall, Thomas, *The Loathsomnesse of Long Haire* (London, 1653)

Hampe, Theodor, *Das Trachtenbuch des Christoph Weiditz von seinen Reisen nach Spanien (1529) und den Niederlanden (1531/32)* (Berlin and Leipzig, 1927)

Hawkins, Richard, *Declaration of the Troublesome Voyadge of Sir John Hawkins to Guynea and the West Indies* [1569] (Amsterdam and New York, 1973)

Heliodorus, *An Æthiopian Historie*, trans. Thomas Underdowne (London, 1569)

Henriquez de Jorquera, Francisco, *Anales de Granada. Descripción del Reino y su ciudad. Crónica de la Reconquista (1482–1492). Sucesos de los años 1588 a 1646* (University of Granada, 1987)

Huarte, Juan de Dios, *The Examination of Mens Wits*, trans. Richard Carew (London, 1594)

Hurtado de Mendoza, Diego, *Guerra de Granada* [Lisbon, 1627], ed. B. Blanco-González (Madrid, 1970)

Ignatius of Loyola, *The Constitutions of the Society of Jesus*, trans. and ed. George E. Ganss (St. Louis, 1970)

Il giornale del banco Strozzi di Napoli (1473), ed. A. Leone (Naples, 1981)

Indagine, Joannes, *Chiromantia*, trans. Fabian Withers (London, 1558)

Jobson, Richard, *The Golden Trade* (London, 1623)

Landi, Giulio, *La descrittione de l'isola de la Madera già scritta nela lingua latina dal molto ill. Signor Conte Giulio Landi, et hora tradotta dal latino ne la nostra materna lingua, dal reverendo M. Alamanio Fini* (Piacenza, 1574)

Lankmann, Nicolaus, *Leonor de Portugal Imperatriz da Alemanha, Diário de Viagem do Embaixador Nicolau Lanckman de Valkenstein*, ed. Aires A. Nascimento (with the collaboration of Maria João Branco and Maria de Lurdes Rosa) (Lisbon, 1992)

Latinus, Johannes, *Austrias carmen* [Granada, 1573] and *De translatione corporum regalium* [Granada, 1576], in *Ad Catholicum pariter et invictissimum Philippum Dei gratia Hispaniarum Regem, de foelicissima serenissimi Ferdinandi Principis nativitate epigrammatum liber* (Nendeln-Lichtenstein, 1971)

Lazarillo de Tormes, *The Life and Adventures of Lazarillo de Tormes, Translated from the Spanish of Don Diego Hurtado de Mendoza. – The Life and Adventures of Guzmán d'Alfarache; or, The Spanish Rogue, by Mateo Alemán*, trans. Thomas Roscoe, 2 vols. (London, 1881)

  Lazarillo de Tormes, ed. Francisco Rico, 2nd edn with bibliography by Bienvenido C. Morros (Madrid, 1986)

  The Life of Lazarillo de Tormes [1586], trans. David Rowland, ed. Keith Whitlock (Warminster, 2000)

Ling, Nicholas, *Politeuphuia* (London, 1597)

Lisle, William, *The Faire Æthiopian* (London, 1631)

Llibre de Memories de Diversos Sucesos e Fets Memorables e de Coses Senyalades de la Ciutat e Regne de Valencia (1308–1644), ed. Salvador Carreres Zacares, 2 vols. (Valencia, 1935)

López de Mendoza, Íñigo (attrib.), *Refranes que dizen las viejas tras el huego* (Seville, 1508)

Lopez, Duarte, *A Report of the Kingdome of Congo*, trans. A. Hartwell (London, 1597)

Lupton, Thomas, *A Thousand Notable Things* (London, 1579)

Lycosthenes, C. (Wolfhardt), *Prodigiorum ac ostentorum chronicon* (Basel, 1557)

Machado, Francisco, *Espelho de Cristãos-Novos e Convertidos* [1541], in *The Mirror of the New Christians*, ed. Mildred Evelyn Vieira and Frank Ephraim Talmage (Toronto, 1977)

Machiavelli, Niccolò, *The Art of War*, trans. Elis Farnesworth (New York, 1965)

Mander, Karel van, *The Lives of the Illustrious Netherlandish and German Painters*, ed. Hessel Miedema, 6 vols. (Doornspijk, 1994–9)

Mandeville, John, *Travels*. Texts and trans. M. Letts, 2 vols. (London, 1953)

Marlowe, Christopher / Dekker, Thomas, *Lust's Dominion* (London, 1657)

Mármol Carvajal, Luis de, *Historia del rebelión y castigo de los moriscos del reino de Granada*, ed. Buenaventura Carlos Aribau (Madrid, 1946)

   Rebelión y castigo de los Moriscos [1600] (Málaga, 1991)

Marques, A. H. de Oliveira, 'Uma descrição de Portugal em 1578–80', in A. H. de Oliveira Marques, *Portugal Quinhentista (Ensaios)* (Lisbon, 1987), pp. 127–245

Mat(t)hesius, J., *Sarepta oder Bergpostill sampt der Jochimßthalischen kurtzen Chronicken* (Nuremberg, 1564)

Medici, Lorenzino de', *Aridosia, Apologia, rime e lettere*, ed. Federico Ravello (Turin, 1921)

Monumenta Historica Societatis Jesu, Litterae Quadrimestres ex universis praeter Indiam et Brasiliam locis in quibus aliqui de Societate Jesu versabantur Romam missae, 4 vols. (1546–56) (Madrid, 1895)

Münster, Sebastian, *Novus orbis regionum ac insularum veteribus incognitarum . . . libellus* (Basel, 1532)

Münzer, Hieronymus, *Intinerário do Dr. Jerónimo Münzer (Extractos)*, trans. Basílio de Vasconcelos (*O Lusitano*, 80; Coimbra, 1931)

Nardi, Jacopo, *Istorie della città di Firenze*, ed. Lelio Arbib, 2 vols. (Florence, 1838–41)

Nebrija, Antonio de, *Gramática de la lengua castellana* (Salamanca, 1492)

Northbrooke, John, *Spiritus est vicarius Christi* (London, 1579)

Officium hebdomadae sanctae, in die Palmorum, usque ad Sabbatum sanctum inclusive, secundum Romanam Ecclesiam novissime impressum (Coimbra, 1576)

Oliveira, Cristóvão Rodrigues de, *Lisboa em 1551: Sumário em que Brevemente se Contêm Algumas Coisas . . . que há na Cidade de Lisboa* (Lisbon, 1987)

Oliveira, (Padre) Fernanado, *Arte da Guerra do Mar*, facsimile of 1555 edn (Lisbon, 1983)

Ordenações Manuelinas (1521) (Lisbon, 1984)

Ortiz de Zúñiga, Diego, *Annales eclesiasticos y seculares de la muy noble y muy leal ciudad de Sevilla* (Madrid, 1677)

Painter, William, *The Palace of Pleasure* (London, 1566)

Palmer Tilley, Maurice, *A Dictionary of the Proverbs in England in the Sixteenth and Seventeenth Centuries* (Ann Arbor, 1966)

Paul, Sir James Balfour (ed.), *The Accounts of the Lord High Treasurer of Scotland* (Edinburgh, 1902)

Pereira, Duarte Pacheco, *Esmeraldo de situ orbis*, ed. and trans. George H. T. Kimble (London, 1937)

Pérez de Hita, Ginés, *Guerras civiles de Granada*, part II (Madrid, 1963)

Pettie, George, *A Petite Pallace, of Pettie His Pleasure* (London, 1578)

Pfandl, Ludwig (ed.), 'Itinerarium hispanicum Hieronymi Monetarii 1494–1495', *Revue hispanique*, 48 (1920), pp. 1–179, 679

Pieruzzi, Antonino, *Summa theologica*, 4 vols. (Verona, 1740)

Pina, Rui de, *Crónica de El-Rei D. João II*, ed. Alberto Martins de Carvalho (Coimbra, 1950)

Poesía lírica y cancionero musical, ed. R. O. Jones and Carolyn R. Lee (Madrid, 1975)

Portugal, Dom Francisco de, 1st Count of Vimioso, *Poesias e Sentenças*, ed. Valeria Tocco (Lisbon, 1999)

Ptolemy, Claudius, *Opus Geographiae noviter castigatum & emaculatum* (Strasbourg, 1522)
Geographicae enarrationis libri octo Bilibaldo Pirkeymhero interprete (Strasbourg, 1525)

Purchas, Samuel, *Purchas his Pilgrimage* (London, 1614)

Quevedo, Francisco de, *Obras completas*, I: *Poesía original*, ed. José Manuel Blecua (Barcelona, 1963)
La hora de todos y la fortuna con seso, ed. Jean Bourg, Pierre Dupont and Pierre Geneste (Madrid, 1987)

Reinosa, Rodrigo de, *Comiençan unas coplas a los negros y negras* (Burgos?, before 1540)

Resende, Garcia de, 'Miscelânea', *Livro das Obras de Garcia de Resende*, ed. Evelina Verdelho (Lisbon, 1994)

Reynosa, Rodrigo de, *Coplas*, ed. María Inés Chamorro Fernández (Madrid, 1970)

Rodríguez-Moñino, Antonio (ed.), *Los pliegos poéticos de la colección del Marqués de Morbecq: siglo XVI* (Madrid, 1962)

Romei, Annibale, *The Courtiers Academie*, trans. John Kepers (London, 1598)

Rosário, A. do (ed.), 'Acordos e Vereações da Câmara de Braga nos Dois Últimos Anos do Senhorio de D. Frei Bartolomeu dos Mártires (1580–1582)', *Bracara Augusta*, 24 (1970), pp. 284–435

Rota, Lorenzo dalla, *Lamento del Duca Galeazzo duca de Milano elqual fu morto da Iovane-andrea da lampognano* (Florence, Bernardo Zucchetta for Piero Pacini, 1505)
Lamento de l'Illustrissimo Sig. Galeazzo Duca di Milano (Venice, 1616)

Rotz, Jean, *The Maps and Text of the Boke of Idrography presented by Jean Rotz to Henry VIII now in the British Museum*, ed. H. Wallis (Oxford, 1981)

Sacrorum conciliorum amplissima collectio, ed. Giovanni Domenico Mansi *et al.*, 53 vols. (Paris, 1901–27)

Sánchez Marín, José A., *La Austríada de Juan Latino* (Granada, 1981)

Sanuto, Marin, *I diarii*, ed. R. Fulin *et al.*, 58 vols. (Venice, 1879–1903)

Sanuto, Marino, *De origine, situ et magistratibus urbis Venetae ovver la città di Venetia (1493–1530)*, ed. A. Caracciolo Aricò (Milan, 1980)

Schedel, Hartmann, *Liber cronicarum* (Nuremberg, 1493)

Segni, Bernardo, *Storie fiorentine di messer Bernardo Segni, dall'anno MDXXVII al MDLV*, ed. Glauco Masi, 3 vols. (2nd edn, Livorno, 1830)

Sousa, D. António Caetano de, *Provas da História Genealógica da Casa Real Portuguesa*, 6 vols. (Lisbon, 1735–49)

Swift, Jonathan, *On Poetry: A Rapsody* (London, 1733)

Synodus diocesana celebrata ab illustrissimo et reverendissimo domino Domino Ioannettino Doria S. R. E. Cardinale et Archiepiscopo Panormitano, Anno Domini M.DC.XV. (Palermo, 1615)

Teles, Baltasar (Padre), *Cronica da Companhia de Jesu em Portugal* (Lisbon, 1645–7)

Tetzel, Gabriel, *Des böhmischen Herrn Leo's von Rožmital Ritter-, Hof- und Pilger-Reise durch die Abendlande, 1465–67* (Stuttgart, 1844)

The Gouernaunce of Prynces [1422] (London, 1898)

Usoz y Río, Luis de (ed.), *Cancionero de obras de burlas provocantes a risa* ('Madrid', i.e. London, 1842)

Varazze, Iacopo da, *Legenda aurea*, ed. Giovanni Paolo Maggioni, 2 vols. (Florence, 1998)

Varchi, Benedetto, *Storia fiorentina*, ed. Gaetano Milanesi, 2 vols. (Florence, 1863)

Vecellio, Cesare, *Degli habiti antichi et moderni di diversi parte del mondo* (Venice, 1590)

Vega, Lope de, *La dama boba*, ed. Diego Marín (Madrid, 1985)

Vicente, Gil, *Copilaçam de Todalas Obras*, ed. Maria Leonor Carvalhão Buescu, 2 vols. (Lisbon, 1983)

  'Farsa dos Almocreves', in *Copilaçam de Todaslas Obras de Gil Vicente*, ed. Maria Leonor Carvalhão Buescu, 2 vols. (Lisbon, 1983)

Vives, Juan Luis, *The Passions of the Soul* [1538], trans. Carlos G. Noreña (Lewiston, NY and Lampeter, 1990)

Weever, John, *Epigrammes in the Oldest Cut and Newest Fashion* [1599] (London, 1911)

Ximénez de Enciso, Diego, *El encubierto. Juan Latino*, ed. Eduardo Juliá Martínez (Madrid, 1951)

Zayas, María de, 'El prevenido engañado' [Zaragoza, 1637], in *Novelas amorosas y ejemplares compuestas por Doña María de Zayas y Sotomayor* (Madrid, 2000)

Zurara, Gomes Eanes de, *Crónica de Guiné*, ed. José de Bragança (2nd edn, Oporto, 1973)

  Crónica dos Feitos Notáveis que se Passaram na Conquista da Guiné por Mandado do Infante D. Henrique, ed. Torquato de Sousa Soares, 2 vols. (Lisbon, 1978–81)

SECONDARY SOURCES

Albaret, Pol de Léon, O. F. M., 'Benedict the Black', in Malachy Carroll and Pol de Léon Albaret, *Three Studies in Simplicity: Padre Pio, Martin de Porres, Benedict the Black* (Chicago, 1974)

Alçada, João Nuno, 'Novo significado da presença de *Todo o Mundo* e *Ninguém* no *Auto da Lusitânia*', *Arquivos do Centro Cultural Português*, 21 (1985), pp. 199–271

Alegria, José Augusto, *História da Capela e Colégio dos Santos Reis de Vila Viçosa* (Lisbon, 1983)

Alencastro, L. F. de, *O Tratado dos Viventes* (2nd edn, São Paulo, 2000)

Allport, Gordon W., *The Nature of Prejudice* (Boston, 1954)

Almeida, Fortunato de, *História da Igreja em Portugal*, 4 vols. (Oporto, 1968)

Almeida, Justino Mendes de, *Edições Seiscentistas Raríssimas de Literatura Popular* (Oporto, 1940)

Amadei, Giuseppe *et al.*, *Il Palazzo d'Arco in Mantova* (Mantua, 1980)

Anderson, Jaynie, *Judith* (Paris, 1997)

Anderson, Ruth Matilda, *Hispanic Costume, 1480–1530* (New York, 1979)

Andree, Richard, 'Menschenschädel als Trinkgefäße', *Zeitschrift des Vereins für Volkskunde*, 22 (1912), pp. 1–33

Angiolini, Franco, 'Schiave', in Angela Groppi (ed.), *Il lavoro delle donne* (Rome, 1996), pp. 92–115

'Slaves and slavery in early modern Tuscany (1500–1700)', *Italian History and Culture*, 3 (1997), pp. 67–86

Anglo, Sydney, 'The court festivals of Henry VII: a study based upon the account books of John Heron, treasurer of the chamber', *Bulletin of the John Rylands Library*, 43 (1960), pp. 12–45

The Martial Arts of Renaissance Europe (New Haven and London, 2000)

Anthiaume, A., *Cartes marines, constructions navales, voyages de découverte chez les Normands, 1500–1650*, 2 vols. (Paris, 1916)

Asseline, David, *Les Antiquités et chroniques de la ville de Dieppe*, ed. M. Hardy *et al.*, 2 vols. (Dieppe, 1874)

Auf's Ohr geschaut. Ohrringe aus Stadt und Land vom Klassizismus bis zur neuen Jugendkultur, Berlin, Museum für Deutsche Volkskunde, Staatliche Museen Preußischer Kulturbesitz (Berlin, 1989)

Aymard, Maurice, 'De la traite aux chiourmes: la fin de l'esclavage dans la Sicile moderne', *Bulletin de l'Institut Historique Belge de Rome*, fascicule XLIV: *Miscellanea Charles Verlinden* (Rome, 1974), pp. 1–21

Azevedo, Lúcio de, *História dos Cristãos-Novos Portugueses* (3rd edn, Lisbon, 1989)

Azevedo, Pedro de, 'Os Escravos', *Archivo Historico Portuguez*, 1 (1903), pp. 289–307

'Os Ciganos em Portugal nos Séculos XVI e XVII', *Archivo Historico Portuguez*, 7 (1909), pp. 42–52

'Os Escravos em Portugal de 1580 a 1816', *Miscelânea Científica e Literária Dedicada ao Doutor J. Leite de Vasconcellos*, 1 (1934), pp. 458–85

Babelon, Ernest, *Catalogue des camées antiques et modernes de la Bibliothèque Nationale* (Paris, 1897)

Babelon, Jean, *Jacopo da Trezzo et la construction de l'Escurial. Essai sur les arts à la cour de Philippe II* (Paris, 1922)

Bacchi, Andrea, *Scultura del '600 a Roma* (Milano, 1996)

Badisches Landesmuseum. Bildkatalog. 400 ausgewählte Werke aus den Schausammlungen (Karlsruhe, 1976)

Balard, Michel, 'Esclavage en Crimée et sources fiscales génoises au XVe siècle', in H. Bresc (ed.), *Figures de l'esclave au Moyen-Age et dans le monde moderne* (Paris and Montreal, 1996), pp. 77–87

Banti, Anna, *Giovanni da San Giovanni, pittore della contraddizione* (Florence, 1977)

Banzato, Davide and Pellegrini, Franca, *Bronzi e placchette dei Musei Civici di Padova* (Padua, 1989)

Bargellini, Piero, *La spendida storia di Firenze dal duca d'Atene a Cosimo I* (Florence, 1964)

Barkindo, B. M., 'Kanem-Borno: its relations with the Mediterranean Sea, Bargirmi and other states in the Chad basin', in *General History of Africa*, 8 vols., v: *Africa from the Sixteenth to the Eighteenth Century*, ed. B. A. Ogot (Berkeley, CA, 1992), pp. 492–514

Barocchi, Paola (ed.), *Il giardino di San Marco: maestri e compagni del giovane Michelangelo* (Florence, 1992)

Baron, Hans, *The Crisis of the Early Italian Renaissance* (Princeton, 1966)

Bartels, Emily C., 'Othello and Africa: Postcolonialism Reconsidered', *The William and Mary Quarterly*, 54: 1 (1997), pp. 45–64

Barthelemy, Anthony Gerard, *Black Face, Maligned Race* (Baton Rouge and London, 1987)

Bassani, Ezio and Fagg, William B., *Africa and the Renaissance: Art in Ivory* (Munich/New York, 1988)

Battaglia, Salvatore (ed.), *Grande dizionario della lingua italiana*, 21 vols. (Turin, 1961–2002)

Beaurepaire, Charles de Robillard de, 'Recherches sur les établissements d'instruction publique et la population dans l'ancien diocèse de Rouen', *Mémoires de la Société des antiquaires de Normandie*, 28 (1871), pp. 225–360

Berardinelli, Cleonice, 'Quatrocentos Anos de Chiado', *Revista da Biblioteca Nacional*, series 2, 6: 1 (1991), pp. 7–19

Berenson, Bernard, *The Study and Criticism of Italian Art. Second Series* (London, 1902)

Berger, Ursel and Krahn, Volker, *Bronzen der Renaissance und des Barock. Katalog der Sammlung. Herzog Anton Ulrich-Museum Braunschweig* (Brunswick, 1994)

Bernard, Alexis, 'Les esclaves à Seville au XVIIe siècle', Ph.D. dissertation, Université de Lyon II, 1998

Bernardes, José Augusto Cardoso, *Sátira e Lirismo: Modelos de Síntese no Teatro de Gil Vicente* (Coimbra, 1996)

Beshah, Girma and Aregay, Merid Wolde, *The Question of the Union of the Churches in Luso-Ethiopian Relations (1500–1632)* (Lisbon, 1964)

Bettini, Sergio, *Botticelli* (Bergamo, 1942)

Biblios: Enciplopédia Verbo das Literaturas de Língua Portuguesa (Lisbon, 1995–)

Bigazzi, Isabella, *Il Palazzo Nonfinito* (Bologna, 1977)

Black, Christopher, *Italian Confraternities in the Sixteenth Century* (Cambridge, 1989)

Blackman, Barbara Winston, '"From time immemorial": historicism in the court art of Benin, Nigeria', in Christian Heck and Kristen Lippincott (eds.), *Symbols of Time in the History of Art* (Turnhout, 2002), pp. 27–39

Blumenthal, Debra G., 'Implements of labor, instruments of honor: Muslim, Eastern and black African slaves in fifteenth-century Valencia', Ph.D. dissertation, University of Toronto, 2000

Bongi, Salvatore, 'Le schiave orientali in Italia', *Nuova antologia di scienze, lettere ed arti*, 2 (1866), pp. 215–46

Bontinck, François, 'Ndoadidiki Ne-Kinu a Mumemba, premier évêque du Kongo (*c.* 1495–*c.* 1531)', *Revue Africaine de Théologie* [Kinshasa], 3 (1979), pp. 149–69

Boose, Lynda E., '"The getting of a lawful race": Racial discourse in early modern England and the unrepresentable black woman', in Margo Hendricks and Patricia Parker (eds.), *Women, 'Race', and Writing in the Early Modern Period* (London and New York, 1994), pp. 35–54

Börner, Lore, *Bestandskataloge des Münzkabinetts Berlin. Die italienischen Medaillen der Renaissance und des Barock (1450–1750)* (Berlin, 1997)

Braga, Isabel Mendes Drumond, 'A Vivência de uma Religiosidade Diferente: os Mouriscos Portugueses entre a Cruz e o Crescente', *Piedade Popular* (Lisbon, 1999), pp. 111–32

Brásio, António, *Os Pretos em Portugal* (Lisbon, 1944)

Bratchel, Michael E., *Lucca, 1430–1494. The Reconstruction of an Italian City-Republic* (Oxford, 1995)

Braude, Benjamin, 'The sons of Noah and the construction of ethnic and geographical identities in the medieval and modern periods', *The William and Mary Quarterly*, third series, 54: 1 (1997), pp. 103–42

Braudel, Fernand, *The Mediterranean and the Mediterranean World in the Age of Philip II*, trans. Siân Reynolds from 2nd rev. edn (New York, 1972)

Bresc, Henri, *Un monde méditerranéen: économie et société en Sicile, 1300–1450*, 2 vols. (Rome and Palermo, 1986)

Bresc-Bautier, Genevieve, Leroy-Jay Lemaistre, Isabelle and Scherf, Guilhem, *Musée du Louvre. Département des Sculptures du Moyen-Age, de la Renaissance et des Temps Modernes. Sculpture française*, II, *Renaissance et Temps Modernes*, 2 vols. (Paris, 1998)

Brodman, James, *Ransoming Captives in Crusader Spain: The Order of Merced on the Christian–Islamic Frontier* (Philadelphia, 1980)

Broglio, Emilio (ed.), *Novo vocabolario della lingua italiana secondo l'uso di Firenze*, 4 vols. (Florence, 1870–97)

Brown, Clifford and Delmarcel, Guy, with Lorenzoni, Anna Maria, *Tapestries for the Courts of Federico II, Ercole, and Ferrante Gonzaga, 1522–1563* (Seattle, 1996)

Brown, Clifford M. and Lorenzoni, Anna Maria, 'Isabella d'Este e Giorgio Brognolo nell'anno 1496', *Atti e Memorie della Academia Virgiliana di Mantova*, n.s., 41 (1973), pp. 97–122

Brown, David Alan, 'Mantegna's Judiths', presentation at 1993 conference, 'Italian art in public and private collections; new attributions/new iconography', Fordham University, New York City

Brown, Peter, *The Cult of the Saints: Its Rise and Function in Latin Christianity* (London, 1981)

Buckland, W. W., *The Roman Law of Slavery: The Condition of the Slave in Private Law from Augustus to Justinian* (Cambridge, 1908)

Bückling, Maraike, *Die Negervenus* (Frankfurt am Main, 1991)

Bugner, Ladislas (general ed.), *The Image of the Black in Western Art*, 4 vols. in 6 tomes (New York, 1976 – Houston, 1989)

Bulliet, Richard W., *The Camel and the Wheel* (Cambridge, MA, 1975)

Burckhardt, Jacob, *The Civilization of the Renaissance in Italy*, trans. and ed. S. G. C. Middlemore (London, Bombay and Sydney, 1929)

Caetano, Joaquim Oliveira, 'O Que Janus Via. Rumos e Cenários da Pintura Portuguesa (1535–1570)', MA thesis, Universidade Nova, Lisbon, 1996

Campbell, Lorne, *Renaissance Portraits. European Portrait-Painting in the Fourteenth, Fifteenth and Sixteenth Centuries* (New Haven, 1990)

Campbell, Malcolm, 'Il ritratto del duca Alessandro de' Medici di Giorgio Vasari: Contesto e significato', in Gian Carlo Garfagnini (ed.), *Girogio Vasari tra decorazione ambientale e storiografia artistica* (Florence, 1985), pp. 339–61

Campbell, Tony, 'Portolan charts of the late thirteenth century to 1500', in J. B. Harley and David Woodward (eds.), *The History of Cartography*, I: *Cartography in Prehistoric, Ancient and Medieval Europe and the Mediterranean* (Chicago and London, 1987), pp. 371–463

Campori, Giuseppe, 'Notizie dei miniatori dei principi Estensi', *Atti e Memorie delle RR. Deputazioni di storia patria per le provincie modenesi e parmensi*, 6 (1872), pp. 245–73

Cappelletto, G., *Storia di famiglie. Matrimonio, biografie famigliari e identità locale in una comunità dell'Italia centrale: Poppi dal XVIII al XIX secolo* (Venice, 1996)

Caraman, Philip, *The Lost Empire: The Story of the Jesuits in Ethiopia 1555–1634* (Notre Dame, 1985)

Caro Baroja, Julio, *Los moriscos del reino de Granada. Ensayo de historia social* (2nd edn, Madrid, 1976)

Carr, Dawson, *Andrea Mantegna: The Adoration of the Magi* (Los Angeles, 1997)

Casini, Bruno, *Aspetti della vita economica e sociale di Pisa dal catasto del 1428–1429* (Pisa, 1965)

Cassandro, Michele, 'Affari e uomini d'affari fiorentini a Napoli sotto Ferrante I d'Aragona (1472–1495)', in *Studi di storia economica toscana nel Medioevo e nel Rinascimento in memoria di Federigo Melis* (Pisa, 1987), pp. 103–23

Castilho, Júlio de, *A Ribeira de Lisboa*, 5 vols. (4th edn, Lisbon, 1981)

Castle, Jo, 'Amulets and protection: pomanders', *Bulletin of the Society of Renaissance Studies*, 27: 2 (May 2000), pp. 12–18

Cecchetti, B., 'La donna nel medioevo a Venezia', *Archivio veneto*, 31 (1886), pp. 33–69 and 307–49

Cerejeira, Manuel Gonçalves, *O Renascimento em Portugal: Clenardo e a Sociedade Portuguesa* (Coimbra, 1974)

Chaplin, Joyce E., *Subject Matter. Technology, the Body, and Science on the Anglo-American Frontier, 1500–1676* (Cambridge, MA, 1991)

Christian IV and Europe (exhibition catalogue), Copenhagen, Rosenborg Castle, Nationalmuseet, Statens Museum for Kunst (Copenhagen, 1988)

Ciabani, Roberto *et al.*, *Le famiglie di Firenze*, 3 vols. (Florence, 1982–92)

Ciletti, Elena, 'Patriarchal ideology in the Renaissance iconography of Judith', in Marilyn Migiel and Juliana Schiesari (eds.), *Refiguring Women: Perspectives on Gender and the Italian Renaissance* (Ithaca, 1991), pp. 35–70

Coates, Timothy, 'State-sponsored female colonization in the *Estado da India*', *Santa Barbara Portuguese Studies*, 2 (1995), pp. 40–56

Cohen, Jeffrey Jerome, 'On Saracen enjoyment: some fantasies of race in late medieval France and England', *The Journal of Medieval and Early Modern Studies*, 31: 1 (2001), pp. 113–46

Colin, Susi, *Das Bild des Indianers im 16. Jahrhundert* (Idstein, 1988)

Congresso Internacional Bartolomeu Dias e a Sua Época: Actas, 5 vols. (Oporto, 1989)

Constable, Olivia Remie, 'Muslim slavery and Mediterranean slavery: the medieval slave trade as an aspect of Muslim-Christian relations', in S. L. Waugh and P. Diehl (eds.), *Christendom and its Discontents* (Cambridge, 1996), pp. 264–84

Conti, Cosimo, *La prima reggia di Cosimo I de' Medici nel palazzo già della Signoria di Firenze descritta ed illustrata* (Florence, 1893)

Conti, L., 'A Igreja Católica e o tráfico negreiro', *O Tráfico de Escravos Negros Sécs. XV-XIX: Documentos de Trabalho e Relatório de Reunião de Peritos Organizada pela UNESCO em Port-au-Prince, Haiti, de 31 de Janeiro a 4 de Fevereiro de 1978*, trans. António Luz Correia (Lisbon, 1979)

Corominas, J., *Diccionario crítico-etimológico de la lengua castellana*, 4 vols. (Berne, 1954)

Cortes, Vicenta, *La esclavitud en Valencia durante el reinado de los Reyes Católicos (1479–1516)* (Valencia, 1964)

Cowhig, Ruth, 'Blacks in English Renaissance drama and the role of Shakespeare's Othello', in David Dabydeen (ed.), *The Black Presence in English Literature* (Manchester, 1985), pp. 1–25

Crollalanza, Giovanni Battista di, *Dizionario storico-blasonico delle famiglie nobili e notabili italiane estinte e fiorenti*, 3 vols. (Pisa, 1886–90)

Cumming, W. P., Skelton, R. A. and Quinn, D. B., *The Discovery of North America* (London, 1971)

Cummins, J. G. (ed.), *The Spanish Traditional Lyric* (Oxford, 1977)

Curtin, Philip D., *Cross-Cultural Trade in World History* (Cambridge, 1984)

d'Essling, Prince, *Les livres à figures vénitiens*, 3 parts in 5 vols. (Florence, 1907–15)

Dalton, Karen C. C., 'Art for the sake of dynasty: the black emperor in the Drake Jewel and Elizabethan imperial imagery', in Peter Erickson and Clark Hulse (eds.), *Early Modern Visual Culture: Representation, Race, and Empire in Renaissance England* (Philadelphia, 2000), pp. 178–214

Davis, Angela, 'The meaning of emancipation according to black women', in Angela Davis (ed.), *Women, Race and Class* (London, 1982)

Debrunner, Hans Werner, *Presence and Prestige: Africans in Europe. A History of Africans in Europe before 1918* (Basel, 1979)

DeCaro, G., 'Burali, Paolo (Scipione)', in *Dizionario biografico degli italiani*, 15 (1972), pp. 370–6

Del Treppo, Mario, 'Aspetti dell'attività bancaria a Napoli nel '400', in *Aspetti della vita economica medievale* (Florence, Prato and Pistoia, 10–14.III.1984) (Florence, 1985), pp. 557–601

Del Treppo, Mario, 'Il re e il banchiere. Strumenti e processi di razionalizzazione dello stato aragonese di Napoli', in G. Rossetti (ed.), *Spazio, società, potere nell'Italia dei comuni* (Naples, 1986), pp. 229–304

Delisle, L. V., 'Le cartographe dieppois Pierre Desceliers', *Journal des Savants* (1902), p. 674

Deschamps, Hubert, *Histoire de la traite des noirs de l'antiquité à nos jours* (Paris, 1971)

Desmarquets, Charles, *Mémoires chronologiques pour servir à l'histoire de Dieppe*, 2 vols. (Paris, 1785)

Deuchler, Florens, 'Eine süddeutsche Hutagraffe um 1600', *Jahrbuch des Bernischen Historischen Museums*, 49–50 (1959–60), pp. 82–90

Devisse, Jean and Labib, S., 'Africa in inter-continental relations', in *General History of Africa*, 8 vols., IV: *Africa from the Twelfth to the Sixteenth Century*, ed. D. T. Niane (Berkeley, CA, 1984), pp. 635–72

Devisse, Jean and Mollat, Michel, *L'image du noir dans l'art occidental*, II, *Des premiers siècles chrétiens aux 'Grandes Découvertes'*, 2, *Les Africains dans l'ordonnance chrétienne du monde (XIVe–XVIe siècle)* (Fribourg, 1979)

  The Image of the Black in Western Art, II, *From the Early Christian Era to the 'Age of Discovery'*, part 2, *Africans in the Christian Ordinance of the World (Fourteenth to the Sixteenth Century)* (New York, 1979)

Devisse, Jean with Courtès, Jean Marie, *The Image of the Black in Western Art*, II, *From the Early Christian Era to the 'Age of Discovery'*, part 1, *From the Demonic Threat to the Incarnation of Sainthood* (New York, 1979)

Di Natale, Maria Concetta (ed.), *Le confraternite dell'arcidiocesi di Palermo: storia e arte* (Palermo, 1993)

Dias, João José Alves (ed.), *Portugal do Renascimento à Crise Dinástica* (Lisbon, 1998)

Dias, José Sebastião da Silva, *A Política Cultural da Época de D. João III*, 2 vols. (Coimbra, 1969)

Díaz Borrás, Andrés, 'Notas sobre los primeros tiempos de la atención valenciana a la redención de cautivos cristianos (1323–1399)', *Estudis Castellonencs*, 3 (1986), pp. 337–54

'Los redentores Valencianos de cautivos sarracenos durante el siglo XV', in Maria Teresa Ferrer i Mallol and Josefina Mutgé i Vives (eds.), *De L'Esclavitud a la Llibertat. Esclaus i Lliberts a L'Edat Mitjana* (Barcelona, 2000), pp. 511–26

Diaz, Furio, *Il granducato di Toscana: I Medici* (Turin, 1976)

Dicionário das Literaturas Portuguesa, Galega e Brasileira, ed. Jacinto do Prado Coelho (Oporto, 1960)

Die Beschwörung des Kosmos (exhibition catalogue), Duisburg, Wilhelm Lehmbruck-Museum (Duisburg, 1994)

Die Kunstdenkmale des Königreiches Bayern, 1, Oberbayern, part 2 (Munich, 1902)

Dielitz, J., *Die Wahl- und Denksprüche, Feldgeschreie, Losungen, Schlacht- und Volksrufe* (Frankfurt am Main, 1887)

Diffie, Bailey W. and Winius, George D., *Foundations of the Portuguese Empire, 1415–1580* (Minneapolis, 1977)

Dillard, J. A., *Black Names* (The Hague, 1976)

Doerig, J. A., 'La situación de los esclavos a partir de las *Siete Partidas* de Alfonso el Sabio (Estudio histórico-crítico)', *Folia humanística*, 4:40 (1966), pp. 337–61

Domínguez Ortiz, Antonio, 'La esclavitud en Castilla durante la Edad Moderna', in C. Viñas y Mey (ed.), *Estudios de historia social de España*, 5 vols. (Madrid, 1949–60), II, pp. 367–428

Domínguez Ortiz, Antonio and Vincent, Bernard, *Historia de los moriscos. Vida y tragedia de una minoría* (Madrid, 1979)

Douglas, Mary, *Purity and Danger: An Analysis of Concepts of Pollution and Taboo* (London, 1966)

Druce, G. C., 'Some abnormal and composite human forms in English church architecture', *Archaeological Journal*, 72 (1915), pp. 135–86

Dutra, Francis A., 'A hard-fought struggle for recognition: Manuel Gonçalves Doria, first Afro-Brazilian to become a Knight of Santiago', *The Americas*, 56 (1 July 1990), pp. 91–113

Ebersole, Alva V., ' "Black is beautiful" in seventeenth-century Spain', *Romance Notes*, 12 (1971), pp. 387–91

Edelstein, Bruce, 'Bronzino in the service of Cosimo I de' Medici and Eleonora di Toledo, together and apart', presentation at the Annual Meeting of the College Art Association, Boston, 1996

Edwards, Paul, 'The Early African presence in the British Isles', in Jagdish S. Gundara and Ian Duffield (eds.), *Essays on the History of Blacks in Britain: From Roman Times to the Mid-Twentieth Century* (Aldershot, 1992), pp. 9–29

Eikelmann, Renate (ed.), *Bayerisches Nationalmuseum. Handbuch der kunst- und kulturgeschichtlichen Sammlungen* (Munich, 2000)

  Der Mohrenkopfpokal von Christoph Jamnitzer (exhibition catalogue), Munich, Bayerisches Nationalmuseum (Munich, 2002)

Ekserdjian, David, *Correggio* (New Haven, 1997)

Elbl, Ivana, 'Prestige considerations and the changing interest of the Portuguese crown in sub-Saharan Atlantic Africa, 1444–1580', *Portuguese Studies Review*, 10 (2003), pp. 15–36

Elias, Norbert, *The Civilizing Process* (New York, 1982)

Epstein, Steven A., *Speaking of Slavery: Color, Ethnicity and Human Bondage in Italy* (Ithaca and London, 2001)

Erben, Dietrich, 'Die Reiterdenkmäler der Medici in Florenz und ihre politische Bedeutung', *Mitteilungen des Kunsthistorischen Institutes in Florenz*, 40 (1996), pp. 287–361

Espanca, Túlio, 'Visitas de Embaixadores Célebres, Reis, Príncipes e Arcebispos a Évora nos Séculos XV–XVIII', *A Cidade de Évora*, 27–8 (1952), pp. 139–246

Eubel, Conrad *et al.*, *Hierarchia catholica medii aevi*, 8 vols. (2nd edn, Padua, 1913–78)

Euw, Antan von and Plotzek, Joachim M., *Die Handschriften der Sammlung Ludwig*, 4 vols. (Cologne, 1979–85)

Evans, William McKee, 'From the land of Canaan to the land of Guinea: the strange odyssey of the "Sons of Ham"', *American Historical Review*, 85 (1980), pp. 15–43

Even, Yael, 'The Loggia dei Lanzi: a showcase of female subjugation', *Woman's Art Journal*, 12 (1991), pp. 10–14

  'Mantegna's Uffizi *Judith*: the masculinization of the female hero', *Konsthistorisk Tidskrift*, 61 (1992), pp. 8–20

Exotisch – höfisch – bürgerlich. Afrikaner in Württemberg vom 15. bis 19. Jahrhundert (exhibition catalogue), Stuttgart, Hauptstaatsarchiv Stuttgart (Stuttgart, 2001)

Fabbri, Maria Cecilia, 'La sistemazione seicentesca dell'Oratorio di San Sebastiano nella Santissima Annunziata', *Rivista d'arte*, 44 (1992), pp. 71–152

Falk, Brigitta, 'Bildnisreliquiare. Zur Entstehung und Entwicklung der metallenen Kopf-, Büsten- und Halbfigurenreliquiare im Mittelalter', *Aachener Kunstblätter*, 59 (1991–3), pp. 171–5

Falke, Otto von, 'Aus dem Jamnitzerkreis', *Pantheon*, 19 (1937)

Féret, P.-J., *Histoire des bains de Dieppe* (Dieppe, 1855)

Ferrai, L. A., *Lorenzino de' Medici e la società cortigiana del cinquecento* (Milan, 1891)

Ferrer i Mallol, Maria Teresa, 'La redempcio de captius a la corona catalano-aragonesa (segle XIV)', *Anuario de estudios medievales*, 15 (1985), pp. 237–97

  'Els redemptors de captius: mostolafs, eixees o alfaquecs (segles XII–XIII)', *Medievalia*, 9 (1990), pp. 85–106

Filesi, Teobaldo, 'Enrico, figlio del re del Congo, primo vescovo dell' Africa nera (1518)', *Euntes Docete*, 19 (1966), pp. 365–85

Le relazioni tra il regno del Congo e la Sede Apostolica nel XVI secolo (Como, 1968)

Filesi, Teobaldo and de Villapadierna, Isidoro, *La 'missio antiqua' dei cappuccini nel Congo (1645–1835): studio preliminare e guida delle fonti* (Rome, 1978)

Fischer, Joseph and Wieser, Franz Ritter von, *Die älteste Karte mit dem Namen Amerika aus dem Jahre 1507 und die Carta Marina aus dem Jahre 1516 des M. Waldseemüller (Ilacomilus)* (Innsbruck and London, 1903)

Fisher, Will, 'The Renaissance beard: masculinity in early modern England', *Renaissance Quarterly*, 54 (2001), pp. 155–87

Fiume, Giovanna, 'Il processo "De Cultu" a Fra' Benedetto da San Fratello (1734)', in Giovanna Fiume (ed.), *Il santo patrono e la città. San Benedetto il Moro: culti, devozioni, strategie di età moderna* (Venice, 2000), pp. 231–52

Fiume, Giovanna and Modica, Marilena (eds.), *San Benedetto il moro: santità, agiografia e primi processi di canonizzazione* (Palermo, 1998)

Fletcher, Jennifer, 'Isabella d'Este, patron and collector', in David Chambers and Jane Martineau (eds.), *Splendours of the Gonzaga* (exhibition catalogue) (London, 1981)

Flores d'Arcais, Francesca, *Guariento* (Venice, 1965)

Floyd-Wilson, Mary, 'Temperature, temperance, and racial difference in Ben Jonson's *The Masque of Blackness*', *English Literary Renaissance*, 28:2 (1998), pp. 183–209

Flynn, Maureen, *Sacred Charity: Confraternities and Social Welfare in Spain, 1400–1700* (Ithaca, 1989)

Fonseca, Jorge, *Os Escravos em Évora no Século XVI* (Évora, 1997)
   'Escravos em Vila Viçosa', *Callipole*, 5–6 (1997–8), pp. 25–50
   Escravos no Sul de Portugal: Séculos XVI–XVII (Lisbon, 2002)

Fra Molinero, Baltasar, 'La formación del estereotipo del negro en las letras hispanas: el caso de tres coplas en pliegos sueltos', *Romance Languages Annual*, 3 (1991), pp. 438–43
   La imagen de los negros en el teatro del Siglo de Oro (Madrid, 1995)

Franco Silva, Alfonso, *La esclavitud en Sevilla y su tierra a fines de la Edad Media* (Seville, 1979)

Freiesleben, Hans-Christian, *Der katalanische Weltatlas vom Jahre 1375* (Stuttgart, 1977)

Friedländer, Max J., *Early Netherlandish Painting from Van Eyck to Bruegel* (London, 1956)
   Early Netherlandish Painting, 14 vols. in 16 tomes (Leiden, 1967–76)

Friedman, Ellen, *Spanish Captives in North Africa in the Early Modern Age* (Madison, 1983)

Friedman, John B., *The Monstrous Races in Medieval Art and Thought* (Cambridge, MA and London, 1981)

Fries, Laurent, *Carta marina universalis 1530* (Munich, 1926)
   Carta marina. Faksimile – Ausgabe einschliesslich der 'Uslegung' (Unterschneidheim, 1972)

Fritz, Rolf, *Die Gefäße aus Kokosnuß in Mitteleuropa, 1250–1800* (Mainz, 1983)

Fryer, Peter, *Staying Power: The History of Black People in Britain* (London, 1984)

Furió, Antoni, *Història del País Valencià* (Valencia, 1995)

Gaborit, J.-R., *Le Louvre. La sculpture européenne* (London/Paris, 1994)

Gaffarel, P., 'Jean Ango', *Bulletin de la Société normande de géographie*, 11 (1889), pp. 262–4

Galluzzi, Riguccio, *Istoria del granducato di Toscana* (Milan, 1974)

García Gallo, Alfonso, 'Las bulas de Alejandro VI y el ordenamiento jurídico de la expansión portuguesa y castellana en Africa e Indias', *Anuario de historia del derecho español*, 27–8 (1957–8), pp. 765–75

Garrad, K., 'The original Memorial of Don Francisco Núñez Muley', *Atlante*, II:4 (1954), pp. 168–226

Garretson, Peter P., 'A note on relations between Ethiopia and the Kingdom of Aragon in the fifteenth century', *Rassegna di studi etiopici*, 37 (1993), pp. 37–44

Gates, Henry Louis, Jr, *The Signifying Monkey: A Theory of African-American Literary Criticism* (New York, 1988)

Gates, Henry Louis, Jr and Wolff, Maria, 'An overview of sources on the life and work of Juan Latino, the "Ethiopian humanist"', *Research in African Literatures*, 29:4 (1998), pp. 14–51

Gaudioso, Matteo, *La schiavitù domestica in Sicilia dopo i normanni: Legislazione, dottrina, formule* (2nd rev. edn, Catania, 1979)

Gemin, Massimo and Pedrocco, Filippo, *Giambattista Tiepolo* (Venice, 1993)

Gensini, Sergio (ed.), *Il cuoio e le pelli in Toscana: produzione e mercato nel tardo medioevo e nell'età moderna* (San Miniato, 21–22.II.1998) (Pisa, 1999)

Genuß & Kunst. Kaffee, Tee, Schokolade, Tabak, Cola (exhibition catalogue), Schloß Schallaburg (Innsbruck, 1994)

George, Katherine, 'The civilized West looks at primitive Africa, 1400–1880', *Isis*, 49 (1958), pp. 62–72

George, Wilma, *Animals and Maps* (London, 1969)

Giglio, Carlo and Lodolini, Elio, *Guida delle fonti per la storia dell'Africa a Sud del Sahara esistenti in Italia*, 2 vols. (Guide des sources de l'histoire de l'Afrique, 5 and 6) (Zug, 1973–4)

Gioffré, Domenico, *Il mercato degli schiavi a Genova nel secolo XV* (Genoa, 1971)

Goddard, Stephen H., 'The Master of Frankfurt and his shop', Ph.D. dissertation, University of Iowa, 1983

Goldthwaite, Richard A., *Private Wealth in Renaissance Florence. A Study of Four Families* (Princeton, 1968)

    The Building of Renaissance Florence (Baltimore, 1980)

Goldthwaite, Richard A. and Mandich, Giulio, *Studi sulla moneta fiorentina (secoli XIII–XVI)* (Florence, 1994)

Gould, Cecil, *The Paintings of Correggio* (Ithaca, 1976)

Goyau, Georges, 'Les débuts de l'apostolat au Congo et dans l'Angola (1482–1590): clergé portugais et apôtres Jésuites. Grandeur et décadence de l'empire chrétien congolais', *Revue d'histoire des Missions*, 7 (1930), pp. 481–514

Graullera Sanz, Vicente, 'Los negros en Valencia en el siglo XVI', *Estudios jurídicos en homenaje al Profesor Santa Cruz Teijeiro*, 2 vols. (Valencia, 1974), I, pp. 391–5

    La esclavitud en Valencia en los siglos xvi y xvii (Valencia, 1978)

Gray, Richard, 'The papacy and the Atlantic slave trade: Lourenço da Silva, the Capuchins and the decisions of the Holy Office', *Past and Present*, 115 (1987), pp. 52–68

Grendler, Paul F. (ed.), *Encyclopedia of the Renaissance*, 6 vols. (New York, 1999)

Griffin, Nigel, ' "Un muro invisible": Moriscos and *cristianos viejos* in Granada', in F. W. Hodcroft, D. G. Pattison, R. D. F. Pring-Mill and R. W. Truman (eds.), *Medieval and Renaissance Studies on Spain and Portugal in Honour of P. E. Russell* (Oxford, 1981), pp. 133–54

Gromicho, António Bartolomeu, 'O Testamento de Garcia de Resende', *A Cidade de Évora*, 13–14 (1947), pp. 3–23

Grosjean, Georges, *Mappa mundi. Der katalanische Weltatlas vom Jahre 1375* (Zurich, 1977)

Grubb, Eileen McGrath, 'Attitudes towards black Africans in imperial Spain', *Legon Journal of the Humanities*, 1 (1974), pp. 68–90

Grundmann, H., *Der Cappenberger Barbarossakopf und die Anfänge des Stiftes Cappenberg* (Cologne/Graz, 1959)

Gruyer, Gustave, *L'art ferrarais à l'époque des princes d'Este*, 2 vols. (Paris, 1897)

Gual Camarena, Miguel, 'Una confradia de negros libertos en el siglo XV', *Estudios de Edad Media de la Corona de Aragon*, 5 (1952), pp. 457–66

Guarnieri, Gino, *I Cavalieri di Santo Stefano nella storia della marina italiana (1562–1859)* (3rd edn, Pisa, 1960)

Gundersheimer, Werner (ed.), *Art and Life at the Court of Ercole I d'Este: The 'De triumphis religionis' of Giovanni Sabadino degli Arienti* (Geneva, 1972)

Habel-Selassie, Sergew, 'The Ge'ez letters of Queen Eleni and Libne Dingil to John, King of Portugal', in *IV Congresso internazionale di studi etiopici*, 2 vols. (Rome, 1974), I, pp. 547–66

Hackenbroch, Yvonne, *Enseignes: Renaissance Hat Jewels* (Florence, 1996)
   Renaissance Jewellery (Munich/New York, 1979)

Hahn, Thomas, 'The difference the Middle Ages makes: color and race before the modern world', *The Journal of Medieval and Early Modern Studies*, 31:1 (2001), pp. 1–37

Hair, P. E. H., 'Black African slaves at Valencia, 1482–1516: an onomastic enquiry', *History in Africa*, 7 (1980), pp. 119–39

Hall, Kim F., *Things of Darkness: Economies of Race and Gender in Early Modern England* (Ithaca and London, 1995)

Hallberg, Ivar, *L'extrême-Orient dans la littérature et la cartographie de l'Occident des XIIIe, XIVe et XVe siècles* (Göteborg, 1907)

Hannaford, Ivan, *Race: The History of an Idea in the West* (Baltimore, 1996)

Harrisse, Henry, *Jean et Sébastien Cabot* (Paris, 1882)
   'The Dieppe World Maps', *Göttingische Gelehrte Anzeigen*, 161 (1899), pp. 437–9

Hartt, Frederick, Corti, Gino and Kennedy, Clarence, *The Chapel of the Cardinal of Portugal, 1434–1459, at San Miniato in Florence* (Philadelphia, 1964)

Haynes, Sybille, *Etruscan Bronzes* (London, 1985)

Hayum, Andrée, *Giovanni Antonio Bazzi – 'Il Sodoma'* (New York, 1976)

Heers, Jacques, *Esclaves et domestiques au Moyen Age dans le monde méditerranéen* (Paris, 1981)

Heikamp, Detlef, *Studien zur mediceischen Glaskunst. Archivalien, Entwurfszeichnungen, Gläser und Scherben* (Florence, 1986)

Hemming, John, *Red Gold. The Conquest of the Brazilian Indians* (rev. edn, London, 1995)

Herculano, Alexandre, *História da Origem e Estabelecimento da Inquisição em Portugal*, 3 vols. (Lisbon, n.d.)

Hervé, Roger, *Mappemonde de Sébastien Cabot . . . 1544* (Paris, 1968)
Découverte fortuite de l'Australie et de la Nouvelle-Zélande par des navigateurs portugais et espagnols entre 1521 et 1528 (Paris, 1982)
'Dieppe, Kartographen von', *Lexikon zur Geschichte der Kartographie*, 2 vols. (Vienna, 1986)

Herzner, Volker, 'Die "Judith" der Medici', *Zeitschrift für Kunstgeschichte*, 43 (1980), pp. 139–80

Hespanha, António Manuel, 'Luís de Molina e a Escravização dos Negros', *Análise Social*, 35 (2001), pp. 937–60

Hieronymus, Frank (ed.), *Basler Buchillustration 1500–1545* (exhibition catalogue) (Oberrheinische Buchillustration, 2), Basel, Universitätsbibliothek, 31 March–30 June 1984 (Basel, 1984)

Hill, John M., 'Notes for the bibliography of Rodrigo de Reynosa', *Hispanic Review*, 14 (1946), pp. 1–21

Hoogland Verkerk, Dorothy, 'Black servant, black demon: color ideology in the Ashburnham Pentateuch', *The Journal of Medieval and Early Modern Studies*, 31:1 (2001), pp. 55–77

Howard, Jean E., 'An English lass amid the Moors', in Margo Hendricks and Patricia Parker (eds.), *Women, 'Race', and Writing in the Early Modern Period* (London and New York 1994), pp. 101–17

Hughes, Diane Owen, 'Distinguishing signs: ear-rings, Jews and Franciscan rhetoric in the Italian Renaissance city', *Past and Present*, 112 (1986), pp. 3–59

Hutchinson, Walter (ed.), *Customs of the World: A Popular Account of the Customs, Rites and Ceremonies of Men and Women of all Countries*, 2 vols. (London, [1912–14])

Inda, Jonathan Xavier, 'Performativity, materiality, and the racial body', *Latino Studies Journal*, 11:3 (2000)

James, M. R., *Marvels of the East. A Full Reproduction of the Three Known Copies, With Introduction* (Oxford, 1929)

Januszkiewicz, B., *Klejnoty i stroje ksiazat Pomorza Zachodniego XVI–XVII wieku* (Warsaw, 1995)

Johnston, Sir Harry *et al.*, *The Living Races of Mankind*, 2 vols. (London 1905, 1906)

Jones, Eldred, *Othello's Countrymen: The African in English Renaissance Drama* (London, 1965)

Jordan, Annemarie, 'Portuguese royal collections (1505–1580): a bibliographic and documentary survey', MA thesis, George Washington University, 1985

'The development of Catherine of Austria's collection in the Queen's household: its character and cost', Ph.D. dissertation, Brown University, 1994

Retrato de Corte em Portugal. O Legado de Antonio Moro (1552–1572) (Lisbon, 1994)

'Queen of the seas and overseas. Dining at the table of Catherine of Austria, Queen of Portugal', in Leonor d'Orey (ed.), *European Royal Tables – International Symposium Acts* (Lisbon, 1996), pp. 14–43

'Exotic Renaissance accessories. Japanese, Indian and Sinhalese fans at the courts of Portugal and Spain', *Apollo*, 150: 453 (1999), pp. 25–35

'Los retratos de Juana de Austria posteriores a 1554: la imagen de una princesa de Portugal, una regente de España y una jesuita', *Reales sitios*, 151 (2002), pp. 42–65

Jordan Gschwend, Annemarie, 'In the tradition of princely collections: curiosities and exotica in the Kunstkammer of Catherine of Austria', *Bulletin of the Society for Renaissance Studies*, 13 (October 1995), pp. 1–9

'Os Produtos Exóticos da Carreira da India e o Papel da Corte Portuguesa na sua Difusão', in *Nossa Senhora dos Mártires: A Última Viagem* (exhibition catalogue) (Lisbon, 1998)

'Los primeros abanicos orientales de los Habsburgos', in *Oriente en palacio. Tesoros asiáticos en las colecciones reales españolas* (Madrid, 2003), pp. 267–71

Jordan Gschwend, Annemarie and Almudena Pérez de Tudela, 'Exotica Habsburgica. La casa de Austria y las colecciones exóticas en el Renacimiento temprano', in *Oriente en palacio. Tesoros asiáticos en las colecciones reales españolas* (Madrid, 2003), pp. 27–44

Kaartinen, Marjo, 'Toinen – vieras. Näkökulmia kolonialistisen toiseuden tutkimukseen', in Kari Immonen and Maarit Leskelä-Kärki (eds.), *Kulttuurihistoria. Näkökulmia tutkimukseen* (Turku, 2001), pp. 387–401

Kabongo, Albert Ndamba, 'Les esclaves à Cordue au debut du XVIIe siècle (1600–1621)', Ph.D. dissertation, Université de Toulouse Le Mirail, 1975

Kamal, Youssouf, *Monumenta cartografica Africae et Aegypti*, 5 vols. (Leiden, 1926–53)

Kammerer, Albert, *La Mer Rouge, l'Abyssinie et l'Arabie depuis l'Antiquité. Essai d'histoire et de géographie historique*, 3 vols. (Mémoires de la Société royale de Géographie d'Egypte, 15–17) (Cairo, 1929–52)

Kaplan, Paul H. D., 'Titian's *Laura Dianti* and the origins of the motif of the black page in portraiture', *Antichità Viva*, 21:1 (1982), pp. 11–18, and 21: 4 (1982), pp. 10–18

'Ruler, saint and servant: blacks in European art to 1520', Ph.D. dissertation, 2 vols., Boston University, 1983

The Rise of the Black Magus in Western Art (Ann Arbor, 1985)

'Sicily, Venice and the East: Titian's *Fabricius Salvaresius with a black page*', in *Europa und die Kunst des Islam: 15. bis 18. Jahrhundert* (Akten des 25. internationalen Kongresses für Kunstgeschichte, 5) (Vienna, 1985), pp. 127–36

'Black Africans in Hohenstaufen iconography', *Gesta*, 26 (1987), pp. 29–36

'The earliest images of Othello', *Shakespeare Quarterly*, 39:2 (1988), pp. 171–86

Kappler, Claude, *Monstres, démons et merveilles à la fin du Moyen Age* (Paris, 1980)

Keniston, Hayward, *The Syntax of Castilian Prose: the Sixteenth Century* (Chicago, 1937)

Keutner, H., 'Über die Entstehung und die Formen des Standbildes im Cinquecento', *Münchner Jahrbuch der bildenden Kunst*, 3rd series, 7 (1956), pp. 138–68

Klapisch-Zuber, Christiane, 'Women servants in Florence (fourteenth and fifteenth centuries)', in B. Hanawalt (ed.), *Women and Work in Preindustrial Europe* (Bloomington, 1986), pp. 56–80

Klemp, Egon, *Africa auf Karten des 12. bis 18. Jahrhunderts* (Leipzig, 1967)

Knight, Alan E., *Aspects of Genre in Late Medieval French Drama* (Manchester, 1983)

Koeppe, Wolfram, 'French and Italian Renaissance furniture at The Metropolitan Museum of Art. Notes on a survey', *Apollo*, 139: 388 (new series) (June 1994), pp. 24–32

Kohlhaussen, Heinrich, 'Der Doppelmaserbecher auf der Veste Coburg und seine Verwandten', *Jahrbuch der Coburger Landesstiftung* (1959), pp. 109–34

Kopplin, Monika, '"Du bist schwarz, doch du bist schön". Zum Bildnis des Mohren in der Kunst des 16. bis 18. Jahrhunderts', *Kunst und Antiquitäte*, 6 (1987), pp. 36–45

Krahn, Volker (ed.), *Von allen Seiten schön. Bronzen der Renaissance und des Barock* (exhibition catalogue), Berlin, Staatliche Museen zu Berlin – Preußischer Kulturbesitz, Skulpturensammlung/Altes Museum (Heidelberg, 1995)

Krausen, Edgar, 'Die Pflege religiös-volksfrommen Brauchtums bei Benediktinern und Zisterziensern in Süddeutschland und Österreich', *Studien und Mitteilungen zur Geschichte des Benediktiner-Ordens und seiner Zweige*, 83 (1972), pp. 274–90

Kris, Ernst, *Goldschmiedearbeiten des Mittelalters, der Renaissance und des Barock*, part I, *Arbeiten in Gold und Silber* (Vienna, 1932) (Publikationen aus den Kunsthistorischen Sammlungen in Wien, V)

Kris, Ernst and Falke, Otto v., 'Beiträge zu den Werken Christoph und Hans Jamnitzers', *Jahrbuch der Preußischen Kunstsammlungen*, 47 (1926), pp. 185–207

Kuehn, Thomas, *Illegitimacy in Renaissance Florence* (Ann Arbor, 2002)

L'Archivio Gonzaga di Mantova, 2 vols. in 1, I ed. Pietro Torelli (Ostiglia, 1920), II ed. Alessandro Luzio (Verona, 1922)

La Corte-Cailler, Gaetano, 'Burle del secolo XVII agli schiavi in Messina', *Archivio per lo studio delle tradizioni popolari: rivista trimestrale diretta da G. Pitrè e S. Salomone-Marino*, 20 (Palermo, 1901), pp. 202–8

La Roncière, Charles de, *La découverte de l'Afrique au moyen-âge. Cartographes et explorateurs*, 2 vols. (Mémoires de la Société royale de Géographie d'Egypte, 5–6) (Cairo, 1925)

Lahusen, Götz and Formigli, Edilberto, *Römische Bildnisse aus Bronze. Kunst und Technik* (Munich, 2001)

Lambert-Gorges, Martine and Postigo, Elena, 'Santiago et la porte fermée: les candidatures malheureuses à l'habit', *Les sociétés fermées dans le monde ibérique (XVI–XVIIIe s.)* (Paris, 1986), pp. 139–68

Langdon, Gabrielle, 'Pontormo and Medici lineages: Maria Salviati, Alessandro, Giulia and Giulio de' Medici', in *Racar, revue d'art canadienne*, 19 (1992), pp. 20–40

Lange, D., 'The kingdoms and peoples of Chad', in *General History of Africa*, 8 vols., IV: *Africa from the Twelfth to the Sixteenth Century*, ed. D. T. Niane (Berkeley, CA, 1984), pp. 238–65

Langedijk, Karla, *The Portraits of the Medici, Fifteenth to Eighteenth Centuries*, 3 vols. (Florence, 1981)

Lawrance, Jeremy, 'The Middle Indies: Damião de Góis on Prester John and the Ethiopians', *Renaissance Studies*, 6 (1992), pp. 306–24

Le Dressoir du Prince. Services d'apparat à la Renaissance (exhibition catalogue), Château d'Écouen, Musée de la Renaissance (Paris, 1995)

Le Siècle de Bruegel: la peinture en Belgique au XVIe siècle (Brussels, 1963)

Lefevre, Renato, 'Roma e la comunità etiopica di Cipro nei secoli XV e XVI', *Annali Lateranensi*, 11 (1947), pp. 277–94

Levack, Brian P., *The Witch-Hunt in Early Modern Europe* (London, 1995)

Levenson, Jay A. (ed.), *Circa 1492: Art in the Age of Exploration* (exhibition catalogue), Washington, National Gallery of Art (New Haven and London, 1991)

Levenson, Jay, Oberhuber, Konrad and Sheehan, Jacquelyn, *Early Italian Engravings from the National Gallery of Art* (Washington, DC, 1973)

Lightbown, Ronald, *Sandro Botticelli*, 2 vols. (Berkeley and London, 1978)
   Mantegna (Berkeley, 1986)
   Sandro Botticelli. Life and Work (New York, 1989)

Lightbown, R. and Tietze-Conrat, E., *Mantegna: Paintings Drawings Engravings* (London, 1955)

Litchfield, R. Burr, *Emergence of a Bureaucracy: The Florentine Patricians, 1530–1790* (Princeton, 1986)

Litta, Pompeo, *Famiglie celebri italiane*, series I, 7 vols., series II, 2 vols. (Milan, 1819–83)

Livi, Ridolfo, 'La schiavitù medioevale e la sua influenza sui caratteri antropologici degli italiani', *Rivista italiana di sociologia*, 11 (1907), pp. 557–81
   La schiavitù domestica nei tempi di mezzo e nei moderni: Ricerche storiche di un antropologo (Padua, 1928)

Lloyd, Joan Barclay, *African Animals in Renaissance Literature and Art* (Oxford, 1971)

Loomba, Ania, *Gender, Race, Renaissance Drama* (Delhi, 1989)

Lopez, Pasquale, *Clero eresia e magia nella Napoli del Viceregno* (Naples, 1984)

Lowe, K. J. P. (ed.), *Cultural Links between Portugal and Italy in the Renaissance* (Oxford, 2000)

Luzio, Alessandro and Renier, Rodolfo, 'Buffoni, schiavi e nani alla corte dei Gonzaga ai tempi d'Isabella d'Este', *Nuova Antologia*, 19 (1891), pp. 112–46

'La coltura e le relazioni letterarie di Isabella d'Este Gonzaga', *Giornale storico della letteratura italiana*, 33 (1899), pp. 1–62

MacDonald, Joyce Green, *Women and Race in Early Modern Texts* (Cambridge, 2002)

Magalhães, Joaquim Romero, 'O Enquadramento do Espaço Nacional', in José Mattoso (ed.), *História de Portugal* (Lisbon, 1993)

Malacarne, Giancarlo, *Il Palazzo Ducale di Mantova* (Mantua, 1996)

Mariani, Ludovico Maria, *San Benedetto da Palermo, il moro Etiope, nato a S. Fratello* (Palermo, 1989)

Marín Ocete, Antonio, *El negro Juan Latino. Ensayo biográfico y crítico* (Granada, 1925)

Mark, Peter, *Africans in European Eyes: The Portrayal of Black Africans in Fourteenth- and Fifteenth-Century Europe* (Syracuse, NY, 1974)

Marrone, Giovanni, *La schiavitù nella società siciliana dell'età moderna* (Caltanissetta, 1972)

Martín Casares, Aurelia, 'La hechicería en la Andalucía Moderna ¿una forma de poder de las mujeres?', in Mary Nash and María José de la Pascua (eds.), *Pautas históricas de sociabilidad femenina: Rituales y modelos de representación* (Cadiz, 1999), pp. 101–12

La esclavitud en la Granada del siglo XVI: género, raza y religión (Granada, 2000)

'Cristianos, musulmanes y animistas: identidades religiosas y sincretismo cultural', in Berta Ares Queija and Alessandro Stella (eds.), *Negros, mulatos, zambaigos: derroteros Africanos en los mundos ibéricos* (Seville, 2000), pp. 207–21

Martin, Peter, *Schwarze Teufel, edle Mohren. Afrikaner in Geschichte und Bewußtsein der Deutschen* (Hamburg, 1993)

Martineau, Jane (ed.), *Andrea Mantegna* (New York, 1992)

Martínez López, Enrique, *Tablero de Ajedrez. Imágenes del negro heroico en la comedia española y en la literatura e iconografía sacra del Brasil esclavista* (Paris, 1998)

Martini, Ferruccio, *Lorenzino de' Medici e il tirannicidio nel rinascimento* (Rome, 1972)

Martins, Mário, *Peregrinações e Livros de Milagres na nossa Idade Média* (Lisbon, 1957)

'O Original em Castelhano do "Flos Sanctorum" de 1513', *Estudos de Cultura Medieval*, 3 vols. (Lisbon and Braga, 1969–83), I, pp. 255–67

Marzal Palacios, Francisco Javier, 'El ciclo de la esclavitud sarracena en la Valencia bajomedieval: esclavización, rescate y vuelta a casa de los esclavos de Cherchell (1409–25)', in Maria Teresa Ferrer i Mallol and Josefina Mutgé i Vives (eds.), *De L'Esclavitud a la Llibertat. Esclaus i Lliberts a L'Edat Mitjana* (Barcelona, 2000), pp. 493–509

Massing, Jean Michel, 'Early European images of America: The ethnographic approach', in J. A. Levenson (ed.), *Circa 1492: Art in the Age of Exploration* (exhibition catalogue), Washington, National Gallery of Art (New Haven and London, 1991), pp. 515–20

'Observations and beliefs: the world of the Catalan Atlas', in J. A. Levenson (ed.), *Circa 1492: Art in the Age of Exploration* (exhibition catalogue), Washington, National Gallery of Art (New Haven and London, 1991), pp. 27–33

'The quest for the exotic: Albrecht Dürer in the Netherlands', in J. A. Levenson (ed.), *Circa 1492: Art in the Age of Exploration* (exhibition catalogue), Washington, National Gallery of Art (New Haven and London, 1991), pp. 115–19

'Hans Burgkmair's depiction of native Africans', *RES Anthropology and Aesthetics*, 27 (1995), pp. 39–51

'La mappemonde de Pierre Desceliers', in Hervé Oursel and Julia Fritsch (eds.), *Henri II et les arts* (Paris, 2003), pp. 231–48

Mauro da Leonessa, P., *Santo Stefano Maggiore degli Abissini e le relazioni romano-etiopiche* (Città del Vaticano, 1929)

McCartney, Eugene S., 'Modern analogues to ancient tales of monstrous races', *Classical Philology*, 36 (1941), pp. 390–4

McHam, Sarah Blake, 'Donatello's bronze *David* and *Judith* as metaphors of Medici rule in Florence', *Art Bulletin*, 83 (2001), pp. 32–47

McKee Evans, William, 'From the land of Canaan to the land of Guinea: the strange odyssey of the "Sons of Ham"', *American Historical Review*, 85 (1980), pp. 15–43

Medeiros, François de, *L'Occident et l'Afrique (XIIIe–XVe siècle)* (Paris, 1985)

'Une structure de domination. La mentalité sous-jacente à la traite négrière et le propos de l'évangélisation au XVIe siècle', *Église et histoire de l'Église en Afrique. Actes du colloque de Bologne, 22–25 octobre 1988*, ed. Giuseppe Ruggieri (Paris, 1988), pp. 29–40

Meillassoux, Claude, *Anthropologie de l'esclavage* (Paris, 1986)

Mendes, Isabel Ribeiro, 'O "Deve" e o "Haver" da Casa da Rainha D. Catarina (1525–1557)', *Arquivos do Centro Cultural Português*, 28 (1990), pp. 191–6

Menéndez Pidal, Ramón, *Los romances de América y otros estudios* (Buenos Aires, 1939)

Meyerson, Mark D., 'Slavery and the social order: Mudejars and Christians in the Kingdom of Valencia', *Medieval Encounters*, 1 (1995), pp. 144–73

'Slavery and solidarity: Mudejars and foreign Muslim captives in the Kingdom of Valencia', *Medieval Encounters*, 2 (1996), pp. 308–9

Miele, Michele, *Die Provinzialkonzilien Süditaliens in der Neuzeit* (Paderborn, 1996)

Miguel, Juan Blázquez, *Herejía e heterodoxia en Talavera y su antigua tierra* (Talavera, 1989)

Miller, Konrad, *Mappaemundi. Die ältesten Weltkarten*, 6 vols. (Stuttgart, 1895–8)

Minnich, Nelson H., 'The Orator of Jerusalem at Lateran V', *Orientalia christiana periodica*, 40 (1974), pp. 364–76

Mirot, Léon, 'L'hôtel et les collections du connétable de Montmorency', *Bibliothèque de l'Ecole des Chartes*, 79 (1918), pp. 311–413, and 80 (1919), pp. 152–229

Molho, Anthony, 'The Italian Renaissance, Made in the USA', in Anthony Molho and Gordon S. Wood (eds.), *Imagined Histories: American Historians Interpret the Past* (Princeton, 1998), pp. 263–94

Mollat du Jourdin, Michel and Habert, Jacques, *Giovanni et Girolamo Verrazano, navigateurs de François 1er* (Paris, 1982)

Mollat du Jourdin, Michel and La Roncière, Monique de, *Sea Charts of the Early Explorers. Thirteenth to Seventeenth Century* (New York, 1984)

Mondovi, Guido (ed.), *Per le fauste nozze Rimini – Todesco – Assagioli 9 Settembre 1883* (Mantua, 1883)

Morabito, Giuseppe, 'Benedetto il moro', in *Bibliotheca Sanctorum*, ed. Filippo Caraffa and Giuseppe Morelli, 12 vols. + index (Rome, 1961–87), II, cols. 1103–4

Morgan, Ronald J., 'Jesuit confessors, African slaves and the practice of confession in seventeenth-century Cartagena', in Katharine Jackson Lualdi and Anne T. Thayer (eds.), *Penitence in the Age of Reformations* (Aldershot, 2000), pp. 222–39

Moses, Wilson Jeremiah, *The Wings of Ethiopia: Studies in African-American Life and Letters* (Ames, IA, 1990)

Mota, A. Teixeira da, 'Entrée d'esclaves noirs à Valence (1445–82): le remplacement de la voie saharienne par la voie Atlantique', *Revue française d'histoire d'Outre-Mer*, 66 (1979), pp. 195–210

Mottà, Giovanna Anastasi, 'La schiavitù a Messina nel primo Cinquecento', *Archivio storico per la Sicilia Orientalia*, 70 (1974), pp. 305–42

Müller, T., 'Original und Nachbildung', *Pantheon*, 20 (1962), pp. 208–12

Müntz, Eugène, *Les collections des Médicis au XVe siècle* (Paris, 1888)

'Les miniatures françaises dans les bibliothèques italiennes', *La Bibliofilia*, 4 (1903), pp. 73–83, 219–34

Nardi, Gennaro, 'Due opere per la conversione degli schiavi a Napoli', *Aspernas: Organo dell'Accademia ecclesiastica napoletana*, 13:2 (1966), pp. 170–205

'Nuove ricerche sulle istituzioni napoletani a favore degli schiavi. La congregazione degli schiavi dei PP. Gesuiti', *Aspernas: Organo dell'Accademia ecclesiastica napoletana*, 14 (1967), pp. 294–313

Nickel, Helmut, 'Two falcon devices of the Strozzi: an attempt at interpretation', *Metropolitan Museum Journal*, 9 (1974), pp. 229–32

'The graphic sources for the *Moor with the emerald cluster*', *Metropolitan Museum Journal*, 15 (1980), pp. 203–10

Niermeyer, J. F., *Mediae Latinitatis lexicon minus* (Leiden, 1976)

Norman, A. V. B., *The Rapier and Small-Sword, 1460–1820* (London and Melbourne, 1980)

Norwich, Oscar I. and Kolbe, P., *Norwich's Maps of Africa. An Illustrated and Annotated Carto-Bibliography* (Norwich, VT, 1997)

'Notizie di un archivio privato utili alla storia pisana', *Bullettino pisano d'arte e di storia*, 1 (November 1913), pp. 217–19

O'Dell-Franke, Ilse, 'Zu Zeichnungen von Christoph Jamnitzer', *Niederdeutsche Beiträge zur Kunstgeschichte*, 22 (1983), pp. 91–112

O'Dell-Franke, Ilse and Szilágyi, András, 'Jost Amman und Hans Petzolt. Zeichnungsvorlagen für Goldschmiedewerke', *Jahrbuch der Kunsthistorischen Sammlungen in Wien*, 79 (1983), pp. 93–105

O'Malley, John W., 'Fulfillment of the Christian Golden Age under Pope Julius II: text of a discourse of Giles of Viterbo, 1507', *Traditio*, 25 (1969), pp. 265–338

    The First Jesuits (Cambridge, MA, 1993)

Oberhummer, E., *Die Weltkarte des Pierre Desceliers von 1553* (Vienna, 1924)

Oliveira, Eduardo Freire de, *Elementos para a História do Município de Lisboa*, 17 vols. (Lisbon, 1882)

Oliveira, Nicolau de, *Livro das Grandezas de Lisboa* (Lisbon, 1991)

Origo, Iris, 'The domestic enemy: the Eastern slaves in Tuscany in the fourteenth and fifteenth centuries', *Speculum*, 30 (1955), pp. 321–66

    The Merchant of Prato (London, 1957)

Os Negros em Portugal – Séculos XV a XIX (exhibition catalogue), Mosteiro de Belém (Lisbon, 1999)

Pabst, Arthur, 'Weitere Werke des Christoph Jamnitzer', *Kunstgewerbeblatt*, 1 (1885), pp. 129–30

Pagnini, Francesco, *Il castello medievale dei Conti Guidi oggi Palazzo Pretorio di Poppi* (Arezzo, 1896)

Pampaloni, Guido, *Palazzo Strozzi* (Rome, 1963)

Panero, Francesco, *Schiavi, servi e villani nell'Italia medievale* (Turin, 2000).

Pappalardo, Cardinal Salvatore, Archbishop of Palermo, *S. Benedetto 'il moro': un fiore esotico sbocciato in Sicilia. Lettera dell'arcivescovo nel IV centenario della morte del santo* (Palermo, 1989)

Parker, K. T., *Catalogue of the Collection of Drawings in the Ashmolean Museum*, 3 vols. (Oxford, 1938–80)

Partridge, Loren and Starn, Randolph, *A Renaissance Likeness: Art and Culture in Raphael's Julius II* (Berkeley, Los Angeles and London, 1980)

Pastor, Cristóbal Peréz, 'Inventarios de los bienes que quedaron por fin y muerte de Doña Juana, Princesa de Portugal, Infanta de Castilla, 1573', *Memorias de la Real Academia Española*, 9 (1914), pp. 135–380

Pastor, Ludwig von, *The History of the Popes from the Close of the Middle Ages*, 40 vols., trans. Frederick Ignatius Antrobus *et al.* (St. Louis/London, 1923–53)

Patterson, Orlando, *Rituals of Blood: Consequences of Slavery in Two American Centuries* (New York, 1998)

Pechstein, Klaus, *Bronzen und Plaketten vom ausgehenden 15. Jahrhundert bis zur Mitte des 17. Jahrhunderts* (Berlin 1968) (Staatliche Museen Preußischer Kulturbesitz, Kataloge des Kunstgewerbemuseums Berlin, III), no. 76

    Goldschmiedewerke der Renaissance (Berlin, 1971) (Staatliche Museen Preußischer Kulturbesitz, Kataloge des Kunstgewerbemuseums Berlin, V)

'Von Trinkgeräten und Trinksitten. Von der Kindstaufe zum Kaufvertrag: Pokale als Protokolle des Ereignisses', *Das Schatzhaus der deutschen Geschichte. Das Germanische Nationalmuseum*, ed. R. Poertner (Düsseldorf/Vienna, 1982)

Pereira, Daniel A., 'Cabo Verde. Catequização e Baptismo de Escravos (1690–1700)', *Estudos da História de Cabo Verde* (Praia, 1986), pp. 103–50

Pérez de Tudela, Almudena and Annemarie Jordan Gschwend, 'Luxury goods for royal collectors: exotica, princely gifts and rare animals exchanged between the Iberian courts and Central Europe in the Renaissance (1562–1612)', *Exotica. Portugals Entdeckungen im Spiegel fürstlicher Kunst- und Wunderkammern der Renaissance. Die Beiträge des am 19. und 20. Mai 2000 vom Kunsthistoriischen Museum Wien veranstalteten Symposiums*, ed. Helmut Trnek and Sabine Haag, *Jahrbuch des Kunsthistorischen Museums Wien*, 3 (2001), pp. 1–127

Petrioli Tofani, Anna Maria and Forlani Tempesti, Anna, *I grandi disegni italiani degli Uffizi di Firenze* (Milan, n.d.)

Petrzilka, Meret, *Die Karten des Laurent Fries von 1530 und 1531 und ihre Vorlage, die 'Carta Marina' aus dem Jahre 1516 von Martin Waldseemüller* (Zurich, 1970)

Phillips, Tom (ed.), *Africa: The Art of a Continent* (exhibition catalogue), Royal Academy of Arts, 4 October 1995–21 January 1996 (London, Munich and New York, 1995)

Picchio, Luciana Stegagno, *História do Teatro Português*, trans. Manuel de Lucena (Lisbon, 1964)

Pignatti, Terisio and Pedrocco, Filippo, *Veronese*, 2 vols. (Milan, 1995)

Pike, Ruth, 'Sevillian society in the sixteenth century: slaves and freedmen', *Hispanic American Historical Review*, 47 (1967), pp. 344–59

'The *converso* origins of the Sevillian dramatist Diego Jiménez de Enciso', *Bulletin of Hispanic Studies*, 67 (1990), pp. 129–35

Pistarino, Geo, 'Tratta di schiavi da Genova in Toscana nel secolo XV', in *Studi di storia economica toscana nel Medioevo e nel Rinascimento in memoria di Federigo Melis* (Pisa, 1987), pp. 285–304

Planiscig, Leo, *Die Bronzeplastiken. Statuetten, Reliefs, Geräte und Plaketten* (Vienna, 1924) (Kunsthistorisches Museum in Wien, Publikationen aus den Sammlungen für Plastik und Kunstgewerbe, 4)

'Der "Zwerg auf der Schnecke" als Repräsentant einer bisher unbeachteten naturalistischen Richtung des venezianischen Cinquecento', *Jahrbuch der Kunsthistorischen Sammlungen in Wien*, new series 13 (1944), pp. 243–54

Plazolles Guillén, Fabiana, 'Trayectorias sociales de los libertos musulmanes y negroafricanos en la Barcelona tardomedieval', in Maria Teresa Ferrer i Mallol and Josefina Mutgé i Vives (eds.), *De L'Esclavitud a la Llibertat. Esclaus i Lliberts a L'Edat Mitjana* (Barcelona, 2000), pp. 593–613

Ploss, H. H., Bartels, Max and Bartels, Paul, *Woman. An Historical, Gynaecological and Anthropological Compendium*, 3 vols. (London, 1935)

Plummer, John, *The Hours of Catherine of Cleves* (New York, n.d.)

Poeschel, Sabine, *Studien zur Ikonographie der Erdteile in der Kunst des 16.–18. Jahrhunderts* (Munich, 1985)

Poeschke, Joachim, *Die Sieneser Domkanzel des Nicola Pisano* (Berlin, 1973)

Polica, Sante, 'Le famiglie del ceto dirigente lucchese dalla caduta di Paolo Guinigi alla fine del Quattrocento', in *I ceti dirigenti nella Toscana del Quattrocento* (Florence, 10–11.XII.1982 and 2–3.XII.1983) (Florence, 1987), pp. 353–84

Polizzotto, Lorenzo, *The Elect Nation: The Savonarolan Movement in Florence, 1494–1545* (Oxford, 1994)

Poole, Julia E., *Italian Maiolica and Incised Slipware in the Fitzwilliam Museum* (Cambridge, 1995)

Pope-Hennessy, John, *Italian High Renaissance and Baroque Sculpture*, 3 vols. (London, 1963)

Popham, A. E., *Italian Drawings Exhibited at the Royal Academy, Burlington House, London, 1930* (London, 1931)

Porçal, Peter, 'Le allegorie del Correggio per lo studiolo di Isabella d'Este a Mantova', *Mitteilungen des Kunsthistorischen Institutes in Florenz*, 28 (1984), pp. 225–76

Prager, Carolyn, '"If I be Devil": English Renaissance response to the proverbial and ecumenical Ethiopian', *Journal of Medieval and Renaissance Studies*, 17:2 (1987), pp. 257–79

Pressouyre, Sylvia, *Nicolas Cordier: Recherches sur la sculpture à Rome autour de 1600* (Rome, 1984) (Collection de l'École Française de Rome, 73)

Prince Henry the Navigator and Portuguese Maritime Enterprise (exhibition catalogue), London, British Museum, September–October 1960 (London, 1960)

Princely Magnificence: Court Jewels of the Renaissance (exhibition catalogue), London, Victoria and Albert Museum (London, 1980)

Privitera, Marta, *Girolamo Macchietti: un pittore dello Studiolo di Francesco I (Firenze 1535–1592)* (Milan/Rome, 1996)

Quaderni storici, 107:2 (2001) ('La schiavitù nel Mediterraneo')

Radulet, Carmen, 'An outsider's inside view of sixteenth-century Portugal', *Portuguese Studies*, 13 (1997), pp. 152–8

Ragghianti Collobi, Licia, *Il libro de' disegni del Vasari* (Florence, 1974)

Ramos y Loscertales, José, *Estudios sobre el derecho de gentes en la Baja Edad Media. El cautiverio en la Corona de Aragon durante los siglos XIII, XIV y XV* (Saragossa, 1915)

Randles, W. G. L., 'South-East Africa as shown on selected printed maps of the sixteenth century', *Imago Mundi*, 13 (1956), pp. 69–88

    'South-East Africa and the Empire of Monomotapa as shown on selected printed maps of the sixteenth century', *Centro de Estudos Históricos Ultramarinos. Studia*, 2 (July 1958), pp. 103–63

Rasmussen, Jorg, *The Robert Lehman Collection*, x, *Italian Majolica* (New York/Princeton, 1989)

Rau, Virginia, 'Notes sur la traite portugaise à la fin du XVe siècle et le Florentin Bartolomeo di Domenico Marchionni', *Bulletin de l'Institut Historique Belge de Rome*, 44 (1974), pp. 535–43

Reid, Jane Davidson, 'The true Judith', *Art Journal*, 28 (1969), pp. 376–84

Révah, I. S., 'O "Auto de Sam Vicente" de Afonso Álvares', *O Século*, 1 January 1951, pp. 13, 19

Richter, Ilona, 'Das Kopfgefäß. Zur Typologie einer Gefäßform', MA thesis, University of Cologne, 1967

Ridolfi, Roberto, *Lorenzino, sfinge Medicea* (Florence, 1983)

Rietstap, J. B., *Armorial général*, 2 vols. (Gouda, 1884–7)

Romagnoli, Ugo, *I Medici profili e vicende* (Bologna, 1939; 2nd edn 1944)

Romano, Dennis, *House and Statecraft: Domestic Service in Renaissance Venice, 1400–1600* (Baltimore, 1996)

Romano, Serena, 'Giuditta e il Fondaco dei Tedeschi', in *Giorgione e la cultura veneta tra '400 e '500. Mito, allegoria, analisi iconologica* (Rome, 1981), pp. 113–25

Rosand, David, 'Venetia figurata: the iconography of a myth', in David Rosand (ed.), *Interpretazioni veneziane. Studi di storia dell'arte in onore di Michelangelo Muraro* (Venice, 1984), pp. 177–96

Rosenberg, Marc, *Jamnitzer. Alle erhaltenen Goldschmiedearbeiten. Verlorene Werke. Handzeichnungen* (Frankfurt am Main, 1920)

Rubiés, Joan-Pau, 'Giovanni di Buonagrazia's letter to his father concerning his participation in the second expedition of Vasco da Gama', *Mare liberum*, 16 (1998), pp. 87–112

Rubinstein, Nicolai, 'The formation of the posthumous image of Lorenzo de' Medici', in Edward Cheney and Neil Ritchie (eds.), *Oxford, China and Italy* (London, 1984), pp. 94–106

Rubio Vela, Augustín, 'Sobre la población de Valencia en el cuatrocientos (Nota demográfica)', *Boletín de la sociedad castellonense de cultura*, 56 (1980), pp. 158–70

Rückert, Rainer, 'Zur Form der byzantinischen Reliquiare', *Münchner Jahrbuch der bildenden Kunst*, 3rd series, 8 (1957), pp. 7–36

Ruddock, Alwyn, *Italian Merchants and Shipping in Southampton, 1270–1600* (Southampton, 1951)

Russell, P. E., 'Towards an interpretation of Rodrigo de Reinosa's *poesía negra*', in R. O. Jones (ed.), *Studies in Spanish Literature of the Golden Age Presented to Edward M. Wilson* (London, 1973), pp. 225–45

'La *poesía negra* de Rodrigo de Reinosa', in P. E. Russell, *Temas de 'La Celestina'* (Barcelona, 1978), pp. 377–406

'*Veni, vidi, vici*: some fifteenth-century eyewitness accounts of travel in the African Atlantic before 1492', *Historical Research*, 66 (1993), pp. 115–28

'White kings on black kings: Rui de Pina and the problem of black African sovereignty', in P. E. Russell (ed.), *Portugal, Spain and the African Atlantic,*

1340–1490: Chivalry and Crusade from John of Gaunt to Henry the Navigator (Aldershot, 1995)

Prince Henry 'The Navigator': A Life (New Haven and London, 2000)

Ruzafa García, Manuel, 'La esclavitud en la Valencia bajomedieval: mudéjares y musulmanes', in Maria Teresa Ferrer i Mallol and Josefina Mutgé i Vives (eds.), *De L'Esclavitud a la Llibertat. Esclaus i Lliberts a L'Edat Mitjana* (Barcelona, 2000), pp. 471–91

Ryder, Alan, *The Kingdom of Naples under Alfonso the Magnanimous: The Making of a Modern State* (Oxford, 1976)

Saalfeld, G. A., *De Bibliorum sacrorum vulgatae editionis graecitate* (Quedlinburg, 1891)

Sabugosa, Antonio Maria José de Mello Silva Cesar e Menezes, Conde de, *Bobos na Corte* (Lisbon, 1924)

Saldern, Axel von, *German Enameled Glass. The Edwin J. Beinecke Collection and Related Pieces* (New York, 1965)

Sale, J. Russell, 'Filippino Lippi's Strozzi Chapel in Santa Maria Novella', Ph.D. dissertation, University of Pennsylvania, 1976 (New York/London 1979)

San Juan, Rose Marie, 'The court lady's dilemma: Isabella d'Este and art collecting in the Renaissance', *Oxford Art Journal*, 14:1 (1991), pp. 67–78

Sänger, Reinhard W., *Die Greifenklaue der Domherren zu Speyer aus der Kunstkammer der Markgrafen von Baden* (Berlin/Karlsruhe, 2001)

Santos, Maria Emília Madeira, *Mulatos, sua Legitimação pela Chancelaria Régia no Século XVI* (Lisbon, 1994)

Saraiva, António José and Lopes, Óscar, *História da Literatura Portuguesa* (4th edn, Oporto, n.d.)

Saunders, A. C. de C. M., 'The life and humour of João de Sá Panasco, o negro, former slave, court jester and gentleman of the Portuguese royal household (fl. 1524–1567)', in F. W. Hodcroft, D. G. Pattison, R. D. F. Pring-Mill, R. W. Truman (eds.), *Medieval and Renaissance Studies on Spain and Portugal in Honour of P. E. Russell* (Oxford, 1981), pp. 180–91

A Social History of Black Slaves and Freedmen in Portugal, 1441–1555 (Cambridge, 1982)

'The legacy of black slavery in Renaissance Portugal', *Camões Center Quarterly*, 4: 1/2 (1992), pp. 14–19

Scheicher, Elisabeth, 'Ein Fest am Hofe Erzherzog Ferdinands II.', *Jahrbuch der Kunsthistorischen Sammlungen in Wien*, 77 (1981), pp. 119–53

Scher, Stephen K. (ed.), *The Currency of Fame: Portrait Medals of the Renaissance* (exhibition catalogue), New York, Frick Collection (London/New York, 1994)

Schiesari, Juliana, 'The face of domestication: Physiognomy, gender politics, and humanism's others', in Margo Hendricks and Patricia Parker (eds.), *Women, 'Race', and Writing in the Early Modern Period* (London and New York, 1994), pp. 55–70

Schmidt, Leopold, *Der Männerohrring in Volksschmuck und Volksglaube mit besonderer Berücksichtigung Österreichs* (Vienna, 1947)

Schneider, Rolf Michael, *Bunte Barbaren: Orientalenstatuen aus farbigem Marmor in der römischen Repräsentationskunst* (Worms, 1986)

'Coloured marble: the splendour and power of imperial Rome', *Apollo*, 154:473 (new series), (July 2001), pp. 3–10

Schreiber, Georg, *Deutsche Weingeschichte. Der Wein in Volksleben, Kult und Wirtschaft* (Cologne, 1980)

Schürer, Ralf, 'Markenzeichen. Nürnberger Beschaumarken zur Zeit Christoph Jamnitzer', in R. Eikelmann (ed.), *Der Mohrenkopfpokal von Christoph Jamnitzer* (exhibition catalogue), Munich, Bayerisches Nationalmuseum (Munich, 2002), pp. 125–133

Seelig, Lorenz, *Studien zu Martin van den Bogart, gen. Desjardins (1637–1694)*, Ph.D. dissertation, Munich 1973 (Altendorf, 1980)

'Kunst und Kultur des Trinkens. Ein Kemptener Silberbecher der Renaissance als Spiegelbild bürgerlicher Tafelsitten', *Allgäuer Geschichtsfreund*, 98 (1998)

' "Ein Willkomme in der Form eines Mohrenkopfes von Silber getriebener Arbeit". Der wiederentdeckte Mohrenkopfpokal Christoph Jamnitzers aus dem späten 16. Jahrhundert', in R. Eikelmann (ed.), *Der Mohrenkopfpokal von Christoph Jamnitzer* (exhibition catalogue), Munich, Bayerisches Nationalmuseum (Munich, 2002), pp. 19–123

Seipel, Wilfried (ed.), *Exotica. Portugals Entdeckungen im Spiegel fürstlicher Kunst- und Wunderkammern der Renaissance* (exhibition catalogue), Vienna, Kunsthistorisches Museum (Milan/Vienna, 2000)

Selwyn, Jennifer D., ' "Schools of mortification": theatricality and the role of penitential practice in the Jesuits' popular missions', in Katharine Jackson Lualdi and Anne T. Thayer (eds.), *Penitence in the Age of Reformations* (Aldershot, 2000), pp. 201–21

Serrão, Vitor, 'O Retábulo-Mor do Mosteiro dos Jerónimos (1570–1572) pelo Pintor Lourenço de Salzedo', in *História e Restauro da Pintura do Mosteiro dos Jerónimos* (Lisbon, 2000), pp. 17–77

Shiels, W. Eugene, *King and Church: The Rise and Fall of the Patronato Real* (Chicago, 1961)

Shirley, Rodney W., *The Mapping of the World: Early Printed World Maps, 1472–1700* (London, 1993)

Sicroff, Albert, *Les controverses des statuts de 'pureté de sang' en Espagne du XVe au XVIIe siècle* (Paris, 1960)

Los estatutos de limpieza de sangre – controversias entre los siglos XV y XVII (Madrid, 1985)

Siebmacher's Großes Wappenbuch, reprint, 35 vols. (Neustadt an der Aisch, 1972–86)

Signorini, Rodolfo, *Opvs hoc tenve: La Camera Dipinta di Andrea Mantegna* (Mantua, 1985)

Lo zodiaco di Palazzo d'Arco in Mantova (3rd edn, Mantua, 1989)

Silverberg, Robert, *The Realm of Prester John* (New York, 1972)

Smyth, W. H., 'On certain passages in the life of Sir John Hawkins, temp. Elizabeth', *Archaeologia: or Miscellaneous Tracts relating to Antiquity published by the Society of Antiquaries*, 33 (1849), pp. 195–208

Snowden, Frank M. Jr., *Blacks in Antiquity: Ethiopians in the Graeco-Roman Experience* (Cambridge, MA, 1970)

Before Color Prejudice: the Ancient View of Blacks (Cambridge, MA, and London, 1983)

Somers Cocks, Anna and Truman, Charles, *The Thyssen-Bornemisza Collection. Renaissance Jewels, Gold Boxes and Objets de Vertu* (London, 1984)

Sommerbrodt, E., *Die Ebstorfer Weltkarte . . . Herbei ein Atlas von 25 Tafeln in Lichtdruck* (Hannover, 1891)

Sparti, Barbara, 'Dancing in fifteenth-century Italian society', in Guglielmo Ebreo of Pesaro, *De pratica seu arte tripudii* (*On the Practice or Art of Dancing*) (Oxford, 1993), pp. 47–61

Spratlin, Velaurez B., 'The negro in Spanish literature', *Journal of Negro History*, 19 (1934), pp. 60–71

Juan Latino: Slave and Humanist (New York, 1938)

Sricchia Santoro, Fiorella (ed.), *Da Sodoma a Marco Pino: pittori a Siena nella prima metà del Cinquecento* (Siena, 1988)

Stefanini Sorrentino, Matilde, *Arazzi medicei a Pisa* (Florence, 1993)

Stella, Alessandro, '"Herrado en el rostro con una S y un clavo": l'homme-animal dans l'Espagne des XVe–XVIIIe siècles', in Henri Bresc (ed.), *Figures de l'esclave au Moyen-Age et dans le monde moderne* (Paris, 1996), pp. 147–63

Histoire d'esclaves dans la péninsule ibérique (Paris, 2000)

Stevenson, E. L., *Marine World Chart of Nicolo de Caverio Januensis, 1502 (circa) . . . with Facsimile* (New York, 1908)

Stocker, Margarita, *Judith: Sexual Warrior; Women and Power in Western Culture* (New Haven, 1998)

Straten, Adelheid, *Das Judith-Thema in Deutschland im 16. Jahrhundert* (Munich, 1983)

Strieder, Jakob, 'Deutscher Metallwarenexport nach Westafrika im 16. Jahrhundert', in Heinz Friedrich Deininger (ed.), *Das reiche Augsburg. Ausgewählte Aufsätze Jakob Strieders zur Augsburger und süddeutschen Wirtschaftsgeschichte des 15. und 16. Jahrhunderts* (Munich, 1938), pp. 155–67

Swarzenski, Hanns, *Monuments of Romanesque Art: The Art of Church Treasures in North-Western Europe* (London, 1954)

Tait, Hugh, *Catalogue of the Waddesdon Bequest in the British Museum*, I: *The Jewels* (London, 1986)

Tamrat, Taddesse, 'The Horn of Africa: The Solomonids in Ethiopia and the states of the Horn of Africa', in *General History of Africa*, 8 vols., IV: *Africa from the Twelfth to the Sixteenth Century*, ed. D. T. Niane (Berkeley, CA, 1984), pp. 423–54

Tanner, Marie, 'Chance and coincidence in Titian's *Diana and Actaeon*', *Art Bulletin*, 56 (1974), pp. 535–50

Tardieu, G. Jean-Pierre, *L'Église et les noirs au Pérou (XVIe et XVIIe siècles)*, 2 vols. (Lille, 1987)

Tavares, Maria José, *Judaísmo e Inquisição* (Lisbon, 1987)

Tedeschi, Salvatore, 'Etiopi e copti al concilio di Firenze', *Annuarium historiae concilio-rum*, 21 (1989), pp. 380–97

Tenenti, Alberto, 'Gli schiavi di Venezia alla fine del Cinquecento', *Rivista storica italiana*, 67 (1955), pp. 52–69

Terpstra, Nicholas (ed.), *The Politics of Ritual Kinship: Confraternities and Social Order in Early Modern Italy* (Cambridge, 2000)

Terra, José da Silva, 'De João de Barros a Jerónimo Cardoso: o Terramoto de Lisboa de 1531', *Arquivos do Centro Cultural Português*, 23 (1987), pp. 373–416

Teyssier, Paul, *La langue de Gil Vicente* (Paris, 1959)

The William and Mary Quarterly, third series, 54:1 (1997) ('Constructing race: differentiating peoples in the early modern world')

The World Encompassed: An Exhibition of the History of Maps (exhibition catalogue), Baltimore, Baltimore Museum of Art, 7 October–23 November 1952 (Baltimore, 1952)

Thiébaut, Dominique, *Botticelli* (Cologne, 1992)

Thiersch, Hermann, *Artemis Ephesia. Eine archäologische Untersuchung. Teil I. Katalog der erhaltenen Denkmäler* (Berlin, 1935)

Thomaz, Luis Felipe, *Le Portugal et l'Afrique au XVe siècle: les débuts de l'expansion* (IICT, separate series n. 221) (Lisbon, 1989)

Thompson, Lloyd A., *Romans and Blacks* (London and Oklahoma, 1989)

Thornton, John, *Africa and Africans in the Making of the Atlantic World, 1400–1680* (Cambridge, 1992)

Tieze-Conrat, E., *Mantegna: Paintings Drawings Engravings* (London, 1955)

Tinhorão, José Ramos, *Os Negros em Portugal. Uma Presença Silenciosa* (Lisbon, 1988)

Toderi, Giuseppe and Vannel, Fiorenza, *Le medaglie italiane del XVI secolo*, 3 vols. (Florence, 2000)

Tognetti, Sergio, *Il banco Cambini. Affari e mercati di una compagnia mercantile-bancaria nella Firenze del XV secolo* (Florence, 1999)

   'Uno scambio diseguale. Aspetti dei rapporti commerciali tra Firenze e Napoli nella seconda metà del Quattrocento', *Archivio storico italiano*, 158 (2000), pp. 461–90

   'Attività industriali e commercio di manufatti nelle città toscane del tardo Medioevo (1250 ca.–1530 ca.)', *Archivio storico italiano*, 159 (2001), pp. 423–79

Tognoli Bardin, Luisa, 'La Giuditta biblica nelle arti figurative: una ricerca', *Arte Cristiana*, 83 (1995), pp. 219–26

Tokson, Elliott H., *The Popular Image of the Black Man in English Drama, 1550–1688* (Boston, 1982)

Tooley, Ronald V., *Collector's Guide to Maps of the African Continent and Southern Africa* (London, 1969)

Torelli, Mario (ed.), *The Etruscans* (exhibition catalogue), Venice, Palazzo Grassi (Milan, 2001)

Torres Fontes, Juan, 'La hermandad de moros y cristianos para el rescate de cautivos', in *Actas del I simposio internacional de Mudejarismo* (Madrid-Teruel, 1981), pp. 499–508

Trasselli, Carmelo, 'Considerazioni sulla schiavitù in Sicilia alla fine del Medioevo: Documenti e rassegne', *Clio*, 1 (1972), pp. 67–90

Siciliani fra quattrocento e cinquecento (Messina, 1981)

Trexler, Richard C., *The Journey of the Magi: Meanings in History of a Christian Story* (Princeton, 1997)

'The foundlings of Florence, 1395–1455', in R. C. Trexler (ed.), *The Children of Renaissance Florence* (reprinted Asheville, NC, 1998) [originally printed in *History of Childhood Quarterly*, 1:2 (1973), pp. 259–89]

Triolo, Julia, 'Il servizio Pucci (1532–1533), di Francesco Xanto Avelli. Un catalogo', *Faenza*, 74 (1988), pp. 32–44, 228–84

'*L'Urbs e l'Imperatore*: a proposal for the interpretation of the Pucci Service by Xanto Avelli', in T. Wilson (ed.), *Italian Renaissance Pottery: Papers Written in Association with a Colloquium at the British Museum* (London, 1991), pp. 36–45

Trollope, T. Adolphus, *A History of the Commonwealth of Florence from the Earliest Independence of the Commune to the Fall of the Republic in 1531*, 4 vols. (London, 1865)

Turner, Jane (ed.), *The Dictionary of Art*, 34 vols. (London, 1996)

Upton, Arvin, *Lorenzino* (New York, 1977)

Vandamme, Erik *et al.* (eds.), *Koninklijk Museum voor Schone Kunsten – Antwerpen, Departement Oude Meesters. Catalogus Schilderkunst Oude Meesters* (Antwerp, 1988)

Vannel, Fiorenza, and Toderi, Giuseppe, *La medaglia barocca in Toscana* (Florence, 1987)

Vansina, J. (based on a contribution by T. Obenga), 'The Kongo kingdom and its neighbours', in *General History of Africa*, 8 vols., v: *Africa from the Sixteenth to the Eighteenth Century*, ed. B. A. Ogot (Berkeley, CA, 1992), pp. 546–87

Varese, Ranieri (ed.), *Atlante di Schifanoia* (Modena, 1989)

Vasconcellos, José Leite de, *Antroponímia Portuguesa: Tratado Comparativo da Origem, Significação, Classificação e Vida do Conjunto dos Nomes Próprios, Sobrenomes, e Apelidos, Usados por nós Desde a Idade-média até Hoje* (Lisbon, 1928)

Vaughan, Alden T. and Mason Vaughan, Virginia, 'Before Othello: Elizabethan representations of sub-Saharan Africans', *The William and Mary Quarterly* 54:1 (1997), pp. 19–44

Veit, Ludwig, 'Der Königskopf mit der Stirnbinde auf Münzen und Siegeln der Stauferzeit und des ausgehenden Mittelalters. Ein Herrschaftszeichen und heraldisches Symbol', *Anzeiger des Germanischen Nationalmuseums* (1976), pp. 22–30

Verberckemoes, Johan, *Laughter, Jestbooks and Society in the Spanish Netherlands* (Basingstoke, 1999)

Verborgene Schätze der Skulpturensammlung (exhibition catalogue), Dresden, Staatliche Kunstsammlungen (Dresden, 1992)

Vercoutter, Jean, Leclant, Jean, Snowden, Frank M. and Desanges, Jehan, *L'Image du noir dans l'art occidental, I, Des Pharaons à la chute de l'Empire romain* (Fribourg, 1976)

Verheyen, Egon, *The Paintings in the 'Studiolo' of Isabella d'Este at Mantua* (New York, 1971)

Verlinden, Charles, 'L'esclavage en Sicile au bas moyen âge', *Bulletin de l'Institut Historique Belge de Rome*, 35 (1963), pp. 13–113

   'Les débuts de la traite portugaise en Afrique (1433–1448)', in *Miscellanea medievalia in memoriam Jan Frederik Niermeyer* (Groningen, 1967), pp. 365–77

   'L'esclavage dans le royaume de Naples à la fin du moyen âge et la participation des marchands espagnols à la traite', *Anuario de historia economica y social*, 1 (1968), pp. 345–401

   'Le recrutement des esclaves à Venise aux XIVe et XVe siècles', *Bulletin de l'Institut Historique Belge de Rome*, 39 (1968), pp. 83–202

   L'esclavage dans l'Europe médiévale, 2 vols., I: *Péninsule ibérique – France* (Bruges, 1955), II: *Italie, colonies italiennes du Levant, Levant latin, Empire byzantin* (Ghent, 1977)

   'Schiavitù ed economia nel Mezzogiorno agli inizi dell'età moderna', *Annali del Mezzogiorno*, 3 (1983), pp. 11–38

Vickers, Nancy, 'Diana described: scattered women and scattered rhyme', *Critical Inquiry*, 8 (1981), pp. 265–79

Vincent, Bernard, 'L'esclavage en milieu rural espagnol au XVIIe siècle: l'example de la région d'Almería', in Henri Bresc (ed.), *Figures de l'esclave au Moyen Âge et dans le monde moderne* (Paris, 1996), pp. 165–76

   'Les noirs à Oran aux XVIe et XVIIe siècles', in Berta Ares Queija and Alessandro Stella (eds.), *Negros, mulatos, zambaigos: derroteros Africanos en los mundos ibéricos* (Seville, 2000), pp. 59–66

Vinyoles i Vidal, Teresa, 'Integració de les lliberts a la societat Barcelonina baixme-dieval', in Maria Teresa Ferrer i Mallol and Josefina Mutgé i Vives (eds.), *De L'Esclavitud a la Llibertat. Esclaus i Lliberts a L'Edat Mitjana* (Barcelona, 2000), pp. 615–42

Vitet, Louis, *Histoire des anciennes villes de France. Haute-Normandie. Dieppe*, 2 vols. (Paris, 1833)

   Histoire de Dieppe (Paris, 1844)

Vogt, John, 'The Lisbon Slave House and African trade, 1486–1521', *Proceedings of the American Philosophical Society*, 117:1 (1973), pp. 1–16

Washburn, W. E., 'Representation of unknown lands in fourteenth-, fifteenth- and sixteenth-century cartography', *Revista de Universidade de Coimbra*, 24 (1971), pp. 305–22

Watson, Katherine, *Pietro Tacca: Successor to Giovanni Bologna* (New York/London, 1983)

Weber de Kurlat, Frida, 'El tipo cómico de negro en el teatro prelopesco: fonética', *Filología*, 8 (1962), pp. 139–68

 'Sobre el negro como tipo cómico en el teatro español del siglo XVI', *Romance Philology*, 17 (1963–4), pp. 380–91

Weihrauch, Hans R., *Die Bildwerke in Bronze und in anderen Metallen* (Munich, 1956)

 'Ein Bronzekopf aus dem Rubenskreis', *Pantheon*, 33 (1975), pp. 121–4

Weinstein, Donald, *Savonarola and Florence: Prophecy and Patriotism in the Renaissance* (Princeton, 1970)

Wenzel Jamnitzer und die Nürnberger Goldschmiedekunst, 1500–1700 (exhibition catalogue), Nuremberg, Germanisches Nationalmuseum (Munich, 1985)

Wethey, Harold, *The Paintings of Titian*, 3 vols. (London, 1969–75)

Whishaw, Bernard and Ellen M., *Arabic Spain: Sidelights on her History and Art* (London, 1912)

Winkler, Friedrich, *Die Zeichnungen Albrecht Dürers*, 4 vols. (Berlin, 1936–9)

Witte, Charles-Martial de, 'Henri de Congo, évêque titulaire d'Utique (+ *c.* 1531), d'après les documents romains', *Euntes Docete*, 21 (1968), pp. 587–99

 'Les lettres papales concernant l'expansion portugaise au XVIe siècle', *Neue Zeitschrift für Missionwissenschaft*, 40 (1984), pp. 1–25, 93–125, 194–205; 41 (1985), pp. 41–68, 118–37, 173–87, 271–87

Wittkower, Rudolf, *Allegory and the Migration of Symbols* (London, 1977)

Wolff, Hans, *America. Das frühe Bild der Neuen Welt* (exhibition catalogue), Munich, Bayerische Staatsbibliothek, 10 April–27 June 1992 (Munich, 1992)

Woodbridge, Linda, 'Black and white and red all over: the sonnet mistress among the Ndembu', *Renaissance Quarterly*, 40:2 (1987), pp. 247–97

Woods-Marsden, Joanna, *The Gonzaga of Mantua and Pisanello's Arthurian Frescoes* (Princeton, 1988)

Woodson, C. G., 'Attitudes of the Iberian Peninsula', *Journal of Negro History*, 20 (1935), pp. 190–243

Woodward, David, 'Medieval Mappaemundi', in J. B. Harley and David Woodward (eds.), *The History of Cartography*, I: *Cartography in Prehistoric, Ancient and Medieval Europe and the Mediterranean* (Chicago and London, 1987), pp. 286–370

Wyss, Robert L., *Handwerkskunst in Gold und Silber. Das Silbergeschirr der bernischen Zünfte, Gesellschaften und burgerlichen* [sic] *Vereinigungen* (Bern, 1996)

Young, G. F., *The Medici* (New York, 1923)

Zajadacz-Hastenrath, Salome, 'Fabelwesen', in *Reallexikon zur deutschen Kunstgeschichte*, 6 (Munich, 1973), cols. 739–816

Index

Please note that people to whom a nickname has become attached (e.g. Jorge Bocall, Elen More or Juan Latino) have been indexed under their first name.

Abdul, slave from Meknès, 39
Abyssinia, 59
Aethiops, 282
Afonso, Álvaro, bishop of Silves, 33
Afonso, Bartolomeu, 219
Afonso de Portugal, bishop of Évora, 346, 348
Afonso, João, 218
Afonso I, king of Congo, 294
Afonso, prince of Portugal, 120
Africa. *See also* East Africa; North Africa; West Africa
  and eighteenth-century Anglophone black writers, 341
  Desceliers map, 57–69
  English texts, 95
  European geographical ignorance, 6
  maps, 54–69
  monstrous inhabitants, 59
  royal families, 275
  and trade, 68
  travellers' accounts, 18, 61–3
Africans
  ambassadors to Europe, 2, 43–7
  black servants in Italian courts, 127–30, 139
  colour endogamy, 257
  Desceliers map, 60
  description on maps, 56
  executioners, 132, 137, 256
  free-born black Africans in Europe, 20
  as honorary Europeans, 18
  lip-plated, 60, 62, 63, 65–7, 68, 69
  occupations in Europe
    carpenters, 185
    carriers, 26, 256, 276
    craftsmen, 256–7
    emancipated slaves, 255–8

    divers, 35
    farmers, 258
    fencing master, 33
    labourers, 256
    musicians, 38, 40, 148, 158
    slaves in Portugal, 113–21, 155–79
    soldiers, 33, 77, 148
    stable workers, 255–6
    stereotypes, 32–41, 46
    swimming instructors, 34
    wrestlers, 34
  in Portugal, 113–21
  and Renaissance Spain, 247–9
  sculpture featuring, 194–209
  and Spanish literature, 71–93
  terminology, European, relating to, 2, 9, 248–9
Agagi, 105
aigrettes, 208
Aigues-Mortes, 222
Albanians, 214
Albizzi, Giovanni degli, 217
Albrecht V, duke of Bavaria, 194
Albuquerque, Afonso de, 222
Alentejo, 157, 171
Alexander VI, Pope, 281
Alfieri, Vittorio, 324
Alfonso I of Naples and V of Aragon, 'il magnanimo', 9, 128, 241
Algarve, 10, 115, 117, 157, 216–19, 261, 358
Alhambra, 327
Alighieri, Dante, 348
Allen, Cardinal William, 9
Almeirim, 155, 173, 174, 179
Almería, 250
Alpujarras, War of the Alpujarras, 327, 328

Álvares, Afonso
  Auto de Santa Bárbara, 356
  Auto de Sant'Iago, 349
  Auto de Santo António, 346
  Auto de São Vicente, 348–9, 350–1, 353–60
  biographical information, 275, 345–9
  and Jews, 349, 351, 354, 357–8
  described as mulatto, 275, 347
  paternity, 347–8
  plays, 345, 346, 348–60
  poems, 348
  reputation, 351–2
Álvares, Francisco, 35
America, 61, 207, 248, 249
Amerindians, 7, 21, 155, 162
Ammirato, Scipione, 306, 307, 310
Amyctyrae, 64, 69
Andalusia, 70, 250, 256
Andrade, Mécia de, 174
Ango, Jean, 48–51
Angola, 72, 160, 248
Antonino, Sant' (Antonio Pierozzi), 293
António, D., prior of Crato, 117
António Luís, Moor, 117
Antwerp, 154
apes, 58
Arabia, 21, 56, 61
Arabic, 334
Arabs, 249, 250, 282
Aragon, 127–8, 226
archers, 36, 37
Arguim, 161
Ariosto, Ludovico, 303
Aristotle, 97, 247, 316, 331
Armenians, 214
armlets, 24, 25
Arques, 51, 52
Arrais, Amador, bishop of Portalegre, 277–8
Arronches, 346
Asia, 50, 52, 61, 178
asps, 58
Asseline, David, 51
asses, 58
Au am Inn, 191, 192
auctions, slave, 10–11
Augustine of Hippo, 316
Augustinians, 166, 191, 231, 345, 346, 351–2
Azores, 33
Aztecs, 331

Baeza, 330
Balbi, Giovanni, 20
Balkans, 215
ballads, 105–6
barbarism
  Renaissance concept, 316–17
  Roman concept, 317
Barce, 283
Barcelona, 70, 226, 242
Barcelona, treaty of, 304, 320
Barros, João de, 33, 43–4, 46, 264, 350
Bartholomeus Anglicus, 71
basilisks, 58
beauty
  cultural potency, 110
  and love, 102
  Renaissance concept, 96–100, 108
  and virtue, 102
Beja, João de, 169
Belém, 275
Bellarmine, St Robert, 297
Beloso, Baltasar, 171
'Bemoim', prince, from Senegambia, 33, 44
Benedetto il moro, San, 8–9, 298–9
Benedictines, 191
Benghazi, 283
Benin, 19, 22, 157
Bening, Simon, 169, 170
Berbers, 71, 215, 219, 250, 282, 283, 303
Berry, Jean de, 127
Best, George, 104, 108, 109
bestiality, 71–2, 98, 121
bestiaries, 65, 66
Bible
  and *Auto de São Vicente* (Álvares), 357, 359
  and conversion of Muslims, 293
  David and Goliath, 132, 179
  Day of Judgement, tau on forehead of
    blessed, 207
  Egypt and Ethiopia in, 339, 344
  Holofernes, 132, 134, 136
  injunction to preach the Gospel, 281
  Judith, 127, 132–4, 136–47
  Lamentations of Jeremiah, 354–5
  lip-plates, alleged reference to, 65
  Manasseh, 134
  Moses and the crossing of the Red Sea, 59
  Noah's curse, 71, 109
  Parable of mote and beam, 79

Samson and Delilah, 141
Song of Songs, 105, 106
bishops, black, 294–6. *See also* Henrique, D.,
    bishop of Utica
black confraternities
    and Jesuits, 297
    Lisbon, Nossa Senhora de Rosário, 265–74
    Southern Italy, 296–9
        Naples, 287, 297
    Spain, 70, 255
        Granada, 253
        Valencia, 227, 231–46
Black Death, 213
black Diana, 205
Black Magus. *See* Magi
black musicians, 35, 40, 158–9
Black Sea, 7, 12, 54, 213, 215
black women
    artistic representation, 125–54
    Catalina de Soto, embroideress, 260
    early images, 130
    emancipated slaves, 257–8, 260
    Isabella d'Este's court, 125–54
    Italian slave trade, 214–15, 223–4
    page, 176
    portraits of servants, 168
    portraits of slaves, 177
    Portuguese slaves, 116–17, 118–19, 165–73
    Valencia lawsuits, 233–41
blackness
    and Bible, 71, 105
    black/white dichotomy, 99–100
    and cartography, 56
    causes, 107
    climatic theory, 108
    curse (of Ham, Noah), 71, 97, 109
    demonisation, 20, 106
    equated with slavery, 20–1
    gradations, 11–12, 99
    heredity theory, 108
    intellectual debate, 12
    Juan Latino and, 328, 336, 342
    negativity, 20–5
    Renaissance England, 94–112
    and sex, 100–5
    Spanish terminology, 248–9
    theories of race, 107
    and ugliness, 96–100, 262
Blemmyae, 59, 68

Bobenhausen, Heinrich von, 191
Boccaccio, Giovanni, 320
body markings, 22–3, 46
Boemus, Johannes, 100
Bordoni, Francesco, 201, 202
Bormelli, King, 24
Bornu, 283
Bosch, Hieronymus, 272
Botticelli, Sandro, 133–4, 185
bozal, 83, 230, 251
Brabant, 171, 173
Braga, 41, 113, 116, 275
Bragança, duke of, 118, 348
Brandão, Pedro, bishop of Cape Verde, 277, 278
branding, 22–3
Brazil, 155, 162, 164, 172, 173, 333
Breu the Younger, Jörg, 33, 34
Briosco, Andrea, 141
Brito Pestana, Álvaro de, 350
Brittany, 173
Brognolo, Giorgio, 134, 135
Brome, Richard, 100–1
Bronzino, Agnolo, 310, 311
Brunelleschi, Filippo, 222
buffaloes, 58
Bulwer, John, 98, 106
Buontalenti, Bernardo, 189
Burali, Paolo, Archbishop of Naples, 287
Burgkmair, Hans, 50

Cabot, Sebastian, 54
Cabra, count of, 329
Cabral, Pedro Álvares, 222
Caccini, Giovanni Battista, 190
Calderón, Alonso, freed slave, 258
Calderón, Francisco, master, 258
Calicut, 55, 57
Calixtus III, Pope, 281
camels, 56, 58, 60, 61
cameos, 204–6
Campagnola, Giulio, 141
Canary islands, 71, 139, 227, 248, 253
Candia, 189
cannibalism, 105
canon law, 214
Cape Verde, 55, 61, 216, 274
Capello, Bianca, 136
Caporale, Francesco, 203–4
Carafa, Cardinal Alfonso, 291

caricature, black Africans in Spanish literature,
74
Carleton, Dudley, 101
Carlos, Infante of Spain, 174
Carrara of Padua, 127, 132
Cartier, Jacques, 54
cartography
Africa, 54–69
Catalan Atlas, 54, 55, 56, 59
Caverio map, 56
Desceliers world maps, 52–5
Dieppe cartographers, 52
Ebstorf map, 67
lip-plated Africans, 65–7
Miller Atlas, 56
monstrous Africans, 59
Portuguese maps, 54–5
sea charts, 51, 54
Walsperger map, 65
Carvalho, Diogo, 173
Carvalho, Jorge, 117
casa dels negres, 226–46
Casavecchia brothers, 221
Castile, 25, 26
castration, 76
Catalan Atlas, 54, 55, 56, 59
Catalan Revolt, 242
Catherine of Aragon, queen of England, 39
Catherine of Austria, queen of Portugal
acquisition of slaves, 159, 161–2
dispensary, 162–5, 172
emancipated slaves, 172
imperial self-image, 156
marriage, 48, 157, 158
slaves as commodities, 174–6
slaves as imperial symbol, 175–9
treatment of slaves, 162–75
Catholic Church. See also Christianity; papacy;
Dominicans; Franciscans; Jesuits
care of black Africans in Italy, 279, 280–300
exclusionary practices, 8–9
official attitude to Africans, 281
and slavery, 12–13
Ceccheregli, Alessandro, 320
Cervantes, Miguel de, 77–8, 328, 332–3
Cerveira, Afonso, 10
Chad, lake, 283
chains, 24–5, 26
Charles IV of Luxembourg, 127

Charles V, emperor
and Alessandro de' Medici, 303, 309, 322–3
cultural programme in Spain, 327
daughter Margherita, 309, 318, 319
heraldry, 179
North African campaigns, 161, 322, 323
Spanish politics, 328
Treaty of Barcelona, 304, 320
chess, 41
Chiado, António Ribeiro, 345, 346–7, 348
Christianity. See also Catholic Church; papacy;
Dominicans; Franciscans; Jesuits
baptism of Italian slaves, 288–93
conversion of Brazilian Indians, 173
conversion of slaves, 165, 254–5, 263, 284,
288–93
and Portuguese slaves, 261, 263, 264–74
sacraments to Italian slaves, 293–6
and 'savages', 21
and slavery, 12–13, 71, 214, 249–52
cinnamon, 58
Circassians, 214, 215, 226, 282
circumcision, 21–2
Cistercians, 166
civilisation. See also barbarians
and black 'savages', 21–2
and nudity, 21
Renaissance notions, 7–8, 18
rules, 25, 27, 28
self-control, 35
and sexual promiscuity, 29
Claramonte, Andrés de, 76
Clement VII, Pope, 31, 269, 304, 305, 307, 309,
313, 315, 318, 320–1, 322, 324
Cleynaerts, Nicholas
bibliography, 114
biography, 113
personal slaves, 120
and Portuguese slaves, 114–21
racism, 120–1
Cochin, king of, 48–50
cochineal, 217
collars, 25
Colle Vecchio, 303, 306, 308
Columbus, Christopher, 139
confraternities. See black confraternities
Congo, 22, 248
ambassador to papacy, 203
ambassador to Portugal, 43

barbarism, 8
black bishop, 261, 295
body markings, 22
cartography of, 55, 58, 59
diocesan authority, 295
kings of (also known as the Manicongo), 5,
        279, 294
    João I (Nzinga Nkuwu), 5, 173
    Afonso I (Nzinga Mbemba), 173
and papacy, 300
royal family of, 5, 173
royal household in, 160
Constantinople, fall of, 282
convents, 165–7, 174, 175, 292, 297
Copley, Anthony, 104
Cordier, Nicolas, 202, 203, 204
Córdoba, 72, 250
Cornejo, Baltasar, 167, 174
Correas, Gonzalo, 76–7
Correggio, Antonio, 145–6, 147, 149–54
Corsi, Pierpaolo, 34–5
Councils of the church
    Basel, 226, 284
    Fifth Lateran, 294
    Trent, 272, 273, 284, 293
Coutinha, D. Guiomar de, 174
creole, slave, 72
Crete, 189
criminality, stereotype, 23, 28–9, 31, 46, 79, 310
crocodiles, 56, 58
Cruz, Catarina da, 172–3
Cyranaica, 283

D' Annebaut, Claude, Admiral de France, 52, 54
Da Cepperello, Lisabetta, 320
Da Filicaia, Baccio, 26
Da Mosto, Alvise (known as Cadamosto), 22,
        35, 61–3, 216
Da Randaczo, Antonino, 299
Da San Giovanni, Giovanni (Giovanni
        Mannozzi), 185, 186
Da Sangallo, Francesco, 319
Da Trezzo, Jacopo, 175
Da Verrazzano, Giovanni, 48
dance, 35, 40–1, 42, 72, 158–9, 242
Datini, Francesco, 306
De Barchi, Cesare, 229
De Bry, Theodor, 208
Dekker, Thomas, 103, 106

Del Cossa, Francesco, 129
Della Marca, Giacomo, 24
Desceliers, Pierre
    Africans, 60
    life, 51
    lip-plated Africans, 60, 62
    map of Africa, 57–9
    world maps, 52–5
Desliens, Nicolas, 51
Desmarquets, Charles, 51
D'Este, Alfonso I, duke of Ferrara, 50, 138
D'Este, Borso, duke of Ferrara, 128, 129
D'Este dynasty, 128
D'Este, Ercole I, duke of Ferrara, 128, 138
D'Este, Isabella
    black servants, 134–5, 149
    character, 137–9
    Correggio's patron, 149
    court, 125–54
    family, 50, 128
    Mantegna's patron, 135–6
    marriage, 130
D'Este, Luigi, 52, 282
devil, and blackness, 20, 106
Deza, Pedro de, 334
Di Buonagrazia, Giovanni, 28
Diana of Ephesus, 149, 150
Dianti, Laura, 152, 154
Dias, Bartolomeu, 55
Dias, Captain Francisco, 33
Dias, Dinis, 54
Dias, Isabel, 275
Dias, Luís, 275
Diaz, João, 162
Dieppe, 48, 49, 51
Diest, 113
dispensaries, 162–5, 172
Dominicans
    black Dominicans, 259
    black Dominican confraternity, 13, 266,
        268–9, 273
    Portugal, 173, 265, 267, 273
    Sant' Antonino, 293
Donatello, 132, 133
Donzelli, Giovanni, archbishop, 289
dragons, 56, 58, 62
dress, 21, 46–7, 50, 72, 207–8
drinking vessels, 183, 190–3, 195
dromaderies, 58

drunkenness, 28–9, 46
Duarte, prince of Portugal, 120
Dumas, Alexandre, 324
Dunbar, William, 98, 101
Dürer, Albrecht, 50, 137, 153, 154

ear-rings, 24, 33, 41, 46, 182, 206
East Africa, 59
Ebersberg, Benedictine abbey, 191
Eça, Catarina d', 174
Eça, Joana d', 169, 173, 174
Eden, Richard, 23, 24, 95
Edinburgh, 37
Edo of Benin, 22
education
    Moriscos, 334
    Portuguese court slaves, 165–7
    slaves, 119–21
Eleanora of Aragon, 135
Eleanora of Toledo, 136
Elen More, 98
elephants, 56, 58, 61–2, 96, 207
Elizabeth I, queen of England, 9
emancipated slaves
    black confraternity in Valencia, 231–46
    Catherine of Austria's household, 172,
        175
    and Christianity, 13
    craftsmen, 256–7
    farmers, 258
    Granada, 252–60
    labourers, 256
    and literacy, 20
    numbers, 20
    occupations, 255–8
    Portuguese court, 169
    possessions, 255
    social prominence, 258–60
    Spanish society, 252–60
    stable workers, 255–6
    status, 161
        proof of, 254
    thieves, 258
    Valencia lawsuits, 233–41
    women, 257–8
emancipation
    contracts, 227, 230, 237–8
    early Spanish emancipations, 251
    Italian slaves, 284, 308

Portuguese practices, 268
Portuguese regulations, 266, 270–1
redemption fees, 233, 235, 253
role of black confraternity in Valencia,
    233–46
Sicilian law, 297
England
    black population, 94
    and blackness, 94–112
    court, 39, 40
    images of Africa, 95
    proverbs, 94
Enrique IV, king of Castile, 72
entertainers, 35, 43
Erasmus, 27
Esperança, Margarida da, 171
Estremoz, 117
Ethiopia
    alliances, 9
    Biblical country, 326
    cartography, 55, 57, 58, 59, 60
    circumcision, 21
    Guma people, 64
    imaginary country, 333, 337
    Jesuits, 286
    and Juan Latino, 333, 337–8, 339–42, 344
    monastery, 294
    musical instruments, 35
    and papacy, 300
    rulers, 9, 59, 128
    saints, 70
Ethiopians, 76, 79, 94, 104, 194
    characteristics, 261–2
    facial stereotypes, 98
    monstrous people, 64
    musicians, 35
    pilgrims to Europe, 2, 138, 297
    terminology, 282, 303
Etruscans, 193, 194
Évora
    bishop, 346, 347
    black population, 115
    convent, 166
    court, 113, 155
    slave market, 162
    slaves, 115, 119
    university, 121
executioners, black Africans as, 132, 137, 256
exotica, 175–6, 178, 223

Fabrizio, Giuseppe, 297
face markings, 22–3
fairness, and beauty, 96–7
Falconetto, Giovanni Maria, 149, 150
falcons, heraldry, 187–8
Fali people, 64
Famagusta, 213
fans, 177, 178
Fascism, 4, 305
Ferdinand II, king of Aragon, the Catholic, 139,
    231, 250
Ferdinand, prince of Spain (son of King
    Philip II), 342
Féret, Amédée, 49
Fernandes, Garcia, 158, 168
Fernandes, Valentim, 264
Fernandes, Vasco, 163
Fernandez, Pero, 165, 166
Fernández de Córdoba family, 329
Fernández de Córdoba, Gonzalo, 329
Ferrara, 24, 128–30, 135, 139
Fez, 60
Figueiredo, Cristóvão de, 158
Fiorentino, Niccolò, 187
Flanders, 198, 199
Florence
    fifteenth-century slave trade, 213–23, 229
    and Alessandro de' Medici, 303–4,
        320–1
    Cambini bank, 216–18, 221–2
    civic virtues, 318
    Fortezza da Basso, 322
    liberty, 304, 324
    merchant bankers, 216
    Palazzo Nonfinito, 189
    Palazzo Pucci, 185
    Palazzo Strozzi, 187
    Pucci family, 185
    republicanism, 303–4, 320–1, 322, 323
    S. Miniato al Monte, church, 33
    Santissima Annunziata, church, 189–90,
        203
flytings, 73, 74
Fondi, count of, 221
fools, 22, 29, 37, 42, 193
foundlings, 220
foundry workers, 256
Fournier, Georges, 51
Francavilla, Pietro, 199, 201

France
    bestiary, 65
    and Canada, 54
    cartography, 52
    medieval drama, 352, 353
    and trade monopolies, 48
Franciscans, 24, 165, 298–9, 346
Frankfurt, Master of, 36, 37
Fraunces, Jacobus, 34–5
Frederick I (Barbarossa), emperor, 207
Frederick II, emperor, 127, 128
Frederick II, king of Sicily, 284
Frederick III, emperor, 32
Fries, Laurent, 54
Frois, Duarte, 162, 164
Frorença, Domingos de, 158
Frutuoso, Gaspar, 33
Funchal, 295
Funta, Antonio Emmanuele, 203

Gabriello, Ridolfo di ser, 217
Gainsh, Robert, 96
Galen, 97
galley slaves, 199, 223, 253, 254
Gama, Vasco da, 28, 55
Garamantes people, 61
Genoa, 23, 213–14, 215, 282, 283, 307
Germany, 50, 191–3, 208
Gesta Romanorum, 65
Ghinetti, Piero, 219
Giachas, 105
Ginori, Tommaso, 221
Giorgione (Giorgio da Castelfranco), 146
Giovio, Paolo, 294
giraffes, 58
Giraldi, Giambattista Cinzio, 317–18
Glockendon, Georg, 50
Goa, 172
gold, 24–5, 41, 46, 67, 68, 206
gold mines, 58, 60
goldsmiths, 8, 162, 167, 278
Gomes, Diogo, 24
Gonneville, Binot de, 50
Gonzaga dynasty, 128, 130, 149
Gonzaga, Ercole, 154
Gonzaga, Francesco, 148
Gonzaga, Federigo, 149
Gonzaga, Maddalena, 136
Good Hope, Cape of, 55

Granada
  Albaicín, 251
  Anales, 258
  archbishop, 259
  black confraternities, 13, 253
  cathedral, 334
  church history, 259
  civil conflict, 327, 334, 336
  conquest of, 327
  corsairs, 226
  emancipated slaves, 252–60
  kingdom of, 250
  Morisco quarter, 251
  Renaissance poetry, 327
  university, 247, 327, 329
Gratian's *Decretum*, 291
Grazzico of Africa, il Moretto, 33
Greece, Ancient, 59, 68, 194
Greeks, 214, 226
Guanches, 71
Guardi, Benedetto di ser Francesco, 218
Guariento, 132, 133
Guerrero, Pedro, archbishop of Granada, 334, 335, 343
Guicciardini, Francesco, 307, 308, 322, 323
Guidetti, Giovanni di Bernardo, 216, 217, 218–24
guilds, 8, 36, 37, 185, 242, 256–7, 287
Guinea, 12, 34, 50, 61, 73, 216, 217, 248, 251
Guma people, 64
gypsies, 21

Haarlem, 44
'habla de negros', 72–3, 77, 78
Habsburg dynasty, 44, 47, 178, 326, 336, 337
Hall, Thomas, 96
Halle, Our Lady of, pilgrimage church and shrine, 46
Hannibal, 317
Hawkins, John, 25, 27, 94
Henri II, king of France, 52
Henrique, Prince, first cardinal regent then Henrique II, king of Portugal, 113, 117, 267, 269, 272–3
Henrique, D., bishop of Utica (Ndoadidiki Ne-Kinu a Mumemba), 8, 279, 280, 294–5, 300

Henrique, D., nephew of the king of Congo, 173
Henrique, D., prince of Portugal, the Navigator, 11, 216
Henriques, Francisco, 163
heraldry, 184–9, 190–1
heredity, 108
Hereford map, 67
heresy, 331
Herrera, Fernando de, 335, 336
Heywood, Thomas, 104
hierarchy, 43, 104, 110
Higden, Ranulf, 65
Hohenstaufen dynasty, 127
Holanda, António de, 157
Holbein, Hans, 61, 62, 67
Holofernes, 132, 134, 136
Holy Roman Empire, 320
Honfleur, 50, 54
horsemanship, 33
Hottentots, 50
hunting, 170
hyenas, 58

Iannis, Lopo, 218
Ibiza, 234, 237, 239
iconography
  black Africans in Portugal, 30, 31, 160, 168, 170, 276
  black Africans in Spain, 71
  black dancing, 42
  black Diana, 205
  black martial skills, 34, 36
  black musicians, 38, 40, 158–9
  black prisoners, 196
  black sculpture, 194, 196, 198, 200, 201, 202, 204, 205
  black Venus, 195–8
  enlarged lips, 60, 63, 68, 69
  fabulous beasts, 66
  Italian black female servants, 125–54
  Italian black pages, 152
  Magi, 23, 127, 130, 131, 148, 163
  Moors, 45, 181–209, 303
  sexuality, 76
  slaves, 26, 72, 153, 157, 177, 200, 201
identity, Africans in Europe, 13–14, 46–7
Ignatius de Loyola, St, 286, 289
Ilha, Lançarote da, 11
Incas, 331

India, 50, 55, 139, 171, 248
Indian Ocean, 55
Innocent VIII, Pope, 281
Inquisition, 174, 257, 263, 349
intellectual skills, 41, 48
Ireland, 217
Isabella I, queen of Castile, 70, 138, 139, 250
Ishaq, emperor of Ethiopia, 9
Isidore of Seville, 64–5, 67
Italy
   black confraternities, 296–9
   black servants in courts, 127–30, 139
   branding of slaves, 23
   Catholic Church's care of black Africans,
      279, 280–300
   concept of 'race', 313–16
   ethnicity, 317–18
   Jesuits in, 285–9
   musicians, 39
   navigators, 139
   sculpture of Africans, 194, 195, 196
   slave trade, 213–16, 217–18, 223, 282
   slaves, 282–4, 307
   status of slave children, 306
ivory, 25, 56, 96, 206

jackals, 58
Jaime of Portugal, cardinal, 33
James IV, king of Scotland, 37
James, St, 132
Jamnitzer, Christoph, Moor's Head, 181–209
Jesuits, 173, 273, 285–9, 297
jewellery, 23–5, 46
Jews
   Álvares's plays, 349, 351, 354, 355, 357–8
   circumcision, 21
   conversions, 262–3
   culture, 331
   emancipation of slaves, 297
   female jewellery, 24
   Ferrara, 24
   impure race, 277
   inferiority, 77
   pecking order of discrimination, 10
   Pesaro, 136
   Portugal, 263, 349–50
   Spain, 77, 349, 356
   treatment of, 21
Joana of Portugal, queen of Castile, 72

João II, king of Portugal, 44, 271
João III, king of Portugal, 113, 156, 157, 158,
   263, 349
João, prince of Portugal, son of King João III,
   176, 179
João Baptista, bishop, 173
Johan, Anthoni, master, 238, 239–41, 244–5
Johan, Anthoni, slave, 239–40, 244–5
John Blanke, 39, 40
Jones, Inigo, 208
Jonson, Ben, 101, 208
Jorge Bocall, 165
Jorquera, Francisco Henríquez de, 258
Juan Blanco, 252
Juan de Austria, 326, 327, 328, 330–1, 332, 335,
   336, 337, 344
Juan de Mérida, 77
Juan Latino
   Austrias carmen, 326–36, 338–9, 343–4
   biography, 330
   birth, 330
   cultural politics, 328
   eminence, 258–9
   and Ethiopia, 333, 337–8, 339–42, 344
   and Granada, 327
   humanism, 247, 327, 331
   Latin writing, 326, 331–3, 341–3
   marriage, 76, 259
   names, 329, 337, 340, 343
   patronage, 330
   Ad Catholicum . . . elegia, 332, 333–4, 336–8,
      339, 342–3
   and race, 328, 336, 342
Juana of Austria, wife of Prince João, 176–9
Judith, 127, 132–4
Julius II, Pope, 294
Jurgurtha, 317
just war, 277, 284

Kilwa, king of, 59

La Roque de Roberval, Jean-François de, 54
labourers, 256
ladinos, 251, 332–3
Lagos, 10, 11, 264
Lamego, 295
Landi, Conte Giulio, 31–2
languages, 41–3, 72–3, 77, 78, 251
Lankmann of Falkenstein, Nicolaus, 32

Las Casas, Bartolomé de, 264
Latin
    education, 165, 334
    and Juan Latino, 326, 331–3, 341–3
    Renaissance language, 42
Latomus, 113, 118, 120
laughing blacks, 26–8, 115
Lazarillo de Tormes, 78–80
laziness, 28, 46
Le Testu, Guillaume, 51
Leal, Jorge, 168
leather trade, 217
Lefebvre, Maître Nicolas, 51
Leo Africanus, 29, 100, 105
Leo X, Pope, 271, 294–5, 348
Leonor of Portugal, empress, 32
leopards, 58
Lepanto, battle of, 328, 329, 335, 344
Levant, 213
Libya, 58, 60, 68
Limpopo, river, 55
Ling, Nicholas, 99
lions, 58, 61
Liperotto Falconi, Girolamo, 221
lip-plated Africans, 60, 62, 63, 65–7, 68, 69
Lisbon
    African dancers, 41, 42
    Alfama district, 29, 30, 31, 40, 42, 159
    Álvares's play, 354–5, 356
    archdiocese, 278
    black ambassador to, 44
    black confraternities, 13, 51
    black population, 114, 116
    Casa da Índia, 159
    Casa da Mina, 159
    Casa dos Escravos, 70, 159, 222
    cathedral, 358
    celebrations, 32, 33
    Chafariz d'el Rei, 29, 116, 159, 160, 276–7
    College of Orphans, 174
    convents, 174
    court, 42, 113
    earthquake, 346, 350, 353, 354–5
    goldsmiths, 8
    Nossa Senhora da Conceição, church, 271
    Nossa Senhora da Esperança de Boa Vista,
        Franciscan convent, 165
    Nossa Senhora do Rosário, confraternity
        attached to Dominican monastery,
        265–74
    palaces, 155
    plague, 162, 346, 350, 353, 354–5
    Poço dos Negros, 272
    Santo Elói, monastery of Augustinian
        canons, 294
    São Vicente de Fora, church, 345, 352, 358
    slave trade, 70, 216–19, 230
    Xabregas, 164
literacy
    and barbarism, 331
    barrier, 41–3
    Portuguese slaves, 119–21, 162, 164, 165, 166
    and Renaissance, 2
    and slaves, 20
    women, 332
Livorno, 199, 200, 202, 217, 218–19, 221–2, 303
Lobi people, 64
Lok, John, 23, 25, 95
Lombardy, 11, 41
Loronha, Maria de, 171
Lorraine, 203
Louvain, 113
Lucca, 20, 220–1
Luís, infante of Portugal, brother of King
        João III, 161
Luís, Mestre, 173
Lust's Dominion, 103, 106
Luther, Martin, 113
lynxes, 58

Macchietti, Girolamo, 310–13
Machado, Barbosa, 346, 347
Machado, Francisco, 350
Machiavelli, Niccolò, 317
Madagascar, 57
Madeira, 31, 295
Madrill, Diogo de, musician, 157
Madrill, Pedro de, slave, 157
Magi, 4, 23, 127, 130–1, 148, 163, 281
Mair, Paulus Hector, 33, 34
Makonde people, 64
Málaga, 250
Malindi, 55
Malines, 44, 46
Malta, 292
Mandeville, John, 64, 95
Manetti, Giannozzo, 220
Mantegna, Andrea
    Adoration of the Magi, 130, 131, 148
    black African servants, 125–54

Camera picta, Palazzo ducale, Mantua, 129, 130, 137
funerary chapel, 145, 146
Isabella d'Este as patron, 135–6
Judith copies, 141–7
Judith monochrome paintings, 139–41, 142
Judith Uffizi drawing, 125–7, 136–41
Ovetari Chapel, Eremitani church, Padua, 131–2
Pallas expelling the vices, 136
Samson and Delilah, 141
Triumphs of Caesar, 148
Mantua, 128–30, 149
Manuel, king of Portugal, 271, 272, 294–5, 349
Marchionni, Bartolomeo di Domenico, 139, 216, 221–3, 229
Margalho, Pedro, 120
Margaret of Austria, regent of the Netherlands, 44
Maria, black (of three Marias), 276
Maria of Portugal, princess, later wife of Philip II of Spain, 169, 174
Marino, Giambattista, 195
Marlowe, Christopher, 103, 106
marriage
    black dress, 178
    colour endogamy between Africans, 257
    discrimination, 9
    emancipated female slaves, 257
    slaves in Italy, 306
    black/white marriages in Renaissance England, 104–5
    slaves in Portugal, 119, 346
Martellus, Henricus, 55
Marti, Jacme, 245
martial skills, 32–5, 36
Martinez, Francesch, 225–6, 233–4, 237, 240, 243, 244
Martins, Ignácio, 273
martyrs, 356–8
Mary of Hungary, regent of the Netherlands, 175
Masinissa, 317
Mauritania, 60, 303
Mazzinghi, Niccolò, 218
medallions, 48
medical treatment, 225, 233

Medici
    bank, 220
    court, 33
    palace, 133
Medici, Alessandro de'
    biography, 304
    blackness, 325
    historiography, 305, 324–5
    image, 319–22
    literary representations, 319–20, 324
    Moorishness, 304–8, 313
    mother, 303–4, 305–7, 308
    murder, 304, 323, 324
    nobility, 318
    paternity, 305, 306, 307, 308–9, 313
    physical appearance, 304–5, 310–13
    portraits, 309–13, 314, 315, 319
Medici, Cosimo de', 'il vecchio', 305, 318
Medici, Cosimo I de', duke then grand-duke of Tuscany, 39, 203, 305, 308, 318–19, 324
Medici, Ferdinando I de', grand-duke of Tuscany, 189, 199, 200, 202, 303
Medici, Ippolito de', 305, 309, 318, 322–3
Medici, Lorenzino de', 304, 306, 308–9, 324–5
Medici, Lorenzo de', duke of Nemours, 305, 308, 309
Medici, Lorenzo de', 'il magnifico', 133, 305, 318, 321
Medici, Piero de', 305
Medina Sidonia, duke of, 255
Mediterranean Sea, 54, 203, 214, 254
Melli, emperor of, 62
Meneses, Cristóbal de, 259
Menil Foundation, 4
Mercedarians, 227
merchant bankers, 216
Meroe, 58, 59
Messina, 283, 285–7, 288, 290, 292, 293, 296, 297
Milan, 130, 139, 205
Mina (or Elmina), 23, 25, 61, 265
Miralles, Melchior, 241–2
Mocetto, Girolamo, 141, 144
Molina, Luís de, 121
Moliner, Johan, 236
Mombasa, 55
monkeys, 56
Monpalau, Jofre de, nobleman, 236
Monpalau, Johan, former slave, 236
monstrous people, 59, 64, 68, 95

Montaigne, Michel de, 333
Montemor-o-Novo, 118
Monti Barca, 283
Montmorency, Connétable Anne de, 52
Moors (*mori*)
  cameos, 206
  cartography, 58
  iconography, 45, 181–209, 303
  impure race, 277
  Italian slave trade, 215, 282
  Jamnitzer's Moor's Head, 181–209
  Mannozzi figure, 185, 186
  mauresque style, 181
  slaves, 156
  terminology, 6, 56, 282, 303
Mor, Anthonis, 176, 179
Morais, Cristóvão de, 176, 177
Moriscos
  defeat, 328
  education, 328–34
  expulsion, 331
  meaning, 248
  pirates, 254
  rebellions, 252, 253, 327
  slave owners, 250–2, 256
Mormile, Scipione, 287
Moses, 59
Mostaert, Jan, 44–7
Mountains of the Moon, 58
Mozambique, 55
Mucini, Stefano, 218
mulattos
  Afonso Álvares, 275, 347
  classification, 11
  freed slaves, 20
  legal treatment, 11
  legitimation in Portugal, 274–5
  numbers, 11
  Portugal, 347
  Portuguese slaves, 156
mulberry trees, 258
Münster, Sebastian, 61, 62
Münzer, Hieronymus, 71, 165
Murillo, Bartolomé, 71
musicians
  drummers, 36–8, 241–2
  paintings of black musicians, 36
  Portuguese court slaves, 158–9

Portuguese slaves, 118
  stereotypes, 35–40
  trumpeters, 39, 40
  West Africa, 19
Muslims
  and Catholic Church in Italy, 285, 288
  circumcision, 21–2
  conversion of slaves, 13, 288
  culture, 331
  emancipation of slaves, 270
  and Juan Latino, 344
  and Moors, 56
  polygamy, 29
  Portuguese slaves, 156, 261
  slave solidarity, 228
  slaves, 227
  Spain, 238, 248, 249–52, 328, 330
  treatment, 21
Musset, Alfred de, 324
mystery plays, 106

names
  and Juan Latino, 329, 337, 340, 343
  naming practices, 5, 12
  nicknames, 12, 121, 252
  Spanish slaves, 251
Naples
  baptism of slaves, 288, 292
  black confraternities, 287, 297
  Charles V in, 322
  court, 39
  kings, 128
  Epifania del Signore, Jesuit confraternity, 287–8
  S. Arcangelo a Baiono, church, 287
  slaves, 221, 283, 284
  synods, 291
Nardi, Jacopo, 308, 323, 324
Nero, emperor, 307
Netherlands, 44, 195
Nicholas V, Pope, 12, 161, 271, 281
Nicosia, 2
Niger, river and valley, 55, 58, 60, 283
Nile, river and valley, 55, 57, 58–9, 283
North Africa, 55, 155, 161, 202–3, 226
Nubia, 59, 60, 283
nudity, 21, 71, 72
Nunez, Jerónimo, 275
Nuñez Muley, Francisco, 251, 335

Nuremberg, 190, 209
Nuremberg Chronicle, 67, 68

Oelhafen family, 190
oil lamps, 194, 195
Olivares, count-duke of, 9, 330
Oliveira, Cristóvão Rodrigues de, 115, 265
Oliveira, Fernando, 273
Onesti, Nastagio degli, 185
Orders
    Christ, 278, 279
    Santiago, 43, 160, 161, 276
    Santo Stefano, 203
    Teutonic, 190–1
Ordinações Manuelinas, 7
ordination, slaves, 291, 293
Organa, 61
Orléans, duke of, 41
Orsini, Alfonsina, 305, 308
Orthodox Church, and slavery, 12
Ortíz, Licenciado, 259
ostriches, 56, 58, 60
otherness
    and Portuguese slaves, 262–3, 264
    and skin colour, 111–12
    stereotypes, 10
Ottomans, 215, 327, 328, 335, 341

Paços da Ribeira, Muge, 155
Paços da Serra, 155, 169
Padua, 132, 141, 194, 195
Palermo, 20, 39, 285, 289, 292, 293, 296,
    298–9
Panasco, João de Sá, 22, 29, 42–3, 160–1
panthers, 58
papacy. See also individual popes
    and Africa, 280, 300
    and black bishops, 294–5
    Lepanto, 328
    and ordination of slaves, 294
    and slavery, 12, 281–2
Paris, 113, 120, 171, 199
Paul III, Pope, 281–2
Paul V, Pope, 297
Pedraza, Francisco Bermúdez de, 259
Pedro, Don, infante of Aragon, 9
Pedro, Master, 33
Pereira, Duarte Pacheco, 22, 28
Peres, Luís, 160

Perpignan, 171, 172
Pestana, Álvara de Brito, 350
Petrarchism, 97, 101
Philip II, king of Spain, 9, 117
    and black Africans, 242–3
    and Granada, 327
    and Juan Latino, 328, 336, 344
    King of Portugal, 41, 275
    and Moriscos, 328–9, 334, 338
    relatives, 169, 326, 342
Philip III, king of Spain, 242, 299, 331
physiognomy, 71–2, 96, 97, 107, 310
Pigafetta, Antonio, 139
Pina, Rui de, 43–4, 46
Pinheiro, Diogo, 295
pirates, 199, 202–3, 226, 254
Pirez, Ines, 169
Pisa, 214, 217, 218, 219, 221
Pisanello (Antonio Pisano), 129
Pisculo, Giuseppe, bishop of Catanzaro, 291
Pius II, Pope, 281
Pius IV, Pope, 298
place names, 251
Plato, 316
Pliny the Elder, 59, 64, 68, 317
Po valley, 128
Polites, 113
Polo, Marco, 59
polygamy, 29
Poppi, 185
porcupines, 58
Portugal
    circumnavigation, 139
    Congolese ambassador, 43
    convents, 165–7, 174, 175
    court, 113
    court fools, 22, 29, 160
    court slaves, 155–79
    'discoveries', 222, 263, 264
    female slaves, 116–17
    historiography, 3
    leather trade, 217
    male slaves, 116–17
    maps, 54–5
    national character, 26
    racial purity, 263, 274–9
    royal family, 5
    slave trade to Spain, 253
    slave trade with West Africa, 11, 12, 17

Portugal (*cont.*)
  slavery code, 7
  trade monopoly, 48
Pory, John, 100, 105
Prague, 189
precious stones, 58, 60
Prester John, 58, 59, 68, 128, 341
priests, sex with slaves, 119, 347
Prosimo, Giovan Benedetto, 293
proverbs, 76–7, 94, 99
Ptolemy, Claudius, 58, 67, 69
Pucci, Alessandro, 189–90
Pucci family, 184–5, 186, 188–90
Pucci, Maria, 188
Pucci, Roberto, 189–90, 203
Pugeriol, Gaspar, 245
purity of blood, 9, 263, 274–9, 339, 341

Quelimane, 55
Quevedo, Francisco de, 77

Rabanus Maurus, 64
race. *See* skin colour
racism
  attitudes, 6
  Cleynaerts, 120–1
  exclusionary practices, 8–10
  and historiography, 4
  and medieval belief in physiognomy, 71
  scientific racism, 7–12, 111
reason, and Africans, 95, 106–7
Red Sea, 59
redondilhas, 346
Reinosa, Rodrigo de, 73–6, 80–93
Resende, André de, 113, 120, 121
Resende, Garcia de, 114, 120
Reubeni, David, 358
rhinoceroses, 56, 58, 61
Ribeiro, Isabel, 171
Riccio, Andrea, 194
Ringhiadori, Leonardo, 222
Rio Grande, 22
Roman law, 7, 11, 35
Romanus Pontifex, 12, 281
Rome, 2, 68, 202, 203, 282, 294, 297–8
Rosales, Cristóvão de, 161
Rotz, Jean, 51
Rouen, 171, 172
Roxburgh ballads, 105–6

Rožmitál, Leo of, 41
Rubens, Peter Paul, 199
Rudolph II, emperor, 189
Ruiz, Fernão, 171
Rumanians, 214
Russians, 214, 215, 226

Sá, Mem da, 173
Sahagún, Bernadino de, 331
Sahara, 55
saints, 8, 70, 191–3, 288–9, 298–9, 356–8
Salamanca, 78, 113, 120
Salema, Diogo, 155
Salviati, Giuliano di Francesco, 218
Salviati, Piero di Francesco, 218
Salzedo, Lourenço de, 276
Santa Auta Retable (attributed to Cristóvão de Figueiredo and Garcia Fernandes), 158
Santa Maria, Clemencia de, 172–3
Santarém, 350
Sanuto, Marin, 24
São Tomé, 70, 274, 275
Saracens, 214, 215, 219
Saro people, 64
Sassetti, Francesco, 220
satyrs, 195
scars, 22–3
Schedel, Hartmann, 67, 68
scolding-match, 73
Scotland, 37, 98, 105–6
sculpture
  featuring Africans, 194–209
  marble sculpture, 203–4
Sebastião, king of Portugal, 269
Segni, Bernardo, 306, 307–8, 310, 321, 324
Senegal, 55, 63, 156, 161, 216, 217, 230, 256
Senegambia, 22, 33, 35, 73
Sessa, duke of, 259, 329, 332, 335, 342
Seville, 70, 71, 73, 76, 250, 330
Seville, duke of, 32
sex
  black virility stereotype, 75, 76
  and blackness, 100–5
  and Italian slaves, 220
  and Portuguese female slaves, 118–19
  Portuguese masters and slaves, 348
  Portuguese priests, 119, 347
  promiscuity, 29–32